D0335156

A FIELD GUIDE TO THE
RARE BIRDS
OF BRITAIN AND EUROPE

A FIELD GUIDE TO THE
RARE BIRDS
OF BRITAIN AND EUROPE

Illustrated by
Ian Lewington

Text by
Per Alström and Peter Colston

HarperCollins*Publishers*

Dedicated to the memory of

PETER GRANT

by three of his many friends

First edition, 1991
Reprinted, 1992

© in the illustrations, Domino Books Ltd, 1991
© in the text, Per Alström and Peter Colston, 1991
© in this edition, Domino Books Ltd, 1991

ISBN 000 219917-3

A **Domino Books** production. All rights reserved. No part of this publication
may be reproduced, stored in a retrieval system, or transmitted in any form or by
any means – electronic, mechanical, by photocopying, recording or otherwise –
without permission from Domino Books Ltd., 7 Bond Street, St Helier, Jersey.

Printed and bound in Spain by Heraclio Fournier, Vitoria

Contents

Preface   7

Introduction   9

The Birds   27-425

GAVIIDAE
Divers   27

PODICIPEDIDAE
Grebes   28

DIOMEDEIDAE
Albatrosses   29

PROCELLARIIDAE
Petrels and Shearwaters   31

HYDROBATIDAE
Storm-petrels   34

PHAETHONTIDAE
Tropicbirds   36

SULIDAE
Gannets and Boobies   37

PHALACROCORACIDAE
Cormorants and Shags   38

PELECANIDAE
Pelicans   39

FREGATIDAE
Frigatebirds   40

ARDEIDAE
Bitterns and Herons   41

THRESKIORNITHIDAE
Ibises and Spoonbills   47

PHOENICOPTERIDAE
Flamingoes   48

ANATIDAE
Swans, Geese and Ducks   49

ACCIPITRIDAE
Hawks and Eagles   74

FALCONIDAE
Falcons   88

TURNICIDAE
Button-quails   94

RALLIDAE
Rails, Crakes etc   95

GRUIDAE
Cranes   98

OTIDIDAE
Bustards   100

GLAREOLIDAE
Coursers and Pratincoles   101

CHARADRIIDAE
Plovers and Lapwings   103

SCOLOPACIDAE
Sandpipers and allies   115

STERCORARIIDAE
Skuas   146

LARIDAE
Gulls   147

STERNIDAE
Terns and Noddies   161

ALCIDAE
Auks   169

PTEROCLIDIDAE
Sandgrouse   170

COLUMBIDAE
Doves and Pigeons   173

CUCULIDAE
Cuckoos   175

CONTENTS

STRIGIDAE
Owls   176

CAPRIMULGIDAE
Nightjars   177

APODIDAE
Swifts   179

ALCEDINIDAE
Kingfishers   181

MEROPIDAE
Bee-eaters   182

PICIDAE
Woodpeckers   183

TYRANNIDAE
New World Flycatchers   184

ALAUDIDAE
Larks   185

HIRUNDINIDAE
Swallows   189

MOTACILLIDAE
Pipits and Wagtails   189

MIMIDAE
Mockingbirds, Thrashers etc   328

PRUNELLIDAE
Accentors   329

TURDIDAE
Robins, Chats etc   330

SYLVIIDAE
Warblers, Goldcrests etc   352

MUSCICAPIDAE
Old World Flycatchers   372

PARIDAE
Tits   373

SITTIDAE
Nuthatches   374

LANIIDAE
Shrikes   374

CORVIDAE
Crows   378

STURNIDAE
Starlings   378

PASSERIDAE
Sparrows   380

VIREONIDAE
Vireos   381

FRINGILLIDAE
Finches   382

PARULIDAE
American Wood Warblers   388

THRAUPIDAE
Tanagers   403

EMBERIZIDAE
Buntings and allies   404

ICTERIDAE
Bobolink, Grackles etc.   422

Colour Illustrations   between pages 192 and 321

British Rarities   426

Appendix: Divergences from the Voous nomenclature   431

Bibliography   433

Index of English names   444

Index of Scientific Names   446

Authors' Preface

There are now several good guides to the common and regular European birds (about 380 species), still led by the evergreen *Field Guide to the Birds of Britain and Europe* of Peterson, Mountfort and Hollom, whose forthcoming new edition will be a major event. Since its first publication in 1954, a number of other excellent guides have appeared, notably the Heinzel/Fitter/Parslow *Birds of Britain and Europe with North Africa and the Middle East.*

All these books, however, have had to give short shrift to the 300-odd far rarer species which irregularly reach Britain and Europe from North America, Asia, Africa – some even from subantarctic islands and Antarctica itself. In the regular guides, these birds are often either omitted altogether, or banished to a mere list of names at the back. That is understandable, for to give them the full treatment in a guide to our native or regular birds would not only double its length and cost: it would make life much harder for the beginner or casual user.

This is ironic, for these rarer birds are precisely the most interesting and exciting for the keen birdwatcher, and those which can present the greatest challenge for sure identification. Of all bird species one may see in Europe, these are the most in need of a full and accurate guide. Yet no such book has ever existed! So when Domino Books presented us with the idea, we all three jumped at it – as surely would have any other "twitchers" or rarity-hunters from Shannon or Spitsbergen to Moscow or Malaga. Our brief was to make the best possible guide, irrespective of length or cost, to make it completely up-to-date on publication and to keep it revised thereafter for a new edition every 2-3 years. If a bird other than a breeder or regular visitor had been reliably recorded in Europe *at all* it was to be in the book. The colour plates were to be accurate as well as beautiful, and where sensible to show plumages in which further records might well be seen, as well as those already sighted. The descriptions were to be full and to concentrate on field recognition. The number and dates of sightings were to be indicated, and where appropriate the places.

It proved a bigger and longer task than any of us foresaw. How well or otherwise we have succeeded the birdwatching world will doubtless mercilessly decide. But one thing is certain: we could not possibly have done this job alone. In general terms we have drawn on the whole corpus of collected knowledge built up since the beginnings of modern ornithology. More specifically, we have benefitted directly or indirectly from the expertise, enthusiasm and helpful criticism of more people than it is possible to mention here.

In particular though, we have to mention with quite special thanks the following individuals, for most valuable help in different ways:

Thomas Alerstam; Reino Andersson; Roland Asteling; Norbert Bahr; Kevin Baker; Peter Barthel; Arnoud van den Berg; Ingvar Byrkjedal; Duncan Brooks; Francis Buckle; Simon Cook; David Cottridge; Graham Cowles; Philippe Dubois; Jöran Ekström; Carl Edelstam; Johan Elmberg; Bob Emmett; Jon Fjeldså; J.Y. Frémont; Dick Forsman; the late Peter Grant; Martin Hallam; Hermann Heinzel; Alistair Hill; Erik Hirschfeld; Tim Inskipp; Ingemar Johansson; Stefan Johansson; Lars Jonsson; Hannu Jännes; Eduardo de Juana; Mikael Käll; Nils Kjellén; Alan

Knox; Peter G. Lansdown; Lars Larsson; Richard Lewington; Brian Little; Trevor Lloyd-Evans; Tim Loseby; Ed Mackrill; John Marchant; Krister Mild; John Mather; Urban Olsson; Kiyoaki Ozaki; A.M. Paterson; Roger Tory Peterson; Gunnlaugur Pétursson; Viggo Ree; George Reszeter; Lennart Risberg; M.J. Rogers; Bart J. de Schutter; J.T.R. Sharrock; Yoshimitsu Shigeta; Hadoram Shirihai; Richard Snell; Koichiro Sonobe; Lars Svensson; Andy Swash; John Tomkins; Magnus Ullmann; Anne Vale; F. Vasic; Johan Wallander; Peter Wheeler; P.A. Whittington; Dan Zetterström.

We are also most grateful to the Sub-Department of Ornithology at the British Museum (Natural History), Tring; the Universitetets Zoologiske Museum, Copenhagen; the Naturhistoriska Riksmuseet, Stockholm; and the American Museum of Natural History – all for allowing us to study their collections of bird skins and to use their libraries.

It is a cliché, but true and needs saying, that while the book would have been the worse without the kindness and help of all the above, such shortcomings as do remain are ours alone. As said above, we intend continually to improve and update it. We would therefore be grateful for all comments, criticisms, corrections and new data, whether on the text or illustrations or the book's general arrangement. Please write to Domino Books Ltd., c/o Natural History Dept., HarperCollins Publishers, 77-85 Fulham Palace Road, London W6 8JB.

Introduction

Area and species covered

The *area* covered by this book includes all European countries, from Iceland and the Faeroes south to Portugal and Spain. It extends eastwards to Finland and those countries bordering the Baltic, then southwards through eastern Europe to mainland Greece, Bulgaria, and Rumania. We have also included the Azores archipelago (*c.* 800 miles west of Portugal) which has a greater affinity with the European avifauna than with Africa. For completeness, records from Malta have also been included but only where a vagrant species has also been recorded elsewhere in Europe. We have not included species which have occurred *only* on Malta, e.g. Temminck's Horned Lark *Eremophila bilopha* or Tristram's Warbler *Sylvia deserticola.* The species covered are:

1. true vagrants, not breeding in Europe and which are only rarely recorded, and
2. very rare breeding birds (generally less than 100 pairs), and not seen in large numbers on migration.

In some cases the choice of species is apparently at odds with point 2 above. Relatively numerous species, such as Audouin's Gull (*c.* 6,000 pairs), Eleonora's Falcon (*c.* 3,500 pairs), and Brünnich's Guillemot (a few million pairs), are included, whereas uncommon species such as Black Vulture (200-250 pairs) are left out. The reason for including Audouin's Gull and Eleonora's Falcon is that both are endemic to the Mediterranean and extremely local. Brünnich's Guillemot only occurs in extremely peripheral northern areas, which are very rarely visited by birdwatchers. In the rest of Europe it is a first-rate rarity. It is possible that certain other rare breeding birds will be included in future editions, together, of course, with newly recorded vagrants.

We have included a few vagrant subspecies, when these are very distinctive and easily recognized in the field.

The British Isles, lying at the crossroads of different winds, currents, seaways and migration routes, are in a fortunate position for recording bird rarities, and in particular have more than their fair share of wind-blown American migrants.

However, here at the extreme westerly edge of the European landmass, various birds which regularly occur in other parts of Europe – particularly in the south – are either unrecorded or are exciting rarities when they do appear. These species do not qualify for inclusion in the main part of the book, and are anyway all covered in the standard guides. They are, however, listed on p. 428, with notes on their occurrence in Britain and Ireland.

Text

SEQUENCE AND NAMES ADOPTED

The taxonomic order and nomenclature basically follow Voous (1977). The few cases where our treatment differs from Voous' are summarized in the Appendix (see p. 432).

The *English* names are those that are normally used in recent literature, i.e. those adopted by the British Ornithologists' Union.

Status Codes

For each species a letter code indicates its occurrence in Europe:

A = 1-10 individuals recorded
B = 11-50
C = 51-100
D = over 100
R Br = Rare breeder
*   = Endangered or globally threatened species (see *Birds to Watch* 1988. The ICBP World Checklist of Threatened Birds).

The descriptions

MEASUREMENTS

The *length* (L) of a bird is the measurement taken (with the bird flat on its back) from the tip of the bill to the tip of the tail. In some cases (with birds more frequently seen in flight than perched) the *wingspan* (WS) is also given. The measurements are generally those in *Birds of the Western Palearctic (BWP)* for the species covered by the volumes already published. In other cases, the measurements adopted are taken from a variety of other sources. All measurements are given in centimetres and inches.

PLUMAGE AND BARE PARTS

The descriptions generally start with characters common to all plumages. The different plumages follow, starting with adult male. For practically all passerines, and some other groups as well, juvenile plumage is normally moulted before the autumn migration and is thus unlikely to be seen in these birds in Europe. However, for the sake of completeness the juvenile plumage has been described, though *only* when distinguishable in the field. The text complements the illustrations, pointing out important characters for identifying species, age or sex. Some species are extremely difficult to identify in the field but relatively simple to distinguish in the hand. For these the wing-formulae or other measurements are given. The primaries are numbered in *descending* order, i.e. starting with the innermost. Wing-length is given from the carpal joint to the wing-tip, with the hand flattened and straightened, except for the sand plovers, in which the wings are flattened but not straightened. For techniques of measuring the bill see Svensson (1984).

The topography of a bird is illustrated on p. 14, and plumage and moult terminology is explained on p. 13.

VOICE

Voice transcriptions are given for most species, but not for those seabirds, ducks, gulls and others that are extremely unlikely to be heard in Europe, and where the voice is of little or no use for identification. For the waders, only the normal (not alarm) calls are described, since their songs are very unlikely to be heard here. Since most vagrant passerines are recorded in the autumn, it would have been enough to describe their calls, but as some have actually been heard singing in Europe we thought there would be no harm in describing the songs of most of them.

Transcribing bird voices is of course difficult, and the perception of a given call or song by different people varies greatly. There are published recordings of most of the songs and calls described in this book.

Note that *i* should be pronounced as in 'it', *sch* as in 'schnapps', *u* as in 'juice', *y* like German 'ü'. Pauses between notes are marked in the following way:

tee-tee – very short pauses

tee tee – normal pauses, as in ordinary conversation

tee, tee – longer pauses

tee...tee – even longer pauses.

In some cases, capital letters have been used, for example in the transcription of the song of Dupont's Lark: *HUU HEE trueeduee grrdu-EE*. This means that the components written in capital letters are considerably louder than the others.

RANGE

A synopsis of the species' range is given for summer and winter. Nearctic species which have reached Greenland, Madeira or the Canary Islands are briefly mentioned, as potential vagrants to Europe.

STATUS

The countries in Europe for which there are records which have been accepted by the national 'Rarities Committee' (or equivalent) are listed. Where known, the *number of individuals* recorded in each country is also given (see Bibliography). In a few cases very interesting records up to the date of publication have also been included, even if not yet accepted by the Rarities Committee for the country concerned; these are marked with an asterisk (*). In many European countries, running totals of rare species are published annually in a *Report on Rare Birds* (see Bibliography). However, in some cases the current figure is unknown or we only know approximately how often a species has occurred in a particular country.

We are also aware that a few earlier records are perhaps now unacceptable. Improved knowledge has led to reassessment of many previously accepted records, and it is always possible that some earlier records may be rejected in the future.

Localities and dates are given for some of the more important records, and the main months of occurrence.

NOTE

Under this heading at the end of a species text we have sometimes drawn attention to further possible identification problems: for example, the risks of confusion with species not yet recorded in Europe but which might well reach us in the near future.

Colour illustrations

Paintings are of *adults*, except where otherwise indicated; where no sex symbols
are given, the reader may take it that the sexes are indistinguishable in the field. If
the sexes are very different, male and female are also usually illustrated. Summer
and winter plumages are also generally shown, if they differ significantly. Distinctive immature plumages are usually shown, although it was not practicable to show
the full range of variation in, for example, eagles. Common European species are
sometimes shown for comparison on the caption page.

It is important to refer to the descriptive text as well as the paintings. The two
are complementary. For some species important characters are also shown in line-
drawings in the text.

Bird topography

A thorough knowledge of the arrangement of the different groups of feathers,
which is more or less the same in all flying birds, is crucial for identification and
for making accurate plumage descriptions. The terms used in this book are shown
in the following figures. Note that throughout the text "coverts" refers to upper
innerwing-coverts and "primary coverts" denotes greater primary coverts for smaller birds.

The following terms are also used throughout the text:

Arm: the inner part of the wing.

Cere: bare skin at the base of the upper mandible in raptors.

Gular feathering: a wedge of feathers on the underside of the bill.

Gular stripe: a dark stripe extending down the centre of the throat.

Hand: the outer part of the wing.

'*Jizz*': a combination of characters which identify a bird in the field.

Mirror: subterminal white spot (one to two) on the tips of the outermost primaries
of gulls.

Nail: the small nail-like shape found at the tip of the upper mandible in ducks and
geese; the colour is usually different from that of the rest of the bill.

Primary projection: the distance from the wing-tip to the tip of the longest tertials
on the folded wing.

Rectrices: tail-feathers.

Remiges: flight-feathers – primaries and secondaries.

Scapular crescent: white tips to the longest scapulars in gulls, forming a white
crescentic mark.

Speculum: usually irridescent panel on the secondaries in dabbling ducks.

Tertial crescent: as scapular crescent, but on the tertials.

Trousers: loosely hanging feathering on tibia of e.g. raptors.

Miscellaneous terms

The following are some more general terms:

Albinistic: an aberration, a complete lack of feather pigmentation resulting in a wholly white or, if partially albinistic, a partly white plumage.

Contour feathers: the predominant type of feather (excluding down and certain other small feathers). Characterized by the presence of largely firm webs.

Endemic: a species occurring only in one stated area is said to be endemic to that area.

Leucistic: a pigmentation deficiency, resulting in unusually pale plumage.

Morph: a normal but distinct plumage variant which is not related to sex, age or season.

Pneumatized: the skull roof of many birds initially consists of a single layer of bone. This gradually develops into a double layer with air in between, with numerous supporting pillars.

Polymorphic: a species occurring in several morphs (see above).

Race: synonymous with subspecies.

Subspecies: a population of a given species which differs more or less obviously in appearance from one or more other populations of the same species. The border between species and subspecies is often arbitrary. The *nominate* subspecies is the one first named: its scientific name has the second and third terms identical, e.g. *Anthus rubescens rubescens*.

Moult, ageing and plumages

The plumage of a bird is replaced, moulted, at least once a year. Understanding moult strategies is often essential for correct ageing and sometimes identification. The following is a brief account of the different plumages that occur.

JUVENILE PLUMAGE

The first true plumage (with contour feathers and not only down) is called *juvenile*. In most birds this is clearly different from that of subsequent plumages. In some, however, the juvenile plumage differs very little from that of the adult.

In late summer the juvenile plumage is fresh, with all feathers the same age. At this time of year adults are normally quite heavily worn and often showing feathers of different generations, and are thus easily told from juveniles.

Especially in passerines, the juvenile feathers (notably on head and body) are slightly looser and more brittle than post-juvenile feathers, which often makes the juvenile look distinctly fluffier than later plumages.

In juvenile waders, the scapulars are smaller. In juvenile geese, the scapulars, coverts and feathers on the underparts (notably flanks) are smaller and more rounded and the side of the neck is less distinctly 'water-combed'. Juvenile ducks can be distinguished by the projecting shafts and slightly forked tips to the tail-feathers. In some large birds, for example most medium-sized to large raptors, the complete juvenile plumage is usually retained until the summer of the second year (i.e. approximately until the bird is 1 year old). The moult then progresses very slowly, and it can take a few years until the last juvenile feathers are shed.

13

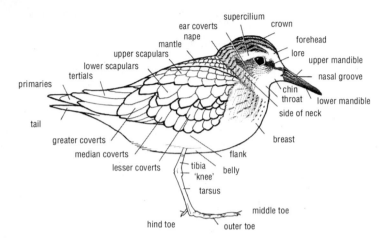

ear coverts
supercilium
crown
nape
forehead
mantle
lore
upper scapulars
upper mandible
lower scapulars
nasal groove
tertials
primaries
chin
throat
lower mandible
tail
side of neck
greater coverts
breast
median coverts
flank
lesser coverts
tibia
'knee'
belly
tarsus
middle toe
hind toe
outer toe

Plumage of a non-passerine (wader)

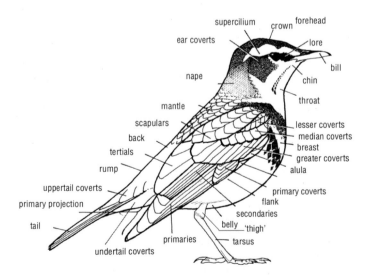

supercilium
crown
forehead
ear coverts
lore
bill
nape
chin
throat
mantle
scapulars
lesser coverts
back
median coverts
tertials
breast
rump
greater coverts
uppertail coverts
alula
primary projection
primary coverts
flank
tail
secondaries
belly
'thigh'
primaries
tarsus
undertail coverts

Plumage of a passerine (thrush)

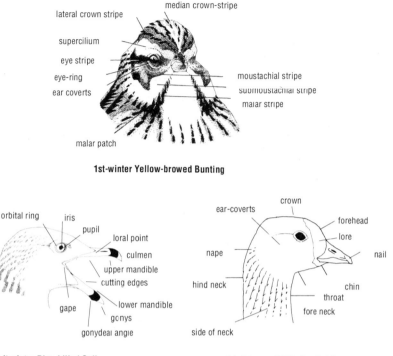

1st-winter Yellow-browed Bunting

Adult winter Ring-billed Gull

Adult Lesser White-fronted Goose

Most birds replace the juvenile plumage rather quickly with a *first-winter plumage* (1st-winter) or *first breeding plumage* (1st breeding). Some moult straight to adult plumage. The moult from juvenile to the next plumage is called a *post-juvenile moult*.

FIRST-WINTER PLUMAGE

For most waders, gulls and passerines the term 1st-winter is used. In passerines and many gulls, the post-juvenile moult takes place at the breeding grounds before the migration, often already when the bird is only about a month old. Waders usually moult to 1st-winter during the autumn migration or in the winter quarters. In a few gulls and passerines the juvenile plumage is retained until they reach the winter quarters.

In most birds the post-juvenile moult includes the feathers of the head and body, often also a number of coverts and tertials and sometimes a few or all tail-feathers (central pair first). It is thus a *partial moult*, as opposed to a *complete moult*, which

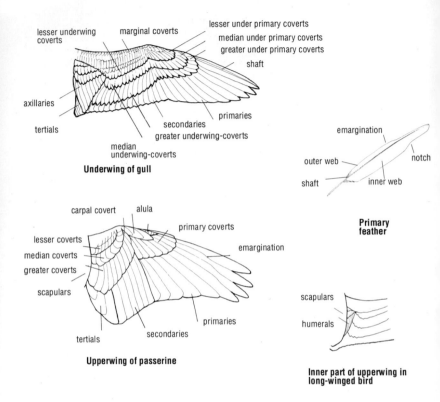

Underwing of gull

lesser underwing coverts
marginal coverts
lesser under primary coverts
median under primary coverts
greater under primary coverts
shaft
axillaries
tertials
primaries
secondaries
greater underwing-coverts
median underwing-coverts

Primary feather

emargination
notch
outer web
shaft
inner web

Upperwing of passerine

carpal covert
alula
primary coverts
lesser coverts
median coverts
greater coverts
emargination
scapulars
tertials
secondaries
primaries

Inner part of upperwing in long-winged bird

scapulars
humerals

also includes the remiges and rectrices. Juvenile woodpeckers usually moult the tail-feathers and primaries but not the secondaries.

First-winter birds which have gone through a partial moult can usually be told from subsequent plumages by the mostly retained juvenile wings and tail. In gulls, the primaries are usually slightly more pointed than in the adult. The same applies to the tail-feathers of some passerines and others, although this is often very subtle.

In passerines, a *moult contrast* can often be seen between on the one hand a variable number of newly moulted, adult-type coverts and tertials, and on the other a variable number of retained juvenile coverts and tertials. Frequently the lesser, median and inner greater coverts and some tertials are new and the rest of the greater coverts and tertials are retained juvenile. The newly moulted feathers are fresher, often slightly longer (often only evident on the greater coverts), and show a slightly or strikingly different pattern compared to the juvenile feathers. In adult passerines moult contrasts are only found in the autumn in those species which have a partial post-breeding moult. However, in these the remiges and rectrices and any unmoulted coverts/tertials are much more heavily worn than in 1st-winter birds.

In North American wood warblers and buntings and a few others, *all* of the coverts and tertials are usually moulted during the post-juvenile moult. It is often apparent that the primary coverts are slightly more pointed and more frayed at the tips than in adult (in other passerines as well). In the former group a subtle moult contrast can often be seen between the newly moulted greater coverts and carpal covert, and the juvenile primary coverts and alula.

1st-winter woodpeckers can be told from adults by the presence of a contrast between the new primaries and the slightly more worn juvenile secondaries.

The iris colour often differs between adult and 1st-year birds (most noticeable during the first autumn). In some species, such as buntings, this requires experience to be appreciated (best with a $10 \times$ magnifying lens in good light). In others, such as gulls, the difference is normally obvious even in the field. In many birds, eg. buntings, the colour is generally rather dark grey-brown in young birds and more deep brown or reddish-brown in adults. In e.g. *Acrocephalus*-warblers the iris is also distinctly darker in young birds than in adults. In most large gulls, the iris is initially dark, usually becoming pale during the summer/autumn of the 2nd year.

In many passerines, the palate/inside of the upper mandible is pinkish or yellowish in young birds and blackish in adults. This is sometimes useful even in spring of the 2nd year.

FIRST BREEDING PLUMAGE

In ducks the juvenile plumage is moulted during the first autumn-winter to 1st breeding plumage. This moult is partial, although the tail-feathers and tertials are usually renewed. (Apparently, there is generally a limited moult prior to the moult to 1st breeding, but that moult does not significantly alter the appearance of the bird).

FIRST ADULT PLUMAGE

In e.g. bustards, sandgrouse (most), pigeons, doves, larks and starlings, the post-juvenile moult is complete and usually takes place at the age of one to three months (except in the Rose-coloured Starling, which moults in the winter quarters). In those species the plumage is usually inseparable from the adult once the moult has been completed. Sometimes (mainly in non-passerines, such as Houbara Bustard) the complete moult is 'arrested' before all of the remiges have been renewed, and 1st-years (see below) can then usually be identified by the shape, degree of wear and, sometimes, pattern of the retained juvenile remiges.

Passerines with a complete post-juvenile moult (as well as most other passerines) can still usually be aged in the first autumn as they show a partially pneumatized (ossified) skull roof, but note that some species (e.g. Isabelline Wheatear) may become fully pneumatized very early in the autumn. Moreover, in a few species (e.g. some buntings) adults also normally have incompletely pneumatized skull roofs.

FIRST-SUMMER PLUMAGE

In most waders, gulls, terns and passerines a 1st-summer plumage can be recognized. In most species this plumage is attained through a partial *pre-breeding moult* (spring moult) in late winter of the first year to early spring of the second year. The extent of this moult is very variable – from very few feathers, to all of the feathers of the head and body plus a variable number of coverts, tertials and tail-feathers (often the central pair). Some waders also normally renew the outer primaries, and most terns usually moult the inner primaries.

The shape of the juvenile remiges and rectrices is more difficult to judge than in the first autumn, since the feathers are rather heavily worn. The degree of wear can be helpful; 1st-summers are generally more worn than adults.

In waders which have renewed the outer primaries, these are fresher than the inner primaries. The resulting moult contrast resembles that seen in adults which have completed their moult after a suspension (see below). However, the inner primaries are much more worn than in adults and contrast more with the outers.

In terns the stage of the moult of the primaries generally differs between 1st-year birds and adults (see the species descriptions).

In pipits and wagtails, as well as in some wood-warblers, ageing by moult contrasts among the coverts and tertials is more complicated than in autumn, since both 1st-summer birds and adults usually have a number of new coverts and tertials and thus show moult contrasts. Moreover, the pattern of any retained juvenile coverts is more difficult to judge because they are heavily worn.

In a small number of species, e.g. Franklin's Gull, Sabine's Gull, Black-billed and Yellow-billed Cuckoos, several warblers, Brown and Isabelline Shrikes, Bobolink and some individuals of some waders, the moult to 1st summer is complete (as in adults of these species). In those, except Franklin's and Sabine's Gulls, 1st-summer birds are generally inseparable from the adult by plumage.

Many passerines have no or only a very limited pre-breeding moult (spring moult), yet they attain a summer plumage which is very different from the winter plumage. In these the summer plumage is revealed as the pale fringes of the winter plumage gradually wear narrower (see adult).

The term *first-year* (1st-year) denotes a bird during its first approximately 12 months of life, thus covering juvenile, 1st-winter and 1st-summer.

SUBSEQUENT IMMATURE PLUMAGES

Many gulls have one or a few more distinguishable immature plumages, called *second-winter* (2nd-winter), *second-summer* (2nd-summer) and *third-winter* (3rd-winter).

The various immature plumages in some seabirds, ducks, birds of prey and cranes are less clearly defined, since the moult is very protracted. It is therefore irrelevant to talk about second-winter, etc. Also, the knowledge about these plumages is often imperfect.

It is important to realize that the considerable individual variation makes it impossible to age older immatures with 100% certainty. They are thus better termed '2nd-winter type', '3rd-summer type' etc. The term *subadult* refers to a bird that is older than first-year but still not adult, as opposed to *immature* meaning any non-adult plumage.

The adult plumage is the final plumage. Many birds have only one adult plumage throughout the year, while others have a *summer plumage* and a *winter plumage*. For ducks we refer to a *breeding plumage* and an *eclipse plumage* instead, since the breeding plumage ('summer plumage') is attained during the late autumn, whereas the female-like eclipse plumage ('winter plumage') is worn during a short period in the summer. Most adult birds have one of the following moult strategies.

1. One complete *post-breeding moult* (autumn moult) per year.

2. A complete post-breeding moult and a partial *pre-breeding moult* (spring moult).

3. A partial post-breeding moult and a complete pre-breeding moult.

4. Two complete moults per year.

1. In many species (e.g. seabirds, geese, raptors, most sandgrouse, doves/pigeons, owls, nightjars, swifts and many passerines) adult birds have only one moult per year, a complete post-breeding moult. However, in larger seabirds and large raptors, the moult is almost continuous (slows down or is suspended during migration in migratory species; also in winter in birds wintering far to the north).

Seabirds and raptors have a so called *serial moult* of the flight feathers, i.e. there are several active moult series at a time (see figure, p. 20). This strategy ensures that the flight ability is only a little affected by the moult.

Black Lark, Stonechat, Pied Wheatear, Rose-coloured Starling and many buntings have only one moult per year, yet they display pronounced differences between summer plumage and winter plumage. In the autumn-winter the summer plumage is concealed by broad fringes of a different colour. The summer plumage is gradually attained as these fringes wear off. At least some buntings also need to moult some feathers on the face to attain complete summer plumage.

2. Most ducks, waders, skuas, gulls, terns, auks, some passerines and others also have a partial pre-breeding moult in order to attain summer (breeding) plumage.

The ducks are peculiar in that the post-breeding moult takes place in mid summer (earlier in males than in females), followed almost immediately by the pre-breeding moult.

Many waders and terns and some passerines have a *suspended* moult of the flight-feathers, i.e. they moult only some flight-feathers before the migration and the rest in their winter quarters. Some do not moult at all until in the winter quarters, while others moult completely on the breeding grounds. Long-distance migrants usually moult fewer feathers before the autumn migration than short-distance migrants. This applies to different species as well as to different populations of the same species.

3. Many warblers and others go through a partial post-breeding moult prior to the autumn migration and a complete pre-breeding moult in the winter quarters in late autumn to early spring (timing variable and for most species imperfectly known). The species that have this moult strategy are usually long-distance migrants.

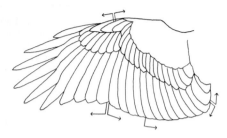

Moult pattern of a bird of prey of the family *Accipitridae*. Arrows show origin and direction of moult waves. After Edelstam (1984).

4. Very few species usually have two complete moults per year (in the Holarctic, as far as is known, only Franklin's Gull, Willow Warbler, Tiger Shrike, *Lanius tigrinus*, and Bobolink and apparently many Pallas's Grasshopper Warblers).

Rare birds

As will be evident from the species accounts, many of the species that are now rare as breeding birds in Europe were once more widespread in the region. These birds have usually declined as a result of human activities: overhunting, habitat destruction, the use of pesticides, etc. It is beyond the scope of this book to discuss this, but we recommend *Save the Birds* (Diamond *et al* 1987).

The vast majority of the species covered, however, are true vagrants. Most come from North America and Northern Asia (together referred to as the Holarctic region) and a few from Africa and even Subantarctic islands or the Antarctic continent.

A large proportion of the Holarctic birds are migratory, some undertaking extremely long flights from the northern hemisphere to the southern and back again. These long-distance migrants are the most likely ones to turn up as vagrants in Europe. More southern species are generally less migratory and thus less likely to straggle to Europe.

Most North American and Asiatic vagrants are much more numerous in Europe in autumn than in spring. This is probably at least partly explained by the fact that the total population is larger in autumn than in spring, with the bulk usually made up of first-year birds, which are less experienced than adults and seem less likely than adults to have a well adjusted navigational sense. Birds that have once successfully navigated to their species' traditional winter quarters are probably less likely to lose their bearings on the return spring migration. Of the vagrants that reach Europe in the autumn there are probably very few which survive to be recorded on their return migration the following spring (particularly passerines). Moreover, as far as North American migrants are concerned, these usually choose a considerably more westerly route for their northward journey in spring than they used in coming south in autumn (see figure, p. 21).

For some reason, North American sparrows and Dark-eyed Junco are more numerous in spring than in summer. The Killdeer also has an aberrant vagrancy pattern, since most of the records are from November-March.

As has already been indicated, for most species a greater proportion of the records normally relate to first-years than to older birds.

NORTH AMERICAN VAGRANTS

Many North American species migrate down the Atlantic coast to South America in the autumn. Several species are regularly known to cover this distance by undertaking non-stop flights from staging areas in SE Canada and NE USA (a distance of 3000-4000km covered in 3-4 days and nights!). It has been shown that the main flights take place immediately after a cold front has passed, when the birds usually have a fresh tail-wind (northwesterly), which is advantageous from an energy-cost point of view. The initial direction of flight is thus southerly to southeasterly (generally more southeasterly in waders than in passerines). The course is changed to southwesterly or southerly when the birds reach the region where the easterly trade winds prevail. However, should they start too close to the centre of the depression, they may be driven off-course, towards Europe, by strong

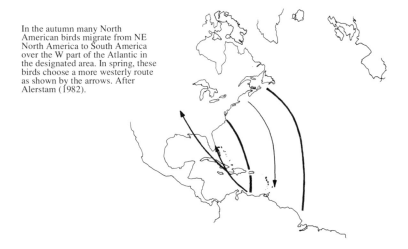

In the autumn many North American birds migrate from NE North America to South America over the W part of the Atlantic in the designated area. In spring, these birds choose a more westerly route as shown by the arrows. After Alerstam (1982).

westerlies. Also, the birds normally have to cross the 'tail' of the cold front, where the winds may be westerly and very strong. The risk of being pushed towards Europe is then great.

Probably the majority of the birds that are driven off-course finally suffer from fatigue and drown well out in the Atlantic. Many exhausted birds land on ships in the west Atlantic, and some of the few that survive may unknowingly hitch a lift into Europe.

Pectoral Sandpiper, Buff-breasted Sandpiper, White-rumped Sandpiper, Long-billed Dowitcher, Wilson's Phalarope, Lesser Yellowlegs, Baird's Sandpiper and American Golden Plover are the most frequently recorded waders in Europe (listed in frequency order; we assume that practically all of the unidentified dowitchers have been Long-billed). All, except Wilson's Phalarope and Lesser Yellowlegs breed extremely far north, tending towards northwest; Pectoral Sandpiper and Long-billed Dowitcher also breed in northernmost Siberia. Lesser Yellowlegs has a basically northwesterly range, although not arctic. Wilson's Phalarope breeds mainly in NW USA and SW Canada. All, except Long-billed Dowitcher and Lesser Yellowlegs, almost exclusively winter in South America and are uncommon or even rare on the Atlantic coast of the USA. Long-billed Dowitcher and Lesser Yellowlegs are more numerous on the east coast of the USA, but still relatively sparse (more numerous in autumn than in spring). These species probably undertake non-stop flights from NE North America to South America more regularly than most other waders. Almost the entire population of the Hudsonian Godwit flies non-stop to South America, yet there are only three records from Europe. The explanation is probably that the total population is comparatively small.

In Europe there are more records of larger species, e.g. wildfowl, waders, gulls and terns than passerines. This is probably mainly because the former are stronger than the latter and thus more likely to survive a transatlantic crossing. Moreover, the former groups are better adapted for long sea crossings and are also capable of settling on the sea.

Not very surprisingly there are significantly more North American vagrants recorded in Britain and Ireland than in Fennoscandia. Of North American passerines there are more than four times as many species recorded in Britain and Ireland as in Fennoscandia! The number of North American duck species recorded in the British Isles and in Fennoscandia respectively is practically the same, and there are only five more species of waders from Britain and Ireland than from Fennoscandia. However, the number of individuals is much higher for the British Isles.

In Fennoscandia there are relatively more spring records of North American birds than in the British Isles. This can be explained by the fact that those birds that arrive in the autumn and survive the winter on this side of the Atlantic migrate north in spring. Larger birds survive to a greater extent than do small birds, which is a further reason why there are more records of ducks, waders and gulls than of passerines in Fennoscandia.

ASIATIC VAGRANTS

Many N Asiatic species are true long-distance migrants, wintering in S Asia. Several different hypotheses have been proposed to explain why some individuals of some species in the autumn migrate west instead of south or south-east. There are probably several factors involved. Possibly, a small part of the population is genetically programmed to migrate in a different direction from the usual. Defects in the navigational sense, either genetic or caused by external factors such as magnetic anomalies in the area of hatching, are other possible explanations. There is probably some dispersion in all directions. This supposition is supported by the fact that Asiatic migrants regularly turn up in other far-out places in the autumn, such as W North America. There are also many examples of European/west Asiatic species which have migrated east instead of south or south-west; for example there is one record of Wood Warbler from the Aleutians in October 1978 and one from Japan in October 1984 (the breeding range extends east to the Urals and the winter quarters are in tropical Africa).

The number of Asiatic vagrant species recorded in the British Isles and in Fennoscandia respectively is not very different, unlike North American species (see above). The number of individuals is often higher in Britain than Fennoscandia, but this could be mainly a reflection of the higher number of active birdwatchers in Britain.

Some species are noted for their irruptive occurrence pattern. Pallas's Sandgrouse and Rose-coloured Starling are two examples of species that have occurred and even bred in Europe in comparatively large numbers in certain years, the former possibly as a result of a shortage of food in its normal range, and the latter as a result of the migrations of its staple food, such as locusts.

For Pallas's Warbler and Yellow-browed Warbler it has been shown that they normally arrive slightly earlier in the northern than the southern parts of Sweden and Britain. This may be at least partly explained by the slightly shorter distances from the breeding grounds.

AFRICAN VAGRANTS

Many African species undertake weather-related movements; in the dry season they migrate to areas where water can be found. Presumably, some of the birds migrating like this are caught by strong southerly winds and 'blown' to Europe, e.g. Allen's Gallinule.

SUBANTARCTIC AND ANTARCTIC VAGRANTS

Many seabirds breeding on Subantarctic islands and on the Antarctic continent spend the southern winter partly in the north Atlantic, e.g. Wilson's Petrel. Others sometimes straggle far north e.g. Black-browed Albatross.

To seabirds the Atlantic represents no obstacle in itself. However, there are two zones (by the Equator and at $30°$ south) where calm conditions or very light winds prevail. For large seabirds which have difficulties flying under such conditions, these zones probably act as effective barriers for northward migration.

Where do vagrant species turn up?

Actually, they can turn up anywhere. Species that are obliged to cross large bodies of water before they reach Europe (mainly Nearctic species) will naturally drop down on to the first piece of suitable land, cover or pool, etc. This is one of the reasons why isolated islands, such as the Isles of Scilly or Fair Isle, hold such an attraction for vagrants. The proportion of non-European to European birds is often comparatively high on such isolated islands. Of course, the actual number of vagrants must surely be larger on the mainland than on these tiny islands, but there the few rarities are swamped by the large numbers of common birds and are thus more difficult to find – less likely to be recorded.

Naturally, the number of vagrants noted in one study area depends to a great extent on the intensity with which the area is being watched. The greater number of North American vagrants recorded in the British Isles, compared to Portugal, for example, is partly a reflection of the much larger number of birdwatchers in Britain and Ireland than in Portugal. However, the strategic position of the British Isles for Nearctic vagrants is perhaps unsurpassed in Europe. Conversely, in the Mediterranean there are a number of small to quite large islands that act as magnets for more southerly or eastern vagrant species.

Has the number of rare birds increased?

Where there has been a dramatic increase in the number of records of a certain species it is often difficult to say whether this is an actual increase or whether it is merely a reflection of the larger number of birdwatchers and their greater expertise in identification. Ring-billed Gull is a good example of a species which belongs in this category, although it seems more likely that the noted increase is mainly accounted for by the increased knowledge about the identification of the species and the greater 'awareness' of it. However, in some species where there has been a recent westward expansion in the USSR, such as Terek Sandpiper, Citrine Wagtail and Greenish Warbler, the increase is almost certainly at least partly real.

Watching rarities

IDENTIFICATION

When an unfamiliar bird is found the observer should always consider first the possibility that it might be an aberrant individual of a more common species. Over the years abnormal individuals of even quite common species have occasionally misled groups of birdwatchers, even experts. A thorough knowledge of the common European birds is fundamental in order to correctly identify any suspected rarity. It is important to ask oneself questions like: "What does a Tree Pipit actually look like? How variable is the head pattern, the streaking on the upper and underparts and the coloration? Can I be 100% sure that the bird I am watching is an Olive-backed Pipit and not just an aberrant Tree Pipit?"

Taking careful fieldnotes and making sketches – no matter how simple – is essential. Remember that characters you think of at the time as unimportant may later prove to be of the utmost importance. Accordingly, try to make your notes as detailed as possible, and try to look at the bird as objectively as possible. "Is it really larger than a Little Stint, or am I fooling myself?" If you carry a camera fitted with a decent telephoto lens, then try to get some photographs, as these are invaluable. Tape-recordings are, of course, also very valuable.

You should quickly summon other birdwatchers, especially those with previous experience of the species concerned. If you are alerted by someone who claims to have discovered a rarity, or if you go on a 'twitch', try to look at the bird as critically as if you had just found it yourself. Don't just assume that the bird has been correctly identified. It is important to remember that the identification of a certain species is not necessarily safer because it has been seen by a large number of people. 'Mass hallucination' has fooled groups of birders many times in the past. However, it is not easy to query the identification of a bird that perhaps hundreds of others have already looked at and agreed what the species is. The important thing is to correctly identify the bird for yourself. There is no merit gained in adding it to your life list or year list, if you have not reached an honest appraisal of all the facts which could lead you to a correct identification.

The fascination of birds, including the rarer species, continues to attract more people to the ranks of serious birdwatchers every day. News of a rarity often spreads quickly, and travelling to see a rare bird – twitching, as it is now called – has become an increasingly popular pursuit. However, it is essential that every one of us takes seriously our responsibility to avoid any harm either to birds or to the environment. The following codes of behaviour have been published by the magazine *British Birds*, both on discovering a rarity in the first place and in "twitching" it afterwards.

Code for rarity-finders

1. The finder should feel no obligation to spread the news of a rarity, whatever the circumstances.

2. Even if inclined to tell others, the finder should first assess the likely number of interested observers, and consider whether the site can cope – without risk of trespass, disturbance or harm to bird, habitat or people's privacy – with such an influx.

3. The landowner, tenant farmer, local people or other birdwatchers should be consulted as appropriate. An explanation of the situation will often prompt an interested and helpful reaction, and allay the understandable concern which may be caused by an unexplained invasion of the area. If highway obstruction is a potential problem, the police may welcome prior warning. On a reserve, the warden should always be among the first to be told.

4. News should not be spread until appropriate arrangements have been made; these may include special wardening, roping-off the viewing site, posting of advisory or directional signs, and arrangements for car parking.

5. Once the decision has been made to spread the news, and preparations made, the message should contain clear instructions for reaching the site and any special arrangements which have been made.

Code for twitchers

1. If you are among the first to hear of a rare bird, satisfy yourself that the site can cope with the likely influx of observers before spreading the news.

2. Respect confidential information.

3. Especially if you have previous experience of visiting rare bird sites, offer advice on any special arrangements which may need to be made, and offer on-site assistance if you are able.

4. Before setting out, ensure that you are fully informed as to how to reach the site, and any special arrangements which have been made.

5. If you pass on the message, do so carefully and in full.

6. At the site, park sensibly and safely, follow any instructions responsibly, and always put the welfare of the bird first.

7. Never turn a blind eye to any misdemeanours committed by others.

8. Do not try to get closer than anyone else to view or – especially – to photograph the bird: let binoculars, telescopes and telephoto lenses cover the distance.

9. Be tactful, informative and friendly towards non-birdwatching onlookers or local people: they will probably be interested to know what is going on.

10. Be patient and restrained, especially if the bird moves suddenly to a new site nearby: give time for a new plan to be devised to cope with the situation.

11. Observe the Country Code at all times.

Rarities Committees

Records of rare birds are vetted annually in at least a dozen European countries by a national Rarities Committee. This consists of a variable number of experts (e.g. 10 in Britain and 6 in Sweden). The observer(s) must submit a detailed description of the bird(s) and the circumstances surrounding the record. The Rarities Committee usually publishes an annual report on rare birds (see Bibliography, p. 433).

Recording a rarity

The following information is necessary when submitting details of any rarity:

- Species name.
- Place of observation (including details of habitat).
- Date, time and length of observation; duration of bird's stay.
- Name(s) of observer(s) finding the bird, who first identified it, and any other observers who are likely to report it.
- Details relating to other forms of observation, such as trapping, discovery of dead bird, or photograph, including name and address of ringer, holder of specimen, or photographer.
- Estimated distance from bird(s). Also give details of type of binoculars and/or telescope used.
- Weather and quality of light during observation.
- Supply a full account of the observation, including details of other species present in the vicinity. Where possible make direct comparison regarding size, habits or detailed comparison of plumage. A full description based on field notes should be written, preferably before consulting the literature. A drawing of the bird(s) is very useful (even if only simple basic sketches).
- Supply summary of previous experience of same or similar species.
- Observer's opinion on the certainty of the identification (100% or not), with discussion on any puzzling character.
- Declaration of any disagreement on the identification (including name(s) of observer(s) who do not concur).

Family GAVIIDAE   Divers

WHITE-BILLED DIVER   *Gavia adamsii*   D **1**

L 76-91cm (30-36"). An arctic species. Winters in fair numbers along N and NW coasts of Norway. Regularly seen in Denmark, Sweden, and Finland – mainly on passage.

All plumages: Largest of the divers, only slightly larger on average than Great Northern Diver, which it closely resembles in all plumages. The colour and pattern of the bill is usually the most reliable character for separating the two species. In summer, the bill is all pale with a distinctive yellowish tinge. In Great Northern the bill is all black; sometimes, however (especially in early spring), the outer part, exceptionally the entire bill, is pale greyish.

In immature and adult winter plumages the bill is pale yellowish. Frequently the inner half of the culmen is dark (exceptionally up to 2/3) and there is often a bluish to dark grey tinge to the sides of the basal part of the bill. Great Northern in corresponding plumage has bill pale greyish, usually with a distinct bluish cast, and invariably the culmen is dark to the tip; also shows darker cutting edges along the distal part of the bill.

The upper mandible tends to be straighter, while the lower mandible shows a more distinct gonydeal angle than in most Great Northerns. But there is some variation, so that 'upturned bill' is only of minor importance in identification. More important is the general carriage of the bill. Habitually swims with the bill pointing slightly upwards, whereas Great Northern holds the bill more level. However, each species may adopt the typical stance of the other for short periods. In the spread wing, the primary shafts are seen to be mostly pale (dark in Great Northern).

Adult summer: Differs from Great Northern in having slightly larger white chequers on the scapulars, also fewer and slightly larger white stripes on the necklace. The gloss on head/neck is purplish rather than greenish, but there is often a faint greenish gloss especially on the crown and ear-coverts.

Adult winter: The sides of the head and neck are generally much paler than in Great Northern, and the contrast between dark and pale areas is less pronounced and more diffusely defined. In Great Northern the head/neck generally looks slightly darker than the upperparts, which is not the case in White-billed. Even birds with exceptionally dark head and neck typically show a diffuse pale area on the sides of the nape and a darker area on the rear ear-coverts, either as an isolated patch of varying shape or just as a downward extension of the dark crown (this pattern is not shared by Great Northern). Full winter plumage is often not reached until late in the autumn/early winter. The moult to summer plumage is usually completed in Apr-May (birds in 'winter' plumage in late spring/summer are thus immature).

Juvenile: Readily distinguished from the winter adult by having contrasting pale fringes to the scapulars; also shows distinctly paler fringes to the mantle, coverts and breast sides. Adults are more uniformly patterned on these areas (under favourable conditions the scapulars can be seen to show slightly paler blocks), although most of the coverts show small white spots, and a few summer scapulars are often retained.

Differs from juvenile Great Northern in much the same characters as described for adults (see above). However, the differences are usually even more striking, as juvenile Great Northern tends to be more extensively dark on the head than adults, and often shows a very indistinct pale eye-ring (always prominent in White-billed). When viewed from behind, usually shows extensive pale areas to the sides of the head and neck (Great Northern usually shows entirely dark head/neck when viewed from behind). The head and neck never appear darker than the upperparts, as is usually the case in Great Northern. Furthermore, tends to show slightly broader and more conspicuous pale fringes to the scapulars than juvenile Great Northern.

Subsequent immature plumages: Juvenile plumage is slowly moulted during the course of the 2nd year to a plumage resembling a winter adult, but lacks the white spots on the coverts. The head and neck progressively become even paler during the spring.

In spring of the 2nd year, plumage sometimes becomes rather pale on the sides of the head and neck, and is thus more similar to White-billed. However, the characteristic head pattern (see adult winter above) is probably never matched by Great Northern. Pattern, colour and general carriage of bill should identify atypical individuals.

During the spring and summer of the 3rd year, the plumage still resembles a winter adult, although it is considerably darker and shows signs of adult summer plumage (Great Northern is normally in full adult summer plumage by this age). In this plumage, bill characters are even more important for distinguishing from immature Great Northern.

Range: Breeds N Siberia, N Alaska and arctic Canada. Has probably bred on Varanger in N Norway. Migratory, wintering at sea south to NW Norway, N Japan and British Columbia.

Status: Rare winter visitor and scarce passage migrant. Approximately 200 individuals winter annually in Norway. In recent years regularly found wintering in small numbers on Baltic coasts. There is a small but regular passage of birds in the Skagerrak and Kattegat and along both the Gulfs of Finland and Bothnia during May.

Many records from Sweden (*c.* 430, with 88 in 1988), Finland (*c.* 200), Denmark (*c.* 130), and British Isles (131). Elsewhere, there are records from the Faeroes (June 1976, June 1982), France (9), Belgium (Dec 1979,Mar-Apr 1987), Netherlands (28), East Germany (6, Mar-Apr, Oct), West Germany (*c.*20), Poland (9), Czechoslovakia (3), Austria (6), Hungary (Nov 1987), Switzerland (Dec 1973, Jan-Mar 1982), Yugoslavia (2), Italy (3), and Spain (2 in Dec 1985).

Family PODICIPEDIDAE   Grebes

PIED-BILLED GREBE   *Podilymbus podiceps*   B **1**

L 30.5-38cm (13.5"). North and South America. Accidental.

All plumages: Distinctly larger than Little Grebe (near size of Slavonian and Black-necked Grebes) with a larger, squarer head, and a proportionally much deeper bill. Lacks 'clown-like' gape of Little.

Adult summer: Unmistakable. Shows black central throat and pale bill with conspicuous black band, and plumage lacks the bright colours shown by European grebes.

Adult winter: Plumage rather similar to Little Grebe, but has a less distinct and less extensive dark cap (paler above-behind eye, unlike Little). Often shows a conspicuous pale eye-ring, which is lacking in Little. Also, the bill is usually more diffusely patterned, and often shows a trace of a dark band. Readily distinguished from Little by its robust size and chunky bill.

Juvenile: Strongly striped on head/neck. However, this plumage is quickly lost and is thus unlikely to be encountered in Europe. Traces of juvenile plumage are sometimes seen in 1st-winter birds.

Range: Breeds North, Central and South America. Mainly sedentary, but inland North American birds are migratory.

Status: Rare transatlantic vagrant to Britain (11). Mainly seen in winter but has been recorded in all months. Some birds long staying, with some individuals returning to the same localities in several consecutive years. Also recorded in Ireland: Co Wexford (May-June 1987) and Co Donegal (Apr 1988), Iceland (Oct 1976) and the Azores (Oct 1927, Oct 1954, Oct 1964, Jan 1969, Oct 1985).

Family DIOMEDEIDAE   Albatrosses

BLACK-BROWED ALBATROSS *Diomedea melanophris*   B **2**

L 83-93cm (32.5-36.5"). WS *c*. 240cm (94.5"). Pelagic. S Hemisphere. Very rare (mainly Mar-Oct).

All plumages: Huge, long-winged seabird with typical flight action of such. In fresh winds, glides in up and down wheeling arcs on stiff wings, revealing upper and underside alternately, and only occasionally flapping. In light winds, flaps wings more often, but prefers to settle on sea in calm conditions. When taking off, runs into wind with outstretched wings, usually flapping until clear of waves.

Dark mantle/scapulars and upperwings, broad dark margins to the underwings, and grey tail. Blackish eyebrows give characteristic 'frowning' look. The distinctive plumage combined with size, silhouette, and flight action should readily separate it from any European species. Some young subadult Gannets might be confused by the beginner, but they have a quite different shape and have a buff crown and nape, white leading edge to the upperwings, dark on the rump, and a different underwing pattern. See Yellow-nosed Albatross, p. 30.

Adult: Has bright yellowish-orange bill and immaculate white head/neck and underparts.

Juvenile: Bill is greyish or horn coloured with blackish tip. Shows a partial or complete greyish band on foreneck and greyish nape/hindneck, and also has less white on the central underwing.

Subsequent immature plumages: Intermediate between juvenile and adult. The bill gradually attains adult coloration, starting with the sides of the upper mandible, and in later stages becoming dull yellowish with dark tip. Full adult plumage is only acquired after several years.

Note: Juvenile could be confused with juvenile Grey-Headed Albatross *D. chrysostoma* (circumpolar, S Oceans), which could possibly occur in Europe. However, the latter generally has a darker head, an even darker underwing, and a blackish bill.

Range: Breeds on islands off S South America, on South Georgia, Kerguelen, Heard, Antipodes, Macquarie, and Campbell Is. Ranges at sea in S Oceans generally north to the Tropic of Capricorn. Accidental in Morocco.
Status: Rare vagrant to Europe. The majority of records are from the British Isles (26 identified from a total of 47 albatrosses). There are a few others from Iceland (July 1966), Faeroes (2), Norway (May 1943, May 1979), Spitsbergen (June 1878), West Germany (Oct 1988) and Spain (July 1984, Dec 1987). A few individuals have summered at gannetries for a number of years. One female returned each summer to the Faeroes for 34 years up to May 1894. More recently, an adult has been present each summer at Hermaness on Unst, Shetlands (1972-July 1987, then unexpectedly returned on 27th March 1990 and present for about 12 days). There are also a few additional records in Europe of albatrosses not specifically identified (June-Oct) from France (June 1988), Belgium (Dec 1980, Sept 1983), Denmark (4), Norway (Oct 1988), West Germany (Sept 1988), Spain (3) and Gibraltar (Mar 1987).

YELLOW-NOSED ALBATROSS   *Diomedea chlororhynchos*   A **2**

L 71-81cm (28-32"). WS 178-205cm (70-81"). Pelagic. S Hemisphere. One or two records presently under consideration.
All plumages: Resembles Black-browed Albatross, but is slightly smaller and slimmer, with a proportionally longer bill, neck and tail. Dark margins to the underwings (especially to leading edge) are usually much narrower.
Adult: Further characterized by blackish bill with yellow culmen turning pinkish at the tip. Nape and sides of the head suffused pale greyish.
Juvenile: Resembles the adult, but head all white and bill wholly blackish. The underwing pattern is similar, but a few may show a wider black leading edge, approaching pattern of Black-browed.
Subsequent immature plumages: Intermediate juvenile/adult.
Note: Both adult and immature can be confused with adult and subadult Grey-headed Albatross. This shows a wider dark leading edge to the underwings, and the adult has a yellow ridge not only to the upper, but also to the lower mandible.
Range: S Atlantic and Indian Oceans, east to E Australian seas. Breeds Tristan da Cunha, Gough, St Paul, Amsterdam, Prince Edward Is, and Crozets. Strays north to E USA and has been reliably identified at least 13 times on Atlantic coast of North America. Otherwise rarely seen N of Lat. 20° S.
Status: A record from Iceland (*c*. 1844) preserved as a skeleton is either Yellow-nosed or Grey-headed Albatross. Britain: adult reported 80km S of the Lizard, Cornwall (29th Apr 1985*).

WANDERING ALBATROSS   *Diomedea exulans*   A **2**

L 107-135cm (42-53"). WS 254-351cm (100-138"). Pelagic. S Hemisphere. Accidental.
All plumages: Huge; on wing-span one of the very largest species in the world. Shape/flight similar to the previous two species. Massive, pinkish bill.
Adult: Mostly white with blackish remiges. Unlikely to be confused with any European species. Females are slightly smaller and tend to

show more dark markings than males, but subadult males also show a similar plumage.

Juvenile: Plumage very different from the adult, but still unmistakable: all-brown with white face and largely white underwings.

Subsequent immature plumages: Adult plumage is progressively attained over a period of many years (perhaps up to 20-30). Accordingly, there are a large number of subadult plumages, intermediate between juvenile and adult.

Range: Circumpolar in S Oceans, north to Tropic of Capricorn. Breeds South Georgia, Inaccessible, Gough, Amsterdam, Marion, Prince Edward, Crozet, Kerguelen, Macquarie, Auckland, Campbell, and Antipodes Is.

Status: Accidental in France (1830); Belgium (near Antwerp – dead, Sept 1833; Blankenberg, West Vlaanderen – dead, 27th Apr 1887); Sicily (Oct 1957); and *c*. 80km off Portugal (Oct 1963).

Family PROCELLARIIDAE   Petrels and Shearwaters

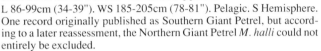

SOUTHERN GIANT PETREL *Macronectes giganteus*   A **2**

L 86-99cm (34-39"). WS 185-205cm (78-81"). Pelagic. S Hemisphere. One record originally published as Southern Giant Petrel, but according to a later reassessment, the Northern Giant Petrel *M. halli* could not entirely be excluded.

All plumages: Very large. Resembles the smaller albatrosses, but has a proportionally stouter body and shorter wings. Also has less graceful flight with more wing-flapping. Superficially resembles a giant dark-phase Fulmar and has a huge fulmar-like bill.

Adult dark morph: Basically dark with a pale head and breast and some pale mottling on the rest of the underparts. Also shows a pale leading edge to the underside of the wing.

Adult pale morph: Wholly white with scattered dark patches.

Juvenile dark morph: Wholly dark (lacks pale face and pale underwing of juvenile Wandering Albatross).

Juvenile pale morph: Similar to adult white morph (see above).

Subsequent immature plumages of dark morph: Gradually acquires adult plumage over a long period of time, first apparent on the head.

Note: Northern Giant Petrel (Circumpolar, S Hemisphere) is very similar to the dark morph of the Southern Giant Petrel (white morph is unknown in Northern). Adult Northern usually (but not always) has a darker head (only face whitish), paler underparts and dark leading edge to the underwing, but note that subadult Southern can be very similar in these respects. Immatures are very difficult to identify. However, at all ages, the colour pattern of the bill is diagnostic: Northern has reddish tip to upper and dark tip to lower mandible, whereas Southern has both mandibles greenish-tipped.

Range: Breeds in Antarctica and on subantarctic islands, and ranges at sea throughout the S Oceans.

Status: Accidental in France: One seen off Ouessant (Nov 1967), subsequently accepted as *Macronectes sp.* as species not fully determined. Britain: Humberside, an individual reported off Flamborough Head on 4th July 1988*, could not be attributed to either the northern or southern species.

BLACK-CAPPED PETREL *Pterodroma hasitata* A* **3**

L 35-46cm (14-18"). WS 89-102cm (35-40"). Pelagic. W Atlantic. Two records.

All plumages: Has diagnostic pattern and is unlikely to be confused with any European species. Theoretically confusable with Great Shearwater which is larger, with a proportionally longer and slimmer bill, dark forehead, usually narrower white collar, less white at the base of the tail above, paler upperparts, less distinct dark diagonal underwing-bar, and dark belly patch (latter often difficult to see).

Black-capped is said to have characteristic flight and jizz: in light to moderate winds it rises with a few quick wingbeats and then declines on stiff, bowed and angled wings – thus flying with a characteristic rising and falling action. In strong winds, glides almost continuously in high sweeping arcs, often reaching considerable height. Ageing apparently very difficult.

Range: Caribbean, breeding at a few sites in the Dominican Republic, Cuba and Haiti. Disperses to adjacent sea areas along the western edge of the Gulf Stream, south to NE Brazil and north to central E USA. Although numbers have declined (formerly bred on several islands in West Indies), recent pelagic surveys off the Atlantic coast of the USA (Florida-Maryland) have shown that, especially in spring and autumn, Capped Petrels are far from rare over the inner edge of the Gulf Stream.

Status: Accidental in Britain: One found inland Norfolk in Mar or Apr 1850; 1st-year female found, long dead, on tideline at Barmston, Humberside on 16th Dec 1984.

BULWER'S PETREL *Bulweria bulwerii* B **3**

L 26-27cm (10"). WS 65-70cm (26.5"). Pelagic. Nearest breeding area – Azores and off NW Africa. Accidental.

All plumages: Distinctly larger than storm-petrels but smaller than shearwaters (except for Little). General appearance rather intermediate between these two groups. It is long-winged and long-tailed, with the tail typically looking pointed (wedge-shaped when fanned). The pale upperwing bar may be difficult to see at long range, so that the bird then appears wholly dark. In light winds the flight is weaving and erratic, the bird giving a few wingbeats interspersed by short glides low over the surface. In fresh winds the flight is more direct, with the bird gliding more and beating the wings less often. Ageing apparently very difficult.

Note: There is a record of Jouanin's Petrel *B. fallax* (numerous in Arabian Sea, but main nesting areas still remain undiscovered) from Italy (see below). Jouanin's is blackish-brown and most birds show a pale upperwing diagonal bar like Bulwer's. However, it is distinctly larger with a shorter/thicker bill, and has a proportionally larger head and broader wings/tail (latter less pointed and shorter).

A specimen, one of three reported seen during a storm, was collected on 2nd Nov 1953 at Cimadolmo, Treviso, Italy. Cramp and Simmons (1977), mention that 'identity certain but record so extraordinary that unnatural origin, such as release by a sailor, must be regarded as possibility (Jouanin)'. However, it has since straggled to the NW Hawaiian chain (Clapp 1971), so may have a larger distribution or vagrancy potential than suspected.

Range: In the Atlantic breeds on the Azores, Desertas, Madeira, Salvage, Canary and Cape Verde Islands. Also breeds in the Pacific. Dispersive in the non-breeding season. Accidental in Morocco.

Status: Accidental in Britain (May 1837, Feb 1908), Ireland: Cape Clear, Co Cork (Aug 1975), France (May 1967, June 1977, Jan 1986). France/Italy: one on a lightship between Corsica and Genoa (June 1898). Spain: Vigo (June 1983), and a remarkable record of 14 birds seen off the Costa Brava (29th Apr 1984).

LITTLE SHEARWATER *Puffinus assimilis*   C 3

L 25-30cm (11"). WS 58-67cm (25"). Pelagic. Nearest breeding areas – Azores and off NW Africa. The majority of records are from the British Isles (Apr-Oct).

All plumages: Closely resembles Manx Shearwater (form found breeding in N Atlantic), but is distinctly smaller, with proportionally shorter and more rounded wings, and shorter bill. Flight action is characteristically more fluttering, showing less gliding and banking than demonstrated by Manx. Jizz and flight action often combine to give rather auk-like appearance. Also differs from Manx in having a whiter face, which is most pronounced in the race *baroli*, where the eye is normally encircled by white (in race *boydi* and in some *baroli* dark crown intrudes down to lower edge of eye, but not well below eye as in Manx). Further, *baroli* has a less extensive dark tip to the underwing than shown by Manx, while *boydi* usually has much dark on the under-tail-coverts (all white in both Manx and *baroli*). Ageing apparently very difficult.

Voice: At the breeding colony, gives a repeated, soft, whistling *whi-whiririri-huu*, which is higher pitched, less harsh and coarse, with more regular rhythm than corresponding calls of Manx Shearwater (calls given at night).

Note: Audubon's Shearwater *P. lherminieri* (with the nearest breeding grounds in the W Atlantic) which is only slightly larger, could possibly occur in Europe. It is very similar to the Little Shearwater, particularly the race *boydi* (considered by some authorities to be better placed with Audubon's). Audubon's has a proportionately longer tail (probably only compared to *baroli*); no white encircling the eye (as in many Little); generally has dark on the distal undertail-coverts (also shared by *boydi*); a broader dark tip to the underwing (especially when compared with *baroli*); and flesh coloured, not bluish legs/feet.

Range: *P. a. baroli* breeds on the Azores, Desertas, Salvage, and Canary Is. *P. a. boydi* breeds on Cape Verde Islands. Other races occur in the S Hemisphere. There are some 20 records from the E coast of North America. Accidental in Morocco.

Status: Rare vagrant. The British Isles' unique position for pelagics accounts for the vast majority of European records (80), mainly Apr-Oct. Also, France (15+), Belgium (Sept 1990*), Denmark (Sept 1912), West Germany (*c.* 5), Austria (3), Italy (3), Gibraltar (2) and Spain (3).

There is one extraordinary British record of at least one bird calling from a burrow among a Welsh breeding colony of Manx Shearwaters (June-July 1981-82).

The Little Shearwater is not known for any definite migratory patterns, which are typical of many of the larger *Puffinus* species. However, a more recent assessment of the movements of Little Shearwaters in the Atlantic has shown a greater dispersal in some birds than had previously been suspected. It has been suggested that small numbers may circulate in British waters as does Cory's Shearwater.

Family HYDROBATIDAE   Storm-petrels

WILSON'S PETREL *Oceanites oceanicus*   D **3**
L 15-19cm (6-7.5"). WS 38-42cm (16"). Pelagic – mainly antarctic species. The recent interest shown in pelagic trips in the 'S W Approaches' has shown Wilson's to be a regular visitor in late summer.
All plumages: Typical small, dark storm-petrel showing a conspicuous white patch at the base of the tail. Distinctly larger than Storm Petrel but rather smaller than Leach's Petrel. Differs from Storm in prominent pale upperwing bar and lack of a white patch on the underwing.

Differs from Leach's in shorter wings (particularly the arm), which are usually held straighter and less angled when gliding (less bend at carpal joint and almost straight trailing edge), and the tail is squarely cut-off (forked in Leach's). The pale upperwing bar is not as prominent as shown by Leach's, and does not extend to the carpal joint. The white patch at the base of the tail is more prominent, as rump lacks Leach's dark central division, and there is also more white to the sides of the rear flanks/undertail-coverts.

Under favourable conditions the tips of the toes can be seen to project beyond the tail tip – a further distinction from both Storm and Leach's. Under exceptional conditions the webs of the toes can be seen to be yellowish (blackish in Storm and Leach's).

The flight differs from both Storm and Leach's Petrels. The travelling flight is stronger, more forceful, with fewer and less fluttering wingbeats and more gliding than in Storm Petrel (reminiscent of Swallow, whereas Storm Petrel is more similar to small bat). Compared to Leach's it is generally less veering, with slightly faster, shallower wingbeats and less gliding. When feeding the flight is bounding and bouncing, with the wings often raised in a shallow V and the legs dangling, feet pattering the surface, giving the impression of almost 'walking on the water'. See also Madeiran Petrel p. 35. Ageing apparently very difficult.
Voice: Harsh, grating, stuttering *kerr kerr kerr kerr* given by adult at breeding colonies (at night).
Range: Breeds on many subantarctic islands and antarctic coastlines. After breeding (which takes place in northern winter), migrates far north into the Atlantic, Indian, and Pacific Oceans, where it often occurs in large numbers (Apr-Sept). During the northern summer some occupy waters in the Cape Verdes, Azores and Madeiran Seas up to the Bay of Biscay.
Status: Wilson's is known to occur well off-shore in late summer (e.g. sea areas adjacent to continental shelf of Europe). A few may also enter the Mediterranean, exceptionally east to Sardinia.

Accepted records up to 1988 are as follows: British Isles (14) Aug-Oct, mainly from SW Britain/SW Ireland (plus many more found in the Western Approaches – see below). Also reported from Portugal (e.g. 65 noted 10-15km NW of Cape St. Vincent on 22nd Aug 1984, and *c.* 40 nearby on 29th Aug 1989), Spain (32), France (5), Italy/Sardinia (2), West Germany (2) and Denmark (Sept 1988).

In Iceland, an adult was caught in a breeding colony of Storm and Leach's Petrels on 31st July 1988. There is another interesting record of a bird which landed on a ship west of Spitsbergen on 25th Nov 1980.

The recent interest shown in pelagic trips off SW Britain during the month of August has produced many more records of this species e.g. 1986 (8), 1987 (70), 1988 (*c.* 100), and confirms that Wilson's is a regular visitor in European waters well off-shore in late summer. There are also earlier records at sea off Ireland with an exceptional 46 seen 40km SW off Dursey Is. Co Cork on 23rd Aug 1974; also 23 seen *c.* 50km S of Cape Clear, Co Cork on 18th-19th July 1981.

WHITE-FACED PETREL   *Pelagodroma marina*   A **3**

L 20cm (8"). WS 42cm (16.5"). Pelagic. Nearest breeding area is off NW Africa. Very few records.

All plumages: Unmistakable. A grey-brown storm-petrel with a contrasting pale greyish upperwing-bar and grey rump, distinctly patterned face and white underparts (including underwing-coverts). Has characteristic wing shape, and feet project well beyond the tip of the almost square tail. The travelling flight is erratic and weaving. When feeding has a distinctive fast low flight, darting from side to side and bouncing over the water (skips off surface with both feet), on stiff-winged glides.

Ageing apparently very difficult.

Range: In the N Atlantic, breeds on Salvage and Cape Verde Islands. In 1987, the first recorded breeding was reported from the eastern islets of the Canary Is. Also breeds in S Hemisphere. Probably disperses into C Atlantic in non-breeding season; vagrants have occurred along the east coast of the USA (at least 47 records since 1885 in western Atlantic). Accidental in Morocco.

Status: Accidental in the Azores (May 1912); Britain: Colonsay, Inner Hebrides, one caught (Jan 1897); France, Bay of Biscay (Aug 1963); Netherlands, Monster (Nov 1974); and several reported off the coast of Portugal (Aug 1962).

MADEIRAN PETREL   *Oceanodroma castro*   R Br **3**

L 19-21cm (8"). WS 42-45cm (17"). Pelagic. Breeds Azores, Farilhõe Is off Portugal, and off NW Africa (also in the Pacific). Very few records from the rest of Europe.

All plumages: Closely resembles Wilson's and Leach's Petrels. Size intermediate between these two. The wings are shorter and slightly broader than Leach's but longer and, when gliding, more angular than Wilson's, and the tail has a shallow fork or may look square. The pale upperwing-bar is less conspicuous than in Leach's, and generally slightly less prominent than in Wilson's. The white patch at the base of the tail extends more onto the sides of the rear flanks/undertail-coverts than in Leach's, but less than in Wilson's. The feet do not project beyond the tip of the tail like Wilson's.

The travelling flight is said to be more direct, less erratic, than in Leach's Petrel, with slightly quicker and shallower wingbeats. In fresh winds it glides more than in light winds. When feeding it often hangs motionless against the wind with wings slightly raised, legs dangling, feet pattering the surface. Ageing apparently very difficult.

Voice: Calls uttered at breeding colony, after sunset, given as *kerr wheecha wheecha wheecha wheeeechuh* and interspersed with *cheeve-cheeve* sounds at intervals.

Range: Breeds Azores, Madeira, Tenerife, Cape Verde Islands, St Helena, and Ascension Is. In July 1980 it was discovered breeding on the Farilhões, 17.5km off the coast of Portugal (more recently 50 pairs found breeding close by on the Berlengas Is.). It may also have a fairly wide dispersal into the mid-Atlantic or even further west, as indicated by several records from the east coast of North and South America. Also breeds in the Pacific. Accidental in Morocco.

Status: Accidental in the rest of Europe. Britain (Nov 1911, Sept 1984*), Ireland (Oct 1931), France (Oct 1984, Aug 1988), and Spain (Feb 1970, Jan 1982). The difficulty of distinguishing this storm-petrel satisfactorily in the field probably accounts for the great rarity of its European records.

Family PHAETHONTIDAE   Tropicbirds

RED-BILLED TROPICBIRD   *Phaethon aethereus*   A **4**

L 46-50cm (19") + 46-56cm (20") tail streamers in adult. WS 99-106 (39-42"). Pelagic. Nearest breeding area is off W Africa. Accidental in Azores and Portugal.

All plumages: A tern-like seabird and unlikely to be confused with any European species. Mainly white, with black on the outer wings, black mask through the eye, and blackish barring on the upperparts and coverts. Flight is usually rather high above the surface, with regular wingbeats, interspersed by occasional glides. Feeds by plunging vertically, often after hovering.

Adult: Red bill and very long, white tail streamers.

Juvenile: Differs from the adult in having a yellow bill with dark tip, slightly more coarsely barred upperparts and the tail feathers have dark spots at their tips but lack streamers.

Note: Requires to be separated from the White-tailed Tropicbird *P. lepturus* which could conceivably reach Europe from its nearest breeding grounds in the W Atlantic. This is readily separated from Red-billed by its all-white upperparts, broad black diagonal band on the inner-wings, less black on the hand (lacks black on primary coverts), and has an orange bill. Juvenile White-tailed is best told from juvenile Red-billed by the white primary coverts (black outer greater and partly black outer median primary coverts in Red-billed).

Range: Breeds on Cape Verde Islands, islets off Senegal, St Helena, West Indies and in the E Pacific. Also in the Red Sea, Persian Gulf and Arabian Sea. Somewhat dispersive in the non-breeding season. Vagrants have reached Madeira (3, Aug-Sept) and Canary Is. (2, Mar 1989).

Status: Accidental in the Azores. Portugal: an individual reported 162km due west of Cabo Sardão on 13th Aug 1988. Netherlands: Egmond aan Zee, male found dead on 27th Jan 1985, but record now considered of uncertain provenance.

Family SULIDAE   Gannets and Boobies

RED-FOOTED BOOBY *Sula sula*   A **4**

L 66-77cm (26-30"). WS 91-101cm (36-40"). Pelagic. Tropical Oceans. One record from Norway.

Adult pale morph: Rather small. Plumage resembles Masked Booby. Black patches on the under primary coverts and bare part coloration are diagnostic features. Also occurs in both dark and intermediate morphs.

Juvenile: Like adult dark morph but dark bill and yellowish-grey legs/feet.

Range: In the Atlantic breeds Caribbean, and islands off Venezuela and Brazil and on Ascension. Also in the Pacific and Indian Oceans. Somewhat dispersive outside the breeding season. Vagrant to Madeira.

Status: Accidental in Norway: Immature seen Mølen, Vestfold on 29th June 1985.

MASKED BOOBY *Sula dactylatra*   A **4**

L 81-92cm (34"). WS *c.* 150cm (60"). Pelagic. Nearest breeding in West Indies. Two records from Spain.

Adult: Readily separated from adult Gannet by the black secondaries and tail but, rarely, subadult Gannets are similar in this respect. From these it differs in having more extensive black on the inner wing (black greater coverts, humerals, and tips to longest scapulars); all-white head, yellowish bill, more extensive, dark grey-blue facial mask, and paler grey legs/feet.

Juvenile: Distinctly different from immature Gannet. The head/neck, upperparts and coverts are brown, without white spots. The underparts, including collar around the neck, and most of the underwing-coverts, are white. Bare part coloration as in the adult, but bill duller and more greenish. Can be confused with adult Brown Booby (see below).

Subsequent immature plumages: Intermediate juvenile/adult.

Range: Largely coincides with Red-footed Booby. Vagrant in Morocco.

Status: Accidental in Spain: adult in Puerto Sotogrande, Cádiz (10th Oct 1985) and an adult at Torremolinos (14th Dec 1985).

BROWN BOOBY *Sula leucogaster*   A **4**

L 64-74cm (25-29"). WS 132-150 (52-59"). Nearest breeding in West Indies, off W Africa and in the Red Sea. Three records.

Adult: Basically resembles a small, mostly dark Gannet. The plumage is all dark brown, except for white lower breast to undertail-coverts and central inner part of the underwing. Bare part coloration varies seasonally and geographically. The colour of the orbital ring also varies between the sexes (blue in male, yellowish with dark spot in front in female), cf. juvenile Masked Booby.

Juvenile: The pale parts are sullied with brownish, and the bill and facial skin is greyish.

Subsequent immature plumages: Transitional plumages between juvenile and adult can be seen during the approximately 1½ years that it takes to reach adult plumage.

Range: Breeds widely in the tropics in the Atlantic, Indian and Pacific Oceans. Vagrants have reached Morocco (3).

Status: Accidental in Azores: off São Miguel, summer 1966. Spain: Benalmádena, Málaga, adult on 28th May 1983; Torremolinos, immature on 9th Sept 1986.

Family PHALACROCORACIDAE   Cormorants and Shags

DOUBLE-CRESTED CORMORANT   *Phalacrocorax auritus*   A **4**

L 66-81cm (26-32"). WS 135cm (54"). North America. Recently in Britain (winter).

All plumages: Very similar to Cormorant but is slightly smaller, with a slightly smaller bill. The nape/hindneck is usually fuller, which is often obvious also in flight. Cormorant frequently shows typical 'angular nape'.

The bare skin at the base of the lower mandible is very similar to that of the *sinensis* subspecies of Cormorant in extent and shape, but slightly more extensive and slightly differently shaped than the nominate subspecies of Cormorant (see figure). There is no gular feathering; Cormorant has a prominent wedge of gular feathering (see figure). However, note that in Cormorant the gular feathering can be very difficult to discern in the field.

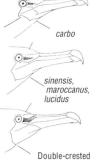

carbo

sinensis,
maroccanus,
lucidus

Double-crested
Cormorant

The upper part of the lores is contrastingly pale orange, forming a distinct pale orange stripe (sometimes this stripe is less well-defined, since the lower part of the lores is pale orange with small dark feathers, and in some juveniles the stripe is rather poorly marked). In immature and non-breeding adult Cormorants the lores are pale yellow or orange, with a variable number of tiny, dark feathers. In breeding Cormorant the lores are dark grey. The gular skin is orange, while on average it is more yellow in Cormorant. The lower mandible is frequently largely yellow (at least in immatures), whereas in Cormorant it is usually ivory (perhaps rarely with pale yellow tinge).

There are only 12 tail-feathers (14 in Cormorant), although this is very hard to see. Also beware of birds moulting the tail.

The Shag is slightly smaller, with slightly thinner bill, and shows distinctly smaller areas of bare skin on the lores and at the base of the lower mandible, and there is a short wedge of gular feathering. The Shag's lores are either all dark, or the lower part is brownish-buffish.

Adult breeding: All-dark, with the mantle, scapulars and wings slightly contrastingly tinged bronzy-brown, similar to Cormorant. It does not show extensively white head/neck as in breeding Cormorant. Never shows any white on "thigh", as in breeding Cormorant.

Adult non-breeding: Like adult breeding, but less glossy on the head/neck. Shows very little or no pale on throat and ear-coverts, unlike many adult non-breeding Cormorants.

Juvenile: Similar to juvenile Cormorant but is typically medium brown to brownish-whitish on throat, foreneck, breast and upper belly/flanks, gradually turning darker brown on the lower belly/flanks and 'thighs' (throat and upper foreneck can be rather dark brown, with a narrow pale margin to the upper throat). In immature Cormorants the belly is whitish, contrasting with darker foreneck/breast and flanks, and the upper throat often shows a large pale patch. Older subadult and a few juvenile Cormorants show only very little whitish on the centre of the belly. In some juvenile Cormorants the breast and most of the foreneck are whitish (as a rule in African subspecies *lucidus* and *maroccanus*), but unlike in Double-crested the *entire* belly is whitish.

Juvenile Shag is uniformly brown below, with darker 'thigh' and usually a thin pale stripe running down the centre of the foreneck and belly and a pale patch on the rear belly (Mediterranean subspecies *desmarestii*, as well as some strongly bleached northern birds in their 1st spring/summer, are extensively whitish below). Shag also usually shows a slightly or conspicuously paler panel on the upperwing-coverts, and the insides of the tarsi as well as the webs between the toes are pinkish or brownish-yellow.

Subsequent immature plumages: From the spring of the 2nd year the plumage starts to change appearance, but full adult plumage is not attained until in the 3rd or 4th year. Young subadults are told from juvenile by often showing a mixture of feathers of different generations, notably on the scapulars and wings. Adult-type scapulars and coverts are more rounded at the tips and slightly more distinctly patterned than juvenile. The belly shows rather large dark spots instead of indistinct dark streaking as in juvenile, and the iris is emerald green (dark greenish-grey in juvenile).

Subadult Double-crested Cormorants are characterized by the whitish breast/lower foreneck (often entire foreneck and throat whitish), contrasting with dark rest of the underside. This pattern is not shown by European Cormorants, but subadult African Cormorants can be very similar in this respect.

Range: Breeds along the coast of North America and in the interior of N USA/S Canada. NE coastal and inland populations are migratory.

Status: One immature at Billingham, Cleveland, Britain from at least 11th Jan-29th Apr 1989, and a similar individual reported on the Isles of Scilly in Nov 1990*.

Family PELECANIDAE   Pelicans

DALMATIAN PELICAN   *Pelecanus crispus*   R Br* **4**

L 160-180cm (67"). WS 270-320cm (116"). SE Europe to Asia. Accidental elsewhere.

All plumages: Could only be confused with White Pelican. Easily identified in flight, when the pale underwing with diffuse darker tips to the remiges can be seen. Adult White has a white underwing with sharply contrasting blackish remiges, and juvenile shows dark remiges and pale underwing-coverts with dark bands (see figure).

Dalmatian Pelican

It shows an untidy, curly crest on the nape as opposed to a loosely hanging crest in White (can be very indistinct in adult non-breeding and immature of both species). The bare part coloration also differs: The legs are grey (flesh-coloured in White), and the iris is pale (dark in White). Note also the smaller amount of bare skin around the eye and the different shape of the feathering on the forehead and at the base of the lower mandible (see figure, p. 40).

White Pelican

Adult: The plumage is basically duskier, without the often prominent pinkish tinge of adult White Pelican. The bare skin around the eye is pale yellowish or whitish, apparently turning purplish for a short period

White Pelican
(m below)

during breeding (pinkish in White), and in the breeding season the gular pouch is orange (yellow in White).

Juvenile: Much paler on the head/neck, upperparts and upperwing-coverts than juvenile White Pelican.

Subsequent immature plumages: Gradually attains adult plumage over a period of probably approximately three years.

Range and status: In Europe, breeds in Albania (10+ pairs), Yugoslavia (15+ pairs), Bulgaria (30-90 pairs), Greece (55-200 pairs), and in the Rumanian Danube delta (now only 25-40 pairs). Also locally and sparsely in Turkey, Iran, USSR, Mongolia and possibly in China. Has declined dramatically since the last century, from probably some millions of pairs to a total world population estimated at 500-1400 pairs. However, this is obviously an underestimate as in Jan 1988, 2,900 discovered wintering in Pakistan. It has disappeared from former breeding colonies on the Rhine, the Scheldt and the Elbe, and from Hungary and from 7 out of 9 breeding colonies in Greece. It winters mainly in Greece, Turkey, northern parts of the Indian subcontinent, a few in China. Accidental in West Germany, Czechoslovakia, Italy (9), Israel, Cyprus and N Africa. Records farther north may be escapes.

Dalmatian Pelican   White Pelican

Family FREGATIDAE   Frigatebirds

MAGNIFICENT FRIGATEBIRD *Fregata magnificens*   A **4**

L 89-114cm (35-45"). WS 217-244cm (85-96"). Tropical Atlantic and E Pacific Oceans. A few records (Mar-Nov).

All plumages: Very large. Dark plumage, long, narrow, kinked wings, and long, forked tail impart unique jizz. A formidable flier, spending virtually all its time in the air, only exceptionally alighting on the sea. Glides and soars effortlessly, often at considerable height. The occasional wing-beats are slow and deep, and it often performs remarkable aerial manoeuvres. Snatches food from surface or, rarely, ground and sometimes steals food from other seabirds.

Adult male: All-black, with a red throat pouch which is inflatable (only blown up when displaying in breeding season).

Adult female: Blackish with a large, whitish patch on the breast, and also has a paler, diagonal upperwing bar.

Juvenile: Resembles the adult female, but has slightly more white on the underparts, and a whitish head.

Subsequent immature plumages: Adult plumage probably attained in four to six years, during which time the plumage changes progressively. Plumage variation thus considerable.

Note: There are four other *Fregata* species in the world. Although they are probably unlikely candidates for the European list, they should be considered when a frigatebird is encountered in Europe (see Harrison 1983 for identification).

Range: Breeds in W Atlantic, from lower Florida Keys (USA) down to S Brazil, and in E Pacific from Baja California, south to Galapagos and Ecuador. A few pairs breed Cape Verde Islands (Boa Vista). Vagrants have reached the Canary Is.

Status: Accidental. There are about a dozen records of frigatebirds for Europe, however, only six safely identified as Magnificent: France

(Oct 1852, Mar 1902); Britain, Inner Hebrides (July 1953); Denmark (Mar 1968); Spain (Sept 1985); Azores (Nov, before 1903).

Unidentified frigatebirds have also occurred in Britain (Aug 1960), Ireland (Aug 1973, June 1988), Belgium (July 1975, Aug 1978), Norway (Sept 1983), Sweden (Oct 1983), and Spain (May 1983).

Family ARDEIDAE   Bitterns and Herons

AMERICAN BITTERN   *Botaurus lentiginosus*   C 5
L 60-85cm (24-33.5"). WS *c.* 110cm (43"). North America. Vagrant (more frequent in past), mainly in late autumn.

Adult: Very similar to closely related Bittern, although is slightly smaller, and has a proportionally longer bill, generally with darker culmen. Forehead and crown are dull chestnut (blackish in Bittern). There is normally a distinct dark eye-stripe, usually lacking in Bittern. The neck shows more stripes, and the sides of the neck and hindneck lack the distinct fine barring of Bittern. There is also a prominent blackish stripe on the sides of the neck (continuation of moustachial stripe). Mantle, scapulars and coverts are generally less coarsely marked than in Bittern, which shows more chevron-like markings, particularly on the coverts.

In flight, the remiges and primary coverts appear uniformly dark with rather broad, rufous tips to the inner primaries, outer secondaries and greater primary coverts. In Bittern the remiges and primary coverts can be seen to be distinctly barred.

Juvenile: Similar to the adult but lacks the blackish continuation of the moustachial stripe on the side of the neck.

Voice: Usually silent except in the breeding season, when the male is said to call *gloup, gloup...* followed by a pumping *oonk KA-lunk, oonk KA-lunk, oonk KA-lunk*.

Habitat and behaviour: Similar to Bittern, hiding in dense vegetation of ponds, lakes, marshes etc. Usually difficult to see unless flushed, but like Bittern often flies from one spot to another at dusk and dawn. Like Bittern it can freeze with its bill pointing straight up when alarmed.

Range: Most of North America (except far north and some southern parts). After breeding migrates or disperses south (mainly Sept-Oct) to S USA, Mexico and West Indies. Vagrants have reached Greenland and the Canary Is.

Status: Rare vagrant. The majority of records are from the British Isles (60), of which *c.* 75% before 1914 (only 10 records since the end of 1957, of which 5 have been in Ireland), all months Sept-Mar, mainly Oct-Nov. There are also a few records from Iceland (6), Faeroes (2), Norway (Aug 1956), Denmark (Nov 1961), Channel Islands, Spain (Jan 1961, Oct 1982), and the Azores (10).

LEAST BITTERN   *Ixobrychus exilis*   A 5
L 28-36cm (11-14"). WS 40-45cm (16.5"). North and South America. Accidental.

All plumages: Even smaller than Little Bittern, which it resembles in all plumages. Shows diagnostic, contrasting deep rufous greater coverts, leading edge to the arm and tips to the alula, greater primary coverts and most of the trailing edge of the wing. The tertials are mostly deep rufous. Apart from the greater coverts and tertials, the rufous pattern of the wing is normally only seen in flight. Little Bittern lacks rufous on the wings.

Adult male: Further differs from adult male Little Bittern by deep rufous on the ear-coverts (just below black crown), and on the hind-neck and sides of the neck. Also, by a narrow pale stripe on either side of the mantle.

Adult female: The black parts of the adult male's plumage are replaced by dark brown, and the neck and underparts are more streaked. Further distinguished from adult female Little Bittern by the uniformly dark mantle and scapulars, with a narrow pale stripe on either side of the mantle (Little shows distinct pale edges to the feathers of the mantle and scapulars). Little can be rather rufous on the upper ear-coverts and hind-neck/sides of neck, but it is not quite as deeply coloured as Least.

Juvenile: Resembles the adult female but is distinguished by its more rufous mantle and scapulars, usually with distinct pale tips and darker centres. Also tends to be slightly more heavily streaked on the neck, especially in juvenile female. Juvenile female normally shows distinct, dark triangular markings on the centres of the lesser and median coverts (lacking in juvenile male, which also tends to be more blackish on crown). Apart from the wing pattern it also differs from juvenile Little Bittern in more rufous-brown mantle/scapulars with pale tips rather than fringes. The neck is, on average, more finely streaked.

1st-winter/-summer: The juvenile plumage is moulted sometime during the 1st autumn/winter to an adult-like plumage, but it is often recognizable by the retained, worn coverts (in immature female with distinct dark triangular markings).

Voice: In the breeding season, gives a low *coo-coo-coo*, which is repeated at fairly frequent intervals; mainly heard at dawn.

Habitat and behaviour: See American Bittern, above.

Range: North and South America. North American birds are migratory, wintering from S USA and Caribbean islands, south to Panama and Colombia.

Status: Accidental in the Azores (5, Sept-Nov). Britain: specimen reported from York (autumn 1852*). Iceland (Sept 1970).

SCHRENCK'S LITTLE BITTERN   *Ixobrychus eurhythmus*   A 5

L 35cm (13.5"). WS 55-59cm (22.5"). E Asia. Accidental.

Adult male: Readily distinguished from both Least and Little Bitterns by the dark chestnut upperside and ear-coverts, the latter sharply contrasting with the pale buffish throat/foreneck with a prominent dark gular stripe. In flight, note in particular the underwing pattern which shows less contrast between flight feathers and coverts than in either Least or Little.

Adult female: Unmistakable, with brown mantle, scapulars and coverts, sprinkled with prominent white markings. Has browner ear-coverts than male, and the neck is heavily streaked both in the centre and on the sides. In flight, shows less contrasting pale patches on the coverts than the male.

Juvenile: Resembles the adult female, but juvenile male shows adult male-like wing-pattern.

1st-winter/-summer: The juvenile plumage is very quickly moulted to 1st-winter, which is like the adult of its respective sex. In the hand, 1st-years are best told from the adult by distinct whitish tips to the greater primary coverts (very ill-defined greyish or rufous tips in adult, sometimes with a little whitish on the inner web).

Voice: During the breeding season the male's call is reported to sound like *gup-gup-gup*.

Habitat and behaviour: See American Bittern, above.

Range: Breeds in E China, Korea, Japan and SE USSR. Winters from southernmost China to Indonesia.

Status: Accidental in Italy: Piemonte, 1st-winter female caught on 12th Nov 1912.

GREEN HERON *Butorides striatus virescens*   A 5

L 40-48cm (16-19"). WS 52-60cm (22"). North American race of Green Heron, sometimes regarded as separate species. A few records (Oct-Dec).

All plumages: Small, usually compact-looking, dark heron (neck can be extended though) and unlikely to be confused with any species on the European list. In flight, readily distinguished from both Least, Schrenck's and Little Bitterns by the dark wings.

Adult: Has dark cap and long, lanceolated, bluish-edged feathers on the mantle and scapulars and dark coverts with distinct, paler fringes. Shows rich rufous-chestnut sides to the head/neck.

Juvenile: Readily distinguished from the adult. Shows brown upperparts with shorter, broader and more rounded feathers. The neck and sides of the head are less deep rufous-chestnut and the neck is more heavily streaked. Also, the coverts have pale triangular marks on the tips.

Bears some resemblance to juvenile Night Heron, but the latter is distinctly larger, with a proportionately shorter and thicker bill and shows more heavily pale-spotted upperparts and coverts.

1st-winter/-summer: Juvenile plumage is moulted sometime in the 1st autumn/winter. In the spring of the 2nd year the plumage is basically like the adult. Some individuals show a substantial number of retained juvenile coverts, whereas others have renewed all of the coverts and even a number of the flight-feathers (normally inner primaries and inner secondaries). Retained juvenile alula and greater primary coverts show broad white tips (none or very thin in adult).

Note: Other races of Green Heron could reach Europe (one race breeds as near as the Red Sea). All plumages of these races are easily distinguished from North American birds as they show a pale grey neck and sides to the head. The North American form is often considered a distinct species – *B. virescens*.

Range: Breeds in North America, mainly in E USA. Also in Central America (to E Panama), in the West Indies and on islands off Venezuela. Winters from southernmost USA to N South America. Vagrant in Greenland. Grey-headed forms occur in South America (from E Panama), Africa and Arabia and from India to Japan and Australia.

Status: Accidental in the Azores (Oct 1978, Oct 1979, Oct 1985 two). Britain: Cornwall, adult (27th Oct 1889), Humberside, adult (27th Nov-6th Dec 1982), and Lothian, 1st-winter found dead (25th Oct 1987).

CHINESE POND HERON   *Ardeola bacchus*   A 5

L 45cm (18"). WS 80-90cm (33.5"). Eastern Asiatic species. One record.

All plumages: Similar in size and build to the closely related Squacco Heron.

Adult summer: Readily distinguished from Squacco by unstreaked red-brown head and neck (lower part often tinged more greyish), and has dark slaty mantle and scapulars.

Adult winter: The head and neck are pale and heavily striped and the mantle/scapulars are dark brown. Extremely similar to winter Squacco but appears to be more heavily streaked and less rich buffish on the head and neck, and the mantle and scapulars tend to be a darker, deeper brown.

Juvenile: Differences from adult winter unknown to us.

Subsequent immature plumages: Individuals that are in winter plumage or moulting from winter to summer plumage as late as late spring-summer should be 1st-years.

Habitat and behaviour: Much as Squacco, favouring marshy areas. Often remains motionless for lengthy periods and can then be surprisingly difficult to spot.

Note: The Indian Pond Heron *A. grayii*, breeding as near as Iran, could possibly straggle to Europe (one reported in Belgium, July 1988*). In summer plumage this species has the head and neck unstreaked pale yellowish-buff, and mantle/scapulars deep reddish-brown. However, in adult winter and immature plumages it is probably not safely separated from Chinese Pond.

Range: Breeds E China to NE India. Winters in south of breeding range and in SE Asia, south to Borneo.

Status: Accidental in Norway: Hellesylt, Co Møre and Romsdal, adult (autumn 1973).

LITTLE BLUE HERON   *Egretta caerulea*   A 6

L 61-74cm (24-29"). WS 104cm (41"). North and South America. One record from the Azores.

Adult: Medium-sized heron. Entirely slaty, with the head and neck tinged purplish, brighter in the breeding season. Note the bare part coloration: lores and bill are pale blue-grey, the latter with blackish tip, and the legs/feet are yellowish-green in the non-breeding season and dark in the breeding season.

Juvenile: White plumage. The bill is pale greyish/pinkish with a dark tip, the lores are pale greyish or pale yellowish-green, and the legs/feet are pale yellowish-green. Best distinguished from Little and Snowy Egrets by slightly stouter bill, different bare part coloration (cf. Snowy Egret, below), and normally dark tips to the primaries.

Subsequent immature plumages: In the spring of the 2nd year, the plumage is blotchy, as slaty feathers are moulted in.

Range: Breeds in E and SE USA. Winters along the coasts in much of the breeding range. Notable post-breeding dispersal, mainly of young birds. Also breeds in the West Indies and in much of South America.

Status: Accidental in the Azores: Flores, where a ringed bird was recovered on 28th Nov 1964 (ringed as nestling in late June 1964, New Jersey, USA).

TRICOLORED HERON *Egretta tricolor* A **6**

L 60-70cm (24-28"). WS 90cm (36"). Americas. A recent record from the Azores.

Adult: A very characteristic, medium-sized heron with a relatively long thin neck and bill. Shows mainly dark blue-grey plumage with mostly white underparts and underwings. There is a white stripe on the chin, throat and foreneck which is bordered with rufous. The colour of the lores and basal part of the bill varies between greenish-yellow (non-breeding) to bright blue (breeding).

Juvenile: Similar to the adult but shows largely pale rufous neck and sides of the head and pale rufous tips to the coverts.

Subsequent immature plumages: Juvenile plumage is replaced during the spring/summer of the 2nd year. In the autumn of the 2nd year it is mostly like the adult.

Range: Breeds E and S USA, Central America, N South America, and West Indies. Most northerly populations move south of USA in winter.

Status: Accidental in the Azores: immature at Lajes, Pico on 22nd-24th Oct 1985.

SNOWY EGRET *Egretta thula* A **6**

L 56-66cm (22-26"). WS *c.* 100cm (41"). Americas. Recently reported from Azores and Iceland.

All plumages: Very similar to Little Egret. Main distinctions (except in breeding plumage – see below) relate to differences in coloration of the lores and legs/feet. The bare skin on the lores is bright yellow (usually bluish-grey or greenish-grey in Little, but sometimes yellowish). Rarely the lores are more greyish (only in young birds?). During the mating period the lores become bright reddish-pink (orange-red in Little). In summer plumage the rear of the legs are often yellowish, and in adult winter and immature birds this is practically always the case, and sometimes the entire legs are yellowish apart from a dark stripe down the front. In Little, the legs are usually blackish, with contrasting yellow feet (birds with mainly yellowish legs have been recorded). Compare with juvenile Little Blue Heron (p. 44).

Adult summer: A further distinction from Little Egret are the shorter, fuller head plumes (forming loose crest), consisting of several feathers (only two or three in Little).

Adult winter: Similar to adult summer, but lacks or shows rudimentary plumes on head and breast and aigrettes on rear mantle/scapulars. Lower mandible is usually paler on the basal part.

Juvenile: Similar to adult winter and apparently difficult to distinguish. Completely lacks plumes and aigrettes.

Range: Breeds USA (mainly on E coast), W Indies, Central and South America. Northerly breeding birds migrate south in winter. Vagrants have reached Tristan da Cunha in the Atlantic on at least nine occasions.

Status: Accidental in Iceland: An undated record; also one collected on 6th June 1983, and another found dead on a ship a few miles south of Iceland in May or June 1985. Azores: two reported at Santa Cruz, Flores on 10th-11th Oct 1988.

WESTERN REEF HERON   *Egretta gularis*   B **6**

L 55-65cm (21.5-25.5"). WS 86-104cm (34-41"). W Africa, Red Sea east to India. Vagrant in S Europe.

All plumages: Very similar and closely related to the Little Egret, with which it is sometimes treated as conspecific under that name.

The bill is distinctly thicker than in Little and usually obviously paler. In western birds the bill is pale brownish (non-breeding) or dark brown (breeding). In eastern birds, at least distally, the bill is usually yellowish or yellowish-brown all year. Little Egret's bill is usually blackish, but non-breeding birds have the basal part of the lower mandible paler (flesh coloured or greyish), and only very rarely is the bill colour the same as in Western Reef.

The lores are generally pale greenish or yellowish, turning pale orange for a short period during mating. In Little Egret, the lores are generally greenish-grey or bluish-grey, rarely yellowish, turning orange-red during the mating period.

It has a proportionately slightly shorter tarsus than the Little Egret. In winter plumage, western birds usually have brown legs, and eastern birds' legs have been recorded as pale brown, or partly greenish, yellowish or orangey. In summer plumage both western and eastern birds usually have darker brown legs (feet still yellowish or greenish). Little Egret has blackish legs and yellow feet (aberrant birds with brown, yellowish or greenish legs have been recorded).

It occurs in both a dark and a white morph, as well as intermediates. In plumage, apparently not separable from Little Egret (dark morph rare in latter).

Adult summer: Shows ornamental feathers on head, breast and rear mantle/scapulars similar to Little Egret.

Adult winter: Lacks plumes and aigrettes. For coloration of bare parts see above.

Juvenile: See Snowy Egret, above.

Range: Nominate race breeds W African coast (Mauritania south to Gulf of Guinea). Vagrants have reached Nantucket Is. Massachusetts, USA (Apr-Sept 1983) and the West Indies (at least 2 birds variously recorded between Jan-Apr 1984, June-July 1985 from Barbados and St Lucia). Has also been observed ten times in Morocco between 1983-86. The eastern race *E. g. schistacea*, breeds from the Red Sea coasts to India and Sri Lanka

Status: *c.* 30 records, more than half since 1976. The majority are from France (24), mainly Apr-Nov, most recent in Camargue in Aug-Sept 1988. Also, recorded in the Azores, Spain (3+, May-June), Sicily (May 1976), Sardinia (June 1986), Yugoslavia (Apr 1975), and Greece (three between 1982-85; May-Aug). There are also a number of records from C Europe (e.g. 5-6 from Switzerland), but these are considered probable escapes from parks in Austria and West Germany.

GREAT BLUE HERON   *Ardea herodias*   B **6**

L 97-137cm (38-54"). WS 180cm (72"). Mainly North and Central America. Accidental in Azores and Spain.

Adult: Distinctly larger than Grey Heron which it closely resembles. The neck is darker than in Grey Heron and shows a brownish-pink tinge lacking in Grey. Also, the marginal coverts and 'thighs' are rufous unlike in Grey Heron.

Also occurs in an all-white morph 'Great White Heron' and an intermediate morph 'Wurdemann's Heron' with a white head. 'Great White Heron' could be confused with Great White Egret, but is larger, heavier, and has a heavier bill and paler legs.

Juvenile: Similar to the adult, but is duller with less pinkish tinge to the neck, shows some rufous markings on the tips of the coverts, and has an entirely blackish crown. Also shows much shorter head plumes and lacks the distinctive elongated feathers on the rear scapulars and breast of the adult. Differs from juvenile Grey Heron in rufous marginal coverts, 'thighs', and markings to coverts.

Subsequent immature plumages: See Tricolored Heron, p. 45.

Range: Breeds North and Central America, Caribbean and Greater Antilles, and on the Galapagos. Majority of North American populations are migratory, wintering from Florida and the Caribbean to South America. Vagrant in Greenland.

Status: Accidental in the Azores. Approximately ten birds observed on the Azorean islands of São Miguel, Pico and Faial during the first week of April 1984 (last on 24th June). An earlier record concerned an individual which landed on an east-bound ship in the North Atlantic on 29th Oct 1968, staying aboard and only captured after the ship had passed the Azores. Spain: immature at Gijón, Asturias from 5th Dec 1988-15th Feb 1989*.

Family THRESKIORNITHIDAE   Ibises and Spoonbills

BALD IBIS *Geronticus eremita*   A* **6**

L 70-80cm (30"). WS 125-135cm (51"). Breeds extremely rarely in Morocco and E Turkey. Threatened by global extinction. Accidental in Azores and Spain.

Adult: Unmistakable. Distinctive shape includes 'mane' of narrow elongated feathers. Blackish plumage has faint green gloss and purplish patch on the lesser coverts. Head 'bald', mainly reddish, and bill and legs reddish. In flight, larger and heavier than Glossy Ibis with shorter neck and legs not projecting beyond tail. Male slightly larger than female.

Juvenile: Differs from the adult in having a dark, feathered head, and lacks elongated feathers on the nape. Also lacks purple-red patch on the coverts. Bill, legs, and iris duller, more greyish. Quite different from Glossy in both colour and shape.

Subsequent immature plumages: During the spring of the 2nd year the elongated nape feathers and the purple-red patch on the lesser coverts start to appear, but the head is still usually mainly feathered. Full adult bare part coloration is probably not attained until the 3rd year.

Habitat: Unlike Glossy Ibis it breeds in mountainous areas, usually nesting on rocks. Normally forages in dry areas, rarely visiting the marshy habitats favoured by Glossy Ibis.

Range: The Bald Ibis is one of the few birds to have become extinct in Europe in historical times; until the 16th or 17th century it bred in S Germany, Austria and Switzerland, and possibly elsewhere too. It now only occurs in two relict, disjunct populations. One largely resident in Morocco where there are a handful of dwindling colonies. The other breeds at a single site at Birecik on the upper Euphrates, Turkey and migrates to Ethiopia and (presumably) North Yemen. It was formerly more widely distributed in N Africa and the Middle East.

The world population is steadily and rapidly decreasing. In Morocco there were less than 250 breeding pairs in 1975. In 1988 only 54 of these remained. In Turkey there were 530 pairs breeding 1953, 65 in 1964, 23 in 1973 and 5 in 1988. In 1989 the Turkish breeding population became extinct and the Moroccan apparently decreased dramatically. However, there are still some non-breeding birds left (mainly immatures), both in Turkey and Morocco.

Status: Accidental in the Azores (one in Feb, before 1905), and Spain (Andalusia July 1958).

Family PHOENICOPTERIDAE Flamingoes

LESSER FLAMINGO *Phoenicopterus minor*   A **6**
L 80-90cm (34"). WS 132cm (52"). Africa S of Sahara and SW Asia. Accidental in S Europe.

All plumages: Resembles Flamingo but is much smaller, with a proportionately shorter neck and legs. However, there is considerable variation in both species (males are larger than females, and juveniles have shorter necks and legs than adults). The bill is also distinctly shorter, darker (looking blackish at a distance) and differently patterned.

Adult: The bill is actually dark crimson, becoming paler red towards the tip of the lower mandible, while the blackish area at the tip is less extensive than in Flamingo. The plumage is generally a deeper pink than in Flamingo but may appear quite pale when worn. Males at least, sometimes show some crimson on the upperparts and breast (unlike Flamingo). The coverts are not uniformly pink as in Flamingo, but show a more contrasting crimson patch. The underwing is similar to Flamingo except for contrasting crimson axillaries. Male considerably larger than female.

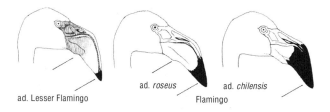

ad. *roseus*   ad. *chilensis*
ad. Lesser Flamingo   Flamingo

Juvenile: Readily distinguished from the adult by dusky plumage, lacking any pink or crimson, and has dark legs. Very similar to juvenile Flamingo, but the bill is distinctly darker, purple-brown with black tip (grey with more extensive dark tip in Flamingo). Size and structural differences are also important aids to identification.

Subsequent immature plumages: Worn juveniles become very pale, even whitish. Full adult plumage is attained in three to four years.

Voice: Like Flamingo gives various hooting, grunting and rather goose-like notes. Calls are generally slightly higher pitched than those of Flamingo.

Range: Saline and alkaline lakes/lagoons of Africa south of the Sahara, and apparently irregularly also in Mauritania, Persian Gulf, Pakistan and NW India (Rann of Kutch). Vagrant in Morocco (8).

Status: Accidental in Spain: Malaga, Laguna de Fuente de Piedra, 31st May 1966 (1 individual), 21st June 1972 (6 individuals), with at least 4 still present one month later. Mallorca (June-Dec 1988*). France: Berre, Bouches-du-Rhône (June 1989*). Other reports of birds found elsewhere in N Europe (e.g. Belgium, W Germany, Poland, Norway) are generally regarded as escapes.

Family ANATIDAE   Swans, Geese and Ducks

FULVOUS WHISTLING DUCK   *Dendrocygna bicolor*   A **7**

L 45-53cm (18-21"). Americas, tropical Africa and S Asia. Accidental in SW Europe.

Adult: Clearly different from other species of European wildfowl. It is extremely long-legged for a duck, and in flight the feet project well beyond the tail tip. Mainly rich yellowish-brown on the head, neck and underparts with a dark stripe running down the centre of the nape/hindneck. Shows prominent white stripes on the flanks. The upperparts are dark with rich yellowish-brown bars. In flight the wings appear very dark both above and below, and the uppertail-coverts are white, forming a white crescent.

Juvenile: Similar to the adult but is duller below, and the scapulars are narrower and rounder with duller, less contrasting tips. Also has slightly reduced flank markings and grey-mottled uppertail-coverts. In the hand can be aged by the shape of the tail feathers (see American Wigeon, p. 54).

Habitat and behaviour: Favours shallow waters, preferably with surface vegetation. Usually feeds by dabbling but sometimes dives for short periods.

Voice: Very vocal, both when feeding and on the wing (perhaps only when in flocks). A loud, whistling *kweeoo*, or *tsoo-ee* usually repeated.

Note: Confusion may arise with other species of *Dendrocygna*, which are kept in captivity and escape from time to time – for differences see Madge and Burn (1987).

Range: Africa south of the Sahara. India to Burma. Also S USA, Central and South America. In Africa, has wandered to Morocco (flock of 12 in Apr 1977 and 2 in Sept 1980).

Status: Accidental in France (Apr 1929, Sept 1970), and Spain (Sept 1971). Commonly kept in captivity, so origin of French and Spanish birds is hard to assess with certainty.

'TUNDRA SWAN'   *Cygnus columbianus columbianus*   A 7

L 115-127cm (45-50"). North American race of Bewick's Swan. Also known as Whistling Swan. Accidental.

Adult: Differs from adults of the 'European' race *bewickii* in having bill mostly black with a small yellow spot in front of the eye (yellow may even be absent). Adult *bewickii* shows an extensive yellow base to the black bill.

Juvenile: Easily distinguished from adult by the pale greyish-tinged plumage and mostly pink bill. Not distinguishable from juvenile *bewickii*.

Subsequent immature plumages: During the 1st winter and spring the plumage and the bill gradually become as in adult. Resembles the adult by the 2nd winter.

Range: Breeds in Alaska and Canadian low Arctic. Winters along the Pacific coast from SE Alaska to California and along the Atlantic coast from New Jersey to North Carolina.

Status: Accidental in winter: British Isles (6), Netherlands (Feb 1976, Feb 1980, Nov 1986) and Sweden (Apr 1979).

LESSER WHITE-FRONTED GOOSE   *Anser erythropus*   R Br* 7

L 53-66cm (21-26"). Rare breeder in N Scandinavia/Finland. Winters in SE Europe – rare elsewhere on migration and in winter.

All plumages: Very similar to White-fronted Goose, but is distinctly smaller, with shorter (often thicker-looking) neck. This, in combination with usually strikingly high forehead/forecrown and noticeably shorter, deep-based, conical bill, give it a very distinctive appearance. These same characters may be evident in flight, if seen together with White-fronts, but observers should beware of exceptionally small White-fronts. The wings project well beyond the tip of the tail when folded (wings reaching to or only slightly beyond the tail tip in White-fronted).

The head and neck are usually slightly darker and contrast slightly more with the breast than in White-fronted. The yellow orbital ring is usually obvious even at moderate range and is slightly more prominent in adult birds (some White-fronts show a narrow yellowish orbital ring, only visible at close range).

Adult: Also differs from adult White-fronted in usually showing a more prominent white blaze, usually extending backwards to above the eye, which is probably never the case in White-fronted; occasionally, however, shows a rather small white blaze. The underparts tend to be less heavily marked with black, but there is much overlap.

Juvenile: Readily distinguished from the adult by lack of white on the head; finely scalloped rather than white-barred scapulars and flanks (due to slightly smaller and rounder feathers with duller pale fringes); lack of black markings on the belly; and usually dark nail on the bill.

Subsequent immature plumages: From late autumn onwards juveniles moult partially, gradually attaining adult plumage. Inseparable from adult by the 2nd winter.

Voice: The calls are generally higher-pitched and more shrill than those of White-fronted, but this may be difficult to judge, especially in a mixed flock.

Behaviour: It normally has a quicker feeding action than White-fronted, and this can be an eye-catching feature when scanning through flocks of White-fronts (stray individuals regularly mix with the latter in W Europe).

Habitat: Breeds on scrubby tundra, usually not far from water.

Range: Breeds from N Scandinavia/Finland eastwards in a narrow belt to easternmost USSR. Western populations winter in SE Europe (Hungary, Yugoslavia, Greece, Rumania, and Bulgaria), but the majority are now mainly found in the southern Caspian lowlands. Greece: Evros delta, 116 in Jan 1988 was the fourth largest number recorded.

In N Scandinavia, numbers have declined dramatically during recent decades (from *c.* 10,000 individuals at the turn of the century to *c.* 60-90 pairs 1940-1984). During a census in N Sweden in 1987 only two breeding pairs were found. In recent years some 50 individuals have been recorded annually in Sweden. A reintroduction-programme has been in operation in Sweden since 1981 (*c.* 110 colour-ringed birds were released up to and including 1984). In Finland, first breeding records since 1976 occurred in summer 1989.

Status: Rare winter visitor to the British Isles (122, Nov-Mar), France (13), Belgium (*c.* 60), Netherlands (100+), Denmark (*c.* 55), East Germany (rare but rather regular migrant in north, almost annual since 1975), West Germany, Poland (very scarce migrant), Estonia, Czechoslovakia (regular in spring before 1960), Austria, Switzerland (19th century), Italy, and Spain.

SNOW GOOSE *Anser caerulescens*   D **7**

L 65-80cm (25.5-31.5"). North American species, rather frequently recorded in NW Europe, although most probably refer to birds escaped from captivity.

Adult: Unmistakable. All-white with black primaries and has pink bill and legs. There is also a dark colour morph, 'Blue Goose' which is rare in the E part of the range. This is dark grey with a white head and upper neck, and has grey coverts and often also greyish to whitish stern. Bare part coloration as in Snow Goose. Intermediates between the two morphs are fairly common.

Juvenile: Juveniles can also be assigned to either colour morph. Each is easily distinguished from the adult of its respective colour morph: Snow is brownish-grey on crown, hindneck, mantle and scapulars. 'Blue' is totally dark slaty-brown. In both, bill and legs/feet are dark.

The Snow Goose is readily separated from other geese by its paler plumage. Both morphs are easily told from 'grey geese' by their bare part coloration.

Subsequent immature plumages: Adult plumage is gradually acquired from late in the 1st autumn.

Voice: Single or double, rather high pitched notes, *eh, eh-onk* or similar are often given. A wide range of calls can be heard, especially from flocks.

Note: Adult 'Blue Goose' bears a superficial resemblance to adult Emperor Goose *A. canagicus* (Alaska and easternmost USSR), which sometimes escapes from captivity. The latter is easily distinguished by e.g. small bill, paler grey upper and underparts with black and white barring, black chin/throat and foreneck, coverts concolorous with the rest of the upperparts, white tail, and orange legs/feet. Juvenile could perhaps be confused with juvenile 'Blue Goose', but distinctive scaliness, small bill, and paler, often yellowish-tinged, legs/feet should prevent confusion.

Both adult and immature Snow Goose are very similar to Ross's Goose *A. rossii* (breeds arctic Canada, winters S and SW USA), which could possibly turn up either as a genuine vagrant or as an escape. There have been recent reports of 1-2 birds of unknown origin in the Faeroes, Scotland, Belgium, Netherlands, and West Germany. Ross's is distinctly smaller (about the size of Lesser White-fronted), with a proportionately shorter neck, rounder head and obviously shorter bill. The bill lacks the prominent blackish 'lips' of Snow Goose (only narrow black along the cutting edges). Unlike Snow the bill shows bluish or greenish warty protuberances at the base (not in juvenile and some adult females), only visible at very close range. Juvenile is considerably paler than juvenile Snow Goose. Blue phase is extremely rare. Hybridization with Snow Goose has occurred.

Range: Breeds arctic Canada and Alaska, NW Greenland; easternmost USSR. Winters chiefly in the SW parts of the USA and in N and C Mexico.

Status: Frequent vagrant. Records from many countries (including the Azores), east to Poland and the Baltic States, and south to Spain – especially from Iceland (75, 1979-1987), Britain/Ireland, and the Netherlands (625 since 1900). Also France, Belgium, East and West Germany and Scandinavia. In recent years, it has even bred successfully in Sweden and Finland a few times. The true status of most of these birds is uncertain, since it is commonly kept in captivity. However, genuine vagrants do turn up: a flock of 18 in the Netherlands in April 1980 included one bird ringed in Manitoba, Canada in 1977. In Ireland and W Scotland, seen fairly regularly with White-fronted Geese from Greenland and usually considered wild.

'BLACK BRANT' *Branta bernicla nigricans*   D 7

L 56-61cm (22-24"). Arctic E USSR and W North American race of Brent Goose. Since mid-1970s increasingly recorded in winter from the British Isles and Netherlands.

Adult: Similar to the dark-bellied race of Brent Goose *B. b. bernicla* (wintering NW Europe), but has a broader necklace, usually meeting in front. The underside is even darker (shows less contrast between breast and belly), and there is an even more contrasting white patch on the flanks. The upperparts are slightly darker.

Juvenile: Differs from the adult in lacking white necklace. Shows broad pale tips to the greater, median and lower lesser coverts; also has darker flanks. It is probably very difficult to separate from juvenile of the dark-bellied race.

Subsequent immature plumages: The white necklace and white flank patches begin to show from late in the 1st autumn. The pale-tipped coverts are retained until the complete moult in the summer of the 2nd year.

Voice: Apparently similar to other races of Brent Goose, a comparatively faint, growling *r-r-rot* or *pr-r-rak*.

Range: Breeds on tundra in E USSR (from the Taymyr Peninsula eastwards), Alaska and W Canada (east to about Perry River and W Arctic islands). Winters on both sides of the Pacific Ocean, but primarily along North American coast.

Status: Annual in W Europe since 1974. The number of records has increased dramatically since the mid-1970s, with over 100 sightings (Sept-May), principally from Britain, Ireland, and the Netherlands. It is likely that those wintering around the North Sea arrived with dark-bellied Brent Geese from the Palearctic. In Finland, single birds were recorded migrating ENE with flocks of dark-bellied Brent Geese in May 1982 and 1984. However, in Ireland 'Black Brants' are presumed to be of Nearctic origin, having arrived with pale-bellied Brent Geese *B. b. hrota* from Canada.

Records of 'Black Brant' are given as follows: British Isles (48), Netherlands (*c.* 50), with smaller numbers elsewhere – Iceland (May 1980), Channel Islands (Jersey: single returning individual wintering nearly every year, 1982-88), France (5 Nov-Mar), Belgium (Mar 1988*), West Germany (9), Sweden (4), and Finland (2). Nearly all records are of singles, rarely two birds together.

RED-BREASTED GOOSE   *Branta ruficollis*   D* 7

L 53-56cm (22"). Breeds arctic Siberia. Winters in fair numbers in SE Europe, but very rare elsewhere on migration and in winter.

Adult: Unmistakable. Smallest European goose, with strikingly colourful pattern of black, white and brownish-red on the head, neck and breast. Also has a black belly, mostly white flanks, a narrow white breast band, and broad white tips to the median and greater coverts.

Juvenile: Resembles the adult, but the black areas are duller and slightly brownish-tinged. The head pattern is also slightly less sharply defined, the whitish tips to the median and greater coverts are slightly more diffuse and the lower lesser coverts are pale-tipped. The rear flanks are not so distinctly barred as in adult, because of smaller and more rounded feathers than in adult.

Subsequent immature plumages: The immature is recognizable on retained juvenile coverts until the complete moult in the summer of the 2nd year.

Voice: The common call is a high pitched, slightly harsh, nasal double staccato *ki kwei*. A wide selection of calls can be heard from flocks.

Range: Breeds on Taymyr, Gydan and Yamal Peninsulas in arctic USSR. The winter ranges are shifting (Caspian formerly main area, now apparently few birds there; numbers in Greece recently showing signs of an increase). The majority now winter along the western shore of the Black Sea in the Dobrogea region of Rumania and N Bulgaria. Altogether the world population seems to be declining strongly.

Status: Rare visitor to C and W Europe, although recently showing signs of a slight increase in the number of birds found on migration and wintering in NW Europe.

Most of the records are from the Netherlands (387 since 1900) and Sweden (58, annual since 1972). More records from Britain (*c.* 40), and Finland (23) in recent years. Also recorded from France (19), Belgium (*c.* 50), Denmark (18), Norway (2), Estonia, Latvia, Poland (11 records, 9 in 20th century), East Germany (*c.* 45 since 1930), West Germany, Austria, Hungary, Czechoslovakia, Yugoslavia, Italy (13), and Spain.

RUDDY SHELDUCK   *Tadorna ferruginea*   R Br **7**

L 61-67cm (25"). Mainly Asiatic species. Breeds in very small numbers in SE Europe – now rarely recorded from the rest of Europe (but escapes not infrequent).

Adult male breeding: Size and general build similar to Shelduck, but lacks male Shelduck's bill-knob. Easily recognized by rich orange-brown plumage with contrasting paler head, separated by a narrow black necklace. Shows diagnostic large white patches on the coverts in flight.

Adult male eclipse: Similar to breeding male, but the narrow black neck-ring is faint or absent.

Adult female: Usually noticeably smaller than the male. Also lacks male's black neck-ring and shows a white area at the base of the bill and around the eyes.

Juvenile: Like the adult female but is slightly duller, and the scapulars (especially the rear ones) are brown with diffuse, pale rufous fringes. The tertials are narrower, more pointed and darker. In the hand, identified by the shape of the tail feathers (see American Wigeon, below).

Voice: The calls include a rolling, honked *aakh*, an abruptly-trumpeted *pok-pok-pok-pok*, and rolling *porrr porrr porrr*.

Range: Breeds in SE Europe in Rumania, Bulgaria and Greece, where it used to be common, but now only some 200 pairs breed. Also occurs eastwards across much of C Asia to N China and Mongolia, and locally in NW Africa and in the highlands of Ethiopia. Northern populations, at least, winter south of the breeding range. Vagrants have reached Greenland and Madeira.

Status: Vagrants have been reported from most European countries, but as western populations have declined considerably this century, most reports now are considered to be escapes from wildfowl collections.

Genuine vagrancy was more common during the last century, as shown by the large invasion during the summer of 1892, when birds were reported widely throughout Europe, a few even reaching Iceland. Now only rarely reported from Mediterranean Spain, S France and Italy during post-breeding dispersal (formerly, NW African birds regularly wintered in SW Spain). Poland: many records probably of escapes, but an individual with a Kirghisian ring was found dead near Konin on 30th Oct 1979.

In NW Europe this species has long been common in waterfowl collections. Since 1969 has bred ferally in the Netherlands, also in East and West Germany. With an increasing number of escapes it is difficult to assess any true vagrancy pattern, but records should continue to be kept.

AMERICAN WIGEON   *Anas americana*   D **8**

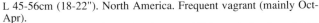

L 45-56cm (18-22"). North America. Frequent vagrant (mainly Oct-Apr).

All plumages: Differs from closely related Wigeon in having whitish axillaries and central underwing-coverts (grey in Wigeon, as rest of underwing, although may be slightly paler).

In female-type birds, the pattern of the greater coverts generally differs (see figure, p. 55), but there is some overlap, particularly between 1st-year female American and adult female Wigeon.

ad. ♀ Wigeon
(untypical)

juv. Wigeon

Typical greater coverts

ad. ♀/juv. ♂/some juv. ♀
American Wigeon

juv. ♀ American
Wigeon

Adult male breeding: Basically resembles an adult male Wigeon, but is easily identified by its pale, heavily black-peppered head and neck. It also has a broad, dark (glossed green) band on the sides of the head, and a white forehead and crown centre (Wigeon has uniformly reddish-brown head/neck with yellowish forehead/crown centre). The flanks are brownish-pink (often uniformly patterned), and there is usually a brownish-pink cast to the mantle and scapulars (Wigeon has grey, densely and finely barred upperparts and flanks).

Adult male eclipse: Resembles the adult female and juvenile but is generally more richly coloured, especially on the breast/flanks. A few scapulars and mantle feathers are often similar to breeding plumage. The tertials are more contrastingly patterned than in other female-type plumages, having black outer webs with white edges and grey-brown inner webs. It can always be distinguished by the presence of large, immaculate white patches on the coverts (usually concealed when swimming).

Adult female: Extremely similar to female-type Wigeon. Classic individuals show greyish head and neck with contrasting, diffuse, dark shade around the eye (generally extending backwards to the nape), and rather rich rufous-brown flanks. Wigeon is usually more brownish on the head/neck, contrasting less with the flanks, and generally shows less contrasting dark patch around the eyes. Sometimes, however, American females show a more brownish head and neck, and Wigeon females can sometimes be rather grey; also, the dark patch around the eyes can be missing in American and distinct in Wigeon. The great variability shown by both species makes them extremely difficult to distinguish with certainty, unless the axillaries can be seen properly.

Juvenile: Very similar to the adult female, but is basically duller, and showing a darker and less barred breast. The coverts tend to show less distinct pale fringes. The juvenile female generally shows the dullest speculum and has darker greater coverts than either the juvenile male or adult female. In the hand, the juvenile can easily be distinguished by the presence of notched tips to the tail feathers with the shaft projecting (slightly pointed rectrices in adult without projecting shaft). See figure.

juv.

ail feathers

1st breeding male: The juvenile male begins to acquire breeding plumage in its 1st autumn. Some birds reach nearly full 1st breeding plumage by the late autumn/early winter, others not until the spring of the 2nd year. The 1st breeding plumage is often not quite as bright and crisp as an older male. It can be distinguished with certainty by its dusky coverts, but note that they are sometimes rather extensively whitish.

Note: Apparent hybrids between American Wigeon and Wigeon have been recorded on several occasions. The plumage of hybrids is intermediate. Some are very similar to American Wigeon but show some intermediate characters, e.g. some reddish-brown on the head and some grey on the flanks in male breeding plumage. Hybrids between Chiloe Wigeon *A. sibilatrix* (S America; commonly kept in captivity) and Wigeon have also been recorded and may be similar to American Wigeon.

Range: Breeds in North America. Winters mainly in the southern parts, south to Central America. Vagrant to Greenland and Morocco.

Status: The second commonest North American dabbling duck in Europe. Regularly seen in Iceland (60+) and the British Isles (205, with largest flock of 13). Fewer records from the Faeroes (June 1984), Norway (3), Sweden (12), Finland (6), West Germany, Denmark, Netherlands (17), Belgium (2), France (11), Channel Islands (3), Spain (2), and the Azores (9). Escapes are always a possibility, since this species is widely kept in captivity. Ringing recoveries have shown that true transatlantic vagrancy has occurred at least four times, so it seems likely that most of the records are of wild origin.

In Britain and Ireland there are records from all months with a peak in late Sept-Oct, whereas all except one of the Swedish and all of the Finnish are from spring. It seems likely that the Swedish and Finnish spring records refer to birds which came across to W Europe the previous autumn.

FALCATED DUCK *Anas falcata*   A **8**

L 48-54cm (19-21"). E Asia. Accidental, (some obviously escapes).

Adult male breeding: Unmistakable, beautifully coloured duck. Note that the white throat can be difficult to see, and the yellow patch on the sides of the undertail-coverts is often concealed by the tertials. At a distance it generally looks grey with darker head. The head shape and the extremely long sickle-shaped (falcated) tertials are also very typical. In flight it is further characterized by dark, green-glossed, speculum with rather broad and diffuse pale bar in front and no distinct pale trailing bar.

Adult male eclipse: Very similar to the adult female, but basically darker, and shows less prominent pale internal markings to the scapulars and flank feathers. The tertials are longer than in the female (but shorter than in breeding plumage and only slightly sickle-shaped), with noticeably broader, pale grey edges, especially basally, and blacker outer webs to the longer feathers. Also shows paler grey, more uniformly patterned forewing.

Adult female: Has a characteristic, slender, dark grey bill and a uniformly patterned head and neck. Also, nape often looks rather full (trace of male's crest). Wing pattern basically similar to male's, which is useful for flight identification. If the speculum cannot be seen (as is often the case when swimming), it may closely resemble an adult male Gadwall in eclipse (which sometimes has all-grey bill as in breeding plumage), but shows more plain head pattern and dark grey legs and feet (Gadwall shows orange-tinged legs/feet). It could perhaps also be confused with female-patterned Pintail, but Falcated is much more compact, and the head and neck are usually greyer than the body (Pintail generally shows browner head than body). Female-type Wigeon and American Wigeon have bi-coloured bill with hardly any markings on the flanks.

Juvenile: Closely resembles the adult female, but is darker, with uniformly dark forehead-crown (heavily streaked in adult female); shows dark mantle/scapulars with pale fringes and sometimes faint barring, but lacks the usually prominent pale internal markings of the adult female. Also, shows more spotted breast with less prominent 'horseshoe' markings than the adult female; and less distinct or no pale internal markings on the flanks. In the hand the shape of the tail feathers differs between juvenile and adult (see American Wigeon p. 54).

Juvenile male has slightly paler grey-brown coverts than females (all ages), and the tertials resemble those of the adult male in eclipse but are slightly shorter.

1st breeding male: Begins to develop during its 1st autumn/winter (variable). When the moult is completed (late autumn to winter), it is like the adult male, but has slightly more grey-brown coverts. Often also shows some pale mottling, particularly on the inner median and greater coverts, only visible at very close range. Sometimes, the inner greater coverts are renewed and are then contrastingly paler than the rest of the coverts. The outer part of the speculum is slightly less glossy than in the adult male.

Range: Breeds in the southern half of E Siberia, E Mongolia and NE China. Winters mainly further south in China, with small numbers reaching as far west as NE India. Records of individuals reported even further west may also be genuine vagrants: e.g. Turkey in Nov 1968, Jordan in Jan 1969, and Iraq in Mar 1916, and winter 1968/69.

Status: European records remain somewhat problematical in view of the escape risk (probably reasonably frequent in wildfowl collections). There have been reports from Britain (Dec 1975-Mar 1976, Oct-Dec 1981, and winters of 1986/8), France (Camargue, Nov-Dec 1986), Netherlands (May 1985), West Germany, Sweden (Apr 1853, Dec 1916-Feb 1917, May 1987*), Finland (Aug 1976, May 1988), Czechoslovakia, Austria, Bulgaria (Feb 1978) and Malta (Oct 1979).

BAIKAL TEAL *Anas formosa*   C* 8

L 39-43cm (16"). E Asia. Very rare vagrant.

Adult male breeding: Unmistakable with its striking facial pattern. A white vertical band divides the breast from the flanks, and it also has a few, very long, narrow, and distinctively patterned scapulars. In flight, the upperwing pattern is characteristic (see adult female).

Adult male eclipse: Resembles the adult female but is basically darker and more rufous-tinged. The dark-framed pale spot at the base of the bill is generally slightly less well-defined, and the crown and sides of the head tend to be less streaked.

Adult female: Easily confused with females of similarly-sized Garganey and Teal, particularly the latter. The bill is often even slightly thinner than in Teal (thus distinctly smaller than in Garganey) and entirely dark grey, lacking the usually obvious orange-brown basal lower corner present in Teal.

Has characteristic head pattern differing from Teal's in the following way: shows a rather small, dark-framed, pale spot at the base of the bill. The lores tend to be paler just in front of the eye and the throat is usually whiter, often extending upwards as a pale wedge to just below/behind the eye. There is normally a pale crescent (eye-ring) below the eye, bordered below by a dark mark, occasionally forming a vertical dark streak. The head is not strongly 'striped' as in Garganey, which shows much more prominent supercilium, more distinct dark eye-stripe, with a broad pale stripe below (to bill) and a strong dark stripe below that. Rarely, however, Garganey shows rather uniformly dark ear-coverts with a contrastingly pale spot at the base of the bill, but this pale spot is not dark-framed as in Baikal Teal, and the supercilium is still much more conspicuous.

The wing pattern differs from both Garganey and Teal. The trailing edge to the speculum is broad and white, whereas the bar in front of the speculum is narrow and orange-brownish. In Garganey the bars in front of and behind the speculum are of approximately equal width, and both are white. In Teal the bar in front is usually obviously wider than that behind the speculum and mainly whitish.

Juvenile: Probably resembles the adult female but can presumably be aged by the tail feathers (see American Wigeon, p. 54).

1st breeding male: When the post-juvenile moult has been completed (late in the 1st autumn-winter), the plumage seems to be exceptionally difficult to distinguish from the adult male.

Range: Breeds C to E Siberia. Winters mainly in China, Korea and Japan. The numbers of birds present in the winter quarters have declined dramatically and give cause for serious concern. From being abundant in some areas in winter only a few decades ago, the Baikal Teal could possibly now be threatened with extinction. The reasons for this exceptional decline are unknown, but they make future vagrancy to Europe highly unlikely.

Status: Very rare vagrant (some are probably genuine records, others more obviously escapes from European wildfowl collections). There are records from the British Isles (11), France (9), Belgium (6), Netherlands (7), Norway (Mar-Apr 1979), Sweden (5, considered escapes), Finland (Nov 1950), Poland (May 1987), West Germany, Italy (10), Malta, and Spain (Jan 1983).

From *c.* 1840 birds were imported, at the beginning of the 20th century in rather large numbers (rarer in collections since World War II), confusing the subsequent assessment of records of birds that have periodically appeared in Europe. Young birds are more likely to be vagrants, as the species is reported to breed only exceptionally in captivity.

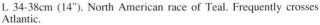

'GREEN-WINGED TEAL' *Anas crecca carolinensis*   D **8**

L 34-38cm (14"). North American race of Teal. Frequently crosses Atlantic.

Adult male breeding: Differs from male Teal mainly in showing a white vertical stripe separating the breast from the flanks. Also lacks the horizontal white stripe on the lower scapulars.

Other plumages: Identical to Teal.

Range: Breeds in North America. Winters mainly in S USA and Central America. Vagrants have reached Greenland and the Canary Is.

Status: The second most commonly recorded North American duck (commonest dabbling duck). Annual in the British Isles (306), Sept-June. Also recorded from Iceland (24), Faeroes (May 1981), France (5), Belgium (4), Netherlands (9), Denmark (2), East Germany (1), Sweden (27), Norway (3), Finland (5) and Spain (Jan-Feb 1989*).

In the British Isles most of the records are from the autumn, as opposed to Sweden, where all records are from spring (cf. American Wigeon, p. 54).

AMERICAN BLACK DUCK   *Anas rubripes*   B **9**

L 53-61cm (21-24"). North America. Accidental in Europe.

All plumages: Resembles female-type Mallard, but it is much darker, lacking pale internal markings to the feathers of the scapulars and flanks, paler belly and whitish outer tail-feathers. The head and neck are contrastingly pale.

The bill is never orange with extensive black markings as in adult female/juvenile Mallard. The speculum is also a deeper violet, and there is no white bar in front of the speculum and only a very narrow (if any) white trailing edge. There is usually a dark crescent on the median under primary coverts, lacking in Mallard.

Adult male: Has greenish-yellow bill (similar to adult male Mallard's) and bright red-orange legs/feet. Bare parts are duller during summer.

Adult female: Has pale greyish-green bill with some dusky markings on the culmen and more brownish-orange legs/feet than adult male.

Juvenile: Plumage very similar to the adult. In the hand the shape of the rectrices is a good feature (see American Wigeon, p. 54). The male is said to have a pale olive bill and orange-brown legs/feet. The female has a rather dusky bill and brownish legs/feet. Adult bare part coloration is gradually attained during the 1st winter.

Note: Black Duck and Mallard frequently hybridize in North America, producing offspring which show intermediate characters.

Range: Breeds in E Canada and NE USA. Winters in E USA.

Status: Rare vagrant. British Isles (16). Many of these individuals have been long-staying, and two or three have even paired with Mallard and produced hybrid offspring; on the Isles of Scilly, one female is known to have bred six times and produced a total of 22 young. Also recorded from the Azores (4), Iceland (13), France (Nov 1972, Dec 1976), West Germany, Denmark (Oct 1988), Norway (Apr 1981), and Sweden (Nov 1973). Some of these records may refer to escapes. There is one transatlantic ringing recovery, showing that true vagrancy is possible.

BLUE-WINGED TEAL   *Anas discors*   D **9**

L 37-41cm (14.5-16"). North America. Frequent vagrant in NW Europe.

All plumages: Shows blue forewing and distinct white bar (doubled in female) in front of, but not behind, the speculum. Both Teal and Garganey show obvious pale bands both in front of and behind the speculum (never double in front), and only adult male Garganey shows bluish-tinged forewing, although paler and greyer than in Blue-winged Teal.

Adult male breeding: Unmistakable. Has dark blue-grey head with a bold white facial crescent, and pale brownish, heavily spotted breast and flanks.

Adult male eclipse: Resembles the adult female and juvenile. Compared to female, it shows a slightly brighter blue forewing, distinctly greener speculum, and broader, not doubled, white bar in front of the speculum. The eclipse plumage is generally retained unusually long, and full breeding plumage is often not attained until late winter.

Adult female: Closely resembles female-type Teal and Garganey. It is slightly larger, with a proportionately longer, heavier and more spatulate bill, and unlike most Teal the bill is all-grey (sometimes shows very little yellowish at the very base of the lower mandible). The legs/feet are yellowish-brown or dull yellowish (brownish-grey or grey in Teal and Garganey). The plumage is normally slightly greyer than in Teal. There is usually a rather distinct whitish spot at the base of the bill, and the chin and throat are generally whiter than in Teal. The pale eye-crescents (broken eye-ring) are frequently quite obvious, which is not usually the case in Teal.

The head is typically less striped than in Garganey, lacking the pale and dark stripe below the eye and showing less prominent pale supercilium and dark eye-stripe. However, some Garganey show more uniformly patterned ear-coverts with a contrasting pale spot at the base of the bill, but the supercilium is still usually clearly more prominent.

In female-type Baikal Teal, the pale spot at the base of the bill is characteristically dark-framed, and the wing pattern is different.

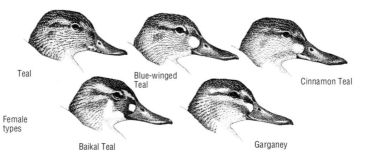

Teal

Blue-winged Teal

Cinnamon Teal

Female types

Baikal Teal

Garganey

Juvenile: Closely resembles the adult female and adult male in eclipse. The feathers of the breast tend to be more spotted than in the adult female (less horseshoe-shaped markings), and the flank feathers generally show less distinct internal pale markings. However, these differences are difficult to judge in the field. The same in-the-hand characters as described for American Wigeon can be used for ageing (p. 54).

Sexing of juvenile is easy on wing pattern, which resembles that of the adult of its respective sex (see adult male eclipse).

1st breeding male: Develops during the 1st winter. When the moult is completed it is very difficult to distinguish from the adult male.

Note: The Cinnamon Teal *A. cyanoptera* (W North America) is kept in captivity in many places in Europe. Female-type birds are very similar to Blue-winged Teal, and some are perhaps not safely separable. The bill tends to be slightly larger and more spatulate. The plumage is basically warmer in coloration. Also, the head is usually more uniform (less prominent pale spot at base of bill, darker throat and less distinct supercilium and eye-stripe, but some Blue-winged very similar in these respects). Adult male eclipse Cinnamon Teal can be identified by orange to red eyes; juvenile males more than two months old are said to have red-orange eyes (dark in Blue-winged Teal of all plumages). Blue-winged and Cinnamon Teals have been reported to hybridize occasionally in the wild.

Range: Breeds across C North America, Winters in the S parts of the USA to N South America. Vagrants have reached Greenland, Morocco (6) and Canary Is (2).

Status: The third most frequently recorded North American dabbling duck. As with most other North American species, the majority of the records are from the British Isles (163). Also, Iceland (3), Faeroes (Nov 1972, Nov 1980), France (16), Channel Is (Alderney, 3 in Sept 1983), Belgium (2), Netherlands (13), Denmark (6, also breeding pair which successfully reared young in 1986), Sweden (10), Finland (5), Poland (Apr 1984), West Germany (2), Switzerland (3), Italy (3), Greece (Apr 1986), Spain (Apr 1987), Portugal, and the Azores (5).

In the British Isles there are records from all months, especially Sept-Oct. All Swedish records are from spring (cf. American Wigeon and 'Green-winged Teal'). Popular in aviculture: some of the above records may relate to escapes. At least ten individuals have certainly crossed the Atlantic as shown by ringing recoveries.

MARBLED TEAL   *Marmaronetta angustirostris*   R Br* 8

L 39-42cm (16"). Breeds in S Spain. Also N Africa, Middle East and W Asia. Few records outside normal breeding range in Europe.

All plumages: A rather small, slim and long-necked duck with rather full nape in most birds (shaggy crest at least in adult male). Plumage very pale sandy-brown with blackish patch around the eyes and shows diagnostic, large, pale spots on the upperparts and flanks. Has long and slender, blackish bill. The wings are very pale, both above and below. At long range, could be confused with female-type Pintail, but when seen close at hand it is highly distinctive.

Adult male: Shows a narrow, whitish band across the bill near the tip and a blue-grey band along the cutting edge of the upper mandible.

Adult female: Said to differ from the adult male in generally shorter or no crest and all-dark bill, with dull greenish area on the sides of the base of the upper mandible (apparently not always reliable).

Juvenile: Resembles the adult female but shows less distinct pale spots on the upperparts and flanks. Also, lacks barring on the breast, has practically unstreaked sides to the head and lacks or only shows an extremely short crest.

Habitat: Breeds on small, relatively shallow lakes with extensive fringe and emergent vegetation.

Range: In Europe, breeding is confined to a few places in S and SE Spain. In the late 1800's several thousand pairs were breeding in Guadalquivir, but it has since declined dramatically, and in 1984-5 only 150-200 pairs were estimated as breeding there. It formerly bred also in France, Italy, Yugoslavia, Crete, Cyprus and Canary Is. Also breeds locally in N Africa, the Middle East and W Asia.

Some post-breeding dispersal and migration apparently takes place, some birds migrating quite far (e.g. across the Sahara). In Spain, it is reported to perform seasonal movements across the Strait of Gibraltar, which may be related to changing water levels.

Status: Vagrants reported from a number of European countries, but most records are old, when population more numerous and range more extensive. Recorded France (*c.* 20), especially from the Camargue (Aug-Sept, Feb-May). East Germany (July 1968), West Germany (4, origin uncertain), Poland (Mar 1989*), Czechoslovakia (4), Hungary (24), Rumania, Bulgaria (June 1979), Albania, Greece (5th in May 1984), Italy, Sicily (6 records, last in Dec 1892), Malta (3), and Portugal. Some recent records from NW Europe may relate to escapes rather than genuine vagrants.

CANVASBACK *Aythya valisineria*   A **9**

L 48-56cm (21"). North America. Two recent records.

All plumages: Similar to Pochard, but is slightly larger, with strikingly different bill shape, and, less obviously, head shape. The bill is all-blackish, lacking Pochard's pale subterminal band (rarely missing in female-type Pochard). The wings show even less of a wing-bar than in Pochard.

Adult male breeding: The crown and anterior part of the head is dark brown to blackish, unlike male Pochard and the 'mid-body' is even paler grey than in that species.

Adult male eclipse: Apparently duller and browner than breeding plumage.

Adult female: The 'mid-body' tends to be paler than female Pochard.

Juvenile: Apparently similar to the adult female. In the hand, can be told by the shape of the tail feathers (see American Wigeon, p. 54). Juvenile male is reported to attain yellowish iris when very young.

1st breeding male: The juvenile plumage is moulted during the 1st autumn-early winter. When the moult is completed (normally already in Dec), it is very difficult to distinguish from the adult male in the field. Under exceptionally good conditions it can be seen that the coverts are darker, browner and less vermiculated. Often a few inner greater coverts are new, contrasting with the rest of the coverts. Retained juvenile tertials are narrower, more pointed, darker and less vermiculated, but all of the tertials are usually renewed. In the hand the greater primary coverts and alula are dark, lacking the distinct grey vermiculations on the tips of adult.

Range: Breeds in NW North America. Winters chiefly in the USA, mainly in the SE.

Status: Accidental in SW Iceland: female collected on 11th Apr 1977. West Germany: male on Saar River near Saarbrücken in Jan-Mar 1987, regarded as escape.

RING-NECKED DUCK *Aythya collaris*

L 37-46cm (14.5-18"). North America. Frequent transatlantic vagrant, mainly autumn/winter.

All plumages: Rather similar to the corresponding plumages of Tufted Duck. Head profile is noticeably different from Tufted, and shows obvious peak to rear crown (shows no trace of a loose crest on nape). The bill is longer and slightly narrower, especially distally, and thus looks more pointed. The wing-bars are grey, not white as in Tufted.

Adult male breeding: Further differs from adult male Tufted Duck in showing two distinct white bands across the bill. Also shows a white vertical wedge on the side of the breast (white reaching higher up than in Tufted), and has uniformly grey flanks. Under ideal conditions a chestnut collar can be seen around the lower neck. Note that moulting immature and adult eclipse male Tufted can show greyish, usually irregularly patterned, flanks.

Adult male eclipse: Resembles the adult female but is more blackish-brown on the head/neck, breast and upperparts. Usually shows some grey flank feathers and has a yellow iris.

Adult female: Has different head pattern to Tufted Duck. Normally shows a distinct white eye-ring (broken in front), and the throat, upper neck, lores and ear-coverts are largely rather pale (usually with a dark area below the eye). In some the head is darker, with only a pale area at the base of the bill (as in many Tufted), but has diagnostic white eye-ring and often a whitish streak behind the eye. Usually shows a rather conspicuous pale band across the bill near the tip, more distinct than in most Tufted. The iris is brown (yellow in Tufted, but note that juvenile female Tufted Duck initially shows a brown iris).

Especially individuals with darker sides to the head and a contrasting pale area at the base of the bill could also be confused with Scaup or Lesser Scaup. However, the characters separating Ring-necked from Tufted Duck also distinguish it from Scaup and Lesser Scaup.

Another possible confusion risk is female Pochard. However, Pochard is larger, shows a distinctly different head/bill shape, less whitish at base of bill, and paler and greyer 'mid-body'.

Juvenile: Closely resembles the adult female but tends to show less well-defined head markings. In the hand the shape of the tail feathers is a good distinction from the adult (see American Wigeon, p. 54).

1st breeding male: Gradually acquired from late in the 1st autumn. When the moult is completed, usually during the 1st winter but sometimes not until the spring of the 2nd year, it is very similar to the adult male, although often fractionally duller (a few scattered juvenile feathers are often retained), with more worn wings.

Range: Breeds in S and C Canada and northernmost USA. Winters chiefly in W and E USA down to Central America. Vagrants have reached Greenland and even Algeria and Morocco (6).

Status: The third most commonly seen North American duck. The majority of the records are from the British Isles (265, since first recorded in 1955), many individuals long-staying, some reappearing in the same sites in successive winters. There was a notable influx to the UK between 1977 and 1980, and since then birds have also increasingly occurred in other areas of Europe. There are records from Iceland (13), Faeroes (Sept 1984), France (14), Belgium (10), Netherlands (12), Denmark, Sweden (13), Norway (21), Finland (Apr 1989*), West Germany (*c.* 10), Austria (pair, Nov 1989), Switzerland (9), Spain (4), Portugal, and the Azores (12, including 3 males and 2 females in Nov 1979).

Most of the records are between Nov-May, with individuals regularly joining flocks of Tufted Ducks. There are very few records from earlier in the autumn.

It is possible that some of the records refer to escapes. However a male ringed at Slimbridge, UK in Mar 1977 was recovered in SE Greenland in May of the same year, providing clear evidence of a bird returning across the Atlantic.

LESSER SCAUP   *Aythya affinis*   A **11**

L 38-46cm (15-18"). North America. A few very recent records.

All plumages: Closely resembles corresponding plumages of Scaup, but is slightly smaller, with a proportionately marginally smaller bill and distinctly peaked rear crown (Scaup has smoothly rounded crown). The wing-bar is white on the secondaries, becoming greyer across the primaries (white wing-bar extends to outer primaries in Scaup).

Adult male breeding: In good light, normally shows purplish gloss to the blackish head. (Scaup shows greenish gloss). However, from certain angles a faint greenish gloss can often be seen, as well as a faint purplish gloss in Scaup. The scapulars are generally a little more coarsely marked than in Scaup, giving the upperparts a marginally darker shade. Flanks usually appear pale grey-tinged because of some fine dark barring (flanks whiter in Scaup as very little or no barring).

Adult male eclipse: Resembles the adult female but usually has a darker head/breast, greyer upperparts and flanks, and shows less white at the base of the bill.

Adult female: On plumage, not safely separable from female Scaup. Structural differences and wing-bar pattern are the best characters. Female-types are easily confused with Tufted Ducks showing much white at the base of the bill and an abnormally short crest. Best distinguished by narrow black nail (bill broadly tipped black in Tufted) and grey wing-bar on the primaries. See Ring-necked Duck (p. 63).

Juvenile: Closely resembles the adult female but generally shows less white at the base of the bill. The iris is initially more brownish, especially in juvenile female. In the hand the shape of the tail feathers is a good distinction from the adult (see American Wigeon, p. 54).

1st breeding male: See Ring-necked Duck (p. 63); apparently acquisition of adult plumage is slightly slower than in that species.

Note: Beware hybrids of other *Aythya* species (e.g. Pochard, Tufted Duck), which are not infrequently encountered and can closely resemble an adult male Lesser Scaup. Hybrids often have upperparts more finely vermiculated and paler tertials.

They usually have a blue-grey bill, lightening distally, with a broad, black terminal band, while Lesser Scaup has all blue-grey bill with a small black nail at the tip.

Habitat: Lesser Scaup is more of a freshwater species in the non-breeding season than Scaup.

Range: Breeds chiefly in the NW parts of North America. Winters over much of the southern half of the USA (further north along the W coast) down to Central America. Vagrant in Greenland (May 1985).

Status: Accidental. Britain: Chasewater, West Midlands, 1st-year male (8th Mar-26th Apr 1987). Ireland: Co Down, adult male (13th Feb-at least 12th Mar 1988); Armagh and Co Down (27th Dec 1988-3rd May 1989), presumably same (21st Dec 1989-21st Apr 1990).

KING EIDER *Somateria spectabilis*   D **10**

L 47-63cm (18.5-25"). Circumpolar on arctic coasts (not breeding Europe). Winters in fairly large numbers on coasts of N Norway. Small numbers regular elsewhere in Scandinavia and Iceland. Very rare elsewhere in Europe.

Adult male breeding: Unmistakable. Readily distinguished from Eider in breeding plumage by striking red bill with large orange shield, blue-grey crown/nape and black scapulars. Note curious triangular 'sails' on rear scapulars.

Adult male eclipse: Predominantly dull blackish-brown, usually with some white on the breast and mantle. The orange bill shield is noticeably reduced in size, but is still very distinctive. Distinguished from subadult males by its immaculate white upperwing-covert patches.

Adult female: Closely resembles female Eider, but is slightly smaller and more compact, with different head and bill profile. The bill is smaller, forehead more rounded and nape fuller, giving a less triangular head shape than in Eider.

Further, the feathering at the base of the bill differs distinctly from Eider: The feathering on the top of the bill reaches much further down (to nostrils), while the feathering at the side is much shorter (not reaching to nostrils). Also differs in its 'happy-looking' corners to the mouth, contrasting pale chin and tips to feathering on the side of the bill, and darker, blackish-looking bill.

Plumage generally more rusty-tinged than Eider, and the flank markings are distinctly crescent-shaped (flanks more barred in Eider). The scapulars look rather scalloped (more barred in Eider), usually with distinct internal pale markings (lacking or only poorly marked in Eider). Sometimes shows small 'sails' on scapulars.

Juvenile: Resembles the adult female, but the plumage is basically paler and duller. The pale fringes to the scapulars, coverts and tertials are distinctly narrower and duller and the wing-bars are much less distinct. The feathers of the breast/flanks are basically dark with pale fringes, lacking the rich coloration and prominent dark crescents of the adult female. The juvenile male differs from the juvenile female in showing whitish centres to the breast feathers.

Differs from juvenile Eider by much the same characters as described for adult female, although the differences in scapular and flank pattern are not valid.

Subsequent immature plumages of male: Distinct adult male characters start to appear during the 1st autumn/winter, usually starting with the development of a paler breast and darkening to the scapulars and flanks. During the 1st winter, the bill turns pale orange, especially on the inner-upper part, where the shield begins to develop. Some 1st-year males (in late spring to early summer) are in a fairly advanced male plumage, but they can always be distinguished from 2nd-year and adult males by their all-brown, juvenile coverts.

From late autumn of the 2nd to autumn of the 3rd year the plumage is generally similar to the adult male in corresponding plumage (breeding and eclipse respectively), but it can probably always be identified by the presence of dark flecking on the coverts. In breeding plumage also usually shows a variable amount of dusky on the head and breast. Full adult plumage is acquired during late autumn of the 3rd year.

The bill colour will instantly separate from Eider from late in its 1st/early 2nd year onwards. It is also worth remembering that the scapulars never acquire any white, which is typical of Eider.

Subsequent immature plumages of female: Adult characters start to develop in the 1st autumn. In the spring of the 2nd year, distinguished from the adult by its more irregularly patterned plumage (juvenile and adult feathers mixed, usually obvious on flanks), and narrow, not white wing-bars. From late autumn of the 2nd year, the plumage is essentially similar to the adult female.

Note: Hybrids between King Eider and Eider have occasionally been encountered (especially noted Iceland, where King does not normally breed). Hybrids are somewhat intermediate in appearance, sometimes similar to King and sometimes more close to Eider.

Range: Breeds along almost entire arctic coast except in Scandinavia and on Iceland. In Europe, winters off coasts of N Norway (probably some 10,000 individuals) and E Iceland (in small numbers). A few also move down the Norwegian coast and sporadically enter the North Sea.

Status: Mostly a vagrant in the rest of Europe. In Sweden over *c.* 665 individuals have been recorded 1961-1988 (no data compiled before that). There has been a considerable increase in the number of birds, from 1-2 per year in the early 1960s, then *c.* 10 per year in the late 1960s/early 70s and still increasing (the highest annual total, *c.* 90 in 1986 and *c.* 100 in 1988). Most of the records are from Feb-May, with a distinct peak in April (coinciding with the spring migration of Eider). There are also many records from Finland (mainly along coast): *c.* 500 to 1986. As in Sweden the numbers have increased in recent years, and from the late 1970's 30-50 birds have been recorded annually. There is a notable peak in May. Increasingly recorded Iceland (330 individuals noted between 1979-87). British Isles (210), majority from Scotland/Shetland Isles, with some long staying/returning individuals (Oct-June). Also recorded from the Faeroes (rare visitor throughout year), France (4), Belgium (Dec 1984, Jan 1986), Netherlands (4), Denmark (61), East Germany (5 in Nov-Feb, 3 in Apr-June), West Germany (10+), Poland (records doubled in the winter of 1985/86, with ten records from Gdansk Bay), Estonia, Hungary (1875, Jan 1973, Apr 1986), Italy (6), and Spain (June 1987).

SPECTACLED EIDER *Somateria fischeri* A **10**

L 52-57cm (20-22.5"). Alaska and E Siberia. Very rare vagrant in N Norway.

All plumages: Distinctly smaller than Eider, near size of King Eider. The feathering at the base of the bill is very different from either. A cloak of feathers covers the inner part of the bill to above (or just beyond) the nostrils.

Adult male breeding: Basically resembles adult male Eider, but the head is mostly greenish with large, white, black-rimmed 'spectacles', and the breast is black. Additionally, the bill is orange.

Adult male eclipse: Mainly dark brown with little barring and mottling and some white. The paler grey 'spectacles' are still obvious. The immaculate white upperwing-patches are a good distinction from other plumages (although often concealed when wings folded).

Adult female: Resembles adult female Eider but shows diagnostic pale 'spectacles'. The scapulars are more broadly barred than in Eider, and normally so is the breast. The bill is usually more bluish than in Eider.

Juvenile: Differs from adult female in much the same characters as described for King Eider (p. 65). Differs from juvenile Eider and King Eider by obvious spectacles.

Subsequent immature plumages: Both sexes gradually acquire adult plumage, apparently in a similar way to that described for King Eider.

Range: Breeds along the arctic coast of E USSR and N Alaska. Winters mainly in the Bering Sea.

Status: Accidental in Norway: male at Vardø, Varanger (Dec 1933); also single males at different localities on arctic and Atlantic coasts (May, June and Sept 1970).

STELLER'S EIDER   *Polysticta stelleri*   D 10

L 43-47cm (17-18.5"). Arctic species (not breeding Europe). Winters in large numbers in N Norway, with smaller numbers in Baltic. Very rare elsewhere in Europe.

Adult male breeding: Unmistakable. White head shows greenish spot in front of eye and tuft on side of nape, and has black chin, throat, neck collar and central upperparts. Has dark orangey-coloured underparts (becoming blackish on belly) and shows a conspicuous black spot just above the waterline on either side of the breast.

Adult male eclipse: Resembles the adult female and is best distinguished by the large, white wing panels (usually concealed when swimming).

Adult female: Much smaller than Eider and King Eider with a very different head profile. The crown is rather flat and the rear crown/nape is distinctly angular, giving the head a square-looking outline. The bill is rather long and 'triangular', without any feathering extending onto the sides – looking as if it has been tacked on. The plumage is less strongly patterned and slightly darker than female Eider or King Eider, and the speculum is violet-blue with broad, white bars in front and behind.

mantle feathers

Juvenile: Basically paler and duller than the adult female. The mantle has narrower and less rufous tips and the breast is more finely barred with pale. The belly is finely barred with pale (uniformly dark in adult female). Under ideal conditions, the pattern of the individual feathers of the mantle and breast can be seen to differ (see figure). Most easily distinguished from the adult female by the wing pattern. The speculum shows little or no violet-blue, and the pale bars are clearly narrower and less distinct. The tertials are shorter and straighter and lack whitish or pale greyish tips to the inner webs. In the hand also differs from the adult by the shape of the tail feathers (see American Wigeon, p. 54).

ad. ♀

breast feathers

    The juvenile male has a slightly more glossy speculum and marginally wider wing-bars than the juvenile female.

Subsequent immature plumages of male: Traces of male plumage, e.g. dark throat, dark spot on nape and white-mottled breast, can be seen from late in the 1st autumn/winter, and this progressively becomes more apparent. By the 2nd winter it resembles the adult male but usually shows some dusky markings on the otherwise white wing panels and sometimes elsewhere in the plumage.

Subsequent immature plumages of female: In the first year, best recognized by the retained juvenile wing. Inseparable from the adult after the moult in the summer of the 2nd year.

Habitat and behaviour: Prefers shallower waters than Eider and King Eider, and is usually found close to the shore. It readily dives, but more frequently up-ends when foraging than most other diving ducks.

Range: Breeds along the arctic coast of the USSR from E of the Taymyr Peninsula to Alaska. Occasionally breeds further west and has probably bred in Varangerfjord in N Norway. Main wintering area is in S Bering Sea, but fairly large numbers winter in N Norway (i.e. 10,925 in Varangerfjord on 7th Apr 1984), where many (mostly immatures) remain in summer (numbers vary between 80-1,000).

Status: It was a regular winter and spring visitor to the Baltic in the 19th century. In the first half of the 20th century the numbers went down, but from the 1960's the numbers increased again. In Sweden a total of *c.* 1,970 individuals were recorded in 1961-1988 (most in the Baltic, mainly around the islands of Öland and Gotland), with the highest counts 225 in 1985, 280 in 1986 and 220 in 1987. In Finland the total was 5,495 individuals in 1974-86, with the top counts of 850 in 1983 and 1,669 in 1986. Also, Poland recorded its highest ever total, with 97 in winter/spring 1987, including max of 65 at Cape Rozewie, and 350 were seen in Estonia in 1984. Lithuania: in 1989, *c.* 350 wintered at Palanga (sole wintering site), where regularly present in recent years.

Elsewhere, there are records from Latvia (2 in Apr 1989), East Germany (22, all from Baltic coasts), West Germany (*c.*15), Denmark (46), Netherlands (May-Aug 1980-1982, Apr 1986, Feb 1987), Belgium (Dec 1983), France (Feb 1855), British Isles (13, mostly in N, including one long-staying male 1972/84), and Iceland (June 1981, July 1986).

HARLEQUIN DUCK *Histrionicus histrionicus* R Br **11**

L 38-45cm (15-17.5"). Breeds Iceland, also North America and E USSR. Very rare visitor to the rest of Europe.

Adult male breeding: Unmistakable. The striking multi-pattern of blue-grey, brownish-red and white is unlike any other duck. At a distance it looks fairly dark, but the white stripes and facial crescent are still conspicuous.

Adult male eclipse: Resembles the adult female but usually shows traces of male plumage, i.e. dark grey cast to the head and upperparts, some brownish-red on the flanks, and a trace of the white band dividing the breast/flanks. The belly is uniformly dark, unlike female (both adult and immature) and most immature males. It further differs from both female and immature male in having dark blue-grey coverts with prominent white tips to the inner greaters (sometimes also on some medians) and white shaft-streaks to the tertials.

Adult female: Noticeably small in size. When swimming it looks all dark with a conspicuous white area on the anterior part of the head (more or less clearly divided into two patches by a dark stripe on the lores), and shows an isolated white spot on the ear-coverts. When standing or in flight, the belly can be seen to be paler with dark mottling. The wings are all dark. Female-type Long-tailed Duck is always much more extensively pale on the head/neck and also pale on the belly, flanks and sides of the stern. Female-type Velvet Scoter is much larger, with less white on lores, and shows white secondaries (though often completely concealed when swimming).

Juvenile: Difficult to separate from the adult female in the field. In the hand the tail feathers can be seen to be notched with the bare shaft projecting (see American Wigeon, p. 54).

1st breeding male: Begins to develop from late in the 1st autumn, usually starting on the head, which turns blue-grey with white markings as in the adult male breeding. In the spring and summer of the 2nd year it sometimes resembles the adult male breeding but can be told by the brown wing without white markings, and paler, mottled belly.

Habitat: Prefers rapidly flowing rivers in summer. In winter, found mainly along rocky coasts.

Range: In Europe, breeds only in Iceland (resident). It also breeds in Greenland, North America (NW and NE) and E USSR, where it is partly migratory, usually only dispersing to the coast. Vagrant in Spitsbergen.

Status: Very rare visitor to Europe (mainly Nov-Apr). Recorded from the Faeroes (4), British Isles (11), Netherlands (Dec 1982-Mar 1983), Norway (6), Sweden (3), Poland (5 near Slupsk on 8th Mar 1875, male in Karpaty Mts in May 1887, male near Poniec, Leszno Prov. on 29th Mar 1987), East Germany (4 since 1930), West Germany (c. 5), Czechoslovakia (Feb 1867), Austria (Mar 1924), Switzerland (19th century), and Italy.

Since it is resident or mainly a short-distant migrant, it seems unlikely that all of the European records refer to genuine vagrants. However, many are from the 19th century – before it was introduced to European waterfowl collections.

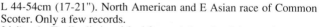

'BLACK SCOTER' *Melanitta nigra americana*   A 11

L 44-54cm (17-21"). North American and E Asian race of Common Scoter. Only a few records.

Adult male: Easily distinguished from adult male of the nominate subspecies (occurring Europe etc) by its large, swollen yellow knob at the base of the bill (extends more than halfway along the bill). Beyond the knob, the bill is all black. In the nominate form the knob is much smaller (approximately or slightly over one third of the bill length) and mainly black on the sides. Beyond the knob, there is a yellow central stripe, reaching to the nail. See figure.

'Black Scoter'

Other plumages: Inseparable from corresponding plumages of the nominate subspecies. Immature males generally develop the adult bill colour and shape from early in their 2nd year.

Range: Breeds in arctic North America and E USSR. Winters in N Pacific and W North Atlantic.

Common Scoter

Status: Accidental. British Isles (5, Sept-Mar), Netherlands (Dec 1954, Nov 1967, Nov 1977), and Spain (Nov 1986).

SURF SCOTER *Melanitta perspicillata*

L 45-56cm (18-22"). North America. Frequent vagrant, mainly to NW Europe in winter.

All plumages: Shows dark wings as Common Scoter (Velvet Scoter has obvious white secondaries).

Adult male: Unmistakable. All black plumage with two, large white patches on the head. Also has a large, strikingly multi-coloured bill. The eclipse plumage is apparently little different from the breeding plumage.

Adult female: Resembles both Velvet and Common Scoters. Differs from female-type Velvet in having a distinctly larger and differently shaped bill, often with a dark spot on the side. Lacks feathering to the sides of the bill unlike Velvet. The sides of the head are distinctly paler, contrasting with the dark cap, and most individuals show a pale patch on the nape/hindneck. The iris is often pale. Differs from female-type Common Scoter in the size and shape of the bill. There is a short wedge of feathering on the culmen of the bill lacking in Common. Also, the sides of the head are not as pale as in a normal Common Scoter, which also lacks the pale spots on the head.

Juvenile: Similar to the adult female, but is usually quite easily distinguishable by the whitish belly (although difficult to see when swimming). A few have a darker, pale brownish belly, approaching a pale adult female, but normally less mottled. Does not show a pale patch on the nape/hindneck, and the iris is always dark. In the hand the shape of the tail feathers is conclusive (see American Wigeon, p. 54). Some juveniles have very pale sides to the head, with very poorly marked pale spots, and are very similar to adult female/juvenile Common Scoter (see figure). Best distinguished by the size, shape and feathering of the bill.

1st breeding male: From late in the 1st autumn, black feathers start to appear on the head and body. Some birds are largely black by the spring of the 2nd year and show a white patch on the nape (usually smaller than in adult) but lack the white patch on the forehead. Colours of bill, legs/feet also start to develop during the 1st autumn/winter. By the 2nd winter, the plumage is similar to the adult.

Range: Breeds across N North America (from Alaska to Labrador). Winters along the coasts S to California and Florida, some also on the Great Lakes. Vagrants have reached Greenland.

Status: Rare winter visitor. Most frequent in the British Isles (*c*. 350), with a recent increase noted in the number of birds found wintering (max 35 in 1984). Also recorded from Iceland (16), Faeroes (4), Norway (26), Sweden (24), Finland (20), Estonia, France (24), Netherlands (4, Apr, Nov-Dec), Denmark (5), West Germany, Czechoslovakia, Spain (5), and the Azores (Oct 1985).

ad. ♀/juv.
Common Scoter

juv. Surf Scoter with very poorly marked pale spots on side of head

BUFFLEHEAD *Bucephala albeola*

L 32-39cm (12.5-15"). North America. Accidental.

All plumages: Reminiscent of a small Goldeneye in general appearance. In both sexes, the wing pattern is similar to that found in the respective sex of Goldeneye.

Adult male breeding: Basically resembles an adult male Goldeneye, but is readily distinguished by a large white patch on the sides and rear of the head. The black portions of the head are glossed dark green and purplish (green in Goldeneye), the sides of the rump and uppertail-coverts are grey (black in Goldeneye), and the scapulars lack black stripes. Also, has pale grey bill (blackish in Goldeneye) and dark iris (pale yellow in Goldeneye).

Adult male eclipse: Resembles the adult female, but can always be distinguished as it shows more white on the upperwings, although this may be difficult to see in a swimming bird.

Adult female: Easily distinguished from female-types of both Goldeneye and Barrow's Goldeneye by its conspicuous oval patch on the ear-coverts. Furthermore, the bill is pale grey and the iris is dark (dark bill, often with variable brownish-yellow pattern, and pale iris in Goldeneye and Barrow's Goldeneye).

Juvenile: Difficult to separate from the adult female in the field. In the hand the shape of the tail feathers is a reliable character (see American Wigeon, p. 54).

1st breeding male: Gradually attained from late in the 1st autumn onwards, but full adult plumage is apparently not reached until the 2nd winter. Pattern on upperwing-coverts resembles that of female.

Range: Breeds mainly in Alaska and Canada. Winters both inland and along the coasts down to Central America. Vagrant in Greenland.

Status: Accidental. Iceland (Nov 1956), British Isles (7, Jan-Mar, June), Channel Islands (Nov 1967), France (Mar 1980, Jan 1987), Belgium, Finland (adult male, Dec 1987), and Czechoslovakia (Mar 1885). Some of these may relate to escapes.

BARROW'S GOLDENEYE *Bucephala islandica*   R Br **12**

L 42-53cm (16.5-21"). Resident in Iceland (also Greenland and North America). Accidental.

All plumages: Female-types especially are very similar to Goldeneye in corresponding plumages, but head/bill profile is distinctly different. The forehead is steeper and the nape/hindneck is fuller, producing a less peaked head shape than in Goldeneye. Also, the bill is relatively shorter and deeper at the base, and the culmen is normally less straight (see figure).

Adult male breeding: Relatively easy to distinguish from adult male Goldeneye by a number of characters. The white patch in front of the eye is more drawn-out and crescent-shaped, reaching to above the level of the eye. Note that a slightly crescent-shaped spot can be seen in some moulting immature male Goldeneyes, not, however, reaching above the level of the eye. The pattern of the upperparts differs in showing more black, reducing the white area to a row of isolated white rectangles on the scapulars. Also, the black of the mantle extends down onto the sides of the upper breast and along the flanks, unlike Goldeneye. The upperwing shows less white than in male Goldeneye; the white patch on the lesser and median coverts is smaller and separated from the white 'speculum' by a black bar on the greater coverts. Under excellent conditions it can be judged that the head is glossed violet not green.

Adult male eclipse: Very similar to the adult female but darker above (especially on back – uppertail-coverts, which are blackish) and generally paler on the breast. Best told by more extensive white upperwing panels.

rrow's Goldeneye

Goldeneye

Adult female: Difficult to separate from female-type Goldeneye. The head is marginally darker, and, when the neck is stretched, the dark can be seen to extend slightly further down the neck. The bill tends to show more extensive brownish-yellow than in Goldeneye, although there is much overlap. N American birds often have the bill almost entirely brownish-yellow. Head and bill profile are the most important characters.
Juvenile: Very similar to the adult female. Initially, the iris is tinged brownish (mainly in female), but it gradually becomes pale yellow like the adult. In the hand it can be distinguished by the shape of the tail feathers (see American Wigeon, p. 54).
1st breeding male: Starts to develop from late in its 1st autumn. Advanced individuals are much like adults by the spring of the 2nd year, except for the retained juvenile wings. After the complete moult in the summer of the 2nd year, the immature male is generally like the adult; some are apparently still identifiable by the not completely adult wing pattern.
Range: In Europe confined to Iceland, where resident. Also breeds in SW Greenland, NE Labrador and NW North America. North American populations winter on adjacent Pacific and Atlantic coasts. Vagrant to Spitsbergen.
Status: Accidental in the Faeroes (4), British Isles (8, origin uncertain), France (1829, 1834, Jan 1972, Feb 1983), Norway (4), Poland (Mar 1957), East Germany (Jan 1960, May 1970), West Germany (all records under review), Austria (Nov 1988*) and Spain.

A number of other records obviously relate to escapes from wildfowl collections. Possibly, even probably, some of the above also belong in this category.

HOODED MERGANSER *Mergus cucullatus*   A 12

L 42-50cm (16.5-19.5"). North America. Accidental.

Adult male breeding: A strikingly beautiful small sawbill. Has large, erectable, fan-shaped crest and small, thin, bill giving it a very distinctive shape. The large white patch on the sides of the head, white breast with double black bands, orange-brown flanks and black upperparts with white shaft-streaks to the tertials immediately distinguish it from all other ducks.
Adult male eclipse: Resembles the adult female, but the yellow iris (dark, reddish-brown in female) and paler coverts still make identification possible.
Adult female: Bears some resemblance to female-types of the much larger Red-breasted Merganser, but is readily distinguished by e.g. size, small bill, and larger, fuller crest. Shows rufous-brown iris.
Juvenile: Very similar to the adult female, but the crest is distinctly shorter and the iris is grey-brown. In the hand, further distinguished by the shape of the tail feathers (see American Wigeon, p. 54).
1st breeding male: Gradually acquired from late in the 1st autumn/winter. Some birds are quite similar to the adult in the spring of the 2nd year (plumage normally less bright, with shorter crest, no pale panel on lesser coverts and usually less white on greater coverts), whereas others are less advanced but show some definite signs of male plumage.
Habitat: Prefers freshwater pools, lakes and rivers.

Range: Breeds in NE USA/SE Canada and NW USA/SW Canada. Winters mainly in coastal areas south to N Mexico.

Status: Accidental in the British Isles (6, Dec-Jan), West Germany (adult male, 1906, 10 records in 1980's relate to escapes), Norway (Sept 1985, June 1986), Finland (May and Oct-Nov 1989*), and Iceland (summer 1988*). Reports from France and Luxembourg since 1983, also Sweden (May 1985) were considered probable escapes. It has recently become well established in many wildfowl collections in Europe so the origin of the European records is not entirely clear.

WHITE-HEADED DUCK *Oxyura leucocephala* R Br* **12**

L 43-48cm (17-19"). Mainly resident in very small numbers in S Spain and E Rumania. Breeds further east to C Asia; also N Africa. Few records N of breeding areas.

Adult male breeding: Only likely to be confused with adult male Ruddy Duck (introduced to England from America), but has a much larger bill with swollen base, and the head is obviously more extensively white. Also, the body is not so deep reddish-brown and is generally more barred, and the undertail-coverts are dark (white in Ruddy).

Adult male eclipse: Similar to breeding plumage but said to be more greyish-buff on the neck and underparts, and the white head has some dusky markings. The bill is slightly smaller and greyer.

Adult female: More closely similar to female-type Ruddy Duck, but is slightly larger and has a distinctly more swollen base to the bill. Normally shows a more distinct dark stripe on the ear-coverts. Also, has more rufous general coloration and more vermiculated upperparts.

Juvenile: Very similar to the adult female, but is said to be more grey-brown in general coloration.

Subsequent immature plumages of male: Progression from juvenile to adult plumage varies individually – some apparently change almost straight to full adult, others are said to attain varying degrees of blackish, covering much of the areas which will eventually become white (black-headed males occur not infrequently), and which is sometimes retained until 2 years old. By the spring of the 2nd year most apparently resemble the adult male but have duskier head pattern. Blue bill attained during 1st winter/spring.

Habitat and behaviour: Freshwater species, preferring rather shallow ponds and lakes with dense vegetation. Dives readily, rarely flies.

Range: Breeds very locally in S Spain, Tunisia, Rumania, and C Turkey. Main breeding areas are in S USSR and eastwards to NW China and NW Mongolia.

Formerly more widespread in S Europe – has bred Hungary, Yugoslavia, Italy (Apulia, Sicily, Sardinia), Corsica, and probably Albania and Greece. Numbers have declined and its range has contracted, now being confined to S Spain and E Rumania. The relict Spanish population is at last showing some signs of an increase (following hunting ban in 1977 and subsequent purchase of the best breeding lagoon as a reserve in 1983). In 1985 the first breeding for decades was reported in the Guadalquivir Marismas, also in 1988 four pairs bred near the SE coast. A re-introduction programme has recently started in Hungary.

Recently there has been some increase in the number of birds found wintering in SE Europe: Greece recorded its largest number ever, with *c.* 400 at Porto Lagos (Jan 1988), and Bulgaria recorded flocks of up to 214 (Jan 1983).

Status: Very rare outside the above mentioned areas. There are records from Portugal, France (4), Belgium (Dec 1986, Nov 1989), Netherlands (*c.* 10), West Germany (5), East Germany (6, Sept-Mar), Poland (5), Czechoslovakia (6th record included a flock of 41 in Nov 1974), Austria (7), Switzerland (7 in 20th century), Sicily (7 records since 1930), and Malta (2). Some birds have been suspected of being escapes, although it is rather rare in captivity.

Family ACCIPITRIDAE   Hawks and Eagles

BLACK-SHOULDERED KITE   *Elanus caeruleus*   R Br **14**

L 31-35cm (12-13.5"). WS 75-87cm (29.5-34"). In Europe resident in small numbers in Portugal and Spain. Very rare vagrant elsewhere. Also in Africa and Asia.

All plumages: Rather small raptor with characteristic shape. Has rather long and broad, but still pointed wings. Also shows a large, rather owl-like head and a shortish tail. The mainly pale grey and white plumage, with mostly black primaries below and large black patch on the upper-wing-coverts make it strikingly different from any other European raptor. It flies with soft wing beats, interspersed with glides on distinctly raised wings. Also frequently hovers.

Adult: Plumage lacks any brownish colours, and the iris is red.

Juvenile: Has brownish-grey crown, hindneck and mantle/scapulars (the latter with broad pale fringes). Also shows pale orange-brown sides to the breast, conspicuous pale tips to the greater coverts and remiges, and a dark subterminal bar to the tail. The iris is initially dark.

Subsequent immature plumages: During the 1st autumn, juvenile plumage is gradually moulted and the iris turns reddish. Shows pale tips to the retained juvenile greater coverts and remiges, separating it from adult until these feathers have all been renewed (probably in summer/autumn of 2nd year).

Habitat: Favours open, dry areas with scattered trees and bushes.

Range: In Europe, breeds only in Spain (100+ pairs) and Portugal (150-200 pairs), where resident. The numbers appear to be increasing. There are interesting records of single individuals observed flying north at Gibraltar on 14th May 1977, 6th Apr 1986 and 8th May 1988 apparently having arrived from Morocco.

It also has a scattered distribution in Africa (including N) and Asia. (American and Australian Black-shouldered Kites are often treated as conspecific with European, African and Asian birds).

Status: Very rare vagrant outside limited breeding range. France (10, a pair in SW in June 1983-Oct 1984, and 1-2 birds again in 1985; first definite breeding occurred in Pyrénées-Atlantiques in summer 1990, and others may be breeding in SW France). Netherlands (May 1971), West Germany (4, origin uncertain), Poland (May 1984), Czechoslovakia (Mar 1938), Austria (May 1986), Italy (3), Rumania, and Bulgaria (Apr 1980).

PALLAS'S FISH EAGLE *Haliaeetus leucoryphus*

L 76-84cm (30-33"). WS 175-220cm (69-86"). Asiatic species. Accidental.

Adult: Easily recognized by large size, all-dark plumage with pale head and neck, and mostly white tail with broad, black terminal band. Has distinctive flight silhouette characterized by its long, comparatively narrow wings, strongly protruding head and neck, and moderately long tail. Female distinctly larger than male (up to 20%).

ower lesser covert

Juvenile: Very different from adult and resembles an immature White-tailed Eagle. As in that species, the inner wing is broader and the tail is longer, creating a noticeably different shape from the adult. Compared to immature White-tailed Eagle, it is basically paler grey-brown and more uniformly patterned on the body and upperwing-coverts. The mantle/scapulars and upperwing-coverts are dark grey-brown with diffuse paler fringes, slightly wider on the coverts. In juvenile White-tailed, these areas are strikingly different: pale rufescent brown with large, 'diamond-shaped', blackish markings on tips (see figure). The underparts are rather uniformly grey-brown, often with a slightly darker breast, but no heavy streaking as in juvenile White-tailed (in the latter, feathers are patterned much as on mantle and coverts). There is a unique, contrasting dark face-mask. The plumage of subadult White-tailed Eagle is blotchier and more variegated than immature Pallas's.

scapular

juv.
White-tailed
le   Eagle

In flight, it has a distinctive underwing-pattern: shows a broader and more conspicuous pale central band than is found in White-tailed, also has a diagnostic, large, pale patch on the inner primaries. The paler panel on the central upperwing seen in juvenile and some subadult White-tailed Eagles is lacking (but is often seen in subadults). The tail is all-dark and the uppertail-coverts pale. In White-tailed the rectrices are partly pale on the inner webs, and the uppertail-coverts are dark (with pale mottling in some subadults).

Subsequent immature plumages: The following two plumages (2nd-year autumn/3rd-year spring and 3rd-year autumn/4th-year spring) are basically similar to juvenile. These can be distinguished from juvenile by showing feathers of different generations, resulting in an uneven trailing edge to the wings, and more irregularly patterned plumage. The plumage progressively becomes more adult-like, and full adult plumage is presumably reached in the autumn of the 5th or 6th year.

Habitat and behaviour: Similar to White-tailed Eagle, inhabiting areas with lakes, ponds and rivers. Lethargic, spending much of its time perched, watching for prey (fish, waterfowl).

Range: Widely distributed in C and S Asia. In W Palearctic has disappeared as a breeding bird, formerly bred in the region N of the Caspian Sea (last bred 1947).

Status: Accidental in Norway (July 1949), Finland (*c.* 1910 and June 1926), and Poland (June 1943). An adult present West Germany/Denmark/Netherlands (Sept-Oct 1976), was possibly an escape.

LAMMERGEIER *Gypaetus barbatus*

L 100-115cm (39-45"). WS 266-282cm (105-111"). Rarest of Europe's vultures. Breeds S Europe to C China; also in Africa.

All plumages: Huge vulture with diagnostic shape. Young immatures look broader winged and shorter tailed than adults, and may look more eagle-like, especially when soaring but none the less still show very characteristic shape.

Adult: The rusty (sometimes almost whitish) head/neck and underparts and all dark upperparts, wings and tail are unlike any other European species. At close range the black face mask and loosely drooping black 'moustaches and beard' are diagnostic.

Juvenile: Easily distinguished from adult by the browner upperside, mostly blackish head/neck, grey-brown underparts and paler underwing. Plumage is typically fresh, with all feathers the same age, thus differing from young subadults.

Subsequent immature plumages: Gradually attains adult plumage over 4-5 years. Subadults are often rather tatty-looking and frequently show paler areas on the coverts and the upperside of the body.

Habitat and Behaviour: Breeds in mountains, in Europe typically between 1,000-3,000m, in parts of Asia normally much higher. Frequently seen patrolling mountain slopes at surprisingly slow speed. Takes bones and meat from freshly killed mammals, tortoises and birds. Bones form a substantial part of the diet and can be swallowed whole. Larger bones may be shattered by dropping from *c.* 50-80 m at favoured rocky areas. Where food is scarce it will scavenge from older carcasses. Unlike other vultures does not normally compete for food at a carcass, preferring to wait until other vultures have finished.

Range: Formerly more widespread in Europe. Population now estimated at 65-80 pairs for mainland Europe. France, Pyrenees (10 prs), Corsica (15 prs). Spain, Pyrenees (45 prs), Greece (35 prs, mainly in Crete). Yugoslavia (1 pr). Basically resident. Also, breeds Middle East, SW and C Asia to Mongolia and C China. Also in N, E and S Africa.

Status: Very rare vagrant in Austria, Czechoslovakia, West Germany, Switzerland, and Portugal.

With the recent reintroduction experiments in the region of Austria and France (Alps), there has been a corresponding increase in the number of observations from Switzerland with 8 records in 1987-88.

PALLID HARRIER   *Circus macrourus*   R Br **14**

L 40-48cm (16-19"). WS 95-120cm (37-47"). Breeds extreme E Europe (also further E to C Asia). Rare visitor to rest of Europe on migration.

All plumages: Resembles Hen Harrier, but is distinctly smaller and slimmer with narrower and decidedly more pointed wings (see figure, p. 77). On shape, it is very similar to Montagu's Harrier, but some adult females look broader-winged than Montagu's and may actually recall Hen Harrier. In the hand the wing formula can be seen to differ slightly from Montagu's (wing point made up of 3 primaries, as opposed to 4 in Hen; see figure, p. 77).

Adult male: Readily distinguished from an adult male Montagu's. Shows much paler plumage, less black on the wing-tip, lacks black bars on the secondaries, and lacks brownish-red markings on the underparts and underwing.

It is also distinctly paler than an adult male Hen Harrier, sometimes appearing whitish on the throat and breast. The uppertail-coverts are greyish or white-flecked and do not form a conspicuous white patch as in Hen. The black pattern on the primaries is also less extensive,

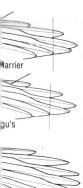

Harrier

Montagu's

Harrier

margination on
primary is often
scaled by the
greater coverts in
Pallid and Hen Harriers.

forming a characteristic black wedge in the wing-tip, and there is no distinct darker band along the trailing edge of the underwing as in Hen (but see subsequent immature plumages of male). The male is 10% smaller than the female.

Adult female: Best distinguished from female-type Hen Harrier by the differences in size and structure described above.

It differs from adult female Montagu's mainly by its wing pattern. The secondaries are uniformly dark above (faint bars can be seen under optimum conditions), whereas in Montagu's a distinct dark band at the base of the secondaries can usually be seen, and there is often another one (generally slightly less distinct) on the trailing edge.

The pattern on the underside of the secondaries also differs significantly between the two species. Both usually show three dark bars (the most forward one eventually disappearing under the greater coverts) and two pale bars in between. In Pallid, the rearmost pale bar is comparatively narrow (narrower than the dark trailing bar), and the pale bars become narrower and darker towards the body, generally making the secondaries look rather dark. In Montagu's, the rearmost pale bar is obviously broader (of approximately the same width as the dark trailing bar), and the pale bars do not become narrower and darker towards the body. In Pallid the dark bars are all equally dark, whereas in Montagu's the dark trailing bar is not quite so blackish as the two dark bars in front.

The axillaries and greater underwing-coverts are rather dark with pale spots (looking chequered). In Montagu's, the axillaries (and often the greater underwing-coverts) are distinctly and coarsely barred, providing another useful distinguishing mark.

The head pattern is also slightly different, although this may be of limited value. The pale collar is narrow but rather conspicuous (similar to Hen Harrier). In Montagu's it is normally lacking, but note that there may seem to be a rather distinct pale collar. The dark stripe behind the eye is generally slightly more prominent, and there is on average less white over the eye.

The markings on the 'trousers' and undertail-coverts are usually clearly different in the two species, which can be a useful character when observing a perched individual. Pallid usually shows rufous, broad 'double spots', which are sometimes rather diffuse and extensive, making the 'trousers' and undertail-coverts look almost entirely rufous. Montagu's shows rather narrow, normally sharply defined, rufous streaks. See figure.

Juvenile: Easily separated from the adult female by e.g. the unmarked, rufous underparts and dark secondaries below. Males can be distinguished from females by their smaller size and paler, grey, iris (dark brown in female).

Juvenile Hen Harrier is usually distinctly streaked and less rufous below. However, some (usual case in the Nearctic (sub)species *hudsonius*) are only streaked on the upper breast and are rather rich rufous below and also have more Pallid-like head/neck pattern, but the size and silhouette should ascertain their identity.

From juvenile Montagu's, it differs in the head pattern, which is even more contrasting in Pallid. There is a broad, unmarked pale necklace, enhanced by a prominent dark area below, which extends onto

♀ Pallid Harrier

Montagu's Harrier

'trousers' and
undertail-coverts.

the sides of the neck in the shape of a dark semi-collar (almost complete in some individuals). In Montagu's, the pale collar is only rarely rather conspicuous, and the dark semi-collar is never so uniformly dark, clear-cut and prominent. Other differences in head pattern as described for adult females are also valid for juveniles.

Subsequent immature plumages of male: The juvenile plumage is retained in the spring of the 2nd year, although paler due to bleaching and wear. Some individuals moult into a plumage with distinct male characters (i.e. some grey on the head, breast and upperparts, occasionally also grey central tail feathers). This plumage resembles the corresponding plumage of Montagu's, but the latter shows darker grey feathers to the upperparts and head/breast and usually has the grey on the breast more well-defined. The iris is yellow from the 1st winter/spring.

From the autumn of the 2nd year to the spring of the 3rd, the plumage basically resembles that of the adult male. However, it still shows some definite immature characters, e.g. darker and more brownish-tinged upper surface to the body and wings, with less clear-cut dark wedge on primaries, darker grey throat and breast; some indistinct streaks on the underparts; and often a narrow dark trailing edge to the wings, dark tip to the outermost primary and darker mottling to the under primary coverts.

During the complete moult in the autumn of the 2nd year, it could also be confused with male Hen Harrier in the corresponding plumage. Size and structure are often the best means of identification. Advanced Hen Harriers in this plumage could also be remarkably similar to adult male Pallid; if the outermost two primaries have not yet been moulted, from below these may look pale and unmarked (heavily worn and bleached), contrasting markedly with the newly moulted, black adjacent primaries to create a rather Pallid-like pattern. From above, the outermost primaries usually look darker, and normally a few secondaries are also unmoulted and clearly darker.

Subsequent immature plumages of female: The juvenile plumage is retained in the spring of the 2nd year, but is paler and generally shows a few streaks on the upper breast.

From the autumn of the 2nd year to the spring of the 3rd, the plumage is more like the adult female but generally shows a more contrasting head pattern, darker secondaries, and a darker iris. These are usually more difficult to separate from the corresponding plumage of Montagu's than juveniles and adults because the secondaries are often so dark in both that the differences in pattern (both above and below) is of little value. The differences in the head pattern are generally not as clear as in juveniles (but still more pronounced than in adults). Fortunately the characteristic pattern of the axillaries has normally developed at this age.

Range: In Europe, only breeds regularly (but sparsely) in E Rumania. Has occasionally bred in East and West Germany (including invasion year of 1952) and Sweden (5-6 pairs in 1952). Occasionally breeding also suspected in Finland, Austria, Hungary, Czechoslovakia and Bulgaria.

The range continues in a belt across the USSR to C Asia. Winters chiefly in Africa and S Asia, a few also in Greece and the Middle East.

Status: Rare visitor outside breeding areas. Recorded from the British Isles (3), France (16), Belgium (14), Luxembourg (3), Netherlands (8),

Denmark (40), Sweden (143, majority in May, Aug-Sept), Norway (23), Finland (70), Poland (12 since 1946), Estonia, East Germany (c. 15), West Germany, Austria, Hungary (Apr, Aug-Oct), Switzerland (10 in 20th century), Italy (scarce migrant), Yugoslavia, and Spain. Elsewhere: Greece, noted as uncommon but quite regular in spring but less common in autumn; Malta, generally scarce spring migrant (late Feb-May), rare/irregular in autumn (Aug-Oct).

DARK CHANTING GOSHAWK   *Melierax metabates*   A **14**

L 38-48cm (15-19"). WS 95-110cm (37-43"). Africa. Only one record.

All plumages: Medium-sized *Accipiter*-like hawk slightly smaller than Goshawk. Wings rather long, broad and rounded, and tail long. Long legs are distinctive when perched.

Adult: Unlikely to be confused with any European raptor. In flight it is pale below with black wing tips and has grey head/neck and breast. The upperside is grey with largely pale, black-tipped wings, pale uppertail-coverts and dark central pair of tail feathers (other tail feathers barred). At close range the underparts (except the breast) can be seen to be finely barred. The legs/feet, cere and base of the bill are red. Female 5% larger than male.

Juvenile: Noticeably darker than the adult. Upperparts brown with a large, paler area on the primaries, and pale uppertail-coverts. Also, the underside of the body and wings are brown-barred (more coarsely than in adult) with a contrasting dark breast. Bare parts are yellower than in the adult.

Subsequent immature plumages: In the spring-summer of the 2nd year, some grey feathers start to appear on the head, neck, breast and upperparts, and there is some grey barring below.

In the spring-summer of the 3rd year, the plumage is like the adult's but generally browner both above/below.

Note: There is another very similar species, the Pale Chanting Goshawk *M. canorus* in E and S Africa.

Habitat and behaviour: Favours arid bushlands and drier woodlands. Often seen on a prominent perch, watching for prey (mainly smaller reptiles, rodents, insects etc.).

Range: Breeds in much of Africa S of the Sahara and on neighbouring coastal parts of Arabia. In Morocco, a small resident population is restricted to a few dozen pairs at most on the Sous Plain.

Status: Accidental in Spain: one near Algeciras, Cádiz Provence on 13th July 1963.

SWAINSON'S HAWK   *Buteo swainsoni*   A **16**

L 43-55cm (17-22"). WS 120-137cm (47-54"). North America. Recently observed in Norway.

All plumages: The wings are long and relatively pointed compared to Buzzard and are held markedly uplifted when soaring. The flight feathers are rather dark-looking, with the bases of the outer primaries paler. The greater under primary coverts show dark tips, but the primary coverts are never all-dark, except in some dark morph individuals. The upperside is mostly dark, usually with a pale U on the uppertail-coverts.

Adult pale morph: Distinctive plumage. When seen in flight from below, more reminiscent of a pale morph of the Booted Eagle than of Buzzard. Distinguished from former by e.g. the lack of a pale nape/hind-neck, pale central upperwing-bar, and a white spot at the very base of the leading edge of the wing. Note head pattern. It is variably heavily marked on the underside of the body.

Adult dark morph: May be confused with dark or intermediate morphs of Booted Eagle, but the pattern of the nape/hindneck and upperside and leading edge to the wings differ. The undertail-coverts are pale and banded.

Adult intermediate ('rufous') morph: Intermediate between pale and dark morph, generally showing pale rufous underwing-coverts and a dark rufous body.

Juvenile: Rather pale, heavily streaked head, streaked/spotted underparts (of variable prominence) and normally rather distinct pale edges to the upperparts and coverts distinguish from the adult. Most birds are rather pale, but some are quite dark.

Some pale and some dark plumaged individuals can be very similar to some Buzzards. The flight feathers are normally darker below, but there seems to be some overlap (at least inner primaries are probably always darker than in Buzzard). Pale Buzzards usually show very pale upperwing-coverts and often rather prominent dark under primary coverts, which are not features of Swainson's. Dark birds do not show the usually distinct pale band on the central underwing-coverts and across the breast as is usually obvious in Buzzard. The wing shape is clearly different.

Subsequent immature plumages: Swainson's is reported to take two years to attain adult plumage.

Range: Breeds on the plains of W USA and SW Canada, rarely further NW. Winters in S South America. Regularly strays to E USA.

Status: Accidental in Norway: Røst, Nordland, 2nd-year on 6th May 1986.

LONG-LEGGED BUZZARD *Buteo rufinus*   R Br **13**

L 50-65cm (20-25"). WS 126-148cm (50-58"). Breeds SE Europe in small numbers (also further E in Asia and in N Africa). Rare visitor outside breeding area.

All plumages: Very similar to Buzzard of the eastern race *vulpinus*, the 'Steppe Buzzard', but is considerably larger and heavier, with proportionately longer wings, slightly longer tail and usually has a more protruding head/neck. When soaring and gliding, the 'arm' is raised and the 'hand' is held more level. The silhouette is thus more reminiscent of Rough-legged Buzzard, but is even larger.

Plumage very variable, as in Steppe Buzzard. A classic individual shows a pale head and breast, contrasting with a darker lower body and 'trousers'; rather pale underwing-coverts with a large, contrasting blackish carpal patch; pale rufous upperwing-coverts; rather large pale patch on the basal parts of the primaries above; and a rufous (more whitish basally), unmarked tail. The plumage shows a decidedly rufous ground colour.

The Steppe Buzzard is generally darker on the head/breast, usually with a contrasting pale breast-band and a pale band on the median underwing-coverts. Adults normally show distinct barring on the breast/belly and sometimes on the undertail-coverts and 'trousers' (at the most a trace of barring and paler breast-band in adult Long-legged). The carpal patch is usually less pronounced and often reduced to a dark 'comma'. The mantle/scapulars and upperwing-coverts are normally darker, and the pale patch on the primaries above is generally less conspicuous. The tail is usually barred (at least distally) and in the adult shows a distinct, broader, dark subterminal bar.

Some adult Steppe Buzzards are deep rufous below with a slightly darker lower body (lacking barring and a pale breast band), and show broad, pale rufous edges to the mantle/scapulars and upperwing-coverts. These individuals are extremely similar to more normally plumaged Long-legged Buzzards and even more similar to darker rufous birds, especially birds showing a barred tail (not too uncommon). In Steppe the leading edge to the upperwing-coverts is usually darker, although there is some overlap. The dark carpal patches below are only occasionally prominent. The tail is usually more uniformly rufous (rather whitish basally on the inner webs in Long-legged, visible from above when tail fanned), and the dark bars (at least the outermost one) are generally more distinct in Steppe, especially on the inner webs. Note that the pale patch on the primaries above is not always more prominent in Long-legged. Great care must be taken when identifying such birds, and it is necessary to use a combination of characters. Size and shape are of the utmost importance.

Some rufous, streaked, juvenile Steppe Buzzards are exceptionally similar to the 'classic' Long-legged Buzzard. They can usually be distinguished by the same characters described in the previous paragraph.

Juveniles are sometimes very similar to normal juvenile Steppe Buzzards. In both, the tail frequently lacks any trace of rufous and shows distinct barring throughout its length. Prominent dark carpal patches and contrastingly dark lower body are good indications of Long-legged, but size and structure are sometimes the only safe way of distinguishing between them.

Some individuals are very pale whitish with a pale rusty suffusion on the head, body and upper– and underwing-coverts. Unlike similarly plumaged pale Buzzards, they normally – but far from always – show large, dark carpal patches, dark 'trousers' (flanks and band across belly often dark in Buzzard, but 'trousers' normally pale) and a larger pale area on the primaries above.

There is also a dark, blackish-brown, morph (probably only in Asiatic populations), which seems to be identical in plumage to the dark morph of the Steppe Buzzard.

Adult: Broad, clearcut dark trailing edge to the wings. The tail is usually unbarred or with a few, generally indistinct, dark bars distally. In those with barred tail, the outermost bar is usually (not always!) distinctly wider than the others. Iris deep brown. Female 5-10% larger than male.

Juvenile: Differs from the adult chiefly in showing a narrower, paler, and more diffuse dark trailing edge to the wings. The tail is also more frequently barred, but the terminal dark bar is never distinctly broader than the other bars. The plumage is generally not so rufous as the adult. Pale iris.

Subsequent immature plumages: Juvenile plumage is little changed by the spring of the 2nd year. After completion of the moult in the autumn of the 2nd year, the plumage is basically similar to the adult, but a few juvenile remiges are often retained.

Range: In Europe, breeds only in Bulgaria (50+ pairs), Yugoslavia (Macedonia *c.* 20 pairs) and Greece (*c.* 60 pairs), and possibly in Albania. Also breeds in Asia Minor east to C Asia, and in N Africa. Northern birds are predominantly migratory, wintering south to NE Africa, Arabia, and eastwards to N India.

Status: In autumn small numbers occur fairly regularly north to Hungary; of 180 dated records for C Europe (mainly Hungary), two-thirds occurred during Aug-Oct, but it has been seen in all months. Scarce migrant to Italy (*c.* 40 to 1983), but very rare elsewhere outside breeding range.

Vagrants have reached France (Sept 1878, Oct 1902, Apr-June 1972, July 1979), Netherlands (Dec 1905), Denmark (4), Norway (Sept 1986), Sweden (Dec 1973-May 1974, Sept 1987, June-July 1989 and Sept 1989), Finland (Sept 1987), Poland (11), East Germany (Mecklenburg 3), West Germany (14), Switzerland (9), Austria (20+), and Czechoslovakia (27 to 1974). Records from Spain (4, May-Aug) and Gibraltar (2nd record in May 1989), where very occasionally has wandered across the Strait from N Africa; also Portugal (seldom recorded, but 2 in spring 1986, and at least one in winter 1986/87).

SPOTTED EAGLE   *Aquila clanga*   R Br **16**

L 65-72cm (27"). WS 155-180cm (61-71"). Breeds in Poland and further E to E Asia. Rare in the rest of Europe, but regular winter visitor to SE Europe.

Adult: A medium-sized, comparatively compact-looking, dark eagle, with a paler area at the base of the inner primaries above, usually a pale U on the uppertail-coverts and sometimes also a pale spot on the back. Resembles Lesser Spotted Eagle in size and shape. However, Spotted is generally slightly heavier, with broader wings and a fuller 'hand' (slightly longer 4th primary), but this distinction is tricky.

It is normally much darker and more uniformly coloured than Lesser Spotted. The underwing-coverts are roughly as dark as the remiges, often slightly darker or even slightly paler (or, exceptionally, considerably paler, see Note below). In Lesser Spotted the underwing-coverts are normally distinctly paler than the remiges. However, in some individuals the underwing-coverts are hardly any paler than the remiges and may thus be impossible to distinguish between Spotted and Lesser Spotted by this character alone.

The lesser and median coverts and upperside of the head and body are usually distinctly darker than in adult Lesser Spotted, contrasting much less with the flight-feathers. Also, the larger part of the mantle/scapulars is the same colour as the coverts, whereas a large part of the mantle/scapulars is usually contrastingly dark in adult Lesser Spotted. The pattern from above in flight is thus normally clearly different from Spotted. However, some Lesser Spotted are darker than usual, with reduced contrasts, and in some otherwise normal individuals the rear mantle/scapulars are not contrastingly dark. Spotted is, apparently, exceptionally very similar to normal Lesser Spotted in the colour and pattern of the upperside (see Note below).

Only the shafts of the primaries are pale, thereby lacking a distinct pale patch at the base of the inner primaries above which is typical of Lesser Spotted (which also shows pale on webs). However, at a distance the pale shafts often coalesce to form a paler area, and in this case the pale area is more extensive than shown by Lesser Spotted (in which it is centred on the inner primaries).

Although most individuals are readily distinguished from Lesser Spotted Eagle, some are extremely tricky, and some might be better left unidentified. In the hand, or on good photographs, the barring of the secondaries is a useful additional clue to be used on difficult individuals: the dark bars are usually narrower than the paler bars, whereas in Lesser Spotted, they are approximately the same width as the paler bars or even marginally wider.

See also adult and subadult Steppe Eagle (p. 84). Female slightly larger than male.

Juvenile: Differs from subsequent plumages by the obvious fresh appearance of its plumage (with all feathers the same age). The trailing edge to the wing is even, also slightly curved, and evenly pale-tipped. The pale 'drops' on the scapulars and upperwing-coverts immediately distinguish from old immatures and adults. The underside of the body is usually striped, sometimes quite prominently. Subadults and adults show more uniformly broad wings (due to shorter secondaries), with uneven trailing edge (due to a mixture of different generations of feathers and often also moult gaps), and lack the pale trailing bar. The remainder of their plumage is generally paler than the juvenile, and they show little or no distinct streaking to the underside.

Easily distinguished from other eagles by its very dark, blackish plumage with a variable number of rows of pale spots on the upperwing-coverts and scapulars. The underwing-coverts are usually conspicuously darker than the remiges, and the anterior upperwing-coverts are almost as dark as the flight-feathers (the white-spotted rear ones often form a pale panel at a distance).

Subsequent immature plumages: Juvenile plumage is retained during the spring of the 2nd year, but is generally slightly paler with less obvious pale markings due to wear.

From the autumn of the 2nd year to the spring of the 3rd: inner primaries and one or two outer secondaries (usually the 5th, sometimes also the 1st) are new, and the rest of the plumage consists of a mixture of worn juvenile and fresh, newly moulted, feathers. The rows of pale spots on the coverts and scapulars are mostly worn off, but newly moulted feathers show pale spots as in the juvenile. Thus shows two generations of feathers.

From the autumn of the 3rd to the spring of the 4th year: plumage usually more adult-like and usually lacks distinct pale spots on the coverts. The outermost 2-4 primaries and a few secondaries (usually the 4th and one to all of the 8th-10th) are still retained from the juvenile plumage (very worn), and the remiges renewed the year before are also retained. There are thus three generations of remiges.

Subadults could be confused with immature Lesser Spotted Eagles. They can usually be distinguished by the same characters as described for adults. However, they are even more likely to be confused with subadult and adult Steppe Eagles (see p. 84).

Note: The plumage variation is enormous, the palest examples referred to as '*fulvescens*'. True '*fulvescens*' is so pale that it could only be confused with a pale Tawny Eagle (see under Steppe Eagle, below), whereas more moderately pale birds can be difficult to separate from some Lesser Spotted and subadult Steppe Eagles and could even be confused with immature Imperial Eagle. These pale birds are (fortunately!) rare and probably only occur in immature plumages. The plumage is mostly pale buffish to pale reddish-brown, both above and below. The head (particularly around base of bill) and breast are usually darker, and there is often some darkening along the leading edge of the wing (both above and below) as well as elsewhere on the underwing and body. They lack the pale central underwing bar found in most young immature Steppe Eagles, and the remiges are neither coarsely barred nor show a broader dark terminal bar like subadult Steppe. They also lack the streaked pectoral band and diagnostic pale inner primaries typical of young immature Imperial Eagles (a few dark streaks can sometimes be seen on the breast). Great care must be taken when separating some pale birds from some Lesser Spotted Eagles: dark areas on the head and upper-/underwing-coverts are important pointers.

Range: In Europe, breeds Poland (10-20 pairs), Estonia, Latvia (nesting in 1980-84 unconfirmed, bred 1987), and Rumania (5 pairs 1981). Also breeds further eastwards in a wide belt across the USSR to the Pacific. It has been recorded breeding in Sweden (1973, failed 1974), Finland (a few pairs have bred more or less annually since the 1880's – more recently breeding confirmed only in the late 1970's), Hungary (1949-51), Czechoslovakia (1877; possibly bred 1945-50 and 1956), and Yugoslavia (1905, 1954 and in 1976-81). It winters mainly in the Middle East to S Asia. In SE Europe, small numbers winter in the Balkans, Greece (normally fewer than 10 but 25+ winter 1984/85) and N Italy (Po Valley).

Status: The majority of the records are from Sweden (*c*. 205, mainly in Sept-Nov) and Finland (102, mainly since 1975). Rare vagrant elsewhere: British Isles (12, but recorded only twice in 20th century – Apr 1908 and Nov 1915), France (30+, where fairly regular Camargue), Belgium (10), Luxembourg, Netherlands (10), Denmark (33), East Germany (10 since 1930), West Germany, Switzerland (18 since 1900), Austria, Spain, Gibraltar (Mar 1987), Portugal and Sicily (16+ records of immatures).

In Sweden and Finland most of the records are from the autumn (mainly in Sept-Nov), in Sweden it has also wintered many times.

STEPPE EAGLE *Aquila nipalensis* C **15**

L 65-80cm (25-31.5"). WS 160-215cm (63-84"). Asia. Vagrant, normally immatures only.

All plumages: The plumage variation is enormous because of the number of years taken to reach maturity, combined with extensive individual variation. A thorough knowledge of the various plumages and of the confusion species, Spotted, Lesser Spotted and Imperial Eagles, is often essential for a correct identification to be made. It is larger than either Spotted or Lesser Spotted Eagles, with a proportionately heavier bill, more protuding head/neck and longer wings with more square tips and longer 'fingers' (proportionately longer 4th primary, especially when compared to Lesser).

In a good view perched, it can be seen that in Steppe the gape reaches as far as the rear edge of the eye, whereas it ends level with the centre of the eye in the two Spotted Eagles. At very close range the nostril can be seen to be 'kidney-shaped' and vertically placed (round in the two Spotted Eagles).

Adult: In flight, looks rather uniformly dark brown above and below. There is usually a pale patch of varying prominence on the crown and nape, and a noticeable pale patch at the base of the inner primaries above. There is often a pale spot on the back and some pale on the up-pertail-coverts. The central throat is normally contrastingly pale.

It is most similar to adult and old subadult Spotted Eagles but can be distinguished if seen reasonably well by its paler and coarsely barred remiges (especially secondaries) and rectrices, with a broader dark terminal bar to the secondaries and rectrices and contrastingly dark 'fingers'. In Spotted the remiges and rectrices look uniformly dark grey; under ideal conditions barring can often be seen, but the barring is denser (showing 9-11 dark bars on outer secondaries, as opposed to 7-8 in Steppe), and the outermost dark bar is not distinctly broader. Very rarely the remiges and rectrices of Steppe can look uniform, and these birds are very difficult to tell from Spotted. The shafts and the outer webs of the inner primaries are distinctly paler above, usually forming a pale patch at the base of the inner hand. Spotted only has shafts paler, and so lacks any obvious pale patch, but when seen from a distance the paler shafts may appear to coalesce into a pale patch. A trace of the white central underwing-bar can often be seen even in adult or near-adult Steppe. See also adult Imperial (p. 86).

Female slightly larger than male.

Juvenile: In flight, distinguished from older birds by even, more 'S-shaped' trailing edge to the wing (all remiges same age), with all of the secondaries and inner primaries tipped broadly whitish. In subadult and adult birds the wings are of more uniform width (mainly because of shorter secondaries), and there are several different generations of feathers, creating an uneven, ragged trailing edge, frequently with moult gaps, and lacking an even white trailing bar. Also elsewhere, there is more than one generation of feathers.

It is relatively easy to distinguish from other eagles because of the broad white band on its central underwing. Rarely, however, this band can be virtually lacking, and confusion with juvenile Imperial Eagle may then arise (see p. 86).

Subsequent immature plumages: Juvenile plumage retained in spring of 2nd year, although slightly more worn. Adult plumage is usually acquired over a period of on average five years. Subadults usually show at least a trace of the white band on the central underwing.

Older birds, which either lack or only have a narrow pale central band, as well as having contrasting pale coverts above/below, can easily be misidentified as Lesser Spotted Eagles. Such birds are best told by their paler and coarsely barred remiges and rectrices, with a distinctly broader dark terminal bar and contrastingly dark 'fingers'. In Lesser Spotted the secondaries look uniformly dark grey. Very close views sometimes reveal 9-11, equally wide, dark bars on outer secondaries (7-8 in Steppe). In most pale subadults the head and most of the mantle/scapulars and upperwing-coverts are of the same general coloration, whereas in most subadult and adult Lesser Spotted the rear mantle/scapulars are contrastingly dark. Some individuals are, however, patterned like typical Lesser Spotted and vice versa.

Darker subadults are very similar to subadult Spotted Eagles, see above for differences. See also subadult Imperial (below).

Note: Tawny Eagle *A. rapax* (resident in Africa and W Asia; often considered conspecific with Steppe under the scientific name of the former, see Appendix) have been recorded in some European countries, but are generally considered to be escapes. It is very variable, but is generally paler and more buffish or rufous than Steppe, and normally shows pale inner primaries below and pale back, rump and uppertail-coverts. In adults and subadults the remiges and rectrices are usually either unbarred or more finely barred than in the corresponding plumages of Steppe and usually lack distinct, broad terminal bar. The gape is slightly shorter than in Steppe, ending level with the centre of the eye, and the iris of older birds is apparently yellowish (dark brown to yellowish-brown in Steppe). Some young birds are apparently very similar to young Iberian Imperial Eagle. Further research into the differences between Tawny and Steppe and immatures of both Tawny and Iberian Imperial would be desirable.

Range: The race *orientalis* breeds from W USSR (E of 41°, but possibly a few pairs left in Ukraine) to C Asia, and is a long distance migrant wintering in E and S Africa. The nominate race occurs E of *orientalis* to E Mongolia/NE China and in Tibet.

Status: Rare vagrant on migration (most birds probably relating to race *orientalis*). France (May 1960), Belgium (Dec 1983, immature – origin uncertain), Netherlands (May 1967, Jan-Feb 1984), Denmark (9), Norway (Aug 1973, June 1984), Sweden (17), Finland (11), Poland (5), East Germany (May 1960, July 1982), Czechoslovakia (5), Hungary (May 1929, May 1952), Rumania, Bulgaria, Yugoslavia (Oct 1928), Greece (11), Italy (7), and Spain.

IMPERIAL EAGLE   *Aquila heliaca*   R Br* **15**

L 72-83cm (28-33"). WS 190-210cm (75-83"). Rare breeding bird in Iberia (*adalberti*) and SE Europe (*heliaca* also to E Asia). Rare visitor outside breeding range, almost exclusively in immature plumage. The two forms are sometimes treated as separate species.

All plumages: Resembles Steppe Eagle in size and shape, although in subadult and adult plumage generally looks slightly longer-tailed and often longer-necked. When gliding and soaring the wings tend to be held flatter, or even slightly raised, but this is a variable feature and consequently of little importance. The bill is massive.

Adult: Mainly brownish-black with a very pale crown, nape and hindneck and also has a pale grey tail with broad, dark terminal band. Also shows whitish patches on the scapulars, on average more prominent in Iberian birds, which also show a white bar along the leading edge of the wing both above and below.

Adult Golden Eagle is paler, although this may not always be obvious from below. When viewed from above, the pale panel on the central upperwing is a good distinction; usually, the remiges are also distinctly paler. Golden shows darker, more yellowish-brownish crown/ hindneck and lacks the whitish patches on the scapulars, also lacks white forewing of Iberian race.

Some adult Steppe Eagles have very dark plumage and show a prominent pale patch on the crown/nape, and could be confused with Imperial. The pale patch on the crown/nape is much smaller and does not extend onto the hindneck. There is also a pale patch at the base of the inner primaries above, and the remiges are usually more distinctly barred and show a more well-defined dark terminal bar. The tail is darker, with narrower dark terminal bar, and the uppertail-coverts are often pale. Also, never shows white patches on the scapulars nor white forewing. Female slightly larger than male.

Juvenile: Has very characteristic and contrastingly patterned plumage; *adalberti* is more rufous than *heliaca* and lacks the distinct streaking of the latter. It could possibly be confused with rare examples of juvenile Steppe Eagle which lack a pale bar on the central underwing. However, from below, it shows a diagnostic pale wedge on the inner primaries, which is much more prominent than in any Steppe. In *heliaca* the breast shows a diagnostic broad band of dark streaks; at closer range the upper– and underwing-coverts, mantle, and scapulars can also be seen to be streaked. The entire back/rump/uppertail-covert area is often pale, although in many only the uppertail-coverts, and often a patch on the back, are pale as in Steppe.

Subsequent immature plumages: Juvenile plumage retained in spring of 2nd year, although more worn than in the 1st autumn. Subsequent plumages basically like juvenile to spring/summer of 3rd year when development of adult plumage accelerates. In the autumn of the 2nd/spring of 3rd year, differs from juvenile by more worn plumage with some newly moulted fresh feathers, e.g. inner primaries. In the autumn of the 3rd/spring of 4th year, more feathers have been renewed, and, since both a number of primaries and secondaries have been moulted, the trailing edge to the wings is uneven. Later immature plumages are heavily blotched because of a mixture of younger imma-ture, pale feathers, and newly moulted, blackish feathers. Full adult plumage is usually reached in the autumn of the 6th year.

Older subadults could be confused with some subadult Steppe Eagles, but are blotchier, both above and below, typically with the breast darker than the belly. Additionally, much the same characters as described for distinguishing adults are also valid for subadults, except that there is often still some pale at the base of the inner primaries above in subadult Imperial, although generally less than in Steppe.

Range: Western subspecies is mainly resident in Spain (showing signs of population recovery – at least 104 pairs 1986), with one or a few more pairs in Portugal. Eastern subspecies breeds in SE Europe. In the 20th century numbers have greatly decreased, and the breeding popu-lation is now rather small: Czechoslovakia (25 pairs); Hungary (27 pairs); Yugoslavia (*c.* 20 pairs); Greece (2-6 pairs), Rumania (*c.* 60 pairs) and Bulgaria (*c.* 10 pairs). It also breeds further E to the area around Lake Baikal in the E USSR. Winters mainly in NE Africa, the Middle East and S Asia.

Status: Rare vagrant elsewhere in Europe. France (*c.* 5 in 19th century, Oct 1989*), Denmark (14), Sweden (8), Finland (June 1981, May

1982), Poland (13), East Germany (Aug 1930), Austria (also bred 1810 and 1818), and Italy (10).

Family FALCONIDAE   Falcons

AMERICAN KESTREL   *Falco sparverius*   A **17**
L 22-27cm (8-11"). WS 52-61cm (20-24"). The Americas. Accidental.
All plumages:. Small, about the size of Merlin, but less heavy and compact with slightly narrower-based wings and slightly longer and narrower tail. The flight is much more Kestrel-like than Merlin-like. Has diagnostic multi-patterned head.
Adult male: Unmistakable. Has orange-brown, coarsely barred upperparts (sometimes more finely and sparsely marked), and greyish-blue, usually black-spotted coverts and tertials. Also, has orange-brown uppertail with broad, black subterminal band (outer pair of tail feathers paler, normally with several bars), and sparsely spotted underparts. In flight shows a characteristic subterminal row of pale spots on the primaries and a broad, pale trailing edge to the secondaries.
Adult female: Patterned rather like a female-type Kestrel, but deeper rufous on the upperparts and coverts, with denser and more regular barring, and strikingly different head markings. In flight the upperwing shows less contrast, and the terminal dark tail bar is narrower.
Juvenile male: Very similar to the adult male, but the head pattern tends to be slightly duller, the mantle more heavily barred, and the underparts more heavily marked, with streaks on the (upper) breast. The juvenile plumage is moulted during the 1st autumn, and 1st-years are inseparable after the moult has been completed, except by their slightly more worn wings/tail. Some juvenile body feathers are sometimes retained in the spring of the 2nd year.
Juvenile female: Apparently very difficult to distinguish from the adult female. The outermost dark tail-bar is generally slightly narrower than in the adult female, and is often the same width as the other dark bars (outermost dark bar is distinctly broader than others in adult). After the post-juvenile moult has been completed some individuals show a contrast between some fresh, newly moulted coverts, and more worn/bleached tertials and some other coverts.
Habitat and Behaviour: Resembles Kestrel, i.e. generally found in open habitats, often perched on wires, poles etc as well as hovering.
Range: Breeds over much of North, Central and South America. N North American populations are migratory, while S birds are resident.
Status: Accidental in the Azores (Feb 1968, 1970, Mar 1980). Britain: Fair Isle, Shetland (May 1976), Cornwall (June 1976). Denmark (autumn 1901), and Malta (Oct 1967).

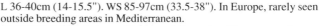

ELEONORA'S FALCON   *Falco eleonorae*   R Br **17**
L 36-40cm (14-15.5"). WS 85-97cm (33.5-38"). In Europe, rarely seen outside breeding areas in Mediterranean.
All plumages: Size between Hobby and Peregrine. Shows very characteristic, elegant shape, with strikingly long, narrow and pointed wings

(proportionately even longer than Hobby's) and relatively long tail. Wing-beats are often characteristically slow in normal flight.

Adult pale morph: Plumage resembles adult Hobby, but generally gives a darker impression. Unlike Hobby, usually has a decidedly rufous-tinged breast and belly. The dark streaking on the underparts is variable, ranging from clearly finer to distinctly broader and more diffuse than in any Hobby ('intermediate morph'). Some individuals are untypically pale on the breast and belly, with contrasting rufous 'trousers' and undertail-coverts and are very similar to adult Hobbys with more warmly coloured underparts. The underwing pattern is diagnostic: Has rather dark (uniform or lightly mottled) underwing-coverts, contrasting with unbarred, paler basal parts to the flight-feathers (contrast most pronounced between primary coverts and basal parts of primaries). In Hobby the flight-feathers are distinctly barred and not contrasting with the similarly patterned underwing-coverts. Female approximately 10% larger than male.

Adult dark morph: Unmistakable. Plumage all-dark with the same (or even more pronounced) contrast on the underwing as in pale birds. Easily told from an adult male of the smaller Red-footed Falcon, which shows rather uniformly dark underwings, paler flight-feathers above and rufous 'trousers' and undertail-coverts. 1st-summer male Red-footed has dark upperwing, but the underwing is much paler than in Eleonora's, with heavily barred remiges and coverts.

Dark morph birds constitute approximately 25% of the population.

Juvenile: Basically resembles an adult pale morph, but shows distinct pale fringes to all of the upperside and some coarse barring on the underparts (at least on the flanks, although not always easily seen). It also has more distinctly barred underwing-coverts and barred basal parts to the flight-feathers below. Adults rarely show some barring on the underside of the remiges, at least on the outer primaries, and in some juveniles the same are indistinctly mottled with pale rather than distinctly barred. The streaking on the underparts is somewhat variable, and it seems likely that the most heavily streaked individuals will become dark morph as adults.

The plumage is extremely similar to juvenile Hobby, and is best distinguished by the distinct contrast between darker underwing-coverts and paler basal parts to flight-feathers.

It could also be confused with juvenile Lanner, see p. 90.

Subsequent immature plumages: Birds in the spring to autumn of the 2nd year can be told from adults by the generally large number of juvenile feathers still present on the upper– and underparts (pale fringes above worn off, though). When perched, some heavily worn tertials and rear scapulars with pale-notched edges are usually apparent. The juvenile remiges and rectrices are apparently not moulted until in the winter-quarters, when more than one year old, so in the 1st summer they are rather heavily worn.

Note: Sooty Falcon *F. concolor* (breeding Middle East, Arabia and NE Africa) has been recorded from Malta (Nov 1968, Aug 1970, June 1971) and could conceivably turn up in Europe. It is smaller than Eleonora's Falcon. Adults resemble an adult dark morph Eleonora's, but are paler grey, with a contrastingly darker outer wing above and lack the contrast on the underwing. Juvenile is paler grey above than juvenile Eleonora's and shows fainter and broader dark markings on the underparts; these markings are often more concentrated on the breast and form a dark 'breast shield'. From below the tail shows a very broad, dark subterminal bar, not seen in Eleonora's. The wing pattern differs in much the same way as between adults of the two species.

Habits: Does not breed until late summer/autumn, then taking advantage of the strong passage of passerine migrants through the Mediterranean. Nests in colonies. Superb flier, catching birds and also insects in the air.

Range: Breeds on rocky islands in the Mediterranean, mainly the Balearics and Italian and Greek islands and NW Africa. European population some 4,000 pairs, most of which occurs in Greece (c. 3,000 pairs). In autumn migrates eastwards through Mediterranean and down Red Sea to winter quarters in E Africa and Madagascar.

Status: Rare/scarce passage migrant elsewhere in S Europe. France (80+), in south reported as regular every year (19 in 1987), especially in spring (Camargue/Iles d' Hyères/Sète area and Corsica), and noted in autumn as late as the end of Oct. Scarce passage migrant at Gibraltar (Mar-Oct), 32 recorded between 1981-87, maximum of 5 on 14th Apr 1975. Malta: scarce passage migrant and non-breeding summer visitor (mid Apr-late Oct).

Accidental in Britain (Aug 1977, Oct 1981, June 1985), Sweden (2 in July-Aug 1983, 2 in Aug-Sept 1988), Hungary (c. 5), Poland (Sept 1982, Sept 1984), Bulgaria (2nd in June 1984), and Portugal (Sept 1981).

LANNER *Falco biarmicus* R Br **17**

L 34-50cm (13.5-19.5"). WS 90-115cm (35-45"). Rare and declining breeding species in S/SE Europe. Accidental outside breeding range. (Elsewhere in Africa, Arabia, Middle East).

All plumages: Differs from similarly sized Peregrine by its proportionately longer, slightly more blunt-tipped wings and longer tail. All plumages are very difficult to tell from Saker (p. 91).

Adult: European race, *feldeggii*, is rather pale grey-brown to more bluish-grey above, with some barring. The underside is pale with some irregular spotting and barring on the body and underwing-coverts, often forming a contrastingly darker band on the central underwing; wingtips are also darker. Shows rufous to buffish, streaked crown/nape and rather narrow, dark moustachial stripe. Often the crown is so dark that the rufous is only apparent on the supercilium and nape.

Adult Peregrine shows more blue-grey upperside with less barring, more blackish head pattern with broader moustachial stripe, more barred underparts, and rather uniformly barred underwing. See 'Barbary Falcon' (p. 93).

Some adult (grey) Gyrfalcons are very similar, but are obviously larger, lack rufous on crown/nape and often show pale barring on the outer webs of the primaries and primary coverts.

Female up to 15% larger than male.

Juvenile: Differs from the adult in darker, neatly pale-fringed upperside without barring, and heavily streaked underparts and underwing-coverts. The central pair of tail feathers are frequently unbarred, and occasionally the entire tail shows very few pale markings.

Juvenile Peregrine usually shows a darker and less streaked crown and has a broader moustachial stripe. It also has a rather uniformly patterned underwing, lacking the obvious contrast between the dark coverts and paler flight-feathers of Lanner.

Juvenile Eleonora's Falcon shows a dark crown with pale fringes rather than a pale crown with dark streaks as in Lanner, and the moustachial stripe is never as poorly marked as in some Lanners. Smaller size, more slender build, and longer/narrower wings are the best distinctions.

Subsequent immature plumages: The plumage changes little until the summer of the 2nd year, when it is moulted. After the moult has been completed, the plumage resembles the adult. A few retained juvenile feathers are sometimes found, particularly on the coverts.

Note: Other races of Lanner could possibly turn up in Europe, including falconers' escapes. Adults of these show mainly unstreaked rufous crown, and the underparts are less heavily marked, usually with only a trace of or even no barring. Juveniles appear to be inseparable.

Habitat: In Europe, occurs in grasslands and breeds usually inland in rocky places with steep cliffs. In N Africa typically breeds in semi-desert and dry savanna country.

Range: In Europe a small and, since approximately 1960, strongly declining population breeds in Italy (100-150 pairs 1982), Sicily (20-40 pairs 1982), Yugoslavia (very few) and Greece (30 pairs 1983); has bred in Albania and possibly breeds in SW Bulgaria. There is evidence for breeding in Spain (probably irregularly in a limited area in S) in the 19th century. Mainly resident, but apparently there is some dispersal. Also breeds in Turkey, a few places in the Middle East and Arabia, and in much of Africa.

Status: Very rarely recorded outside breeding range. A few individuals have been reported from Gibraltar (*c.* 15, Mar-Sept), also neighbouring Spain and Portugal, and are presumably birds originating from Morocco. There are also a few other records from France (*c.* 10), West Germany, Czechoslovakia (2), Rumania, and Malta (3). Reports of individuals seen in NW Europe from time to time are usually considered to relate to falconer's escapes.

SAKER *Falco cherrug* R Br* **17**

L 45-55cm (18-21.5"). WS 102-126cm (40-50"). Small numbers breed E/SE Europe. Rarely recorded outside breeding and regular wintering ranges.

All plumages: Very similar to corresponding plumages of Lanner, but distinctly larger and heavier (near size of Gyrfalcon) with broader wings.

Adult: Normal individuals from the western part of the range are quite readily distinguished from European Lanners. The crown is generally paler, and probably never as uniformly dark as in many Lanners and apparently always lacks the distinct dark bar across the fore-crown often seen in Lanner (usual pattern of the two subspecies of Ethiopian Africa). The crown shows at the most a trace of rufous. The moustachial stripe and eye-stripe tend to be less distinct. Some individuals show a very pale, almost whitish, and very poorly marked head, which is a pattern probably never seen in adult Lanner (but occasionally

91

shown by juvenile, at least of Middle East/NE African race *tanypterus*).

The upperparts are usually distinctly rufous-brown with no, or very little, barring and contrast more with the primary coverts and flight-feathers than in Lanner (reminiscent of female-type Kestrel). The basal parts of the primaries often show small, pale spots on the outer webs, which does not seem to be found in Lanner (except sometimes on the outermost primary). The central pair of tail feathers are unmarked or show regular pale spots on each side of the shaft – as in many juvenile Lanners, but unlike adults. The lower flanks and 'trousers' are streaked, generally heavily, whereas in Lanner the flanks, and normally also the 'trousers', and sometimes the undertail-coverts, are usually rather barred, and the 'trousers' tend to be less heavily marked.

Some individuals (normal in E populations) show prominent barring above, on the flanks, 'trousers', and central tail-feathers. They may be decidedly greyish especially on the back, rump, uppertail- coverts and uppertail, and the crown is also sometimes rather dark. Such individuals are exceptionally difficult to distinguish with certainty from Lanner, but are generally more rufous above.

The plumage of these barred birds is virtually identical to adult (grey) Gyrfalcons, except for the difference in general coloration above (distinctly rufous-tinged in Saker, greyish in Gyr). However, normal western Sakers are rather easily separated from Gyrfalcon. The latter shows decidedly greyer and usually finely barred upperparts; less streaked underparts, generally with spotted breast/belly, barred flanks and undertail-coverts; and rather densely barred central tail feathers.

Female distinctly larger than male.

Juvenile: Generally more heavily patterned below than the adult, although there is some overlap in the amount of dark markings. The dark streaks are less drop-shaped than in adult (generally most noticeable on the breast – slight overlap, though). The central pair of rectrices show more regularly than adult distinct, rounded, pale spots on both the outer and inner webs. The cere, orbital ring and legs/feet are bluish-grey (yellow in adult).

It is extremely similar to juvenile Lanner and best told (with care!) by size and shape. The 'trousers' are usually clearly darker than in Lanner, normally appearing mostly dark (usually pale with dark streaking in Lanner, sometimes, however, in Saker too). Lanner sometimes shows a trace of coarse barring on the flanks, which is not a feature of Saker. Some Sakers are distinctly rufous-tinged above, unlike Lanner. Also, legs/feet are not yellowish-tinged as is normally the case in Lanner.

It also closely resembles juvenile (grey) Gyrfalcon, and some individuals are very difficult to separate. Gyrfalcon generally shows a darker crown, more prominent moustachial stripe, and duskier ear-coverts, but there is much overlap. Gyr is generally more grey-brown above and never rufous-tinged. Some individuals show distinct pale barring on much of the upperparts and upperwings, others show just a trace of this pattern, and in some it is lacking altogether. Saker never shows any pale bars. The 'trousers' tend to be less dark in Gyr, and the undertail-coverts are distinctly streaked, rarely barred (unmarked or very finely streaked in Saker). The tail tends to be more densely and distinctly barred in Gyr, but this is a variable feature, and the central pair of tail-feathers are sometimes virtually unmarked. Also, it apparently never shows the distinct, rounded spots on both webs of the central tail-feathers frequently seen in Saker.

Subsequent immature plumages: See Lanner (p. 90).

Habitat: Breeds in various types of steppe, where it feeds primarily on small to medium-sized rodents, especially susliks.

Range: European population estimated at maximum 150 breeding pairs. Breeds in small numbers (has declined in recent decades) in Czechoslovakia (25 pairs), Austria (5 pairs), Hungary (*c.* 65 pairs), Rumania, Bulgaria (*c.* 12 pairs) and Yugoslavia (*c.* 40 pairs). More numerous further east to E Asia. N populations migratory. The European population is partly migratory; many winter in the S parts of the range, whereas others winter in e.g. SW Yugoslavia and S Italy some also crossing the Mediterranean to NE Africa.

Status: Rare outside breeding range. There are records for France (5, Aug-Dec), West Germany (15), East Germany (5), Poland (21, including 9 between 1968-87, mostly in South), Norway (June 1980), Sweden (Nov 1900), Albania, Greece (12-15 post-war records of which 9 were in winter), Sicily (6 since 1967) and Malta (very rare and irregular). There are also a few other records in NW Europe which are perhaps more likely to relate to falconer's escapes.

'BARBARY FALCON' *Falco peregrinus pelegrinoides* B **16**

L 34-40cm (13-15.5"). WS 80-100cm (31-39"). N Africa to C Asia. A few records from S Europe. 'Desert race' of Peregrine Falcon, often considered separate species (see Appendix).

All plumages: Extremely similar to other subspecies of Peregrine Falcon, especially *brookei* subspecies (S Europe). Although slightly smaller than Peregrine this is of little importance in the field.

Adult: Paler above than nominate and *brookei* and more rufous-tinged and more sparsely marked below. The moustachial stripe is narrower, and the nape and supercilium are rufous.

Easily confused with adult Lanner. Shape typical of Peregrine and thus noticeably different from Lanner (see under latter, p. 90). Crown never mainly rufous; occasionally the anterior part is rufous-tinged and the rear part dark, which is the reverse pattern to that shown by Lanner. Also, the moustachial stripe is usually more distinct, especially at the base. The underparts are generally more rufous-tinged, with finer barring (never lacking altogether). The underwing lacks the distinct contrast between dark (central) coverts and paler, dark-tipped flight-feathers as shown by many Lanners. Furthermore, the tail gradually darkens towards the tip, and the dark terminal bar is distinctly wider than the rest (best seen from above). In Lanner, the tail shows distinct pale bars throughout its length, and the dark terminal bar, at the most, is only a fraction broader than the others.

The female is considerably larger and tends to be more rufous below with more dark markings.

Juvenile: Similar to juvenile nominate and *brookei* subspecies, but the underparts tend to have narrower dark streaks, particularly on the 'trousers'. Distinguished from juvenile Lanner by same characters as separate juveniles of Lanner and Peregrine (see Lanner, p. 90).

Subsequent immature plumages: See Lanner (p. 90).
Habitat: Semi-desert areas with rocky hills, preferring drier and more barren country than other Peregrines.
Range: Breeds mainly in inland areas in Morocco, Tunisia, Algeria, Egypt, S Middle East, S Arabia and from Iran to the Tien Shan.
Status: Accidental. Italy (12), Malta (at least 2) and Greece (Apr 1987*), also possibly Portugal and Spain.

Family TURNICIDAE Button-quails

ANDALUSIAN HEMIPODE *Turnix sylvatica* R Br **18**

L 15-16cm (6"). Now very rare resident in a few places in S Spain and Portugal. Also known as 'Little Button-quail'.
Adult: Only likely to be confused with Quail which it resembles in general appearance, habits and often habitat choice. It is slightly smaller and has a proportionately longer bill. If seen well on the ground, easily distinguished by plainer face; rather large, triangular or arrow-head-shaped, dark marks on the sides of the breast/flanks; orange-brown centre to the breast; coarsely marked coverts (often concealed by flank and scapular feathers); and pale, whitish to yellow iris (dark in Quail).

In flight, upperwings show a distinct contrast between darker (uniform) remiges/primary coverts and paler coverts (upperwing rather plain in Quail; remiges barred). The wings are also slightly shorter and more rounded than in Quail.

Female is larger than male (up to 15%), with brighter plumage.
Juvenile: Said to differ from the adult in having more spotted underparts, rows of whitish spots on the upperparts and less marked coverts. Juvenile plumage moulted when very young (normally before age of *c.* 7 weeks). Sometimes juvenile flight-feathers retained.
Voice: During the breeding season a series of rather low-pitched, hooting *hoooooo* repeated every 1-3 seconds, recalling the distant hooting of a mist-buoy. Heard mainly at dawn/dusk. Note that these calls are given by the female, which plays the leading role in mating, unlike most other birds.
Habitat and behaviour: Inhabits dry, open habitats with grass, scrub, low thickets, stubble etc. It is extremely secretive and difficult to see and prefers to run away from an intruder rather than fly. However, if flushed, normally flies fast and low only for a short distance, then without warning suddenly drops into low ground cover. Unlikely to be flushed a second time.
Range and status: Extremely rare resident in S Portugal and SW Spain, where it has declined markedly. In Spain, several were observed at Coto del Rey in Apr 1989, while others were reported in the Coto Doñana reserve. Formerly bred commonly in Sicily up to 1880 but now extinct (*c.* 1920). Also breeds in N Africa (where now extremely rare), but mainly in Africa (S of the Sahara), India and SE Asia.

Family RALLIDAE   Rails, Crakes, Gallinules, Coots

SORA   *Porzana carolina*   B **18**
L 20-25cm (8-10"). North America. A little more than a dozen records.
All plumages: Closely resembles Spotted Crake. Shows uniformly
chestnut crown with blackish central stripe (latter not normally seen in
side-view), not heavily streaked crown as in Spotted. The supercilium,
neck and breast are uniformly patterned, lacking the small, distinct
whitish spots of Spotted. The pattern of the tertials and inner greater
coverts usually differs significantly (see figure).

Adult: Further differs from Spotted Crake (and all other European
crakes) by showing a diagnostic black mask which extends onto the
throat, foreneck and breast. Bill greenish-yellow (red base in Spotted).
   In winter, the black feathers are narrowly grey-tipped. Female tends
to show slightly less black on the head/neck and more heavily spotted
upperparts and coverts.

Juvenile: Duller than the adult, lacking grey on head/neck and the contrasting black mask. The base-colour of the breast, neck and sides of
the head are paler and more buffish than in juvenile Spotted. The bill is
initially rather dark but gradually becomes paler from the base out-
wards. The same is true for juvenile Spotted, but some red has generally developed at the base of the bill by the autumn.

ttted   **Sora**
ke

ertial and inner
reater covert

   The plumage is reminiscent of the clearly smaller juvenile Little
Crake. It differs in e.g. darker and more evenly patterned mantle/sca-
pulars, without broad dark and paler stripes as in Little; more varied
whitish markings on the upperside, coverts and tertials; and uniformly
buffish undertail-coverts (barred blackish and whitish in Little). Further, crown pattern is diagnostic (uniformly streaked in Little), and the
primary projection is much shorter.
   Adult plumage is usually attained during the 1st autumn to winter.
Voice: The territorial call, usually heard only in the breeding season
(mainly dusk/dawn), is a characteristic *ke-eep* with the second syllable
inflected and with the quality of a synthesizer. Also gives 'laughing'
trills which decrease in pitch and speed towards the end, recalling
Little Grebe.
Habitat and behaviour: Similar to other crakes.
Range: Breeds in much of North America (excluding extreme N and S
areas). Winters from the S parts of the USA to the N parts of South
America. Vagrant to Greenland and Morocco (Mar 1989).
Status: Accidental in the British Isles (11, Aug-Dec, once in Apr), in-
cluding five since 1981. France (Jan 1963), Spain (Dec 1975) and
Sweden (June 1966, two in June-July 1987).

ALLEN'S GALLINULE   *Porphyrula alleni*   B **18**
L 22-24cm (9"). Africa S of Sahara. Accidental, mainly in late autumn-
winter.
Adult: Distinctly smaller and slimmer than Moorhen. Has distinctive,
iridescent blue and green plumage, Moorhen-like white lateral under
tail-coverts, and bright red legs/feet. Only likely to be confused with
the American Purple Gallinule (see p. 96).
Juvenile: Lacks adult's bright colours. Unlike young crakes it lacks any
distinctive whitish markings above or dark barring below. It has

bluish– and greenish-tinged coverts, dull blue-green remiges, and bluish primary coverts. See also juvenile American Purple Gallinule.

Subsequent immature plumages: Resembles the adult from after the moult in the 1st autumn/winter. Some show signs of immaturity on the upper and/or underparts.

Habitat and behaviour: Dense vegetation in marshy areas. More skulking and retiring than most moorhens, and less inclined to swim any distance from thick cover. Climbs reeds and walks on floating vegetation.

Range: Africa (S of Sahara). At least the N populations move south in the dry season (Dec-Mar). Vagrant to N Africa (Morocco, Tunisia, Egypt), Cyprus, Madeira, and Canary Is.

Status: Accidental in the Azores (4), and Italy (10) with a scattering of records from Britain (Jan 1902), France (Oct 1895, Dec 1951), Denmark (Dec 1929), Finland (May 1979), West Germany (Feb 1936, Dec 1986); Spain (5), and Portugal (May 1973).

Except for the two May individuals, the records are from Oct to early Feb, with an obvious peak in December. This fits well with the time of migration in W Africa. Four of the N European records were during or shortly after anticyclonic conditions with strong southerly winds from NW Africa. There are a few more records of immatures than of adults.

AMERICAN PURPLE GALLINULE   *Porphyrula martinica*   A **18**

L 30-36cm (13"). Americas. Accidental.

All plumages: Resembles Allen's Gallinule, but is obviously larger (approximately the size of Moorhen).

Adult: Further differs from Allen's by all white undertail-coverts, yellow tip to the bill and yellow legs/feet.

Juvenile: Easily told from juvenile Allen's by uniformly patterned upperparts. Bill tip and legs/feet turn yellowish after some time.

Subsequent immature plumages: See Allen's Gallinule above.

Habitat and behaviour: See Allen's Gallinule.

Range: Breeds from SE USA (sporadically much further north), Central America and the West Indies south to N Argentina. Highly migratory: some winter in southeasternmost USA but the majority continue to Central and South America.

It is an inveterate wanderer. In the S Atlantic, vagrants have reached Tristan da Cunha (almost regular), Ascension Is, St Helena, and it is more or less regular in South Africa (10 records 1962-1974).

Status: Accidental in the Azores: (Nov 1957, May 1966, July 1969, Dec 1978), at sea off Flores (8th Apr 1961); Iceland (Sept 1976, June 1983); Britain: immature on Isles of Scilly (7th Nov 1958); Norway (autumn 1883); and Switzerland: adult female (Dec 1967).

PURPLE GALLINULE   *Porphyrio porphyrio*   R Br **18**

L 45-50cm (18.5"). In Europe: limited breeding in SW Spain, S Portugal, and Sardinia. Rare vagrant elsewhere.

All plumages: Easily recognized by very large size (almost twice the bulk of Moorhen), and very large bill.

Adult: Further characterized by deep blue plumage, with white undertail-coverts and red bill/shield and legs/feet.

Juvenile: Much duller, more grey than adult, with paler central underparts. The bare parts are initially darker and browner but rather quickly turn reddish.

Subsequent immature plumages: During the 1st autumn the juvenile slowly acquires adult-like plumage. However, it is still duller and usually shows mottled underparts. The juvenile wing feathers are retained. Full adult plumage is attained after the complete moult in the summer of the 2nd year.

Voice: Has a wide range of calls, including a 'ghost-like' hooting. Also gives various grunting and *chuck* notes.

Note: Escapes of non-European subspecies have been recorded. These are normally slightly differently coloured compared to European birds; e.g. some have green– or brown-tinged upperparts and wings.

Habitat and behaviour: Occurs in dense vegetation, often reed beds, in marshy areas. Usually very secretive, but sometimes seen feeding in the open.

Range: Formerly bred in many places in Portugal, Spain, Italy (both on mainland and Sardinia) and probably elsewhere, but now breeds only in small numbers in S Portugal, SW Spain and in Sardinia. Mainly resident. Some individuals wander, especially late summer (July-Aug), as a result of breeding areas drying out in S Europe. Accidental in Cyprus.

Also breeds in a few places in N Africa and W Asia and more extensively in Africa (S of Sahara), Madagascar, and from S/SE Asia to Australasia.

Status: Rare vagrant, although position in N and C Europe has in the past been clouded by escapes of various races. Probably genuine vagrants have been recorded from France (24), mainly July-Oct (also Feb, Dec); Belgium (6), Netherlands (Nov-Dec 1988), West Germany (5, origin uncertain), Norway (2), Poland (2), Czechoslovakia (3), Austria, Switzerland (Aug 1933, Aug-Sept 1983), Hungary (Oct 1967), Yugoslavia (2), Greece, and Italy (30) – excluding Sardinia where breeds.

AMERICAN COOT *Fulica americana* A 18

L 31-37cm (12-14.5"). Americas. Accidental.

Adult: Immediately distinguished from Coot and Crested Coot by dark (actually deep red) band across the bill, and has white sides to under-tail-coverts (Moorhen-like). Note the reddish-brown upper shield (appearing blackish at a distance) and the contrast between black head/neck and greyer body.

Juvenile: Much paler and greyer than the adult especially on throat/fore-neck. Differs from juvenile Coot and Crested Coot by Moorhen-like pattern of undertail-coverts. Usually shows a trace of a dark band across the bill (which juvenile Coot and Crested Coot may also have). Note the Crested Coot-like feathering at the base of the bill, and the dark upper shield. It is very unlikely to be seen in juvenile plumage in Europe, since this plumage is rather quickly shed.

Subsequent immature plumages: Similar to the adult from 1st autumn, but at least in 1st summer shows more worn and browner wings.

Note: Hybrids between Coot and Moorhen superficially resembling American Coot have been reported.

Habitat and behaviour: Very similar to Coot.

Range: Breeds in North, Central and South America. N-C North American populations are migratory, moving to the coasts and S parts in winter. Many recorded wandering N of breeding range, in summer/autumn even reaching S Greenland.

Status: Accidental in Iceland (Nov 1969, Mar 1971), Faeroes (Nov 1985), Ireland (Feb-Apr 1981), and one reported Azores (14th Oct 1988*).

CRESTED COOT   *Fulica cristata*   R Br **18**

L 38-42cm (15-16.5"). Rare resident in S Spain. Also breeds in Africa and Madagascar.

All plumages: Distinguished from Coot by the different shape to the feathering at the side of the bill and lack of white on the leading and trailing edges of the wing (usually only seen in flight).

Adult: The bill is distinctly bluish tinged, whereas it is tinged pale pinkish in Coot. In the breeding season the red knobs are diagnostic, but they are generally very inconspicuous in the non-breeding season. However, they often make the top of the shield look less rounded than in the Coot.

Juvenile: Easily distinguished from the adult by paler areas on the head, neck and underparts. Juvenile plumage lost very early.

Subsequent immature plumages: See American Coot, above.

Voice: Like Coot it has a range of different calls. However, they are generally lower-pitched and include a typical groaning *euh*, somewhat reminiscent of the call of a female Mallard.

Habitat and behaviour: Similar to Coot, but less often on land. It is more strictly a freshwater species.

Range: Very rare in small area in S Spain, where resident. The numbers have gone down markedly. In 1984/85 breeding was proved for the first time for decades. Also breeds in Morocco, where it is still locally common (but has also declined there). Formerly more widespread in N Africa. Also breeds in E and S Africa, and Madagascar.

Status: Rarely recorded outside its limited breeding area, but there are old records from France (5), Italy (7), Malta (4); Portugal (said to have bred) and more recently an individual observed on Faro Marshes (late May 1989*).

Family GRUIDAE   Cranes

SANDHILL CRANE   *Grus canadensis*   A **19**

L 88-95cm (36"). WS 175-195cm (69-77"). North America. Only 3 records.

Adult: Resembles Crane but is easily distinguished by different pattern on the head and neck. Plumage rather more 'scaly'. In flight the remiges are slightly less contrastingly dark than in Crane.

Juvenile: Differs from the adult in lacking a red patch on the head. The head/neck, upperparts and tips of coverts are usually more or less brown (plumage of adult often brown-stained in breeding season, though). Apparently distinctly browner on especially upperparts and coverts than juvenile Crane.

Subsequent immature plumages: Juvenile plumage is gradually replaced during the autumn of the 1st year and spring of the 2nd by a more adult-like plumage. Some juvenile feathers (including remiges) are often retained until the summer/autumn of the 3rd year, sometimes perhaps for an additional year.

Voice: The calls are slightly lower-pitched and more drawn-out than those of Crane. Juveniles give high-pitched, thin, rolling whistles.

Range: Breeds in arctic E USSR and in North America, mainly in N Canada and Alaska, but also in some parts of the USA and in Cuba. Winters in S USA to Central America (including Soviet population).

Status: Accidental in the Faeroes (14th Oct 1980). Britain: Shetland, Fair Isle (26th-27th Apr 1981). Ireland: Castlefreke, Co Cork (11th-14th Sept 1905).

SIBERIAN WHITE CRANE   *Grus leucogeranus*   19

L 120-140cm (47-55"). WS 230-260cm (90-102"). W and E Siberia. No acceptable record in Europe.

Adult: Unmistakeable. All white, with bare red skin on the face and contrasting black primaries. The legs are flesh-coloured.

Juvenile: Shows largely orange-brown head/neck, upperparts and coverts (only tips to median and greater coverts).

Subsequent immature plumages: See Sandhill Crane (p. 98).

Voice: The calls are appreciably higher-pitched than Crane. Juvenile gives high-pitched thin whistles.

Range: Breeds only in two areas in the USSR, one small population in the Ob-Irtysh basin and another, larger, between lower Yana and Alazeya Rivers in Yakutia. Now very rare, total world population probably just over 2,650 individuals. Very few winter S Caspian (Iran) and in N India (Bharatpur) respectively, remainder in SE China (Poyang Lake; 2,626 counted in Nov 1988).

Status: Estonia: a report of 7 flying SW on 30th Sept 1984 has recently been rejected.

DEMOISELLE CRANE   *Anthropoides virgo*   D* 19

L 90-100cm (35-39"). WS 165-185cm (65-73"). Asia. Rare visitor.

Adult: Unmistakable, showing elongated, black foreneck feathers, white head tufts and very long tertials.

Juvenile: Mostly grey on the head/neck. The foreneck feathers and tertials are shorter than in the adult.

Subsequent immature plumages: An adult-like plumage is gradually acquired during the autumn of the 1st year to the spring of the 2nd. The general coloration is browner, the black parts are duller, and the feathers on the foreneck and tertials are shorter than in the adult.

Voice: The calls are slightly higher-pitched than in Crane, usually with a harder, 'drier' and more 'wooden' quality. Juvenile calls with thin, rolling whistles.

Range: Breeds from N of the Black Sea in a belt across Asia to E USSR, Mongolia and N China. Formerly bred Rumania and in N Africa (a few pairs apparently still left in Morocco). W populations migrate to Africa, whereas E populations winter chiefly in India/Pakistan. In Cyprus, it is a passage migrant (mainly late Mar-mid Apr, and mid Aug-early Sept).

Status: Rare vagrant (but origins of some uncertain due to escapes). Has been recorded in France, Netherlands (pair Aug-Sept 1989*), Denmark (5), Norway, Sweden (8), Finland (6), West Germany, Poland (3), Austria (pair Oct 1989*), Czechoslovakia, Yugoslavia, Greece, Bulgaria, Rumania, Italy (6), Malta, Portugal, and Spain (where more regular in 19th century). In Hungary there were 9 records (1858-1984) totalling 63 birds, of which six records only involved single individuals (June 3, Aug-Sept 3), but on three occasions, small flocks have joined larger groups of migrating Common Cranes, ie. 40 on 15th Apr 1980, 5 on 22nd Oct 1977, and 12 from 13th-15th Nov 1981.

Family OTIDIDAE Bustards

HOUBARA BUSTARD *Chlamydotis undulata* C* **19**

L 55-65cm (22-25"). WS 135-170cm (53-67"). Asia and N Africa. Rare vagrant mainly Oct-Dec (majority of records in 19th century).

Adult: Large, but still distinctly smaller than Great Bustard, while much larger than Little Bustard, and easily told from both by the black frills on the sides of its neck. In flight also shows less white in the upperwings: the greater primary coverts and flight-feathers are basically dark with a large white patch on the primaries and the coverts are brownish. It further differs from Great by e.g. less rufous and less strongly barred upperparts.

N African, nominate, race slightly deeper brown and more heavily marked above (dark markings forming bars rather than spots), shows all-white (not black tipped) crest and more extensively black frills than Asian *macqueenii.*

Male shows a slightly longer crest (often concealed) and neck frill than the female. In practice, sexes very difficult to separate by plumage, but male is *c.* 10% larger than the female.

Juvenile: Very similar to the adult, but shows only a trace of the black neck frill and lacks crest. The remiges and rectrices are slightly narrower, more pointed and browner, often with subterminal buff markings to the outer primaries (shape and pattern only possible to judge in the hand).

Subsequent immature plumages: Acquires adult plumage surprisingly quickly for a bird of this size. The juvenile commences a complete moult shortly after fledging, so that in the 1st autumn/winter the plumage is generally very difficult to distinguish from that of the adult. The crest and neck frill are usually still slightly shorter than in the adult, but in practice this is difficult to judge. The outer primaries are retained, so that in the hand, their shape, pattern, and relative wear are an aid to identification. (cf. the other primaries).

Range: Resident in N Africa, E Canary Is, and the Middle East. Also breeds from E and S of the Caspian Sea east to Mongolia, wintering around the Persian Gulf and in Afghanistan, Pakistan and NW India. The total world population has declined markedly in the 20th century, mainly as a result of excessive hunting (E population, particularly in winter quarters).

Status: Rare vagrant, (majority in 19th century). Britain (5, most recent in Nov-Dec 1962), France (Dec 1807, Feb 1833), Belgium (Nov 1842, Dec 1844, Dec 1845), Netherlands (Dec 1850), Denmark (Oct 1892), Sweden (Feb 1847, Oct 1933, Oct 1974), Finland (Sept 1861), Latvia, Poland (5, most recent in Dec 1977), East Germany (1836, 1847), West Germany (6), Czechoslovakia (Sept 1889), Hungary (Apr 1931), Switzerland (May 1839, Nov 1840, Nov 1916), Italy (10), Yugoslavia (Nov 1934, Nov 1970), Greece (June 1841), Rumania, Malta (3), and Spain. Most of the records probably refer to the Asian race.

Family GLAREOLIDAE   Coursers and Pratincoles

CREAM-COLOURED COURSER   *Cursorius cursor*   D **20**

L 20-24cm (8-9.5"). WS 51-57cm (21.5"). Desert species of N Africa, Middle East and W Asia. Vagrants have been seen as far as NW Europe.
All plumages: Sandy-isabelline, plover-like wader with striking head pattern, short decurved bill and whitish legs. In flight shows contrasting black remiges above, white trailing edge to the secondaries, largely blackish underwing, and characteristic shape and flight (rather well-spaced and somewhat jerky wingbeats interspersed with irregular glides). Capable of running very fast, often preferring to run away rather than fly if approached too closely.
Adult: Has diagnostic head pattern, with blue-grey crown contrasting with long white supercilium and black eye-stripe, the latter two meeting on nape to form an obvious V when viewed from behind.
Juvenile: Shows more indistinct head pattern. The upperparts and breast are lightly speckled. The primaries and primary coverts have distinct pale fringes (all black in adult).
1st-winter: Juveniles often moult completely in the summer to early autumn and are then indistinguishable from the adult (which moults in a similar way). In birds that fledge late, the moult is often suspended, and they can be distinguished from adults on a variable number of retained juvenile feathers.
Voice: Most commonly heard call is a penetrating, usually repeated, rather nasal *uet*, often alternated by a short, frog-like *quar*.
Range: Breeds N Africa, Canary Is, Middle East to Iraq and Iran. Migratory or dispersive in winter.
Status: Rare vagrant. British Isles (33, Sept-Dec), France (15), Channel Is (Oct 1896), Belgium (Aug 1881), Netherlands (Oct 1933, Oct 1986), Denmark (4), Norway (Oct 1915), Sweden (3), Finland (Oct 1893, Sept 1989), East Germany (8), West Germany (18), Czechoslovakia (5), Hungary (Sept 1882, Sept 1930), Austria (Oct 1899), Switzerland (5), Italy, Sicily (28, Feb-June, Sept-Nov), Yugoslavia (5), Greece (2), Spain (3) and Portugal (2). Malta recorded a notable influx in June 1916 with flocks of 20 and 30+; more recently 32 records between 1968-86.

ORIENTAL PRATINCOLE *Glareola maldivarum*   A **20**

L 23-24cm (9.25"). S and E Asia. Two recent records.
All plumages: Resembles both Collared and Black-winged Pratincole.
The colour of the underwing-coverts is like adult of the former, while
the colour of the upperside and lack of a white trailing edge to the sec-
ondaries is similar to adult of the latter. In adult, the tail streamers are
obviously shorter than in either. Plumage variation and ageing as in
Black-winged Pratincole, below.
Range: Breeds in S and E Asia, from Pakistan to NE China. N popula-
tions migratory, wintering south to Australia. Accidental in Aleutian
Is, Mauritius and Seychelles.
Status: Two recent records in Britain: Suffolk/Essex from 22nd June-
11th Oct 1981 and from Kent, third week of June to early Oct 1988.

BLACK-WINGED PRATINCOLE *Glareola nordmanni*   R Br **20**

L 23-26cm (10"). WS 60-68cm (25"). Breeds in small numbers in
extreme E Europe, also further E in the USSR. Rare visitor to the rest
of Europe.
All plumages: Closely resembles the corresponding plumages of Collared Pratincole. Has slightly broader wings, a slightly shorter tail with
shallower fork (only in adult) and slightly longer legs. When folded,
the wings usually project clearly beyond the tail tip (in adult Collared
wing tips and tip of tail are approximately equal, tail sometimes longer;
juvenile Collared does not differ from Black-winged in this respect).
    The upperside is slightly darker, showing less contrast between the
coverts and the remiges/primary coverts. There is no white trailing
edge to the secondaries as in Collared (but beware heavily worn Collared, in which the white trailing edge can be narrow). The underwing-
coverts and axillaries are black, while in Collared they are mostly
brownish-red, but this colour can be difficult to discern under certain
conditions. See also Oriental Pratincole, above.
Adult summer: Further differs from Collared by the smaller amount of
red at the base of the bill (not reaching to the nostril as in Collared).
Adult winter: Shows narrow pale fringes to much of the plumage, most
obvious on the head, neck and breast. The black border to the pale
throat patch is very ill-defined. The dark on the lores and the red on the
bill is reduced (in Collared also).
Juvenile: Easily distinguished from the winter adult as it shows broad,
pale fringes with blackish subterminal marks on the upperparts and
coverts. A few brown tips are sometimes present on the underwing-
coverts, and the secondaries show very narrow pale tips which are
usually not visible in the field.
1st-winter/-summer: Usually resembles the adult after the complete post-
juvenile moult in the 1st autumn. A few juvenile feathers (e.g. inner
secondaries) are often retained to the summer of the 2nd year.
Voice: A variety of calls are given, e.g. short, sharp *kett* or *kytt*; rather
hard, nasal *ky-re*, *kerret*, *tyrr*, etc. The calls are generally slightly
lower-pitched than in Collared. In the breeding season, the repertoire is
further expanded to comprise multisyllabic calls, and the alarm call is
said to be a short *pwik* and *pwik-kik-kik*, often repeated and different
from the alarm call of Collared (a rolling *kirr* or *kirrrik*).

Note: Hybridization with Collared Pratincole has occurred on a few occasions. Hybrids show intermediate characters and are more difficult to determine.

Range: Breeds from Rumania and Ukraine in a belt across the USSR to just E of Lake Balkash. Winters in W and S Africa.

Status: Rare vagrant. Iceland (Oct 1979, Oct 1983, June 1987), British Isles (25, mainly July-Oct), France (9, incl. one paired to a Collared Pratincole in 1970), Belgium (Aug 1949), Netherlands (22), Denmark (4), Norway (Aug 1884, June 1974), Sweden (11, May-Sept, 1 in Oct/Nov), Finland (12), East Germany (12, May-Sept), West Germany (failed breeding in 1966; Nov 1981, Aug 1989), Poland (6), Czechoslovakia, Austria (2), Hungary (has bred several times), Switzerland (June 1974), Italy (6), Yugoslavia, Bulgaria (bred 1890), Greece (13 to 1969), and Spain (Oct 1982).

Family CHARADRIIDAE   Plovers and Lapwings

SEMIPALMATED PLOVER   *Charadrius semipalmatus*   A **20**
L 17-19cm (7"). North America. Accidental.

All plumages: Extremely similar to the corresponding plumages of Ringed Plover, but shows partial webbing (palmations) between all three fore-toes, whereas Ringed only shows partial webbing between the outer and middle toe. It is also marginally smaller, more compact, and has a fractionally stubbier bill. The yellow orbital ring is usually more prominent, especially in breeding plumage (but less prominent than in Little Ringed Plover). In flight the white wing-bar is generally slightly shorter, but this is difficult to appreciate in the field.

Adult summer: Tends to show browner rear ear-coverts, less pronounced white patch above/behind the eye, and a narrower breast band than in Ringed Plover. However, there is much overlap, and females of both species generally show browner ear-coverts and a narrower breast band than their respective males. Moreover, at least in males in spring-summer the white forehead does not normally reach the eye, which is normal in Ringed Plover, but again there is overlap.

Adult winter: Black areas on head and breast are replaced by dark brown, and the bill is mostly dark.

Juvenile: Differs from winter adult in showing narrow, pale (buffish when fresh) fringes and narrow dark subterminal bands to the upperparts, coverts and tertials (pattern rather quickly becoming difficult to see). Never shows a darker bar across the forehead as in many adults.

1st-winter: Difficult to distinguish from the adult, unless the presence of retained juvenile feathers can be determined with certainty.

1st-summer: Many birds show less-black markings than adults. Flight-feathers more worn than in adult.

Voice: The flight call distinguishes from Ringed Plover: a *tew-it*, almost monosyllabic and recalling a subdued Spotted Redshank, or a more drawn out *tu-éét* or *tew-éé*. The call of Ringed is more mellow, softer and more distinctly disyllabic, with the stress on the first syllable.

Range: Breeds Alaska and N Canada. Winters along the coasts of S USA, Central America and most of South America.

Status: Accidental in the Azores: adult recovered on 25th Sept 1972, which had been ringed two months earlier at Grindstone, Canada. Also one reported from Flores on 8th Oct 1988*. Britain: juvenile on Isles of Scilly from 9th Oct-9th Nov 1978.

KILLDEER   *Charadrius vociferus*   C **20**

L 23-26cm (9.5"). North America etc. Rare vagrant, mainly in late autumn/winter.

Adult: Unmistakable. Much larger than other ringed plovers with long, dark bill and long tail. It shows two blackish bars across the breast. The back, rump and uppertail-coverts are bright orange-brown. In flight shows prominent white wing-bar and wedge-shaped tail with black-and-white surround.

Juvenile: Very similar to the fresh-plumaged adult, but the fringes to the upperparts and coverts are normally paler (adults show rufous fringes when fresh and may also show indistinct, narrow, dark submarginal lines like juvenile). Fresh juveniles show prominent hair-like tufts on the tips of the central pair of tail-feathers and uppertail-coverts. The juvenile plumage is moulted early.

1st-winter: Difficult to tell from the adult, but a few retained juvenile coverts and sometimes tertials can often be detected, clearly more worn than and contrasting with the new feathers.

Voice: A very characteristic, loud, penetrating, shrill *ty-EE*; *ty-EE-dee-dee*; *dee*; *dee-dee-dee* and similar.

Habitat and behaviour: Prefers drier and grassier habitat than ringed plovers. Moves like other plovers.

Range: Breeds over much of North America (except arctic parts), Central America, N South America and West Indies. Migratory in N half of range.

Status: Rare vagrant. Mainly recorded in the British Isles (44), with a scattering of records elsewhere: Iceland (3), Faeroes (Sept 1939), Norway (Apr 1974), Channel Islands (Jan 1971, Sept 1973), France (6, May, Sept, Nov-Dec), Switzerland (May 1974, Dec 1977), Hungary (Nov-Dec 1986), Rumania (Sept 1985), Spain (Sept 1988) and the Azores (Jan 1928, up to 4 in Jan-Feb 1945; May 1966 and Dec 1977).

Differs from all other Nearctic waders in its late autumn-winter arrival in Europe (most occur Nov-Mar), perhaps due to late autumn and winter storms, which sometimes result in northward movements on the American Atlantic coast.

KITTLITZ'S PLOVER   *Charadrius pecuarius*   A **21**

L 12-14cm (5"). Africa. Only one record.

All plumages: Slightly smaller than Kentish Plover, but generally appears slightly larger because of its proportionately longer bill and legs. The upperparts usually show diffuse pale fringes, giving a more variegated pattern than found in other ringed plovers. The lesser coverts are contrastingly dark but are generally only seen in flight.

Adult summer: Has diagnostic head pattern, also lacks dark breast band (only diffuse patches at sides of breast), and has rather richly coloured breast and belly.

Adult winter: Could be confused with Kentish and Lesser Sand Plovers in non-breeding plumages, but has diagnostic long supercilia that meet the pale neck collar, unlike the other two species.

Juvenile: Very similar to winter adult but said to show more distinct paler fringes to the upperparts and coverts.

1st-winter/-summer: See Semipalmated Plover, p. 103.

Voice: Gives short *trip*, *pip-ip*, etc in flight.

Range: Resident in Africa, mainly S of Sahara, but also in Egypt. Vagrant to Israel (a few in Oct-Nov 1986 and 6 from Nov 1988-Mar 1989). Morocco (4 between Jan-Mar 1990).

Status: Accidental in S Norway (May 1913). A most extraordinary record in view of the species' distribution and apparently non-migratory behaviour.

LESSER SAND PLOVER *Charadrius mongolus*   A 21

L 19-21cm (7.5-8.25"). Asiatic species. Only recorded a few times (June-Sept).

Adult male summer: Shows distinctive plumage with black-and-white head pattern and a broad, rufous breast band, usually extending onto the nape and often onto the sides of the crown. It could only be confused with the very similar Greater Sand Plover (see p. 106).

Adult female summer: Similar to the male, but the black areas of the male are usually replaced by dark grey-brown, and the breast band is generally less rufous.

Adult winter: Mainly greyish-brown above and white below with large, greyish-brown patches on the sides of the breast. Plumage very similar to the Greater Sand Plover, below. It could also be confused with the slightly smaller and proportionately shorter-legged Kentish Plover. Kentish always shows a distinct white neck collar, but note that the collar may seem to be missing when the neck is retracted. Some Lesser Sand Plovers (more common in juvenile) show a very faint paler neck collar. The bill usually looks more pointed in Kentish, and the sides of the tail show much white (very little in Lesser Sand), normally only visible in flight.

Juvenile: Differs from the winter adult in showing narrow pale fringes (buffish when fresh) and narrow, indistinct dark subterminal bands to the upperparts and coverts (both pale and dark markings usually worn off/moulted rather quickly). When fresh, face and breast usually show a warm buffish tinge.

1st-winter: Difficult to distinguish from the winter adult. A few, contrastingly worn, pale-fringed juvenile coverts can sometimes be found.

1st-summer: Normally resembles a winter adult; some individuals attain partial summer plumage and then resemble adult female summer. The flight-feathers are usually more worn than in adult. Most seem to remain in their winter quarters.

Voice: Apparently the calls differ between different populations. See under Greater Sand Plover, p. 106.

Note: There are two different subspecies-groups (comprising 5 races), the NE *mongolus*-group and the C Asian *atrifrons*-group. The 2 races in the former group show a comparatively long wing and short bill and tarsus (wing/tarsus ratio of adult more than 4.1), also male has a mainly white forehead and a narrow, black band to the upper border of the rufous breast band. The 3 races in the *atrifrons*-group show a relatively shorter wing and longer bill and tarsus (wing/tarsus ratio less than 4.1), and mainly have a black forehead but lack a black border above the breast band in the breeding adult male.

Range: The *atrifrons*-group breeds in C Asia and winters along the coasts of E and S Africa and S Asia to the Sunda Islands. The *mongolus*-group breeds in E USSR and winters in SE China to Australia. Vagrant in E Mediterranean.

Status: Accidental in Sweden (adult 29th-30th June 1988), Denmark (adult male 2nd-3rd July 1988), Norway (July 1973), Poland (June 1977), Austria (Sept 1964), and Spain (June 1981).

GREATER SAND PLOVER *Charadrius leschenaultii*   B 21

L 22-25cm (8.5-9.75"). Asia. Rare vagrant.

All plumages: Very similar to the corresponding plumages of Lesser Sand Plover. Individual and geographical variation within each species further complicates the problem of distinguishing between the two species, and great care must always be taken when identifying sand plovers.

It is usually distinctly larger than Lesser, although this can be difficult to judge when the two are not seen together; the body of Greater is considerably bigger than Ringed Plover's, Lesser's only slightly, but this must be used with caution. The bill is usually obviously longer than the bill of Lesser and usually distinctly longer than the distance between the base of the bill and the rear edge of the eye, whereas in Lesser (and a few Greater, at least of subspecies *columbinus*) the bill is usually shorter than, or approximately equal to, that distance (see figure, measurements taken from the loral point). This measurement can normally only be taken on good photographs with the head in profile. The bill (exposed culmen) measures 20-28mm compared to 15-21mm in Lesser. Also the bill often (but not always!) looks considerably stronger than in Lesser. The outer end of the bill generally tapers off rather smoothly. In Lesser the outer end is usually more swollen, and the angle at which the two mandibles meet is steeper, thus giving a blunter and stubbier impression. Differences in the length and shape of the bill are most pronounced between Greaters of E populations and Lessers of the *mongolus*-group. Differences are less pronounced (but still usually perceptible) between Greaters of W origin (race *columbinus* and Lessers of the *atrifrons*-group).

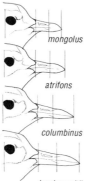

mongolus

atrifons

columbinus

leschenaultii

Another difference from the *atrifrons*-group of Lesser is that the swollen outer end ('nail') is generally proportionately longer, usually slightly longer than the distance from the loral point to where the nail begins (although deciding where the nail begins may be rather arbitrary). In Lesser the 'nail' is usually slightly shorter than that distance (see figure). There is some overlap though, and young Greaters especially, sometimes have the 'nail' shorter than the inner part of the bill. In the field it is difficult to determine with certainty which part of the bill is longer, but sometimes it is actually quite obvious. In the *mongolus* group the bill is generally closer to Greater in this respect.

To conclude, the bill usually differs significantly between the two species. It is, however, of the utmost importance to remember that some Greater Sandplovers of the race *columbinus* are as small-billed as Lesser Sandplovers of the race *atrifons*.

Usually shows proportionately longer legs than Lesser, especially when compared to the *mongolus*-group. The tarsus measures 34-41mm as opposed to 27-38mm in Lesser. Its legs are generally rather pale, usually with a distinct greenish or yellowish tinge. Rarely are they dark-looking, though. In Lesser the legs are generally quite dark greyish, but they sometimes show a distinct greenish tinge, especially in juveniles. Altogether, the Greater Sandplover generally looks rather 'disproportionate', sometimes even grotesque, while the Lesser Sandplover has more 'ordinary' proportions.

Adult male summer: E populations generally show a narrower, rufous breast band than Lesser. However, in W populations (*columbinus*) the breast band is frequently as wide as in a typical Lesser (some variation in Lesser also). The upperparts generally show some rufous mottling, sometimes very extensive in *columbinus*. Lesser only exceptionally shows any rufous on the mantle and scapulars.

There is a complete overlap in the head pattern between the two species. Greater also sometimes shows a narrow, dark band bordering the breast band above, as in the *mongolus*-group of Lesser Sand Plover.

Adult female summer: Differs from the male in the same way as in Lesser Sand Plover (see above).

Other plumages: Are homologous with those of Lesser Sand Plover (p. 105), and apparently do not differ from the corresponding plumages of Lesser.

Voice: The flight call is a trilling *kyrrr; kirr; trrr* or similar, often repeated. It is very similar, but usually slightly deeper than the call of Lesser Sand Plovers passing through and wintering in E and SE Asia. Lesser Sand Plovers wintering in Africa are said to give quite different calls, *chitik*.

Range: Breeds from C Turkey, rather patchily across Asia to Mongolia and SE of Lake Baikal. Winters along the coasts of E and S Africa, and in S and SE Asia to Australia. Vagrant in Morocco and Tunisia.

Status: Rare vagrant. Britain (9, Apr-Sept, Nov-Feb), France (June 1969, May 1970, May 1980), Belgium (July 1954, 1972 and 1986), Netherlands (July 1977, Aug 1984, Aug 1985), Norway (Aug 1984), Sweden (4, May-Aug), Finland (2), Poland (4, Sept-Oct, Apr), East Germany (Sept 1931), West Germany (July 1988*), Austria (June 1979), Greece, Bulgaria (June 1984), and Malta (6). In N Europe there has been a notable increase in the number of observations, especially during the last decade (mainly July-Oct, rarer in spring).

CASPIAN PLOVER *Charadrius asiaticus*   B **21**

L 18-20cm (7.5"). Central Asia. Very rare vagrant (spring/autumn).

Adult male summer: Shows distinct head pattern and a broad, rufous breast band with a narrow, black lower border, readily separating it from both sand plovers.

Adult female summer: Shows same basic pattern as male but lacks rufous or may occasionally show a little dull rufous on the grey-brown breast; lacks neat black lower border to breast band.

Adult winter: Basically similar to the summer-plumaged adult female. Males sometimes show some rufous on the breast. Resembles the sand plovers, but is generally more attenuated at the rear end, and the bill is comparatively thin, especially at the tip. The head pattern is distinctive: the supercilium is usually more prominent than in sand plovers; the anterior lores are always pale (often in sand plovers also, but more frequently lores are dark from eye to base of bill); and the dark band on the ear-coverts tends to be narrower. The entire face is generally buffish-washed (whiter in sand plovers). The breast band is distinctly broader and more complete than in the sand plovers, and unlike these, the upperparts and coverts show distinct pale fringes when not too worn (rufous when fresh). Also shows a less distinct wing-bar and has a duskier underwing.

Juvenile: Similar to the fresh adult winter. The breast band tends to be less complete, and is rather more like the patches found in the sand plovers, although normally more extensive on the lower breast. The juvenile plumage is usually moulted early.

1st-winter: Can usually be told from the adult by the contrast shown between some retained juvenile coverts (mainly greaters) and sometimes tertials and some fresher and newer ones. Note that the pattern of the juvenile and the new feathers is very similar.

1st-summer: Apparently shows more worn primaries than in adult.

Voice: The most frequently heard call is a short, rather sharp *kytt.*

Habitat: Favours drier and grassier areas than the sand plovers.

Note: The Oriental Plover *C. veredus* of E Asia (formerly considered conspecific with Caspian), might possibly stray to Europe. The breeding adult male is easily distinguished from male Caspian by its largely pale head and sides to the neck (often whitish with darker crown) and more brownish-orange breast band. Other plumages are more similar to Caspian, but the wing-bar is even fainter or lacking altogether, the underwing is all dark, and the legs are generally slightly longer and more yellowish or even pale orangey (Caspian has pale greyish, olive-grey or pinkish-grey legs).

Range: Breeds in the arid steppes and semi-deserts of C Asia. Winters in E and S Africa. Migrates through the Middle East and Arabia. Surprisingly, only recently recorded in Cyprus (Aug 1984, Apr 1987).

Status: Very rare vagrant. Britain: Norfolk, two (22nd May 1890); Isles of Scilly, male (21st May 1988); Lothian, Aberlady Bay, (12th-13th July 1988). France: (20th Aug 1980), adult (26th Apr 1985, 6th Aug 1988*). West Germany: Heligoland (Nov 1850, May 1859). Norway: Finnmark (9th-15th June 1978). Italy: Marche (1887), Puglia (1898), and Sicily (Mar 1978). Greece: Evros delta (23rd July 1988), Bulgaria (1879), Rumania (May 1979), and Malta (7, Mar, May, July-Nov).

AMERICAN GOLDEN PLOVER *Pluvialis dominica*   D **22**
L 24-28cm (9.5-11"). North America. Rare vagrant to mainly W Europe, especially in autumn.
All plumages: Very similar to corresponding plumages of the Pacific Golden Plover. Until recently, these two were usually considered conspecific (under the name of Lesser Golden Plover *P. dominica*), but

now they are more often regarded as separate species (see Appendix). See Pacific for differences (p. 110).

It also requires to be separated from Golden Plover, but is appreciably smaller, slimmer, with proportionately longer legs, and has longer and narrower wings. The primary projection is more prominent, and the wing-tips usually reach further beyond the tail tip. The underwing-coverts are greyish, and the axillaries are a darker shade of grey. In Golden the underwing-coverts are largely whitish, and the axillaries are pure white. The whitish wing-bar is also slightly less prominent than in Golden.

In all plumages, differs from Grey Plover by e.g. fainter wing-bars, dark rump and uppertail-coverts and grey underwing (mainly whitish underwing with black axillaries in Grey Plover).

Adult summer: The black stripe on the foreneck is distinctly wider than in Golden (particularly obvious when viewed head on), and the white stripes on the forehead, supercilium and sides to the neck are slightly broader. On the sides of the lower neck/upper breast the white stripe widens into a prominent patch, cut off by the usually black flanks (recalling Grey Plover in this respect). This pattern is not seen in Golden, in which the sides of the lower neck/upper breast are more extensively spangled, and the flanks show a broad white stripe (see figure). The undertail-coverts are entirely or largely black, which is never the case in Golden. It also shows more coarsely spangled and normally slightly less 'golden' upperparts and coverts (spots generally larger and more widely spaced and tend to have a higher proportion of white marks).

The sexes are very similar and are difficult to separate due to individual variation. The female usually has the black areas slightly more brownish-black, and there is usually at least a little pale mottling on the face. Some females show more extensive pale mottling below. In a breeding pair the female is perhaps always less brightly and contrastingly coloured.

ad. ♂ in summer plumage

Pacific Golden Plover

American Golden Plover

Golden Plover

Adult winter: Distinguished from Golden Plover by its much greyer plumage with less distinctly marked upperparts, coverts and tertials (sometimes almost plain), more distinct head pattern, and generally less spotted breast. See Pacific Golden Plover (p. 110) for further differences from Golden Plover.

Juvenile: Easily distinguished from the winter adult by its more evenly patterned and more brightly coloured upperparts, coverts and tertials.

Also, shows more distinctly marked underparts with some barring. The warm coloration may be very faint in worn plumage, but it is usually still obvious on the back, rump and uppertail-coverts (areas which are normally concealed when bird standing and thus less subject to wear and bleaching). Adults rarely acquire full winter plumage until established in their winter quarters. In the autumn, they usually show a mixture of summer and winter feathers, often making the plumage look very blotchy.

Differs from juvenile Golden Plover by its generally noticeably greyer plumage, with darker crown and mantle/upper scapulars (contrasting clearly with paler nape/hindneck, lower scapulars and coverts). It also has a more prominent, whitish, supercilium. However, occasionally very fresh individuals are as brightly coloured above as Golden, but the mantle/scapulars and coverts are normally slightly less finely and densely spangled. These are best distinguished by the lack of a distinct yellowish tinge to the supercilium, face, neck and breast and by the differences in structure and underwing pattern described above.

1st-winter: Difficult to distinguish from the winter adult, unless some retained juvenile coverts, tertials etc can be detected.

1st-summer: Apparently rather similar to the breeding adult, and the birds normally return to their breeding areas.

Voice: The flight call is readily distinguished from Golden Plover by being usually di-or trisyllabic, also thinner and higher-pitched (see fuller description under Pacific Golden Plover). Monosyllabic notes are sometimes given.

Range: Breeds in Alaska and N Canada E to Baffin Island. Winters in the interior of South America. Vagrant to Greenland and W Africa.

Status: Rare vagrant. The two forms *dominica* and *fulva* have not always been separated, and the combined totals for 'Lesser Golden Plovers' are therefore given where known: Iceland (6), British Isles (151, 12 identified as Pacific), France (6), Netherlands (15), Denmark (2), Norway (8), Sweden (16, 4 identified as American), Finland (13, all Pacific), Poland (4, all Pacific), East Germany (Aug 1973), West Germany (10, 2 identified as American), Greece, Italy (19), Malta (6), and Spain (5). The American Golden is the more frequent in NW Europe, e.g. British Isles, especially Sept-Oct.

PACIFIC GOLDEN PLOVER *Pluvialis fulva*   C 22

L 23-26cm (9-10"). Asia/Alaska. Formerly considered conspecific with American Golden Plover but now regarded by most authors as a separate species (see Appendix). Very rare vagrant, mainly in autumn.

All plumages: Very similar to American Golden Plover and Golden Plover. Differs from Golden Plover by much the same characters as described for American, but the differences in primary projection and projection of wing-tips beyond tail-tip are not valid. The difference in leg length is even more pronounced. In flight the tips of the toes project clearly beyond the tail tip, unlike in Golden. Also, the bill is proportionately longer and heavier than in Golden.

Compared to American, it shows a proportionately slightly larger bill and longer legs (toes often do not project beyond tail tip in flight in American). The primary projection is usually considerably shorter; as a rule, there are three primary-tips visible beyond the tertials on the folded wing, as opposed to four in American (note that the space between the outermost two is small in both species; beware of birds with one or more missing tertials!). This is at least partly a reflection of the longer tertials, which usually end close to the tip of the tail, whereas in American they normally end well short of the tail tip. These structural differences are very important.

Adult summer: The basic pattern is rather like a bright male 'northern' Golden Plover. In full summer plumage, birds showing a pale face and a poorly marked blackish stripe on the foreneck are apparently less frequent than in Golden Plover (particularly females, and more frequent in southern populations in Golden).

It differs from Golden Plover by mostly the same characters as described for American. However, the flanks and undertail-coverts are rarely black. Usually the flanks are rather coarsely barred and the undertail-coverts rather heavily marked with black. In Golden the flanks are generally more sparsely patterned with finer and fainter dark bars, and the undertail-coverts show no or very little black.

The plumage is very similar to that of the American Golden Plover. A 'classic' individual differs from a typical American in showing a rather broad, white, coarsely black-barred stripe on the flanks; less of a white patch on the sides of the lower neck/upper breast; and whitish undertail-coverts with coarse black markings (not completely black). However, there is much individual variation in both, and many individuals may be indistinguishable by plumage alone. Some males show no white flank stripe at all, and the undertail-coverts sometimes appear all black. Conversely, some male American show some white mottling on the undertail-coverts. There is even more overlap between female American and male Pacific. It is apparently very rare for the flanks to show any white in American, except when in moult. The white patch on the sides of the lower neck/upper breast is generally slightly less prominent than in American, even in birds with black flanks. The crown and mantle tend to be paler due to, on average, slightly larger golden spots, but again there is overlap. Sexing – see American (possibly generally more differences between the sexes).

Adult winter: Very similar to Golden Plover in non-breeding plumage. The breast is usually less distinctly spotted than in Golden, and there is a tendency for the upperparts, coverts and tertials to be less regularly and distinctly spotted; often at least some of these feathers show rather even pale fringes rather than neatly pale-spotted fringes as in Golden. The head pattern is also slightly different (see juvenile, below).

It is readily distinguished from winter plumaged American by the more buffish tinge to its face, neck and breast. The supercilium is less prominent and contrasting. Also, the upperparts, coverts and tertials are usually more yellowish, with more distinct spotting; unlike Pacific, some American are virtually plain above. Overall, the general plumage coloration is nearer to Golden Plover, whereas American more resembles Grey Plover. However, beware of heavily worn individuals which are less yellowish.

Juvenile: Differs from the winter adult by its more evenly patterned upperparts, coverts and tertials (feathers all of same age); however, some adults very similar to juveniles above. The underparts are more distinctly patterned, with some fine barring. In the autumn, adults are usually in transitional plumage and show a mixture of summer and winter feathers.

Very similar to juvenile Golden Plover. The supercilium is generally better defined, there is usually a distinct pale patch at the base of the upper mandible ('goggles', uncommonly seen in Golden), and the 'sub-moustachial area' is normally paler and less spotted. In Golden Plover, the face looks comparatively plain and featureless. The centre of the breast and upper belly are generally less strongly patterned than in Golden. Also, upperparts and coverts are not quite so finely and densely spangled as in Golden, and the coverts are often contrastingly paler than the mantle/scapulars, which is not normally the case in Golden.

The pattern of the uppertail-coverts and central pair of tail feathers usually differs distinctly from Golden, although this is of limited value in the field. These feathers show pale spots along their edges (usually also in American), whereas in Golden they show pale transverse bars.

It is normally quite distinct from juvenile American, which in general coloration is usually more like a juvenile Grey Plover.

The entire upperside and coverts are rather evenly coloured, unlike American, which, except when very fresh, usually shows contrastingly darker crown, mantle and upper scapulars. The supercilium, face, neck and breast are distinctly yellowish. In American the supercilium is whitish, and the face, neck and breast have a pale brown-grey base colour. The supercilium is usually less prominent and less contrasting with the crown than in most American. Note that heavily worn individuals can be rather dull, and that some fresh-plumaged American are very brightly coloured above, without contrastingly darker crown, mantle and upper scapulars. These yellowish American can still usually be identified by the lack of yellowish on the supercilium, face, neck and breast (a very faint yellowish tinge to the supercilium, face and (hind) neck is sometimes present when very fresh).

1st-winter: See American Golden Plover (p. 108).

1st-summer: Many remain in their winter quarters in a non-breeding plumage, but apparently many also attain breeding plumage and return to their breeding grounds. These birds have their primaries more worn than adults.

Voice: The flight calls are usually very different from Golden Plover and also normally clearly different from American as well. The normal flight calls of Pacific are a *chu-it*, much resembling the call of Spotted Redshank; a more drawn-out *chu-eet* or *chu-ee(uh)*, with the stress more on the second syllable than on the first, and a similar but even more drawn-out *chu-EE* or *chu-EE(uh)*, with the stress very clearly on the second syllable. The last (two calls) type is normally given when flushed. Other less commonly heard calls include distinctly trisyllabic calls, *chu-i-uh* or *chu-ee-uh* and monosyllabic calls.

The commonly heard flight calls of American include a *tyy-ee*, or, differently transcribed, *klee-i*, with the stress on the *first* syllable or with the second syllable faint or even missing, *klee(-i)* or *kleep*. Also *tyy-y-ee*, *ty-yy-ee*, *qú-li-u* or *qu-lí-u* or *klú-i-lip*, with the stress either on the first or second syllable, often with the second slightly vibrant (the first two syllables are not always clearly separated). The calls of American are usually slightly higher-pitched than those of Pacific.

Range: Breeds from the Yamal Peninsula in N USSR eastwards to W Alaska, where it overlaps with American Golden Plover. Winters chiefly in S Asia to Australia, New Zealand and Pacific Ocean islands. Also occurs on passage and in winter in Oman, Aden, Seychelles and a few regularly winter in East Africa. Vagrant to Algeria, W and S Africa.

Status: Very rare vagrant in Europe (mainly autumn). There are a few records from Norway (3), Sweden (5), Finland (13), Poland (4), West Germany (8, but one in July-Aug 1988 is only the second this century), Denmark (2), Netherlands (14), west to the British Isles (12) and south to Italy, Sicily (2), Malta and Greece. Combined totals of *dominica* and *fulva* are given under the previous species. Note that the Pacific Golden Plover is much rarer than American Golden in the British Isles.

SPUR-WINGED PLOVER   *Hoplopterus spinosus*   R Br **22**

L 25-27cm (10"). Rare breeding bird in Greece (also Turkey, Middle East and Africa). Accidental outside breeding range.

Adult: Easily recognized by the characteristic black-and-white pattern of its head, neck and underparts, and its grey-brown upperparts. In flight, all blackish flight feathers contrast with a pale band across the upperwing-coverts, and it also shows a contrast between mostly black tail and white uppertail-coverts and rump.

The peculiar spur at the carpal joint, which has given the bird both its English and scientific name, is usually difficult to see. Male averages slightly larger and shows a slightly longer spur than female. See also Sociable and White-tailed Plovers (p. 114 and p. 115).

Juvenile: Similar to the adult but shows duller, brown-tinged black areas with some pale fringes, particularly on the crown and chin. The upperparts, coverts and tertials also show pale fringes and dark subterminal bands, and the scapulars are distinctly shorter. The iris is browner and the spur is shorter and blunter.

1st-winter: The juvenile rather quickly becomes indistinguishable from the adult, unless retained juvenile coverts or browner iris can be seen.

Voice: Usually very noisy on the breeding grounds, and often heard calling at night. The display call is a repeated, rather harsh, grating *ki-ki-ki-kIlerrik*. The alarm call is a short, sharp, penetrating, *kitt*, recalling Common Tern.

Habitat: Favours wetter areas, such as irrigated farmland, lake-sides, salinas, marshes etc.

Range: Breeds in N and E Greece (< 80 pairs in 1986, where it bred for the first time in Europe in 1959). Also breeds more widely in Turkey, the Middle East and NE and C Africa. Greek and Turkish birds are migratory, presumably wintering in Africa. Regular in Crete and Cyprus on migration.

Status: Accidental in West Germany (Apr 1964, May 1971, Sept 1978, origins uncertain), Czechoslovakia, Rumania (1964, Aug 1977), Bulgaria (1962), Yugoslavia (5, May-Aug), Italy (Sept 1989), Malta (3), and Spain. In Britain and elsewhere in N Europe, a few further individuals are known to have escaped from captivity.

SOCIABLE PLOVER *Chettusia gregaria*

L 27-30cm (11"). W Asia. Rare vagrant, mainly autumn/winter, also spring.

All plumages: This eye-catching plover is well marked and should not be confused with any other wader. In flight, it could possibly be mistaken for either Spur-winged or White-tailed Plovers. From the former, it differs in showing white secondaries and lacking the broad, pale band across the coverts. From the latter, it differs in showing less white on the wings above and a black tail band, and the legs project far less beyond the tail tip and are blackish, not yellow.

Adult summer: Easily recognized by its striking head pattern with prominent supercilia meeting on the nape and by its black and chestnut belly-patch. The male tends to be blacker on the crown/belly and more extensively chestnut on the belly than the female.

Adult winter: Lacks the belly-patch, and the breast usually shows coarse markings. The prominent supercilium is still a very distinctive feature. In fresh plumage, the upperparts and coverts show pale fringes.

It could perhaps be confused with non-breeding Dotterel and Caspian Plover, but is much larger with proportionately longer, dark legs and has a different pattern both on the upperparts, underparts, and on wings/tail.

Juvenile: Apparently very similar to the winter adult. At the time of the year when juveniles can be seen, adults usually still show some traces of summer plumage and some very worn feathers mixed in with the newly moulted winter feathers. See below.

1st-winter: Can usually be distinguished from the adult winter by at least some retained juvenile coverts (particularly outer medians). These are contrastingly worn and show rather sharply defined pale fringes and dark subterminal bands. Adult (and newly moulted coverts) show diffuse pale tips and lack dark subterminal bands (note that dark subterminal bands to scapulars can sometimes be seen in adult winter).

1st-summer: Generally not quite so distinct and colourful as the adult. Some individuals are apparently still rather pale on the belly with darker patches only.

Voice: Usually silent outside breeding season.

Habitat and behaviour: Favours rather dry, grassy areas or ploughed fields. In W Europe, stragglers almost always join flocks of Lapwings.

Range: Breeds in the steppe region of C Asia. Winters chiefly in NE Africa (scarce), Pakistan and NW India, some also in the Middle East and Transcaucasia. Numbers have gone down markedly in recent years. Accidental in Morocco.

Status: Rare vagrant in the British Isles (32), France (20), Belgium (4), Netherlands (18), Denmark, Sweden (3 in May-Aug 1989), Finland (Apr-May 1951, Aug 1988), East Germany (7 since 1967, June, Sept-Oct), West Germany (>20, Apr-June, Aug-Oct), Poland (4), Czechoslovakia (6th record included three, Apr 1985), Austria, Switzerland (5), Hungary (Sept 1900), Italy, Sicily (2), Yugoslavia (Mar 1967, Apr 1983), Greece, Rumania, Malta (3), Spain (5) and Portugal.

The majority of the British records have occurred during autumn/winter, while most records from the Continent have occurred in spring/summer.

WHITE-TAILED PLOVER   *Chettusia leucura*   B 23

L 26-29cm (11"). West C Asia. Accidental (spring/summer).

Adult: Diagnostic, long, yellow legs prevent confusion with all other similar waders. Also, shows striking wing pattern and all white tail, but has rather poorly marked head unlike its relatives.

Juvenile: Readily distinguished from the adult by its strongly marked upperparts and coverts.

1st-winter: Usually indistinguishable from the adult unless some retained juvenile coverts and/or very narrow, darker subterminal tail bar can be detected.

Voice: Usually silent away from the breeding areas, but occasionally various squeaky notes with a somewhat Lapwing-like quality are given, e.g. *ket.*

Habitat: Prefers wet areas, such as ponds, ditches, and marshes.

Range: Breeds in W Asia, mainly in the Caspian/Aral area and the lower Euphrates/Tigris region. Range may be expanding slightly westwards, since breeding pairs have been found in Turkey and Syria in recent years, and breeding has also been suspected in Jordan. Vagrant in Cyprus (10, Mar-June) and Morocco.

Status: Accidental in Britain (4, May-July), France (Nov 1840), Netherlands (July 1975, June 1984, July 1984), Sweden (May 1975), Finland (May 1975, May 1990*), East Germany (May 1976), West Germany (July 1984, May 1989*), Poland (Apr 1975), Austria (Aug 1968, Mar-Apr 1975), Hungary (May 1975, Nov 1987), Rumania (May 1977), Greece (Apr 1958, Aug 1966), Italy (Sicily, Apr 1975), and Malta (4). There were 25 European records up to 1987, although 8 in 1975 presumably represented a small influx.

Family SCOLOPACIDAE   Sandpipers and allies

GREAT KNOT   *Calidris tenuirostris*   A 23

L 26-28cm (10.5"). E Siberia. Accidental.

All plumages: Recalls Knot in general size and structure but is noticeably larger (not always apparent unless seen side by side). It has a proportionately longer bill, which looks more broad-based and fine-tipped and with a trace of decurvature. Also, looks proportionately smaller-headed, longer necked and more attenuated at rear than Knot.

Adult summer: Unmistakable and unlikely to be confused with any other *Calidris* wader. White underparts have large, blackish spots on the breast and flanks, often coalescing to form an almost solidly dark breast. Also, shows a rather featureless, heavily streaked head and usually at least a few, diagnostic, largely bright rufous and black, white-tipped scapulars.

Adult winter: Very similar to winter Knot, but crown, hindneck and upperparts tend to be more streaked. The flanks are usually patterned with rather large, somewhat drawn-out triangular or rounded marks. Quite frequently there are also some large blackish spots on the breast. A similar pattern can occasionally also be seen in Knot, but the flanks generally show many distinct V-marks (a few sometimes seen in Great Knot), and the spots on the breast and flanks are usually smaller.

The head pattern is usually noticeably different from that of Knot. The lores show a rather large, diffuse, darker area, whereas Knot usually shows a more distinct dark loral stripe. The supercilium is usually less well-defined, and the ear-coverts are normally not contrastingly darker than the nape/hindneck, which is often the case in Knot. The rump/uppertail-coverts are almost unmarked whitish and contrast clearly with the upperparts and tail. In Knot this contrast is less apparent, because its rather more strongly marked rump and uppertail-coverts look pale grey.

Juvenile: Much darker and more boldly patterned than the winter adult. Differs from worn summer adults by its fresher plumage with all feathers the same age and has differently patterned upperparts.

The plumage is very distinctive and bears only a superficial resemblance to juvenile Knot. It is considerably darker, with darker centres to the feathers of the upperparts, coverts and tertials. The scapulars and usually the distal parts of the inner greater coverts and tertials show pale-spotted fringes. In Knot, the upperparts, coverts and tertials are rather pale grey with distinct pale fringes and darker subterminal bands, giving a distinctly more scalloped appearance.

The head/neck are usually more heavily streaked than in Knot, and the face pattern differs in much the same way as for the winter adult. The breast and flanks show large dark spots, often coalescing to form a dark pectoral shield. The pattern of the underparts thus resembles a summer adult and is very different from that of Knot. The pattern of the rump/uppertail-coverts is similar to that of the adult.

1st-winter: Similar to the winter adult, but at least some juvenile coverts and tertials are usually retained. There is no moult of the remiges in the autumn/winter as in adults (usually in their winter quarters).

1st-summer: Generally shows a basically winter-like plumage with some scattered summer feathers. Some attain a more advanced summer plumage. Most remain in their winter quarters.

Voice: Like Knot, it is usually silent in the non-breeding season. Muffled *gryt* or *kryt* notes are sometimes heard.

Range: Breeds in easternmost Siberia. Migrates south along easternmost Asia to winter chiefly in Australia, E Indonesia and Papua New Guinea. Some winter as far W as Pakistan; also recently discovered wintering in Oman and the United Arab Emirates. Vagrants have reached Morocco (Aug 1980), Oman (Sept 1982 and flock of 119 in winter 1988/89!), Saudi Arabia (2 in May/June 1984) and Eilat (Oct 1985).

Status: Accidental in Spain: Ebro delta, adult (7th Apr 1979); East Germany: Langenwerder Island, Wismar, adult (1st Aug 1987). Britain: Shetland, adult (15th Sept 1989*). Norway: Rossholmen, Nordre Øyeren (12th Sept 1987).

SEMIPALMATED SANDPIPER   *Calidris pusilla*   C 24

L 13-15cm (5.5"). North America. Rare vagrant, majority found in British Isles (mainly autumn).

All plumages: Fractionally larger and stouter than Little Stint, with a thicker, more blunt-tipped bill; also has a slightly shorter primary projection. Bill length variable – in some it is comparatively short (male on average has shorter bill than female), whereas in others it is strikingly long (eastern populations tend to have longer bills than western birds). The toes are partially webbed (most pronounced between middle and outer toes), which is a character shared only with Western Sandpiper among the stints. See also Western Sandpiper (p. 118) and Red-necked Stint (p. 119).

Adult summer: Plumage is generally drab-looking, lacking the rufous colours of most other stints. Some birds (especially when more worn in late spring/summer), are warmer in general coloration, but never approach the typically rich foxy coloration of Little Stint. The comparatively pale centred coverts and tertials without rufous fringes/edges will always distinguish a bright individual from an exceptionally pale Little. It also lacks the prominent white V on the sides of the mantle, typical of Little Stint. See 1st-summer Red-necked Stint (p. 119).

Adult winter: Plumage is very similar to other stints. Compared with Little Stint, it seems slightly paler and more uniform above. In Little, often all, sometimes only the rearmost (and sometimes perhaps none) of the scapulars have obviously more extensively dark centres. Structure (particularly palmations) and call are of more importance. A rather high proportion of the feathers on the head and body are generally moulted during the autumn migration, but the wings are not moulted until in the winter quarters.

Juvenile: Readily distinguishable from an autumn adult by its comparatively fresh plumage with all feathers the same age. Adults usually show a mixture of heavily worn summer feathers and newly moulted winter feathers, while juveniles do not usually start moulting until they reach their winter quarters. It is more delicately patterned above, and less coarsely marked on breast.

It is generally rather dull and evenly patterned above, and is usually much less richly coloured than juvenile Little Stint. However, some fresh birds are quite brightly coloured and may be confused with Little. They may be distinguished by e.g. (1) Usually extensively pale grey lower two rows of scapulars with distinct dark 'anchor-shaped' marks (in some, the lower scapulars appear to have more uniformly dark centres without obvious 'anchor-marks', but the dark centres, particularly of the lowest row, are probably never as blackish as in Little). (2) Distinctly paler centres to coverts (particularly innermost greater coverts) and tertials, with less contrasting and less rufous fringes/edges. (3) Never has such a distinct white V on mantle as 'classic' Little. (4) Generally has less coarsely marked breast sides. Also, structure and call are important field marks to be taken into account.

1st-winter: Similar to the winter adult but can be distinguished under ideal conditions by at least some retained juvenile coverts and tertials with distinct pale fringes.

117

1st-summer: Apparently usually like the winter plumage with only a few feathers of the breeding plumage showing. Usually remains in the winter quarters.

Call: Usual flight calls are comparatively low-pitched; gives a rather coarse, short *krrit* and *krryt* (slightly variable pitch). Also, slightly higher-pitched calls sounding more like *kit* are often heard, usually in combination with the typical calls. Typical flight calls are very different from the rather high-pitched sharp *tit* notes of Little Stint. Compare also calls of Western Sandpiper and Red-necked Stint.

Range: Breeds Alaska, C and E Canada. Winters mainly in coastal South America, north to West Indies and Pacific coast of Central America. Vagrant in Greenland and Madeira.

Status: Rare vagrant. British Isles, annual since 1980, (58, mainly Aug-Oct, with a peak in Sept). Also noted in Iceland (Oct 1989*), Norway (Aug 1987), France (3, Sept), Netherlands (June 1989*), West Germany (only record under review), Austria (Nov 1985), Portugal (Oct 1989*), and the Azores (*c.* 10). Most of the records refer to juveniles.

WESTERN SANDPIPER *Calidris mauri*   B 24

L 14-17cm (5.5"). Alaska and NE Siberia. Accidental.

All plumages: Structurally resembles Semipalmated Sandpiper, but has proportionally slightly longer legs and usually a strikingly longer bill. Although there is a slight overlap (approximately 2mm) between the shortest-billed male Western and the longest-billed female Semipalmated, probably at least 90% are immediately separable on bill length alone. Further, the bill is usually slightly decurved and finer-tipped than in Semipalmated. In general appearance, often recalls a miniature Dunlin. Toes are partially webbed as in Semipalmated.

Adult summer: Bright rufous on the sides of the crown – nape, ear-coverts and at least some upper scapulars (often also on bases of at least some lower scapulars). Has whitish breast with strong streaking, usually in the shape of 'arrowheads' or triangles on the sides of the breast and usually extending down the flanks. In worn plumage, the breast sometimes looks very dark. The coverts are dull grey-brown as in Semipalmated Sandpiper and Red-necked Stint.

Adult winter: Plumage very similar to Semipalmated Sandpiper, but is marginally purer grey above and usually shows a band of fine streaks across the breast (lacking in Semipalmated, which has breast sides obscurely streaked). Structure and call are of more help in identification.

Juvenile: Easily told from an autumn adult in the same way as in Semipalmated Sandpiper, but note that the moult to 1st-winter plumage usually starts significantly earlier than in Semipalmated Sandpiper – usually during the migration.

Similar to juvenile Semipalmated Sandpiper but is more contrastingly patterned. The most important character is that the upper scapulars show deep rufous fringes, usually forming a contrasting rufous stripe along the upper scapulars. In very fresh individuals, the central mantle is also rufous, diminishing the effect slightly. In Semipalmated Sandpiper the mantle/scapulars are more homogeneously patterned/coloured, also in unusually bright individuals, and never showing a contrasting rufous stripe on upper scapulars. Another important character is that the crown is dull compared to the upper scapulars, generally with the sides of the crown paler, greyer and more finely streaked than the centre of the crown. In Semipalmated Sandpiper the crown is at least as brightly coloured as the mantle/scapulars and is rather evenly coloured/streaked (accordingly, there is a rich rufous 'cap' in individuals with rich rufous mantle/scapulars, which is never the case in Western). The face and breast (especially sides) usually look 'cleaner' and whiter than in Semipalmated. See also juvenile Red-necked stint, below.

1st-winter: Similar to the winter adult, and differs in the same way as described for 1st-winter Semipalmated Sandpiper.

1st-summer: Mostly like winter plumage, with only a few breeding plumage feathers showing. Usually they remain in their winter range.

Voice: Calls similar to Semipalmated, but generally higher-pitched, more shrill and drawn-out: *krreep* or *krreet*. Also, gives high-pitched *kirrp* and *kirr* and even higher-pitched notes, lacking 'r'-sound.

Range: Breeds W Alaska and tip of NE Siberia. Winters mainly S USA, West Indies, and Central and South America south to Peru and Surinam. Vagrant in the Canary Is and Madeira.

Status: Accidental in the British Isles (May-June 1956, Aug 1969, July 1973, Sept 1973, 1975 and 1988), France (Sept 1973), Denmark (May 1976), Sweden (Aug 1988), Spain (Sept 1979), and the Azores (Oct 1978*).

RED-NECKED STINT *Calidris ruficollis* A 24

L 13-16cm (5.5"). E and NE Siberia. A few records, all quite recent.

All plumages: Very similar to Semipalmated Sandpiper in general shape, but bill and legs on average shorter and the primary projection is usually noticeably longer; often the entire rear end looks more drawn-out. Compared to Little Stint, the bill is on average slightly shorter and blunter-tipped, the legs slightly shorter, and it is slightly more robust with more attenuated rear (primary projection similar though). Compared to Western Sandpiper, the bill is much shorter and straighter. Toes are unwebbed as in Little Stint.

Adult summer: Only likely to be confused with Little Stint or an abnormally small, brightly coloured Sanderling. In typical individuals most of the ear-coverts, sides of neck, throat, foreneck and central upper breast are unmarked bright rufous, and the base colour of the breast-sides is whitish. In Little Stint the throat is always white, and the breast-sides normally have a rufous base colour. In Little Stint the rufous of the breast is strongly dark-spotted, unlike in Red-necked.

Another important distinction is that the coverts and tertials are grey-brown, with indistinct, narrow, whitish fringes/edges, whereas in Little most have blackish centres and distinct rufous fringes/edges. Occasionally, the odd covert and/or tertial is patterned much as in Little. The scapulars usually stand out as the most rufous area on the upperside, whereas Little has the mantle, scapulars and wings the same general coloration. There is also a tendency to show a less pronounced white V on the mantle than Little, but there is some overlap.

At times, small adult summer Sanderlings can be confused with Red-necked Stint. Sanderling usually shows a rufous base colour to the breast-sides, and the rufous ear-coverts, throat, foreneck and breast show dark streaks/spots. The coverts and tertials often show blackish centres and pale rufous fringes and are then of the same general coloration as the mantle/scapulars. The blackish markings on the scapulars are frequently irregularly 'serrated' at the tips, unlike in Red-necked, and the scapulars generally show more prominent pale rufous markings on the centres than in Red-necked. Often also some coverts and tertials show distinct internal pale rufous markings. Sanderling's longer bill is usually apparent, and the lack of a hind toe is diagnostic.

Adult winter: Plumage is extremely similar to Little Stint, but is usually slightly paler and a purer grey above, usually with less extensive dark centres to the scapulars (sometimes shows more prominent dark centres, though, and Little sometimes looks like typical Red-necked in this respect). Structure and call are more important.

Juvenile: Readily distinguished from autumn adults. See under juvenile Semipalmated Sandpiper (p. 117), but notice that, like juvenile Western, it usually starts moulting earlier than juvenile Semipalmated.

Many individuals are rather bright rufous above and could be confused with juvenile Little Stint, but are usually quite easily separated by: (1) extensively pale-centred lower two rows of scapulars with dark subterminal 'anchor'– or 'drop'-shaped marks (recalling pattern of Semipalmated and Western Sandpiper); (2) paler-centred coverts and tertials without distinct rufous fringes/edges; (3) fainter, smaller and often more diffuse spots/streaks on breast sides (often virtually unmarked); and (4) usually less prominent white V on mantle. However, some birds are much more Little Stint-like, with extensively dark lower scapulars and distinctly rufous-fringed coverts and tertials. Such individuals can be distinguished from Little by: (1) centres of lowest row of scapulars often not quite as blackish as in Little; (2) centres of coverts paler with less contrasting and more diffuse pale fringes, rufous usually mainly on tips (often rufous edges and whitish tips in Little); (3) tertials and innermost greater coverts grey-brown with less contrasting and more diffuse fringes/edges, never blackish with rather sharply defined and strongly contrasting rufous fringes/edges as in Little (note that under certain conditions blackish centres may seem to be paler and grey-brown centres darker than they actually are, so it is important to study these feathers from more than one angle); (4) usually more greyish-tinged breast, often forming pectoral band, with different streaking (see above); (5) usually no distinct narrow pale fork to supercilium above the eye; (6) ear-coverts more uniformly dark, lacking the slightly paler patch just behind the eye seen in most Little; (7) usually less prominent white V on mantle. Structural differences and particularly call are also important features.

Many individuals, particularly when in rather worn plumage, are often very similar to juvenile Semipalmated Sandpiper. The scapulars tend to be more contrasting rufous than in Semipalmated, although this is not always so. By far the best plumage character is the head pattern. The sides of the crown are paler and more finely streaked than the centre, usually creating a distinct dark central ridge, whereas in Semipalmated the crown is uniformly streaked and coloured (often very brightly, unlike Red-necked), creating a distinct cap. However, some Semipalmated show slightly paler sides to the crown. The supercilium, particularly at its upper border, tends to be less prominent and less well-defined. The shorter bill and legs and the usually longer primary projection are often useful clues, and the absence of webbing between the toes is a definitive character. The call can be helpful to the experienced ear.

Juvenile Western Sandpiper may be quite similar in plumage, but usually shows even more contrastingly rufous upper scapulars; generally has a 'cleaner-looking' face (usually more prominent supercilium, wider in front of eye, and generally narrower dark loral stripe); and usually paler breast with more sharply defined streaks. Western should never present a real problem, since the bill is distinctly longer and more decurved, and the toes are partially webbed.

1st-winter: See Semipalmated Sandpiper, p. 117.

1st-summer: Apparently rather variable, with some birds resembling winter-plumaged individuals, and others more like the summer adult. Some are very similar to fresh summer adult Semipalmated, but show little or no streaking on the lower ear-coverts/sides of throat, sides of neck, foreneck and uppermost part of the breast. Some rufous on the head and scapulars is also usually present. If seen, the lack of palmations will eliminate Semipalmated Sandpiper.

Voice: The most commonly heard flight calls are rather similar to the calls of Semipalmated and Western: *kreet*, *kreep* or *chreek*. Compared to Semipalmated, the voice is generally more shrill, slightly more 'cracked', and often slightly higher-pitched, and the 'r'-sound tends to be a little less distinct. It is generally slightly lower-pitched and slightly less drawn-out than the calls of Western. It is very different from the calls of Little Stint. Other frequently heard calls are e.g. *krep*, *kiep* and *klyt*; these calls are normally mixed with the ones first described.

Range: Breeds in E Siberia, also sporadically in W Alaska. Winters from S China and Burma, south to Australasia, with a few birds reaching as far as South Africa. Vagrant in Israel (May 1977, Nov 1984).

Status: Accidental in Britain (July 1986), Belgium (Aug 1988*), Netherlands (May 1987), Denmark (Aug 1986), Sweden (Aug 1985, two in July 1986), and East Germany (July 1979). All records relate to adults.

LONG-TOED STINT *Calidris subminuta*   A 25

L 13-15cm (5.5"). Siberia. Accidental.

All plumages: Very similar to the corresponding plumages of Least Sandpiper – which see for differences (p. 122). It differs from Little Stint and Semipalmated and Western Sandpipers by e.g. pale, usually yellowish or greenish-tinged, legs. Note that the legs sometimes become covered by mud and may look dark. Temminck's Stint has a different shape (notably shorter legs) and white outer tail feathers.

Adult summer: Rather dark, richly coloured and strongly patterned. It is much more richly coloured than Temminck's Stint, with more heavily streaked breast and usually shows a more distinct head pattern.

Adult winter: Plumage lacks any bright colours and is basically brownish-grey and white, similar to other winter stints. The upperparts show a browner cast and stronger pattern than in the dark-legged stints. Temminck's is much plainer both on the head, breast and upperparts.

Juvenile: Readily distinguished from a winter adult by its more richly coloured plumage. Compared to autumn adults in summer plumage, the plumage is much fresher, the head pattern is slightly more distinct, the breast is slightly more finely streaked, and the scapulars are patterned slightly differently. It is superficially similar to a juvenile Little

Stint but differs in e.g. more heavily streaked breast. In plumage and general appearance it is actually very similar to Sharp-tailed Sandpiper, but is much smaller.

1st-winter: Similar to adult winter but can be told by the presence of some (usually many) retained juvenile coverts and tertials, with distinct, rather clearcut paler fringes.

1st-summer: Similar to the adult summer, although the primaries are generally more heavily worn.

Habitat and behaviour: On migration and in winter, favours much the same habitat as Temminck's Stint and Least Sandpiper, i.e. inland waters, such as muddy pools, lagoons, and river banks, but is occasionally found on mudflats, shores and similar habitats. When alert, frequently adopts a rather characteristic, upright posture with craning neck, suggesting a miniature Ruff or small *Tringa* rather than a stint.

Voice: The flight call is a soft, rolling *kyrrit*, reminiscent of the calls of Pectoral and Curlew Sandpiper.

Range: Breeds in E and South C Siberia westwards to the River Ob area. Winters from S Asia to Australia.

Status: Accidental in Sweden: Ottenby, Öland, juvenile on 4th Oct-5th Nov 1977. Britain: Cleveland, juvenile on 28th Aug-1st Sept 1982; South Uist, Western Isles, juvenile from 4th-7th Sept 1990*.

LEAST SANDPIPER *Calidris minutilla* B 25

L 11-13cm (4.75"). North America. Rare vagrant (mainly autumn).

All plumages: Very similar to corresponding plumages of Long-toed Stint, but is slightly smaller, more compact, with a shorter neck and generally more crouching appearance. Legs and toes are distinctly shorter, and the bill is often appreciably longer. However, these differences are not always very striking. In flight the toes do not project clearly beyond the tail tip as in Long-toed. In the hand the middle toe can be judged to be approximately the same length as the bill (whereas it is distinctly longer than the bill in Long-toed). The bill is completely blackish, and the base of the lower mandible is only rarely paler. In Long-toed the base of the lower mandible is usually pale orange-brownish. The wing-bar is slightly more prominent than in Long-toed, because most of the primary shafts are pale, whereas only the outermost is pale in Long-toed.

Adult summer: Rather difficult to tell from Long-toed in corresponding plumage. Head pattern differs as follows. The supercilium tends to be less prominent (however, rather poorly marked in many Long-toed as well). The supercilium usually (but not always) extends thinly across the forehead, and there is only exceptionally a narrow, pale lateral crown-stripe ('split supercilium'). In Long-toed, the dark of the forehead usually reaches to the base of the bill, meeting the dark loral stripe, and most individuals show a distinct split supercilium. The loral stripe tends to be broader, and the malar region, particularly immediately below the loral stripe, is generally more heavily streaked.

The upperparts are normally distinctly duller than in Long-toed, usually only with narrow, rather pale rufous edges to the scapulars and tertials. However, there is overlap, as some Least are rather brightly coloured and some Long-toed quite dull. The tertials and inner greater and median coverts often show slightly scalloped pale edges, which is apparently never the case in Long-toed.

The breast tends to show a more complete band than Long-toed's (but there is much overlap), and the streaks are usually noticeably coarser and more triangular on the sides. Also, the streaking tends to end higher up on the lower breast/upper flanks.

Adult winter: Very similar to winter Long-toed. The differences in head pattern described above also apply to winter plumage (generally more pronounced). The dark centres to the scapulars are usually less extensive and less clearcut than in Long-toed.

Juvenile: Differs from winter and summer adults in the same way as for Long-toed Stint (p. 121). Differences between Least and Long-toed are usually much more pronounced than in other plumages. The head pattern differs from juvenile Long-toed in much the same way as in the adult, although the differences are usually more obvious and consistent. The supercilium is generally less prominent, notably in front of the eye, where it usually bulges noticeably in Long-toed. The supercilia meet thinly across the forehead, while in Long-toed the forehead is dark to the base of the bill and connects with the loral stripe. The loral stripe is broad and prominent; in Long-toed it is narrower, especially in the centre, where it is often broken. The dark patch on the ear-coverts is generally more 'diagonally' placed than in Long-toed, in which it is normally more 'horizontal'. Unlike the summer adult, juvenile Long-toed only occasionally shows a distinct split supercilium, but when present it is characteristic.

The sides of the breast are usually more coarsely streaked, and the streaking normally does not extend as far down as in Long-toed. Also, the feathers in the centre of the mantle show paler fringes, if not too worn, giving a rather scalloped appearance when seen well. In Long-toed the mantle usually looks distinctly striped. The pale V on the sides of the mantle tends to be less distinct than in Long-toed.

The coverts are usually approximately of the same general coloration as the mantle and scapulars, and the fringes are usually complete. In Long-toed, the fringes to the coverts are generally more whitish and thus distinctly paler than the upperparts, and the fringes are broken at the tips (also rarely in Least, when worn).

1st-winter and 1st summer: See Long-toed Stint, above.

Habitat and behaviour: The habitat preference is rather similar to that of Long-toed Stint. Does not normally adopt the very upright posture frequently shown by Long-toed.

Voice: The usual flight call is a high-pitched, thin *brreeep*, the *eee* sound often inflected slightly upwards. The call is usually distinctly thinner and more high-pitched than in Long-toed.

Range: Breeds over much of Alaska and N Canada. Winters in the S parts of the USA to South America.

Status: Rare vagrant in Iceland (2), British Isles (32, mostly Aug-Oct, and has exceptionally wintered), France (6, Aug-Oct, Feb), West Germany (Sept 1985), Austria (two in June 1976), Norway (June 1988), Finland (June 1847), Spain (Oct 1987*), and the Azores (5).

WHITE-RUMPED SANDPIPER *Calidris fuscicollis* D **25**

L 15-18cm (6.5"). North America. Rather frequent vagrant (mainly late summer/autumn).

All plumages: Slightly smaller than Dunlin, with a proportionately shorter, straighter bill, shorter legs and longer wings. The primary projection is notable, and the wings normally project well beyond the tail tip, making the rear end look distinctly attenuated. The uppertail-coverts are contrastingly white, a character shared only with Curlew Sandpiper among similarly sized sandpipers, although the band is wider in that species. Main risk of confusion is with Baird's Sandpiper, which see for differences.

Adult summer: Rather dull in general coloration, usually with a little rufous on crown, ear-coverts, mantle and scapulars. The most notable feature is the whitish, rather strongly streaked breast, with the streaking extending onto the flanks in the shape of arrowheads. The supercilium is generally rather distinct. General coloration and pattern may recall Western Sandpiper, which is smaller with a proportionately longer bill.

Adult winter: Shows rather dark brownish-grey upperparts, with dark shaft-streaks of variable prominence. Has a greyish, finely streaked breast, often a few streaks on the flanks, and a distinct supercilium.

Frequently, nearly complete winter plumage is acquired during the autumn migration, except for the wings which are not moulted until in the winter quarters.

Juvenile: Rather brightly and contrastingly patterned and in the autumn easily separated from heavily worn and moulting adults. It could perhaps be confused with juvenile Dunlin with reduced spotting on the belly/flanks, but the structural differences described above, and the white upper tail-coverts, should readily separate them.

1st-winter/-summer: Much as Long-toed Stint (see p. 121), but apparently some individuals moult the outer primaries or all of the flight feathers in the 1st winter/spring. Birds showing fresh outer primaries which contrast with more worn inners are readily aged as 1st-summers.

Voice: The call is a diagnostic, short, sharp, high-pitched, squeaky *jeet* or *tzeet*, often with a trace of an 'r'-sound, *tzreet* and frequently repeated in short, quick series; recalling sounds produced by some insects or bats.

Range: Breeds in arctic Canada and Alaska. Winters in S South America. Vagrants have reached Greenland (including 20-25 on 25th July 1975), Spitsbergen, Franz Josef Land, and the Canary Is.

Status: The third most numerous North American vagrant. Iceland (33), British Isles (322, annual, mostly July-Oct), France (6), Netherlands (Oct 1977), Denmark (5), Norway (4 June-July), Sweden (6), Finland (Aug 1980, May 1982), West Germany (6), Austria (4), Switzerland (3), Spain (5) and the Azores (*c*. 15).

BAIRD'S SANDPIPER *Calidris bairdii* D **25**

L 14-17cm (6"). North America, tip of NE Siberia, NW Greenland. Regular vagrant.

All plumages: Most resembles White-rumped Sandpiper which is of similar size/shape. Shows a broad, dark central stripe to the rump and uppertail-coverts, but other differences are usually so obvious that this is of subordinate value. The bill tends to be slightly straighter and finer tipped, and is blackish, whereas that of White-rumped usually shows some orange-brown at the base of the lower mandible.

Adult summer: More buffish in general coloration than White-rumped and lacks this species' rufous tones on the crown, ear-coverts, mantle and scapulars. In very fresh White-rumped the rufous tones are not always apparent; in these, the tips to the scapulars are generally rather brownish-grey (more buffish in Baird's). The entire head shows a buffish base-colour, and the supercilium is therefore usually less prominent than in White-rumped. The breast also normally shows a distinct buffish tinge (whitish in White-rumped, sometimes with a faint buffish wash), and generally the sides of the breast are more coarsely marked than the centre of the breast (usually the breast is more uniformly streaked in White-rumped). Unlike in White-rumped, the flanks are unmarked or sometimes show just a few indistinct streaks.

Adult winter: Differs from White-rumped in its more buffish-tinged upperparts and darker and more buffish breast with less distinct streaking. The flanks are unmarked (usually with at least a few distinct streaks in White-rumped).

Juvenile: Readily distinguished from adult in the autumn by fresh and evenly patterned plumage (actual pattern is also different). The plumage is less variegated than in juvenile White-rumped. The head and neck (except chin/throat) are usually rather buffish, and the supercilium not very contrasting. In White-rumped the crown and ear-coverts are usually at least slightly rufous-tinged, contrasting with a greyish hindneck and a well-defined, whitish supercilium. The mantle and scapulars are regularly white-tipped and buffish-edged, giving a neatly scalloped impression and a warm general coloration. In White-rumped the mantle and upper scapulars are mainly rufous-fringed, contrasting with a whitish V on the sides of the mantle, and white tips to the lower scapulars. The lower scapulars generally do not show distinctly contrasting pale bases, which is often the case in White-rumped.

The coloration and pattern of the underparts differs in much the same way as in summer adults, but in both species the markings are finer than in summer plumage. Post-juvenile moult normally starts in the winter quarters, unlike in White-rumped, which begins to moult during migration.

1st-winter/-summer: See White-rumped Sandpiper, p. 124.

Voice: The flight call is a slightly harsh but still rather soft, rolling *krrt*; *kyrrt*; *kirrp* or *kyrrp*, recalling Pectoral and Curlew Sandpipers, but very different from the call of White-rumped.

Habitat: Unlike White-rumped often found far from water, on pastures, meadows, grassy air-fields etc., but also visits shores, mud-flats and shallow pools of coastal marshes.

Range: Breeds from NE tip of Siberia to St Lawrence Island, N Alaska and N Canada, E to Baffin Island and NW Greenland. Winters in W and S South America.

Status: Rare autumn vagrant. Majority of records are from the British Isles (153, annual, mainly Aug-Oct, with a distinct peak in Sept, exceptionally wintering). Also, France (5), Netherlands (Sept 1980, Aug 1981), Sweden (Aug 1982, Oct 1983, Oct-Nov 1989*), Norway (two in May 1975), Finland (1962), Poland (Aug 1978), West Germany (1), East Germany (May 1986), Austria (Oct-Nov 1985), Czechoslovakia

(Sept 1981), Greece (Aug 1986), Spain (Aug 1988*) and the Azores (Jan 1979).

PECTORAL SANDPIPER   *Calidris melanotos*   D **26**

L 19-23cm (7.5-9"). North America and E Siberia. Regular vagrant, mainly late summer/autumn.

Adult summer: Its comparatively large size, moderately long bill with yellowish-brown or greenish-brown basal third, generally pale yellowish or greenish-tinged legs, and sharp division between streaked pectoral band and remaining whitish underparts should make this species fairly easy to identify. See also Sharp-tailed Sandpiper (p. 127).

The male tends to be darker on the breast than the female, particularly in worn plumage. Unlike most other waders (with some exceptions, e.g. lapwings) the male is larger than the female, and this is sometimes appreciable in the field.

Adult winter: Noticeably duller than the summer plumage.

Juvenile: Rather similar to adult summer female, but is more regularly and distinctly patterned and generally brighter. In the autumn the plumage is also fresher than the adult.

1st-winter/-summer: See White-rumped Sandpiper, p. 124.

Voice: The flight call is a characteristic, reedy *kyrrt*, *kirrp* or *tiyrrp*, resembling the call of Baird's and Curlew Sandpipers.

Habitat: Favours marshy freshwater areas with some vegetation, such as wet grasslands, pools, lagoons etc.

Range: Breeds in the arctic from the Taymyr peninsula in Siberia across to Alaska and Canada to the S part of Hudson Bay. Winters mainly in S half of South America but a few also regularly winter in SE Australia and New Zealand. Vagrants have reached Greenland (where first breeding recorded in July 1983), Spitsbergen, Madeira and the Canary Is.

Status: Annual in the British Isles: over 1,400 noted between 1958-1985 (often 25+ a year, but 150 in 1984). The largest parties recorded have been 11 at Akeragh Lough, Co Kerry, and 6 at Ballycotton, Co Cork, in Sept 1971. There are also many other records: Iceland (14), Faeroes (May 1984, Oct 1987), France (*c.* 120), Channel Islands (15), Belgium (13), Netherlands (*c.* 40), Denmark (11), Norway (34), Sweden (51), Finland (21), East Germany (12, May-Oct), West Germany (*c.* 80), Poland (9), Czechoslovakia (5), Austria (*c.* 20), Hungary (Sept-Oct 1987), Switzerland (13), Italy (5), Malta, Portugal (2), Spain (28), and the Azores (5).

Numbers reported have increased in recent years, presumably as a result of more observation. Now annual in France (30 in 2 years: 1984-85) and Sweden since 1976 (except 1981). In the British Isles and France, most of the records fall during Sept-Oct. In Sweden, a high proportion of the records are from May, and in Finland the majority of the records are in spring. This pattern may indicate that the majority arrive in the autumn, winter somewhere in Europe or Africa and then migrate N-NE with other arctic waders in the spring.

The geographic distribution of records over the British Isles would seem to indicate that the majority have a Nearctic origin, but possibly many also come from Siberia. If this assumption is correct, it may seem rather surprising that it is still by far the most numerous transatlantic vagrant in Europe considering the relative scarcity of this species along the E coast of the USA in autumn. However, many Pectorals are known to use SE Canada/NE USA as a staging area in the autumn, prior to a direct flight to South America along the W Atlantic. Many birds are presumably caught up in eastbound depressions that are prevalent in this area at this time of year.

SHARP-TAILED SANDPIPER   *Calidris acuminata*   B **26**

L 17-21cm (7-8.5"). E Siberia. Very rare vagrant (mostly autumn).

All plumages: About the same size and general build as Pectoral Sandpiper, with which it is most likely to be confused. However, usually shows more contrasting head pattern than Pectoral, with brighter rufous cap (not in winter), which contrasts markedly with a whiter and more distinct supercilium. Also, has a more prominent eye-ring and usually a darker and better defined band on the ear-coverts. The bill is usually dark with a pinkish base to the lower mandible (cf. Pectoral), although some have the base of both mandibles pinkish.

Adult summer: Very distinctly patterned and easily distinguished from Pectoral by its strongly marked underparts, showing bold dark chevrons on the sides of the breast/flanks and spear-shaped markings on the undertail-coverts. Occasionally these markings are less prominent. As in Pectoral, the male is slightly larger than the female.

Adult winter: Differs further from Pectoral in winter plumage in pattern of underparts, lacking Pectoral's well-defined breast band and usually showing some markings on the flanks (sometimes in Pectoral also).

Juvenile: Easily distinguished from an adult by its brightly and distinctly patterned plumage without strong markings to the underparts. Also differs from juvenile Pectoral by the rather bright orange-buff (paler when worn) foreneck and breast, with a band of fine streaks across the foreneck and only a few streaks on the sides of the breast. The sides of the rear flanks and undertail-coverts normally show some fine streaks, unlike Pectoral.

1st-winter/-summer: See White-rumped Sandpiper, p. 124.

Voice: The flight call is a very characteristic, soft, rather subdued *ueep* and *ueep-ueep*, often repeated several times.

Habitat and behaviour: Similar to Pectoral Sandpiper.

Range: Breeds in N Siberia. Winters mainly in Australia, also in New Guinea and W Pacific south to New Zealand. Regularly straggles to (W) North America, mainly in autumn.

Status: Very rare vagrant in the British Isles (20, mainly Aug-Oct), France (Sept 1972), Belgium (Sept 1989*), Netherlands (Sept 1989*), Denmark (Aug 1989*), Norway (Aug 1984, May 1986, June 1986), Sweden (July 1975, Sept 1976, Aug 1977, July 1985), and Finland (Aug 1984).

STILT SANDPIPER   *Micropalama himantopus*   B **26**

L 18-23cm (8"). North America. Rare vagrant (mainly autumn).

All plumages: Its comparatively large size (like a small *Tringa*), slender build, long, slightly drooping bill (with swollen end), and long, yellowish or greenish legs make this species rather easy to identify. It lacks a distinct wing-bar, and the rump and uppertail-coverts are whitish (with some dark markings in summer adult).

Adult summer: Unmistakable. The ear-coverts and sides of the crown are rufous, the supercilium is rather distinct, the remainder of the head and neck are heavily streaked, and the underparts are strongly barred.

Adult winter: Grey above, with a distinct pale supercilium, and some grey mottling and streaking on breast/flanks.

Juvenile: Readily distinguished from other plumages by combination of regularly and distinctly patterned upperparts and obvious lack of barring on the underparts. Note the distinctly pale-fringed coverts and tertials. Moult to 1st-winter plumage starts rather early, so that it is unlikely to be encountered in Europe in full juvenile plumage.

It could possibly be confused with juvenile Curlew Sandpiper, but Curlew Sandpiper is distinctly smaller and has shorter, dark legs. Curlew Sandpiper shows paler-centred lower scapulars, and is less rufous on the mantle and upper scapulars. Also it is more sparsely streaked on the neck and breast and lacks dark markings on the flanks and undertail-coverts.

1st-winter/-summer: Much as White-rumped Sandpiper (see p. 124), but apparently the outer primaries are *usually* moulted in the 1st winter.

Voice: Usually silent away from breeding grounds. A subdued, soft *dju* is sometimes heard, and a soft rattling trill *kirr* has also been described.

Habitat and behaviour: Prefers freshwater ponds, lakes, and lagoons, where it often wades in belly-deep water (even swims for brief spells).

Range: Breeds in N Alaska and Canada E to W Hudson Bay. Winters mainly in C South America, some also in S USA.

Status: Rare vagrant in Iceland (June 1985), British Isles (22, mainly July-Oct, also Apr-May), France (July 1989*), Belgium (Sept 1984), Norway (June 1987), Sweden (July 1963), Finland (June 1983), Austria (Aug 1969), and Spain (Majorca, May 1983).

BUFF-BREASTED SANDPIPER   *Tryngites subruficollis*   D **26**

L 18-20cm (7.5"). North America. Frequent vagrant (mainly autumn).

Adult: Rather similar to a juvenile female Ruff, but is obviously smaller, with a distinctly shorter bill. The face is typically very plain, often showing a diffuse paler surround to the eye, but no trace of a dark eye-stripe as in most Ruff. Further differs from juvenile Ruff in more distinctly spotted sides to the breast and brighter yellowish legs. Ruff often shows slightly scalloped and striped tertials, inner greater and median coverts, a feature lacking in Buff-breasted. In flight, differs from Ruff as it lacks a prominent white wing-bar and white sides to the rump and uppertail-coverts, and shows dark to the leading edge and greater primary coverts below. Also, the flight-feathers show dark vermiculations below, diagnostic in the hand.

In winter plumage the buffish-brown edges to the feathers of the upperparts tend to be broader and browner than in summer. The male is larger than the female, often appreciably so in the field.

Juvenile: Resembles the adult but can be distinguished by the dark subterminal bands or spots on the coverts and, less obviously, on the scapulars. Also the fringes to the scapulars and coverts are more whitish than in the adult. Indistinguishable from the adult after the complete moult in the 1st winter-spring.

Voice: Usually silent outside the breeding season.

Habitat: Favours dry, grassy areas away from water.

Range: Breeds in N Alaska and Canada and easternmost Siberia (Wrangel Island). Winters in South America (chiefly C Argentina and Paraguay). Vagrant in Spitsbergen, Canary Is (4), N Africa, Sierra Leone, Kenya and S Africa.

Status: This is the second most numerous of the Nearctic autumn vagrants in Europe (very rare in spring). Annual in the British Isles (525 to 1985, with more than 65 records in 1975 and again in 1977). Some of the largest parties recorded have been up to 15 together on the Isles of Scilly (Sept 1977), and 9 at Tacumshin, Co Wexford (Sept 1980). There are also records from Iceland (5), Faeroes (Apr 1977), France (60+), Channel Islands (8), Belgium (3), Netherlands (9), Denmark (8), Norway (13), Sweden (12), Finland (5), East Germany (5), West Germany (c. 20), Poland (5, including one wintering 1982/83), Austria (4), Switzerland (5), Italy (9), Bulgaria, Malta (3), Spain (5), and the Azores (6 on 9th Oct 1979).

Most of the records are from late Aug-early Oct, with a peak in early-mid Sept.

It may seem rather surprising that this species should occur in W Europe each autumn in fairly good numbers, as it is a rather uncommon migrant along the Atlantic coast of North America. It is probable that some birds regularly diverge from the main passage route through C North America, moving more south-east and arriving in New England states before making a direct flight to South America. Some of these birds are then probably driven off course by the frequent depressions passing across the Atlantic in autumn (cf. Pectoral Sandpiper).

SHORT-BILLED DOWITCHER *Limnodromus griseus* A **27**

L 25-29cm (10.5"). North America. Very few authenticated records.
All plumages: Extremely similar to Long-billed Dowitcher (see latter, below, for differences, p. 130). Both dowitchers are easily distinguished from other waders by combination of distinctive plumage, medium size, long, straight bill (with slightly swollen tip) and greenish-tinged legs. In flight, show a pale trailing edge to the secondaries and inner primaries, and a whitish back like Spotted Redshank (beware latter untypically flying with legs drawn up underneath body).
Adult summer: Plumage is rather variable, partly because of subspecific variation. Nominate *griseus* is orange-rufous on face/neck and underparts, with a whitish belly and frequently also whitish flanks and undertail-coverts. It is heavily barred and spotted on the breast sides, flanks and undertail-coverts. The race *hendersoni* is often entirely orange-rufous below with rather sparse spotting and little or no barring. The westernmost subspecies *caurinus* is somewhat intermediate.
Adult winter: Basically grey above and whitish below. Some barring and spotting is usually evident on the underparts, especially on the flanks.
Juvenile: Compared to adult summer, much less heavily patterned below and lacks rufous. Pattern of scapulars, coverts and tertials also differs. In the autumn, shows much fresher plumage than the adult, with all feathers the same age (in adult, even in full breeding plumage the coverts are usually a mixture of both summer and winter feathers).
1st-winter: Usually distinguishable by at least some retained scapulars, coverts and tertials.

1st-summer: Most birds remain in a winter-like plumage throughout their first year. Some apparently more like adult summer, but show more worn flight-feathers.

Voice: The flight call is diagnostic: a soft, fast, slurred, rattling *chu-du-du*, often double, *chu-du* or with four or more syllables, somewhat reminiscent of one of the calls of Turnstone.

Range: Breeds in S Alaska (subspecies *caurinus*), C Canada (*hendersoni*) and E Canada (*griseus*). Winters from S USA to N South America. Vagrant in Greenland.

Status: Accidental. Improved identification criteria of the two dowitchers (which were considered a single species until the 1950s) has lead to a reassessment of many old records. Many Long-billed Dowitchers were misidentified as Short-billed in the past.

The recent records, from West Germany: Niedersachsen, juvenile from 9th-16th Oct 1981, and Ireland: Tacumshin, Co Wexford, juvenile from 30th Sept-2nd Oct 1985, are certain. Other records are currently claimed from Britain (Norfolk in Oct-Nov 1957, and 3 old specimen records in autumn 1862, Sept 1872 and Oct 1902), Norway (July 1971, Aug 1976), Spain (three in Apr 1964), and Azores. All British records and some elsewhere are under review.

LONG-BILLED DOWITCHER *Limnodromus scolopaceus* D **27**

L 27-30cm (11.25"). NW North America and NE Siberia. Frequent vagrant in the British Isles (mainly autumn), rarer elsewhere in Europe.

All plumages: Very similar to the corresponding plumages of Short-billed Dowitcher, and they are often very difficult to distinguish. It is slightly larger and heavier, with a proportionately longer bill, but this is useful only for a minority of individuals because of much overlap (females of both species are on average larger and longer-billed than their respective males). The tail feathers are neatly cross-barred, with the dark bars a little wider than the white ones (sometimes twice as wide). In Short-billed the bars are of variable width and not all feathers are regularly barred, but the white bars are generally wider than the dark ones. There is much overlap, though.

Adult summer: Resembles nominate race of Short-billed, which is similarly barred/spotted on the underparts. However, on average Long-billed shows more barring on the upper breast, above the wings, and the belly is unspotted, unlike in most Short-billed. In worn plumage (July-August) the flanks are usually less barred than in the nominate race of Short-billed. Often only the rear flanks and sides of the upper breast appear to be barred, while in nominate Short-billed the entire flanks are heavily barred. The main distinction is that the entire underparts are rufous (noticeably whitish-fringed when fresh), whereas nominate Short-billed shows whitish belly and often whitish flanks and undertail-coverts. The rufous colour tends to be slightly deeper and less orange-tinged than in Short-billed (not always obvious).

Compared to Short-billed Dowitcher of the race *hendersoni*, the best character is that the underparts are clearly more heavily spotted (especially on foreneck and breast) and barred. Also, the scapulars normally show narrower and less buffish tips, giving a darker impression than in *hendersoni*, and the rufous colour on the underside still averages deeper and less orange-tinged (colour may be indistinguishable). Many *hendersoni* show some whitish on the belly and undertail-coverts.

Sometimes very difficult to distinguish from the race *caurinus* of Short-billed, which is more like Long-billed on the scapulars and which may show strongly marked underparts with little or even no white. However, as a rule, the more strongly marked individuals of *caurinus* also show the greatest amount of white on the underparts, and the belly is generally marked.

Adult winter: Generally slightly darker and more 'dirty' grey above than Short-billed. The foreneck and breast are usually rather dark and uniformly patterned and quite sharply defined against the whitish belly. In Short-billed the foreneck and breast are generally paler and finely streaked/speckled. Some Short-billed show a darker breast, but in these, the dark area usually does not extend as far down on the breast as in Long-billed. However, many are best left unidentified if diagnostic calls are not heard.

Juvenile: Usually relatively easy to separate from juvenile Short-billed. It is basically darker and duller. In fresh plumage, the fringes to the scapulars are deeper rufous, and the fringes are often spotted, unlike in the majority of Short-billed. Generally shows less distinct pale markings to the centres of the scapulars than in Short-billed, but there is much variation in both species. The tertials and inner greater coverts are dark brown-grey – paler than centres to scapulars – with narrow pale fringes (rufous at the tips when fresh). In Short-billed these feathers show blackish centres – almost as dark as centres to scapulars – and buff fringes and internal markings. Occasionally, in Long-billed the tertials and inner greater coverts show pale internal spots near their tips (usually one on each web), exceptionally even a few more submarginal pale markings on the outer web. Conversely, very rarely the tertials of Short-billed are brown-grey with very indistinct pale internal markings. See figure.

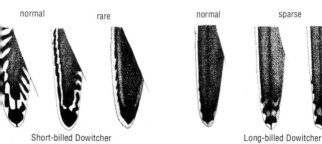

normal   rare   normal   sparse   extremely rare

Short-billed Dowitcher   Long-billed Dowitcher

Although the vast majority are easily identified by the pattern of the scapulars, inner median and greater coverts and tertials, the following minor differences may be of importance when confronted with an atypical individual. The foreneck and breast generally show a darker, greyer base colour and normally contrast more with the pale belly than in Short-billed. However, some fresh individuals are rather deep rufous-tinged, particularly on the sides of the breast (slightly deeper than in a normal Short-billed). The foreneck and centre of the breast are very faintly and diffusely streaked or even virtually plain, whereas in Short-billed these areas usually show rather distinct but fine dark streaks and spots. Also, the sides of the breast are usually more faintly marked than in Short-billed. The forehead and crown are slightly paler grey with less distinct brown streaks than in Short-billed (often looks rather uniformly grey, unlike in reasonably fresh Short-billed). Those untypical individuals should not be identified unless heard.

The plumage is usually moulted during the migration, and most vagrants to Europe show a mixture of both juvenile and 1st-winter feathers (usually first apparent on the scapulars). Juvenile Short-billed normally does not moult until in its winter quarters.

1st-winter: See Short-billed Dowitcher. Since the coverts/tertials and usually at least a few scapulars are retained well into the early winter, these birds are readily told from Short-billed by the pattern.

Voice: Has diagnostic flight call, very different from Short-billed. It gives a short, sharp, rather high-pitched *keek*, reminiscent of one of the calls of Oystercatcher. When flushed, the call is frequently repeated in quick series, *keek-keek-keek*. This has led to some confusion in the past over the call as a diagnostic feature. However, even multiple calls differ distinctly in tone and quality from those of Short-billed.

Note: The Asiatic Dowitcher *L. semipalmatus* (long-distance migrant of C and E Asia) could possibly reach Europe as a vagrant. It is much larger than the other dowitchers (near size of Bar-tailed Godwit, with which it could also be confused), with proportionately longer legs. In all plumages, bill and legs are blackish (bill often shows a pinkish base to the lower mandible at least in juvenile). In summer plumage it is rufous on face/neck and underparts, usually with most of the belly and undertail-coverts whitish, and the underparts are very poorly marked. The upperparts, coverts and tertials are dark with pale (usually a mixture of rufous and whitish) fringes/edges and lack the barring found in the other two dowitchers. The winter plumage usually shows a more patterned crown and mantle/scapulars and more streaked/barred foreneck and breast than the other dowitchers. The juvenile is distinctive: dark on the mantle/scapulars, coverts and tertials with broad, pale fringes, and pale on the underparts. In flight, differs in having a much wider and more extensive pale trailing edge to the upperwings (reaching clearly further out on the primaries), mainly unmarked pale underwings (looking grey in other dowitchers due to heavily barred underwing-coverts/axillaries and mostly grey flight-feathers), and an obscurely barred, not pure whitish back.

Range: Breeds NE Siberia, W and N Alaska, N Yukon and NW Mackenzie. Winters further N than Short-billed, generally from Oregon on the Pacific and S Carolina on the Atlantic coasts down to S Mexico and Guatemala. Accidental in Morocco.

Status: Vagrant, but virtually annual in British Isles (146 Long-billed identified from a total of *c.* 270 dowitchers). Also recorded from Iceland (Aug and Oct 1980), France (15+ of *c.* 40 dowitchers), Channel Islands (Sept 1975, Mar-Apr 1982), Belgium (May 1989*), Netherlands (6, May, July-Aug), Denmark (4 of 11 dowitchers), West Germany (Sept 1984, Oct 1988), East Germany (Sept 1986), Norway (5), Sweden (9 of 19 dowitchers), Finland (4), Italy (Sept 1985), Greece (May 1962), and Spain (3). A number of other unidentified dowitchers have also been recorded from some of the above countries as well as from Portugal (Oct 1985), East Germany (Aug 1973, Aug 1979, plus six together in Sept 1978), and Poland (4).

Most of the British records concern juveniles, which usually appear from mid/late September onwards, reflecting the rather late migration in North America. Wintering is not uncommon.

It is surprising that the Long-billed Dowitcher is much more numerous than the Short-billed as a vagrant in Europe, since the latter is more numerous in autumn along the Atlantic coast of North America. However, many Long-billed migrate SE in the autumn, and are more numerous then along the E coast of North America than in spring. It seems likely that some birds accidentally overshoot into the paths of eastbound depressions.

HUDSONIAN GODWIT Limosa haemastica   A* 27

L 37-42cm (15.5"). North America. Accidental.

All plumages: Resembles both Black-tailed Godwit and Bar-tailed Godwit. Size and shape more similar to latter, being marginally smaller than Black-tailed with slightly uptilted and more pointed bill, and has shorter legs (legs slightly longer than in Bar-tailed, though). The wing pattern is diagnostic, with the axillaries and most of the underwing-coverts blackish, and the wing-bar and white band at the base of the tail are narrower than on Black-tailed.

Adult summer: The underparts are deep chestnut, deeper than in either Black-tailed or Bar-tailed and clearly more extensive than in the former. Unlike in Bar-tailed there is some heavy barring on the flanks and breast, and generally some distinct, rather fine barring on the belly. The face and usually the neck are contrastingly greyish and heavily streaked, unlike both the other godwits (some female Bar-tailed may have a rather heavily streaked neck, though).

The male is slightly smaller with a proportionately shorter bill and generally brighter plumage than the female.

Adult winter: Very similar to winter Black-tailed Godwit, i.e. less streaked on the upperparts, coverts, head, neck and breast, with a shorter supercilium than in Bar-tailed.

Juvenile: Readily distinguished from other plumages by combination of comparatively fresh plumage with neatly and distinctly patterned upperparts and lack of chestnut and barring on the underparts. It is very similar to juvenile Black-tailed Godwit, and both show an equally variable pattern on the mantle/scapulars, coverts and tertials. Hudsonian shows a much more grey-brown, less buffy, neck and breast, but beware of worn and bleached Black-tailed.

1st-winter: See Short-billed Dowitcher, p. 129.

Voice: The call is a rather shrill, nasal *ket*, often repeated.

Range: Breeds in W and S Alaska, NW Canada and S end of Hudson Bay (Canada). Winters in South America, chiefly in Argentina.

Status: Accidental in Britain: Humberside, adult (10th Sept-3rd Oct 1981); Devon (22nd Nov 1981-4th Jan 1982); again in Humberside (26th Apr-6th May 1983); Grampian (26th Sept 1988). Denmark: adult (Sept 1986). All British records possibly refer to one individual.

In the autumn, almost the entire population gathers in S Hudson Bay and James Bay before making a non-stop flight to South America. In view of this, these few records for Europe may seem surprising (cf. Pectoral Sandpiper).

LITTLE WHIMBREL *Numenius minutus*   A* 27
L 29-32cm (12"). C and NE Siberian species. Accidental.

Adult: Resembles Whimbrel, but is much smaller, with a proportionately shorter, thinner and straighter bill. The plumage is basically buffier, and the underparts are less heavily patterned, and flanks almost unmarked. The loral stripe is incomplete, unlike in Whimbrel, giving it a more bare-faced expression.

In flight the back, rump and uppertail-coverts are concolorous with the rest of the upperparts, and the underwing-coverts are dark (brownish and strongly barred), thus differing markedly from Whimbrel. The remiges are uniformly dark, not distinctly barred as in Whimbrel, and the upperwing shows a contrastingly pale central panel absent from Whimbrel. See 'Hudsonian Whimbrel' and closely related Eskimo Curlew (below) for differences; also Upland Sandpiper (p. 136).

Juvenile: Differs from the autumn adult in its fresher plumage, and also showing smaller pale spots to the scapulars and tertials, with more distinct pale marks but less distinct dark ones.

1st-winter: Can sometimes be distinguished by retained juvenile coverts and tertials. The flight-feathers are normally not moulted, unlike in adults, which moult completely in their winter quarters; sometimes, however, the outer primaries are renewed in spring in 1st-years.

1st-summer: Can often be separated from the adult by its more worn primaries or contrast between fresh outer primaries and worn inners.

Voice: Flight call resembles Whimbrel but is shorter, slightly more metallic and higher-pitched, *ty-ty-ty*.

Range: Breeds in C and NE Siberia. Winters mainly on plains of N Australia and perhaps also S Papua New Guinea (where common migrant).

Status: Accidental in Britain: Mid Glamorgan (30th Aug-6th Sept 1982), and Norfolk (24th Aug-3rd Sept 1985). Norway: Varangerhalvøya (14th July 1969).

'HUDSONIAN WHIMBREL' *Numenius phaeopus hudsonicus*   A 27
L 40-46cm (16-18"). North American race of Whimbrel. Accidental.

All plumages: Differs from nominate race of Whimbrel (Europe-W USSR) in showing dark rump, uppertail-coverts and underwings (white in nominate), and the plumage is slightly warmer brownish.

Voice: Similar to European race.

Range: Breeds Alaska and N Canada. Winters S USA, S to South America. Vagrant in W Africa.

Status: Accidental in Britain: Fair Isle (May 1955), Shetland (July-Aug 1974). Ireland (Oct 1957, Sept 1980). Azores (Oct 1985).

ESKIMO CURLEW *Numenius borealis*   A* 27
L 29-34cm (13"). North America. A few 19th century records for Britain. This species is now close to extinction, and future records seem highly unlikely.

Adult: Very similar to Little Whimbrel, but is slightly larger with a marginally longer, more decurved bill, and longer wings with a longer primary projection (wings project well beyond tail tip when folded, hardly at all in Little Whimbrel). It also has slightly shorter legs, not projecting beyond the tip of the tail in flight, as do those of Little Whimbrel. The plumage is a little darker, more cinnamon than in Little Whimbrel, particularly on the underwing-coverts. The underparts are more heavily marked, often with Y-like marks on the flanks, which are lacking in Little Whimbrel. The loral stripe apparently reaches to the base of the bill, and in the hand, the rear tarsus shows a reticulate pattern (both front and rear are scutellated in Little Whimbrel).

Juvenile and subsequent immature plumages: Ageing probably as in Little Whimbrel (p. 134).

Range: Formerly bred in NW Canada and Alaska, wintering in SE South America (chiefly S Brazil, C Argentina). Once abundant (said to have been one of the most numerous North American shorebirds!), but excessive hunting caused it to decline dramatically, and by the early 20th century it was feared extinct. However, since 1945, one or two birds have usually been seen annually on migration, but never more than 6 at a time, except for 23 in Texas in May 1981. In Alaska, an adult was reportedly seen with a youngster in Aug 1983. Perhaps there may still be hope for this species.

Status: Accidental. 6 records of 7 individuals for the British Isles: Suffolk (2 in Nov 1852), Kincardine (Sept 1855), Ireland (Oct 1870), Aberdeen (Sept 1878, Sept 1880), and Isles of Scilly (Sept 1887).

SLENDER-BILLED CURLEW *Numenius tenuirostris*   D* **28**

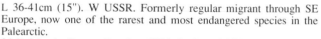

L 36-41cm (15"). W USSR. Formerly regular migrant through SE Europe, now one of the rarest and most endangered species in the Palearctic.

Adult: Marginally smaller than Whimbrel, and bill about the same relative size, but the outer end is strikingly thin, without any expansion at the tip. Head pattern close to Curlew's, but the crown tends to be slightly darker, the supercilium slightly paler and more contrasting, and the loral stripe more distinct. It lacks Whimbrel's clearly marked pale median crown stripe (like some Curlews, may occasionally show an ill-defined but clearly visible paler median crown stripe).

The foreneck and breast are distinctly whiter with more sharply defined blackish streaks and spots than in either Curlew or Whimbrel. The markings on the flanks are typically very distinct and clearcut and rather rounded in shape, whereas both Curlew and Whimbrel usually show at least some, usually many, anchor-shaped markings or bars on the flanks. In flight the upperwing normally shows more contrast between the darker outer wing and paler inner wing than in Curlew and Whimbrel. Also, tail and underwings are generally whiter than in the other two.

Female slightly larger and longer-billed than male. Very little seasonal variation, but there are generally fewer dark spots on the flanks in winter.

Juvenile: Differs from the adult in showing streaks instead of spots on the flanks. In the autumn the plumage is also fresher, and particularly the inner greater coverts and tertials show more distinct triangular pale markings along their edges and less distinct dark bars.

1st-winter: Distinguished from adults by at least some retained juvenile coverts and tertials.

Voice: The flight call is a Curlew-like *cour-lee*, but it is sweeter, faster and higher-pitched.

Range: Breeds N Kazakhstan and taiga zone of W Siberia in extensive marshlands and peat bogs, but now in serious decline. Formerly wintered regularly in NW African coastal sites, mainly in Morocco and Tunisia. Commonly reported until 1960s, drastic decline noted in 1970s. In Morocco: *c.* 10 records (1976-87) concerned small groups of 3-12 birds. During the winters of 1987/88 and 1988/89 up to 4 were present at Merja Zerga in northwest Morocco. In Tunisia since 1970 there have been 8 records from coastal areas and 4 from inland sites; one bird was reported in Feb 1984. Vagrant in the Canary Is and Cyprus.

Status: Formerly migrated through Turkey, Balkans, S Hungary and Italy (including Sicily) in Aug-Nov and Mar-May (occasionally also found in winter). The highest counts in recent years are: Greece, 150 Evros delta (Oct 1978); Rumania, 28 Danube delta (Sept 1971); Yugoslavia, 15-20 River Tisza (Oct 1969); and Hungary, 36 near Kardoskút (Oct 1969).

Accidental: France (9, most recent – singles in Vendée in Feb 1968 and Camargue in Apr 1988), Belgium (6), Netherlands (7 between 1856-1947, Nov-Feb), West Germany (3-4, no records since 1945), East Germany, Poland (5), Latvia, Czechoslovakia (4), Austria (11), Switzerland (5), Spain (up to 7 in Coto Doñana, Jan-Mar 1966), Majorca (May 1989*), Portugal, Malta, Bulgaria and the Azores.

UPLAND SANDPIPER *Bartramia longicauda* C 28

L 28-32cm (11.75"). North America. Rare autumn vagrant.

Adult: A distinctive, slim, graceful sandpiper, typically showing a rather small head and a long, comparatively thin neck. Superficially resembles Little Whimbrel, but the bill is shorter and practically straight. The tail is much longer (reaching well past tips of folded wings), and the face is plainer. The underparts, notably the flanks, are much more heavily marked, and the remiges are barred, particularly below. Note the difference in leg colour (yellow-ochre in Upland; greenish-grey in Little Whimbrel). In flight back, rump, uppertail-coverts are very dark.

Juvenile: Differs from the adult in showing well-defined pale fringes (often slightly scalloped) and dark subterminal bands or spots on the scapulars and particularly on the coverts and tertials. In the adult, these feathers are paler with diffuse paler fringes and dark cross-bars.

1st-winter: Can be distinguished from adult by at least some retained juvenile coverts and tertials.

1st-summer: Primaries more worn than in adult.

Voice: Not especially vocal on migration or in winter, but a piping *quip-ip-ip-ip* (last syllable lower in pitch) and soft, double notes have been described.

Habitat and behaviour: Favours dry grassy areas, e.g. pastures, harvested fields, airfields etc. Noted for habit of perching on fence posts and telephone poles in the breeding season. When alarmed it frequently bobs its rear end up and down, like Common Sandpiper.

Range: Breeds over much of C North America. Winters in South America, chiefly from S Brazil to S Argentina.

Status: Rare vagrant. The majority of the records are from the British Isles (41, July-Dec, once in Feb and Apr), with a scattering of records from Iceland (3), France (4, Sept), Channel Is (Guernsey, Oct 1988), Denmark (Nov 1920), West Germany (Hessen, one in 1811), Italy (7), Sicily (Sept 1969), Malta (2), Portugal (Sept 1977), and the Azores (Jan 1966, Feb 1979).

MARSH SANDPIPER *Tringa stagnatilis* D 28

L 22-24cm (9"). USSR. Regular visitor which has bred a number of times.

All plumages: Most likely to be confused with Greenshank, but is markedly smaller, near size of Green Sandpiper, and has a more slender build, a distinctly thinner, usually straighter (can be very slightly uptilted), darker bill, and proportionately longer legs.

Adult summer: Differs from Greenshank in its paler and greyer upperparts with bold dark markings more widely scattered on the scapulars, and generally more boldly patterned coverts and tertials; note also the difference in the shape of the dark markings. The breast is generally less coarsely, irregularly and densely marked and the supercilium is usually more distinct behind the eye and the lores paler.

Adult winter: Basically grey above and white below. Generally more uniform on the upperparts, coverts and tertials than Greenshank (latter normally shows dark subterminal bands and spots to these feathers), and the breast is usually less streaked. The head pattern is also noticeably different: the crown is distinctly less streaked, and the lores are pale or with a dark smudge just in front of the eye (Greenshank shows a distinct dark loral stripe – often not reaching to the eye). Also, the supercilium is distinctly longer and more pronounced (usually does not reach past the eye in Greenshank), and the forehead is paler.

Juvenile: Readily distinguished from other plumages. Juveniles usually moult very early, so that birds in full juvenile plumage are not frequently seen in Europe. The head pattern differs from that of juvenile Greenshank in the same ways as in adult winter, except that the crown is heavily streaked. Further, the ear-coverts are generally darker than in Greenshank and stand out more as a dark patch because of the almost unstreaked malar area and ear-coverts below the eye (these parts usually heavily streaked in Greenshank).

The upperparts, coverts and tertials (notably the last) are more heavily marked, with a more intricate pattern of irregular bold dark markings and buffish internal markings, than in Greenshank. These areas thus generally look more buff. Also, the breast is rather finely streaked at the sides and usually unmarked in the centre, unlike in Greenshank.

1st-winter: The juvenile feathers of the head, neck, breast and upperparts are usually lost quickly, leaving only the wing juvenile (contrasting strongly with the new, rather plain grey winter feathers). Usually, at least some of the coverts and tertials are retained throughout the winter, enabling ageing.

1st-summer: Many individuals are patterned much as in winter and generally remain in their winter quarters. Others attain full or nearly complete summer plumage and migrate north in spring. These differ from adults by their more worn primaries or contrast between fresh outers and worn inners.

Voice: The flight call is a short, yelping *kio* or *kiu*, usually uttered singly, but when flushed sometimes quickly repeated and then recalling the call of Greenshank.

Range: Breeds in a rather broad belt across the USSR from Ukraine to E of Lake Baikal. In the latter part of the 19th century bred in good numbers in Hungary and Rumania. In Hungary, last known regular breeding was in 1906, but reported to have bred in 1913, and possibly in other years. A few probably still breed in Rumania. Has also bred in Austria (1914), Latvia (4 times since 1974), Finland (7 times 1978-1988), Poland (1988) and probably in Czechoslovakia until *c.* 1930.

Winters in Africa (mainly S of Sahara) and S Asia to Australasia. Regularly passes through E Czechoslovakia, Hungary, Balkans, Italy, and Spain on migration.

Status: Vagrant/rare transient in the rest of Europe: British Isles (64, mid Apr-early Oct), France (20-30 annually, but 44 in 1988), Belgium (120+), Luxembourg, Netherlands (*c.* 90, now annual), Denmark (13), Norway (4), Sweden (69, almost annual since 1973), Finland (233 with 30+ in 1984), Estonia (3), Poland (*c.* 80, almost annual), East Germany (50+ since 1930), West Germany (100+), Austria, Switzerland (100+, mainly Apr-May), Malta, and the Azores. A few regularly winter in S Spain. Most records from N and W Europe are from May-Sept.

GREATER YELLOWLEGS *Tringa melanoleuca* B 28

L 29-33cm (12.25"). North America. Very rare vagrant (mainly autumn).

All plumages: Very similar to Lesser Yellowlegs (see p. 139). It could also be confused with Greenshank, but is more slender and has proportionately longer legs, which are bright yellow, sometimes pale orange (greenish in Greenshank as implied by name; however, beware abnormal individuals showing yellow coloured legs). Also, the upperparts, coverts and tertials are more white-spotted (less noticeable in winter) than in Greenshank. The most reliable character is that there is no white wedge up the rump and back as in Greenshank, which is immediately apparent in flight.

Adult summer: Strongly patterned both on the upper and underparts. Further differs from summer Greenshank in prominently barred flanks.

Adult winter: Mainly grey and white. The upperparts, coverts and tertials usually show small whitish or pale greyish spots or notches and dark spots or bars in-between.

Juvenile: Mostly resembles winter plumage, but is distinctly darker on the upperparts, coverts and tertials, with neat, pale buffish spots/notches, fading to whitish rather quickly. The dark spots and bars in between hardly contrast with the centres of the feathers, and the pale spots and notches are more clearcut and contrasting than in winter. The underparts are much less heavily patterned than in the summer adult, and the upperparts are more neatly and more evenly patterned. The moult to 1st-winter plumage starts comparatively early, and is usually first apparent on the mantle and scapulars. Moulting adults in the autumn show much more contrast between new and old feathers above/below, and the pattern of the summer feathers is clearly different from that of juvenile.

1st-winter: Very similar to adult winter, but can usually be distinguished by the presence of at least some retained juvenile coverts and tertials and by the flight feathers being more worn.

1st-summer: Full summer plumage is not usually attained, many individuals remaining in a mostly winter-like plumage. The primaries are obviously more worn than in the adult.

Voice: The flight call is very similar to Greenshank's, a clear, usually trisyllabic *chew-chew-chew*, often with the last syllable slightly lower-pitched. Multisyllabic as well as disyllabic calls are often heard also, occasionally even single notes.

Range: Breeds from S Alaska across S-C Canada to Newfoundland. Winters from C-S USA to S South America. Vagrant in Greenland.

Status: Very rare vagrant in Iceland (2), British Isles (29, mainly July-Nov, also Mar-May), France (Aug 1987, Nov 1989*), Denmark (Aug 1988), Sweden (adult, Aug 1976), Poland (Aug 1986, Sept 1987), Spain (Sept 1983), and the Azores (3).

LESSER YELLOWLEGS   *Tringa flavipes*   D **28**

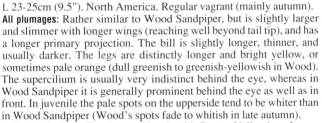

L 23-25cm (9.5"). North America. Regular vagrant (mainly autumn).

All plumages: Rather similar to Wood Sandpiper, but is slightly larger and slimmer with longer wings (reaching well beyond tail tip), and has a longer primary projection. The bill is slightly longer, thinner, and usually darker. The legs are distinctly longer and bright yellow, or sometimes pale orange (dull greenish to greenish-yellowish in Wood). The supercilium is usually very indistinct behind the eye, whereas in Wood Sandpiper it is generally prominent behind the eye as well as in front. In juvenile the pale spots on the upperside tend to be whiter than in Wood Sandpiper (Wood's spots fade to whitish in late autumn).

The major identification problem is with Greater Yellowlegs. Lesser is smaller, but size can be difficult to judge without comparison (Lesser is between Wood Sandpiper and Redshank in size, whereas Greater is the size of a Greenshank). The other main feature is the bill, which is proportionately shorter, thinner and straighter than in Greater (bill-length normally clearly shorter than tarsus in Lesser, while slightly shorter to slightly longer than tarsus in Greater, but this cannot normally be judged in the field; tarsus measured to hind toe). Further, the bill is usually all-dark or with a brownish tinge to the very base; occasionally, the inner third or so of the bill is paler, greyish or greenish-tinged. In Greater the inner third, sometimes half of the bill is distinctly paler, usually greyish or greenish-tinged, although the whole bill often looks quite dark in summer plumage.

The primaries and secondaries are entirely dark, whereas in Greater the inner primaries and the secondaries show small, pale notches along their edges, but this is usually difficult to discern in the field.

Adult summer: Plumage differs from Greater in flanks being less barred and belly unmarked. Greater is usually heavily barred on the flanks and often rather heavily spotted on the belly, but some may lack spots on the belly.

Adult winter: Plumage very similar to Greater. There is a tendency for the breast to be greyer and less heavily streaked and the flanks to be less marked, but there is overlap.

Juvenile: Differs from other plumages in the same way as described for Greater Yellowlegs. Unlike Greater, the juvenile plumage is not usually moulted until the bird has reached its winter quarters. It is very like juvenile Greater. The streaking on the breast tends to be fainter and less coarse, with a slightly more brownish-tinged base colour.

There is a slight risk of confusion with a juvenile Redshank showing pale orange legs, but Redshank is larger and stockier, with shorter legs, and the underparts are much more strongly patterned. The broad, white trailing edge to the secondaries and inner primaries and white wedge up the back of Redshank are immediately obvious in flight.

1st-winter/-summer: See Greater Yellowlegs, p. 138. Apparently most attain full summer plumage in their 1st-summer, but can be distinguished by their more worn primaries or contrast between worn inners and newer, fresher outers.

Voice: The usual flight call is distinctly different from that of Greater Yellowlegs, a rather high-pitched, flat *tew*, usually uttered singly, but sometimes in short series, particularly when flushed.

Range: Breeds in Alaska, NW and C Canada eastwards to James Bay, having more of a north-western distribution than Greater. Winters from S USA to S South America, generally further south in the USA than Greater. Vagrant in Greenland and Morocco (2).

Status: The majority of the records are from the British Isles (203, annual, average 7 per year 1976-85, seen in every month, but mainly in Aug-Oct). Much rarer elsewhere: Iceland (8), France (19, especially Finistère), Belgium (Aug-Sept 1983, May 1986), Netherlands (Nov 1979), Denmark (3), Norway (5), Sweden (3rd in Nov 1985), Finland (Oct 1978), Austria (Aug 1975, Oct 1978), Hungary (Sept 1959), Italy (Oct 1978), Greece (Aug 1986), Spain (9), and the Azores (16).

It may seem strange that the Lesser Yellowlegs should be so much more regular in Europe than the Greater, in view of the latter being the more eastern breeder of the two. The Greater Yellowlegs is by far the more numerous of the two species in New York State, USA in the autumn. However, many Lessers migrate SE in the autumn, and it seems likely that some birds fly into the paths of Atlantic depressions. That Lesser is even more of a long-distance migrant, and is generally passing through the USA at a greater speed than Greater, further indicates that it is the more likely of the two to straggle to Europe.

SOLITARY SANDPIPER   *Tringa solitaria*   B 28

L 18-21cm (7.5"). North America. Accidental (mainly autumn).

All plumages: Intermediate between Wood Sandpiper and Green Sandpiper in some respects, although much more similar to the latter. It is slightly smaller, slimmer and more attenuated at the rear than Green. It usually has a longer primary projection, and the folded primaries protrude further beyond the tail tip. Can show slightly larger pale spots to upperparts, coverts and tertials than Green, although not in worn birds.

In flight, immediately separated from both Green and Wood Sandpipers by its dark rump, uppertail-coverts and central tail feathers, leaving only the outer tail white with blackish barring. The underwing-coverts and axillaries show slightly wider pale barring than in Green, making the underwing slightly paler than in this species (underwing still essentially dark). The wings are also slightly longer and clearly narrower than in Green Sandpiper.

Adult summer: Distinctly pale-spotted above and rather streaked on head, neck and breast, the breast and flanks often showing some barring.

Adult winter: Generally shows smaller pale spots above and more uniformly patterned head, neck and breast than in summer plumage.

Juvenile: Resembles the adult winter, but shows more distinct, and more buff-coloured spotting on the upperparts, coverts and tertials. Generally, it has a less plain neck and breast, which when fresh shows a distinct warm brownish tinge. Plumage fresher than autumn adult.

1st-winter/-summer: Difficult to distinguish from the adult, but the primaries either are more worn, or show contrast between new and fresh outers and old and worn inners.

Voice: The calls are rather similar to those of Green Sandpiper, generally giving a double *peet-veet*, *peet-peet* or *ueet-veet*, but when flushed, often tri– or multisyllabic calls, *peet-peet-peet*, apparently– without the typical drawn-out and inflected first syllable of the corresponding calls of Green (*tlUUeet- veet-veet*).

Habitat and behaviour: Much like Green Sandpiper in favouring muddy ditches, and tiny shallow pools etc. Usually found singly (always so in Europe) or a few together, and generally not with other waders.

Range: Breeds in much of Alaska and Canada. Winters in Central and South America and the West Indies.

Status: Accidental in Iceland (2), British Isles (27, July-Oct), France (4, Aug-Sept, Jan), Sweden (May 1987), and Spain.

TEREK SANDPIPER *Xenus cinereus* R Br **28**

L 22-24cm (9"). Breeds in Finland and eastwards in Asia. Rare vagrant elsewhere in Europe.

All plumages: Unmistakable. The rather small size (comparable to Wood Sandpiper), long, uptilted bill and rather short, yellow legs immediately identify this species. In flight, shows diagnostic wing pattern, with dark leading edge, primaries, primary coverts and bar on the greater coverts, and a distinct whitish trailing edge to the secondaries. Note also the all-grey back, rump and tail.

Adult summer: Shows distinct blackish markings on the scapulars.

Adult winter: Plainer above and on the breast than in summer plumage, with very indistinct dark markings on the scapulars.

Juvenile: Differs from the summer adult by its warmer brown coloration due to narrow buff tips to the upperparts, coverts and tertials, also shows slightly less well-marked dark scapular markings and less streaked neck and breast.

1st-winter/-summer: See Solitary Sandpiper, above.

Voice: The flight call is a clear, musical, fast *uee-uee-uee; uee-uee-uee-uee*, etc, somewhat recalling Whimbrel.

Range: Breeds in a broad belt across the USSR. Some westward expansion has been noted recently, and has bred annually in Finland since the mid 1950s (*c*. 30 pairs in 1980). Bred Norway in 1967, and first breeding confirmed in Latvia in 1986 (two successful pairs in 1988), where it has probably occurred since 1980. Winters in Africa, Arabia, and from S Asia to Australasia. Vagrant in Canary Is and Cyprus.

Status: There has been a notable increase in records, particularly in spring, but also in autumn (exceptionally overwintering), There are records from the British Isles (35, mainly May-Sept, twice overwintering), France (*c.* 35, Apr-Oct), Belgium (4), Netherlands (8, May-Sept), Denmark (12, May-Sept), Norway (5), Sweden (61, May-Sept), Estonia, Poland (28), East Germany (15+), West Germany (*c.* 20), Czechoslovakia (4), Austria (5), Hungary (9), Switzerland (2), Greece (Apr-May, Aug-Sept), Rumania, Bulgaria (Aug 1980), Italy (*c.* 30), Spain (3) and Malta (2).

SPOTTED SANDPIPER *Actitis macularia* D 29

L 18-20cm (7.5"). North America. Rare vagrant (mainly autumn).

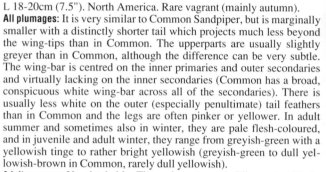

All plumages: It is very similar to Common Sandpiper, but is marginally smaller with a distinctly shorter tail which projects much less beyond the wing-tips than in Common. The upperparts are usually slightly greyer than in Common, although the difference can be very subtle. The wing-bar is centred on the inner primaries and outer secondaries and virtually lacking on the inner secondaries (Common has a broad, conspicuous white wing-bar across all of the secondaries). There is usually less white on the outer (especially penultimate) tail feathers than in Common and the legs are often pinker or yellower. In adult summer and sometimes also in winter, they are pale flesh-coloured, and in juvenile and adult winter, they range from greyish-green with a yellowish tinge to rather bright yellowish (greyish-green to dull yellowish-brown in Common, rarely dull yellowish).

Adult summer: Unmistakable. The underparts are boldly spotted black, recalling Mistle Thrush. The upperparts and tertials show bolder and more widely spaced dark markings and less streaking than in Common Sandpiper. The bill is flesh-coloured with contrasting dark tip. The female averages slightly larger, and can show larger and blacker spots.

Adult winter: Lacks black spotting on the underparts and is more uniform above, closely resembling Common Sandpiper in winter plumage. The upperparts, coverts and tertials are more coarsely and generally more sparsely marked than in Common. The patches on the sides of the breast are generally less prominent and less well-defined, and the foreneck and central breast lack the very fine dark streaks usually shown by Common.

Juvenile: Differs from the autumn adult in having plumage all fresh with no trace of spotting on the underparts. From the winter adult, differs in having more contrastingly patterned median and lower lesser coverts, tertials and scapulars; the individual coverts normally show two distinct pale bars and usually also two distinct dark bars. Generally the adult shows only one dark and one pale bar, sometimes two pale bars, less broad and less distinct than in juvenile. The number of bars can usually only be judged in the hand.

It is very similar to Common Sandpiper. Generally there is less distinct pale fringing on the upperparts (fringes are more even and usually more spotted in Common). The coverts are typically barred more boldly than in Common and generally contrast more with the plainer upperparts. The tertials and tail feathers (except outer two pairs) are usually plain with a few dark and pale markings at their tips only, whereas Common shows regularly pale– and dark-spotted edges; very rarely is there overlap in this respect. For differences in breast and foreneck patterns see adult winter (above).

1st-winter: Difficult to distinguish from the adult unless some juvenile coverts can be detected.

1st-summer: May show a contrast between fresh outer primaries and worn inners, not found in adult. Many go through a complete moult and are then not safely separable from the adult.

Habitat and behaviour: Similar to Common Sandpiper.

Voice: The calls include piping, single or double, *peet* and *tueet-ueet-ueet* notes, often drawn-out into series when flushed (the latter resembling most the call of Green Sandpiper, lower-pitched and clearly different from typical *hee-dee- dee*, or *hee-dee-dee-dee* of Common Sandpiper).

Range: Breeds over much of USA and Canada (except most northerly parts of Alaska and Canada and most southerly parts of USA). Winters in small numbers along the coasts of the USA (mainly in the S), but mainly from Central America and West Indies to South America. Vagrants have reached Greenland, Spitsbergen, Madeira, and the Canary Is.

Status: As with other Nearctic vagrants the vast majority of the records are from the British Isles (93), including a pair which nested unsuccessfully in Scotland in 1975. Recorded all months (most Aug-Nov), occasionally wintering. Also, recorded from Iceland (2), France (Sept-Nov 1987), Channel Islands (May 1988), Belgium (4), Netherlands (July 1975, Aug 1980), Finland (June 1982, May 1989*), East Germany (Oct-Dec 1966), West Germany (2 in 20th century), Switzerland (June 1891, May 1970), Italy (Apr 1986), Spain (4), and the Azores (5).

GREY-TAILED TATTLER *Heteroscelus brevipes* A 29

L 26-29cm (10-11.5"). Asiatic species. Accidental.

All plumages: Medium-sized *Tringa*-type wader with comparatively short, yellow legs. Rather uniform grey upperside and underwing are characteristic.

Adult summer: Further characterized by heavily streaked neck and barred breast and fore-flanks.

Adult winter: The parts that are barred and streaked in summer are uniformly grey in winter.

Juvenile: Resembles the winter adult, but shows pale (buffish when fresh) and dark spots to the edges of the scapulars, coverts and tertials.

1st-winter: Can usually be distinguished from the adult by at least some retained juvenile coverts and/or tertials.

1st-summer: Generally shows primaries more worn than the summer adult or a contrast between fresh outers and worn inners (all primaries are evenly worn in adult). Some birds do not attain summer plumage and remain in their winter quarters.

Voice: The flight call is a double, clear whistle *tuee-dee*, sometimes tripled, *tuee-dee-dee*.

Note: The closely related Wandering Tattler *H. incana* of NW North America, could possibly, although not very likely, occur in Europe. It is marginally darker and greyer above and generally shows a darker bill. In summer, the belly, rear flanks and undertail-coverts are distinctly more barred than in Grey-tailed (these areas show very little or no barring in Grey-tailed). In juvenile and winter plumages, the flanks are usually more extensively grey than in Grey-tailed. The juvenile has the scapulars, coverts, tertials, uppertail-coverts and tail generally less distinctly marked than in Grey-tailed (although this feature may be of little value when plumage more worn). In all plumages, the nasal groove on the upper mandible extends almost ¾ of the length of the bill, and the rear of the tarsus is reticulated. In Grey-tailed, the nasal groove ends just over half-way to the bill tip, and the rear of the tarsus is scutellated. The bill and tarsus differences can usually only be judged in the hand, though. The call of Wandering is a multi-note trill, very different from the call of Grey-tailed. Outside breeding areas, Wandering is found almost exclusively on rocky coasts, Grey-tailed usually on muddy shores, estuaries, and beaches.

Range: Breeds in E Siberia, E of Lena river and also around the upper Yenisey. Winters from Malaysia and the Philippines south to Australia and New Zealand.

Status: Accidental in Britain: Dyfed/Gwynedd, Dyfi Estuary (13th Oct-17th Nov 1981).

WILLET *Catoptrophorus semipalmatus* A **29**

L 33-41cm (13-16"). North America. Accidental.

All plumages: A rather large, stockily built wader with a long and comparatively heavy, straight bill and blue-grey legs. The contrasting wing pattern (both above and below) is diagnostic. The supercilium is usually prominent only in front of the eye.

Adult summer: Heavily streaked and spotted on the head and neck and spotted and barred on the breast and flanks. The upperparts and at least some coverts and tertials are heavily patterned with dark anchor-shaped marks and bars.

Adult winter: Predominantly grey and white without heavy dark markings.

Juvenile: Superficially similar to the winter adult, but much browner with buffish and dark notches to the edges of the feathers of the upperparts, coverts and tertials.

1st-winter: Similar to winter adults, but usually show at least some retained juvenile coverts and tertials.

1st-summer: The primaries are generally more worn than in the summer adult.

underwing pattern

Voice: The flight calls include a shrill, rather harsh *veht*, doubled *vee-vet* and hard *kip* and *krep* notes (often repeated).

Range: Breeds along the E coast of the USA, West Indies, also inland in NW USA and S Canada. Winters along the coasts down to N South America. E population thus largely resident.

Status: Accidental in the Azores: São Miguel, one found long dead (12th Mar 1979). France: an undated specimen from near Abbeville (19th century). Finland: Kemi, Kuivanuoro (21st Sept 1983).

WILSON'S PHALAROPE *Phalaropus tricolor* D **29**

L 22-24cm (9"). North America. Regular vagrant, mainly autumn.

All plumages: Distinctly larger and longer-necked than the other phalaropes, with a proportionately longer, very fine bill. In adult winter and immature plumages, the legs are bright yellowish (blackish in adult summer). In flight, differs from other phalaropes in showing white rump/uppertail-coverts and no distinct wing-bar.

Adult male summer: Easily distinguished from other summer-plumaged phalaropes. Shows whitish supercilium, a conspicuous deep chestnut tinge to the side of the neck, pale orange-brown wash to the foreneck, and rather dull grey-brown upperparts and coverts.

Adult female summer: Unmistakable. Unlike most other waders (but like the other phalaropes) it is distinctly more brightly coloured than the male, and shows a much more contrasting pattern on the head, neck and upperparts.

Adult winter: Predominantly uniformally pale grey above and white below. The ear-coverts, forehead and crown are concolorous with the hindneck and upperparts, unlike other phalaropes, which show a blackish or dark grey patch on the ear-coverts and the crown/nape and a white forehead/forecrown, sometimes extending onto most of the crown. Superficially resembles Marsh Sandpiper in winter plumage, but has much shorter, yellower legs and no white wedge up the back.

Juvenile: Basically resembles a summer adult male but lacks the chestnut on the neck, also shows distinct buffish fringes to the upperparts, coverts and tertials. However, juvenile plumage is lost very quickly and most unlikely to be encountered in Europe.

1st-winter: Most juveniles moult the body feathers shortly after fledging but retain the coverts and tertials until sometime in the winter, when many complete their moult, after which they are inseparable from adults. Others apparently moult less completely and retain some juvenile coverts and flight feathers.

1st-summer: Probably a few individuals attain full summer plumage, but many none at all.

Voice: Usually silent.

Habitat and behaviour: Favours fresh and brackish water. Swims less than the other phalaropes and is frequently seen running to and fro along the margins of ponds etc in a very characteristic crouched position, stabbing at insects.

Range: Breeds in the interior of USA/SW Canada. Winters on fresh and brackish waters in South America. Vagrant in Madeira and Morocco.

Status: Regular vagrant. Most are from the British Isles (227 since 1st record in 1954; now on average 11 per annum, but 17 in 1987). Also recorded in Iceland (Sept 1979), France (*c.* 40), Channel Islands (2), Belgium (11), Netherlands (16), Denmark (5), Norway (3), Sweden (6), Finland (4th in Sept 1989), Estonia (Oct 1989*), West Germany (10), Czechoslovakia, Italy (2), Spain (5), and the Azores (Aug 1979).

In the British Isles and France, occurs mainly Aug-Oct, but there are winter records in Britain (Dec 1989), also in France (Jan-Feb 1972, Jan-Feb 1978, and Dec 1974). Some individuals appear to return to the same localities in subsequent springs/(autumn). Records from the Nordic countries are mainly in the spring, indicating a northward migration of birds that had crossed the Atlantic to Europe the previous autumn (cf. Pectoral Sandpiper). 1st-winter birds dominate strongly in numbers in autumn.

Family STERCORARIIDAE Skuas

SOUTH POLAR SKUA *Catharacta maccormicki*   A **30**

L 53cm (21"). WS 127cm (50"). Antarctica. Accidental, but perhaps overlooked.

All plumages: Very similar to Great Skua, but is slightly smaller, with a proportionately marginally smaller bill. The white patch on the upper and underwing tends to be narrower than in Great, but there is much overlap in this respect.

The general coloration is much greyer, notably on the underparts, never showing the usually obvious rufous tones of most Great Skuas.

Pale morph individuals are further characterized by pale head, neck and underparts, contrasting with dark upperparts and wings. Occasionally, there is rather prominent pale streaking on the mantle/scapulars and some fine pale streaks on the coverts, though. Great is normally darker on the head, neck and underparts, and adults usually show heavy pale streaking to the sides of the head/neck and upperparts and generally also on the upperwing-coverts. Apparently, some adult Great may show a more uniformly pale head, neck and underparts but probably never in combination with dark mantle/scapulars and upperwing-coverts. Furthermore, does not normally show a distinct dark cap as do most adult Great Skuas. Intermediate individuals often show an obvious contrast between darker crown and paler hindneck, but on these the sides of the head normally contrast little with the crown.

Dark and intermediate morph also are less streaked than adult Great. The head and neck are uniformly patterned, or there may be some very fine pale streaking to the hindneck and neck sides. The mantle/scapulars and upperwing-coverts are dark. These individuals are easily confused with juvenile Great Skuas. The latter usually shows rufous markings on the scapulars and upperwing-coverts and a distinct rufous tinge to the underparts, but some are uniformly dark, without rufous tones and are then exceptionally similar to darker South Polars. The head/neck are apparently never paler than the mantle and are usually darker than the underparts in these juvenile Great Skuas (opposite to what is normal in South Polar). They also lack the fine pale streaking on the hindneck and neck sides, shown by most darker adult South Polars. However, some juvenile Great Skuas are so similar to dark South Polar Skuas that they cannot be safely separated in the field.

Many dark individuals are easily confused with some juvenile Pomarine Skuas. The latter is slightly smaller and less heavily built. The axillaries/underwing-coverts and upper– and undertail-coverts are only exceptionally unbarred (always so in South Polar). Pomarine also shows less conspicuous white patches at the base of the primaries, notably above. The base of the bill and the legs/feet are probably always paler than in any South Polar Skua.

Adult light morph: Shows pale buffish-grey head/neck and underparts, which contrast with darker upperparts, wings and tail.

Adult dark morph: Rather uniformly dark with very fine paler streaks on the hindneck and sides of the neck.

Adult intermediate morph: Plumage intermediate between light and dark morphs. Generally shows a paler collar on the hindneck.

Juvenile: Difficult to distinguish from the adult of its respective morph, but does not show any pale streaking on the neck and upperparts. The central pair of tail feathers normally project less, but there seems to be some variation. The basal part of the bill is said to be usually slightly paler than the tip, unlike in the adult .

Habitat and behaviour: Resembles that of other skuas; has a pelagic life style in the non-breeding season.

Range: Breeds Antarctic continent/peninsula. Immatures, in particular, regularly undertake a northward migration in the antarctic winter and are seen in small numbers in the Pacific and W Atlantic (e.g. Newfoundland Banks) between May-Oct. In the Atlantic, has exceptionally been recorded as far N as SE Greenland (July 1902, July 1975, both immatures).

Status: Accidental. Faeroes: an immature was reported to have been collected there (Sept 1889). Britain: several recent observations (pending their acceptance) reported since 1982, mainly from the SW between 19th Aug-18th Oct*. Easily overlooked and may occur more regularly in the E Atlantic than has been suspected.

Family LARIDAE Gulls

WHITE-EYED GULL *Larus leucophthalmus*   A* **30**
L 39-43cm (16"). WS 100-115cm (40-45"). Red Sea. Accidental in E Mediterranean.

All plumages: Noticeably darker than other medium sized gulls, with dark underwings. The bill is exceptionally long and thin, and the wings are also comparatively long.

Adult summer: Further characterized by black hood and bib, thick white crescents above and below the eye, white half-collar, grey breast and flanks; bright red bill with black tip, and yellow legs.

Adult winter: Resembles the summer adult, but black hood and bib are heavily white-peppered, and the bare part coloration is slightly duller.

Juvenile: Readily separable from the adult by its grey-brown head/neck, breast and flanks, with paler face and throat. The mantle, scapulars and coverts are grey-brown with paler fringes. The tail is mostly blackish, contrasting with the whitish lower rump and uppertail-coverts. The bill is blackish, and the legs are greenish-grey. This plumage is lost rather quickly through a partial moult.

1st-winter/-summer: Like the juvenile, but has better defined dark head pattern and uniformly dark grey-brown mantle and scapulars.

2nd-winter/-summer: Resembles adult winter and summer respectively but still shows signs of immaturity, e.g. some brown on the coverts, dark outer primary coverts, duller head pattern and often some dark in the tail. The white tips to the secondaries and inner primaries are also generally narrower, and the bare part coloration is usually duller.

Note: All plumages are rather similar to the Sooty Gull *L. hemprichii*, which breeds in much the same area as White-eyed, but which has not yet been recorded in Europe. In all plumages best distinction is the bill, which is much thicker in Sooty and yellowish with a black band and a red tip (adults) or pale greyish with blackish tip (immatures). Sooty is browner in all plumages and shows a dark brown rather than a black hood/bib in adult summer plumage. It also has a paler and less strongly patterned head in both 1st-winter and 1st-summer plumages.

Range: Restricted to the Red Sea south to Somalia and Yemen. Disperses slightly in non-breeding season. Vagrant to Mediterranean coast of Israel (July 1943, June 1971).

Status: Accidental in Greece: 19th century specimen from Piraeus harbour.

GREAT BLACK-HEADED GULL   *Larus ichthyaetus*   B 30

L 57-61cm (23"). WS 149-170cm (58-67"). Asia; reaching E Mediterranean in winter. Rare vagrant.

All plumages: A large gull, approaching Great Black-backed in size. The bill is long and heavy, and the forehead is often characteristically sloping.

Adult summer: Unmistakable – the only large gull with a black hood. Note also the very distinctive wing pattern and bare part coloration.

Adult winter: Shows characteristic head pattern with dark 'half-hood' and white 'eye-lids'. Otherwise as in summer.

Juvenile: Distinctly different from the adult. It could be confused with juvenile/1st-winter Great Black-backed or Herring Gull, but the underside is whitish and almost unmarked except for a partial or complete grey-brown breast band. There is also a dark spot in front of the eye and dark framing to the whitish 'eyelids' (not always apparent above the eye). The scapulars, coverts and tertials show dark centres and rather diffuse pale fringes. Great Black-backed and Herring show more sharply defined and normally obviously scalloped pale fringes and frequently pale cross-bars to the scapulars, coverts and tertials (most of the the greater coverts normally look barred).

In flight it shows a distinct contrast between the comparatively pale greater and median coverts and the darker lesser coverts (little contrast on coverts in Great Black-backed and Herring). Also, the underwing-coverts and axillaries are whitish with darker lines of variable prominence (rather uniformly dark in Great Black-backed and Herring), and the uppertail-coverts and tail are white with a clearcut blackish band on the latter, unlike the other two species (some dark mottling on uppertail-coverts and tail and less clearcut dark tail band in Great Black-backed and Herring). As this plumage is moulted rather early, birds in full juvenile plumage are unlikely to be encountered far from the breeding areas.

1st-winter/-summer: Unlike other large, but like the smaller gulls, attains a grey mantle and scapulars in its 1st winter. The plumage is otherwise like the juvenile, but there is usually a dark patch of variable prominence on the ear-coverts and across the rear crown/nape. The (lower) hindneck is normally more spotted/mottled and usually does not extend so far onto the breast. In 1st-summer birds especially, the inner greater, median and some lesser coverts and the inner tertials are frequently newly moulted grey. When swimming or standing the dark areas on the inner wing are often completely concealed, giving the impression that the bird is older. The bill is pale with a clearcut dark tip (unlike Great Black-backed and Herring Gulls of same age).

Beware confusion with 2nd-winter and 2nd-summer Herring Gulls (particularly race *michahellis* of S Europe), which can look superficially similar. If seen reasonably well, Great Black-headed is easily distinguished by its characteristic pattern of the head (especially whitish, dark-framed 'eyelids'), wings and tail.

2nd-winter/-summer: Resembles the adult in its respective plumage but shows more dark on the primaries, primary coverts, and elsewhere on the wing, and usually has at least a broken tail band. The black hood is usually incomplete in summer.

3rd-winter/-summer: Almost fully adult (some are probably identical to adult), but generally shows slightly less white at the tips of the outer primaries and often a trace of a dark tail band.

Note: Other large immature gulls with patches of oil or other discolorations on the ear-coverts/crown have occasionally been confused with immature Great Black-headed.

Range: Breeds Black Sea and fresh water lakes in S USSR eastwards to Mongolia and N Tibet. Winters from the E Mediterranean along the coasts of NE Africa and S Asia to the Indian Subcontinent. Accidental in Cyprus, but increased vagrancy reported, with possibly 5 different birds present in Mar 1987. Vagrant to Madeira.

Status: Rare vagrant. Britain (5, last recorded in Aug 1932; all records under review), Belgium (June 1936), Netherlands (June 1946, June-Sept 1974-1976), Denmark (adult, Oct 1987), Norway (Mar 1986, Apr 1987), Sweden (2), Poland (5), Austria (Apr 1980), Italy (Sardinia 1901, 1906), Greece (5, Mar-June), Rumania (probably regular) and Malta.

LAUGHING GULL   *Larus atricilla*   C 31

L 36-41cm (15"). WS 100-107cm (39-42"). North America. Rare vagrant (mainly autumn/winter).

All plumages: Very distinctive and only likely to be confused with Franklin's Gull (p. 150). A medium sized, slim gull with long wings and legs, and a comparatively long bill, which often looks slightly drooping. In all plumages, typically gives a rather dark impression.

Adult summer: Identified by combination of blackish hood, dark grey upperparts and upperwing and black outer primaries without prominent white markings. Bill dull red, often with a dark subterminal bar. Legs dull red or dark brown.

Adult winter: Differs from the summer adult by a grey patch of variable prominence on the ear-coverts and usually across the rear crown/nape. The bare parts are usually blackish (tip of upper mandible often red).

Juvenile: Mainly grey-brown on the head/neck, breast and flanks and shows a distinctive scaly pattern to the scapulars, coverts and tertials (dark centres and broad, pale fringes). Plumage otherwise as 1st-winter. Juveniles are unlikely to be seen in Europe, since this plumage is moulted early in the autumn.

1st-winter/-summer: Shows blackish outer wing (inner primaries only marginally paler) and blackish secondaries with distinct white tips. The axillaries, underwing-coverts and under primary coverts show at least some, often very extensive, dark markings. It has a broad, black tail-band and grey sides to the tail, and white uppertail-coverts and rump. The mantle and scapulars are dark grey. The head pattern is similar to the winter adult, but there is also extensive grey on the nape, neck, breast and flanks.

Already in 1st-winter plumage, a fairly large number of the coverts are sometimes new and a perched individual may then sometimes give the impression of being in 2nd winter, although is easily distinguished in flight by the wing and tail pattern. Birds in 1st-summer plumage sometimes develop a nearly full blackish hood.

2nd-winter/-summer: Similar to the adult of its respective plumage, but easily told in flight by the more extensive black on the outer wing, and generally shows some dark in the tail and often also on the secondaries. 2nd-winter birds also show extensive grey on the nape, neck, breast and flanks, unlike the adult, and 2nd-summers may show a less complete hood than the summer adult.

Range: Breeds along the coasts of E USA, Central America, the Caribbean and N South America (to Venezuela). Winters from North Carolina (USA) down to the coasts of NE Brazil, Peru and N Chile. Vagrant in Greenland and Morocco.

Status: As with so many other Nearctic vagrant species in Europe, the majority of the records are from the British Isles (56). Also, Iceland (5, July, Nov-Dec), France (7, Mar-June, Aug-Sept), Denmark (3), Sweden (Jan 1964, Oct 1987, and 2 in Sept 1989), Poland (Mar 1988*), Austria (May 1972), Greece (Aug 1984), Portugal (June 1981), Spain (3) and Gibraltar (Nov 1988*).

All plumages except juvenile have been recorded. British records cover all months, with one or two individuals long-staying and returning to the same sites in successive winters (e.g. one remained in the Newcastle area from Feb 1984-Jan 1986).

FRANKLIN'S GULL *Larus pipixcan* B **31**

L 32-36cm (13"). WS 85-95cm (35"). North America. Rare vagrant; recorded all months.

All plumages: Closely resembles the corresponding plumages of Laughing Gull, but appreciably smaller, more compact, with a proportionately shorter bill, and slightly shorter wings and legs. The tail is pale grey in the centre unlike Laughing, although this may be difficult to see.

Adult summer: Further distinguished from Laughing Gull by diagnostic (although slightly variable) wing pattern most obvious when seen in flight. When perched, the larger white tips to the primaries are still obvious unless very worn, and the white bar across the primaries is often visible as well. Many birds show a conspicuous pale pink flush to the underparts, which is only exceptionally seen in Laughing. Also, the bare parts tend to be more brightly coloured.

Adult winter: Differs from Laughing by its characteristic dark 'half-hood' and even more prominent white crescents above/below the eye.

Juvenile: Resembles 1st-winter (see below) but has brownish mantle and scapulars with paler fringes (less distinct than in juvenile Laughing), and brownish wash to the hindneck and breast sides. Juvenile plumage is rather quickly moulted to 1st-winter plumage and is thus unlikely to be seen in Europe.

1st-winter: Differs from 1st-winter Laughing Gull by its characteristic head pattern (as winter adult), and white or only very faintly grey-washed neck, breast and flanks. In flight, further told by its distinctly paler inner primaries (both above and below) with broader white tips, and by its unmarked underwing-coverts. Also shows a narrower tail band, which does not reach the outer, all white, pair of tail feathers (outer edge of tail looks grey in Laughing). Other minor differences are: distinct white tips to the outer primaries, slightly broader white tips to the secondaries, and less distinct pale fringes to the coverts.

1st-summer: Unlike all other gulls except Sabine's, it goes through a complete moult early in the 2nd year. It then becomes rather similar to the adult winter, but shows more extensive black on the outer primaries, generally reaching onto the primary coverts. The white tips to the primaries are smaller, and the white bar across the primaries is incomplete. A trace of a tail– or secondary bar is sometimes seen. At least two of the 1st-year birds that have turned up in Europe in summer have shown atypical plumage, with most of the juvenile remiges and rectrices retained.

2nd-winter: Resembles a winter adult and is perhaps not always separable. At least some show more extensive black on the outer primaries and smaller white tips and an incomplete white bar across the primaries.

Habitat and behaviour: Franklin's is more of an inland, freshwater species than Laughing, but it is often also found on the coast. It frequently feeds by picking from the surface in flight, which is not commonly seen in Laughing.

Range: Breeds on inland marshes in North America, chiefly in N-C USA and S-C Canada. Winters mainly on the Pacific coast of South America, also in small numbers further north to Gulf of Mexico. Vagrant to Greenland (July 1974, May 1980, May 1983) and Madeira.

Status: Rare vagrant in Iceland (Sept 1984), Faeroes (May 1976), British Isles (15, Jan-Dec), France (5, Oct-Feb), Belgium (June-July 1987), Netherlands (June-July 1987, June 1988), West Germany (Sept 1986), Norway (5, June, Nov-Dec), Sweden (6, Apr-Aug), Spain (May 1978, Oct 1983, May 1989*), and the Azores. Both adults and immatures (except juvenile) have been seen.

The vagrancy pattern is curiously different from Laughing Gull which has been recorded approximately four times as often in the British Isles as Franklin's, whereas the total number of records of Franklin's for the rest of Europe (excluding British Isles) is approximately the same as for Laughing Gull.

SABINE'S GULL *Larus sabini* **D 33**

L 34cm (13"). WS 86-91cm (34-36"). Arctic breeding species. Regularly seen in W Europe – mainly during autumn migration, usually only a few but sometimes in fairly large numbers.

All plumages: Size between Black-headed and Little Gull, with a distinctly forked tail (however, tail shape not always apparent). The tricoloured upperwing pattern is diagnostic at all ages, but note that juvenile/1st-winter Kittiwakes may look remarkably similar at a distance and are easily mistaken for Sabine's.

Adult summer: Further characterized by its dark grey hood (black lower border) and blackish bill with yellow tip.

Adult winter: Differs from the summer adult in having a variable dark patch on the ear-coverts and across the rear of the crown, nape and hindneck. Does not normally moult to winter plumage until in the winter quarters.

Juvenile: The upperparts and upperwing-coverts are grey-brown, but at close range an attractive, neat scaly pattern with dark subterminal bands and pale fringes can be seen. The crown, ear-coverts, nape, hindneck, sides of neck and breast sides are grey- brown. Shows dark tailband, and also has diagnostic dusky greater underwing-coverts, forming a dark bar on the underwing.

Does not moult to 1st-winter plumage until in its winter quarters, unlike juveniles of the other small/medium-sized gulls, which usually moult rather soon after fledging.

1st-winter: Differs from the juvenile by its adult winter-like head/neck pattern and grey mantle, scapulars and some coverts. The hindneck and sides of the breast are sometimes washed with grey.

1st-summer: This is attained through a complete moult in late winter to early spring – a moult strategy only shared by Franklin's Gull (all other gulls having a partial moult in spring). It resembles an adult, but the head/neck pattern mostly resembles a 1st-winter and is apparently never like the summer adult. The white tips to the primaries are smaller, the bill is sometimes entirely dark, and the legs and feet are often paler, fleshy. It usually remains in its winter quarters.

2nd-winter: Generally not safely separable from the adult, unless the age of not-yet-moulted primaries can be determined.

Habitat: Highly pelagic outside breeding season and usually only sighted from land during/after strong on-shore winds that push the birds close inshore, and sometimes (more rarely) even inland.

Range: Breeds locally on tundra from W Alaska to E Greenland, Spitsbergen (rare) and Siberia. Winters off W South America and SW Africa. Part of the Nearctic population migrates across the Atlantic, many apparently using the Bay of Biscay as a staging area before onward migration to S Africa.

Status: Scarce/rare migrant (mainly autumn). In France (autumn), regular in Bay of Biscay, where large flocks can sometimes occur, e.g. hundreds, up to 250 together, on Vendée coast in autumn 1980; up to 2,000 off Le Pertuis, Charente-Maritime on 29th-30th Aug 1981; also Belle Isle has recorded a peak daily figure of up to 1,000 during late August.

Records from other European coasts are usually the result of W/NW gales, e.g. storm-force winds overnight on 15th-16th Oct 1987 wrought havoc on SE England, with an unprecedented inland wreck of Sabine's Gulls snatched up from the Bay of Biscay. About 60 were found on inland waters on 16th/17th and c. 120 were reported 16th-19th Oct on the south coast; most were adults.

Regularly recorded in autumn in Britain/Ireland (c. 70-100 annually, exceptionally 250+ mainly from SW; fewer in North Sea). Also, many coastal records in autumn from Netherlands, West Germany and Denmark. Elsewhere: Iceland (c. 20, mainly July-Sept), Faeroes (3), Channel Islands (Nov 1975), Belgium (c. 150), Norway (44), Sweden (73), Finland (Oct 1929, May 1982), Estonia, Latvia, Poland (12), East Germany (6, July, Sept-Oct, including one bird inland 31st May-4th July 1975), Czechoslovakia (Dec 1985), Hungary (Dec 1941), Switzerland (8), Bulgaria (May 1988*), Rumania, Italy (1959, 1971), Spain (8), Gibraltar (Nov 1987), Portugal, and the Azores.

Most of the records are from mid Aug-mid Nov, with a peak in Sept-Oct. Adults migrate earlier than juveniles and account for the majority of the early records, whereas juveniles make up the bulk of the later records (except in mid-Oct 1987, see above). On the whole the juveniles are more numerous than adults.

BONAPARTE'S GULL *Larus philadelphia* C 31

L 28-30cm (11.5"). WS 81-84cm (32-33"). North America. Rare vagrant (mainly autumn/winter).

All plumages: Closely resembles Black-headed Gull, but is noticeably smaller and of neater appearance, mainly as a result of its slightly smaller bill. The latter is all-blackish, sometimes with red or pinkish to the very base of the lower mandible and sometimes with a brownish tinge to the inner part.

The underside of the primaries are white, with a sharply-defined black trailing edge. In Black-headed, the central primaries are very dark below, but beware of anomalous individuals, in which the dark area can be strongly reduced. The mantle and scapulars are a shade darker than in Black-headed.

Adult summer: Further distinguished by its blackish-grey hood (dark brown in Black-headed).

Adult winter: Shows much the same basic head pattern as winter Black-headed, but the hindneck and breast-sides are grey, like the upperparts, but occasionally this can be less distinct. Adult's legs/feet are usually slightly paler throughout the year than those of Black-headed.

Juvenile: Resembles 1st-winter, but is extensively dark on the crown, hindneck, breast-sides, mantle and scapulars as in juvenile Black-headed, but the plumage is generally less warm in tone. This plumage is quickly shed, so that vagrants to Europe are very unlikely to be seen in full juvenile plumage.

1st-winter/-summer: Differs from similarly aged Black-headed by its basically 'cleaner' and more contrasting appearance. The dark upperwing-covert bar is generally slightly darker than in Black-headed. The dark trailing edge to the wing looks more sharply defined and narrower, especially on the outermost secondaries and inner-central primaries (because the dark tips are clearcut and do not continue diffusely up the inner webs of the feathers as in Black-headed). The inner greater primary coverts are usually plain grey whereas in Black-headed they are dark-centred, enhancing the impression of a broad and diffuse dark trailing edge to the inner primaries. The outer greater primary coverts are frequently strongly patterned with dark, which is only rarely the case in Black-headed. Also, the primaries generally show more conspicuous white spots on their tips than in Black-headed.

In 1st-winter, hindneck and breast-sides are grey, unlike Black-headed. In 1st-summer, often acquires an almost complete hood but with same colour-difference from Black-headed as adult's.

Habitat and behaviour: Much as Black-headed Gull, but Bonaparte's more frequently picks from the surface in flight when feeding. Its unique habit among gulls of nesting low in conifers is peculiar.

Range: Breeds in Alaska and NW-C Canada. Winters mainly in USA to Central America. Vagrant to Greenland.

Status: Rare vagrant (only very exceptionally found far inland). The majority of the records are from the British Isles (63, Jan-Dec). Only a few noted elsewhere: Iceland (5, Apr-July, Oct), France (Mar 1910,

Oct 1987), Belgium (Jan 1982, Aug 1988*), Netherlands (Aug 1985, June 1988-Jan 1989), Denmark (Aug 1988), Norway (Aug 1972), Czechoslovakia (Apr 1988*), Spain (Nov 1982, Feb 1986), and the Azores (8). Both adults and immatures have been seen.

GREY-HEADED GULL   *Larus cirrocephalus*   A **32**

L 39-42cm (16"). WS *c.* 100cm (40"). Africa and South America. Only one record.

All plumages: Resembles Black-headed Gull, but is distinctly larger, with slightly broader wings, marginally longer legs and a slightly longer, heavier bill. The upperparts and upperwings are appreciably darker grey. The wing pattern is clearly different from that of Black-headed, as the outer primaries are much more extensively dark, reducing the white on the leading edge of the hand considerably, and adults and many 2nd-winter birds also show two prominent mirrors. The underwing is much darker than in Black-headed. Note that in extreme cases, 1st-year Black-headed Gull can be closely similar to a 1st-year Grey-headed in the pattern of the primaries above/below. 2nd-winter/-summer birds and adults show a pale iris, unlike Black-headed.

Adult summer: Identified by its pale grey hood with dusky lower border.

Adult winter: Generally shows a distinctly fainter head pattern than winter Black-headed.

Juvenile: Resembles juvenile Black-headed, but is less warmly coloured. The juvenile plumage is quickly lost.

1st-winter/-summer: Differs from the juvenile in the same way as for Bonaparte's Gull, see p. 153. The tail band is slightly narrower and can be less extensive on the outer feathers than in Black-headed. Also, the head pattern is obviously fainter, and often the hindneck is pale grey. Many 1st-summer birds acquire an almost full hood.

2nd-winter/-summer: Resembles the adult, but many at least are separable by the lack of or more reduced white mirrors on the outer primaries. They also show dark centres to the tertials and secondaries, and sometimes also have some dark on the coverts.

Note: Brown-headed Gull *L. brunnicephalus* of E Asia might conceivably reach Europe (has straggled as far W as Israel) and is very similar to Grey-headed in all plumages. Best told by its mostly white underwing. The mantle is paler grey and more similar to Black-headed. In adult summer plumage, the hood is brown. In winter plumages, head pattern is more like Black-headed and thus slightly more distinctly marked than in Grey-headed.

Range: Has a scattered distribution in Africa (nearest breeding in Mauritania) and South America. Resident and dispersive. Vagrant to Algeria (Apr 1981), Morocco (Nov 1988*), Tunisia (two, July-Aug 1988*) and Eilat (3 individuals between Mar-Sept 1989).

Status: Accidental in Spain: an adult present on the Marismas of the Guadalquivir on 30th June, 1st July and 15th Aug 1971.

AUDOUIN'S GULL   *Larus audouinii*   R Br* **32**

L 48-52cm (20"). WS 115-140cm (50"). Endemic to the Mediterranean (a number winter on coasts of NW Africa). Extremely rare outside this area.

All plumages: Slightly smaller and slimmer than Herring and Lesser Black-backed Gulls. With experience, head and bill shape are characteristic. The forehead is long and sloping, often almost concave, and the bill rather stout and of comparatively 'uniform' width. The iris is typically dark (in the other large gulls the iris is pale from the 2nd-winter plumage). The legs and feet are always considerably darker than in either Lesser Black-backed or Herring: grey or dark olive in the adult and even darker in young immatures, in all often appearing blackish at a distance.

Adult: Easily distinguished from Herring Gull by its dark red bill with black band and yellowish tip; at a distance the bill appears blackish. It also shows noticeably paler grey upperparts and upperwings than Herring Gull, and there is only one very small, white mirror on the outermost primary (often not visible from above). When perched the scapular and tertial crescents are inconspicuous. At close range the hindneck, flanks, belly, rump and underwing can be seen to show a diagnostic pale grey suffusion. Unlike in most other large gulls there is no dark mottling to the head/neck in winter.

Juvenile: Very similar to juveniles of both Herring Gull (mainly Mediterranean race *michahellis*) and Lesser Black-backed Gull, especially the latter. The best distinctions are: more uniformly patterned head/neck, breast and flanks (often with a contrasting dark patch on rear flanks); largely pale central underwing-coverts and axillaries with dark bars (much darker in Herring and Lesser Black-backed, particularly the latter); and practically all-dark tail with contrasting pale uppertail-coverts, forming U-shaped patch (Herring and Lesser Black-backed have a broad, dark tail band and barred rump, uppertail-coverts and sides to the tail). The bill is generally paler with a dark tip (darker in Herring and Lesser Black-backed).

1st-winter/-summer: Like the juvenile, but the scapulars are grey with rather extensive and sharply defined dark centres, and the head, neck and underparts are paler, especially in 1st-summer birds. The pattern of the scapulars is diagnostic and unlike that of any other European gull.

2nd-winter/-summer: Plumage is usually more advanced than similarly aged Herring Gull, with the upperparts and a large proportion of the coverts pale grey, strongly contrasting with the dark outer wing and secondaries (inner primaries often paler). The underwing is obviously paler than in Herring, and the dark tail band is generally better defined and slightly narrower. The inner part of the bill is sometimes reddish.

3rd-winter/-summer: Resembles the adult, but shows dark on the outer greater primary coverts, and the white mirror is often lacking or smaller than in the adult.

Habitat: A strictly coastal species, breeding mainly on small, rocky islands. Found off rocky or sandy coasts outside breeding season.

Range: Audouin's Gull is confined to the Mediterranean, mainly W and NE. The total population is estimated to exceed 6,000 pairs, and it is thus one of the rarer gulls of the world. However, it is encouraging to learn that in Spain, a dramatic increase was noted in 1989 with 4,200 pairs present in the Ebro Delta colony (cf 2,860 pairs in 1988). In the non-breeding season, disperses to the Mediterranean coasts of Africa and to the Atlantic coast of NW Africa south to at least Senegal. At

Gibraltar, Audouin's is a regular passage migrant through the Straits (1,737 recorded migrating west in June-Sept 1989).

Status: Accidental in France: Vendée, first records for the Atlantic coast, immature (Oct 1985) and an adult reported from Olonne Marshes (19th Apr 1989*); very few noted in the south (excluding Corsica), with 4 records relating to immature birds (Mar 1952, Sept 1973, Apr 1984, May 1985), but 16 individuals reported from the Camargue and Aude (May-June 1986), only 3 seen in 1987. Also noted Portugal (Apr 1889), and Malta (13, Feb-Nov). From Switzerland there are three exceptional records, 2 adults and 1 immature (Jan 1956, Dec 1983, Dec 1986).

RING-BILLED GULL *Larus delawarensis* D **32**

L 43-47cm (18"). WS 121-127cm (47.5-50"). North America. Frequent transatlantic vagrant.

All plumages: Closely resembles corresponding plumages of Common Gull, but is slightly larger and heavier, with an appreciably heavier bill. The grey on the upperparts is distinctly paler than in Common Gull.

Adult summer: The white mirrors on the two outermost primaries are distinctly smaller than in Common Gull, and when perched the scapular and tertial crescents are more inconspicuous. The bill and legs are bright yellow, the former with a clearcut, broad, black ring. In Common, the bill and legs are dull greenish-yellow, and there is at most a narrow, indistinct black ring on the bill. The iris is pale yellowish, as in e.g. Herring Gull.

Adult winter: As adult summer, but shows distinct dark spotting/streaking on the head/hindneck, also often on the breast sides, and has slightly duller bill and legs. The dark markings tend to be slightly darker and more spotted than in Common Gull, but there is much overlap. Note that Common regularly shows a rather distinct band on the bill.

Juvenile: The scapulars are dark with pale-notched fringes and usually show extensive pale internal markings, at least on the rear feathers. The pattern is more reminiscent of e.g. juvenile Herring Gull, than of juvenile Common Gull, which shows pale fringes of uniform width and lacks internal pale markings. Other differences as in 1st-winter. Juvenile plumage is unlikely to be seen in Europe as it is quickly lost.

1st-winter/-summer: Shows grey mantle/scapulars and less strongly patterned head and underparts than juvenile (especially in 1st-summer when patterning is normally lacking altogether). The grey mantle/scapulars can show more dark subterminal markings and paler fringes than in Common Gull and the breast/flanks are generally more distinctly marked with dark spots, crescents and bars. On average, the nape/hindneck show slightly more distinct, darker spotting than in Common.

The wing pattern is distinctly more contrasting, with the dark parts darker and the pale areas paler and greyer, less brownish-tinged, than in Common Gull. The greater coverts generally show dark subterminal marks (sometimes two or three rows), lacking in Common. Furthermore, the dark centres to the lesser and median coverts are darker, more clearcut and more pointed at their tips and contrasting more with the more distinct pale fringes than in Common. From late autumn, the coverts are often too heavily worn/bleached to reveal any pattern.

The dark tail band is rather variable, but is hardly ever perfectly clearcut, as in Common, and this is a very good character.

1st-year Ring-billed Gull

1st-year
Common Gull

In 1st-winter plumage, the bill is usually pink with a clearcut dark tip, occasionally more extensively dark as in the juvenile. In 1st-summer, the bill is sometimes yellowish and the dark band well developed. In Common, the basal part of the bill is generally more greyish but sometimes pink or yellowish as in Ring-billed; a broad, dark band is sometimes seen in Common too, especially in summer.

Note that small, 2nd-winter/-summer Herring Gulls can be confused with a 1st-winter/-summer Ring-billed, since the general plumage pattern is superficially similar. If the larger size and heavier build of Herring is not apparent, the best distinctions are the rather irregularly mottled and barred greater coverts and tertials, darker and more uniformly patterned underwing, generally broader and more ill-defined tail band, and pale iris.

2nd-winter/-summer: Differs from the adult in having dark primary coverts and alula, also shows slightly more extensive black on the primaries with only one small mirror on the inner web of the outermost primary or no mirror at all. Often shows a trace of a dark secondary bar and, usually, at least some dark in the tail, sometimes a complete dark band. Common Gull shows two distinct mirrors on each wing, although slightly less prominent than in the adult; occasionally there is only one mirror which, however, is larger than in Ring-billed. Common only exceptionally shows dark on the secondaries and/or in the tail, but in extreme cases may even show a complete tail band. The iris is usually pale, unlike in Common. At least in 2nd-summer birds, the bill and legs are often coloured like the adult. Note that 2nd-year Common regularly shows a broad, distinct band on the bill.

Some small, 3rd-winter/-summer Herring Gulls could be misidentified as 2nd-winter/-summer Ring-billed, but their coverts and usually their tertials are more patterned, also the tail band is generally broader and more diffuse. Additionally, in N races of Herring, the legs are flesh-coloured.

Range: Breeds in N USA and S Canada. Winters mainly in the E USA, south to Central America. Vagrants have reached Morocco (5), the Canary Is (7), Madeira (8), Spitsbergen (July 1976), and Greenland (Nov 1976).

Status: An increasingly recorded transatlantic vagrant. The majority of the records are from SW Britain and Ireland. First observed in Britain in March 1973, but since then the number of records have increased dramatically, partly from advances in identification and from more observers actively searching through gull flocks. There has been a dramatic increase in numbers in eastern N America in recent years.

British Isles: *c*. 610 up to 1987; with exceptional numbers recorded in 1981 (55), 1982 (76), 1983 (89), 1984 (84), and 1985 (*c*. 100, with 65 of these recorded in Ireland). Many of the records following the large influx during the winter of 1982/83 are presumed to refer to birds that came across in 1981/82, as indicated by the proportions between the ages in the different years (see below).

Elsewhere, Iceland (21), where first recorded in 1978, and now seen most years. Faeroes (Jan 1981), France, mainly Atlantic coast (30+, annual since 1982), Channel Islands (Jan 1982, Nov 1984, Oct-Nov 1987), Belgium (May 1988*), Netherlands (July 1986), Sweden (Apr 1978, Mar 1984, July 1987), Norway (8), Poland (Apr 1984, Feb 1985, Jan 1987), West Germany (May 1982), Switzerland (Dec 1984, Jan 1985, Dec 1985- Mar 1986), Portugal (Apr 1981, Nov 1986), Gibraltar (Dec 1983), Spain (25 – including the first record for continental Europe in Jan 1951 of a bird earlier ringed in USA); and the Azores (112 to 1987, regularly winters).

For the British Isles there are records from all months, although most from late Dec-Apr, with most 1st-year birds arriving from midwinter and often staying throughout the spring and summer. 2nd-year birds and adults generally arrive in the late autumn and stay throughout the winter. Most depart Mar-Apr (and May for 2nd-years), apparently joined by migrants from farther south, since there is usually a pronounced peak at that time.

Between 1973-1980: 29, 5% were 1st-years, 29, 5% 2nd-years and 41% adults. In 1981: 65% were 1st-years, 22% 2nd-years and 13% adults; In 1982: 21% were 1st-years, 44% 2nd-years and 35% adults; In 1983: 18% were 1st-years, 16% 2nd-years and 66% adults. In 1984: 26% of the British records and 17% of the Irish were of 1st-years. Since inexperienced 1st-years are more likely to straggle off-course than are older birds, this pattern clearly indicates that a large proportion of the birds seen at least in 1982 and 1983 came across the Atlantic with the big influx in the winter of 1981/82.

'KUMLIEN'S ICELAND GULL' *Larus glaucoides kumlieni* B 33

L 52-60cm (20-23"). WS 140-150cm (57"). North American race of Iceland Gull. Accidental.

Adult summer: Identical to nominate subspecies of Iceland Gull in all respects except for wing-tip pattern and iris colour. Typical individuals show a variable amount of dark grey on the outer primaries and often have a distinctly darker, brownish or brownish-flecked iris (pale yellow in Iceland). However, many individuals breeding well within the range of Kumlien's are inseparable from nominate Iceland.

The main confusion risk in Europe is with abnormally pale (leucistic) Herring Gulls or hybrids of Herring Glaucous Gull. These can be eliminated with caution by structural differences (usually larger and heavier and show longer bill and proportionately shorter wings than 'Kumlien's'), the former also usually by the different pattern on the primaries (shows more dark than 'Kumlien's'), and they invariably show a pale iris, never dark-looking as in 'classic' Kumlien's.

Juvenile to 2nd-summer: Not separable with certainty from Iceland. There is considerable individual variation in both subspecies.

3rd-winter/-summer: The characteristic pattern on the outer primaries begins to show, enabling identification. 2nd– and 3rd-year birds with darker outer primaries can be confused with leucistic Herring Gull or hybrids of Herring and Glaucous Gull in corresponding plumage. Structural differences are usually a good guide if used with caution. Traces of a dark secondary and/or tail band are definite Herring and hybrid characters.

Range: Breeds on Baffin Is and NW Ungava Peninsula in NE Canada, wintering along the Atlantic coast from Newfoundland to Virginia.

Status: Accidental in the Faeroes (*c.* 40, Dec-Feb, see below). British Isles (8, Dec-Apr), including one adult returning to same successive wintering site in Banff Bay, Grampian, 1985-89 and again Jan-Apr 1990; Denmark (Feb 1987) and Sweden (May 1985).

Faeroes: In Jan 1983, there was an invasion of *c.* 100 adult Iceland Gulls involving many positively identified as *kumlieni* (at least 24 adults and 14 immatures). These Kumlien's were believed to have originated from the northernmost part of its range. This followed a long period of westerly winds and extremely low temperatures in its normal wintering areas (Greenland and adjacent Canadian waters). The only previous record was in Dec 1905.

ROSS'S GULL *Rhodostethia rosea*   D **33**

L 29-31cm (12"). Arctic species. Rare vagrant mainly in winter, more rarely spring/summer.

All plumages: Size of Little Gull but has longer, more pointed wings and a longer, wedge-shaped tail (central pair of rectrices are even relatively more prolonged than the rest); tail shape is, however, often difficult to discern in the field.

Adult summer: Unmistakable, with a distinct, narrow black neck-ring and often a strong pink suffusion to the underparts. Otherwise as winter.

Adult winter: Plumage is rather similar to an adult winter Little Gull. The slightly wider white trailing edge to the wing is not as in Little, complete, but confined to the secondaries and inner primaries, and the outer web of the outermost primary is blackish, unlike in Little. The crown is never as dark grey as in many Little Gulls. Furthermore, the underwing is mostly grey rather than blackish as in Little, but this may be difficult to judge. The underparts are often pinkish-tinged.

In 2nd-winter Little Gull, the underwing may look greyish, and often the outer web to the outermost primary is blackish, but there are usually distinct blackish subterminal markings on the following one to five primaries. Further, the under primary coverts and underwing-coverts are paler (whitish) than the remiges, unlike in Ross's.

Juvenile: Shows much dark on the head, hindneck, breast-sides, mantle and scapulars as in juvenile Little Gull. See 1st-winter for differences from Little. Juvenile plumage is very unlikely to be recorded outside the breeding areas.

1st-winter/-summer: Resembles the juvenile, but has grey upperparts and a pale (normally partly grey-tinged) head, hindneck and breast-sides. It differs from similarly aged Little Gull in its clean white secondaries and inner primaries, lacking the dark secondary bar and shaded inner primaries of Little. Also shows more white on the inner webs of the outer primaries. From below, the usually grey-washed underwing-coverts contrast with the broad, white trailing edge and distinct black tips to the outer primaries (underwing whitish in Little with dark secondary bar and diffuse dark tips to the outer primaries). It has a paler grey crown (not showing Little's usually distinctive dark cap) and a more restricted black tail band.

In 1st-summer plumage there is no grey on the head, hindneck and breast-sides as in winter. It often shows a blackish necklace and a pinkish tint to the underparts, simplifying separation from Little.

2nd-winter/-summer: Generally like the adult, but some individuals show traces of immaturity on the wings, and some 2nd-summers show hardly any pink and only a trace of the dark neck-ring.

Range: Breeds mainly in NE Siberia (from Khatanga river to Kolyma delta). Has bred occasionally in Canadian arctic, Greenland and Spitsbergen. Probably winters along the edge of the ice in the Arctic Ocean.

Status: Rare vagrant in Iceland (23 records involving 14+ individuals, Feb-Aug, with peak in June, including one adult seen in N nearly every summer 1972-1981). Faeroes (8), British Isles (54, especially Jan-Feb), France (Dec 1913), Netherlands (June- July 1958, Jan 1981), Denmark (Dec 1955, Jan-Feb 1984, May 1988), Norway (5th in May 1981), Sweden (Apr-May 1981, May 1982, Jan 1983 (2), Oct 1984, May 1988), Finland (June 1973, July 1982, Feb 1988), West Germany (Heligoland, Jan 1848, Feb 1858, Aug 1982; Hamburger Hallig, Dec 1953), and Sardinia (Jan 1906). Adults are much more frequent than 1st-years.

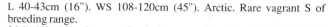

IVORY GULL *Pagophila eburnea*   D **33**

L 40-43cm (16"). WS 108-120cm (45"). Arctic. Rare vagrant S of breeding range.

Adult: All white plumage. Confusion may arise with albinistic individuals of other similarly sized gulls (e.g. Kittiwake), but the bluish– or greenish-grey bill with yellow and orange tip is diagnostic. Note rather stocky, 'pigeon-like' build and comparatively short, blackish legs.

1st-year: Unmistakable, white with a variable number of blackish spots (most in juvenile, fewer in 1st-summer) and dusky face (sometimes lacking in 1st-summer). The basal part of the bill is slightly darker than in the adult.

Habitat and behaviour: Coastal – vagrants usually seen at fishing ports or at carrion on beach. Often picks food from the surface in flight. Noted for its tameness.

Range: Resident in high arctic, only occasionally straggling south.

Status: Rare vagrant in Iceland (93, Oct-May with peak in early Jan, approximately 50% 1st-winter). Faeroes (possibly regular), British Isles (109, mainly Nov-Feb), France (two in 19th cent; and 1st-winter, Finistère-Brest, Dec 1984-Jan 1985), Netherlands (Feb 1987, Feb 1990*), Denmark (5), Norway (55), Sweden (16), Finland (24), Poland (Sept 1989*), West Germany (Jan 1850, Nov 1880, Oct 1963, Apr 1980), Switzerland (Mar 1817), and Italy (Veneto 1958, Liguria 1972).

ROYAL TERN   *Sterna maxima* B **34**

L 45-50cm (19"). WS 106-112cm (42-44"). North America, West Indies and W Africa. Very rare vagrant (mainly summer/autumn).

All plumages: Only slightly smaller than Caspian Tern but is slimmer, less large-headed, with narrower wings, and has a longer, more deeply forked tail and a slightly slimmer bill. Shape (except bill) often recalls Sandwich Tern more than Caspian. The adult's bill is orange, but in very young birds it is more yellowish and may even be greenish-yellow. The bill of Caspian is red in the adult and more orange-tinged in young, at all ages usually with a distinct dark mark near the tip. The underside of the primaries is white with a distinct blackish trailing edge to the outers (not entirely blackish on the outer primaries as in Caspian). It shows more of a shaggy crest than Caspian, most pronounced in the adult.

Adult summer: Shows slightly more white on the lores, and the outer primaries are generally more contrastingly dark than in Caspian. The contrast between dark (older) outer and pale (newer) inner primaries progressively increases until the autumn moult has been completed.

Adult winter: This plumage begins to show already by late spring/early summer. The forehead and usually at least the fore-crown are white, unlike Caspian, which shows a greyish forehead/crown (heavily streaked).

Juvenile: Easily distinguished from the adult by its more boldly patterned upperparts and upperwings and dark-tipped tail. The bill is slightly more yellowish, and the legs/feet are initially dull yellow.

The head pattern differs from juvenile Caspian Tern's in much the same way as described for winter adults. It shows a strikingly different upperwing pattern than juvenile Caspian. The outer wing is dark, and the inner wing is pale with three distinct dark bars, one on the leading edge, one on the greater coverts and one on the secondaries. Juvenile Caspian shows a rather uniformly pale upperwing.

1st-winter: Like juvenile, but with uniformly grey upperparts and some coverts. Sometime in the winter the wing moult commences. The juvenile, dark-centred, greater coverts may be retained for some time. There is only one moult series in the primaries. The legs are usually yellowish with blackish spots.

1st-summer: Similar to the adult (with winter patterned head) but with two active moult series in the primaries (generally only one in the adult). The last juvenile (outermost) primaries are moulted in Aug-Oct. Occasionally, there is some dark on the leading edge of the wing, and the legs sometimes still show some yellow, unlike the adult.

2nd-winter/-summer: In 2nd-winter, not safely separable from adult, unless there is some dark on the leading edge of the wing or some yellow on the legs (rarely, though). In 2nd summer, the forehead normally still shows at least some white.

Voice: Calls resemble Sandwich Tern but are deeper and more musical. The juvenile voice is generally distinctly higher-pitched than the adult's.

Range: In the Atlantic, breeds on the E coast of USA, Mexico and the Caribbean and on the W coast of Africa. Also breeds on the Mexican Pacific coast. Winters from SE USA to Argentina and Peru. African population winters S to Angola. Apparently some northward dispersal takes place in autumn both in America and Africa.

Status: Birds presumably of W African origin occasionally reach S Spain and Gibraltar (10 or more records July-Nov, also Apr). Other records are from Ireland: Dublin (Mar 1954-long dead). Britain: July 1965, Sept 1971, and Nov 1979. Norway (June 1976). At least one N European record is attributable to transatlantic vagrancy (Britain: Kenfig pool, Glamorgan, 1st-winter, 24th Nov 1979), having been ringed on the E coast of the USA.

LESSER CRESTED TERN *Sterna bengalensis*   B **34**

L 40cm (16"). WS 89-94cm (35-37"). Nearest breeding in Libya. Rare vagrant (has bred Italy and Spain).

All plumages: Similar to Royal Tern, but is much smaller, with a thinner bill. Closely resembles Sandwich Tern in size and build, although is slightly larger, with a fractionally deeper base to the bill. The grey tone to the upperparts and upperwing is very close to that of Common Tern and is thus slightly darker grey than in Royal or Sandwich Terns.

Adult: Head pattern much like Royal Tern (summer/winter). However, it normally does not start to moult the head quite so early as Royal. In the spring, the primaries are either silvery above, paler than the rest of the upperwing, or the outers are slightly darker than the inners (the contrast in the latter case is enhanced as the feathers become more worn). The rump, uppertail-coverts and tail are grey, like the upperparts or fractionally paler, which is immediately different from either Royal or the hypothetical Sandwich Tern with an anomalous bill colour.

Juvenile: The basic plumage pattern and bare part coloration is like juvenile Royal and thus easily told from the adult. The pattern of the upperwing is clearly darker and bolder than in juvenile Sandwich Tern which also lacks the dark greater covert bar.

1st-winter: Much like the juvenile but with the upperparts and many coverts unmarked, grey. The flight-feathers are darker due to wear (primary moult starts in Nov-Jan).

1st-summer: Resembles the winter adult but is usually more worn, with some dark on the leading edge of the inner wing and often some yellow on the legs/feet. A second primary moult series starts with the innermost in May-July, before the outermost primaries (now very worn and dark) have been renewed. The adult in spring/early summer has the outer primaries only slightly darker than the inners (or not at all darker). The second series is completed in Sept-Dec, when the outer primaries are obviously worn and dark in the adult.

2nd-winter/-summer: The leading edge of the wing usually shows some dark in 2nd-winter birds also. 2nd-summer resembles the adult summer but there is sometimes some white admixed on the forehead and crown.

Voice: The calls are variable, and apparently very similar to those of Sandwich Tern.

Note: Crested Tern *S. bergii* (nearest breeding area in Red Sea, and a possible candidate for future vagrancy), could be confused with Lesser Crested. However, it is distinctly larger (almost the size of Royal), with a greenish-yellowish bill, usually looking distinctly drooping, and the plumage has a much darker grey tone above. In summer, there is a distinct white band across the forehead. In winter and immatures, the crown shows less white than in Lesser Crested. Juvenile shows even more boldly patterned upperwing, normally also with a dark bar on the median coverts, and has more strongly marked scapulars.

Range: Breeds coasts/islets in Libya, Red Sea, Persian Gulf, Australia and New Guinea. Libyan population migrates to winter along the coasts of NW Africa (passes through S Mediterranean mainly in May-June and Aug-Oct). Other populations disperse to the coasts of E Africa, and S Asia to Australasia.

Status: Very rare vagrant. Has bred a few times in S Europe, and at least twice in a mixed pair with Sandwich Tern. Breeding recorded in Italy (S Po delta) in 1985-86 and in Spain (Ebro delta) in 1979 and in 1985 (2 pairs); a territorial pair was also present in 1981. In Britain, an adult which had returned to the Farne Islands, Northumberland for the sixth successive summer in June 1989, paired with a Sandwich Tern and hatched a single egg. Subsequently, a mixed pair was seen feeding a juvenile (presumed hybrid) at Musselburgh Lagoons, Lothian in Aug 1989 and in June 1990, the female on Inner Farne laid an egg and then shared incubation with a Sandwich Tern (egg hatched on 30th June!). There are additional records from Italy (mainly E Sicily), S France, S Spain and Gibraltar (about a dozen records, max 6 on 2nd Nov 1988).

Accidental in the British Isles (4, May-Sept where first recorded in July 1982). Austria (2 adults Aug 1980, and one individual in July 1983), Switzerland (Sept 1946, Aug 1977) and Greece (June 1987).

ELEGANT TERN   *Sterna elegans*   A **34**

L 39-43cm (16"). WS 86cm (34"). Extreme SW USA and W Mexico. Accidental.

All plumages: Very like Lesser Crested Tern, with bill distinctly longer, thinner and looks slightly drooping (often less distinct in juvenile).

Adult: Shows an even more pronounced, shaggier crest than Lesser Crested. The upperparts and upperwing are marginally paler, without the often contrastingly paler primaries of the latter. Rump, uppertail-coverts and tail are white or very pale greyish, unlike Lesser Crested. In winter, shows slightly less white on crown than in Lesser Crested.

Juvenile: Very similar to Lesser Crested of the same age but is said to be slightly more distinctly patterned on the upperparts and coverts.

Subsequent immature plumages: Presumably attained in a sequence similar to that of Lesser Crested Tern, p. 162.

Voice: Apparently similar to that of Lesser Crested Tern.

Range: Breeds Pacific coasts of Mexico and S California. Winters mainly along the W coast of South America. Accidental in Texas.

Status: Accidental in France: Arcachon, Gironde, one present in a colony of Sandwich Terns in June 1974, then some regular sightings from 1975 onwards (but not every year). Two were seen in 1984, both paired with Sandwich Terns, and at least one individual has been seen every year since then (caught and ringed in 1987). Ireland: Carlingford Lough, Co. Down (22nd June-3rd July 1982), and at Ballymacoda, Co Cork (1st Aug 1982).

ROSEATE TERN   *Sterna dougallii*   R Br* **35**

L 33-38cm (14 in). WS 72-80cm (30 in). Rare and local breeder in
Azores, Britain/Ireland and NW France. (Also breeds elsewhere in the
Atlantic, Indian Ocean and Pacific). Accidental outside breeding areas
and migration routes in Europe.

Adult summer: Very similar to Arctic and Common Terns, but in some
respects more reminiscent of Sandwich Tern (with which it appears to
be more closely related). The bill is longer than in either and mostly
black, showing very little red at the base, except in mid to late summer,
when the inner half often turns red. In flight, the head generally looks
more protruding than in Arctic and Common. The wings appear proportionately shorter and the wing-beats are generally noticeably
quicker and shallower (often recalling Little Tern). The tail streamers
are even longer than in Arctic; also its legs are slightly longer even than
those of Common Tern.

The grey tone of the upperside is distinctly paler than in either Arctic
or Common Tern. The underside is also clearly paler, lacking the grey
tinge of Arctic and Common, and often there is a faint pinkish tinge.
The pale plumage is closer to Sandwich than to either Arctic or Common.

There is no conspicuous dark trailing edge to the underside of the
primaries as in Arctic and Common Terns. Instead, the outer primaries
show comparatively faint and diffuse dark subterminal markings and
distinct white tips (no white tip to the outermost one). The white tips
to the primaries are also conspicuous on the upperwing when perched,
unless the primaries are very worn.

Particularly in late summer and autumn (when worn), the outermost
c. 3 primaries form a dark wedge above. In Common Tern this wedge
is less contrasting and usually broader (normally made up of 5-6 primaries), and in Arctic there is no dark wedge at all. The tail streamers
are all-white, lacking the dark outer web of Arctic or Common.

Adult winter: Shows white on the forehead, anterior lores and also a little
on the crown. It differs from both Common and Arctic Terns by much
the same characters as described above for summer. However, bill colour, moult contrast in the primaries, length of tail streamers, and the
colour of the underparts are no longer applicable.

Juvenile: Easily told from adult winter by e.g. strongly marked scapulars.

Distinctly different from either juvenile Arctic or Common Terns.
Structural differences as described for adults are of less importance.
The forehead is generally more dusky and the lores more extensively
dark than in Arctic and Common, but these differences are lost as the
moult progresses. The scapulars are heavily marked with dark U– or
V-shaped marks and usually also show some dark and some buffish
internal markings. The tertials and innermost greater coverts are often
patterned in the same way. The pattern is clearly different from either
Arctic or Common and more reminiscent of that of juvenile Sandwich
Tern. The pattern of the underside of the primaries and of the outermost
tail feather also differs from Arctic and Common in the same way as
in adults (see above). From Arctic it also differs in showing a distinct
dark bar on the secondaries. As in adult, the grey tone on the upperside
and upperwings is paler that in Arctic and Common.

The bill is all blackish, rarely with a little pinkish at the base of the lower mandible and thus clearly different from most, but not all, Common and some Arctic Terns, which show extensive orange on the base of the lower mandible. Also, the legs are blackish unlike in the other two.

1st-winter/-summer: Unlike Arctic or Common Terns (but like e.g. Sandwich Tern) the post-juvenile moult starts early in the autumn, on the breeding grounds. It is first apparent on the scapulars, which attain scattered pure grey feathers, eventually becoming all-grey. 1st-winter is separable from adult as long as there are some juvenile wing– and tail-feathers left. The primary moult starts later than in the adult (usually in mid-winter; in late summer/early autumn in adult). 1st-summer plumage is basically like the winter adult.

Usually does not return to the breeding quarters until in its 4th year.
Voice: Very distinctive and much closer to Sandwich than to either Arctic or Common Terns. A shrill, grating *kierrik*; *cherrick*; *chy-ree* are commonly heard. Also a rasping *kr-raep* and in juvenile *krrip*.
Note: Has hybridized with Common Tern, giving rise to hybrid offspring with mixed characters.
Habitat and behaviour: More strictly coastal than either Arctic or Common Terns, and very rarely recorded inland. Reported to have different feeding action from the latter two species, generally flying into water from an angle, rather than hovering and diving.
Range: Now very rare in Europe. The breeding population of the British Isles has declined from *c.* 3,500 pairs (1962), 2,500 pairs (1969-70), 800 pairs (1980) to 455 pairs (1984). Similar decline also noted in France, from *c.* 500 pairs (1973) to *c.* 120 pairs (1979). Azores now hold largest number, *c.* 1,000 breeding pairs (1990). In August to mid-Sept, migrates south down the Atlantic coast to winter off W Africa. Arrives on the breeding grounds again in mid-May. It is also distributed patchily in the W Atlantic, Indian Ocean and W Pacific.
Status: Rare outside breeding range or migration routes. Channel Is (Jersey Aug 1987), Belgium (*c.* 12 records; has bred in mixed pair with Common Tern). Netherlands (7, May-Aug, and in 1984 successfully bred with a Common Tern). West Germany (bred rarely in the 19th century, *c.* 5 sightings since 1945), Denmark (*c.* 1900, June 1922, Aug 1988), Norway (June 1984, July 1985), Sweden (June 1949 and June 1984), Poland (adult, 10th Oct 1987), Austria (May 1954), Switzerland (3), Italy (8), Malta (3), and Gibraltar (where an extremely scarce and irregular migrant). In Spain, bred Ebro delta in 1961.

ALEUTIAN TERN *Sterna aleutica* A **34**

L 32-34cm (13"). WS 75-80cm (30"). Easternmost Siberia and Alaska. One record.
Adult summer: Very typical. Shows slaty-grey upperparts and upperwing, contrasting with white rump and tail (latter deeply forked). Also, shows black cap with white forehead; grey foreneck to belly; and conspicuous dark bar on the secondaries below. Reported to be comparatively longer-winged than other similarly-sized terns – with deep, slow, elegant wing-beats (see also Bridled Tern p. 167).
Adult winter: Said to show some white streaking on the forecrown and has white underparts, otherwise like the summer adult.

Juvenile: Very different from the adult. Plumage very characteristic and not really similar to any European tern. Most similar to juvenile Bridled Tern, but has pale grey rump, uppertail-coverts and tail (not concolorous with rest of upperparts as in Bridled) and paler grey, broadly white-tipped, greater coverts (not concolorous with rest of up-perwing as in Bridled). Juvenile Common Tern is much paler on the upperparts and upperwings (except fore-edge of inner wing), and juvenile Whiskered Tern shows much paler upperwings.

Subsequent immature plumages: Little-known. The 1st-summer plumage is said to resemble the winter adult.

Voice: Apparently very different from the calls of European terns – described as a soft, whistling tri– to five-syllabic note.

Range: Breeds locally in E Siberia (Sakhalin, Kamchatka, Sea of Okhotsk) and W, SW and S Alaska. Winter quarters unknown, presumably far to the south.

Status: Accidental in Britain: Farne Is, Northumberland (28th-29th May 1979). As with the recent records of Elegant Tern in NW Europe, this is an exceptional and most unexpected record. The species has not even been recorded in Canada or USA south of Alaska!

FORSTER'S TERN   *Sterna forsteri*   B **35**

L 33-36cm (14"). WS 73-82cm (29-32"). North America. Very rare vagrant (autumn-late winter).

All plumages: Closely resembles the corresponding plumages of Common Tern, but is slightly heavier, with an appreciably thicker bill, has longer legs, and the head usually appears proportionately larger and more 'angular'. The tail is pale grey with a white outer web to the outermost feather (white with a blackish outer web to the outermost feather in adult Common, and pale grey with blackish outer edges in juvenile Common).

Adult summer: Differs from Common Tern mainly in the contrastingly pale, silvery, upper surface to the primaries, with dark tips. When worn, the primaries are darker and contrast less with the rest of the up-perwing. The inner part of the bill and the legs tend to be more orange in colour, and the white area on the lores (below the black cap) is generally slightly broader.

Adult winter: Readily distinguished from Common Tern by its very characteristic head pattern, recalling a winter Gull-billed Tern. The anterior lesser coverts are not dark as in Common.

Juvenile: Initially patterned with brown on the crown, nape, mantle and scapulars (more uniformly than in juvenile Common Tern), but the brown is quickly lost through moult and wear. The head pattern is basically similar to the winter adult – thus clearly different from that of juvenile Common Tern. The upperwing is rather uniformly pale with a slightly darker trailing edge, unlike Common, which shows a prominent dark bar on the leading and trailing edge of the inner wing. The bill is usually nearly all blackish, lacking the distinct orange base to the lower mandible of most Common Terns.

1st-winter/-summer: Attained in a sequence much as in Roseate Tern, see p. 164.

Voice: Variable, but generally more nasal and slightly lower-pitched than Common Tern, including *kyarr*, often rapidly repeated *kek* and a harsh *kerr*.

Range: Breeds mainly inland C North America and along the E coast of USA. Winters in California and along the E coast from Virginia south to Mexico.

Status: Very rare vagrant. British Isles (18, where first recorded in Feb-Mar 1980). Mainly seen in SW Britain, Wales, Anglesey, and Ireland; noted all months, but mainly in autumn/late winter; one or two individuals returning to same successive wintering sites. Also recorded in Iceland (Oct 1959), the Netherlands (Nov 1986) and Straits of Gibraltar (Oct 1987).

BRIDLED TERN   *Sterna anaethetus*   B 35

L *c.* 36cm (14"). WS 77-81cm (31"). Nearest populations: Caribbean, W Africa, Red Sea and Persian Gulf. Accidental.

Adult summer: Reminiscent of Aleutian Tern but easily told by white underparts, darker and browner upperparts, and dark rump, uppertail-coverts and tail (the latter with white outer edge). More difficult to tell from Sooty Tern, (see below).

Adult winter: Similar to adult summer, but shows less distinct head pattern, with white streaking on crown and less distinct dark loral stripe (sometimes lacking), and pale grey fringes to mantle and, less prominently, scapulars.

Juvenile: Clearly different from the adult, showing a much more diffuse head pattern and usually has distinct pale fringes to the upperparts, coverts and tertials. Some individuals are obviously darker on the head and apparently lack the pale fringes to the upperparts and upperwings.

It could possibly be confused with juvenile Black Tern, but this is much smaller and considerably paler above. Also see juvenile Aleutian Tern (p. 165) and juvenile Sooty Tern (below).

Subsequent immature plumages: Reported basically to resemble the winter adult from the 1st-winter plumage until approximately 22 months old, when adult breeding plumage is attained.

Range: Breeds Carribean, NW Africa, Red Sea, Persian Gulf, off E Africa, S India, Australasia and Pacific Ocean. Dispersive and pelagic in non-breeding season.

Status: Accidental in the British Isles (12, Apr-Nov), France (July 1986, July 1987), Belgium (July 1989*), Netherlands (2 in July, with one remaining until early Aug 1989*) and Denmark (July 1987). All relate to adults.

SOOTY TERN   *Sterna fuscata*   C 35

L 43cm (17"). WS 82-94cm (32-37"). Widespread throughout tropical oceans. Rare vagrant.

Adult: Resembles Bridled Tern, but is distinctly darker, blackish, above. Also, white on forehead does not continue past the eye as a white supercilium as in Bridled, and the dark loral stripe is shorter and more tapering than in Bridled. In flight, the undersides of the primaries are clearly darker than in Bridled. There appears to be less seasonal variation than in Bridled Tern.

Juvenile: Very different from the adult. Also, easily separated from juvenile Bridled and other terns by its dark head/neck and underparts, with only the lower belly and undertail-coverts pale. Shows distinct whitish tips to the scapulars and coverts. The underwing is basically similar to the adult, but is suffused with grey on most coverts, (see also juvenile Brown Noddy, below).

Subsequent immature plumages: The first subadult plumage, reported to be attained at the age of *c.* 6 months, mostly resembles the juvenile but is paler on the head, neck and underparts. The second subadult plumage, appearing at the age of approximately 1 year, is similar but even paler below, with the outer primaries generally new and fresh (not juvenile and worn). Subsequent plumages are normally much like the adult but usually with some dark mottling underneath and/or on the head for some time.

Range: Circumequatorial. Nearest breeding areas are in the Carribean, S Red Sea and Persian Gulf. Dispersive in the non-breeding season; highly pelagic.

Status: Rare vagrant. Majority of records are from the British Isles (26, Apr-Oct) and France (10, mostly June-July). Fewer elsewhere: Iceland (June 1969), Norway (two in May 1976), Sweden (two in July 1977), Belgium (July 1988*), Denmark (June 1989*), East Germany (Aug 1979), West Germany (Sept 1929, July 1957), Italy (4, Aug-Oct, Mar), Spain (4), and the Azores. Apparently all records relate to adults.

BROWN NODDY *Anous stolidus*   A **35**

L 38-40cm (15.5"). WS 77-85cm (32"). Circumequatorial. Only 2 records.

Adult: Entirely dark brown except for the white cap. Shows characteristic wedge-shaped tail.

Juvenile: Resembles the adult, but only the forehead is pale, and the upperparts and coverts show paler fringes.

1st-summer: Reported to resemble the adult but shows a less distinct cap.

Note: The Black Noddy *A. minutus*, has a similar distribution in the Atlantic and is thus a possible candidate for future vagrancy to Europe. It is slightly smaller than Brown Noddy and is blackish rather than dark brown. The bill is distinctly longer and more slender. Juvenile shows a whitish cap, similar to the adult's.

Range: Much as Sooty Tern.

Status: Accidental in West Germany (Oct 1912), and Norway (Aug 1974).

Family ALCIDAE   Auks

BRÜNNICH'S GUILLEMOT   *Uria lomvia*   R Br **36**

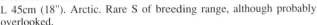

L 45cm (18"). Arctic. Rare S of breeding range, although probably overlooked.

All plumages: Closely resembles Guillemot, but is marginally heavier with a distinctly shorter, deeper bill with more decurved upper mandible. Shows a distinct whitish streak along the base of the upper mandible, lacking in Guillemot (beware Guillemot with fish in bill, seeming to have similar bill pattern and also heavier bill). The head, neck and upperside, especially the former two areas, are blacker than in most Guillemots and close in colour to Razorbill. The flanks are unmarked or show only a few fine streaks, rarely the case in Guillemot. In flight the axillaries and particularly the underwing-coverts are almost unmarked, unlike Guillemot, which has distinct dark markings.

Adult summer: Further distinguished from Guillemot by the white on underparts extending further up the foreneck as a wedge (see figure). The 'bridled' form of Guillemot is not found in Brünnich's.

Adult winter: More extensive dark on the sides of the head than in Guillemot, and lacks the dark streak behind the eye. Rarely, a similar pattern can be seen in Guillemot.

s   Guillemot

ner plumage

It can also be confused with juvenile Razorbill, which may be quite small-billed. However, the bill of Razorbill has more domed culmen and more pronounced gonydeal angle. There is no pale stripe along the cutting edge of the upper mandible. Also, the white on the head reaches higher up the sides than in Brünnich's Guillemot.

Juvenile: Occurs in two different types, one resembling the summer adult and the other resembling winter adult. The juvenile is, even after it has left the breeding colony, initially significantly smaller and more short-billed than the adult but grows quickly. However, unlikely to be seen in juvenile plumage S of breeding range.

1st-winter/-summer: Much like the adult. In the hand, can usually be distinguished by slightly more pointed primaries, browner and more loosely textured greater primary coverts and normally a moult contrast among the greater coverts – a few outers being slightly browner, more loosely textured, more worn and often slightly shorter than the rest.

Range: Circumpolar Arctic. Breeds locally in N and NW Norway (*c.* 3,000 pairs) and Iceland (*c.* 2 million pairs). Disperses in the non-breeding season.

Status: Very rare winter visitor; many records relate to birds found dead on the tide-line. Faeroes (rare in winter). British Isles (26, mainly Oct-Apr, especially N Britain and Orkney/Shetland Is); one present in Shetland on Sumburgh Head cliffs from 16th June-12th July 1989 was only the fourth one to be seen alive in Britain. France (Apr 1978, Jan 1981), Belgium (two before 1842, two in Jan and one in Dec 1981), Netherlands (9, Dec-Mar), Denmark (7, including first live individual seen in Dec 1989), Sweden (18), Finland (including 58 records of exhausted and storm-driven birds found all over the country in late Nov-early Dec 1902; 2 records 1975-88), Estonia, Latvia, Poland (Apr 1964), East Germany (Mar 1966, Aug 1987), West Germany (2), Austria (1882), Rumania, Spain, and the Azores (Dec 1965).

CRESTED AUKLET   *Aethia cristatella*   A **36**

L 24cm (9.5"). Mainly in the Bering Sea. One record.

All plumages: Rather small (slightly larger than Little Auk), with a very short bill, and mostly dark plumage. Has a whitish iris, at least in adults.

Adult summer: Typically shows bright orange-red bill and gape, prominent recurved crest and narrow, white plumes on the sides of the head, forming white streak behind the eye.

Adult winter: Shows pale brownish bill and lacks the 'swollen' gape. The crest is slightly shorter and the white plumes behind the eye are less distinct or absent.

Juvenile/1st-winter: Reported to resemble the winter adult but lacks crest and white plumes.

1st-summer: Resembles the adult summer, but has a slightly shorter crest and plumes and has distinctly more worn and bleached flight-feathers, coverts and some scattered feathers elsewhere.

Range: Breeds on islands in the Bering Sea, also on some of the Kurile Islands. Disperses to sea in winter, south to Japan.

Status: Accidental. An exceptional record of one collected *c.* 45 nautical miles NE off Langanes, NE Iceland in Aug 1912.

PARAKEET AUKLET   *Cyclorrhynchus psittacula*   A **36**

L 27cm (10.5"). Mainly in the Bering Sea. One record.

All plumages: Only slightly larger than Crested Auklet. The peculiarly shaped, bright orange-red to dull brownish-red bill and pale iris differ strikingly from noticeably smaller Little Auk. Also, the head/breast pattern is different, and there is no white trailing edge to the wing or white scapular streaks as in Little Auk.

Adult summer: Shows white mottling on the throat, foreneck and breast and distinct white plume behind the eye.

Adult winter: Has a duller bill, less distinct or no white plume, also a whiter throat, foreneck and breast than in summer. The head is more extensively dark than in Little Auk.

Juvenile: Presumably not very different from the adult winter.

Range: Breeds on islands in the Bering Sea and off SW Alaska. Winters at sea south to N Japan and Canada, generally slightly further east than Crested Auklet.

Status: Accidental. There is one European record, perhaps the most extraordinary of all records of rarities in Europe: one collected on Lake Vättern, S-C Sweden in mid-Dec 1860, after extreme weather conditions with an easterly gale.

Family PTEROCLIDIDAE   Sandgrouse

SPOTTED SANDGROUSE   *Pterocles senegallus*   A **36**

L 30-35cm (13"). WS 53-65cm (21-25.5"). North Africa, Arabia and W Asia. Accidental in Sicily.

All plumages: Typically sandy-coloured, with a distinct pale orange patch on the throat and ear-coverts (except in juvenile), also has an elongated blackish patch on the central belly, which is usually difficult to see when the bird is on the ground. In flight, identified by rather uniformly pale upperwings and pale underwings with contrastingly dark flight-feathers; dark belly patch more easily seen. The central tail feathers are elongated (except in juvenile).

Adult male: Shows grey on the sides of the head, lower foreneck and upper breast. Has large, paler spots on the scapulars and coverts, although these are not easily seen at a distance.

Adult female: Shows distinct dark spots on most of the upperparts, coverts, foreneck and breast.

Juvenile: Resembles the adult female but has fine wavy bars on the upperparts and coverts and fine dark 'horseshoes' on the breast (thus no spots). It also lacks orange on the head and the elongated central tail feathers. The primaries differ from the adult in being paler at the tips with fine dark vermiculations (except the two outermost). Juvenile plumage is moulted quickly after fledging.

1st-winter: Apparently indistinguishable from the adult from after the complete moult in the summer/autumn. Birds which have arrested the moult of the outermost one or two primaries are perhaps always young.

Voice: A very distinctive, far-carrying, almost echoing, soft *quitoo*, usually repeated, normally rapidly when flushed.

Habitat and behaviour: Inhabits desert areas. Like other sandgrouse, normally not seen on the ground except at water holes, because of their rather secretive habits and camouflaged plumage. Small to large flocks (where common) are usually seen flying rapidly to and from water holes in the early morning or evenings, calling frequently.

Range: Resident in N Africa, the Middle East, Arabia and in S Asia to Pakistan/NW India. In the dry season it is nomadic, moving away from dry areas in search of water.

Status: Accidental in Sicily: two near S. Croce Camerina on 26th Apr 1909.

CHESTNUT-BELLIED SANDGROUSE *Pterocles exustus* A **36**

L 31-33cm (12.5"). WS 48-51cm (19.5"). Africa, Arabia to India. Accidental in Hungary.

All plumages: Dark belly and flanks, contrastingly dark flight-feathers and primary coverts above, broad white trailing edge to the secondaries and inner primaries (less distinct in juvenile) and unique dark underwings. Shows elongated central tail feathers in all except juvenile.

Adult male: Mostly greyish-brown, with buffy throat/ear-coverts. Shows narrow, dark tips to the rear scapulars and inner coverts, and has a narrow, dark breast band. The dark patch on the belly/flanks is dark chestnut, becoming blackish in the centre.

Adult female: Differs from the adult male in showing a spotted/streaked crown, hindneck and breast. Also, has barring to the upperside and most of the coverts, and the dark patch on the underparts is pale rufous with dense dark bars.

Juvenile: The pattern is distinctly different from that of the adult female. Neck and breast show fine dark scallops and pale fringes. The upperparts and coverts are warm brown with dark vermiculations, dark subterminal bands and pale fringes. Primaries (except outermost 1 or 2) with pale tips and dark vermiculations. As in other sandgrouse, the juvenile plumage is quickly lost.

1st-winter: See Spotted Sandgrouse.

Voice: The flight call is a characteristic, guttural *uit-kuerr; uit-kerre; uit-kerre-kerre; kuerr; kerre;* or similar.

Habitat and behaviour: Much as other sandgrouse but generally inhabits less dry areas than Spotted.

Range: Resident in a belt across C Africa, S Arabia to much of the Indian Subcontinent. Nomadic in the dry season.

Status: Accidental in Hungary: female obtained from a flock of Pallas's Sandgrouse in Aug 1863.

PALLAS'S SANDGROUSE   *Syrrhaptes paradoxus*   D **36**

L 30-41cm (12-16"). WS 63-78cm (25-31"). C Asia. Rare vagrant, mainly before the 20th century (periodically large irruptions).

Adult male: Distinguished from other sandgrouse by combination of extensive orange on the head; pale brownish upperparts and coverts, especially the former with coarse barring; black patch on the belly (smaller than in Black-bellied but larger than in Spotted); and in flight, rather uniformly pale upper– and underwings (primaries actually paler than rest of upperwing). At close range, diagnostic chestnut greater coverts and elongated outermost primary can be seen.

Adult female: Resembles the adult male but is duller, with dark spots on the sides of the breast and coverts, has streaked ear-coverts, shows a dark band across the lower throat and lacks male's bar across the breast.

Juvenile: Shows brownish-tinged breast with fine dark 'horseshoe-markings'. The upperparts and coverts are less barred, showing more V-shaped marks than the adult. Lacks the orange on the head, black necklace, chestnut greater coverts, and elongated outer primary and central tail feathers. The primaries differ from the adult much as in Spotted Sandgrouse. Juvenile plumage is moulted quickly.

1st-winter: Mostly like the adult, but the outer primaries are apparently usually retained, facilitating ageing in these cases.

Voice: Characteristic *quat* and *quet* and rolling *por-r-r* are given in flight.

Range: Breeds on the steppes of C Asia from approximately the Aral Sea to Mongolia and E USSR. Northern birds migrate south but generally do not winter far south of the southern limits of their breeding range. Large irruptions have occasionally been noted, when even breeding has taken place far outside its normal range (see below).

Status: In 19th century flocks periodically irrupted westwards into Europe, notably after heavy snow fall or where hard snow crust made it difficult for the birds to feed in their breeding area. Some of the largest invasions recorded were in May 1863, May 1888 and 1908, when parties of birds were widespread – reaching the Faeroes, British Isles, Channel Is, France, Belgium, Netherlands, Denmark, Norway, Sweden, Finland, Estonia, Latvia, East and West Germany, Poland (where flocks of up to 400 reported), Czechoslovakia, Switzerland, Austria, Hungary, Yugoslavia, Greece, Bulgaria, Rumania, Italy, and Spain.

In 1888 it was reported from many parts of the British Isles – small parties even reaching the Outer Hebrides, NW Ireland and Cornwall, and it was subsequently recorded breeding in Yorkshire 1888, Scotland 1888/9 and probably Suffolk 1888. Also occurred in at least 10 other years between 1859-1909. Also, nested or attempted to breed in Belgium (1889), Netherlands (1863, 1888), Denmark (many pairs bred Jutland 1888, some possibly nesting 1889), West Germany (1888), Poland, and Austria (possibly bred 1864).

Since the last invasion in May 1908, numbers have been few and widely scattered over Europe. The most recent mini-invasion was in 1969 (May-Dec), when a few were reported from Britain, Netherlands, Sweden and Finland. Also one record from Denmark in Jan 1972. Britain, Isle of May (two in May 1975) and Shetland (male, 19th May-4th June 1990*). Norway, Nord Trøndelag (July-Sept 1990*).

Family COLUMBIDAE   Doves and Pigeons

RUFOUS TURTLE DOVE   *Streptopelia orientalis*   B **37**

L 33-35cm (13.5"). Asia. Rare vagrant (mainly late autumn/winter).
All plumages: Obviously larger and heavier than Turtle Dove, with a slightly shorter primary projection.
Adult: Eastern subspecies *orientalis*: Generally looks distinctly darker than Turtle Dove. The forehead and usually the crown are grey, contrasting with a brown nape and hindneck (approximately same colour as mantle), whereas in Turtle, nape/hindneck are greyish like the rest of the head and clearly contrast with browner mantle. The dark bars on the side of the neck are typically 4-6 (Turtle has 3-4 relatively wider bars; but often difficult to judge). Note that both may show a bluish tinge to the pale patch surrounding the dark bars (normally the case in Rufous, seldom in Turtle). The breast is more brownish-pink, less lilac-tinged, and the colour of the breast extends further down than in Turtle. The belly and undertail-coverts are pale greyish-pinkish, not whitish as in Turtle.

The dark centres to the lesser and median coverts are normally extensive and diffuse and rounded at the tips. This creates a characteristic scaly appearance which is enhanced by usually pale tips. Normally the coverts appear contrastingly paler than the scapulars, and frequently there seem to be at least two pale wing-bars. Turtle shows clearcut, relatively small, triangular dark marks on the otherwise uniformly orange-brown coverts, not contrasting markedly with the scapulars and not showing pale bars. However, beware of juvenile Turtle moulting to 1st-winter, in which unmoulted juvenile coverts may resemble those of adult Rufous and often contrast with the newly moulted scapulars. A closer look should reveal some newly moulted and characteristically patterned coverts, though. The outer lesser, median and greater coverts are not contrastingly blue-grey to the carpal joint, as in most Turtle Doves, most obvious in flight. Unless the feathers are worn, the primaries usually show more distinct pale tips than in Turtle.

The back/rump are usually uniformly dark blue-grey, whereas most (but far from all) Turtle Doves show a lot of brown admixed. The pale tips to the tail-feathers (not central pair) are generally more greyish than in Turtle, but there is some overlap, and the difference is usually difficult to judge. The outermost feather usually shows some dark on the outer web, which is not normally the case in Turtle. Also, the central pair normally contrasts slightly less with the other rectrices than in Turtle.

Western subspecies *meena*: More similar to Turtle Dove than the nominate subspecies. Although most individuals are still quite distinctive, some require a closer scrutiny, and it is important to bear the following in mind. Slightly smaller than *orientalis*; tends to show more Turtle-like pattern on the lesser and median coverts (sometimes little different from less typically patterned Turtle Doves, and rarely even shows rather extensively blue-grey on the outer coverts, reaching the carpal); the colour of the breast is rarely very similar to that of Turtle; normally shows blue-grey only on the back; the belly and undertail-coverts are whitish, as in Turtle (slightly less extensive, though).

Juvenile: Easily separated from the adult by its paler and browner plumage, with fainter dark centres to the scapulars, coverts and tertials, also lacks distinct neck-patch. Extremely difficult to distinguish from juvenile Turtle Dove by plumage, and the following differences are slight and often require experience to be interpreted correctly. It is generally darker-looking, both above and below, most obvious in *orientalis*, in which the belly shows more or less the same pinkish-brown colour as the breast. The back and rump is usually tinged distinctly blue-grey, not at all in Turtle. The crown/nape is the same colour as the mantle, whereas in Turtle it is usually slightly paler and more greyish. Because of the normally darker underparts the pale throat tends to be more contrasting. The dark centres to the scapulars, coverts and tertials are often slightly darker with more contrasting pale tips than in Turtle. The tertials also have narrower and more clearcut rufous edges. The primaries show more sharply defined pale tips and edges. The greater primary coverts show no or very narrow pale tips, but generally rather broad ones in Turtle; there is overlap, though. Fortunately, new feathers appear very soon, facilitating identification.

1st-winter/-summer: Some are inseparable from the adult, whereas others retain some juvenile feathers, particularly the outer primaries, middle secondaries and some tail-feathers.

Voice: The song is a hoarse, usually four-syllabic, cooing *or-DOO doo-doo, hoo-hoo HOO hoaw*, repeated many times, reminiscent of Wood-pigeon and very different from the deep purring notes of Turtle Dove.

Range: Breeds in much of E, C and S Asia, west to approximately the Ural Mountains. The subspecies *meena* breeds in the westernmost part of the range. Northern populations are migratory, wintering in India, Burma, Japan and S China to Indo-China.

Status: Rare vagrant in Britain (8, Oct-Nov, Jan, May), Denmark (9 Oct-Mar, May), Norway (3), Sweden (8) Finland (6), Hungary (Nov 1985), Italy (Veneto 1901), and Greece.

Most of the records are from Oct-Feb. Individuals have occasionally wintered in Scandinavia, e.g. Norway (Feb-Mar 1978). Sweden (Dec 1976-Apr 1977; Feb-Apr 1985, reappearing 1985/1986, 1986/1987 and 1988/1989), and Finland (Jan-Mar 1985). Some of the records may relate to escapes, since it is kept in captivity in many places in Europe

LAUGHING DOVE *Streptopelia senegalensis*   B **37**

L 25-27cm (10"). Africa and SW Asia. A few records from other part of Europe, although status of these unclear.

Adult: Easily recognized. Resembles Collared Dove in general shape but is obviously smaller and much darker and more richly coloured, a

174

well as being more contrastingly patterned above/below. Has diagnostic neck pattern. In flight, note in particular the dark breast and underwing and dark upperside with deep blue-grey outer coverts of the inner wing when compared with Collared. Compared to Turtle Dove (more similar in general colour pattern), Laughing is even darker and shows distinctly shorter, more rounded wings and a longer tail (Collared Dove-like). The flight is also weaker.

Juvenile: Resembles the adult but is duller, and lacks the characteristic neck pattern. Inseparable from adult after the complete moult in the summer/autumn of the 1st year.

Voice: The song is a rapid, somewhat slurred, hollow cooing that initially rises and then falls, *do-do-dou-do-do- do, coou coo-coo-coo-coo-coo*, or similar.

Habitat and behaviour: Much like Collared Dove. Regularly found near human settlements, often behaving like feral pigeon.

Range: Resident in large parts of Africa, S Arabia, W Asia and the Indian Subcontinent. Range apparently expanding into Turkey and the Balkans. Vagrant in Crete, Cyprus and Morocco.

Status: Accidental in Finland (Nov 1969, June 1972, Oct 1987). Sweden (June 1979, May 1988, considered probable escape). Norway (Sept 1987*). France (Oct 1989*), Italy: Pantelleria (Aug 1974), Sicily (Nov 1985), Linosa Is (Apr 1987). Greece (3). Malta (several, as well as 6 singles in 1977). Some records perhaps relate to escapes.

Family CUCULIDAE   Cuckoos

BLACK-BILLED CUCKOO   *Coccyzus erythrophthalmus*   B **37**

L 27-31cm (10.5-12"). North America. Very rare vagrant (mainly Sept-Nov).

All plumages: Has distinctive shape most reminiscent of Great Spotted Cuckoo among European birds. Very similar to Yellow-billed Cuckoo.

Adult: Shows red orbital ring and small, distinct, greyish-white tips and blackish subterminal marks to the grey tail feathers, only visible from below (central pair are uniformly brownish).

1st-winter: Distinguished from the adult by its slightly narrower tail feathers with narrower and more diffuse whitish tips without blackish subterminal marks, and yellowish orbital ring. The edges to the primaries are also more rufous than in the adult. Also, in the autumn, the remiges are normally clearly less worn than in the adult, which usually moult these in the winter quarters.

Voice: The song, mainly heard in the breeding season and thus very unlikely to be heard in Europe, is a chuckling, three-to five-note *diu-chu-chu-chu*, or *un-du-du-du* with a characteristic hollow, and slightly nasal tone. A rattling *cururururu* is sometimes heard.

Behaviour: Rather secretive, usually keeps to dense vegetation.

Range: Breeds in C and E North America. Winters in NW South America. Vagrant in Greenland.

Status: Accidental in Europe (late Sept-early Nov, peak in Oct). Iceland (2nd record in Oct 1982), British Isles (12), France (July 1886), Denmark (Oct 1970), West Germany (Oct 1952), Italy (Toscana 1858, Veneto 1969), and the Azores (3).

YELLOW-BILLED CUCKOO   *Coccyzus americanus*   C 37

L 28-32cm (11-12.5"). North America. Rare vagrant (especially Oct), more often recorded than Black-billed Cuckoo.

All plumages: Closely resembles corresponding plumages of Black-billed Cuckoo. Best distinguishing characters are bill colour and tail pattern. In Yellow-billed, most of the lower mandible is yellow. In Black-billed the basal part of the lower mandible is pale bluish-grey. The bill is also slightly heavier and a little more decurved than in Black-billed. The tail feathers (except the central pair) show much more white than in Black-billed, and are blackish (adult) or dark grey (juvenile/1st-winter) rather than medium grey as in Black-billed. Furthermore, the upperparts are generally slightly more greyish and the throat/breast whiter than in Black-billed, but this may not always be apparent. The primaries and greater primary coverts show a contrasting rufous patch, sometimes, however, this may only be obvious in flight. Adult Black-billed does not normally show any contrasting rufous on its primaries, while young birds often do, but rufous generally less contrasting than in Yellow-billed because of browner upperparts.

Adult: Has yellow orbital ring unlike adult (but like juvenile/1st-winter) Black-billed Cuckoo. Tail feathers are blackish with broad, white tips.

1st-winter: Differs from adult mainly by the dark grey inner part to the tail feathers. Also, the white tips are slightly more diffuse, and the tail feathers are slightly narrower than in the adult. Also, shows less worn remiges (see Black-billed).

Voice: Usually silent outside breeding season, when *cucucucucucu keru-keru-kerueck-kerueck-kerueck-kerueck*or similar notes are heard. The first are hard, rapidly repeated notes and the second part slower.

Behaviour: Like Black-billed Cuckoo, above.

Range: Overlaps with Black-billed Cuckoo but extends further to the S and W but not quite so far N. Winters in South America, generally further S than Black-billed. Vagrant to Greenland and Morocco.

Status: Rare vagrant, majority occurring in mid Sept-mid Nov. Iceland (3rd in Oct 1981), British Isles (53, mid Sept-Dec, peak in Oct), France (Nov 1924, Oct 1957), Belgium (Oct 1874), Denmark (Oct 1936), Norway (Oct 1978, also one found on board ship in late Feb 1982), Italy (8), Sicily (Nov 1932), and the Azores (20+).

The Yellow-billed is more frequently recorded in Europe than the Black-billed. In autumn many birds apparently migrate straight from New England to South America and then easily become caught up in fast-moving NE bound depressions. Black-billed Cuckoos usually take a more westerly route and are less prone to being driven off-course by Atlantic depressions.

Family STRIGIDAE   Owls

MARSH OWL   *Asio capensis*   B 38

L 29-31cm (12"). WS 82-99cm (34"). Africa, nearest in Morocco. Rare vagrant in Portugal and Spain.

Adult: Differs from its European counterpart, the Short-eared Owl, by e.g. distinctly smaller size; much darker and almost uniformly coloured crown, neck, upper breast, upperparts and coverts; barred underparts

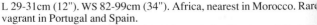

176

and dark eyes. In flight, further identified by the darker secondaries above, contrasting more strongly with the broad, pale tips to the same and with the pale orange-brown patch on the primaries.

Juvenile: Clearly different from the adult, being heavily barred on the upperparts and coverts and almost unmarked below; the whole plumage is very downy. It is moulted soon after fledging – thus it is very unlikely to be encountered in Europe unless breeding.

1st-winter: After the partial post-juvenile moult has been completed it closely resembles the adult. Some strongly barred coverts (particularly outer greaters) may be retained. The secondaries appear to be more distinctly and more densely barred, but this requires more research.

Voice: Harsh cries, *kcheeow*, somewhat reminiscent of a coarse Barn Owl or screaming cat. Also (probably the song) a double, harsh trumpeting *aah-aah*, not unlike a distant Canada Goose.

Habitat and behaviour: Much as Short-eared Owl, but favours marshy areas more than Short-eared.

Range: Nearest breeding occurs in a restricted area in Morocco, where it is apparently resident or dispersive. Also, found scattered over large parts of Africa S of Sahara, mainly in the south; also in Madagascar. Vagrant in Canary Is.

Status: Rare vagrant in Portugal and Spain. There are a number of autumn-winter records from the Spanish Marismas, e.g. 9 birds seen or collected at Casa Vieja in Oct-Nov 1868, Nov 1870, and Dec 1873.

Family CAPRIMULGIDAE   Nightjars

EGYPTIAN NIGHTJAR   *Caprimulgus aegyptius*   B **38**

L 24-26cm (10"). WS 58-68cm (25"). N Africa and W Asia. Rare vagrant mainly to S Europe.

Adult: Resembles Nightjar, but is slightly smaller and much paler, without the bold dark streaks on the crown, mantle and scapulars, and has less barred underparts (especially undertail- coverts). The secondaries and tail are pale with widely spaced, narrow, dark bars. In Nightjar they are darker-looking, with denser, rather diffuse, rufescent barring, except for central pair of rectrices, which are more like in Egyptian. The primaries show whitish bars below (rufous-tinged in Nightjar). In flight, the Kestrel-like contrast between darker outer wing and rather uniformly paler coverts above is characteristic (Nightjar looks more uniformly dark with paler panel on central inner wing). Never shows white patches on the primaries as in male Nightjar. The above should separate Egyptian from an anomalously pale Nightjar.

Juvenile: Resembles the adult, but is less strongly patterned on the upperparts and coverts and very poorly marked on the underparts.

1st-winter: Some outer greater coverts and sometimes other coverts are often retained. These are more worn and bleached with less distinct dark markings than the new coverts.

Voice: The territorial call, given in spring by the male, is a fast hollow, wooden *kow-kow-kow-kow-kow-kow-kow-kow- kow-kow...*, the series repeated at short intervals.

Habitat and behaviour: A desert or semi-desert species, but vagrants could turn up anywhere. Behaviour similar to Nightjar.

Range: Breeds in N Africa and W Asia. Winters in Africa S of the Sahara. Vagrant in Cyprus.

Status: Rare vagrant in Europe. Majority of records are from Italy (*c.* 20) and Malta (14, Mar-May). Fewer elsewhere: Britain (June 1883, June 1984), Denmark (May-June 1983), West Germany (Heligoland, June 1875), and Sweden (May 1972).

COMMON NIGHTHAWK *Chordeiles minor* B **38**

L 23-25cm (9.5"). WS 59-68cm (25"). North and Central America. Accidental in N Europe and Azores (Sept-Oct).

All plumages: Recalls Nightjar but has slightly longer, more pointed wings and an appreciably shorter and distinctly notched tail. The remiges are unbarred, and there is a more prominent and more proximally placed white band across the primaries than in male Nightjar. It is basically slightly darker than Nightjar, with a usually obviously larger, pale throat patch. Also, the underparts are more coarsely barred than in Nightjar. On close inspection, the plumage is actually clearly different in most respects from Nightjar. When perched, the wings reach approximately to or beyond the tail tip, in Nightjar they fall well short of the tip of the tail.

ad.　　juv.

outer tail -feather

Adult male: Shows a white subterminal tail-band (not on central pair of rectrices) and a usually white throat patch.

Adult female: Resembles the adult male, but lacks a white tail-bar and has a slightly narrower, sometimes pale buffish primary-bar and a generally buffish throat patch.

Juvenile: Resembles the adult female, but is basically paler and less strongly patterned, with barred throat patch. The remiges show distinct, narrow, clearcut pale tips unlike the adult. The dark bars on the outer tail-feathers are all of approximately the same width, unlike the adult female, which usually shows a broader dark terminal bar (see figure). In the hand, the pattern of scapulars, coverts (mainly median and rear lessers) and tertials differs clearly from that of adult (see figure).

juv.　　ad.

median
covert

tertial

Similar to the adult after the apparently complete post-juvenile moult, which usually takes place in the winter quarters.

Voice: The territorial call, given in the breeding season, is a metallic, nasal, buzzy *pee* or, differently transcribed, *beerp*, repeated approximately every third second for lengthy periods.

Behaviour: Basically like Nightjar, but becomes active earlier in the evening (usually well before dark) and is more often seen flying around in broad daylight, often hawking insects in higher air space than Nightjar.

Range: Breeds in much of North and Central America, except for the most northern parts, and in the Carribean. Winters mainly in South America. Vagrant in Greenland.

Status: Mainly recorded in the British Isles (14, Sept-Oct), especially on the Isles of Scilly. Other records are from Iceland (1), the Faeroes (Oct 1955), and near the Azores (Sept 1966, Oct 1968).

Family APODIDAE Swifts

NEEDLE-TAILED SWIFT *Hirundapus caudacutus* B 38

L 19-20cm (8"). WS 50-53cm (20"). Asia. Accidental (mainly May-July).

All plumages: Obviously larger than Swift, with a rather thick-set, cigar-shaped body, shortish, slightly rounded tail and characteristic wing-shape (like 'Gurkha knives' when gliding). The prominent white throat, diagnostic white U on the rear underparts and contrastingly pale patch on the mantle/back further make it unmistakable. Under optimum viewing conditions, note white marks on inner tertials and spiny projections to the tail-feathers.

Adult: Shows prominent white forehead and anterior lores, also blue or green gloss to the flight-feathers, coverts and tail when fresh.

Juvenile: Duller than the adult, with little gloss to wings and tail. and a less contrastingly pale mantle/back and grey-brown forehead and lores.

Subsequent immature plumages: The juvenile plumage is retained throughout the 1st winter. In the spring/summer of the 2nd year, the plumage is more like the adult, but flight-feathers are still juvenile and heavily worn. The flight-feathers are moulted in the autumn of the 2nd to early in the 3rd year, after which the plumage resembles the adult.

Range: Breeds in C and E Asia. Northern populations migrate to winter in Australia and Tasmania; southern populations are resident.

Status: Accidental in Britain (7, May-July); Ireland, Cape Clear, Co Cork (June 1964); Norway (May 1968); Finland (May 1933, Apr 1990*); and Malta (Nov 1971).

CHIMNEY SWIFT *Chaetura pelagica* A 38

L 12-13cm (5"). WS 28-30cm (11.5"). North America. A few autumn records (all since 1982).

Adult: Unmistakable. A small swift with grey-brown plumage, slightly paler on the throat and upper breast. Has distinctive silhouette rather similar to Needle-tailed Swift — also shares spiny projections to the tips of the tail feathers with that species.

Juvenile: Difficult to tell from the adult but shows very narrow, distinct whitish tips to the inner primaries, secondaries and tertials.

Range: Breeds in E North America. Winters in South America. Vagrant to Greenland.

Status: Accidental in Britain: Porthgwarra, Cornwall (two, between 21st-27th Oct 1982); Isles of Scilly (one, 4th-9th Nov 1986); Grampound, Cornwall (one, 18th Oct 1987).

PACIFIC SWIFT *Apus pacificus* A 38

L 17-18cm (6.75"). WS 48-54cm (20"). Asia. Only one record.

Adult: Distinctly larger than Swift (but smaller than Alpine Swift), with proportionately even longer wings, and a longer tail with a deeper fork. There is a distinct white band across the rump. The whitish throat-patch is more prominent than in Swift, and the upperside and under-parts typically show distinct paler fringes, visible at close to moderate range. See also White-rumped Swift, below.

Juvenile: Differs from adult mainly in showing all fresh plumage, when adult is worn and often moulting. In the hand, narrow whitish tips to inner primaries and secondaries can be seen. The juvenile flight-feathers are apparently not moulted until the autumn/winter of the 2nd year, so eventually are extremely worn – much more so than in the adult.
Voice: Calls resemble those of Swift, but are usually harsher.
Range: Breeds in C and E Asia. Northern populations winter in SE Asia to Australia.
Status: Accidental in Britain (North Sea), one captured 19th June 1981 on Leman Bank gas platform – taken ashore and released in Norfolk.

WHITE-RUMPED SWIFT   *Apus caffer*   R Br **38**

L 14cm (5.5"). WS 34-36cm (13.5") Breeds Africa and locally in S Spain. Accidental elsewhere in Europe.
Adult: Similar to Pacific Swift, but much smaller and lacks pale scaling. Also, shows whitish tips to secondaries. However, beware of partially albinistic Swift. In flight, the long, deeply forked tail is frequently held closed, appearing long and pointed. See Little Swift, below.
Juvenile: Very similar to the adult but is reported to show narrow, pale tips to the primaries and coverts on the leading edge of the wing.
Voice: Includes a comparatively low-pitched but still shrill, harsh *pree pree-pree-preep-pree-pree.*
Range: Breeds in Africa (S of the Sahara), also locally in small numbers in S Spain, where it was discovered as recently as 1964. Also found breeding in Morocco in 1968. The Spanish population is migratory, usually arriving in late May and departing in Sep-Oct, although there are a few winter records.
Status: Accidental in Finland: Kestiliä, near Oulu (18th Nov 1968). Norway: Jomfruland, Telemark (18th May 1984); Eftang, Larvik (two, 15th June 1986). Malta (25th May 1975). Gibraltar (9th July 1988).

LITTLE SWIFT   *Apus affinis*   B **38**

L 12cm (4.7"). WS 34-35cm (13.5"). Africa and S Asia. Accidental in both N and S Europe (May-Nov).
Adult: Smallest swift, even slightly smaller and more compact than White-rumped. Has rather squarely cut-off tail and shows a distinctly larger white rump-patch than in White-rumped.
Juvenile: Very similar to the adult and generally not separable in the field. Shows less gloss to the upperparts, narrow paler fringes to the underparts, median and greater coverts, and narrow pale tips to the secondaries and inner primaries. The pale fringes quickly wear off.
Subsequent immature plumages: Only tentatively separable from adult in 1st winter/summer by the different timing of the moult of the flight-feathers, mainly in winter/early spring to summer/early autumn in 1st-year birds and late spring/summer to winter in adults.
Voice: A rapid, high-pitched twittering series of notes.
Range: Nearest breeding in Morocco, Algeria, Tunisia and in the Middle East. Also, found over much of Africa (S of the Sahara) and S to SE Asia. Resident over most of its range.
Status: Accidental in the British Isles (9, May-Nov), Sweden (June 1979, Nov 1982, Aug 1985, Oct 1988), Italy (2), Malta (8), and Spain (5).

Family ALCEDINIDAE Kingfishers

WHITE-BREASTED KINGFISHER *Halcyon smyrnensis*   A **39**
L 26-28cm (10.5"). Middle East to Asia. Accidental in Greece.
Adult: Unmistakable, large kingfisher with bright red bill and mainly brown, white and brilliant blue plumage. In flight, shows large white patch at base of primaries.
Juvenile: Slightly duller than the adult, often showing some dark markings on the breast. The bill is paler with some dusky markings.
1st-winter: Hard to tell from adult; more worn flight-feathers is a clue.
Voice: Very vocal in the breeding season. Loud, clear, laughing *tiy-dy-y-y-y-y-y-y-y-y-y*, slowing down and falling in pitch at the end (territorial call?), and a slower, more hoarse *tiy-dy-dy-dy-dy-dy* (alarm?) are often heard. Also gives short, sharp *kit*.
Habitat and behaviour: Favours wet areas with some bushes and trees, but also found in drier areas, often in forests. Often seen sitting on prominent perch, e.g. in trees, on telegraph wires or poles etc. Only rarely plunge-dives for fish.
Range: Breeds in S and SW Turkey eastwards to E China, Philippines and W Indonesia. Resident throughout range. Regarded only as accidental visitor to Cyprus, but 9 sightings between late Jan and early May 1987.
Status: Accidental in Greece (3rd record in Mar 1987).

PIED KINGFISHER *Ceryle rudis*   A **39**
L 24-26cm (9.5"). Africa, Middle East and Asia. Accidental in Greece and Poland.
Adult: Unmistakable, large kingfisher, with complex black and white pattern and slight crest. The male shows two more or less complete black bands across the breast, the female only one, broken, band.
Juvenile: Resembles the adult female but generally shows a complete breast band and some dark markings on the throat.
1st-winter: Usually not safely separated from the adult of respective sex.
Voice: Various shrill, twittering notes, e.g. *cheerry*, usually repeated, and sharp *cheek* are given.
Habitat and behaviour: Lakes, ponds, rivers etc. Dives for fish after hovering or from a perch.
Range: Breeds in Africa (S of Sahara), W Asia (nearest in SW Turkey) and from Pakistan to E China. Resident. Regarded as scarce and irregular winter visitor to Cyprus (only 6 recent records Oct-Jan).
Status: Accidental in Greece: 5th record concerned a single bird seen on several dates in port of Chios (winter 1986/87). One record from Poland (Aug 1859).

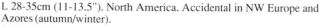

BELTED KINGFISHER *Ceryle alcyon*   A **39**
L 28-35cm (11-13.5"). North America. Accidental in NW Europe and Azores (autumn/winter).
Adult: Easily identified by its large size, blue-grey and white plumage and full crest. The female shows a rufous band below the blue-grey breast band and some rufous on the flanks.
Juvenile: Differs from the adult of its respective sex in having rufous-mottled upper breast band. Male also shows a rufous patch on flank.
1st-winter: Often part of juvenile plumage retained, enabling identification.

Voice: A loud, rattling *ky-r-r-r-r-r-r-r-r-r-r*.

Habitat and behaviour: Much as Pied Kingfisher.

Range: Breeds in most of North America (except northernmost parts). Winters along the coasts and inland in the southern areas, some south to Central and N South America and the West Indies. Vagrant in Greenland.

Status: Accidental in Britain: (Cornwall Nov 1908, Nov 1979-Aug 1980); Ireland: Co. Mayo (Nov 1978-Feb 1979), Co. Down (12th Oct 1980), Co. Clare (Oct 1984-Dec 1985) and Co. Tipperary (Feb-Mar 1985). Also, in Iceland (Sept 1901). Netherlands (Dec 1899), and the Azores (Mar 1899).

Family MEROPIDAE   Bee-eaters

BLUE-CHEEKED BEE-EATER   *Merops superciliosus*   B **39**

L 27-31cm (10.5-12"). WS 46-49cm (18.5"). Africa, Middle East, Asia. Accidental in both N and S Europe (Apr- Sept).

Adult: Similar to Bee-eater, but if seen reasonably well, easily told by its brilliant green plumage with a pale blue forehead and stripes bordering black face-mask. Also has yellow and rufous throat patch. Note that juvenile Bee-eater is more greenish than the adult. When seen from below in flight, best distinguished from Bee-eater by its throat pattern (including lack of black band across lower throat), more rufous underwing, distinctly narrower dark bar on the secondaries and longer central tail feathers.

Juvenile: Slightly duller than the adult, without the pale blue on the head and with the rufous of the throat extending onto the ear-coverts. The iris is dark brown (bright red in adult), and the central tail feathers are not elongated.

1st-winter: Recognizable from the adult as long as there are some retained juvenile feathers, e.g. central tail feathers left, or as long as the iris remains browner.

Voice: Similar to Bee-eater, but more shrill and not quite as soft, *greep* or *diripp*. Also *kyp*.

Range: Patchily distributed in NW and W Africa, the Middle East eastwards to Kazakhstan (USSR) and NW India. Also in SE Africa and on Madagascar, sometimes treated as a separate species (under the name of *M. superciliosus*, northern species then called *M. persicus*). Scarce passage migrant in Cyprus (mainly late Mar-May, rarer autumn).

Status: Accidental in Britain (7, June-Sept), France (4), Netherlands (Sept 1961), Denmark (June 1989*), Sweden (Aug 1961, July 1968, May 1985), Italy (9), Yugoslavia (May 1953), Greece (6), Bulgaria (May 1988), Malta (10, Apr-May, Sept), and Gibraltar (Sept 1973).

Family PICIDAE Woodpeckers

NORTHERN FLICKER *Colaptes auratus*   A **39**
L 28-35cm (11-14"). Mainly North America. Accidental, perhaps only ship-assisted.
All plumages: Unmistakable. Near size of Green Woodpecker, with pale brown upperparts, coverts and tertials with coarse, blackish barring, and black spots on underparts. Has broad, black breast patch, large white rump patch, yellow to pinkish-orange underwing and undertail.
Adult male: Eastern populations show largely greyish-pinkish face and neck with a black moustachial stripe and a red band across the nape.
Adult female: Lacks male's black moustachial stripe.
Juvenile: Resembles the adult male but shows less-black markings.
1st-winter: The primaries are new and contrast slightly with the more worn secondaries. The iris is more grey-brown than in the adult (deep reddish-brown). Most individuals have attained adult iris colour in Oct, however, some not until Dec or even later.
Voice: Includes loud *wek-wek-wek-wek-wek...* and other loud, somewhat squeaky calls.
Range: Breeds over most of North America, on the E coast as far north as Labrador and Newfoundland. Also in Central America and on Cuba. Northern populations are migratory. Frequently noted in weather-related 'ship falls' in the western N Atlantic.
Status: Accidental in Europe. Ireland, Co Cork (13th Oct 1962), one survived an Atlantic crossing aboard a ship without being handled and later seen to fly ashore (one of ten or more flickers which landed on board on 7th-8th Oct 1962, during a crossing from New York to Southampton). Scotland: Caithness (corpse found July 1981 – presumably bird died on ship outside European limits, later brought ashore). One other record, Denmark (18th May 1972).

YELLOW-BELLIED SAPSUCKER *Sphyrapicus varius*   A **39**
L 19-20cm (7.5"). North America. Only three records.
Adult male: Unmistakable, with red forehead, crown and throat and black and white stripes on the head. The red throat patch is framed in black, the black forming a prominent black gorget. Also, has white-mottled mantle, broad white stripe on the coverts, and pale yellowish underparts with streaked/barred flanks.
Adult female: Resembles the adult male, but lacks red on the throat and often also on the forehead/crown.
Juvenile: Easily told from the adult by its mostly brownish head, neck and underparts with some paler mottling. Much of the juvenile plumage is usually retained through the autumn. Sexing is possible when the final throat colour has started to develop.
Range: Breeds in N USA/S Canada and W USA. Winters mainly in the S parts of USA to Central America and the West Indies.
Status: Accidental in Britain: Isles of Scilly (1st-year male, 26th Sept-6th Oct 1975). Ireland: Cape Clear, Co. Cork (1st-year female, 16th-19th Oct 1988). Iceland (one in SE, 5th June 1961).

Family TYRANNIDAE New World Flycatchers

EASTERN PHOEBE *Sayornis phoebe*   A **51**

L 17-18cm (7"). North America. Accidental in Britain in spring 1987* – 2 sightings.

Adult: A rather large, relatively long-tailed flycatcher with brownish-grey upperside, slightly darker on the head. The underside is whitish to dull yellowish (autumn), usually with a darker wash on the breast, especially at the sides. Further characterized by the lack of a pale eye-ring, the blackish lower mandible and the lack of or relatively indistinct wing-bars.

1st-winter: Similar to the adult, but the outermost one or a few greater coverts and the tertials are usually retained from juvenile and are distinctly buff-tipped. The rectrices are as a rule more pointed than in the adult.

Voice: The song is a characteristic, emphatic *fee-bee*, the second syllable often harsh and slightly vibrant; this is the origin of the bird's English name. It calls with a rather loud, slightly metallic *tsyp*.

Behaviour: Normally sits in a rather upright position on a prominent perch, from which it makes regular sorties to catch insects in the air. Has a characteristic habit of frequently pumping its tail.

Range: Breeds in E USA and in Canada. Winters in the southern part of the breeding range south to Mexico.

Status: Accidental in Britain: Slapton, Devon (22nd Apr 1987*) and same or another on Lundy Island (24th-25th Apr 1987*).

ACADIAN FLYCATCHER *Empidonax virescens*   A **51**

L 14-16cm (6"). North America. One record.

Adult: Characterized by rather greenish upperparts; distinct pale eye-ring; two distinct pale wing-bars; and a long, broad bill with convex edges and all yellowish lower mandible. It shows a whitish throat and breast, the latter often with a darker wash, mainly at the sides. When fresh, the underparts are tinged pale yellowish. The legs are grey.

Juvenile: Plumage is typically mottled above. Unlikely in Europe.

1st-winter: Similar to the adult but generally shows more buffish wing-bars (use with care!) and has less worn remiges (adults usually moult all or some of the flight-feathers in their winter quarters).

Voice: The song (unlikely to be heard outside breeding season) is a distinctive, explosive *peet-see*. The call is a characteristic *peet*, like the first note of the song.

Note: There are several extremely similar *Empidonax* flycatchers in North America that could possibly reach Europe as vagrants. Most are best identified by their songs; the song and calls of Acadian are diagnostic. The most similar in plumage is the Yellow-bellied Flycatcher *E. flaviventris*. This generally shows more yellowish underparts, particularly on the throat and breast (the latter often with darker wash as in Acadian); also has a slightly shorter bill, wings (notably primary projection) and tail. It is most safely distinguished by different wing formula: 10th primary > 6th in Acadian, < 6th in Yellow-bellied (counted descendantly); and 2, sometimes 3, emarginations in Acadian: 3, often 4 in Yellow-bellied. See e.g. Whitney and Kaufman (1985-1986) Kaufman (1990) and Pyle et al. (1987) for fuller details.

Range: Breeds in E USA. Winters in Central and South America.
Status: Accidental in Iceland (4th Nov 1967).

Family ALAUDIDAE Larks

BAR-TAILED DESERT LARK *Ammomanes cincturus* A **40**

L 15cm (6"). Africa, Middle East and W Asia. Accidental in S Europe.
Adult: A small, pale and rather plain lark. It differs from the small European larks by the plain upperparts. The breast is unmarked or very indistinctly streaked. The tail is pale rufous with blackish central feathers and blackish tips to the rest. In flight, the remiges and primary-coverts can be seen to be pale rufous, with blackish tips to the outer primaries (secondaries mostly grey-brown in E subspecies, though). The flight is characteristically unsteady, floppy, and the wings are relatively short, broad and rounded, also the tail is rather short.
Juvenile: Similar to the adult but shows indistinct dark subterminal markings to the coverts and tertials. Indistinguishable from the adult by plumage once the complete post-juvenile moult has been completed, usually when very young.
Voice: The song is usually a repeated double note, e.g. *tsi-tuuee* or *t' syy-ii'*. Sings either during undulating song-flight or from the ground or a perch. The flight calls include a soft *jupp*, a slightly metallic, buzzing *djyrrt*, somewhat reminiscent of one of the calls of Lesser Short-toed Lark, and a rather soft *djyrrt*.
Habitat: Inhabits sandy desert areas but as a vagrant could turn up in almost any open habitat.
Note: Desert Lark *A. deserti*, with much the same breeding range as Bar-tailed, has strayed to Cyprus (Apr 1973), and could reach Europe. It is appreciably larger than Bar-tailed, with proportionately larger bill, which is orangey on the basal part of lower mandible (pale pinkish in Bar-tailed). Although geographically very variable, the throat/upper breast is whitish with diffuse streaks on breast, and the rest of the underparts usually more pinkish– or rufous-buff, whereas Bar-tailed shows whitish throat and belly and frequently buffish breast/flanks, and the breast is unstreaked or very indistinctly streaked. Desert usually has rather grey-brown centres to the tertials, while in most Bar-tailed these are pale rufous (some overlap). The tail of Desert is never uniformly pale rufous with a clearcut, narrow blackish terminal bar.
Range: Breeds in N Africa, including Sahara, in the Middle East, Arabia and from Iran to Pakistan. Mainly resident or dispersive.
Status: Accidental in Italy (Molise 1972, Sicily Mar 1975), and Malta (7, Feb-May, Sept).

HOOPOE LARK *Alaemon alaudipes* B **40**

L 18-20cm (7.5"). Africa, Middle East and W Asia. Rare vagrant to Mediterranean.
Adult: An unmistakable, large, slender lark with long, decurved bill and long, strikingly pale legs. It has uniformly grey-brown to more rufous upperparts, bold head pattern and spotted breast. In flight, its striking black-and-white wing-and-tail pattern are obvious.

Juvenile: Shows pale fringes and dark subterminal marks from forehead to uppertail-coverts and on coverts and tertials; also has poorly marked breast. The bill is slightly shorter and less decurved.

This plumage is lost soon after fledging, through a complete moult, after which it is usually indistinguishable from the adult. However, some retain some remiges, rectrices and coverts, which enables ageing.
Voice: The distinctive song consists of whistles of different pitch, e.g. *hue hue hue kyrrrreeee ee ee chu-chu-chu-chu chu chu chu uu uu uue*. The end of the song is often delivered in a short song-flight, with the bird springing up into the air and exposing its striking wing and tail pattern, then dropping down on folded wings. The flight call is a rather low-pitched *grruit*.
Habitat and behaviour: Prefers the same sandy habitat as Bar-tailed Desert Lark. It is capable of running very fast.
Range: The range coincides largely with Bar-tailed Desert Lark's, but is more extensive particularly in Arabia and W Asia. Resident or dispersive, mainly in response to severe weather conditions.
Status: Accidental in Greece, Italy (Toscana 1965), and Malta (17, mostly Oct-Nov, also Apr-May, July-Aug and Dec).

DUPONT'S LARK *Chersophilus duponti* R Br **40**

L 18cm (7"). Breeds locally in Spain. Also in N Africa. Accidental elsewhere in Europe.
Adult: Somewhat reminiscent of Skylark, but easily distinguished by distinctive jizz with long, slightly decurved bill, rather small-looking head with no crest, plump body and rather short and narrow-looking tail. It often adopts a rather upright posture. There is also usually a faint pale median crown stripe. May possibly be confused with Crested Lark with the crest folded or moulting. The bill is longer and more decurved than in European Crested Larks but close to some Asiatic and North African birds. The upperside is more heavily streaked than in Crested Lark, which also lacks the pale crown stripe. In fresh plumage (autumn), the upperside and wings are distinctly scaly.
Juvenile: The upperside is paler than in adult with contrasting blackish subterminal spots and distinct whitish tips, producing a white-spotted appearance. The dark markings on the breast are clearly different from the adult: brownish centres, darker subterminal marks and narrow pale fringes; pattern less strong and more spotty than in the adult. The juvenile plumage is lost quickly after fledging through a complete moult, after which the plumage is indistinguishable from adult.
Voice: The distinctive song consists of clear whistles, mixed with guttural, nasal notes, e.g. *HUU HEE trueeduee grrdu-EE*. It is given in flight or from the ground or a perch. The calls include a subdued soft '*hue*' and an equally subdued '*grryt*'.
Habitat and behaviour: Breeds in dry open areas with scattered, low vegetation. It is very secretive and avoids an approaching intruder by running away, rather than flying off.
Range: Resident in the E half of Spain, where locally rather common; a census in spring 1988 estimated a minimum of 7,000-8,000 pairs, *c.* 70% in the Iberian system highlands and 26% in the Ebro Valley. Also locally in N Africa. Has bred in Portugal in 19th century, no records since.

Status: Accidental in France (3+ records in 19th century, only one since, Crau, Bouches-du-Rhône in 1915), Italy (Toscana 1900, Puglia 1962), and Malta (Nov 1901).

BIMACULATED LARK *Melanocorypha bimaculata* A **40**

L 16-17cm (6.5"). Asia and Middle East, nearest breeding C Turkey. Accidental.

Adult: Very similar to marginally larger Calandra Lark. Tends to have a slightly larger bill, also noticeably shorter wings/tail, giving a more front-heavy appearance when standing. The supercilium is whiter and more prominent and ear-coverts more rufous and more contrastingly patterned, with a more pronounced dark eye-stripe and more distinct white patch in the lower anterior corner. There is much overlap. It is easily distinguished in flight, when less contrastingly dark remiges above, lacking white trailing edge, and broadly white-tipped tail without white edges (see figure) are obvious (but see juvenile), the underwing is also paler because of paler remiges (still looking dark), and shorter wings/tail are now more apparent than when seen on the ground.

lated   Calandra
        Lark

eft half of tail

Juvenile: Easily distinguished from the adult, by e.g. more contrastingly patterned upperparts, coverts and tertials. Most of the upperparts show blackish centres, warm brownish edges and whitish tips. The coverts, tertials and central tail-feathers have brown centres, blackish subterminal bands and whitish fringes. Distinguished from other juvenile larks except Calandra by, e.g. the usually distinct, large dark patches on the sides of the neck (paler than in adult, though). Told from juvenile Calandra by the wing and tail pattern, which is basically as in the respective adult, although in juvenile Calandra, the pale tips to the secondaries and inner primaries are narrower and less distinct than in the adult. Juvenile plumage is moulted soon after fledging, after which the plumage is indistinguishable from adult.

Voice: The song and calls are very similar to those of Calandra Lark. With experience it can be appreciated that the song is slightly less harsh, hard and varied than Calandra's. Also the calls are slightly less harsh. Sings both in flight and from the ground or a perch.

Range: Breeds in the highlands from C Turkey, eastwards to Afghanistan and Tarbagatai (USSR). At least partly migratory, many wintering in Arabia to NW India. Vagrant in Cyprus (Mar-Apr).

Status: Accidental in the British Isles (May 1962, Oct 1975, June 1976), Sweden (May 1982, Dec 1983), Finland (Jan 1960), and Italy (Toscana 1919, Sicily Oct 1978).

WHITE-WINGED LARK *Melanocorypha leucoptera* B **40**

L 18cm (7"). USSR. Rare vagrant.

Adult male: Typically shows a rufous crown (finely streaked) and rear ear-coverts. Has whitish underparts with rufous on the breast sides (more or less streaked), and is comparatively pale grey-brown above with moderately heavy streaking. The wing pattern is diagnostic, showing rufous lesser coverts and primary coverts, contrasting blackish outer primaries and a very broad, white trailing edge to the secondaries and inner primaries. From below, the wing looks whitish with a dark bar on the central inner wing and dark outer primaries. The wings are comparatively long and narrow-looking, the effect enhanced by the broad, white trailing edges.

Adult female: Differs from the adult male mainly in distinctly streaked crown and ear-coverts with little or no rufous, and more distinctly streaked breast/flanks without rufous on breast sides. May show only little rufous on the wings, especially on the lesser and median coverts.

Juvenile: Shows same basic pattern as juveniles of other similar larks (see Bimaculated Lark, p. 187) and is thus easily told from the adult. Readily distinguished from other juvenile larks by the broad, white trailing edge to the secondaries and inner primaries.

Indistinguishable from adult by plumage after the complete post-juvenile moult, which takes place rather soon after fledging.

Voice: The song resembles that of Skylark, but is slower, more deliberate, with more pauses and variations, and it is less continuously and monotonously flowing. Song delivered in flight, from the ground or a perch. The flight calls include a rather harsh *tcher-ee* and a softer, more piping *tser-lee*. Also a thin *sit-sit-sit*.

Habitat: Favours dry, grassy areas.

Range: Breeds on the steppes of Kazakhstan (USSR). Winters chiefly in S USSR and neighbouring areas, mainly S of the breeding range.

Status: Rare vagrant in Europe. Britain (5, 2 each in Aug and Nov and 1 in Oct), Norway (Oct 1961, Oct 1972), Finland (June 1971), Poland (Mar 1932, Oct 1975, Aug 1978), West Germany (Heligoland, Aug 1881, June 1886), Czechoslovakia (Feb 1899), Austria (Apr 1910), Switzerland (Nov 1924), Italy (8, Oct-Mar), Yugoslavia, Greece (3), Bulgaria and Malta (1).

BLACK LARK *Melanocorypha yeltoniensis* B 40

L 19-20cm (7.5"). USSR. Accidental.

All plumages: Largest and heaviest lark occurring in Europe. Has robust bill and rather broad, rounded wings.

Adult male summer: Unmistakable, all-black plumage with some narrow, pale fringes.

Adult male winter: Shows broad, pale fringes to much of the plumage – generally most obvious on crown/nape, upperparts and often on breast.

Adult female: In worn plumage, more heavily patterned above/below than any European lark. Note in particular heavy markings on the breast/flanks, undertail-coverts and belly. In fresh plumage, the dark markings above/below are more obscured, and it may then look very poorly marked, especially above. The upperparts are decidedly greyish-tinged when fresh. In flight, shows dark underwing-coverts and axillaries but no white in wings/tail.

Juvenile: Plumage basically as in juveniles of other similar larks (see Bimaculated Lark, p. 187). Lack of pale outer tail feathers differs from all except Bimaculated, which, however, shows distinct dark patches on the sides of the neck and is distinctly smaller. The juvenile plumage is lost early through a complete moult, after which the plumage is inseparable from adult.

Voice: Song resembles White-winged Lark, but is generally slightly slower and deeper. It is given in flight, sometimes low over the ground with the wings raised and trembling, or from the ground or a low perch.

Habitat: Much as White-winged Lark, but favours wetter areas.

Range: Coincides largely with that of White-winged Lark, but Black Lark is apparently mostly resident or dispersive when forced to move because of severe weather.
Status: Accidental in West Germany (Apr 1874, July 1892, July 1909), Finland (Mar 1989*), Poland (Jan 1988*), Austria (one in 19th century), Italy (autumn 1803, May 1961), Greece (autumn 1930, Apr 1959, Feb 1963, Feb 1964), Rumania (Mar 1897, Mar 1900), and Malta (winter 1929).

Family HIRUNDINIDAE   Swallows

CLIFF SWALLOW   *Hirundo pyrrhonota*   A **38**
L 12.5-15cm (5.5"). North America. Recently in Britain (2 records).
Adult: Resembles Red-rumped Swallow, but shows an almost square tail; whitish forehead; deep rufous ear-coverts, throat and upper breast; and a blackish patch on lower throat/upper breast. Also, shows pale streaks on the mantle and has grey-brown undertail-coverts with paler fringes (not uniformly black as in Red-rumped).
Juvenile: Duller than the adult, lacking strong gloss and only showing a pale rufous tinge to the nape, ear-coverts and throat. It also lacks the blackish patch on the lower throat/upper breast (an indistinct brownish-grey patch is often seen), and the forehead patch is rufous-tinged and less distinct (rufous in adult of a southern subspecies as well). The flight feathers are fresh and the tertials show distinct pale fringes (also in the adult when fresh, but generally not until winter quarters).
Range: Breeds in most of North America, south to C Mexico. Winters mainly in South America. Vagrant in Greenland.
Status: Accidental in Britain: Isles of Scilly, juvenile from 10th-27th Oct 1983; Cleveland, South Gare, juvenile on 23rd Oct 1988.

Family MOTACILLIDAE   Pipits and Wagtails

RICHARD'S PIPIT   *Anthus richardi*   D **41**
L 18cm (7"). Asia. Rare but regular autumn visitor.
All plumages: Extremely similar to Blyth's Pipit (see p. 191). It could also be confused with Tawny Pipit. Slightly larger than Tawny and has a proportionately heavier bill (upper mandible also more decurved at the tip) and longer legs, hind-claw and tail. These structural differences are often, however, of little importance in the field without comparison. It is usually distinctly browner above (unless the plumage is very worn), and is deeper and more contrastingly buffish on the breast and flanks than Tawny (less obvious in juveniles and worn plumage). It also lacks Tawny's dark loral stripe, but note that from certain angles it often *seems* to show one (very rarely it is faint or even lacking in Tawny). Note that in the autumn a correct interpretation of age (plumage) is essential for identification of any large pipit.
Adult: Further distinguished from adult and 1st-winter Tawny Pipit by the obviously heavier streaking on the crown, mantle and scapulars (especially mantle and scapulars almost plain in Tawny); distinctly

streaked breast (scattered streaks are often seen in Tawny, especially on the sides); and generally more distinct malar stripe and malar patch. When fresh, the pale edges to the tertials are clearly narrower and more sharply defined than in fresh adult Tawny (and 1st-winter with new tertials). See note under 1st-winter. In the autumn most birds moult completely on the breeding grounds, but some do not moult all of the remiges before migration and thus show two different generations of flight feathers. A few do not moult any remiges at all before migration. In the spring, a number of coverts and tertials (often all lesser and median and a number of inner greater coverts and all tertials) are renewed; cf. 1st-winter and 1st-summer.

Juvenile: Easily separated from the adult by the blackish centres, brownish edges and narrow, clearcut, whitish (initially pale buffish) tips to the upperside, coverts and tertials. Most of the feather edges often wear whitish rather quickly, creating a distinct scaly appearance above. The breast is spotted rather than streaked. Normally, juvenile plumage is moulted on the breeding grounds before the migration, but many birds that turn up in Europe are still in full or nearly full juvenile plumage. Extremely like juvenile Tawny Pipit, and when somewhat worn, the differences described above in the colour of the upper and underparts are insignificant. However, newly moulted feathers on the upperparts, usually apparent early in the autumn, reveal each species' typical colour and pattern. The pattern of the lores is usually the best character for distinguishing from juvenile Tawny. In fresh plumage, the pale edges to the tertials are narrower than in Tawny.

1st-winter: Resembles the adult, but shows a variable number of retained juvenile coverts and/or tertials. In some birds, all of the juvenile coverts and tertials are retained, whereas many individuals have e.g. all of the lesser and median and a few inner greater coverts and one (per wing) to all tertials new. Rarely, all of the coverts and tertials are new. Juvenile coverts and tertials show narrow, clearcut, whitish fringes (edges brown when fresh) clearly different from the warmly coloured, broad and diffuse fringes/edges of adult and newly moulted adult-type feathers. Those few birds which have moulted all of the coverts and tertials are very difficult to tell from adult. In the hand, they can be distinguished by the contrast shown between the fresh coverts and more worn remiges. Also by the generally whitish-tipped primary coverts and more pointed rectrices (central pair sometimes new). Adults which have only moulted partially (see above) show much more contrast, because the remiges are much more worn. 1st-years do not moult any remiges, so there are never two generations of flight feathers as in some adults (see above).

Beware of juvenile Tawny Pipit and juvenile moulting to 1st-winter, in which the upperparts can look heavily streaked (irregularly when moulting), as well as having a breast pattern which can be very similar to that of Richard's.

1st-summer: More difficult to distinguish from the adult, since the pattern of retained coverts (both in adult and 1st-summer) is harder to determine due to heavy wear and bleaching, and because both adult and 1st-summer normally show moult contrasts among the coverts. With experience it can be seen that the remiges and primary coverts, and any retained coverts are more heavily worn than in adult.

Voice: The song typically consists of a series of monotonously repeated buzzy phrases *tzwee-tzwee-tzwee-tzwee-tzwee-tzwee-tzwee* and is normally delivered in a somewhat circling song flight. The call is often given a few times during a pause between two series. It is a loud, explosive, harsh *dscheep*, or *schreep*, and if heard at any distance, may recall one of the familiar calls of House Sparrow. Slightly shorter and softer versions are often heard. The call is clearly different from the normal *tchilp* and *chup* notes of Tawny Pipit.

Habitat and behaviour: Favours grassy areas, often where rather wet. Richard's is noted for its habit of frequently adopting a very upright posture. However, Tawny Pipit may also adopt a very upright stance, although it is usually not quite so pronounced. Richard's regularly hovers Skylark-like before landing, which is not seen in Tawny.

Range: Breeds in Siberia, Mongolia and China. Winters mainly in the Indian Subcontinent to S China. Other forms, often treated as conspecific with Richard's, occur in Africa, S Asia, and Australasia.

Status: Rare, but regular visitor to Europe, mainly in the autumn (mid Sept-early Nov).

Many records from the British Isles (average 50+ a year: Total of 1,385 up to 1985); in occasional invasion years (e.g. 1967, 1968, 1970 and 1977) up to *c*. 150 seen in one year. Relatively few reach Ireland though (36 up to 1988).

Also recorded from France (*c*. 50), Channel Islands (Jersey, 4th in Oct 1987), Belgium *c*.90, Luxembourg, Netherlands (230 since 1969), Denmark (77, +49 in autumn 1988!), Norway, Sweden (193), Finland (170 between 1975-88), Poland (20+), East Germany (*c*. 30 since 1930). West Germany, annual in autumn (many records from Heligoland); Czechoslovakia (5), Austria (a few are almost annual on migration in Rhine delta), Switzerland (4), Yugoslavia (Mar 1907), Greece, Bulgaria, Italy (including Sicily where rare but possibly regular migrant Mar-Apr, Sept-Oct), Malta (almost annual), Portugal, and Spain (where a few also winter in south).

BLYTH'S PIPIT *Anthus godlewskii* A **41**

L 17cm (6.75"). Asia. Accidental in N Europe (autumn).

All plumages: Extremely similar to Richard's Pipit, but is marginally smaller and more compact, with an appreciably shorter tail and hindclaw, and normally has a noticeably shorter and more pointed bill as well as shorter legs. In general appearance it often recalls one of the smaller pipits rather than Richard's. On average, the second outermost tail feather shows considerably less white on the inner web and more white on the outer web than in Richard's (see figure, p. 321), however there is some overlap as Richard's quite often shows a classic Blyth's pattern on the inner web and the outer is often all-white. This character is only useful in the hand.

Measurements: These usually differ (Richard's in brackets): wing 84- 97cm (89-102cm); tail 59-74cm (64-87cm); bill length from skull 14.3-17.5cm (16.5-21.4cm); bill depth at proximal edge of nostrils 4.2-4.5cm (4.5-5.5cm); tarsus 23.5-28cm (28-33.5cm); and hind-claw 9-15cm (14.5-23.9cm) (After Hall 1961, Svensson 1984, and personal measurements).

Plate 1

juv. (worn)

Great Northern Diver

juv.

WHITE-BILLED DIVER *Gavia adamsii* Arctic

The largest diver. Easily confused with Great Northern Diver. Habitually swims with bill slightly lifted.

Summer: Entirely yellowish-white bill distinguishes from Great Northern.

Winter: Paler sides to the head/neck and more diffuse border between dark and pale than in Great Northern Diver. Yellowish-white bill never dark on tip of culmen or on distal cutting edges.

Juvenile: Distinguished from adult winter by broad, pale fringes to scapulars.

2nd-winter: Like adult winter, but lacks white spots on coverts.

PIED-BILLED GREBE *Podilymbus podiceps* Americas

A rather small grebe, with relatively deep bill.

Summer: Dull compared to European grebes. Distinctive black patch on throat and band on bill.

Winter: Lacks black throat; at most a faint dark band on the bill.

1st-winter: Sometimes a trace of juvenile dark stripes on side of head.

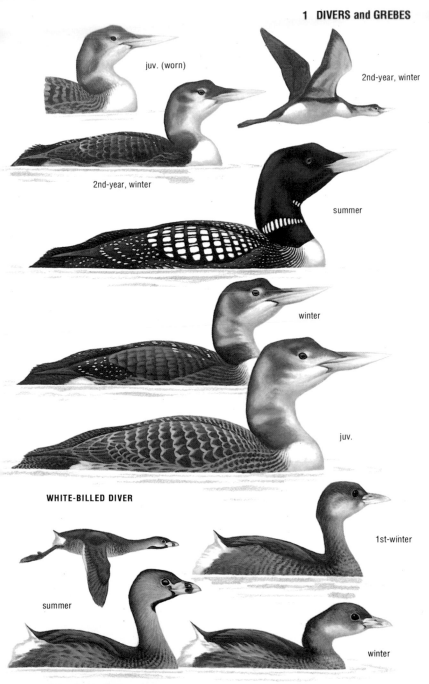

juv. (worn)

2nd-year, winter

2nd-year, winter

summer

winter

juv.

WHITE-BILLED DIVER

1st-winter

summer

winter

PIED-BILLED GREBE

Plate 2

BLACK-BROWED ALBATROSS *Diomedea melanophris* S Hemisphere 29

Black on mantle/scapulars and upperwings, broad dark margins to underwings. Yellow-orange bill. **Juvenile**: Dark bill, less white on underwing, band across foreneck.

YELLOW-NOSED ALBATROSS *Diomedea chlororhynchos* S Hemisphere 30

See Black-browed Albatross. Narrower dark margins to underwings. Bill pattern. Grey-washed head in S. Atlantic race. **Juvenile**: All-blackish bill, all-white head.

WANDERING ALBATROSS *Diomedea exulans* S Hemisphere 30

Unmistakable. Female on average darker than male. **Juvenile**: All brown except for white face mask and mainly white underwings.

SOUTHERN GIANT PETREL *Macronectes giganteus* S Hemisphere 31

Huge pale bill, tipped greenish.
Dark morph: Mostly dark; pale head, neck, breast, some pale mottling elsewhere on underparts.
White morph: All white with some dark mottling.
Juvenile dark morph: All dark.

Albatrosses

YELLOW-NOSED

BLACK-BROWED

WANDERING

juv.

old subad./ad. ♀

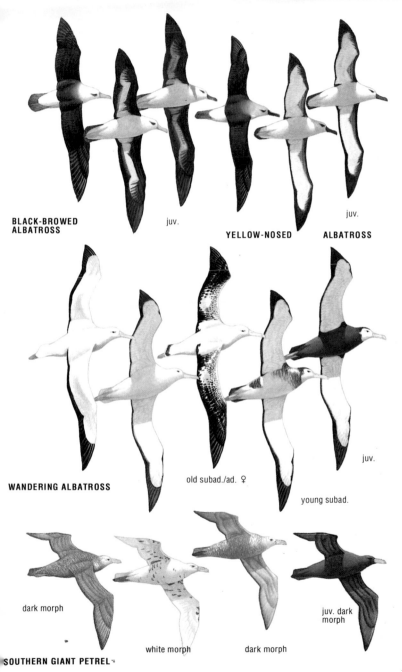

BLACK-BROWED ALBATROSS

juv.

YELLOW-NOSED ALBATROSS

juv.

WANDERING ALBATROSS

old subad./ad. ♀

young subad.

juv.

dark morph

white morph

dark morph

juv. dark morph

SOUTHERN GIANT PETREL

Plate 3

BLACK-CAPPED PETREL *Pterodroma hasitata*
W Atlantic   32

Very distinctive seabird. Blackish cap, prominent blackish diagonal underwing bar, broad white hindneck collar and broad white U on uppertail-coverts.

LITTLE SHEARWATER *Puffinus assimilis*
Nearest Azores and Canary Is.   33

Like Manx Shearwater but smaller with shorter and more blunted wings and more fluttering flight. Also eye encircled by white and less dark on wing tips.

WHITE-FACED PETREL *Pelagodroma marina*
Nearest off NW Africa   35

Unmistakable storm-petrel, with white underside and underwing-coverts, distinctive head pattern and pale grey rump/uppertail-coverts. Very long legs.

Manx Shearwater (not to scale)

BULWER'S PETREL *Bulweria bulwerii* Nearest Azores and Madeira   32

Rather intermediate in size and appearance between storm-petrels and shearwaters, with a typically rather long, tapering tail (wedge-shaped when spread). All dark plumage with paler upperwing-bar.

WILSON'S PETREL *Oceanites oceanicus* S Hemisphere.   34

Storm-petrel with distinctive wing shape. When gliding, rather straight trailing edge and comparatively little bend at carpal. Distinct pale upperwing bar, not reaching fore-edge of wing; underwings all dark. Toes project beyond tip of squarely cut off tail.

MADEIRAN PETREL *Oceanodroma castro* Azores, Madeira and Portugal   35

Storm-petrel with rather long wings, held distinctly angled when gliding. Tail with shallow or no fork, toes not projecting. Moderately distinct pale upperwing-bar.

BLACK-CAPPED PETREL

LITTLE SHEARWATER
baroli

WHITE-FACED PETREL

BULWER'S PETREL

WILSON'S PETREL

MADEIRAN PETREL

Plate 4

RED-BILLED TROPICBIRD *Phaethon aethereus* Tropical oceans 36
    Unmistakable. **Juvenile**: Yellow bill, no tail streamers.

MASKED BOOBY *Sula dactylatra* Tropical oceans 37
    Like adult Gannet, but black secondaries and tail, all white head. Bare part coloration. **Juvenile**: Broad white hindneck collar.

BROWN BOOBY *Sula leucogaster* Tropical oceans 37
    Brown with mostly white underparts and underwing-coverts. Cf. juvenile Masked Booby. **Juvenile**: Underparts sullied pale brownish.

RED-FOOTED BOOBY *Sula sula* Tropical oceans 37
    White morph: Blackish patches on under primary coverts. Bare part colours. **Brown morph**: Mostly dark. **Immature**: Yellowish-grey legs/feet.

MAGNIFICENT FRIGATEBIRD *Fregata magnificens* Tropical oceans 40
    Unmistakable.

DOUBLE-CRESTED CORMORANT *Phalacrocorax auritus* N America 38
    Similar to Cormorant. No gular feathering, prominent orange streak on upper lores. **Immatures**: Pale foreneck/breast, darker belly.

DALMATIAN PELICAN *Pelecanus crispus* SE Europe 39
    Duskier than White Pelican, curly crest on nape. Bare part coloration. **Juvenile** Paler than juvenile White Pelican.

juv.

older subad.

breeding

1st-year, spring

DALMATIAN PELICAN   **DOUBLE-CRESTED CORMORANT**

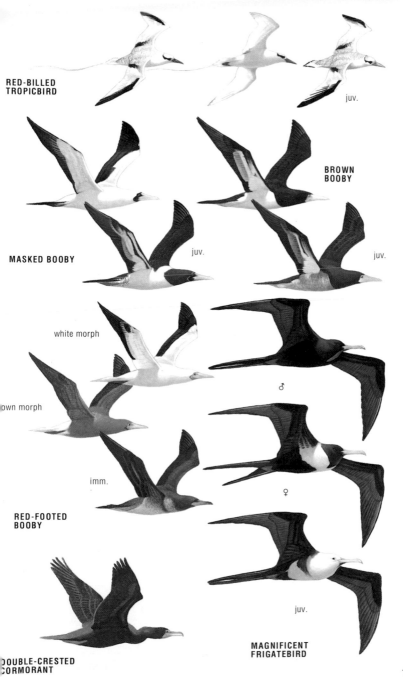

RED-BILLED
TROPICBIRD

juv.

BROWN
BOOBY

MASKED BOOBY

juv.

juv.

white morph

♂

own morph

imm.

♀

RED-FOOTED
BOOBY

juv.

DOUBLE-CRESTED
CORMORANT

MAGNIFICENT
FRIGATEBIRD

199

Plate 5

Birds not to scale.

AMERICAN BITTERN
Botaurus lentiginosus N America   41

Similar to Bittern. Dull chestnut forehead/crown, neck with more stripes but lacking barring.

LEAST BITTERN *Ixobrychus exilis*
Americas   41

Similar to Little Bittern but rufous around pale upperwing patch, trailing edge to wings and tips of greater primary coverts. **Male**: Black cap and upperparts. **Female**: Dark brown cap and mantle/scapulars. Uniform mantle/scapulars, unlike female Little Bittern. **Juvenile female**: Distinguished from adult Least and juvenile Little Bittern by pattern of upperparts.

SCHRENCK'S LITTLE BITTERN
Ixobrychus eurhythmus E Asia   42

Male: Chestnut upperside and pale underside with dark gular stripe. **Female**: Diagnostic pattern of upperparts and coverts.

GREEN HERON *Butorides striatus virescens*
N and Central America   43

Small, mainly dark, with rufous sides of head/neck. **Juvenile**: Lacks large pale areas on wings of small bitterns.

CHINESE POND HERON
Ardeola bacchus E Asia   44

Summer: Rufous head/neck, slaty mantle/scapulars, mainly white wings. **Winter/juvenile**: Very like winter Squacco Heron, but normally more heavily streaked.

Bittern

juv.

Little Bittern

CHINESE POND HERON

winter/juv.

summer

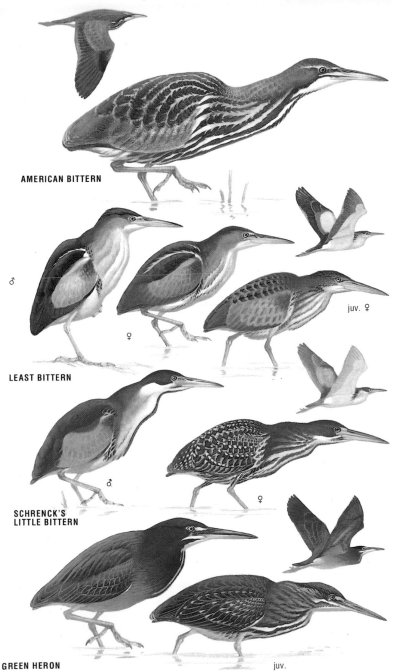

AMERICAN BITTERN

♂

♀

juv. ♀

LEAST BITTERN

♂

♀

SCHRENCK'S LITTLE BITTERN

GREEN HERON

juv.

Plate 6

WESTERN REEF HERON *Egretta gularis* W Africa, Red Sea to India   46
Resembles Little Egret. Bill usually paler and slightly thicker and legs often paler.

SNOWY EGRET *Egretta thula* Americas   45
Distinguished from Little Egret by yellow lores and rear of tarsus, in breeding plumage head plumes of several feathers.

LESSER FLAMINGO *Phoenicopterus minor* Africa and SW Asia   48
Smaller than Flamingo, shorter and darker bill. Crimson areas on upper- and underwings.

BALD IBIS *Geronticus eremita* Morocco and Turkey   47
Unmistakable.

LITTLE BLUE HERON *Egretta caerulea* Americas   44
All dark. **Juvenile**: Bare part coloration and dark tips to primaries distinguish from small white egrets.

TRICOLORED HERON *Egretta tricolor* Americas   45
Mostly dark; white and rufous stripe on foreneck, white underparts. **Juvenile**: Pale rufous sides to head/neck and tips to coverts.

GREAT BLUE HERON *Ardea herodias* Americas   46
Larger than Grey Heron, rufous 'thighs' and marginal coverts, pinkish-grey tinge to neck. **Juvenile**: Rufous markings on some wing-coverts.

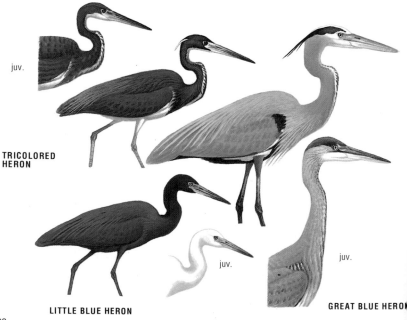

juv.

TRICOLORED
HERON

LITTLE BLUE HERON

juv.

juv.

GREAT BLUE HERON

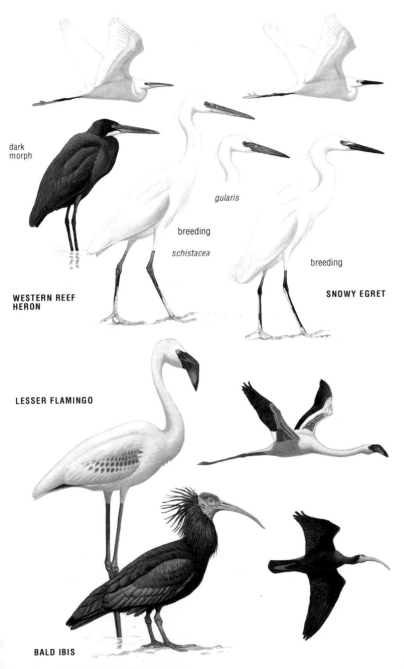

dark
morph

gularis

breeding

schistacea

breeding

**WESTERN REEF
HERON**

SNOWY EGRET

LESSER FLAMINGO

BALD IBIS

Plate 7

FULVOUS WHISTLING DUCK *Dendrocygna bicolor*   Africa, Asia, Americas   49
  Largely rufous head, neck and underparts with whitish flank streaks. Dark
  wings in flight. Noticeably long-legged.

LESSER WHITE-FRONTED GOOSE *Anser erythropus*   N Sweden, Norway, Finland   50
  Smaller than White-fronted, with shorter bill and neck and normally steeper
  forehead. Wings project clearly beyond tip of tail. Distinct yellow orbital ring.
  White blaze usually reaches onto fore-crown, unlike in White-fronted.
  Juvenile: Lacks white blaze and black markings on belly.

SNOW GOOSE *Anser caerulescens*   N America   51
  White morph: Unmistakable.
  Dark morph, 'Blue Goose': Dark grey with whitish head/upper neck and paler
  grey upperwing-coverts.
  Juvenile white morph: Sullied brownish-grey on part of head, neck and
  upperparts. Dark bill and legs/feet.
  Juvenile dark morph: Dark head/neck, bill and legs/feet.

'BLACK BRANT' *Branta bernicla nigricans*   N America/NE Asia   52
  Race of Brent Goose. Like dark-bellied Brent Goose, but with broader necklace
  and more contrastingly pale flanks.

RED-BREASTED GOOSE *Branta ruficollis*   N Siberia   53
  Unmistakable.

'TUNDRA SWAN' *Cygnus columbianus columbianus*   N America   50
  Race of Bewick's Swan. Very little yellow on bill in adult.

RUDDY SHELDUCK *Tadorna ferruginea*   SE Europe   54
  Unmistakable. Note large white wing patches in flight.
  Male: Narrow blackish necklace.
  Female: No necklace, paler face.

'TUNDRA SWAN'

RUDDY SHELDUCK

FULVOUS WHISTLING DUCK

juv.

LESSER WHITE-FRONTED GOOSE

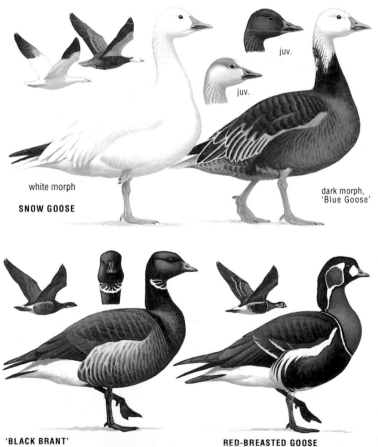

white morph

SNOW GOOSE

juv.

juv.

dark morph, 'Blue Goose'

'BLACK BRANT'

RED-BREASTED GOOSE

Plate 8

AMERICAN WIGEON *Anas americana* N America   54

Male breeding: Diagnostic head pattern. Large white patch on coverts distinguish from 1st breeding male.

Male moulting: Breeding plumage not yet fully developed.

Female: Very like female-type Wigeon, but head usually greyer and axillaries and central underwing- coverts whitish.

FALCATED DUCK *Anas falcata* E Asia   56

Green-glossed speculum with rather broad and diffuse pale bar in front but only very narrow pale tips to trailing edge of secondaries.

Male breeding: Unmistakable. Distinctive pattern and shape of head, also very long, falcated tertials.

Female: Rather compact with normally quite full nape. Comparatively plain head and all dark grey bill.

'GREEN-WINGED TEAL' *Anas crecca carolinensis* N America   58

Race of Teal. **Male breeding**: Like European race, but vertical white stripe on fore-flanks, while lacking white horizontal stripe on lower scapulars.

BAIKAL TEAL *Anas formosa* E Asia   57

Narrow rufous bar in front of speculum.

Male breeding: Multi-patterned head. Often some brown tips when fresh in autumn/winter.

Female: Dark-framed pale spot at base of bill, also white wedge below eye in some individuals.

MARBLED TEAL *Marmaronetta angustirostris*
S Europe   61

Basically pale, with dark patch around eyes. Diagnostic pale spots on scapulars and flanks.

Wigeon ♀

MARBLED TEAL

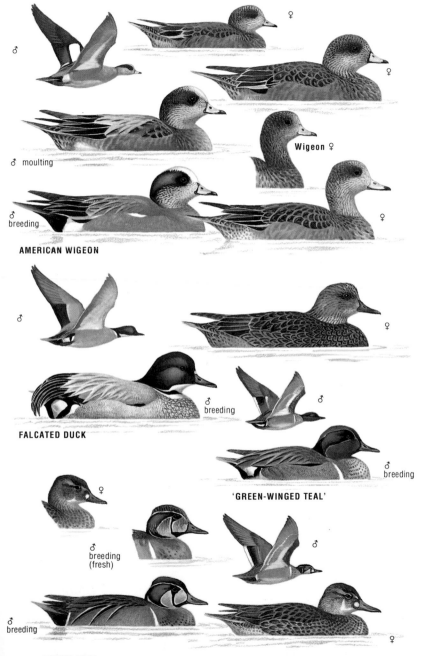

♂

♀

♀

Wigeon ♀

♂ moulting

♂ breeding

AMERICAN WIGEON

♀

♂

♀

♂ breeding

FALCATED DUCK

♂

♂ breeding

'GREEN-WINGED TEAL'

♀

♂ breeding (fresh)

♂

♂ breeding

♀

BAIKAL TEAL

Plate 9

AMERICAN BLACK DUCK *Anas rubripes* N America   59

Resembles female-type Mallard, but much darker, with contrastingly pale head. Speculum deeper violet and lacking white bar in front, only very narrow white trailing bar.

Male: Greenish-yellow bill.

Juvenile female: Dusky greyish-green bill.

BLUE-WINGED TEAL *Anas discors* N America   59

Pale blue upperwing-coverts and one (male) or two (female) white bars in front of speculum but no white on trailing edge of secondaries.

Male breeding: Unmistakable.

Male moulting: Breeding plumage beginning to show.

Female: Like female-type Garganey, but head less striped and different upperwing pattern.

Juvenile: Very like adult female, but breast and flanks normally with less distinct pale internal markings.

RING-NECKED DUCK *Aythya collaris* N America   63

Confusable with Tufted Duck. Distinctly peaked rear crown but no trace of a crest. Diffuse grey wing-bars.

Male breeding: Grey flanks with white wedge at front. Two white bands across bill.

Male moulting: Breeding plumage not yet fully developed. Birds still in incomplete breeding plumage in late winter-early spring are 1st-years.

Female: Resembles female-type Tufted Duck, but note pale eye-ring and stripe behind eye and dark iris. Often paler on side of head.

CANVASBACK *Aythya valisineria* N America   62

Resembles Pochard. Larger, with distinctive shape of head and bill, latter all blackish.

Male breeding: Further differs from Pochard by blackish anterior part of head and paler mid-body.

Female: Tends to have slightly paler mid-body than female Pochard.

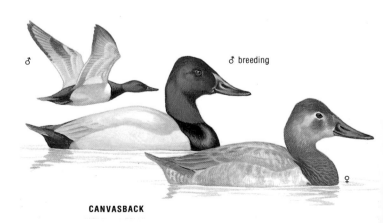

♂   ♂ breeding   ♀

CANVASBACK

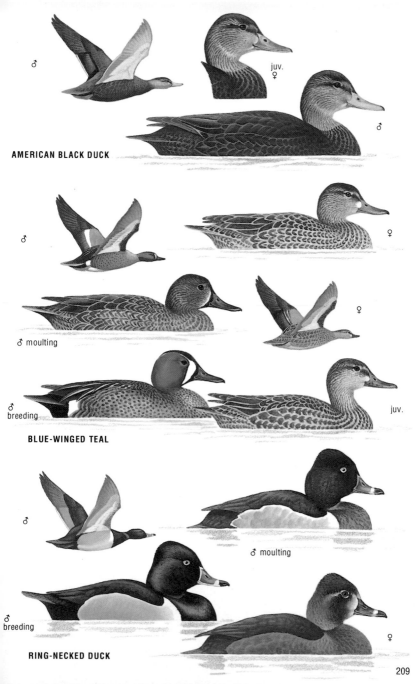

AMERICAN BLACK DUCK

♂

juv.
♀

♂

BLUE-WINGED TEAL

♂

♀

♂ moulting

♀

♂
breeding

juv.

RING-NECKED DUCK

♂

♂ moulting

♂
breeding

♀

209

Plate 10

KING EIDER *Somateria spectabilis* Arctic 65

Male breeding: Unmistakable.

Male eclipse: Immaculate white upperwing patches distinguish from immature males, but are normally concealed when swimming.

Female: Like female Eider. Distinctive head/bill shape and different feathering on bill. Darker bill, 'smiling' corners to mouth, and crescentic dark markings on flanks.

Juvenile male: Like adult female, but no or very indistinct pale internal markings on breast, scapulars and notably flanks and narrower and less rufous fringes. No distinct wing-bars (often difficult to judge on swimming birds). Scapulars and a few breast-side feathers new; pattern of these show bird to be male.

1st-year male, spring: Rather dark (including all dark upperwings). Bill colour distinguishes from Eider.

2nd-year male, spring: Some dusky on head, breast and upperwing-coverts, and not yet fully developed bill shield.

SPECTACLED EIDER *Somateria fischeri* Alaska/E Siberia 66

Diagnostic cloak of feathering on bill.

Male breeding: Unmistakable head pattern. Black breast and orange bill.

Male eclipse: Mostly dark, with some white; white upperwing patches distinguish from other plumages, but are normally concealed when swimming. Pale 'spectacles' and orange bill still obvious.

Female: Diagnostic pale 'spectacles'. More broadly barred scapulars and flanks than female Eider and King Eider.

STELLER'S EIDER *Polysticta stelleri* Arctic 67

Male breeding: Unmistakable.

Male eclipse: Large, white upperwing-covert patches distinguish from other plumages, but are usually concealed when swimming.

Female: Characteristic head/bill shape; no feathering extending onto sides of bill. Plumage little-patterned. Violet-blue speculum with broad, white bar in front and behind.

Juvenile: Less rufous than adult female, and little or no gloss to speculum and narrow, indistinct wing-bars.

Eider

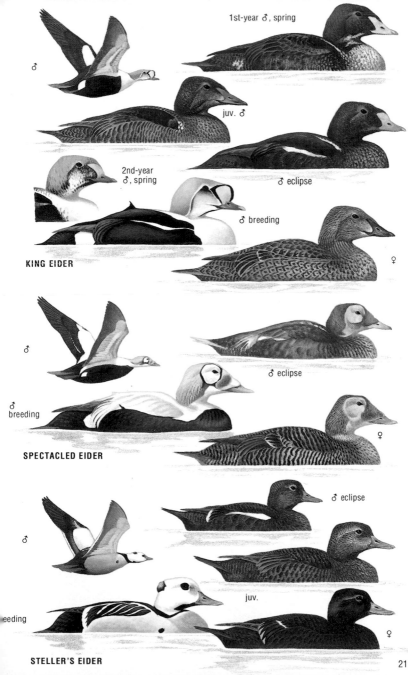

1st-year ♂, spring

♂

juv. ♂

2nd-year ♂, spring

♂ eclipse

♂ breeding

KING EIDER

♀

♂

♂ eclipse

♂ breeding

♀

SPECTACLED EIDER

♂ eclipse

♂

juv.

♀

breeding

STELLER'S EIDER

211

Plate 11

HARLEQUIN DUCK *Histrionicus histrionicus* Nearest Iceland 68

Male breeding: Unmistakable. **Male eclipse**: Differs from females and immature males by broad, white shaft-streaks to tertials. **Female**: Diagnostic whitish spots on sides of head. **1st breeding male**: Still has juvenile wings, lacking white.

'BLACK SCOTER' *Melanitta nigra americana* N America/E Asia. 69

Race of Common Scoter. **Male**: Large, swollen yellow bill knob.

SURF SCOTER *Melanitta perspicillata* N America 70

All dark wings. **Male**: Striking multicoloured bill and two white patches on head. **Female**: Confusable with both Common and Velvet Scoter. Distinctive bill, with feathering on culmen but not on sides. Sides to head pale with two whitish patches and usually also one on nape. **Juvenile**: No whitish patch on nape. **Male moulting to 1st breeding**: (late 1st autumn-spring) Intermediate between juvenile and adult male. **1st breeding male**: Bill not fully adult, and no white on forehead.

BUFFLEHEAD *Bucephala albeola* N America 70

Male breeding: Large white patch on sides/rear of head.

Male eclipse: Extensive white on upperwing distinguish from other female-types, but is often difficult to see when swimming.

Female: White patch on side of head.

LESSER SCAUP *Aythya affinis* N America 64

Very like Scaup, but slightly smaller, with more peaked rear crown and shorter wing-bar.

Male breeding: Head glossed violet, and scapulars and flanks slightly darker than Scaup.

Female: Very like female Scaup.

Male moulting to 1st breeding: Iris duller than adult's. Birds still in incomplete breeding plumage in winter-spring are 1st-years.

♂

Scaup

♂
breeding

♂

♂ moulting to
1st breeding

♂
breeding

♀

LESSER SCAUP

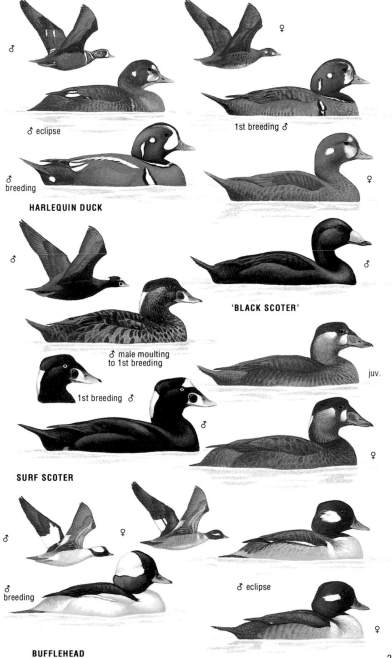

♂

♀

♂ eclipse

1st breeding ♂

♂
breeding

♀

HARLEQUIN DUCK

♂

♂

'BLACK SCOTER'

♂ male moulting
to 1st breeding

juv.

1st breeding ♂

♂

♀

SURF SCOTER

♂

♀

♂

♂
breeding

♂ eclipse

♀

BUFFLEHEAD

Plate 12

BARROW'S GOLDENEYE *Bucephala islandica* Nearest Iceland 71

Male breeding: Like adult male Goldeneye. Distinguished by drawn-out, crecent shaped white patch in front of eye, row of isolated white spots on scapulars, black wedge on fore-flanks and black stripe along flanks.

Male moulting: Breeding plumage starting to appear (different stages shown here). Birds still in incomplete breeding plumage in winter-spring are 1st-years.

Female: Like female Goldeneye, but shorter and deeper-based bill, steeper forehead and fuller nape.

1st-year female: Rather dark iris.

HOODED MERGANSER *Mergus cucullatus* N America 72

Male breeding: Unmistakable. Crest may be lowered as depicted.

Female: Small size. Prominent crest. White shaft-streaks on tertials.

Male moulting to 1st breeding: Adult male moulting from eclipse similar except for iris colour and pattern of lesser coverts. Birds still not in full breeding plumage in late winter-spring are 1st-years.

WHITE-HEADED DUCK *Oxyura leucocephala* S Spain & Rumania 73

Male breeding: Only confusable with male Ruddy Duck, but shows swollen base to bill. White on head reaches above eye, and body less rufous and more barred.

Male eclipse: Less rufous than in breeding, slightly more dark on head and grey bill.

Female: Like female Ruddy Duck, but shows swollen base to bill, more distinct dark stripe on ear- coverts and more rufous body.

Immature male: Smaller bill and more dusky sides to head than adult male.

♀ **Goldeneye**

♀ **Ruddy Duck**

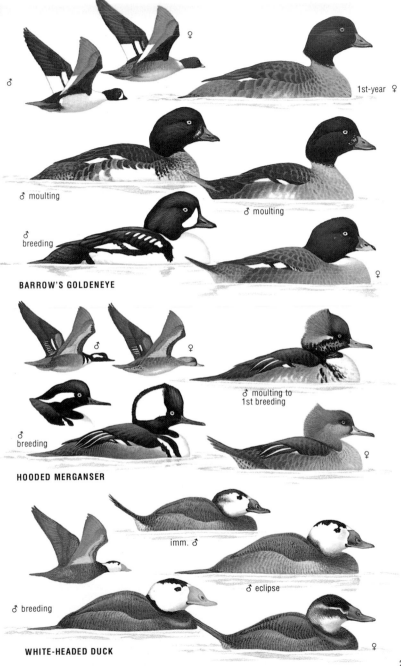

♂

♀

1st-year ♀

♂ moulting

♂ moulting

♂ breeding

♀

BARROW'S GOLDENEYE

♂

♀

♂ moulting to 1st breeding

♂ breeding

♀

HOODED MERGANSER

imm. ♂

♂ eclipse

♂ breeding

♀

WHITE-HEADED DUCK

Plate 13

PALLAS'S FISH EAGLE *Haliaeetus leucoryphus* Asia   75
All dark with paler head/neck and distinct broad white band on tail.
Juvenile: Resembles immature White-tailed Eagle, but white patches on primaries below and much more prominent pale bar on underwing-coverts.

LAMMERGEIER *Gypaetus barbatus* S Europe   75
Huge, with unmistakable silhouette and plumage.
Juvenile: Slightly more compact silhouette than adult. Greyish underwing-coverts and underparts, also darker head.
Subadult: Plumage often rather blotchy.

LONG-LEGGED BUZZARD *Buteo rufinus* SE Europe   80
Like 'Steppe Buzzard', but larger and longer-winged. Tail with no or little barring. Extensive plumage variation in both sometimes makes identification very difficult. Juvenile distinguished from adult by narrower, more diffuse and paler trailing edge to wings, and tail often distinctly barred throughout length.

variation

juv.

'Steppe Buzzard'

ad.

juv.

juv.

PALLAS'S FISH EAGLE

subad.

juv.

subad.

LAMMERGEIER

juv.

typical

variation

LONG-LEGGED BUZZARD

Plate 14

DARK CHANTING GOSHAWK *Melierax metabates*   Africa   7̶9̶

Pale grey wings with dark tips, dark central tail-feathers and pale uppertail-coverts distinctive. Also note red cere and legs.

Juvenile: Dark brown above with paler uppertail-coverts, and barred underparts with darker breast characteristic.

PALLID HARRIER *Circus macrourus*   E Rumania   7̶6̶

Male: Like a small, slim, pale Hen Harrier, with blackish wedge on primaries and lack of dark trailing edge to wings below.

Female: Smaller, slimmer and with more pointed wings than female Hen Harrier. Differs from Montagu's Harrier in pattern on secondaries (above and below) and axillaries.

Juvenile: Unstreaked rufous on underparts. Told from juvenile Montagu's by distinct pale neck collar bordered below by prominent dark semi-collar.

1st-year male in transition: Variable, contrasting pattern during moult in early 2nd autumn.

BLACK-SHOULDERED KITE *Elanus caeruleus*   Iberia   7̶

Rather small, with very distinctive shape and plumage.

Juvenile: Easily distinguished from adult by pattern of upperside.

♀

juv.

Montagu's Harrier

juv.

DARK CHANTING GOSHAWK

juv.

juv.

♂

♂

♀

juv.

♀

♀

juv.

PALLID HARRIER

juv.

1st-year ♂ in transition

juv.

juv.

BLACK-SHOULDERED KITE

Plate 15

IMPERIAL EAGLE *Aquila heliaca* Europe 86

Blackish plumage with very pale nape/hindneck, pale grey basal part of tail, white scapular markings and in race *adalberti* white on forewing.

Juvenile: Contrastingly patterned. Note paler inner primaries below and heavy streaking to much of plumage, notably breast.

Subadult: Very blotchy, typically with rather pale lower body.

STEPPE EAGLE *Aquila nipalensis* Asia 84

Dark plumage. Barred remiges and rectrices with broader dark terminal bar. See Spotted and Lesser Spotted Eagles (see below and Plate 16).

Juvenile: Prominent white bar on central underwing.

Subadult: Much variation. Usually trace of pale bar on central underwing. Older subadults show barred remiges and rectrices like adults'. See immature Spotted and Lesser Spotted Eagles (Plate 16).

SPOTTED EAGLE   STEPPE EAGLE   Lesser Spotted Eagle

adalberti

heliaca

juv. heliaca

juv. heliaca

adalberti

subad.

juv. heliaca

subad.

PERIAL EAGLE

subad.

juv.

subad.

subad.

juv.

subad.

STEPPE EAGLE

juv.

Plate 16

SPOTTED EAGLE
Aquila clanga Asia 82

Unbarred remiges and rectrices, unlike in adult Steppe Eagle. Darker than Lesser Spotted Eagle, on upperside especially. **Juvenile**: Very dark, whitish spots on scapulars and upperwing-coverts. Rare *'fulvescens'* lacks the streaking and pale wedge on underside of inner primaries of juvenile Imperial. **Subadult**: Pale-tipped greater coverts.

ju

juv.

imm.

Lesser Spotted Ea

SWAINSON'S HAWK
Buteo swainsoni N America 79

Rather Buzzard-like in general appearance, but more pointed wings and darker flight-feathers with a little pale on basal parts of outers. Some individuals could be confused with Booted Eagle, but lacks pale upperwing-bar.

Pale morph: Contrastingly pale underwing-coverts. **Dark morph**: Mostly dark rufous. **Intermediate morph**: Intermediate between pale and dark morph. **Juvenile**: Pale fringes above and streaked below.

'BARBARY FALCON'
Falco peregrinus pelegrinoides N Africa-C Asia 93

Race of Peregrine Falcon (often considered separate species). Paler above and less barred below than European Peregrines, rufous nape. Unlike Lanner tail darkens towards tip.

Juvenile: More finely streaked than European Peregrines. Told from juvenile Lanner by rather uniformly pale underwing.

juv.

juv.

juv.

subad.

juv.
'fulvescens'

juv.
'fulvescens'

POTTED EAGLE

pale
morph

pale
morph

dark morph

intermediate
morph

juv.

WAINSON'S HAWK

juv.

juv.

'BARBARY FALCON'

223

Plate 17

AMERICAN KESTREL *Falco sparverius* Americas   88
  Male: Unmistakable. **Female**: Head pattern diagnostic.

LANNER *Falco biarmicus* S Europe   90
  Variable rufous on crown and nape, narrow moustachial stripe, barred above,
  some barring on underparts, often darker on central underwing, evenly barred
  tail. See adult 'Barbary Falcon' (Plate 16) and Saker.
  Juvenile: Grey-brown with pale fringes above, heavily streaked below.
  Underwing-coverts contrastingly dark. Yellowish legs/feet, unlike juvenile
  Saker.

SAKER *Falco cherrug* E-SE Europe   91
  Larger and heavier than Lanner (little difference in size between birds shown
  here indicates male Sakers and female Lanners). Compare adult Lanner,
  especially crown, upperparts, underparts and central tail-feathers.
  Juvenile: More heavily streaked below and on underwing-coverts than adult,
  bluish-grey legs/feet. Browner above than juvenile Gyrfalcon.

ELEONORA'S FALCON *Falco eleonorae* Mediterranean   88
  Resembles Hobby, but is larger, with longer wings and tail. **Pale morph**: Told
  from Hobby by more rufous underparts and contrast between dark
  underwing-coverts and paler, unbarred basal parts to flight-feathers.
  Dark morph: All dark, but still obvious contrast on underwing.
  Juvenile: Paler basal parts to flight-feathers than juvenile Hobby.

ELEONORA'S FALCON   Gyrfalcon

224

♂

♀

♀

♂

♂

♀

AMERICAN KESTREL

juv.

juv.

juv.

erlangeri
(NW Africa)

LANNER

juv.

juv.

juv.

SAKER

Plate 18

ANDALUSIAN HEMIPODE *Turnix sylvatica* SW Spain & S Portugal 9

Told from Quail by orange-brown breast and large blackish spots on flanks. Female larger and more colourful than male. In flight, note contrastingly dark flight-feathers.

SORA *Porzana carolina* N America 9

Diagnostic black face mask. Yellow bill.

Juvenile: Like juvenile Spotted and Little Crakes but chestnut crown with blackish central stripe diagnostic. No white spots on head etc as in Spotted or barring on undertail-coverts as in Little.

ALLEN'S GALLINULE *Porphyrula alleni* Africa 9

Like American Purple Gallinule, but smaller, red legs and tip to bill, blackish central stripe on undertail-coverts.

Juvenile: Lacks pale spots above and dark barring below as in juvenile crakes. 'Scaly' feathers of upperparts differ from juvenile American Purple Gallinule.

AMERICAN PURPLE GALLINULE *Porphyrula martinica* Americas 9

See Allen's Gallinule.

PURPLE GALLINULE *Porphyrio porphyrio* SW Europe 9

Large, with strong, red bill and red legs/feet. Plumage all blue, with white undertail-coverts.

Juvenile: Paler and greyer than adult, with more brownish bare parts.

AMERICAN COOT *Fulica americana* Americas 9

Black band on bill, deep red top of shield and white sides to undertail-coverts.

CRESTED COOT *Fulica cristata* S Spain 9

Lacks Coot's wedge of feathering on side of bill. No white trailing edge to secondaries. Bluish-tinged bill. In breeding season red knobs on forehead.

Coot

non-breedi

CRESTED COOT

juv.

PURPLE GALLINULE

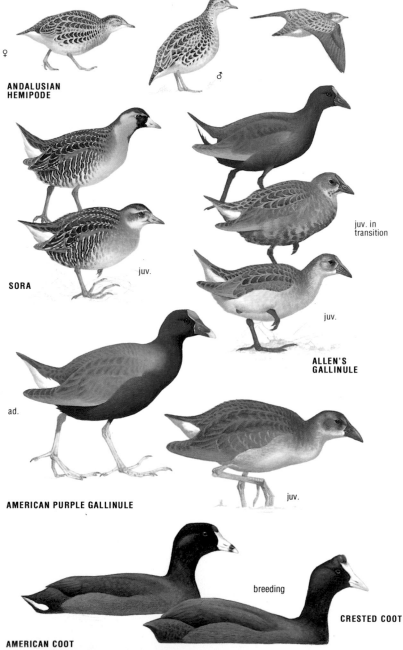

♀

**ANDALUSIAN
HEMIPODE**

♂

SORA

juv.

juv. in
transition

juv.

**ALLEN'S
GALLINULE**

ad.

AMERICAN PURPLE GALLINULE

juv.

breeding

CRESTED COOT

AMERICAN COOT

227

Plate 19

SANDHILL CRANE *Grus canadensis*   N America & E USSR   98
  Grey head/neck and red forehead.
  Juvenile: Extensively rufous-brown – more than in juvenile Crane.

SIBERIAN WHITE CRANE *Grus leucogeranus*   W and E Siberia   99
  All white, with black outer wing and red forehead.
  Juvenile: Rufous-brown and white, with black outer wing. Note also pinkish
  legs.

DEMOISELLE CRANE *Anthropoides virgo*   Asia   99
  Largely black head/neck with white head tufts.
  Juvenile in transition: Adult plumage starting to show.

HOUBARA BUSTARD *Chlamydotis undulata*   Asia & N Africa   100
  Diagnostic black frill on side of neck. In flight, white on upperwing confined to
  large patch on primaries. See Great and Little Bustards.

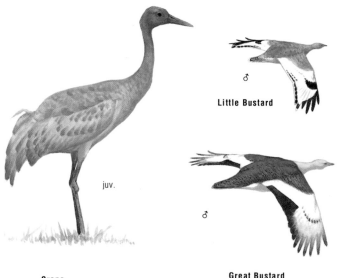

♂
Little Bustard

juv.

♂

Crane

Great Bustard

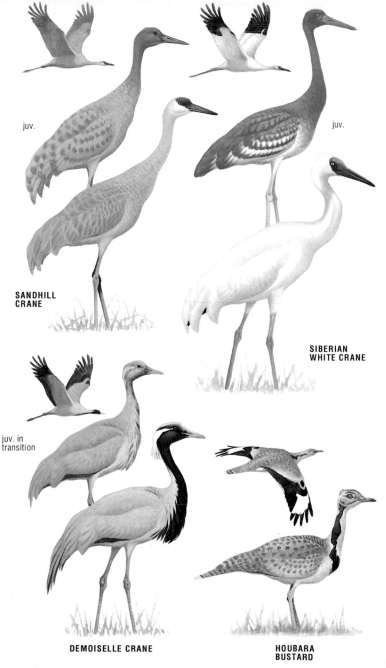

juv.

juv.

**SANDHILL
CRANE**

**SIBERIAN
WHITE CRANE**

juv. in
transition

DEMOISELLE CRANE

**HOUBARA
BUSTARD**

Plate 20

CREAM-COLOURED COURSER *Cursorius cursor*　N Africa & W Asia　　　101

Shape and plumage distinctive both on ground and in flight. In flight, note blackish underwing and outer wing above.

Juvenile: Dark markings on breast and upperparts and less distinct head pattern.

BLACK-WINGED PRATINCOLE *Glareola nordmanni*　Rumania　　　102

Lack of white trailing edge to secondaries and blackish underwing-coverts distinguish from Collared Pratincole.

Summer: Well-defined pale throat patch with narrow dark border.

Winter: Differs from summer plumage in ill-defined dark margin to pale throat and mottled breast.

Juvenile: Differs from adult in broad, pale fringes and dark submarginal markings to much of upperparts and coverts.

BLACK-WINGED PRATINCOLE

ORIENTAL PRATINCOLE *Glareola maldivarum*
　E Asia　　　102

Rather dark above and lack of white trailing edge like Black-winged, but rufous underwing-coverts like Collared. Tail shorter than in either.

Collared Pratincole

SEMIPALMATED PLOVER
　Charadrius semipalmatus
　N America　　　103

Very like Ringed Plover. Webbing between all three fore-toes on each foot and subdued Spotted Redshank-like call.

Juvenile: Narrow pale fringes and dark submarginal lines to much of upperparts and coverts distinguish from adult winter.

KILLDEER *Charadrius vociferus*
　Americas　　　104

Relatively large. Double blackish breast-band. Bright orange-brown back, rump and uppertail-coverts.

summer

　　　ORIENTAL PRATINCOLE

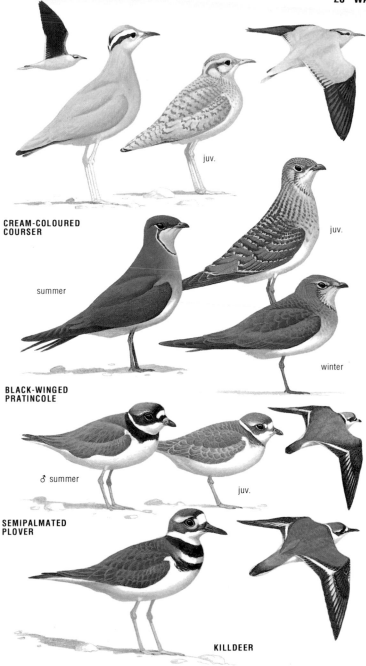

CREAM-COLOURED
COURSER

juv.

BLACK-WINGED
PRATINCOLE

summer

juv.

winter

SEMIPALMATED
PLOVER

♂ summer

juv.

KILLDEER

Plate 21

GREATER SAND PLOVER *Charadrius leschenaultii* Asia   106

Larger than Lesser Sand Plover. Bill longer, more pointed and normally stronger. Legs usually paler.

Male summer: Often prominent rufous mottling to mantle/scapulars, unlike Lesser Sand Plover. Western race shown.

Female summer: Usually duller than male (extreme shown).

Winter: Brownish-grey and white.

Juvenile: Told from adult winter by distinct pale fringes to upperside, coverts and tertials, and by buffish tinge to face and breast when fresh.

LESSER SAND PLOVER *Charadrius mongolus* Asia   105

Sexing and ageing as in Greater Sand Plover.

Male summer: *mongolus*-group: White forehead and narrow blackish upper margin to rufous breast-band.

Male summer: *atrifrons*-group: Mainly black forehead and no dark upper margin to breast-band.

CASPIAN PLOVER *Charadrius asiaticus* C Asia   107

Told from sand plovers by head pattern (difference least obvious in juvenile), finer bill, less distinct wing-bar, duskier underwing.

Male summer: Prominent blackish lower border to rufous breast-band.

Winter: Broader and more complete breast band than in sand plovers. Worn plumage shown. Adult female summer similar or with a little rufous on breast.

Juvenile: Broader pale rufous fringes above and generally more extensive patches on breast than in juvenile sand plovers. Fresh adult winter very similar.

KITTLITZ'S PLOVER *Charadrius pecuarius* Africa   104

Summer: Head pattern. No complete band on breast.

Winter: Long supercilium reaching pale neck collar.

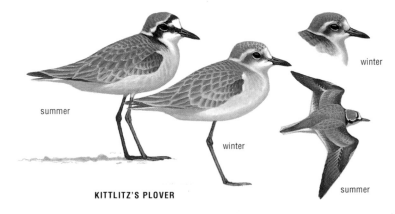

winter

summer

winter

summer

KITTLITZ'S PLOVER

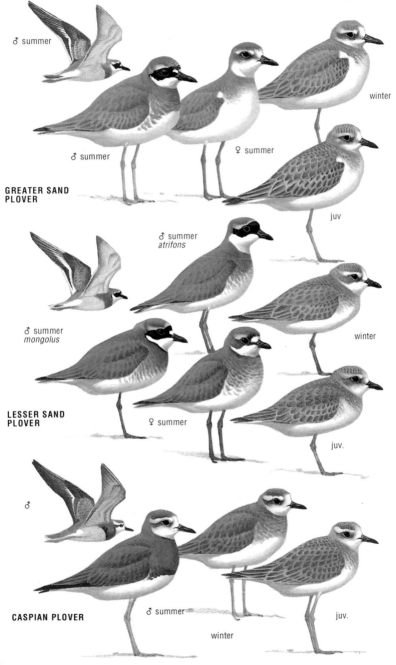

♂ summer

♂ summer

♀ summer

winter

GREATER SAND PLOVER

juv

♂ summer
atrifons

♂ summer
mongolus

winter

LESSER SAND PLOVER

♀ summer

juv.

♂

CASPIAN PLOVER

♂ summer

winter

juv.

Plate 22

AMERICAN GOLDEN PLOVER *Pluvialis dominica* N America   108

Smaller and slimmer than Golden Plover, longer legs and wings and greyish axillaries and underwing-coverts. Longer primary projection and shorter tertials in relation to tip of tail than Pacific.

Summer: Classic male shown, with prominent white patch on breast-side, all black flanks and undertail-coverts. Highly variable, sometimes indistinguishable from Pacific by plumage.

Winter: Generally much greyer than winter Golden and Pacific, lacking yellow on supercilium, face and breast. Normally less distinctly patterned above and on breast than Golden, and supercilium more prominent.

Juvenile: More distinctly and evenly patterned plumage than adult winter. Yellowish on neck and breast. Differs from juvenile Golden and Pacific by lack of yellowish on supercilium, neck and breast.

PACIFIC GOLDEN PLOVER
Pluvialis fulva Siberia and Alaska   110

Very like Golden Plover, but slightly smaller and slimmer; proportionately longer bill and legs, grey axillaries and underwing-coverts.

Summer: Classic male shown. Broader black stripe on foreneck, less spangling on side of breast, more coarsely marked flanks and more black on undertail-coverts than Golden.

Winter: Usually more distinct supercilium and less clearly spotted breast than Golden, and less distinctly patterned upperside and coverts.

Juvenile: Fresh, with distinctly and evenly patterned plumage. Head pattern normally more distinct than in Golden, pale spots above usually slightly larger.

SPUR-WINGED PLOVER
Hoplopterus spinosus Greece   113

Unmistakable. In flight, pale bar on upperwing-coverts and black secondaries and tail band.

Juvenile: Shorter scapulars than adult, with dark markings on coverts and tertials.

bright juv.

AMERICAN GOLDEN PLOVER

dull juv.

PACIFIC GOLDEN PLOVER

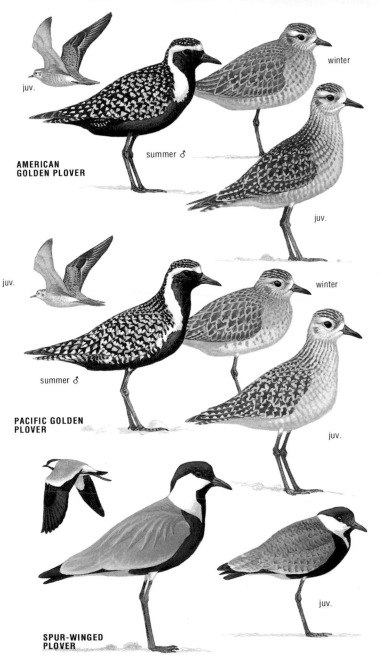

juv.

summer ♂

winter

**AMERICAN
GOLDEN PLOVER**

juv.

juv.

summer ♂

winter

**PACIFIC GOLDEN
PLOVER**

juv.

**SPUR-WINGED
PLOVER**

juv.

Plate 23

SOCIABLE PLOVER *Chettusia gregaria*   C Asia

114

Distinctive black and white wing pattern and white tail with black band. Head pattern distinctive.

Summer: Diagnostic black and chestnut belly patch.

Winter: Variably strongly marked breast. (Lower bird more worn, lacking pale fringes above. Juvenile very similar to top bird.)

WHITE-TAILED PLOVER *Chettusia leucura*   W Asia

115

Long, yellow legs. Rather plain head. Distinctive black and white wings and all white tail.

Juvenile: Easily told from adult by coarsely marked upperparts, coverts and tertials.

GREAT KNOT *Calidris tenuirostris*   NE Siberia

115

Summer: Prominent black spots on breast and flanks. Bright rufous centres to some scapulars.

Winter: Resembles Knot. Slightly larger, with longer bill, more extensively and diffusely dark lores, normally larger dark spots on breast/flanks, and whiter and more contrasting rump/uppertail-coverts.

Juvenile: Heavily streaked head/neck, coarsely spotted breast/flanks and distinctively patterned upperparts, coverts and tertials.

winter

Knot

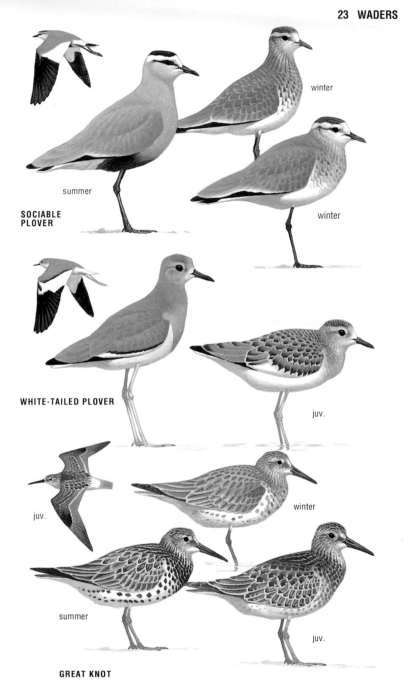

summer

SOCIABLE
PLOVER

winter

winter

WHITE-TAILED PLOVER

juv.

winter

juv.

summer

juv.

GREAT KNOT

Plate 24

SEMIPALMATED SANDPIPER *Calidris pusilla* N America 117

Short to rather long, blunt-tipped bill. Partially webbed toes only shared with Western Sandpiper among stints. **Summer**: Told from Little Stint by lack of rich rufous colours and paler centres to coverts and tertials. **Winter**: Grey and white. Very difficult to identify (see text). **Juvenile**: More distinctly patterned above, less coarsely marked on breast and fresher overall than adult. Usually clearly duller than juvenile Little Stint, with less distinct white stripe on side of mantle, paler lower scapulars with dark 'anchor-shaped' marks, paler centres to coverts and tertials and less distinct dark spots on breast-sides.

WESTERN SANDPIPER *Calidris mauri* N America and NE Siberia 118

Usually considerably longer bill than other stints (often recalling Dunlin's). Partially webbed toes. **Summer**: Rufous ear-coverts and sides to crown and some rufous on upper and usually also on some lower scapulars. Heavily streaked breast, extending onto flanks. **Winter**: Fine streaks across breast. **Juvenile**: Differs from juvenile Semipalmated Sandpiper in contrastingly rufous-fringed upper scapulars.

RED-NECKED STINT *Calidris ruficollis* NE Siberia 119

Summer: Differs from brightly coloured Little Stints in rufous throat, mostly whitish base colour to breast-sides, and paler coverts and tertials without rufous fringes/edges (a few tertials may be new and Little Stint-like). **Winter**: Extremely difficult to identify (see text). **Juvenile**: Very variable and often difficult to distinguish from juvenile Little Stint and Semipalmated Sandpiper. See text.

juv.

winter

Little Stint

summer

bright juv.

RED-NECKED STINT grey juv.

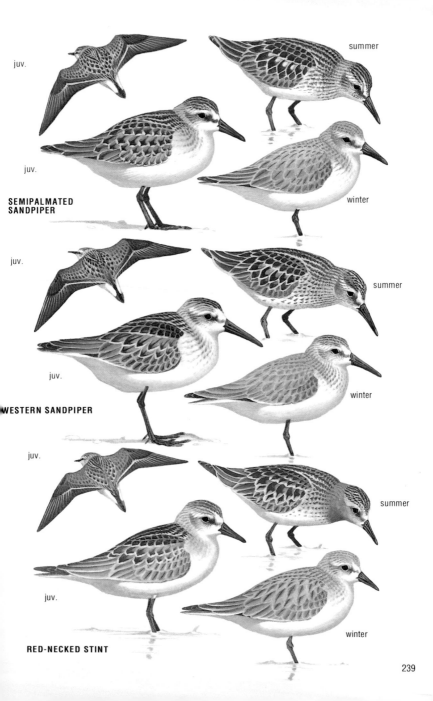

juv.

summer

juv.

SEMIPALMATED SANDPIPER

winter

juv.

summer

juv.

WESTERN SANDPIPER

winter

juv.

summer

juv.

RED-NECKED STINT

winter

Plate 25

LONG-TOED STINT *Calidris subminuta*   E Siberia   121

Longer legs and toes than Least, less chunky build. Head pattern usually differs from Least's in more prominent supercilium, narrower loral stripe and lacking pale 'bridge' across forehead (differences less obvious in summer). Less distinct wing-bar. Pale brown base to lower mandible.

Summer: Usually more rufous on upperside and especially tertials than Least.

Winter: More extensive and more clear-cut dark centres to scapulars than Least.

Juvenile: More distinctly and finely patterned than adult in the autumn. More contrastingly pale-fringed coverts and more finely streaked breast-sides than Least.

LEAST SANDPIPER *Calidris minutilla*   N America   122

See Long-toed Stint.

WHITE-RUMPED SANDPIPER *Calidris fuscicollis*   N America   124

Long wings and rather short bill. Resembles Baird's Sandpiper, but white uppertail-coverts obvious in flight. Also, more distinct, whitish supercilium and pale brown base to lower mandible.

Summer: Differs from Baird's by whitish, heavily streaked breast and flanks, and by some rufous on scapulars.

Moulting to winter: Some summer feathers still left. Rather dark grey above and greyish breast with fine streaking, usually also some streaks on flanks.

Juvenile: Differs from adult summer by less heavily streaked underparts and pattern of upperparts and coverts. Compare with juvenile Baird's and note contrastingly rufous mantle, upper scapulars, crown and ear-coverts, whitish V on mantle and whitish base colour to breast.

BAIRD'S SANDPIPER *Calidris bairdii*   N America   124

See White-rumped Sandpiper.

dull summer   bright summer

LONG-TOED STINT   **LEAST SANDPIPER**

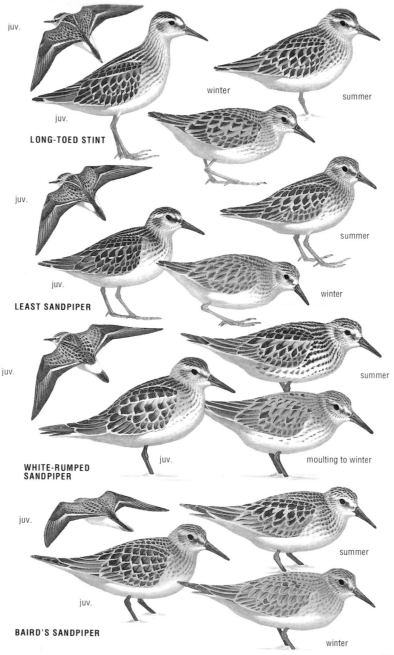

juv.

juv.

LONG-TOED STINT

winter

summer

juv.

summer

juv.

LEAST SANDPIPER

winter

juv.

summer

**WHITE-RUMPED
SANDPIPER**

juv.

moulting to winter

juv.

summer

juv.

BAIRD'S SANDPIPER

winter

241

Plate 26

PECTORAL SANDPIPER *Calidris melanotos*   N America and NE Siberia   126

Relatively sharp demarcation line between streaked pectoral band and remaining whitish underparts characteristic. Pale yellowish or greenish legs.

Female summer: Finer ştreaks on breast than male summer. Smaller.

Winter: Duller than summer.

Juvenile: Slight differences from adult female summer in pattern of particularly scapulars and coverts. In autumn, clearly more fresh than adult.

SHARP-TAILED SANDPIPER *Calidris acuminata*   NE Siberia   127

Summer: Distinctive pattern on underparts and head clearly different from that of Pectoral Sandpiper.

Winter: Duller than in summer, with rather poorly marked underparts. Compared to Pectoral Sandpiper more distinctly patterned head and less well-defined breast pattern.

Juvenile: Distinguished from juvenile Pectoral Sandpiper by head pattern, and by orange-buff foreneck/breast with fine and relatively sparse streaking.

STILT SANDPIPER *Micropalama himantopus*   N America   127

Long, slightly decurved bill and long, yellowish legs. Whitish patch on rump/uppertail-coverts. No distinct wing-bar.

Summer: Heavily barred underparts and rufous ear-coverts.

Winter: Grey above. Rather distinct streaking on underparts.

Juvenile: Strongly patterned above. Usually distinct streaks on breast and flanks.

BUFF-BREASTED SANDPIPER *Tryngites subruficollis*   N America   12

Confusable with juvenile female Ruff but is smaller and shorter-billed, and shows more distinctly dark-spotted breast-sides. In flight, by lack of distinct wing-bar and white sides to rump/upper tail-coverts.

Juvenile: Pattern of scapulars and coverts and colour of scapular fringes differ from adult.

juv. ♀ **Ruff (Reeve)**

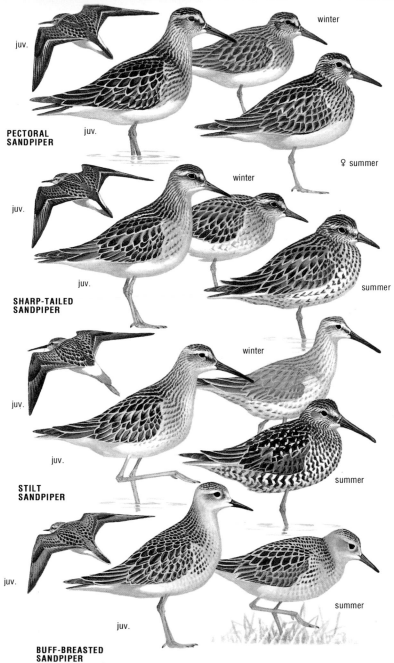

juv.

winter

PECTORAL SANDPIPER

juv.

juv.

♀ summer

juv.

winter

juv.

SHARP-TAILED SANDPIPER

summer

juv.

winter

juv.

STILT SANDPIPER

summer

juv.

juv.

BUFF-BREASTED SANDPIPER

summer

Plate 27

SHORT-BILLED DOWITCHER *Limnodromus griseus* N America   12•

Most easily distinguished from Long-billed Dowitcher by calls. **Summer**, race *griseus*: Differs from Long-billed by whitish belly – and here also flanks and undertail-coverts. **Winter**: Very like Long-billed. Paler above and on breast; finely streaked/spotted on foreneck/breast. **Juvenile**: Differs from adult summer mainly by lacking rufous and heavy barring on underside. Like juvenile Long-billed, but distinct pale internal markings to lower scapulars, tertials and inner greater coverts.

LONG-BILLED DOWITCHER *Limnodromus scolopaceus* N America   13•

See Short-billed Dowitcher.

HUDSONIAN GODWIT *Limosa haemastica* N America   13•

Diagnostic black axillaries and underwing-coverts.

Male summer: Resembles both Black-tailed and Bar-tailed Godwits. Deep chestnut and heavily barred underparts, with contrastingly grey head/neck characteristic. **Juvenile**: Like juvenile Black-tailed Godwit, but is more grey-brown on neck/breast.

LITTLE WHIMBREL *Numenius minutus* C and NE Siberia   13•

Resembles Whimbrel. Distinctly smaller, with shorter, straighter bill. Less patterned underparts, especially flanks. Back, rump, uppertail-coverts and underwing dark (also in 'Hudsonian Whimbrel').

ESKIMO CURLEW *Numenius borealis* N America   13•

Resembles Little Whimbrel. Slightly longer and more decurved bill and longer wings, projecting well beyond tip of tail. More heavily marked underparts.

'HUDSONIAN WHIMBREL' *Numenius phaeopus hudsonicus* N America   13•

Like European Whimbrel, but dark back, rump, uppertail-coverts and tail as well as underwing.

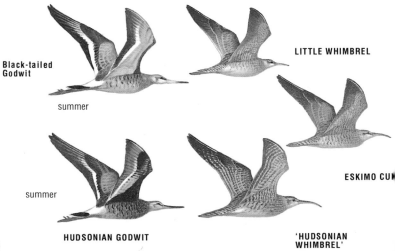

LITTLE WHIMBREL

Black-tailed Godwit

summer

ESKIMO CU•

summer

HUDSONIAN GODWIT

'HUDSONIAN WHIMBREL'

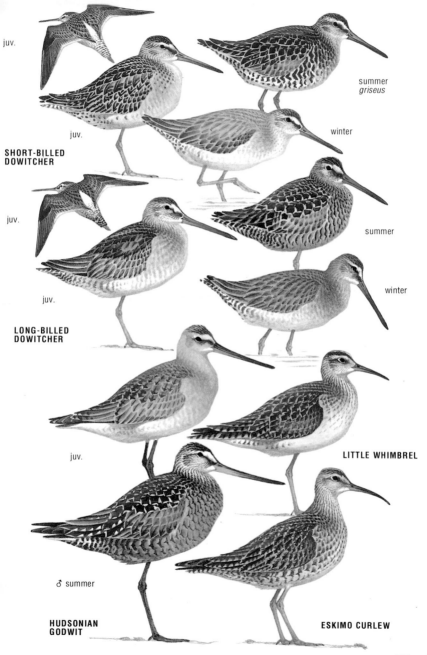

juv.

summer
griseus

winter

**SHORT-BILLED
DOWITCHER**

juv.

juv.

summer

juv.

winter

**LONG-BILLED
DOWITCHER**

juv.

LITTLE WHIMBREL

♂ summer

**HUDSONIAN
GODWIT**

ESKIMO CURLEW

Plate 28

SLENDER-BILLED CURLEW *Numenius tenuirostris* W Asia 135

Confusable with both Curlew and Whimbrel. Close to latter in size. Bill typically with very thin outer end. Foreneck/breast more whitish base, better-defined dark streaks. Dark spots on flanks.

UPLAND SANDPIPER *Bartramia longicauda* N America 136

Shortish, straight bill and long tail. Relatively plain face, heavily barred flanks and contrastingly dark back, rump and uppertail-coverts. Yellowish legs. Juvenile told from adult by more distinct pale fringes to coverts and tertials, with dark subterminal bands.

GREATER YELLOWLEGS *Tringa melanoleuca* N America 138

Told from Greenshank by yellow legs, more spotted mantle and no white wedge on back. Larger than Lesser Yellowlegs, longer, thicker and more distinctly uptilted bill. **Summer**: More heavily barred flanks than Lesser Yellowlegs. **Juvenile**: Less heavily marked underparts.

LESSER YELLOWLEGS *Tringa flavipes* N America 139

See Greater Yellowlegs.

SOLITARY SANDPIPER *Tringa solitaria* N America 140

Like Green Sandpiper, but dark rump, uppertail-coverts and central tail-feathers. Juvenile more fresh overall and more evenly patterned on upperparts, coverts and tertials than adult in autumn.

TEREK SANDPIPER *Xenus cinereus* Finland. 141

Summer: Bill, legs, wing pattern and grey back, rump and tail. **Juvenile**: Narrow buffish tips to upperparts, less prominent dark markings than adult summer.

MARSH SANDPIPER *Tringa stagnatilis* Asia 13

Smaller, slimmer than Greenshank, with finer, straighter, darker bill, longer legs. **Summer**: Paler, greyer and more sparsely dark-spotted above than Greenshank. **Winter**: Less patterned than Greenshank. Pale supercilium and lores. **Juvenile**: Pattern of head, upperparts, coverts, tertials and breast distinguish from juvenile Greenshank.

juv.

winter

summer

juv.

MARSH SANDPIPER

LENDER-BILLED
URLEW

UPLAND
SANDPIPER

juv.

summer

juv.

GREATER
YELLOWLEGS

summer

juv.

LESSER
YELLOWLEGS

summer

juv.

juv.

SOLITARY
SANDPIPER

TEREK SANDPIPER

Plate 29

juv. **Common Sandpiper**

SPOTTED SANDPIPER *Actitis macularia*   N America   142
  Summer: Resembles Common Sandpiper, but black-spotted underparts. **Winter**:
  Very like Common Sandpiper, but distinctly shorter tail and usually more
  yellowish legs. **Juvenile**: Coverts and tertials are more strongly patterned than in
  adult winter. Compared to juvenile Common Sandpiper, upperside more plain,
  while coverts more strongly marked. Tertials lack pale- and dark-spotted edges.

GREY-TAILED TATTLER *Heteroscelus brevipes*   NE Siberia   143
  Rather uniformly grey on upperside, upperwings and underwings. Shortish
  yellow legs. **Summer**: Heavily streaked and barred underside. **Juvenile**: Small
  pale spots on upperparts, coverts and tertials. No barring below.

WILSON'S PHALAROPE *Phalaropus tricolor*   N America   144
  Long, thin, dark bill. Larger than other phalaropes and does not swim so much.
  Whitish rump/uppertail-coverts. Lacks distinct wing-bars. **Female summer**:
  Unmistakable. **Winter**: Lacks other phalaropes' blackish band through eye and
  patch on rear crown/nape. Yellow legs. **1st-winter**: Juvenile, distinctly
  buffish-edged and blackish-centred coverts and tertials retained.

WILLET *Catoptrophorus semipalmatus*   N America   144
  Diagnostic wing pattern, both above and below. Long, comparatively heavy,
  straight bill, and blue-grey legs. **Summer**: Heavily and characteristically marked
  on upper- and underparts. **Winter**: Grey and white.

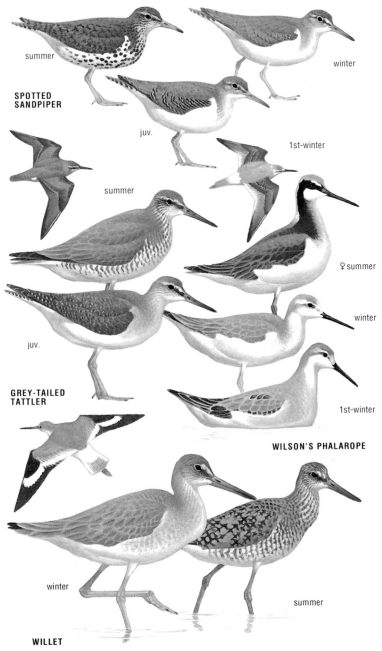

summer

winter

SPOTTED
SANDPIPER

juv.

1st-winter

summer

♀ summer

winter

juv.

1st-winter

GREY-TAILED
TATTLER

WILSON'S PHALAROPE

winter

summer

WILLET

Plate 30

SOUTH POLAR SKUA *Catharacta maccormicki*   Antarctica   146

Very like Great Skua. Plumage greyer, lacking rufous.

Adult pale morph: Rather pale head, neck and underparts, contrasting with dark mantle/scapulars and coverts.

Adult intermediate morph: Somewhat intermediate between pale and dark morph. Often shows pale hindneck-collar.

Adult dark morph: All dark grey-brown. Some juvenile Great Skuas are practically identical, but most show contrastingly dark head and some rufous markings on upperwing-coverts.

WHITE-EYED GULL *Larus leucophthalmus*   Red Sea   147

Gives dark impression; dark underwings. Long, slender bill.

Adult summer: Black hood and bib. Bold white eye-crescents. Dark-tipped red bill and yellow legs.

1st-winter: Largely grey-brown (including underwing). Broad, dark tail-band contrasting with whitish rump/uppertail-coverts.

2nd-winter: Like adult winter, but usually some brown admixed.

GREAT BLACK-HEADED GULL *Larus ichthyaetus*   Asia   148

Adult summer: Unmistakable. Large, with distinctive wing pattern, black hood and characteristic bare part coloration.

Adult winter: Distinctive dark 'half-hood'.

1st-winter/-summer: Could be confused with 2nd-winter/-summer Herring Gull, but note typical dark head pattern and contrasting whitish 'eye-lids'. Pale underwings with dark lines, and white tail with clear-cut blackish band.

2nd-winter: Wing and tail pattern intermediate beween 1st-year and adult.

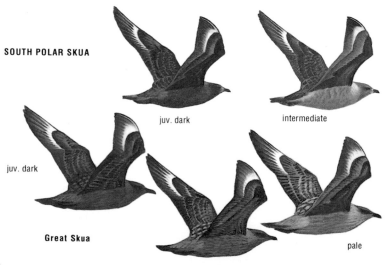

SOUTH POLAR SKUA

juv. dark

intermediate

juv. dark

Great Skua

pale

typical

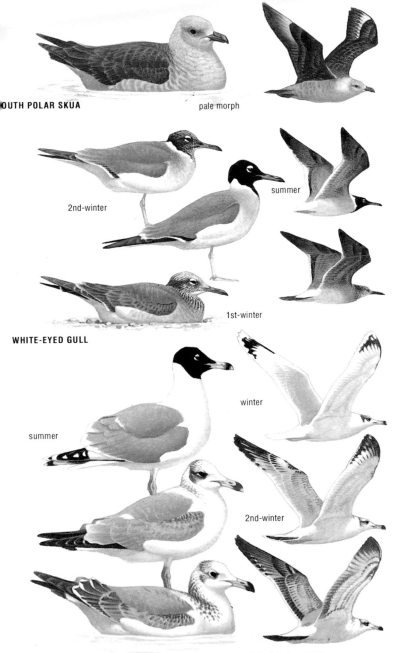

SOUTH POLAR SKUA

pale morph

2nd-winter

summer

1st-winter

WHITE-EYED GULL

summer

winter

2nd-winter

GREAT BLACK-HEADED GULL

1st-winter/-summer

Plate 31

LAUGHING GULL *Larus atricilla*   N America   149

Resembles Franklin's Gull, but distinctly longer billed.

Winter: Compared to adult winter Franklin's Gull the head pattern is less distinct, and there is more black and less white on the primaries.

Summer: Like adult winter, but black hood and reddish bill.

1st-winter: Pattern of wings and tail differ from adult, as well as extensively grey neck, breast and flanks. Differs from 1st-winter Franklin's by less distinct head pattern, grey-washed breast/flanks, darker inner primaries, duskier underwing and broader tail-band.

2nd-winter: Resembles adult winter, but extensively grey neck, breast and flanks, in flight also some dark on primary-coverts and often tail.

FRANKLIN'S GULL *Larus pipixcan*   N America   150

Cf. Laughing Gull in all plumages.

1st-winter: Differs from adult by pattern of wings and tail.

BONAPARTE'S GULL *Larus philadelphia*   N America   153

Like Black-headed Gull, but inner primaries white below instead of dark grey, and bill blackish.

Summer: Blackish-grey hood (dark brown in Black-headed).

Winter: Usually grey suffusion to hindneck and breast-sides, unlike in Black-headed.

1st-winter: Differs from adult by pattern of wings and tail. Wing pattern above more distinct and contrasting than in Black-headed Gull. Grey on hindneck and breast-sides.

1st-winter **Black-headed Gull**

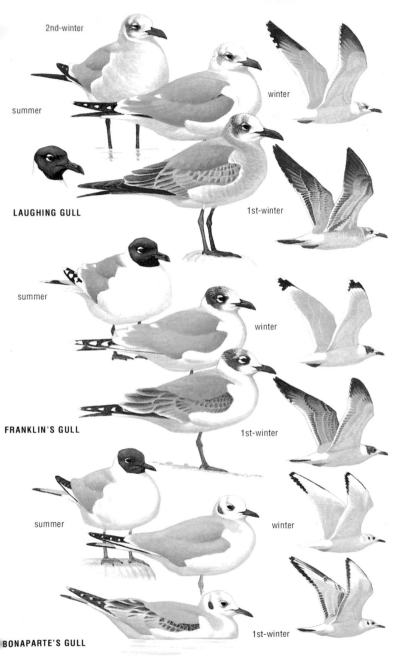

2nd-winter

winter

summer

LAUGHING GULL

1st-winter

summer

winter

FRANKLIN'S GULL

1st-winter

summer

winter

BONAPARTE'S GULL

1st-winter

253

Plate 32

GREY-HEADED GULL *Larus cirrocephalus*   Africa and South America   154
  Like Black-headed Gull, but largely dark underwings and more extensively
  dark outer primaries, with white mirrors in adult.
  Summer: Told from Black- headed by pale grey hood and pale iris.
  Adult winter: Dark spot on ear-coverts normally less distinct than in
  Black-headed Gull.
  1st-winter: Differs from adult by pattern of wings and tail.

RING-BILLED GULL *Larus delawarensis*   N America   156
  Like Common Gull, but is larger, with proportionately heavier bill. Paler grey
  on mantle/scapulars and upperwings.
  Winter: Told from Common Gull by yellow bill with broad, blackish band,
  yellow legs and pale iris.
  Summer: Lacks dark spots on head/neck of the winter plumage.
  1st-winter: Pattern of wings and tail clearly different from adult. Pink bill with
  blackish tip and pink legs. More contrastingly patterned upperwings and less
  well-defined dark tail-band than Common Gull.
  2nd-winter: More dark on hand than adult and usually only one small white
  mirror. Frequently broken tail-band and sometimes traces of a dark bar on
  secondaries. Latter three characters usually not seen in 2nd-winter Common
  Gull.

AUDOUIN'S GULL *Larus audouinii*   Endemic to Mediterranean   154
  Bare part colours tell from Herring Gull; paler grey on mantle/scapulars,
  smaller white mirrors.
  1st-winter: Diagnostic pattern of scapulars. In flight, mostly resembles 1st-year
  Lesser Black-backed Gull, but with distinctly paler underwing.

1st-winter   **RING-BILLED GULL**

1st-winter   **Common Gull**

summer

winter

1st-winter

GREY-HEADED GULL

winter

summer

1st-winter

2nd-winter

RING-BILLED GULL

1st-winter

AUDOUIN'S GULL

Plate 33

'KUMLIEN'S ICELAND GULL' *Larus glaucoides kumlieni*   N America   158

Like nominate race of Iceland, but with variable dark pattern on primaries and usually darker iris.

ROSS'S GULL *Rhodostethia rosea*   Arctic   159

Small, with short, blackish bill and wedge-shaped tail (shape often difficult to judge). Largely grey underwing. **Summer**: Narrow blackish necklace and pinkish below. **Winter**: No necklace and little or no pink. Confusable with adult winter Little Gull, but white trailing edge to wing does not reach outermost primaries. **1st- winter**: Resembles 1st-winter Little Gull, but white secondaries and inner primaries, and cap not blackish.

SABINE'S GULL *Larus sabini*   Arctic   151

Tail forked (not always easy to judge). Very distinctive wing pattern.

Summer: Dark grey hood, with blackish lower border. Yellow tip to bill.

Winter: Slightly variable dark pattern on head.

Juvenile: Largely grey-brown on head, hindneck, breast-sides, upperparts and upperwing-coverts. Blackish tail-band.

IVORY GULL *Pagophila eburnea*   Arctic   160

All white, with yellow-tipped bill and blackish legs.

1st-winter: All white, with dusky face and some dark spots.

1st-w
ROS
GUL

1st-wi
Little

2nd-
Littl

1st-winter **Kittiwake**

winter
**SABINE'S
GULL**

256

'KUMLIEN'S ICELAND GULL'

winter

winter

ROSS'S GULL

summer

1st-winter

1st-winter

SABINE'S GULL

summer

winter

juv.

juv.

IVORY GULL

1st-winter

Plate 34

ROYAL TERN *Sterna maxima*   N America, W Africa   161
Confusable with Caspian Tern, but underside of primaries white with dark tips to outers, and bill all orange or orange-yellow.
Summer: Cap all black for very short period.
Winter: Whiter on forehead/crown than Caspian Tern.
Juvenile: Told from adult by boldly patterned upperwings and dark-tipped tail. Whiter on forehead/crown and much more boldly marked on upperwing than juvenile Caspian.

LESSER CRESTED TERN *Sterna bengalensis*   Nearest Libya   162
Much smaller than Royal Tern, with a thinner bill. Diagnostic grey rump, uppertail-coverts and tail.
Juvenile: Boldly patterned upperwings and dark-tipped tail.

ELEGANT TERN *Sterna elegans*   W N America   163
Long, slender, slightly drooping bill. More prominent and shaggier crest than Lesser Crested Tern. White rump, uppertail-coverts and tail.
Juvenile: Boldly patterned upperwings and dark-tipped tail.

ALEUTIAN TERN *Sterna aleutica*   E Siberia/Alaska   165
Summer: White forehead. Grey wash on much of underparts. Dark bar on secondaries below. Blackish bill and legs.
Juvenile: Very distinctive pattern on upperparts and upperwings, and grey rump, uppertail-coverts and tail.

summer

summer

Caspian Tern

juv.

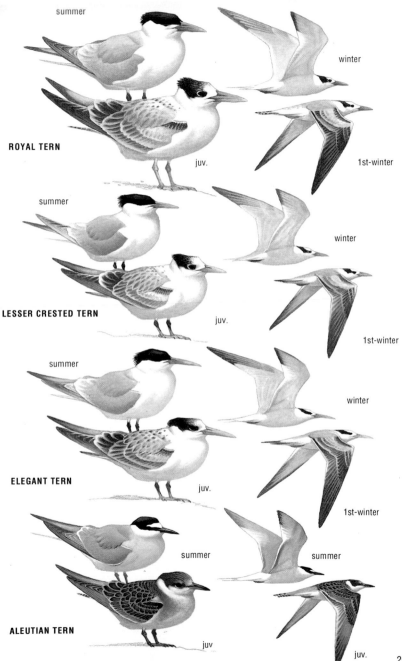

summer

winter

ROYAL TERN

juv.

1st-winter

summer

winter

LESSER CRESTED TERN

juv.

1st-winter

summer

winter

ELEGANT TERN

juv.

1st-winter

summer

summer

ALEUTIAN TERN

juv

juv.

259

Plate 35

FORSTER'S TERN *Sterna forsteri* N America 166
Summer: Paler grey primaries above than Common Tern and lacking contrast between darker outers and paler inners. Tail pale grey with white outer edge. **Winter:** Diagnostic blackish patch on ear-coverts. **1st-winter:** Differs from adult winter by some brown markings on coverts and tertials. Upperwing much paler and more uniform than in juvenile/1st- winter Arctic and Common Terns. Head pattern also very different.

BRIDLED TERN *Sterna anaethetus*   Tropical oceans 167
Dark grey-brown above, including rump, uppertail-coverts and tail.
Summer: White forehead and supercilium. Uniformly broad dark loral stripe.
Juvenile: Less distinct head pattern than adult, and pale tips to upperparts, coverts and tertials.

SOOTY TERN *Sterna fuscata*   Tropical oceans 167
Like Bridled Tern but blackish above, shows tapering loral stripe and lacks white supercilium. **Juvenile:** Unmistakable. Mostly dark, with distinct whitish markings on upperparts, coverts and tertials.

BROWN NODDY *Anous stolidus*   Tropical oceans 168
All dark brown, with whitish cap. Wedge-shaped tail.
Juvenile: Only forehead pale.

ROSEATE TERN *Sterna dougallii*
British Isles, NW France and Azores 164
Like Common and Arctic Terns. Paler grey above. Lacks distinct dark trailing edge to primaries below and black outer web to outermost tail-feather.
Summer: Mostly blackish bill. Longer tail-streamers than Common and Arctic Terns.
Juvenile: Very distinctive pattern on scapulars, tertials and some coverts. Blackish bill and legs.

summer

Common Tern

summer

juv.

summer

ROSEATE TERN   juv.

summer

1st-winter

summer

winter

FORSTER'S TERN

juv.

BRIDLED TERN

summer

juv.

SOOTY TERN

juv.

BROWN NODDY

Plate 36

BRÜNNICH'S GUILLEMOT *Uria lomvia*   Iceland and NW Norway   169
  Summer: Like Guillemot, but bill shorter and deeper, with whitish streak at
  base. Blacker above, no dark streaks on flanks and axillaries.
  Winter: Dark on head reaches further down on sides than in Guillemot; thus
  lacks Guillemot's dark eye-stripe.

CRESTED AUKLET *Aethia cristatella*   Bering Sea   170
  Summer: Recurved crest and peculiar orange bill and gape makes it
  unmistakable. Plumage all dark.
  Winter: Crest shorter and bill browner, lacking 'swollen' gape.

PARAKEET AUKLET *Cyclorrhynchus psittacula*   Bering Sea   170
  Summer: Peculiarly shaped, orange bill and distinctive plumage.
  Winter: Differs from summer plumage in mostly whitish throat/upper breast.

SPOTTED SANDGROUSE *Pterocles senegallus*   Africa & W Asia
                                                                                170
  Rather narrow, elongated blackish belly patch (difficult to see when standing).
  Relatively pale upper- and underwing with blackish secondaries.
  Male: Very distinctive, particularly pattern of upperparts and coverts.
  Female: Characteristic dark-spotted plumage.

CHESTNUT-BELLIED SANDGROUSE *Pterocles exustus*   Africa and W Asia   171
  Large dark patch on belly and flanks. Contrastingly dark outer wing above.
  Underwing all dark.
  Male: Comparatively dull plumage. Note pattern of upperparts and coverts.
  Female: Strongly streaked/spotted neck/breast and heavily barred upperside
  and coverts with some large pale spots.

PALLAS'S SANDGROUSE *Syrrhaptes paradoxus*   C-E Asia   172
  Male: Conspicuous blackish belly patch. Rather heavily barred upperside.
  Wings comparatively pale, both above and below.
  Female: Duller and more patterned on head, neck, breast-sides and coverts than
  male.

summer

winter

winter

BRÜNNICH'S GUILLEMOT

summer

summer

winter

PARAKEET AUKLET

winter

CRESTED AUKLET

♂

SPOTTED SANDGROUSE

♂

♀

♂

♂

ESTNUT-BELLIED NDGROUSE

♀

♂

♂

♀

ALLAS'S SANDGROUSE

263

Plate 37

RUFOUS TURTLE DOVE *Streptopelia orientalis* Asia 173

Race *orientalis*: Larger and heavier than Turtle Dove; overall darker impression. Note brown nape/hindneck; more brownish-pink breast and pale greyish-pink belly (and undertail-coverts). More extensive, less pointed and more diffuse dark centres and generally paler tips to lesser and median coverts; not contrastingly pale blue-grey outer coverts; and less brown admixed on back/rump. **Juvenile** race *meena*: Extremely difficult to tell from juvenile Turtle Dove, but usually darker overall.

LAUGHING DOVE *Streptopelia senegalensis* Africa and SW Asia 174

Small, with shape like Collared Dove. Gives dark impression. Neck pattern diagnostic. **Juvenile**: Lacks adult's neck pattern.

BLACK-BILLED CUCKOO *Coccyzus erythrophthalmus* N America 175

Like Yellow-billed Cuckoo, but from below tail-feathers paler and show less white on tips. Colour of lower mandible differs. Less or no contrastingly rufous patch on primaries. Red orbital ring. **1st-winter**: Yellow orbital ring. Pale tips to tail-feathers even smaller than in adult and lacking black subterminally.

YELLOW-BILLED CUCKOO *Coccyzus americanus* N America 176

See Black-billed Cuckoo. **1st-winter**: From below, tail-feathers dark grey, with slightly narrower and less clear-cut white tips than in adult.

MOURNING DOVE *Zenaida macroura*
Slender body, long pointed tail, black spots on tertials.
1, Isle of Man, 31st Oct 1989*.

Turtle Dove

orientalis

RUFOUS TURTLE DOVE

juv. *meena*

LAUGHING DOVE

juv.

1st-winter

1st-winter

BLACK-BILLED CUCKOO

ad.

1st-winter

1st-winter

YELLOW-BILLED CUCKOO

ad.

Plate 38

MARSH OWL *Asio capensis*   Africa
176
Resembles Short-eared Owl, but is much darker and more uniformly coloured, with more contrastingly patterned upperwing. Dark eyes.

EGYPTIAN NIGHTJAR *Caprimulgus aegyptius*   N Africa and W Asia
177
Distinctly paler than Nightjar, lacking bold dark stripes on crown, mantle and scapulars. In flight, pale upperwing-coverts contrasting with darker flight-feathers.

COMMON NIGHTHAWK *Chordeiles minor*   N and Central America
178
Tail notched and clearly shorter than Nightjar's (wings reach to tip of tail when folded). Flight-feathers unbarred and with a more proximally placed and usually more prominent white band on primaries than in male Nightjar (white band lacking in female Nightjar). Male has subterminal white tail-band.

NEEDLE-TAILED SWIFT *Hirundapus caudacutus*   Asia
179
Large, with characteristic shape and plumage. Note prominent white throat and U on lower body and pale patch on mantle/back.

CHIMNEY SWIFT *Chaetura pelagica*   N America
179
Small, nearly all dark, with characteristic shape.

LITTLE SWIFT *Apus affinis*   Africa and Asia
180
Small, with almost square tail and broad, white patch on rump.

WHITE-RUMPED SWIFT *Apus caffer*   S Spain
180
Small, with forked tail (although normally held closed in flight) and narrow, white band on rump. Note whitish tips to secondaries.

PACIFIC SWIFT *Apus pacificus*   Asia
179
Resembles White-rumped Swift, but is larger (larger than Swift, whereas White-rumped is smaller than Swift). Paler fringes to much of body visible at close range.

CLIFF SWALLOW *Hirundo pyrrhonota*   N America
189
Very distinctive. Somewhat resembles Red-rumped Swallow, but square-tipped tail, rufous throat, blackish patch on breast and lacks black undertail-coverts.

ds not to scale

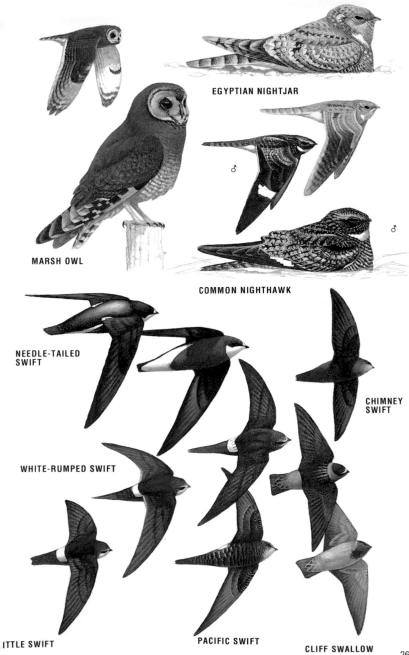

EGYPTIAN NIGHTJAR

MARSH OWL

♂

♂

COMMON NIGHTHAWK

NEEDLE-TAILED
SWIFT

CHIMNEY
SWIFT

WHITE-RUMPED SWIFT

ITTLE SWIFT

PACIFIC SWIFT

CLIFF SWALLOW

Plate 39

WHITE-BREASTED KINGFISHER *Halcyon smyrnensis*   Middle East & Asia   181
   Unmistakable. Rather large. Large white patch on primaries visible in flight.

PIED KINGFISHER *Ceryle rudis*   Africa to Asia   181
   Unmistakable. Rather large. Female has only one dark band on breast, male has
   two.

BELTED KINGFISHER *Ceryle alcyon*   N America   181
   Unmistakable. Rather large. Female differs from male by rufous breast band and
   some rufous on flanks.

BLUE-CHEEKED BEE-EATER *Merops superciliosus*   Africa to Asia   182
   Unmistakable if seen reasonably well. In flight from below confusable with
   Bee-eater, but underwing more rufous and narrower blackish trailing edge on
   secondaries. Throat pattern different, and long central tail-feathers.

NORTHERN FLICKER *Colaptes auratus*   N and Central America   183
   Male: Unmistakable. **Female:** Differs from male in lacking black moustachial
   stripe.

YELLOW-BELLIED SAPSUCKER *Sphyrapicus varius*
   N America   183

   Male: Unmistakable. **Female:** Differs from male in
   lacking red throat, often also lacking red on
   forehead/crown. **1st-winter male:** Usually pale
   mottling to black parts.

Bee-eater

WHITE-BREASTED
KINGFISHER

PIED KINGFISHER

BELTED KINGFISHER

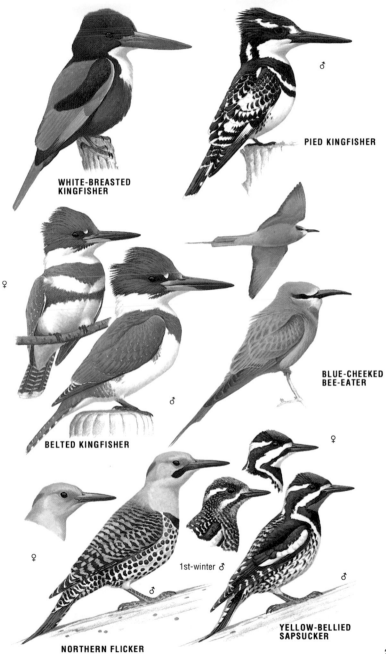

WHITE-BREASTED
KINGFISHER

♂

PIED KINGFISHER

♀

♂

BLUE-CHEEKED
BEE-EATER

BELTED KINGFISHER

♀

♀

1st-winter ♂

♂

♂

NORTHERN FLICKER

YELLOW-BELLIED
SAPSUCKER

Plate 40

HOOPOE LARK *Alaemon alaudipes* Africa and W Asia 185
 Rather large, with distinctive shape. Relatively pale and unmarked on the ground, but very strikingly patterned in flight.

DUPONT'S LARK *Chersophilus duponti* Spain 186
 Distinctive shape, with rather long and slightly decurved bill. No crest. Heavily marked above and on breast, looking scaly on upperparts and wings in fresh plumage (autumn; illustrated). Reluctant to fly; prefers to run away.

BIMACULATED LARK *Melanocorypha bimaculata* W Asia 187
 Very like Calandra Lark and best distinguished in flight by less contrastingly dark flight-feathers above, lack of white trailing edge to secondaries and broadly white-tipped tail lacking white edges. Right bird in more fresh plumage than left one.

BLACK LARK *Melanocorypha yeltoniensis* USSR 188
 Male: Unmistakable.
 Female: Large and heavy. Rather grey-looking and lacking prominent features except for heavily marked underparts (more obvious when worn; quite fresh plumage shown here). Dark underwings. No white in wings and tail.

WHITE-WINGED LARK *Melanocorypha leucoptera* USSR 187
 Male: Wing pattern. Also rufous crown, rear ear-coverts and breast-sides.
 Female: Differs from male mainly by heavily streaked crown and ear-coverts with little or no rufous, and more heavily streaked breast without rufous sides.

BAR-TAILED DESERT LARK *Ammomanes cincturus* Africa and W Asia 185
 Small, pale and virtually unstreaked lark showing rufous tail with clear-cut blackish terminal bar. In flight largely rufous remiges.

Calandra Lark

BAR-TAILED DESERT LARK

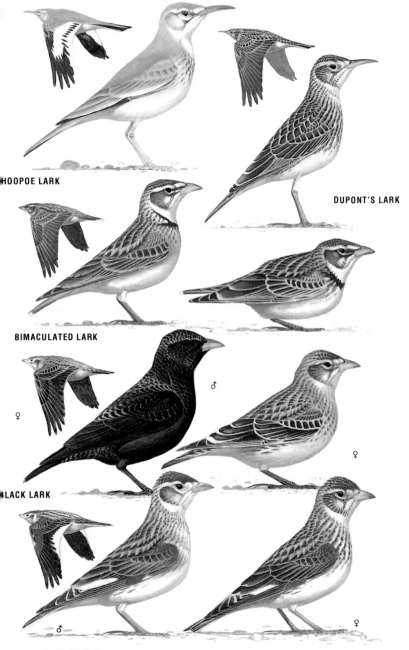

HOOPOE LARK

DUPONT'S LARK

BIMACULATED LARK

♀

♂

LACK LARK

♀

♂

♀

WHITE-WINGED LARK

Plate 41

RICHARD'S PIPIT *Anthus richardi*   Asia

189

Very like Blyth's Pipit. Cf. also Tawny Pipit, especially
colour and pattern above and on lores. Fresh autumn
plumage shown. **1st-winter**: Median coverts, tertials and
two scapulars are unmoulted juvenile and
differ from adult in colour and pattern.

BLYTH'S PIPIT *Anthus godlewskii*
E Asia   191

See Richard's Pipit (1st-winter also has
retained juvenile lesser coverts, but no
juvenile scapulars).

OLIVE-BACKED PIPIT *Anthus hodgsoni*
Asia   322

Very like Tree Pipit, but in fresh plumage
greenish above, with very indistinct
streaking. Head more contrastingly
patterned.

BUFF-BELLIED PIPIT *Anthus rubescens*
N America and E Asia   324

Winter, race *rubescens*: Dark grey-brown above
with indistinct streaking and rather uniformly
deep buff base colour below. Dark legs.
1st-winter, race *japonicus*: Underparts paler,
with larger, blacker and more clear-cut
streaks. Worn plumage shown here (more
streaked above than when fresh).

PECHORA PIPIT *Anthus gustavi*
Siberia   323

See 1st-winter Red-throated. More
rufous-tinged head and upperparts, mantle
more strikingly patterned contrastingly
buffish breast, dark loral stripe and distinct
primary projection.

CITRINE WAGTAIL *Motacilla citreola*
Asia   325

Male summer: Unmistakable. **Female
summer**: Broad yellow supercilium round
ear-coverts. **1st-winter**: Grey and white;
broad supercilium, round ear-coverts, no
loral stripe. **1st-summer male**: Sometimes
duskier head than adult male.

ju
1s

Tawny Pipit

Water Pipit

1st-winter

1st-win
japonic

**BUFF-BELLIED
PIPIT**

1st-winter

Red-throated Pipit

Yellow Wagtail   grey 1st-w

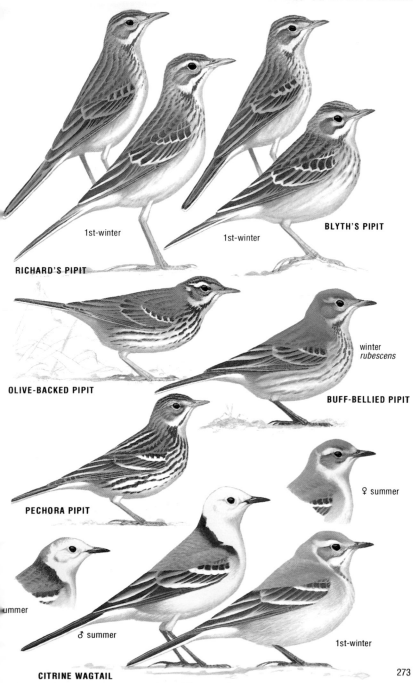

1st-winter

1st-winter

BLYTH'S PIPIT

RICHARD'S PIPIT

OLIVE-BACKED PIPIT

winter
rubescens

BUFF-BELLIED PIPIT

PECHORA PIPIT

♀ summer

ummer

♂ summer

1st-winter

CITRINE WAGTAIL

273

Plate 42

GRAY CATBIRD *Dumetella carolinensis* N America 328
Unmistakable.

BROWN THRASHER *Toxostoma rufum* N America 328
Unmistakable.

BLACK-THROATED ACCENTOR *Prunella atrogularis* Asia 329
Usually unmistakable. Occasionally black bib much reduced (presumably only in 1st-winter females) when confusable with Siberican Accentor, but paler on throat and lacks rufous on upperparts and flanks.

BLACK-THROATED
ACCENTOR

SIBERIAN ACCENTOR

SIBERIAN ACCENTOR
Prunella montanella Siberia 329
Unmistakable. Head shows extremely dull individual.

'EASTERN' STONECHAT
Saxicola torquata maura group Asia 334
Male summer: Rump and uppertail-coverts white and unstreaked (rarely in European birds). **Winter**: All plumages are paler than European, with unstreaked rump and uppertail-coverts. Female lacks dark on throat. **1st-winter male**: Usually some blackish on ear-coverts behind eye, unlike female, but may be indistinguishable in field. Sometimes more definitely male-patterned on head (as here), but lores and chin not completely black. Race *variegata* shown – white basally on outer tail-feathers.

MOUSSIER'S REDSTART
Phoenicurus moussieri N Africa. 334
Male: Unmistakable. **Female**: Differs from female Redstart mainly in smaller size and shorter tail and primary projection.

fresh ♀

fre

'EASTERN'
STONECHAT

Stonechat

GRAY CATBIRD

BROWN THRASHER

atypical winter

summer

BLACK-THROATED ACCENTOR

atypical

typical

SIBERIAN ACCENTOR

♂ summer *maura*

♂ winter *maura*

1st-winter ♂ *variegata*

♀ winter *maura*

'EASTERN' STONECHAT

♂

♀

MOUSSIER'S REDSTART

Plate 43

SIBERIAN RUBYTHROAT *Luscinia calliope* Asia   330

Male: Unmistakable. Grey breast and all black bill indicate spring-summer.

Female: Usually some pink on throat, head pattern less striking than male's.

1st-winter male: Like adult male winter, but buffish tips to retained juvenile outer greater coverts and tertials.

1st-winter/-summer female: Characterized by distinctive jizz and head pattern. Usually no pink on throat. Ageing as in 1st-winter male.

SIBERIAN BLUE ROBIN *Luscinia cyane* Siberia   331

Male: Unmistakable.

Female: Distinctive shape and habit of quivering tail when alerted. Rather featureless, but breast with darker crescents or mottling and rump and uppertail-coverts often show some blue.

1st-winter male: Mainly like female, but usually shows more blue. Note unmoulted, juvenile, outer greater coverts with distinct buffish tips.

RED-FLANKED BLUETAIL *Tarsiger cyanurus* Asia   332

Male: Unmistakable. Some to all remiges may be brown-edged.

Female/1st-year male: Easily identified by blue rump, uppertail-coverts and tail, orange flanks and well-defined, rather narrow white throat.

WHITE-THROATED ROBIN *Irania gutturalis* SW Asia   333

Male: Unmistakable.

Female: Characterized by combination of greyish-tinged upperside, blackish tail, whitish throat and orange flanks.

Bluethroat   **SIBERIAN RUBYTHROAT**

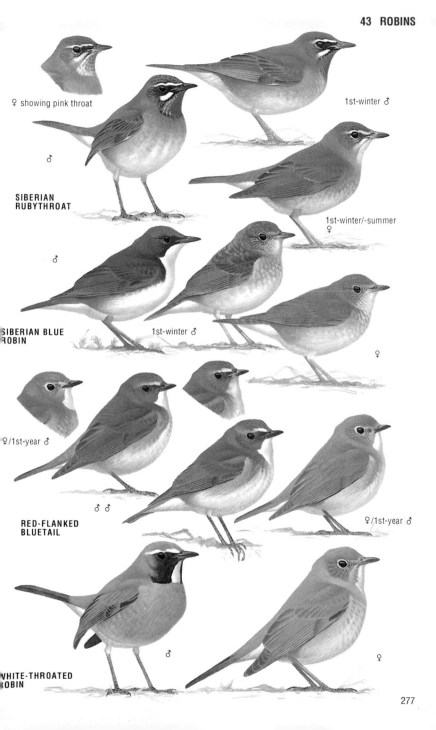

♀ showing pink throat

1st-winter ♂

♂

SIBERIAN
RUBYTHROAT

1st-winter/-summer
♀

♂

SIBERIAN BLUE
ROBIN

1st-winter ♂

♀

♀/1st-year ♂

♂ ♂

RED-FLANKED
BLUETAIL

♀/1st-year ♂

♂

WHITE-THROATED
ROBIN

♀

Plate 44

ISABELLINE WHEATEAR *Oenanthe isabellina* Greece   336

Like some pale female/1st-winter male Wheatears. Identified by paler centres to coverts (paler than alula!), supercilium buffish throughout length or whiter in front of/above eye, broader tail-band and whitish underwing-coverts/axillaries. Wings never distinctly darker than upperparts as in most female Wheatears in spring-summer.

WHITE-CROWNED BLACK WHEATEAR *Oenanthe leucopyga* N Africa to Arabia   341

Unmistakable. **1st-winter/-summer**: All black head or only some white on crown. Black-headed birds differ from male Black Wheatear by white rear belly/rear flanks and narrower and usually broken tail-band.

PIED WHEATEAR *Oenanthe pleschanka*
Rumania and Bulgaria   337

Male summer: Black mantle. **Male winter**: Usually darker and more grey-brown above than male Black-eared and lesser coverts broadly pale-fringed when fresh. Black throat reaches further down than in Black-eared, although this may be difficult to judge because of broad pale fringes. **1st-winter male**: Like adult male winter, but wings more worn and primary coverts have broader, pale fringes. Lores and chin only rarely completely black. Told from 1st-winter male Black-eared by pattern of throat and colour of upperparts (see male winter). **Female summer**: Less warmly coloured than most Black-eared. Grey throat/upper breast frequent. In black-throated individuals, black on throat extends further down than in Black-eared. **Female winter**: Less warmly coloured than majority of Black- eared, with more distinct pale fringes above.

DESERT WHEATEAR *Oenanthe deserti*
N Africa and Asia   339

All-black tail. **Male**: Black throat connected to black on wing, scapulars not black, pale inner coverts. **Female**: Wings show broad, pale fringes in winter plumage. **1st-winter male**: Like adult male winter, but more pale-fringed head and wings.

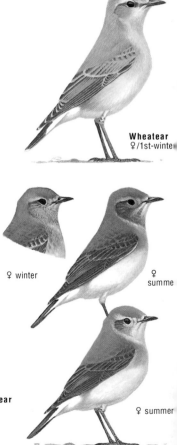

Wheatear
♀/1st-winter

♀ winter

♀ summer

Black-eared Wheatear
melanoleuca

♀ summer

1st-winter/
-summer

1st-winter/
-summer

ISABELLINE WHEATEAR

WHITE-CROWNED BLACK WHEATEAR

♂ summer

♀ summer

♀ winter

♂ winter

♀ summer

1st-winter ♂

PIED WHEATEAR

♂ summer

♀ winter

♀ summer

DESERT WHEATEAR

1st-winter ♂

279

Plate 45

WHITE'S THRUSH *Zoothera dauma* E Asia 341
Unmistakable scaly pattern above and below.

SIBERIAN THRUSH *Zoothera sibirica* Siberia 342
Male: Unmistakable.
Female: Conspicuous supercilium and distinctive pattern on underside.
1st-winter female shows pale tips to greater coverts.
1st-winter/-summer male: A mixture of female-like and male characters.

VARIED THRUSH *Zoothera naevia* N America 343
Male: Unmistakable.
Female: Browner above and with less distinct breast band than male.

juv.

Mistle Thrush

WHITE'S THRUSH

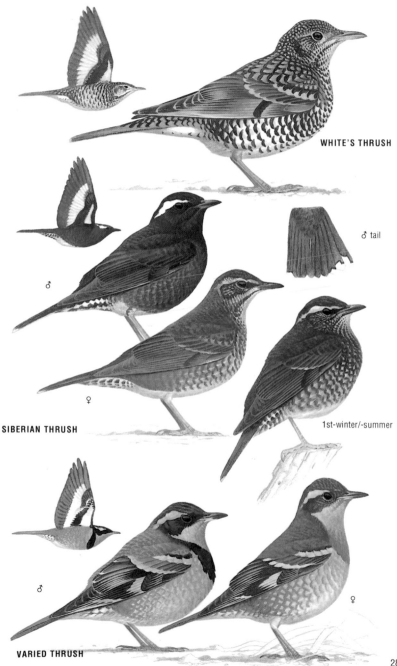

WHITE'S THRUSH

♂ tail

♂

♀

SIBERIAN THRUSH

1st-winter/-summer

♂

♀

VARIED THRUSH

281

Plate 46

WOOD THRUSH *Hylocichla mustelina*   N America   343

Rufous above, brightest on crown/nape and whitish below with rounded blackish spots. Pale tips to retained juvenile greater coverts distinguish 1st-winter/- summer from adult. Note moult contrast.

HERMIT THRUSH *Catharus guttatus*   N America   344

Contrastingly rufous rump, uppertail-coverts and tail diagnostic. Ageing as in Wood (median coverts juvenile in bird shown here).

SWAINSON'S THRUSH *Catharus ustulatus*   N America   345

Much smaller than Song Thrush and unmarked or only faintly spotted flanks. Distinct buffish eye-ring, buffish streak on lores and buffish throat/breast. Ageing as in Wood (but no moult contrast in bird shown here).

GREY-CHEEKED THRUSH *Catharus minimus*   N America   345

Differs from Swainson's by indistinct head pattern and whitish or very pale buffish breast. Ageing as in Wood.

VEERY *Catharus fuscescens*   N America   346

Rufous above and comparatively faintly spotted on breast. Ageing as in Wood (but no moult contrast in bird shown here).

EYE-BROWED THRUSH *Turdus obscurus*   C Siberia   347

Male: Diagnostic head pattern and brownish-orange breast and flanks. **Female:** Browner head and paler throat than adult male. **1st-winter/-summer male:** Distinct whitish tips to outer greater coverts distinguishes from adult. Bright plumage and greyish-tinged head indicates that it is likely to be a male.

TICKELL'S THRUSH *Turdus unicolor*   W Himalayas   346

Male: Mainly grey plumage with whitish belly and undertail-coverts. Yellow bill and orbital ring. **Female:** Note brown breast and flanks with some spots on breast and mainly yellow bill and orbital ring.

TICKELL'S THRUSH

1st-winter/-summer

WOOD THRUSH

1st-winter/-summer

HERMIT THRUSH

1st-winter/-summer

SWAINSON'S THRUSH

1st-winter/-summer

GREY-CHEEKED THRUSH

1st-winter/-summer

VEERY

♀

♂

EYE-BROWED THRUSH

1st-winter/-summer ♂

Plate 47

DUSKY THRUSH *Turdus naumanni eunomus*
Siberia 348
Male: Unmistakable. **Female**: Slightly
duller. **1st-winter/-summer**: Retained
juvenile greater coverts have paler edges
and tips than adult and any new inners.
Sexing only possible with extremes.

NAUMANN'S THRUSH *Turdus naumanni*
naumanni Siberia 348
Sexing and ageing as in Dusky.

BLACK-THROATED THRUSH *Turdus*
ruficollis atrogularis Siberia 350
Male: Unmistakable. **Female**: Usually
shows a blackish gorget on breast.
1st-winter male: Like adult female, but
any retained juvenile greater coverts show
paler edges and tips. **1st-winter/-summer
female**: More streaked. Ageing as in
1st-winter male.

RED-THROATED THRUSH
Turdus ruficollis ruficollis Siberia 349
Like Black-throated Thrush, but rufous
instead of black on throat/breast and
rufous outer tail-feathers.

AMERICAN ROBIN *Turdus migratorius*
North America 351
Male: Unmistakable. **Female**: Browner on
head, paler than male. **1st-winter/summer**:
Whitish spots on tips of outer greater
coverts.

1st-winter

DUSKY
THRUSH

1st-winter

NAUMANN'S
THRUSH

1st-winter

BLACK-THROATED
THRUSH

1st-winter

RED-THROATED
THRUSH

♀

♂

1st-winter

AMERICAN ROBIN

♀ (variant)

♂

DUSKY THRUSH

1st-winter/
-summer

1st-winter/
-summer

♀

♂ (bright)

NAUMANN'S THRUSH

1st-winter/
-summer

1st-winter/
-summer

1st-winter/
-summer

♀

♂

BLACK-THROATED
THRUSH

1st-winter/
-summer
♀

1st-winter ♂

♀

♂

RED-THROATED THRUSH

1st-winter/-summer ♀

1st-winter ♂

285

Plate 48

PALLAS'S GRASSHOPPER WARBLER
Locustella certhiola
E Asia   352

Like Grasshopper Warbler, but
different tail pattern and
unstreaked undertail-coverts.
Juvenile: Yellowish throat and
belly, spotted breast.

very streaky
individual

Grassho
Warbler

LANCEOLATED WARBLER   *Locustella lanceolata*
Siberia   353

Usually heavily streaked below, some practically unstreaked. **Juvenile**: Less
streaked than other plumages.

GRAY'S GRASSHOPPER WARBLER   *Locustella fasciolata*   Siberia   355

Large, but otherwise a typical *Locustella*. **Juvenile**: Olive-tinged breast,
yellowish supercilium, throat and belly.

BLYTH'S REED WARBLER
Acrocephalus du metorum   Finland   *358*

Shorter primary projection than Marsh,
more greyish-tinged above. Darker and
warmer in colour than Olivaceous.

PADDYFIELD WARBLER   *Acrocephalus agricola*
Bulgaria and Rumania   357

Head pattern differs from Marsh and
Blyth's Reed Warblers.

BOOTED WARBLER   *Hippolais caligata*
Asia   361

Paler than Paddyfield Warbler, lacking
rufous. More square- tipped tail with
whitish edge and tip. Smaller body and bill
and more prominent supercilium than
Olivaceous.

**Marsh
Warbler**

AQUATIC WARBLER   *Acrocephalus paludicola*
E Europe   356

Like Sedge Warbler, but more contrasting
pattern.

**Olivaceous
Warbler**

AQUATIC WARBLER

1st-wint

juv.

juv.

**PALLAS'S
GRASSHOPPER
WARBLER**

LANCEOLATED WARBLER

juv.

**GRAY'S
GRASSHOPPER
WARBLER**

**BLYTH'S REED
WARBLER**

variation

PADDYFIELD WARBLER

BOOTED WARBLER

287

Plate 49

THICK-BILLED WARBLER *Acrocephalus aedon*   E Siberia   36●

Large, with short, heavy bill, short primary projection and long, strongly graduated tail. Note lack of supercilium and loral stripe.

DESERT WARBLER *Sylvia nana*   Asia and N Africa   36●

Pale plumage with contrastingly rufous rump, uppertail-coverts and central tail-feathergs. Bare part coloration diagnostic.

MARMORA'S WARBLER *Sylvia sarda*   Endemic to Mediterranean   36.

Male: Easily identified by distinctive shape, bare part coloration and practically all grey plumage.

Female: Tends to be browner.

Juvenile: Browner than adult. Perhaps indistinguishable from juvenile Dartford Warbler.

MÉNÉTRIES'S WARBLER *Sylvia mystacea*   SW to C Asia   36.

Male summer: Like male Sardinian Warbler, but usually pale pink central throat, often also pink breast and flanks. Individuals lacking pink distinguished from Sardinian by overall paler plumage, paler crown and ear-coverts usually merging with grey nape, and less contrastingly patterned tertials.

Female: Paler than Sardinian Warbler, with more contrastingly dark tail and less grey crown, nape and ear-coverts. Usually paler lores, more distinct pale eye-ring and more plain tertials. Difficult to tell from some female Subalpine Warblers, but tail darker (pattern of outer feathers differs; see illustration in text). Flanks usually less deep buff.

1st-winter: Like adult female but darker iris and different pattern on retained juvenile outer tail-feathers.

Sardinian Warbler   ♀ *melanocephala*

THICK-BILLED WARBLER

variation

♂

DESERT WARBLER
nana

♀

MARMORA'S WARBLER

juv.

♂

1st-winter ♂

♀

1st-winter ♀

MÉNÉTRIES'S WARBLER

Plate 50

GREENISH WARBLER *Phylloscopus trochiloides*   NE Europe   365
Differs from Chiffchaff and Willow Warbler by more prominent supercilium and eye-stripe and 1-2 whitish wing-bars.
Race *plumbeitarsus*, 'Two-barred Greenish Warbler': Distinct double wing-bars when fresh. Told from Yellow-browed Warbler by e.g. darker tertials with whitish edges. Race *nitidus*, 'Green Warbler': More or less distinctly yellowish supercilium, ear-coverts and underparts.

ARCTIC WARBLER *Phylloscopus borealis*   N Scandinavia   366
Differs from Greenish Warbler in especially head and bill pattern and colour of legs/feet and breast-sides/flanks.

EASTERN CROWNED WARBLER *Phylloscopus coronatus*   E Asia.   365
Resembles Greenish and Arctic, but crown pattern clearly different.

PALLAS'S WARBLER *Phylloscopus proregulus*   Siberia   368
Small, with very distinctive head pattern and yellow rump.

YELLOW-BROWED WARBLER *Phylloscopus inornatus*   Asia.   368
(Sub)species *inornatus*: Confusable with Pallas's, but less distinct head pattern, and rump concolorous with mantle. Cf. Greenish Warbler. (Sub)species *humei*: Generally more 'washed-out' than *inornatus*. No distinct green tinge on crown, lack of yellow on supercilium, and upper wing-bar less contrasting. Best distinguished by call.

DUSKY WARBLER *Phylloscopus fuscatus*   Asia   370
Darker and browner than Siberian race of Chiffchaff (*tristis*) with paler bill and legs/feet. Like Radde's but finer bill and differently coloured supercilium. Underparts never as yellowish as in some Radde's (right bird), and undertail-coverts rarely as contrastingly rufous-buff. Legs generally darker than in Radde's (though often paler than here).

RADDE'S WARBLER *Phylloscopus schwarzi*   Siberia   370
See Dusky Warbler. Some autumn birds very yellowish below (only 1st-winter?).

RUBY-CROWNED KINGLET *Regulus calendula*   N America   372
Like Goldcrest, but lacks dark lateral crown-stripes (also in juvenile Goldcrest) and shows distinct, broken eye-ring. Male told from female by red crown patch (often concealed).

♂

RUBY-CROWNED KINGLET

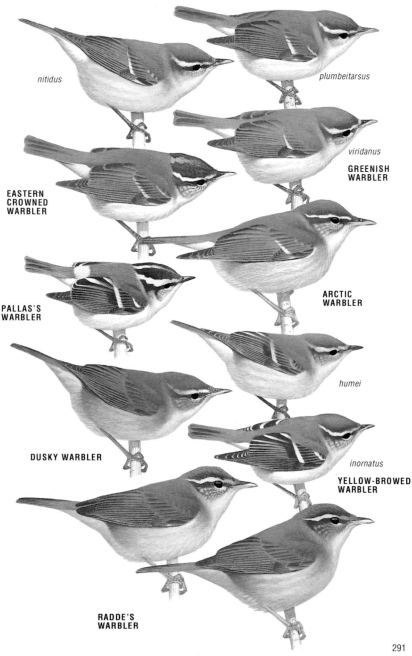

nitidus

plumbeitarsus

viridanus

GREENISH
WARBLER

EASTERN
CROWNED
WARBLER

PALLAS'S
WARBLER

ARCTIC
WARBLER

DUSKY WARBLER

humei

inornatus

YELLOW-BROWED
WARBLER

RADDE'S
WARBLER

291

Plate 51

EASTERN PHOEBE *Sayornis phoebe* N America 184

Rather large, long-tailed and rather dark-looking. **1st-winter**: Has at least some distinctly pale-tipped greater coverts.

ACADIAN FLYCATCHER *Empidonax virescens* N America 184
Very distinctive.

BROWN FLYCATCHER *Muscicapa dauurica* Asia 372

Very distinctive. Large bill, distinctive head pattern. **1st- winter**: Broader pale tips to greater coverts than in adult, forming distinct wing-bar.

AZURE TIT *Parus cyanus* Asia 373

Unmistakable. White throat, distinctive wing and tail pattern.

RED-BREASTED NUTHATCH *Sitta canadensis* N America 374

Unmistakable small nuthatch. Female has paler crown, eye-stripe and underparts.

CORSICAN NUTHATCH *Sitta whiteheadi* Endemic to Corsica 374

Much paler below than Red-breasted Nuthatch. Sexes differ by head pattern as in Red- breasted Nuthatch.

DAURIAN JACKDAW *Corvus dauuricus* Asia 378

Very distinctive, but beware of partially albinistic Jackdaws.

1st-winter/-summer: Darker nape than Jackdaw, thin pale streaks on side of head and faintly outlined dark bib. Dark iris.

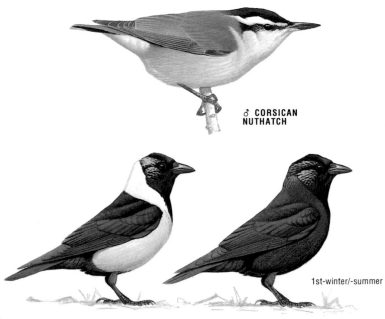

♂ CORSICAN NUTHATCH

1st-winter/-summer

DAURIAN JACKDAW

EASTERN
PHOEBE

1st-winter

ACADIAN
FLYCATCHER

AZURE TIT

1st-winter

BROWN FLYCATCHER

♂

♀

RED-BREASTED NUTHATCH

293

Plate 52

ISABELLINE SHRIKE *Lanius isabellinus* Asia 37!

Like female-type Red-backed Shrike, but usually paler above, with contrasting rufous rump, uppertail-coverts and tail. Ageing as in Brown.

BROWN SHRIKE *Lanius cristatus* Asia 37

Like Isabelline Shrike, but less rufous tail and deeper buff breast/flanks. **Male**: Less contrastingly rufous crown/nape, pale forehead and lack of white on primaries. **Female**: Like male, but usually some dark chevrons on underparts and slightly less distinct mask in front of eye. **1st- winter**: Differs from adult in pattern of head, underparts and coverts/tertials.

LONG-TAILED SHRIKE *Lanius schach* Asia 37

Large shrike with very distinctive plumage. **Juvenile**: Told from other shrikes by combination of size and plumage.

DAURIAN STARLING *Sturnus sturninus* E Asia 37

Male: Unmistakable. **Female**: Especially rear crown and mantle paler and browner than in male. **1st-winter female**: Like adult female, but some wing feathers usually retained juvenile and contrastingly brown with pale edges.

ROSE-COLOURED STARLING *Sturnus roseus* Rumania 37

Male summer: Unmistakable. **Male winter**: Pink parts dusky, and narrow pale fringes to black head. **Juvenile**: Much paler than juvenile Starling, with pale lores, finely spotted breast, paler rump and yellowish lower mandible.

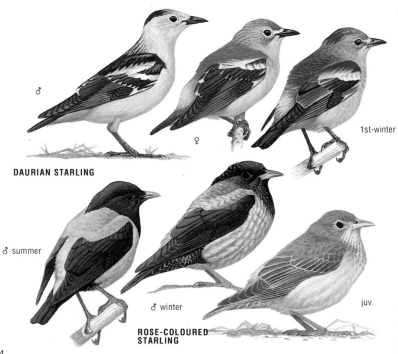

♂

♀

1st-winter

DAURIAN STARLING

♂ summer

♂ winter

juv.

ROSE-COLOURED
STARLING

♂ isabellinus

♀ phoenicuroides

♂ phoenicuroides

♀ isabellinus

1st-winter
isabellinus

bright 1st-winter
♂ phoenicuroides

**ISABELLINE
SHRIKE**

♂

♀

1st-winter

BROWN SHRIKE

juv.

LONG-TAILED SHRIKE

Plate 53

RED-FRONTED SERIN *Serinus pusillus*
  W & C Asia   382

Unmistakable. **Juvenile**: Largely pale rufous head and breast. **1st-winter/-summer**: Sometimes pale chestnut on head.

TRUMPETER FINCH *Bucanetes githagineus*
  SE Spain   385

Male: Unmistakable. **Female**: Less pinkish. **1st-winter male**: Like adult male, but usually some buffish edged primaries and primary coverts.

PALLAS'S ROSEFINCH *Carpodacus roseus*
  Siberia   386

Male: Unmistakable. **Female/1st-year male**: Like female-type Scarlet Rosefinch, but variable amount of pink on head, breast and back/rump. More heavily streaked.

EVENING GROSBEAK *Coccothraustes vespertinus* N America   387

Unmistakable.

ARCTIC REDPOLL *Carduelis hornemanni* N Scandinavia   382

Paler than Redpoll, with less-streaked rump and underparts.

TWO-BARRED CROSSBILL
  Loxia leucoptera
  Finland   383

Distinct, double, white wing-bars and white edges/tips to tertials.

♀/1st-year ♂

SCARLET ROSEFINCH

1st-winter

♂

ARCTIC REDPOLL

♂

♀

TWO-BARRED CROSSBILL

juv.

1st-winter/-summer

1st-winter/
-summer

juv.

RED-FRONTED SERIN

♂ summer

1st-winter ♂

♀

TRUMPETER FINCH

♂

♀/1st-year ♂

♀/1st-year ♂

PALLAS'S ROSEFINCH

♂

♀

EVENING GROSBEAK

297

Plate 54

RED-EYED VIREO *Vireo olivaceus*   N America   381

Identified by very distinctive head pattern. 1st-winter told from adult by brown
iris (bright red in adult).

PHILADELPHIA VIREO *Vireo philadelphicus*   N America   381

Distinctive head pattern and rather yellowish underparts. Bill rather strong, with
slightly hooked tip.

BLACK-AND-WHITE WARBLER *Mniotilta varia*   N America   388

Male summer: Unmistakable. Distinctive habit of creeping along branches and
tree trunks like nuthatch. **Female**: Differs from adult male by paler ear-coverts
and paler streaking on underparts. In summer also by whitish throat. **1st-winter
male**: Head pattern like female, but stronger blackish streaking on underparts.

TENNESSEE WARBLER *Vermivora peregrina*   N America   389

Very pointed bill. **Male summer**: Grey head, whitish supercilium and underside.
Female summer: Differs from male in greenish-tinged crown and more
yellowish-tinged supercilium, ear-coverts and underside. Adult male winter
may be similar. **Female winter/1st-winter male**: More green and yellow.

NORTHERN PARULA *Parula americana*   N America   390

Male summer: Small, with unmistakable, colourful plumage. **1st-winter male**:
Differs from adult male winter by greenish-edged remiges, primary coverts and
alula, contrasting with bluish-edged greater coverts. **1st-winter/-summer female**:
Resembles 1st-winter male, but no blackish or rufous on throat.

GOLDEN-WINGED WARBLER *Vermivora chrysoptera*   N America   388

Male: Unmistakable. **Female**: Grey face mask and throat patch.

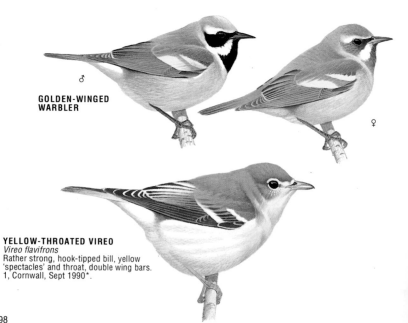

♂

**GOLDEN-WINGED
WARBLER**

♀

YELLOW-THROATED VIREO
Vireo flavifrons
Rather strong, hook-tipped bill, yellow
'spectacles' and throat, double wing bars.
1, Cornwall, Sept 1990*.

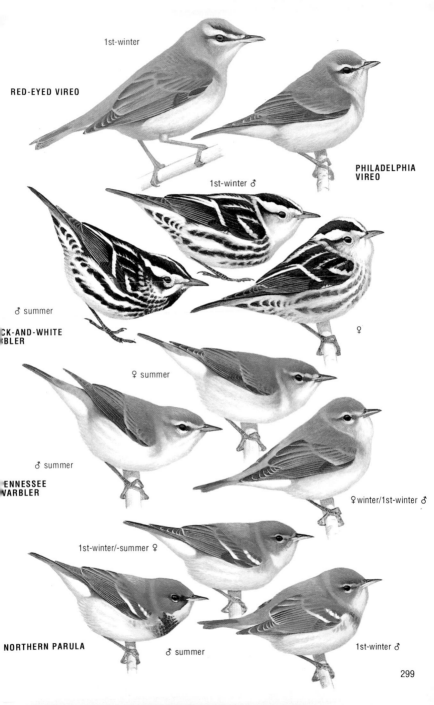

1st-winter

RED-EYED VIREO

PHILADELPHIA
VIREO

1st-winter ♂

♂ summer

CK-AND-WHITE
RBLER

♀

♀ summer

♂ summer

TENNESSEE
WARBLER

♀ winter/1st-winter ♂

1st-winter/-summer ♀

NORTHERN PARULA

♂ summer

1st-winter ♂

Plate 55

YELLOW WARBLER *Dendroica petechia* Americas 390
Male summer: Yellowish-green above and yellow below, with rufous streaking on breast and flanks. From below, tail looks yellow with darker margin. **Female summer**: Shows less or no rufous streaking. **1st-winter female**: Dullest plumage. Tertials usually retained juvenile, with whitish edges.

CHESTNUT-SIDED WARBLER *Dendroica pensylvanica* N America 391
Male summer: Unmistakable. Note especially head pattern and chestnut stripe on flanks. **Female summer**: Duller than male. Some 1st-summer males similar. **Female winter/1st-winter male**: Note 'mild' grey face with whitish eye-ring, indistinctly streaked, greenish upperside, and pale, unstreaked underparts.

MAGNOLIA WARBLER *Dendroica magnolia* N America 395
White subterminal tail band on all except central pair of feathers. Yellow rump. **Male summer**: Unmistakable. Shows distinctive head pattern, blackish mantle, yellow underparts with blackish streaks and white wing panel. **Male winter**: Prominent blackish streaks on flanks (some adult females and 1st-winter males may be similar). **Female winter/1st-winter male**: Characterized by greyish head, greenish, indistinctly streaked mantle/scapulars, largely yellow underside and double whitish wing-bars.

CAPE MAY WARBLER *Dendroica tigrina* N America 394
Yellow to yellowish-green rump. **Male summer**: Unmistakable. Note in particular head pattern. **Male winter**: Less distinct head pattern and less streaked mantle/scapulars than in summer. **Female summer**: Less yellow and less distinctly streaked below than male, shows double wing-bars rather than a panel, and head pattern clearly different from male's. **Female winter**: A dull individual.

BLACK-THROATED BLUE WARBLER *Dendroica caerulescens* N America 392
Male: Unmistakable. **Female**: Distinctive head pattern, plain upperparts, unmarked pale dusky yellowish underside and a usually rather prominent white patch on primaries.

BLACK-THROATED BLUE WARBLER

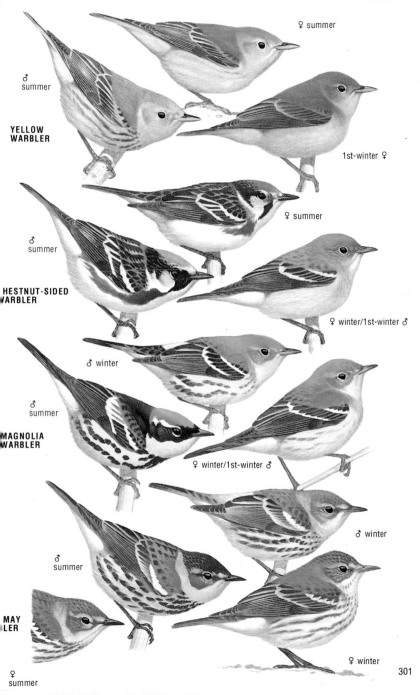

♀ summer

♂
summer

**YELLOW
WARBLER**

1st-winter ♀

♀ summer

♂
summer

**HESTNUT-SIDED
WARBLER**

♀ winter/1st-winter ♂

♂ winter

♂
summer

**MAGNOLIA
WARBLER**

♀ winter/1st-winter ♂

♂ winter

♂
summer

**MAY
LER**

♀ winter

♀
summer

301

Plate 56

YELLOW-RUMPED WARBLER *Dendroica coronata* N America 396

Distinct yellow rump and yellow patch on breast-sides.

Male summer: Very distinctive head pattern and very heavily streaked underparts, forming breast band.

Winter: Brown, distinctly streaked upperside and distinctive head pattern. Variation shown.

BLACK-THROATED GREEN WARBLER *Dendroica virens* N America 393

Male summer: Virtually plain, greenish upperside and very distinctive head pattern.

Female/1st-winter male: Less black on throat and less-blackish streaks on flanks than adult male.

1st-winter female: Indistinctly marked on throat and flanks. Generally not safely distinguished from adult female/1st-winter male.

PALM WARBLER *Dendroica palmarum* N America 397

Summer: Note especially head pattern, yellow underside.

Winter: No chestnut on crown. Often yellow only on undertail-coverts.

BLACKPOLL WARBLER *Dendroica striata* N America 398

Male summer: Very distinctive head pattern.

Winter: Note rather indistinct yellowish supercilium, dull yellowish throat and breast, merging with the remaining whitish underparts. Distinctly streaked upperside, prominent double wing-bars and rather pale legs. More heavily streaked bird likely to be male.

BLACKBURNIAN WARBLER *Dendroica fusca* N America 393

Male summer: Unmistakable.

Male winter: Characterized by very distinctive head pattern and heavily streaked upperparts with pale stripes on mantle.

1st-winter female: An extremely dull individual (most are indistinguishable from adult female in the field and also difficult to tell from males).

1st-winter ♀

♂ summer

♂ winter

BLACKBURNIAN WARBLER

winter

♂ summer

YELLOW-RUMPED WARBLER

winter

♀/1st-winter ♂

♂ summer

BLACK-THROATED GREEN WARBLER

1st-winter ♀

summer

winter

PALM WARBLER

winter

winter

♂ summer

BLACKPOLL WARBLER

winter

Plate 57

AMERICAN REDSTART *Setophaga ruticilla* N America   399

  Male: Unmistakable. **Female/1st-winter male**: Very distinctive tail pattern. Most show yellow wing-patch. Orange instead of yellow patterns, as well as patch on primaries indicates adult female or 1st-winter male.

OVENBIRD *Seiurus aurocapillus* N America   399

  Unmistakable. Walks on the ground, often bobbing its rear body/tail. Skulky.

NORTHERN WATERTHRUSH *Seiurus noveboracensis* N America   400

  Very characteristic. Habits resemble Ovenbird's.

COMMON YELLOWTHROAT *Geothlypis trichas* N America   400

  Male: Unmistakable. **Female**: Characterized by plain olive-brown upperside and wings, yellowish throat-central upper breast, brownish flanks and 'dirty' yellowish undertail-coverts. **1st-winter/-summer male**: Head pattern usually less distinct than in adult male. **1st-winter female**: Sometimes very dull, with more buffish throat (most indistinguishable from adult female in the field).

HOODED WARBLER *Wilsonia citrina* N America   401

  Male: Unmistakable. **Female**: Larger than Wilson's Warbler, and shows white in tail and dark loral stripe.

WILSON'S WARBLER *Wilsonia pusilla* N America   402

  Male: Unmistakable. **Female**: Black cap indistinct or lacking.

CANADA WARBLER *Wilsonia canadensis* N America   402

  Male: Plain blue-grey above including wings and largely yellow below. Distinctive head pattern and 'necklace'. **Female**: Less-blackish head pattern and fainter spots on breast than male.

WILSON'S WARBLER

CANADA WARBLER

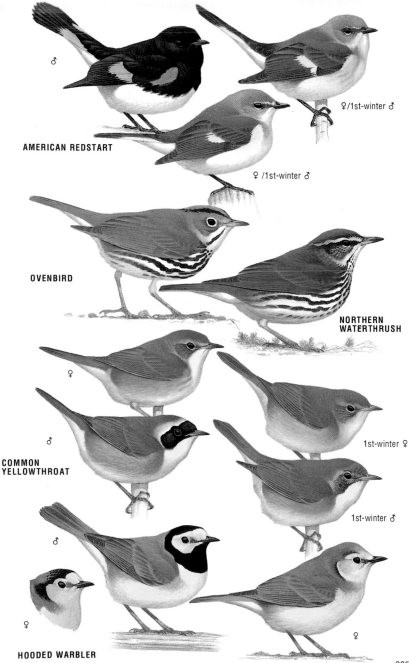

♂

AMERICAN REDSTART

♀/1st-winter ♂

♀ /1st-winter ♂

OVENBIRD

NORTHERN WATERTHRUSH

♀

♂

COMMON YELLOWTHROAT

1st-winter ♀

1st-winter ♂

♂

♀

HOODED WARBLER

♀

Plate 58

SUMMER TANAGER *Piranga rubra*   N America   403
Male: Unmistakable.
Female/1st-winter male: Yellowish-brownish olive above and brownish-yellow below. Some show a variable amount of red.

SCARLET TANAGER *Piranga olivacea*   N America   403
Male summer: Unmistakable.
Female: More greenish above and greenish-yellow below than female Summer Tanager, and the bill is slightly smaller and normally darker.
1st-winter male: Mostly like female, but some black on scapulars and wings.

RUFOUS-SIDED TOWHEE *Pipilo erythrophthalmus*   N America   404
Male: Unmistakable.
Female: Dark brown where male is black. Ageing by red iris.
1st-winter male: Ageing by duller iris and contrastingly browner outer greater coverts, alula, primary coverts and remiges.

DARK-EYED JUNCO *Junco hyemalis*   N America   407
Male: Unmistakable.
1st-winter female: Browner than male. Ageing by retained juvenile tertials and outer greater coverts.

LONG-TAILED ROSEFINCH *Uragus sibiricus*   E Asia   386
Male: Unmistakable.
Female/1st-winter male: Also unmistakable. Pink on back and rump.
1st-winter/-summer male: Usually shows more pink than females, some similar to adult male.

♂ summer

♀/1st-winter ♂

LONG-TAILED ROSEFINCH

1st-winter ♂

SUMMER
TANAGER

♂

♀/1st-winter ♂

♀ /1st-winter ♂

SCARLET
TANAGER

♀

1st-winter ♂

♂
summer

♀

RUFOUS-SIDED
TOWHEE

♂

1st-winter ♂

DARK-EYED JUNCO

♂

1st-winter ♀

Plate 59

FOX SPARROW *Passerella iliaca* N America 405
  Rather large and heavy, with much rufous in plumage. Note also grey supercilium and sides of neck. E race shown.

SONG SPARROW *Melospiza melodia* N America 406
  Differs from most female buntings by pattern on longest and central tertial and by lack of white in tail. Could be confused with Savannah Sparrow, but is larger and longer-tailed, and tail is slightly rounded rather than notched. Darker and more rufous general appearance, and never any yellow in supercilium. E race shown.

WHITE-CROWNED SPARROW *Zonotrichia leucophrys* N America 406
  Very distinctive head pattern. Head shows bird from western part of range.
  1st-winter: Head pattern clearly different from adult's.

WHITE-THROATED SPARROW *Zonotrichia albicollis* N America 407
  Polymorphic. Colour of head and breast variable. 'White-striped' morph resembles White-crowned Sparrow, but yellow fore-supercilium, well-defined white throat (generally dark-framed), and darker bill.
  Some 1st-winters, particularly females, are very dull and may even lack yellow on supercilium (as shown).

SAVANNAH SPARROW *Passerculus sandwichensis* N America 405
  Differs from most female buntings in same way as Song Sparrow. Confusable with Song Sparrow. Yellow on fore-supercilium characteristic, but can be missing in autumn in race *princeps* ('Ipswich Sparrow'). This race is paler and greyer above and more finely streaked below as well as larger than other relevant subspecies.

LARK SPARROW *Chondestes grammacus*
Large bunting-like sparrow with striking chestnut, black and white head pattern. Extensive white on outer feathers of rather longish tail. Black spot in middle of breast not always visible.
1 Suffolk, England, June 81*. 1 Norfolk, England, May 91*.

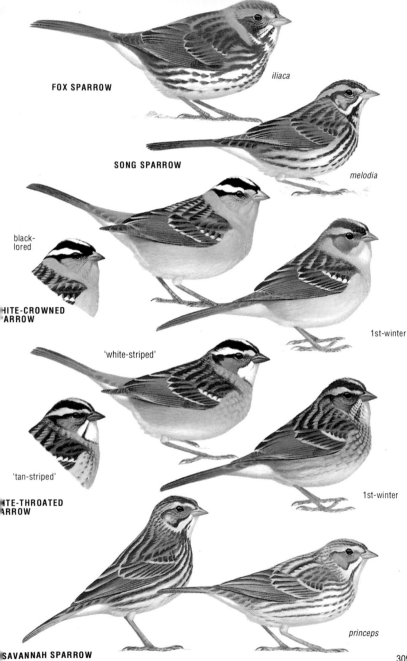

FOX SPARROW

iliaca

SONG SPARROW

melodia

black-
lored

HITE-CROWNED
ARROW

1st-winter

'white-striped'

'tan-striped'

ITE-THROATED
ARROW

1st-winter

princeps

SAVANNAH SPARROW

309

Plate 60

BLACK-FACED BUNTING *Emberiza spodocephala* Asia   408

Male summer: Grey hood and black lores make it unmistakable.

Male winter: Variable. Some, like the bird shown, are rather female-like, but usually more poorly marked supercilium, greyish-tinged sides of neck and crown, the latter spotted rather than streaked on sides and with poorly marked median stripe.

Female: Rather dull and featureless. Note comparatively indistinct median crown stripe and supercilium, distinct malar stripe and malar patch, lack of rufous on coverts as well as on upper- and underparts, and rather indistinct streaking on central breast.

PINE BUNTING *Emberiza leucocephalos* Siberia   409

Male summer: Unmistakable. Head pattern; unstreaked, rufous breast/flanks and back/rump.

Male winter: Head pattern more obscure, but still distinctive.

Female: Very like female Yellowhammer, but completely lacks yellow and green tones.

MEADOW BUNTING *Emberiza cioides* Asia   410

Male: Note unique head pattern and unstreaked, rufous breast/flanks and back, rump and uppertail-coverts. Grey lesser coverts often concealed.

Female: Head pattern slightly variable, but always paler and usually less well-defined than in male. Underparts paler than in male.

♀ **PINE BUNTING** (typical)   ♀ **Yellowhammer**

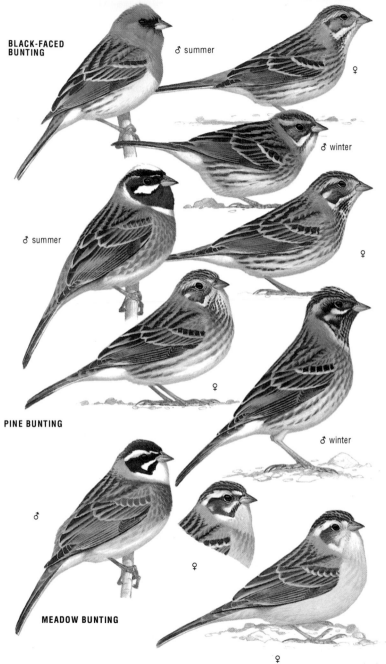

BLACK-FACED BUNTING

♂ summer

♀

♂ winter

♂ summer

♀

PINE BUNTING

♀

♂ winter

♂

MEADOW BUNTING

♀

♀

311

Plate 61

YELLOW-BROWED BUNTING *Emberiza chrysophrys* Siberia   411

Male summer: Unmistakable head pattern. **Female summer**: Less contrasting
head pattern than male. Some 1st-summer males are possibly similar. **Winter**:
Head pattern still very distinctive, although sometimes very little yellow on
supercilium (as illustrated).

CHESTNUT BUNTING *Emberiza rutila* E Asia   413

Male summer: Unmistakable. **Male winter**: Some paler fringes, mainly on head.
Female/1st-winter male: Some rufous on head/breast and lesser coverts (largely
concealed). **Female**: Could be confused with female-type Yellow-breasted
Bunting, but the head pattern, wing-bars and streaking on the underparts less
distinct, more rufous, unstreaked rump and little or no white in tail.

YELLOW-BREASTED BUNTING *Emberiza aureola* Finland   414

Adult male summer: Unmistakable. **Female**: Characterized by distinct head
pattern, with no or only a faint malar stripe, usually largely yellowish underside,
little-streaked breast and usually distinctly streaked rump. **Juvenile**: Like
female, but slightly different pattern on median and greater coverts and more
distinctly streaked central breast.

LITTLE BUNTING *Emberiza pusilla* N Scandinavia   412

Resembles female Reed Bunting (see Plate 62), but head pattern is clearly
different.   Grey-brown lesser coverts and usually paler and more distinct
wing-bars. Variation in head pattern shown (right bird in more fresh plumage).

LITTLE BUNTING

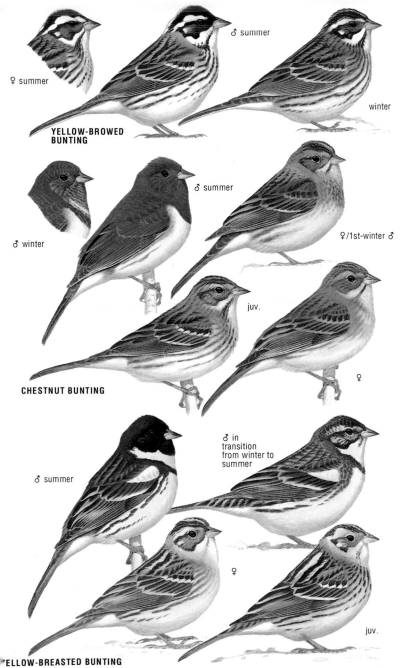

♀ summer

♂ summer

winter

YELLOW-BROWED BUNTING

♂ winter

♂ summer

♀/1st-winter ♂

juv.

♀

CHESTNUT BUNTING

♂ summer

♂ in transition from winter to summer

♀

juv.

YELLOW-BREASTED BUNTING

Plate 62

PALLAS'S REED BUNTING *Emberiza pallasi* Siberia 416

Like Reed Bunting, but is slightly smaller, with straight culmen and pinkish lower mandible. Grey-brown (female) or bluish-grey (most males) lesser coverts. Non-juvenile plumages usually paler above, with less streaking on underparts and usually paler and more distinct wing-bars. **Male summer**: Generally more contrastingly patterned and less brownish than Reed Bunting. **Male winter**: Warm buff nape often distinctive. When fresh, usually indistinguishable from female in the field except by colour of lesser coverts. In the hand told by extensive blackish centres to crown and throat and white central parts to nape-feathers. **Female**: Head pattern usually less contrasting than in Reed Bunting. Right bird in fresh plumage (autumn), left bird in worn plumage (summer). **Juvenile**: Differs from non-juvenile females by darker plumage, with rather heavily streaked underparts and differently patterned median and greater coverts.

RED-HEADED BUNTING *Emberiza bruniceps* C Asia 418

Male summer: Unmistakable. **Female**: Extremely difficult to distinguish from female Black-headed Bunting, and some are probably inseparable. In summer, head pattern sometimes differs – ghosting male's in either species. **Juvenile**: Compared to non-juvenile female, is usually more heavily streaked above and spotted on breast and flanks.

ROSE-BREASTED GROSBEAK *Pheucticus ludovicianus* N America 420

Male summer: Unmistakable. **Female**: Very distinctive head and wing pattern and large bill. **1st-winter male**: Like females, but often some pink on breast and often some extensively black feathers on upperparts. Any newly moulted median coverts more white and any new greater coverts blacker than in females (all median and some inner greater coverts new in illustrated bird).

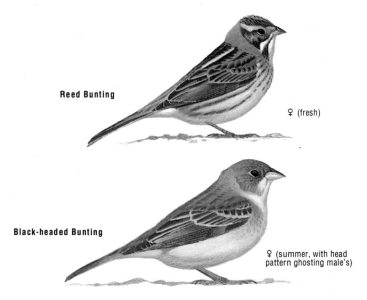

Reed Bunting

♀ (fresh)

Black-headed Bunting

♀ (summer, with head pattern ghosting male's)

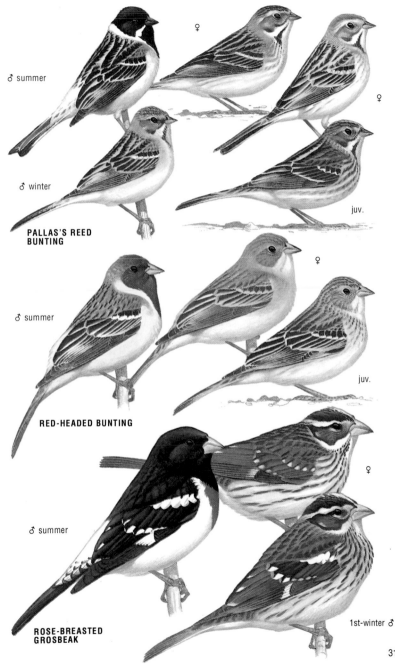

♂ summer

♀

♀

♂ winter

juv.

**PALLAS'S REED
BUNTING**

♂ summer

♀

juv.

♂ summer

♀

1st-winter ♂

**ROSE-BREASTED
GROSBEAK**

RED-HEADED BUNTING

Plate 63

INDIGO BUNTING *Passerina cyanea*   N America   421
  Male summer: Unmistakable.
  Male winter: Blue mainly concealed by brown, but 'shines through' here and there, always obvious on wings.
  Female: Nondescript, rather plain above and indistinctly streaked on breast. Generally some pale greenish-blue on wings and tail.
  1st-winter male: Note unmoulted outer greater coverts with narrower, paler and more clear-cut tips than in adult and newly moulted inner greater coverts. May not show the scattered blue feathers of this individual.

DICKCISSEL *Spiza americana*   N America   419
  Male summer: Unmistakable. Note unique head pattern and rufous lesser and median coverts. Adult male winter similar, but with narrow pale fringes to black throat patch.
  Female: Distinctive head pattern, usually yellowish breast, rather finely streaked underparts and normally at least some chestnut on lesser and median coverts.
  1st-winter male: Differs from adult female by usually retained juvenile tertials, with contrastingly worn and paler edges. More yellow on breast, less streaking on underparts and more chestnut on lesser and median coverts than 1st-winter female and often a few blackish feathers on throat. However, many are probably not safely sexed; extremes shown.
  1st-winter female: See 1st-winter male.

BOBOLINK *Dolichonyx oryzivorus*   N America   422
  Male summer: Unmistakable.
  Female: Note distinctive head pattern, heavily streaked upperparts with pale 'braces', rather sparsely streaked underparts, and buffish general coloration. (Slightly worn individual in spring-summer shown).
  1st-winter: Differs from adult winter in usually retained juvenile tertials, with more worn and paler edges (contrasting with greater coverts).

DEAD SEA SPARROW *Passer moabiticus*   Middle East   380
  Male summer: Unmistakable. **Male winter**: More brownish-tinged plumage and paler bill. **Female**: Resembles a small, rather pale House Sparrow.

♂ winter

♂ summer

♀

DEAD SEA SPARROW

♂ summer

♂ winter

♀

1st-winter ♂

INDIGO BUNTING

♂ summer

1st-winter ♂

♀/1st-winter ♂

1st-winter ♀

DICKCISSEL

♂ summer

♀ summer

1st-winter

BOBOLINK

317

Plate 64

COMMON GRACKLE *Quiscalus quiscula*   N America   423
All glossy black, with pale iris and distinctive tail shape.
Juvenile: Brown, with dark iris. Moult has just started in bird shown (some new coverts).

NORTHERN ORIOLE *Icterus galbula*   N America   424
Male: Unmistakable.
Female/1st-winter male: Rather variable plumage, some adult females very dark. 'Bullock's Oriole' generally greyer above and whiter below than 'Baltimore Oriole'.

YELLOW-HEADED BLACKBIRD *Xanthocephalus xanthocephalus*   N America   424
Male: Unmistakable.
Female: Unmistakable. Distinctly smaller than male.
1st-winter/-summer: Differs from adult female in distinct whitish tips to primary coverts and central alula, often also on outer greater coverts.

♀
'Bullock's'

♀
'Baltimore'

NORTHERN ORIOLE

COMMON GRACKLE

♂

YELLOW-HEADED BLACKBIRD

COMMON GRACKLE

juv.

♂

♀/1st-winter ♂

♀

♀ /1st-winter ♂

NORTHERN ORIOLE

♂

♀

YELLOW-HEADED
BLACKBIRD

1st-winter/-summer

Birds not to scale

SOFT-PLUMAGED PETREL *Pterodroma mollis* - 2 or 3 British Isles, Aug 1989*.

1st-winter

THAYER'S GULL *Larus glaucoides thayeri* - 1st-winter recorded in Ireland, winter 1989/90*.

LEAST TERN *Sterna antillarum* - 1 ad. May-June 1990 in Sussex, England*.

winter

summe

ANCIENT MURRELET *Synthliboramphus antiquus* - 1 ad. spent May-June 1990 and Apr 1991 on Lundy Is*. England.

juv.

♂

TREE SWALLOW *Tachycineta bicolor* - 1 on Scilly Is. June 1990*.

♀

BROWN-HEADED COWBIRD *Molothrus ater* - 1 ad. ♀ in Norway, 1st June 1987.

's   Richard's
          Pipit

typical

's   Richard's
          Pipit

d. patterned
median covert

Adult: Differs from Tawny Pipit by much the same characters as described for Richard's: generally has browner and distinctly more heavily streaked upperside, deeper buff tone to particularly flanks, distinctly streaked breast, more distinct malar stripe and malar patch, unmarked lores and narrower, pale edges to fresh tertials. It is slightly greyer above than Richard's (worn Richard's are practically identical in colour, though). The upperparts are slightly, but generally appreciably, more heavily streaked than in Richard's (although in the easternmost races of Richard's the streaking is practically as heavy as in Blyth's). Mainly as a result of the more buffish belly and throat, the underparts look more uniformly coloured than in Richard's, notably when the bird is viewed head-on; the (rear) flanks can be rather contrastingly deep buff, but not more so than in Richard's. The supercilium tends to be less prominent, especially in front of the eye, but there is much variation in both. The ear-coverts are frequently rather warmly rufous-tinged, contrasting with the greyer upperparts, which is not seen in Richard's.

The best plumage character is the pattern of the median coverts. The dark centres are more 'square', less triangular, and more clearcut than in Richard's (see figure). The same is usually true also for the greater coverts. When fresh, the tips to the median and greater coverts are generally slightly paler, less deep rufous, than in Richard's. As a result of the differences in pattern and colour, the wing-bars generally look more distinct in Blyth's but this must be used with extreme care because of the variation in both species caused by moult, wear and bleaching. Suspended or partial autumn moult, as in many Richard's, is very rare, if it occurs at all. Spring moult is similar to Richard's.

Juvenile: Very similar to juvenile Richard's, but greyer above, often with contrastingly rufous-tinged ear-coverts. Best distinguished from juvenile Tawny by the unmarked lores (but see note under Richard's), when fresh, also by slightly narrower pale edges to the tertials. This plumage is normally moulted before the autumn migration.

1st-winter: The pattern of the retained juvenile coverts and tertials differs from that of the adult in the same way as described for Richard's (p. 189). However, most 1st-winters retain all or most of the coverts and tertials until they have reached the winter quarters, so moult contrasts are less commonly seen in autumn migrants than in Richard's. The pattern of the median coverts can only be used to distinguish Blyth's and Richard's if any of these feathers have been moulted; the pattern of the juvenile feathers is the same in both species.

1st-summer: See Richard's Pipit.

Voice: This is often the best means of distinguishing from Richard's. The song, although unlikely to be heard in Europe, is very different from that of other pipits and more reminiscent of the song of Corn Bunting. It begins with *zret zret zret*..., followed by a characteristic, rattling *sri-sri-serererererereleee- ueh*, or variations on that theme.

There are two different types of flight call, one, usually given when flushed, is very similar to the classic call of Richard's but slightly higher-pitched, softer, more shrill and with a slight drop in pitch at the end, *pscheeo*; it also tends to be a fraction shorter. The other call is a short *chep*, rather similar to one of the calls of Tawny Pipit. The second note is either given in combination with the first or separately, often repeated. The alarm call, unlikely to be heard from vagrants, is clearly different from Richard's, a very harsh *bzrp* or *brzi*.

Habitat and behaviour: These are sometimes additional clues to identification. It prefers drier areas than Richard's and, when in taller vegetation, often 'sneaks' around in a rather Tree Pipit-like manner. It does not normally hover before landing as Richard's frequently does (but is capable of hovering and may do so occasionally).

Range: Breeds in Mongolia and neighbouring parts of China and the Altai. Winters mainly in India and Sri Lanka.

Status: Accidental in Britain: Brighton, Sussex, 1st-winter collected (23rd Oct 1882); Shetland, Fair Isle, 1st-winter (13th-27th Oct 1988*); Cornwall, Skewjack (24th Oct-1st Nov 1990*). Belgium: De Moeren (16th Nov 1986*). Netherlands: Westenschouwen, 1st-winter collected (13th Nov 1983). Finland: Lågskär, 1st-winter collected (10th Oct 1974). Three 1st-winter birds ringed in 1986: Säppi (19th Oct-6th Nov), Porkkala (15th-30th Nov), and Houtskari (23rd-29th Nov); and one ringed in 1988, Säppi (15th-17th Oct).

OLIVE-BACKED PIPIT *Anthus hodgsoni* D **41**

L 14.5cm (5.75"). Asia. Rare vagrant (mainly late autumn).

All plumages: Very similar to closely-related Tree Pipit. The upperparts and edges to the wings/tail are distinctly greenish in fresh plumage. However, the upperparts often wear greyish rather quickly (more grey than in Tree), often contrasting with greenish edges to the remiges. The mantle and scapulars are less streaked than in Tree, and they frequently look virtually unstreaked. Nominate *hodgsoni* (Himalayas and S China) has heavily streaked upperparts. A few individuals with rather prominently streaked mantle have been recorded in Europe. The streaks on the flanks are either fine as in Tree or distinctly bolder, and the breast streaks are sometimes – but far from always – obviously bolder and extend further down than in Tree Pipit.

The head pattern differs from that of Tree in several respects. The crown is slightly less heavily streaked, and shows a bold blackish streak on the sides, bordering the supercilium. In Tree Pipit the crown is more heavily streaked, usually without a broader stripe on side. The supercilium is prominent and buffish in front and whitish above and behind the eye. In Tree Pipit the supercilium is buffish throughout its length and thus much less contrasting. There is, however, some overlap, as the supercilium is occasionally buffish behind the eye in Olive-backed in fresh plumage and pale buffish in front of and almost whitish above/behind the eye in some more worn Tree Pipits. On the rear ear-coverts, there is a prominent whitish and a distinct blackish spot. However, the whitish spot is sometimes very indistinct and may even be lacking altogether, and rarely the dark spot is very poorly marked. In Tree Pipit these spots are usually indistinct or lacking. However, some Tree Pipits show a very prominent whitish spot, and the dark spot can be as distinct as in a normal Olive-backed (see figure). To conclude, the head pattern usually differs significantly between the species, but it is important to remember that there is extensive variation in both species. Additional minor differences from Tree Pipit are: sides of breast and rear flanks often greyish-greenish, belly marginally purer white, tips to median and greater coverts average more buffish when

Tree Pipit
Pale and dark patch on ear coverts extremely prominent

fresh, tertials show slightly paler centres, and the edges of the same usually do not wear so pale as in Tree. Ageing apparently very difficult by plumage.

Voice: The song is distinctly different from Tree Pipit. It is faster, slightly higher-pitched, a little softer, and the trills are slightly harder and 'drier', often recalling Wren. The flight call is, on average, slightly finer and fainter than Tree Pipit's, but in practice the variation in both species makes the flight calls usually inseparable. The alarm call, often heard throughout the year, is distinctly higher-pitched, slightly finer and fainter than in Tree, *sit* rather than *syt* as in Tree.

Habitat and behaviour: Similar to Tree Pipit. Does not pump the tail more than Tree, as seems to be a general misconception.

Range: Breeds in Asia, mainly in Siberia, Mongolia, China and Japan. Winters in S Asia. Vagrant in Israel.

Status: Rare vagrant in Europe. Especially noted British Isles (72); annual since 1973, mostly late Sept-Nov; one wintered in Berkshire (Feb-Apr 1984), also very rarely in spring (Apr 1948, May 1970). Notable influx in Oct-Nov 1987, with 20 records, including at least 8, possibly 11 on Fair Isle, Shetland.

Fewer records elsewhere: Faeroes (Oct 1984), France (Ouessant, Oct 1987, Oct 1988), Netherlands (Oct 1987, Apr 1988, Sept 1988), Denmark (Oct 1982, Nov 1987, Apr-May 1989*), Norway (12), Sweden (Oct 1988, Oct 1989*), Finland (9, Oct-Nov). Poland (*c.* 18), and in 1984 on the Hel Peninsula there was a remarkable influx between 9th-27th Sept, with a peak of 13 birds on 21st Sept (only 3 previous records, e.g. Sept 1978, May 1984, Apr 1985). West Germany, especially on Heligoland (May 1961, Oct 1986, Oct 1987, three in Oct 1988; Apr-May 1989*). Malta (3, Oct-Nov).

PECHORA PIPIT *Anthus gustavi*   B **41**

L 14cm (5.5"). Asia. Very rare vagrant (autumn), possibly overlooked.

All plumages: Very like a 1st-winter Red- throated Pipit and the occasional adult female which lacks a pink throat. The bill is distinctly heavier, with pinkish instead of yellowish on the lower mandible (but colour often difficult to judge in the field). The colour of the head and upperparts is richer, more rufescent (if not too worn), with even blacker streaks and whiter 'braces' on the mantle; the upperparts are thus generally even more contrastingly patterned than in Red-throated. The belly is whitish and contrasts clearly with the buffish breast, unlike Red-throated, which shows rather uniformly coloured underparts (when worn, the underparts of Pechora may be uniformly whitish).

The head pattern differs from that of Red-throated mainly in showing a distinct — although often short and difficult to see — dark loral stripe (to the eye, thus breaking the eye-ring), which is lacking in Red-throated (but note that from certain angles Red-throated may *seem* to show one). Also, usually shows a more poorly marked supercilium and finely streaked ear-coverts.

The wing-bars are on average more prominent than in Red-throated. Although there is some variation in both, the second outermost tail feather usually shows a considerably larger, pale wedge than in Red-throated (see figure, p. 324). The pale wedges on the outer tail feathers are often pale brownish-tinged (perhaps only in adults; always whitish

Pechora
Pipit

Red-throated
Pipit

outer tail-feathers

in Red-throated). Also, the tertials fall clearly short of the primary tips, which is a character unique to Pechora among the pipits (but beware of Red-throated with heavily worn or moulting tertials). Ageing apparently very difficult by plumage.

Voice: The song is very different from other pipits. It usually begins with *tsivi-tsivi*, followed by several mechanical, metallic, buzzing trills of slightly varied pitch, interspersed by a few short squeaky notes. The flight call is diagnostic and very different from that of other pipits, a short, hard, clicking *tsep* or, differently transcribed, *pset*. The call note may be repeated several times. Unfortunately, it is usually silent when flushed (which in itself is an indication of the species – any skulking pipit which remains silent even when flushed several times should be carefully checked). The alarm call *tsyp*, reminiscent of the alarm call of Rock Pipit, is unlikely to be heard from vagrants.

Habitat and behaviour: Prefers wet areas with much vegetation, where is extremely skulking and difficult to observe. This, with an unpipit-like habit of taking off without calling, makes it easily overlooked.

Range: Breeds in N Siberia from the Pechora River to Kamchatka and also in a small area in SE USSR and NE China (possibly linked with the main range). The winter range is imperfectly known but includes the Philippines and Indonesia. The migration routes are puzzling; it appears to migrate mainly along a narrow corridor somewhere between Japan and Hong Kong.

Status: Very rare vagrant in the British Isles (32, late Aug-Nov, mostly Sept-mid Oct, the majority from Fair Isle, Shetland). A few other records from Iceland (1), Norway (Sept 1976), Finland (Sept 1972, May 1973), France (Apr 1987) and Poland (Sept 1983, Apr 1985).

BUFF-BELLIED PIPIT   *Anthus rubescens*   B 41

L 14.5cm (5.75"). North America and Asia. Accidental (mainly Sept-Nov).

All plumages: Very distinctive. Shows some resemblance to the corresponding plumages of Water Pipit, with which it was long considered conspecific (see Appendix). However, it is slightly smaller with a proportionately shorter, finer, Meadow Pipit-like, bill. The lores are unmarked, whereas in Water Pipit they are dark to the eye (breaking the eye-ring; Note that from certain angles there may *seem* to be a dark loral stripe in Buff-bellied). Also, the moustachial stripe is normally more distinct than in Water Pipit. There is generally more white on the second outermost tail feather, but this is difficult to judge in the field.

The Asiatic subspecies, *japonicus*, also usually shows rather pale legs. However, it should be borne in mind that both the nominate race as well as the Water Pipit may show quite pale legs.

Adult summer: Further differs from Water Pipit in its more uniformly coloured underparts with a more orange, less pink, tone. The breast/flanks are more distinctly streaked than in most Water Pipits. The upperparts are also greyer than in a reasonably fresh plumaged Water Pipit. Nominate and *japonicus* subspecies are very similar.

Adult winter: Plumage differs markedly between the nominate and the *japonicus* subspecies. The latter shows bolder, darker and more clear-cut streaks on the underparts than *rubescens*. Also, the underside is whitish or pale buffish in *japonicus* and rich buff in *rubescens* in fresh plumage (although in worn plumage, latter may be whitish below).

The nominate race resembles the Water Pipit with much warmer underparts and smaller, more clearcut and slightly darker streaks.

The subspecies *japonicus* could also possibly be confused with Meadow Pipit. The best feature is the clearly darker and more grey-brown upperparts, with much fainter streaking (streaking more pronounced in worn plumage, but, especially, crown never as prominently streaked as in Meadow).

1st-winter: A variable number of coverts and tertials are renewed. Under ideal conditions (normally only with the bird in the hand) any retained juvenile coverts and tertials can be seen to show more worn and bleached edges, and usually show a slightly more diffuse pattern than in the adult. There is often a contrast between juvenile and newly moulted feathers (moult contrast never seen in the adult).

1st-summer: See Richard's Pipit (p. 189).

Voice: The song is somewhat reminiscent of Rock Pipit. The flight call is most similar to Meadow Pipit but thinner, sharper, more squeaky and slightly more drawn-out.

Habitat: The choice of habitat is generally rather wide, and birds are frequently found in both dry and wet areas.

Range: The nominate race breeds in Greenland, Canada, Alaska and W-C USA. Winters mainly along the coasts and S interior USA, south to Central America. The subspecies *japonicus* breeds in NE USSR and winters mainly in Japan and S China. A small number of the latter race regularly occurs as far west as the Middle East.

Status: Accidental in Europe (majority probably related to *rubescens*; at least one record concerned *japonicus*). Iceland (Oct 1977, Nov 1977, Oct 1983, Oct 1989*). Britain: St Kilda (Sept 1910), Fair Isle (Sept 1953), Isles of Scilly (Oct 1988). Ireland (Oct 1951, Oct 1967). West Germany: Heligoland (Nov 1851, May 1858, Sept 1899). Italy (Nov 1951, Oct 1960), where at least one record concerned *japonicus*.

CITRINE WAGTAIL *Motacilla citreola* D **41**

L 17cm (7"). W USSR to Asia. Rare vagrant, but increasingly recorded in spring/autumn.

Adult male summer: Easily recognized, with bright yellow head (frequently with dark smudge on crown) and underparts, the latter turning whitish at the rear. Has grey upperparts with diagnostic black half-collar and broad, white wing-bars, sometimes forming a white panel.

Adult female summer: Plumage very distinctive and only likely to be confused with *male* Yellow Wagtail of the British subspecies *flavissima* or Asian *lutea*. It differs from these by the usually more prominent supercilium that clearly surrounds the ear-coverts; rarely, the supercilium surrounds the ear-coverts in *flavissima/lutea* as well, although more diffusely. The lores are pale or diffusely darker and lack the distinct dark stripe shown by most (but not all!) Yellow Wagtails (more than 50% of *lutea* show unmarked lores). Also, shows a less prominent and less well-defined yellow stripe on the lower ear-coverts than in most *flavissima* (fewer *lutea*. The upperparts except the crown/nape are grey, often the breast-sides and flanks also. Yellow shows vividly green upperside, although it is very rarely greyish. An important char-

lutea in summer plumage
head pattern of some
♂ and a few ad. ♀

acter is that typically the supercilium, throat and upper breast are bright yellow, the belly and flanks often paler yellowish, and the undertail-coverts always whitish. In *flavissima/lutea* the underside is uniformly yellow. The wing-bars are generally whiter and more conspicuous, but may be narrow when worn, and Yellow Wagtail sometimes shows rather broad, whitish wing-bars. Some adult females are brightly coloured on the head, with yellow forehead/forecrown and yellow ear-coverts; also a trace of a dark hindneck collar. These could be confused with less advanced 1st-summer males. For ageing, see 1st-summer.

Adult winter: Plumage of both sexes basically resembles the summer female. The male is usually yellow on the forehead, ear-coverts (often with dark framing), throat and most of the underparts, and sometimes shows a little blackish on the (sides of) neck. The female usually lacks a yellow forehead and is not so yellow on the ear-coverts and underparts. In some females the yellow is very pale and buffish-tinged.

Juvenile: The plumage is browner above than the adult female and lacks yellow; also shows a conspicuous dark gorget and prominent blackish 'brow' above the supercilium. It is very similar to a juvenile Yellow Wagtail and best told by the characteristic supercilium (see 1st-winter), broader and whiter wing-bars, and whitish rather than yellowish edges to the secondaries. The juvenile plumage is moulted before migration.

1st-winter: Plumage basically grey and white, lacking the adults' yellow coloration and the juvenile's prominent black 'brow' and gorget. Retained juvenile coverts and tertials (generally all or most retained) show more whitish tips/edges and usually slightly more sharply defined dark centres than fresh winter adult (or any newly moulted adult-type feathers in 1st-winters); the latter have a faint brownish-grey tinge to the pale tips/edges. Rather similar to a White Wagtail in general coloration, but is easily distinguished by the lack of a dark gorget and more distinct head pattern.

It closely resembles a grey and white 1st-winter female Yellow Wagtail. Most 1st-winter Yellow Wagtails show greenish-tinged upperparts and at least some yellow on the underparts, particularly on the undertail-coverts. However, some 1st-winter female Yellow Wagtails, particularly Russian *beema* and other more eastern races, show no trace of green above or yellow below and are thus very similar to Citrine. The best distinguishing character is the difference in head pattern (see figure, p. 327). There is frequently a darker margin above the supercilium, which is very rarely seen in 1st-winter Yellow (but usual, although much more prominent, in juvenile!). The forehead is often contrastingly pale brown, unlike in Yellow. The supercilium is broad and conspicuous (often brownish and diffuse in front of the eye) and usually clearly surrounds the ear-coverts. In some birds the pale surround is less distinct, and very rarely it is even lacking. Yellow shows a narrower supercilium that tends to be more distinct and less brownish in front and never surrounds the ear-coverts. The lores are pale or diffusely darker and lack the distinct dark stripe seen in most Yellow Wagtails (although from certain angles, there may sometimes *seem* to be a dark stripe). The ear-coverts do not show such a broad pale stripe on the lower part as in particularly *beema* Yellow Wagtail, and they are never uniformly dark grey as in some Yellow. The bill is practically

inter typical
e
ail

✓ marked pale
und to ear-coverts

nter beema

ιl

flava

all dark, whereas Yellow usually (but not always) shows extensively pale base to the lower mandible.

The wing-bars are generally broader, but when worn may be close to those of Yellow. Any newly moulted coverts show paler, less brownish tips than in corresponding feathers in Yellow. Also, Citrine is fractionally larger, with a slightly longer tail than Yellow Wagtail.

1st-summer: Resembles the adult of its respective sex and generally difficult to distinguish without experience. The flight feathers, primary coverts and outer greater coverts are more worn than in the adult (but note that a moult contrast among the greater coverts is also normally found in the spring adult). Some individuals are in a less advanced stage of plumage than the adults (e.g. some 1st-summer males show a rather indistinct black band on the hindneck and mostly green-grey crown/hindneck, and some females look mostly as in 1st-winter).

Voice: The flight call is a characteristic, sharp, slightly harsh *tzreep*, clearly different from most European Yellow Wagtails. The call of the 'Black-headed' Yellow Wagtail (subspecies *feldegg*) is confusingly similar to Citrine but less sharp and harsh. The calls of some eastern races of Yellow Wagtail are exceptionally similar to Citrine. However, Citrine has very rarely even been heard to give calls similar to those of any of the northwestern races of Yellow Wagtail.

Note: Hybrids between Citrine and Yellow Wagtail, recorded on a few occasions, could be hard to identify, particularly in 1st-winter plumage.

Range: Breeds in central European USSR, NE and E USSR, W Siberia and W and C Asia. The range is expanding westwards, with now a few pairs breeding probably every year in E Turkey. There is a small regular passage through the Middle East and a few winter regularly in Saudi Arabia. Winters mainly in Indian Subcontinent and SE Asia.

Status: Rare vagrant in Europe, but increasingly recorded. The increase noted during the last two decades is probably linked to signs of further westward expansion in the USSR.

There are records from: Iceland (at least two, most recent-29th Oct 1982). British Isles (50) Aug-Nov, annual – virtually all 1st-winter birds; but in Essex, a male was seen feeding nestling wagtails in July 1976. France (Apr 1987, Apr 1989*). Netherlands (Aug-Sept 1984). Denmark (7). Norway (18). Sweden (51), including a male feeding 3 juveniles not specifically identified in July 1977. Finland (47, now annual), also between 1983-87, a male was paired with a female Yellow Wagtail at the same site in the south. Latvia (5, May). Poland (23, Mar-May, also autumn). East Germany (May 1984). West Germany (Heligoland, 5 records 19th century), more recently May 1972, May 1984, May 1985 and Sept 1987; singing male present in Bavaria (May 1986); and one in Apr 1988*. Czechoslovakia (Apr 1921, May 1976, also bred 1977), Austria (7), Hungary (May 1989*), Switzerland (Apr 1980), Italy (3rd record in May 1986), Yugoslavia (Apr 1987), Greece (Apr 1978, May 1981, Apr 1987), Rumania, and Spain (Mallorca, Apr 1987).

Family MIMIDAE Mockingbirds, Thrashers and Catbird

BROWN THRASHER *Toxostoma rufum* A **42**
L 24cm (9.5"). North America. Two European records.
All plumages: Unlikely to be confused with any European bird. The longish bill, long tail and short wings gives it a distinctive shape. The rufous upperparts, double pale wingbars, and distinct dark streaks on the underparts are also very characteristic.
Adult: Shows a yellow to yellow-orange iris.
1st-Winter: Best separated from the adult by its brownish to greyish-yellow iris. The iris usually attains adult coloration in the first part of the 2nd year. A moult contrast is often seen among the greater coverts, but note that the pattern of the different generations is the same.
Voice: The song is not unlike a Song Thrush. The alarm call is a rather sharp, *tchek*.
Behaviour: Usually very skulking, keeping to thickets, scrub etc. Normally observed low down or on the ground.
Range: Breeds mainly in E USA and S-C Canada. Northern populations are migratory, wintering in the S part of its range.
Status: Accidental in West Germany: Heligoland (autumn 1836). Britain: Durlston Head, Dorset (18th Nov 1966-5th Feb 1967).

GRAY CATBIRD *Dumetella carolinensis* A **42**
L 18.5cm (7.25"). North America. Accidental.
All plumages: Typically all grey with black cap and deep rufous under-tail-coverts.
Adult: Has a deep brownish-red iris.
1st-winter: Differs from the adult mainly in having slightly contrasting brownish flight-feathers, primary coverts and often outer greater coverts; also a greyish-brown to dull reddish- brown iris.
Voice: The song is rather varied, consisting of a mixture of squeaky, grating and clear notes, reminiscent of the song of some robins, thrushes etc. The most commonly heard call is a mewing, slightly harsh, somewhat Jay-like *weee* or *wEEeh*. Hard notes are also heard.
Behaviour: Much as Brown Thrasher.
Range: Breeds mainly in E and C USA and S Canada. Winters in SE USA to Central America.
Status: Accidental in West Germany: Heligoland (28th Oct 1840). East Germany: Leopoldshagen (2nd May 1908). Channel Islands: Jersey (mid-Oct-Dec 1975). Ireland: Cape Clear, Co. Cork (4th Nov 1986).

Family PRUNELLIDAE Accentors

SIBERIAN ACCENTOR *Prunella montanella* B **42**

L 14.5cm (5.5"). Asia. Accidental (mainly Oct-Nov).

Adult: Clearly an accentor in shape, general appearance and behaviour. Easily recognized by its very distinctive head pattern. Shows dark crown with a paler centre, prominent, bright buff supercilium, dark ear-coverts with a pale spot at the rear, and has grey sides to the neck. It also has bright buff throat, breast and often flanks. The mantle, scapulars and flanks are variably streaked with rufous, often very prominently on the mantle/scapulars. However, sometimes the streaking is blackish and the rufous tones are almost lacking. In worn plumage, large, dark marks are often evident on the breast.

Juvenile: Said to be much duller overall than the adult, but apparently not rather heavily streaked below as in juvenile Black-throated Accentor (below). Most unlikely to be seen in Europe in this plumage.

1st-winter: Similar to the adult. Probably differs from the adult by iris colour as in Dunnock (grey-brown in young, deep red-brown in adult).

Voice: The song resembles the Dunnock's, but is slightly fuller, harsher and stronger. Thin *see-see-see-see* notes are often heard, similar to the corresponding call of Dunnock but slightly weaker.

Range: Breeds mainly in N Siberia west to the Urals. Winters chiefly in N China and Korea.

Status: Accidental in Europe. Sweden: first recorded in Oct 1976, but in mid-late Oct 1987 there was an unprecedented invasion, with 3 on Öland and one in Uppland. Also one in Västerbotten in mid Oct 1988. There are also records from Finland (Oct 1975, Oct 1976, Oct 1986, Oct 1988), Poland (26th-27th Mar 1988*), Czechoslovakia (Dec 1943), Austria (one reported, early 19th century), and Italy (Nov 1884, Nov 1901, Nov 1907).

BLACK-THROATED ACCENTOR *Prunella atrogularis* A **42**

L 15cm (6"). Urals and C Asia. Two recent records for N Europe.

Adult: Resembles Siberian Accentor, but usually shows a distinct blackish bib, although in winter it is slightly less prominent because of paler fringes. The bib is occasionally rather indistinct or very rarely even virtually lacking altogether (perhaps only in 1st-winter). Birds without distinct dark bib differ from Siberian in paler supercilium and throat (especially centre which is generally whitish). They never show rufous streaking on upper– and underparts as most Siberian Accentors do, but note that some Siberian are very similar to Black-throated in this respect. The ear-coverts (especially below eye) are normally rather pale in those Black-throated, rarely or never the case in Siberian.

Juvenile: Paler on the underparts than the adult, with streaked breast. Head pattern less striking, with at the most a trace of a dark throat patch. Very unlikely to be recorded in Europe in this plumage.

1st-winter: See Siberian Accentor, above. Birds with little black on the throat seem more likely to be 1st-winters than adult.

Voice: The song resembles Dunnock's but is harsher with more buzzing trills, and it has a distinctly different rhythm.

Note: Radde's Accentor *P. ocularis*, breeding chiefly in E Turkey/Iran could possibly reach Europe. It is very similar to rare examples of the Black-throated which show an indistinct or no dark bib. Radde's never shows a dark bib. The throat is whitish or very pale buffish (in Black-throated the warm buffish of the breast extends onto the sides of the throat), and the sides of the throat are usually finely spotted, forming darker malar stripes not seen in Black-throated. Also, the supercilium is whitish (or very pale buffish in fresh plumage).

Range: Breeds in the Urals and in the mountains of W China, W Mongolia and neighbouring parts of the USSR. Ural population migratory, probably wintering mainly in Afghanistan to NW India, together with the S population. Vagrants have reached Israel and Oman.

Status: Accidental in Finland: Helsinki on 19th Oct 1987, and Sweden: Stora Fjäderägg, Västerbotten from 14th-15th June 1988.

Family TURDIDAE   Robins, Chats, Thrushes and allies

SIBERIAN RUBYTHROAT   *Luscinia calliope*   B **43**

L 14cm (5.5"). Asia. Accidental in both N and S Europe (mainly Oct-Nov).

All plumages: Similar to Bluethroat in size, shape and general appearance. Shows a distinct, rather short supercilium.

Adult male: Shows brilliant red throat patch, contrasting with short, white submoustachial stripe and black lores and malar stripes. In fresh plumage (autumn), breast is generally browner than in worn plumage, when usually greyer. The base of the lower mandible is paler in winter.

Adult female: Shows short, pale submoustachial stripe and throat, divided by an indistinct darker malar stripe, thus ghosting the male's pattern. Most individuals show at least a little pink on the throat and the throat pattern is occasionally quite similar to the male's, but probably never quite as deep and extensively red. Such male-like adult females further differ from males in showing a fainter dark margin to the throat, have a browner breast and are not so pure white on the submoustachial stripe or so black on the lores as in the male.

Juvenile: Plumage is heavily pale-spotted above and strongly marked below, and very similar to juvenile Robin or Thrush Nightingale. Compared to the former, it is less buffish on the breast, and shows more rufous-tinged edges to the primaries. From the latter, it differs mainly in less rufous tail and uppertail- coverts. It is unlikely to be recorded in Europe in this plumage, since it is moulted when very young.

1st-winter/-summer male: Similar to the adult male but shows distinct buffish tips to a variable number of retained juvenile tertials and outer greater coverts; these contrast with newly moulted coverts/tertials.

1st-winter/-summer female: Differs from the adult female in the same way as described for 1st-winter male (see above). Only rarely shows a few pink feathers on the throat.

Voice: The song is varied, warbling and built up largely of imitations of other birds. The song is not as strong as that of some other related species. The call note is a loud, clear double whistle, *EE-uh*, which is often the only sign of its presence. The alarm call (heard all year around), is a *schak*, like a miniature Fieldfare.

Habitat and behaviour: In the non-breeding season, favours wetter areas with dense vegetation, e.g. ditches, thickets and reedbeds. Extremely skulking. Behaviour otherwise much as Bluethroat, and like that species, often cocks tail.

Range: Breeds mainly in Siberia, NE and C China and Hokkaido (Japan). Winters in S China, Philippines, and Indo Chinese countries west to India.

Status: Accidental in Iceland: adult male (8th Nov 1943). Britain: Fair Isle, 1st-winter female (9th-11th Oct 1975); Denmark: 1st-winter female (Oct 1985), Sweden (22nd-24th Sept 1990*), Estonia, and Italy (7, Oct-Dec, Mar).

SIBERIAN BLUE ROBIN   *Luscinia cyane*   A **43**

L 13.5cm (5.25"). Asia. Only one record for N Europe.

Adult male: Unmistakable. The upperparts are deep blue and the underparts white. The demarcation line between blue and white on the sides of the head, and on the neck and breast is blackish.

Adult female: Rather featureless. Upperparts are greyish-brown, often with some blue on the uppertail-coverts, rump and sometimes on the tail. Shows a pale buffish throat, slightly deeper buffish breast and usually flanks. Also, the breast normally shows indistinct dark crescents, sometimes diffuse spots. It has a distinctive profile, with a comparatively short tail, and the legs are usually strikingly pale.

Juvenile: Plumage pale-spotted above and more heavily marked with dark scales on the underparts than in the adult female. This plumage is moulted soon after fledging, thus very unlikely to be seen in Europe.

1st-winter male: Plumage variable. The rump, uppertail-coverts and tail are probably always blue, and usually there is some blue on the scapulars and lesser, median and inner greater coverts. Sometimes, most of the upperparts and all of the wing-coverts are blue; such individuals are still easily told from adult male by more female-like head and grey-brown alula, remiges and primary coverts. Any retained juvenile greater coverts are like the corresponding feathers in 1st-winter female.

1st-summer male: Resembles the adult male, but is easily told by retained juvenile alula, flight-feathers, primary coverts and usually outer greater coverts and some tertials (feathers worn and grey-brown as opposed to rather fresh and blue-edged in adult).

1st-winter/-summer female: Resembles the adult female, but less frequently shows blue on the rump, uppertail-coverts and tail. It differs in retained juvenile (outer) greater coverts with rufous/buffish edges and spot on the tip (more difficult to judge in spring). Any new inner greater coverts contrast clearly with the juvenile outers.

Voice: The song usually begins with some fine, hesitant *sit* notes, followed by a rapid series of varied, loud, almost explosive notes, e.g. *tri-tri-tri-tri*; *ueediu-ueediu- ueediu*; *sui-sui-sui* or *tjuree-tiu-tiu-tiu-tiu*. The alarm call is a rather subdued, hard *dack*.

Habitat and behaviour: Forest with dense undergrowth. Extremely shy and skulking. Feeds on the ground. Has a characteristic habit of constantly quivering the tail when alerted.

Range: Breeds in E Siberia, NE China and Japan. Winters mainly in SE Asia and Indonesia.
Status: Accidental in the Channel Islands: Banquette Valley, Sark, 1st-winter female trapped on 27th Oct 1975.

RED-FLANKED BLUETAIL   *Tarsiger cyanurus*   C **43**

L 14cm (5.5"). Asia. Rare vagrant (mainly autumn). Has bred Finland and Estonia.
Adult male: Brilliantly coloured and unmistakable. The blue upperside, relatively narrow white throat and orange flanks are not shared by any European bird. The edges to the flight feathers vary from blue to brownish, with some individuals showing a mixture of both. In winter, the upperparts are slightly brownish-tinged.
Adult female: Distinctively plumaged, with brown upperparts and contrasting blue rump, uppertail-coverts and tail. The flanks are orange, and there is a relatively narrow, white throat patch. Distinctive profile.
Juvenile: Plumage heavily spotted as in juveniles of other small *Turdidae*. Identified by its blue tail. This plumage is very unlikely to be seen outside the breeding area, since it is quickly lost.
1st-winter: Very similar to the adult female. Sometimes shows an obvious moult contrast among the greater coverts and/or tertials, often with a trace of a pale spot on the tips of the juvenile feathers.
1st-summer male: Resembles adult female. Most are not safely separable unless singing. Some show traces of male plumage, e.g. blue on lesser coverts and scapulars (perhaps shown by some adult females also).
Voice: The song is rather short, fast and clear, e.g. *didiu-diu dew dew dew dew*. It calls with a high-pitched *uist*, often alternated by a hard, slightly nasal *track* or alternatively transcribed, *rug*, often repeated, and which is frequently the first sign of its presence.
Habitat and behaviour: Forest with some undergrowth. Not particularly skulking. Has a characteristic habit of twitching its tail with small movements when alerted. Generally seen perched low in bushes, occasionally Robin-like on the ground.
Range: Breeds in a belt from westernmost USSR to Japan and Kamchatka and in the Himalayas and C China. Winters mainly in the Himalayas and S China. Has occasionally bred Finland, and recently in Estonia (June 1980). Accidental in Cyprus and Lebanon.
Status: Rare vagrant in Europe. Britain (11, Sept-Oct, except for one male in May/June). Channel Islands, Sark (31st Oct-2nd Nov 1976). Netherlands, Texel (Oct 1967, Sept 1985). Denmark (May 1976). Norway (May 1969, Aug 1977, Nov 1978, Sept 1987). Sweden (9, May-July, singles Sept, Dec). Finland (westward expansion halted and only a few recorded in recent years). Estonia (a few records) male in May 1977; also male from 24th Apr 1980 and a female later found with 4 newly fledged young in June. Poland (Aug 1987), East Germany (Sept 1972), West Germany (Oct 1956), Czechoslovakia (May 1973), and Italy (3).

L 16.5cm (6.5"). SW Asia. Accidental (mainly May- June).

Adult male: Readily identified by blue-grey upperparts with contrasting blackish tail. Shows distinctive black face pattern and throat sides, which contrast with the white supercilium and central throat. Also, has orange or pale orange-buff breast, flanks and underwing-coverts. Shows narrow, pale fringes to black and orange areas in winter.

Adult female: Rather brownish-grey upperparts with contrasting blackish tail. Shows a relatively plain head with a pale eye-ring and a rather narrow, whitish throat patch. Also, has diffusely mottled breast, and orange-tinged flanks and underwing- coverts, sometimes breast too. Unlikely to be confused with any European species.

Juvenile: Grey-brown, heavily pale-spotted above and pale buffish on the throat, breast and flanks, with fine dark scales or spots. Tail and underwing-coverts as in adult. This plumage is quickly lost and unlikely to be seen in Europe.

1st-winter: Differs from the adult female by the distinct, small, pale (buffish when fresh) spots to the primary coverts and usually to some tertials and outer greater coverts (contrasting clearly with any newly moulted, fresher tertials and coverts, lacking pale spots). Males tend to be more orange-tinged than females, particularly on the breast.

1st-summer male: Differs from the adult male by the retained, brownish and more heavily worn, flight-feathers, primary coverts and often outer greater coverts, which contrast with the fresh, blue-grey remainder of the wing and upperparts. The adult male has blue-grey edges to all of these feathers. The pale spots particularly on the primary coverts are often still visible in 1st- summer male.

1st-summer female: As 1st-winter, but the pale tips are generally more difficult to see in spring. Furthermore, the flight-feathers are generally distinctly more worn than in the adult.

Voice: The song is a rather short warble, built up mainly of rather harsh notes. The call is said to be a loud *chi chyt*.

Habitat and behaviour: In the breeding areas, favours dry, scrubby sites, mainly on mountain slopes and adjoining dry gullies. Not normally seen in the open, except when singing. Has mainly terrestrial habits and often cocks tail.

Range: Breeds in mountainous areas in Turkey, eastwards to Afghanistan and neighbouring parts of the USSR. Winters in NE Africa and Arabia. Vagrant in Cyprus (Apr 1962, Mar 1981).

Status: Accidental in Britain: Isle of Man (male, June 1983), Skokholm Is, Dyfed (female, May 1990*). Netherlands (adult male, Nov 1986), Norway (male, May 1981), Sweden (single males in June-July 1971, May 1977, May 1981, May 1986 and May 1989*), and Greece (May 1966).

MOUSSIER'S REDSTART   *Phoenicurus moussieri*   B **42**

L 12cm (4.75"). N Africa. Accidental, mainly in Mediterranean (spring).

Adult male: Strikingly marked. Upperparts, ear-coverts and wings black, with a contrasting, broad white stripe on the forehead and sides to the head/neck and a large, white wing-patch. The underparts are deep orange-rufous. Pattern of rump, uppertail- coverts and tail as in Redstart. In fresh plumage (autumn), the black areas, notably the upperparts, show paler fringes.

Adult female: Similar to female Redstart, but is smaller, with a shorter tail and primary projection. Also, tends to be slightly deeper and more extensively rufous-tinged below, but there is much overlap. Often shows a rather distinct paler wing patch.

Juvenile: Resembles the adult female but is mottled above and below, but less strongly than in juvenile Redstart. Male shows a prominent white wing patch. Very unlikely to be seen in Europe in this plumage, since it is quickly moulted.

1st-winter/-summer male: Similar to the adult male but shows a distinct contrast between newly moulted, blackish-centred, median and inner greater coverts (number variable) and retained juvenile, more brownish-centred and more worn outer greater coverts, primary coverts, alula and remiges (the juvenile greater coverts are buffish- tipped when reasonably fresh).

1st-winter/-summer female: Differs from the adult female in the same way as described above for 1st-winter/-summer male, but the moult contrast is far more difficult to discern.

Voice: The song is rather short, rapid and built up of a mixture of harsh and clear notes. It calls with a short, soft *hit* and a very harsh *trrrrr*.

Range: Breeds in Morocco, Algeria and Tunisia. Resident or dispersive.

Status: Accidental in Europe. Britain: Dinas Head, Dyfed, male (24th Apr 1988). Italy (Calabria 1906), Sicily (27th Feb 1987). Malta: Dec 1933, Apr 1958, Mar 1974 (*c.* 5), May 1976, and 7th Apr 1982 (3). Greece: male reported from SW tip of Peloponnese on 30th Mar 1988*. Majorca: female reported early May 1988*.

'EASTERN STONECHAT'   *Saxicola torquata maura* group   D **42**

L 12.5cm (5"). Asiatic race-group of Stonechat. Rare but rather frequent autumn vagrant (mainly to N Europe)..

Adult male summer: Similar to European races of Stonechat (*hibernans* and *rubicola*), but is generally more contrastingly patterned, having a white, unmarked rump and uppertail-coverts (latter sometimes with dark shaft-streaks). However, note that European birds are sometimes very similar and may even show a large, unmarked whitish rump patch. On average, the breast shows a more well-defined and smaller orange patch. The underwing-coverts are more blackish than in the European races due to narrower pale fringes.

Adult male winter: Shows the same basic pattern as in summer, but the black parts are partly concealed by broad, pale brownish fringes, and the white on the sides of the neck, rump/uppertail-coverts and underparts is largely clouded by warm brownish- orange. The lores, chin and at least part of the ear-coverts and throat are black. The plumage is basically paler than in European Stonechats, with broader and paler fringes to the head and upperparts and paler fringes to the underparts. The rump/uppertail-coverts are probably never unstreaked nor so pale in European Stonechats in fresh plumage.

Adult female: Similar to European races of Stonechat, but is generally paler both above and below, with unmarked, white (worn, mainly spring/summer) to pale brownish-orange (fresh, mainly autumn/winter) rump/uppertail-coverts. The throat is usually wholly pale, unlike in the European races. In winter plumage, easily mistaken for Whinchat, but the latter shows a more prominent supercilium as well as more "black and white-spotted" mantle/scapulars and dark-spotted rump/uppertail-coverts and often breast sides. The tail pattern is immediately conclusive.

Juvenile: Plumage is distinctly spotted with pale above and dark below. It is quite difficult to separate from juvenile European Stonechats, but the rump/uppertail-coverts are like the fresh adult, except for some faint streaking. Moulted early.

1st-winter male: Somewhat variable. Some individuals are easily sexed in the field, showing distinct male characters on the head, but they are apparently never completely black on the lores and chin as the adult male. They further differ from the adult male in showing a distinct moult contrast between some new, black-centred coverts and some retained juvenile, more brownish-centred ones. Often only the lesser coverts are new, contrasting with the others. Some individuals are similar to the female and not always separable in the field, but they usually show a little blackish on the ear-coverts (especially just behind the eye) and often throat also. In the hand, they show blackish central underwing-coverts with pale fringes (pale buffish-grey in female) and have more extensive, more sharply defined and blacker centres to the crown, mantle/scapulars and any newly moulted coverts than in the female (see figure). Usually some pure white on the sides of the neck and rump and dark grey centres to the throat. 1st-winter male European Stonechat is patterned like the winter adult male on the head/neck.

1st-summer male: Like adult male, but has retained juvenile, worn and brownish, outer greater coverts, primary coverts and flight feathers.

1st-winter/-summer female: Very similar to the adult female in plumage. Moult contrasts are more difficult to discern than in the 1st-year male.

The race *variegata* is basically similar to the respective plumages of *maura* but shows a considerable amount of white on the inner part of the tail (mainly on the inner webs, see figure)

Range: Breeds in Asia from Transcaucasia and W Siberia to E Siberia, Japan and SE Tibet. The subspecies *maura* breeds over most of the range (often separated into two subspecies, the easternmost one called *stejnegeri*). The race *variegata* breeds in N Caspian to E Caucasus. Many other races are described, as the species also extends south from Europe and the Middle East to Africa and Madagascar etc, and further east to China.

Status: Individuals showing characters of the eastern race *maura* (including *stejnegeri*), 'Siberian Stonechat', have been recorded as follows: Faeroes (Sept 1946), British Isles (126, Sept-May, especially

1st-winter
♂

wn and
ntle/scapular
her

t half of tail

335

Oct-Nov), France (10, Oct-Dec, Feb, Apr), Channel Is (Jersey Oct 1984), Netherlands (13), Denmark (18, Sept-Nov, Apr-May), Norway (11), Sweden (53, most in the autumn, but also in spring), Finland (*c.* 130, majority autumn, but several May/July, and first reported case of a hybrid breeding with Whinchat confirmed in summer 1986), West Germany (3), Austria (May 1985), Italy (Oct 1988) and Rumania.

Single examples showing characters of the race *variegata* have been recorded from Britain, Cornwall (1st-4th Oct 1985), and Norway (1 ringed 15th-19th June 1983).

ISABELLINE WHEATEAR *Oenanthe isabellina* R Br **44**

L 16.5cm (6.5"). Breeds locally NE Greece (also further E to E Asia). Very rare vagrant elsewhere in Europe (spring/autumn).

All plumages: Similar to female Wheatear, but is slightly larger, heavier and usually appears to have a proportionately larger head and bill. It also has a shorter primary projection, shorter tail and slightly longer legs. The differences in size and structure are not always very obvious.

The dark tail-bar is distinctly wider than Wheatear's, (see figure) and there is slightly less white on rump, combined with slightly shorter tail, often resulting in the white area on the tail/rump/uppertail-coverts looking obviously smaller than in Wheatear. Axillaries and underwing-coverts are whitish to pale buffish, as opposed to dark grey with pale fringes in Wheatear. See also female Desert Wheatear (p. 339).

Isabelline Wheatear   Wheatear

left half of tail

Adult summer: Paler and more sandy-coloured above than female Wheatear, never appearing distinctly bluish-grey as in many Wheatears. The wings are rather pale with a contrastingly darker alula, and are never uniformly dark – obviously darker than the upperparts – as in most female Wheatears in spring/summer. The ear-coverts are never darker than the crown as in many Wheatears. It is important to remember that some female Wheatears are rather pale and sandy-coloured above, with the wings and ear-coverts no darker than the upperparts, and these are easily confused with Isabelline. See below for further differences. Male tends to show a blacker loral stripe and whiter supercilium in front of/above the eye than the female (much overlap, though).

Adult winter: Easily confused with female/1st-winter male Wheatear. The plumage is usually slightly paler and less richly-coloured than in Wheatear, but some Wheatears are very similar in general coloration. The pale wings with a contrastingly dark alula are matched by many Wheatears, but in these the centres to the coverts are distinctly darker. This is often apparent only on median coverts, since the dark centres of the greater coverts are often entirely covered by pale fringes. In Wheatear, the dark centres to the median coverts show up as a row of dark spots, about as dark as the alula, whereas in Isabelline the dark centres are rather inconspicuous and always clearly paler than the alula.

The supercilium is typically either pale buffish throughout its length or more whitish in front of/above the eye and distinctly more buffish behind; it is often very poorly defined. In Wheatear, the supercilium is normally buffish in front of the eye and whiter above/behind (often slightly dusky at the very rear end), and it is only rarely so poorly marked as in many Isabelline Wheatears.

The throat and ear-coverts below the eye are often contrastingly pale, almost whitish, divided by a buffish malar stripe, creating a distinctive pattern. Wheatear is usually more uniformly buffish on these parts; there is some overlap, however.

Juvenile: Basically resembles the adult but has faintly mottled upperparts and generally shows some dark markings on the breast. The plumage is much less strongly marked than juvenile Wheatear. The juvenile plumage is moulted soon after fledging, so that it is unlikely to be found far away from the breeding areas.

1st-winter/-summer: In the hand, separable from the adult by its more worn wings, generally with one to a few contrastingly fresher new inner greater coverts and/or tertials. The pale edges to the juvenile greater coverts are usually more sharply defined than in the adult, particularly at the tips. In the autumn, there is frequently some pink and/or yellow on the inside of the upper mandible and palate, where the adult is all-blackish. Note that the skull usually becomes fully pneumatized very early (usually before late Aug).

Voice: The song is very variable, consisting of a mixture of hard and harsh notes, clear whistles and masterful imitations. The speed changes are often rather dramatic. Often sings in a short, display flight with the tail fanned. The call is similar to Wheatear.

Range: Breeds in dry, usually mountainous areas from NE Greece, where local and uncommon (under 50 pairs), eastwards to Mongolia and NE China. Winters in Africa, Arabia and S Asia. Regular spring/autumn in Cyprus. Vagrant in Madeira and Morocco.

Status: Accidental elsewhere in Europe. Britain (7, Sept-Nov, May), France (Sept 1970, May-June 1988), Denmark (Sept 1989*), Norway (Sept-Oct 1977), Sweden (Oct 1980), Finland (Sept 1977, Apr-May 1979, Sept 1987, June 1988), Poland (May 1986), Rumania (bred 1975-78), Bulgaria (bred 1972, 1981), Italy, Spain, and Malta (mainly in spring). In Sicily: scarce spring passage migrant, now regular, late Feb-mid Apr (since 1974, 1-20 individuals recorded annually near Siracusa; and is possibly a regular visitor to NW Africa).

PIED WHEATEAR *Oenanthe pleschanka* R Br **44**

L 14.5cm (5.75"). Breeds E Rumania and Bulgaria, also further E to E Asia. Rare vagrant in Europe outside limited breeding area (mainly autumn).

Adult male summer: Basically black-and-white, often with some warm buff on the breast and dusky on the crown. It resembles an adult male of the black-throated morph of the Black-eared Wheatear, but the mantle is black, and the black throat usually extends obviously further down, onto the upper breast, connecting with the black of the upperparts and wings. A white-throated morph, '*vittata*', is very rare. It shows a black band between the ear-coverts and the upperparts/wings.

Adult male winter: Has same basic pattern as in summer (summer plumage attained mainly through wear), but the white of the crown/nape and the black of the mantle/scapulars is largely obscured by brownish-grey (with narrow, pale fringes). The lower part of the throat and the wings show much pale fringing, and the underparts are much more richly coloured. It is darker and more brown-grey above than an adult male Black-eared, generally with less contrastingly dark scapulars (some Black-eared of race *melanoleuca* very similar, though). In the hand (but generally not in the field), the black centres to the mantle are ob-

vious (white in Black-eared). The throat pattern is still normally conclusive, although broad pale fringes to the lower part of the throat may
make the black seem to end higher up than it actually does. When fresh,
the wings generally show more pale fringes than in a fresh adult male
Black-eared, particularly on the lesser coverts which usually lack pale
fringes in adult (but not 1st-winter) Black-eared. The typical male pattern gradually becomes more obvious as the plumage wears.

Adult female summer: Dark brownish-grey above, with a variably dark
throat/breast, and is very similar to many females of the eastern race
melanoleuca of the Black-eared Wheatear. Black-eared usually shows
a warm brown tinge to the upperparts, but some individuals are indistinguishable from Pied in their upperpart coloration. In the hand it can
be seen that Pied lacks whitish on the central part of the mantle-fea-
thers; the majority of female Black-eared shows a tiny whitish spot or
shaft-streak on the centre of these feathers.

The throat pattern is often a very good character. In individuals with
a dark grey or blackish (lower) throat, the dark usually extends clearly
further down than in Black-eared (in both species, the downward extension of the dark throat resembles that of their respective male).
Some are rather uniformly grey on the throat and upper breast with
fine dark shaft-streaks – a pattern apparently not seen in Black-eared.
Very few are rather pale on the throat, but individuals with immaculate
white throat as in many Black-eareds are exceptionally rare (*'vittata'*).

The breast is usually rather cold greyish-buff, darker on the sides.
Black-eared generally shows a warmer, more orange-buff tinge, although sometimes the colour is indistinguishable from that of a normal
Pied. Also, tends to show a less well-defined breast band than Black-
eared, and apparently never shows a broad, rather clearcut orange-buf-
fish breast band (with darker sides) as is frequently found in
Black-eared. The ear-coverts are apparently never contrastingly blackish as in some Black-eared. Black-eared from the eastern part of the
range are often *extremely* similar to Pied; some individuals may be so
similar that they are better left undetermined. Frequent hybridization
in some areas also further complicates the matter (see below).

Adult female winter: Much as summer plumage, but shows pale fringes
to the wing and tail feathers and usually has a paler throat. It is normally even more difficult to tell from Black-eared than in summer. The
throat pattern is only sometimes useful in identification. The general
colour differences are the same as for summer plumage; note that as in
summer plumage some birds are indistinguishable in coloration. When
fresh, the upperparts show distinct pale fringes. Black-eared is usually
plain above, or with paler fringes to the scapulars, but pale fringes are
only rarely found on the crown or mantle. Since some eastern Black-
eared females are practically identical to female Pied in the autumn, it
is very hard (sometimes impossible) to identify a vagrant female Pied
in the autumn with 100% certainty. It seems much less likely that one
of those relatively few Black-eared straggle to Europe than a Pied.

Readily distinguished from Wheatear by, e.g. darker upperparts and
breast, different head pattern (less distinct supercilium, buffish
throughout its length; unmarked, generally pale lores; and frequently
dark markings on the sides of the throat), clearly darker axillaries and
underwing-coverts, more white on the rump and narrower, frequently

f of tail showing
ual variation

broken tail-bar which reaches higher up on the edges (see figure). The shape is also clearly different.

Juvenile: Mottled both above and on the breast. Unlikely to be seen outside breeding areas.

1st-winter male: Rather variable. Most are easily sexed, showing definite male characters. Apparently only very rarely shows completely black lores and chin as in the adult. The centres to the scapulars are often less-black than in adult male. The flight-feathers are generally more worn (white tips to primaries less distinct) and more brownish. The primary coverts show broader pale fringes (almost lacking in adult), and the inner greater coverts are often new, contrasting with browner and more worn outers. Others are more female-like, but in the hand these birds are sexed as they show blackish centres to the throat and mantle/scapulars, and whitish centres to the crown/nape.

Similar to many 1st-winter male eastern Black-eared Wheatears of the black-throated morph, but is even darker and more brownish-grey above (some Black-eared remarkably similar, though), normally with more distinct pale fringes, and usually shows a clearly more extensive dark throat (but see adult male). In the hand, (and occasionally also in the field) it is easily told by the blackish centres to the mantle feathers, as opposed to whitish in Black-eared.

1st-summer male: Generally less clean and bright than the adult male and told with certainty by the mainly juvenile wings (see above).

1st-winter/-summer female: Very difficult to distinguish from the adult female but the wings, notably primary tips, are generally more worn, and moult contrasts among the coverts/tertials are sometimes seen. The inside of upper mandible and palate are apparently pale, yellowish or pinkish as opposed to blackish in adult birds (valid in males also).

Voice: The song is similar to Black-eared Wheatear. It is rather simple, and mainly built up of harsh, rattling notes mixed with some clearer ones. The call is a rather harsh, slightly nasal *chep*, like Black-eared's.

Note: Hybridization with Black-eared Wheatear is frequent in a few areas near the Caspian Sea. Male hybrids normally show intermediate characters, e.g. black mantle and white throat (may be similar to '*vittata*' form of Pied). Female hybrids can be extremely confusing and complicate identification even further.

Range: Breeds locally in E Rumania and Bulgaria and east to Mongolia and neighbouring parts of USSR and China. Winters in E Africa.

Status: Rare vagrant to the rest of Europe. British Isles (20), most late autumn, but one male in May 1978. Netherlands: female on Schiermonnikoog (28th May 1988). Norway (2nd in Nov 1986), Sweden (Oct 1975, Sept 1987, Oct 1987, 3 in Oct 1988), Finland (5, Oct), West Germany (6), Austria (June 1983), Hungary (8), Yugoslavia (bred 1966), Greece (first proof of breeding confirmed in 1989), Italy (7), and Malta (Mar 1968, Apr 1973).

DESERT WHEATEAR *Oenanthe deserti* C **44**

L 14-15cm (5.75"). N Africa, NW Arabia, E to Mongolia. Rare vagrant (mainly from late autumn).

All plumages: Shows diagnostic all black tail (under good conditions a little white can be seen at the base of all but the central pair of feathers; see figure, p. 340).

Adult male summer: Although this plumage is very distinctive, it could be confused with the black-throated form of Black-eared Wheatear, but the black on the throat is connected with the black of the wing. The innermost coverts are at least partly whitish, and usually form a pale line which contrasts both with the rest of the wing and with the upperparts. The scapulars are the same colour as the mantle, not black as in Black-eared.

Adult male winter: Usually shows some pale fringes to the ear-coverts, throat and wings.

Adult female summer: Generally rather paler and more sandy-coloured than other European wheatears, except Isabelline. It could be confused with abnormally pale (leucistic) individuals of other wheatears, but the tail pattern is diagnostic. From Isabelline, it also differs in having much darker wings, contrasting with the upperparts, and the pale innermost coverts generally form a contrasting pale stripe. Sometimes shows some dark on the (lower) throat. Also see under winter plumage.

left half of tail

Adult female winter: Flight feathers and coverts show paler fringes, which obscure the dark centres to many of the feathers, creating an essentially pale wing, with contrasting blackish alula. It may be confused with Isabelline Wheatear, if the tail pattern cannot be seen satisfactorily. Isabelline is slightly larger and heavier, with larger head/bill, is shorter-tailed, has longer legs and adopts a more upright stance.

The head pattern is slightly different from Isabelline's. The supercilium, usually slightly less prominent than in Isabelline (although it can be virtually absent in both) is generally pale buffish throughout its length. Ear-coverts tend to be more uniformly patterned and are sometimes rusty brown, darker than the crown. The throat is either all whitish or with dusky sides, and the lores probably always unmarked, even though from certain angles there sometimes *seems* to be a dark stripe.

The wing pattern also differs. The inner median and inner greater and especially the lesser coverts are often appreciably paler than the upperparts and the rest of the wing (never so in Isabelline), and the centres of the coverts are distinctly darker than in Isabelline, sometimes visible only on median coverts (row of blackish spots; paler, more diffuse and less contrasting spots in Isabelline). Additionally, the pale rump area is distinctly larger (uppertail-coverts and entire rump pale; only uppertail-coverts and distal part of rump in Isabelline), and the whole area is frequently rather rich buffish, unlike in Isabelline.

Juvenile: Basically like the adult female but indistinctly mottled above and on the breast. Quickly moulted.

1st-winter male: The black of the head is partly obscured by broad, pale fringes, but usually 'shines through' (especially on neck sides). Some individuals (particularly in late autumn/winter when more worn) are quite similar to the adult male, but the wings are rather more dark brown than blackish, and the paler fringes/edges to the feathers are more distinct. In the hand, it can be seen that the primaries are more worn than in the adult, and a moult contrast can often be seen among the greater coverts. Differences in the colour of the inside of the upper mandible and palate as described for Isabelline Wheatear, are probably also valid.

1st-summer male: Basically resembles the adult male, but the plumage tends to be less 'advanced'. The flight feathers and usually at least some of the coverts are more worn and browner than in adult males.

1st-winter/-summer female: Probably only separable from adult in the hand, using same in-the-hand characters described for 1st-winter male.

Voice: The song consists of short, slightly varied phrases built up of rather melancholic whistles and trills, e.g. *huee-heurrr*.

Range: Breeds N Africa, NW Arabia, Transcaucasia and Iran, east through C Asia to Mongolia. Winters N Africa, and in Asia from Arabia to NE India. In Cyprus: scarce passage migrant (Mar-mid Apr, rarer autumn). Vagrant to the Canary Is and Madeira.

Status: Rare vagrant in Europe. British Isles (32) Aug-Apr (June), but most from late autumn (13 during Nov-Jan). France (7, Feb, July-Oct); Belgium (Oct 1990*), Netherlands (Nov 1970, Apr 1989*); Denmark (Oct 1987, Nov 1987); Norway (Dec 1984); Sweden (15, Sept-Dec, peak in Nov, also Apr-May); Finland (Nov 1950, June 1954, Nov 1958, Nov 1981, Mar-Apr 1988); West Germany (7, with 5 of these on Heligoland), Italy (including 8 records from Sicily); Malta (7th record in Nov 1977); Spain (Sept 1972, Apr 1985); Gibraltar (Sept 1987); and Greece.

WHITE-CROWNED BLACK WHEATEAR *Oenanthe leucopyga*   A **44**

L 17cm (6.75"). North Africa to Arabia. Accidental (Apr-June).

Adult: Similar to male Black Wheatear, but is slightly smaller with the plumage glossed bluish and shows white crown (perhaps lacking in some). Also, shows more extensive white on the rump as well as on the rear flanks/belly. Has characteristic tail pattern with all but the central pair of feathers either entirely white or marked with black spots on the tips, not forming a complete tail-bar (see figure).

Juvenile: Resembles adult but is browner and lacks white crown.

1st-winter/-summer: Generally lacks or shows very little white on the crown. Tends to show more black in the tail than adult, but only very rarely forming a complete bar (narrower than in Black). The alula, primary coverts, remiges and outer greater coverts are usually obviously browner and more worn than in the adult, and contrast with the remainder of the newer, black plumage. Confusable with male Black Wheatear, but told by same characters as in adult (except for crown).

Voice: The song is very variable, consisting of simple, soft whistles, e.g. *chu-chi-u...chu-chi...chu-chi-u*. It calls with a soft, clear *hue*.

of tail showing ual variation

Range: Resident in North Africa, the Middle East and Arabia. Vagrant to Cyprus (11th-24th Mar 1970).

Status: Accidental in Britain: Kessingland, Suffolk (1st-5th June 1982). West Germany: Buchenhüll near Eichstätt (9th-13th May 1986). Spain: Reserva Biologica de Doñana (two on 28th May 1977). Malta: one collected (18th Apr 1872).

WHITE'S THRUSH *Zoothera dauma*   D **45**

L 27cm (10.5"). Asia. Rare vagrant (mainly from late autumn).

Adult: The striking black crescentic markings to the head and body, and strong upperwing pattern make this species unmistakable. Note the dark tail with prominent white corners and pale brown central feathers – a striking feature when flushed. However, the diagnostic black-and-white underwing pattern is usually difficult to see. Could be confused with Juvenile Mistle Thrush by an inexperienced observer, but Mistle Thrush shows pale streaks and rather indistinct dark markings to the upperparts, spotted underparts (but see juvenile White's) and less striking wing pattern both above and below.

Juvenile: Resembles the adult but is more barred above (less crescentic-shaped dark markings) and shows more spotted underparts, particularly on the breast. Very unlikely to be seen outside of breeding range.

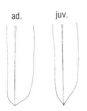

ad.   juv.

outer tail feather

1st-winter/-summer: Similar to the adult, but there is frequently a moult contrast seen in the greater coverts (retained juvenile outers being distinctly shorter and more worn than the new inners). The tail-feathers are typically more pointed (see figure).

Voice: The song is peculiar, the bird producing a soft, drawn-out, single whistle, which is repeated at rather long intervals or two whistles, one distinctly higher-pitched than the other. The latter type may possibly be a duet between male and female. Silent outside the breeding season.

Habitat and behaviour: Forest, especially in damp secluded gullies where there is an accumulation of leaf litter. Extremely secretive and rarely seen in the open. Usually walks deliberately rather than moving in hops like other thrushes.

Range: Breeds mainly in Siberia W to the Urals and Japan and winters in S Asia. Also breeds in the Himalayas, S-C China and neighbouring areas. Vagrant in Greenland (Oct 1954).

Status: Rare vagrant in Europe mainly Oct-Jan. Iceland (Oct 1939, Oct 1982, Nov 1982), Faeroes (Nov 1938, autumn 1974), British Isles (41, Sept-Feb, also May), France (10), Belgium (17), Netherlands (14), Denmark (3), Norway (6), Sweden (6th in Oct 1985), Finland (Sept 1961, Oct 1988), Poland (6, Sept-Dec), East Germany (Nov 1935, Dec 1942), West Germany (c. 25, Sept-Nov, Apr), Austria (3), Italy (20), Sicily (Oct 1974), Yugoslavia, Greece (Feb 1965), Rumania (Sept 1981), and Spain (Balearic Is, 2).

SIBERIAN THRUSH *Zoothera sibirica*   C **45**

L 22cm (8.5"). Asia. Rare vagrant (late autumn-winter).

Adult male: Unmistakable, mostly dark slate-grey (often looking blackish) with a prominent white supercilium. Shows characteristic underwing pattern like White's Thrush, and white corners to the tail.

Adult female: Grey-brown above, and very heavily patterned with dark spots and scales below. The dark markings often coalesce, particularly on the flanks, which often look dark with paler spots. The supercilium is conspicuous and often curves down behind the ear-coverts. Underwing and tail pattern much as in male.

Juvenile: Shows distinct pale shaft streaks above unlike adult female.

1st-winter/-summer male: Easily recognized by showing a mixture of definite male and female-like plumage characters.

1st-winter/-summer female: Difficult to tell from the adult female. The juvenile inner greater coverts typically show buffish triangular markings (more square markings on the outer greater coverts). The adult female often shows buffish 'squares' on the greater coverts, but no wedge-shaped markings. A moult contrast can often be seen among the greater coverts. Also, the tail-feathers tend to be more pointed than in the adult, but this is often difficult to judge.

Voice: The song is very simple. Usually gives a variable, double fluty note, followed by a soft, faint twitter, e.g. *HUEEE-tirrr... HEEEUU-tirrr ...* (cf. Eye-browed Thrush). The calls include a hard, typical thrush call, *jack* and a thin, fine *sit*.

Habitat and behaviour: Forest. Very secretive.

Range: Breeds in Siberia, not as far west as White's Thrush and further NE. Also in Japan, N China and Korea. Winters chiefly in SE Asia.

Status: Rare vagrant in Europe. Britain (Oct 1954, Dec 1976, Dec 1977, Nov 1984). Ireland: Cape Clear, Co. Cork (immature female, 18th Oct 1985), France (4 records 19th century, one in Jan 1982), Belgium (Oct 1901, Oct 1912), Netherlands (Oct 1856), Norway (6, Sept-Oct), Sweden (1st-winter male, 11th Sept 1990*), Poland (10 records, including two flocks of 17-18 individuals on 23rd Jan 1976 and 20th Mar 1978), East Germany (9), West Germany (2), Austria (2), Hungary (Feb 1918 and *c*. 25 on 15th Feb 1947 in Budapest), Switzerland (Dec 1978), Italy (3), and Malta (Oct 1912).

VARIED THRUSH   *Zoothera naevia*   A 45

L 25.5cm (10"). North America. One autumn record for Britain.

Adult male: This handsome thrush is very distinctive and unlikely to be confused with any European species. The dark bluish-grey upperparts, dark breast band, mostly orange underparts and supercilium, and striking wing pattern are very characteristic.

Adult female: Like the male but more brownish-tinged above with a more brownish, less distinct breast band. Rectrices often bluish-tinged.

Juvenile: Basically resembles the adult female but lacks breast band and has a mottled breast. Unlikely to be found outside breeding areas.

1st-winter/-summer male: Differs from the adult male in usually having obviously browner greater coverts (often a few inners new and edged bluish-grey, contrasting with the others). The tail-feathers are more pointed and usually browner than in the adult.

1st-winter/-summer female: Very similar to the adult female, but the tail-feathers are generally more pointed and lack the bluish tinge of many adults. Often shows a moult contrast among the greater coverts (but note that the pattern of new and juvenile feathers is the same).

Voice: The song is similar to White's Thrush, i.e. produces noticeably thin, high-pitched, slightly squeezed, drawn-out notes of varing pitch, at distinct intervals, e.g. *yyyyh...eeeeh...iiiih*. Call low *tuck*.

Range: Breeds in Alaska, W Canada and NW USA. Winters mainly along the W coast of the USA. Regular vagrant to the E coast of the USA, mainly in winter.

Status: Accidental in Britain: Nanquidno, Cornwall: 1st-winter from 14th-23rd Nov 1982.

WOOD THRUSH   *Hylocichla mustelina*   A 46

L 19cm (7.5"). North America. Accidental.

Adult: Easily recognized by its small size compared with Song Thrush, bright orange-brown crown, nape and mantle/scapulars, brightest on the head, and white underparts with distinct, rounded, black spots.

Juvenile: Differs from the adult in showing pale shaft-streaks above and buff spots to coverts. Moulted early.

1st-winter/-summer: Similar to adult but normally shows at least some retained juvenile outer greater coverts, with buffish/pale rufous, usually triangular, markings at tips, lacking in adult and any newly moulted greater coverts. These contrast clearly with juvenile feathers.

Voice: The song usually consists of a three-note whistle often preceded by a fainter, double, hard note and followed by a fainter, slightly metallic trill, *te-te-EE-O-LEHR-tirrr.* The three-note part is generally varied slightly from phrase to phrase. Alarm call, *uit-uit-uit-uit.*

Behaviour: Tends to be rather secretive, as other North American thrushes (except American Robin).

Range: Breeds in E USA and extreme SE Canada. Winters in Mexico and Central America.

Status: Accidental in Iceland (23rd Oct 1967); Britain: Isles of Scilly (7th Oct 1987*); and the Azores (one in 19th century)

HERMIT THRUSH   *Catharus guttatus*   B **46**

L 17cm (6.7"). North America. Accidental in N Europe (spring/autumn).

Adult: Easily distinguished from Song Thrush by obviously smaller size and less heavily spotted underparts, with the flanks unmarked or nearly so. The underwing pattern is reminiscent of White's and Siberian Thrushes, but this feature is generally very difficult to see in the field. Has grey-brown upperparts with contrasting rufous rump, uppertail-coverts and tail (also often rufous on edges of primaries/outer secondaries). It also shows a whitish to pale buffish base colour to the throat/breast and rather plain face with a usually distinct, narrow, whitish eye-ring. The dark spots on the breast tend to be slightly larger and more widely scattered than in the other *Catharus* thrushes; cf. Grey-cheeked Thrush (p. 345), Swainson's Thrush (p. 345) and Veery (p. 346). The wing formula is a reliable in-the-hand character. The 6th primary is distinctly longer than the 9th; the 8th, 7th and 6th are distinctly emarginated, and the 5th slightly less distinctly; cf. the other *Catharus* thrushes.

Juvenile: Shows distinct pale markings to the upperparts and coverts; moults soon after fledging.

Catharus underwing

1st-winter/-summer: Distinguished from the adult by its generally more pointed rectrices (see figure). Most birds also show small, buffish triangular marks to at least some outer (retained juvenile) greater coverts, sometimes to some medians. Adult and any newly moulted coverts lack this pattern, and the latter contrast clearly with juvenile feathers.

Voice: The song consists of a few, clear, fluty notes, the first one more drawn-out and the last ones fading, followed, after a short pause, by a series of similar but higher– or lower-pitched notes. Call, a rather Blackbird-like *chuck,* often repeated. Also said to give a whiny *wee.*

Behaviour: See Wood Thrush (p. 343). It has a characteristic habit of rapidly cocking and slowly lowering the tail when alerted.

Range: Breeds in S Alaska, Canada (not northernmost parts) and NE and W USA. Winters mainly in S USA to Central America. Vagrant to Greenland (4).

Status: Accidental in Iceland (7); Britain: Fair Isle (June 1975), Isles of Scilly (Oct 1984, Oct 1987); Luxembourg (Aug 1975), West Germany (3 in 19th century); East Germany (Dec 1825); Sweden: Höganäs, Skåne (27th April 1988).

SWAINSON'S THRUSH   *Catharus ustulatus*   B **46**

L 18cm (7"). North America. Rare vagrant (mainly autumn).

Adult: Very similar to Grey-cheeked Thrush (below). Also compare with Veery (p. 346) and Hermit Thrush (p. 344); the latter also for differences from Song Thrush). Characterized by uniformly olive-grey-brown upperparts, buffish lores (often only present as a streak on the upper lores), obvious buffish eye-ring and buffish throat and breast. The wing formula is also distinctive, but this can only be judged in the hand. The 9th primary is distinctly longer than the 6th, and the 8th and 7th are emarginated, extremely rarely the 6th is also faintly emarginated; cf. the other *Catharus* thrushes.

Juvenile and 1st-winter/-summer: See Hermit Thrush.

Voice: The song is a short series of clear, fluty, rising notes that fade to a faint, squeaky twitter; sometimes it is less clear, the notes sounding more blurred. The common call is a soft, liquid *wheit*. Also gives a rather soft *whup*.

Behaviour: See Wood Thrush (p. 343).

Range: Breeding range much as Hermit Thrush. Winters from Mexico to South America. Vagrant once recorded in the Ukraine, USSR (Nov 1893).

Status: Rare vagrant in Iceland (Oct 1978), British Isles (13, Sept-Oct, once in May), France (Feb 1979), Belgium (4, Oct), West Germany (1886, and one in Oct 1869 on Heligoland), Norway (Sept 1974), Finland (Oct 1974, Nov 1981), Austria (Salzburg Mar 1878), and Italy (3 records in 19th cent, one in Oct 1929).

GREY-CHEEKED THRUSH   *Catharus minimus*   B **46**

L 18cm (7"). North America. Rare vagrant (mainly Oct-Nov).

Adult: Very similar to Swainson's Thrush, but the lores and indistinct eye-ring are pale grey, and so is the mottling on the ear-coverts. The throat and breast are whitish to very pale yellowish (not buffish as in Swainson's, but note that worn Swainson's may look whitish). The upperparts and flanks tend to be marginally greyer than in Swainson's. The wing formula is similar to Swainson's, but the 6th primary is distinctly emarginated (although slighter than the 7th and 8th).

Juvenile and 1st-winter/-summer: See Hermit Thrush (p. 344).

Voice: The song is rather nasal and squeaky, clearly different from other *Catharus* thrushes. The calls include a nasal *bzeit*, often given between two song phrases, and a thin *seee*.

Behaviour: See Wood Thrush (p. 343).

Range: Breeds mainly in Alaska and N Canada, generally further north than Hermit and Swainson's Thrush. Winters in the West Indies, Central and South America. Vagrants have reached Greenland.

Status: Rare vagrant in Iceland (2nd record on 30th Oct 1983). British Isles (34, all Oct-Nov, including at least 12 individuals in Oct-Nov 1986, from SW Britain – Cornwall/Isles of Scilly/Lundy Is etc), France (Oct 1974, Oct 1986), West Germany (Heligoland, Oct 1937), Norway (Oct 1973, Sept 1974), and Italy (Nov 1901).

VEERY *Catharus fuscescens*   A **46**

L 17cm (6.7"). North America. Accidental in Britain and Sweden (autumn).

Adult: Shows much more rufous upperparts and obviously fainter spots on the breast than other *Catharus* thrushes. Note the buffish base colour of the breast, the rather plain face, without a distinct eye-ring, and also its rather greyish flanks.

Juvenile and 1st-winter/-summer: See Hermit Thrush (p. 344).

Voice: The song is a wheeling *tiu veery-veery-veeeru*, or similar, with typically, rather thin, squeaky, mouth-organ-like voice. Call, *brscheit*.

Behaviour: See Wood Thrush (p. 343).

Range: Breeds mainly in a band across C North America. Winters in Central and South America.

Status: Accidental in Britain: Porthgwarra, Cornwall (6th Oct 1970); Devon, Lundy Is (10th Oct-11th Nov 1987). Sweden: Svenska Högarna (26th Sept 1978).

TICKELL'S THRUSH *Turdus unicolor*   A **46**

L 21cm (8.25"). W Himalayas. One autumn record from Heligoland.

All plumages: Shows brownish-orange underwing-coverts and axillaries.

Adult male: Easily identified by its rather small size, rather uniformly bluish-grey plumage with whitish belly to undertail-coverts. It also has a yellow bill, orbital ring and yellowish legs.

Adult female: Shows grey-brown upperparts (sometimes, however, rather bluish-grey, especially on back/rump, uppertail-coverts and rectrices), greyish-brown breast, normally with some distinct dark streaks/spots, and greyish brown or warm ochre-brown flanks. Shows a rather plain face and lacks a supercilium. Also, has a mainly yellow bill, yellow orbital ring and yellowish to pinkish legs.

Juvenile: Resembles the adult female, but shows distinct pale shaft-streaks to the upperparts, pale-tipped coverts and heavily spotted underparts. The bill is all-dark.

1st-winter male: Plumage very similar to a greyish adult female. Differs in showing distinct pale tips to the retained juvenile greater coverts (the inners often newly moulted, lack pale tips and usually show greyer edges). The shape of the tail- feathers can be very similar to the adult. The bill gradually becomes paler during the 1st autumn.

1st-summer male: Apparently mainly like the adult male, but has mostly juvenile, worn and brown wings.

1st-winter/-summer female: Similar to adult female, but at least the outer greater coverts are usually unmoulted, juvenile, and show pale tips.

Voice: The song resembles Blackbird, but the phrases are much shorter, usually only a few notes. The deep, frequently repeated, *chuck* call is also rather similar to the corresponding call of Blackbird.

Note: Female/1st-winter male Pale Thrush *T. pallidus* of E Asia (one trapped on Heligoland, 16th July 1986, but thought to have been an escape), could be confused with female Tickell's. However, it is larger; more chestnut-tinged on the upperparts with the crown, nape and ear-coverts often greyer; never streaked on the breast; shows white corners to the tail and brownish-grey underwing-coverts; and has a wholly dark upper mandible and tip to the lower.

Range: Breeds in the W Himalayas. Winters mainly in E India.
Status: Accidental in West Germany: Heligoland, adult male collected on 15th Oct 1932.

EYE-BROWED THRUSH   *Turdus obscurus*   C **46**

L 23cm (9"). Asia. Rare vagrant (mainly autumn/winter).

All plumages: Shows distinctive head pattern, with obvious whitish supercilium and crescent below the eye extending to the bill base. The breast and flanks are rich to pale brownish-orange, the former often more brownish-grey, particularly in 1st-winter/- summer female. The breast and flanks are unmarked (except in juvenile). The axillaries and underwing-coverts are brownish-grey.

Adult male: Further identified by grey hood and isolated white spots on the chin. The outermost rectrices usually show distinct whitish tips.

Adult female: Resembles the adult male, but is browner on the head/neck and shows a whitish throat with a dark malar stripe.

Juvenile: Differs from other plumages in heavily pale-spotted above and dark-spotted below. Very unlikely outside breeding areas.

1st-winter/-summer: Resembles the adult female, but at least the outer greater coverts are retained, juvenile, and show whitish markings. Any new inners lack pale markings. The rectrices are usually obviously more pointed than in the adult, and the outermost feathers show no, or only ill-defined, whitish tips. It is usually not possible to sex 1st-winter/-summer birds with certainty, although there is a tendency for males to be greyer on the head with less white on the throat, particularly in spring; the extremes may be reliably sexed.

Voice: The song is very simple and similar to Siberian Thrush, but the voice is slightly fuller and softer, and the notes are generally trisyllabic rather than usually disyllabic. The flight call is a sharp, slightly metallic *dzeee* and a less sharp *tsreee*, reminiscent of Redwing. Alarm calls, *chuck* and when very anxious at nest, an explosive, shrill *xixixixixixi*.

Note: There are two other similar species in E Asia that could possibly straggle to Europe. The Brown-headed Thrush, *T. chrysolaus*, is very similar, but lacks the whitish supercilium and whitish crescent below the eye and never shows a grey head. The Grey-sided Thrush *T. feae*, has the same head pattern as Eye-browed, but is warmer brown above, particularly on the forehead/crown and usually shows a greyish breast and flanks (sometimes with a warm brown cast).

Range: Breeds mainly in the central parts of Siberia. Winters chiefly in S China to SE Asia.

Status: Rare vagrant in Britain (11, Sept-Dec, Apr-May), France (Jan 1962, Oct 1986, plus 7 records-all Nov, in 19th century), Belgium (6, Oct-Nov), Netherlands (4), Norway (Nov 1961, Dec 1978, Oct 1981), Finland (June 1978, Dec 1984), Poland (8), East Germany (10), West Germany (8), Czechoslovakia (3rd record – two near Prague 15th Mar 1980), Hungary (Oct 1988*), Italy (*c.* 20), and Malta (Oct 1966, Oct 1975).

L 23cm (9"). Asia. Rare vagrant (mainly autumn/winter).

All plumages: Shows grey-brown upperparts, usually with some rufous admixed, particularly on the uppertail-coverts. The underparts are extensively rufous with pale fringes (fringes narrow or lacking in worn plumage). Usually shows a rather distinct head pattern, with an often rufous-tinged supercilium, and shows largely rufous underwing and outer tail-feathers. Some individuals could be confused with female Red-throated Thrush (see p. 349).

Adult male: Tends to be brighter and more extensively rufous than the other plumages. The greater coverts are uniformly greyish-brown or show pale rufous on the edges and tips, often slightly paler on latter.

Adult female: Appears to be very difficult to tell from the adult male, but tends to be slightly duller below (especially on throat, which is generally paler) with, on average, more distinct malar stripes and also less rufous on the scapulars and central pair of tail-feathers.

Juvenile: Reported to be quite different from the adult: shows pale spotting above and pale, heavily dark-spotted underparts. Most unlikely to be encountered outside breeding areas.

1st-winter/-summer: Resembles the adult female but can usually be told by the retained juvenile outer (sometimes all) greater coverts. These show narrower, paler and less rufous edges and more distinct whitish spots on the tips than adult greater coverts. Any newly moulted inner greater coverts are patterned like adult and are also more fresh and slightly longer than the juvenile and create a distinct moult contrast. The rectrices are more pointed than in adult. The extremes seem possible to sex; very brightly coloured birds with unstreaked underparts being males, dull and indistinctly marked individuals with prominently spotted breast (and often flanks), females.

Voice: The song is rather similar to some dialects of Redwing, a few descending clear notes immediately followed by a faint twitter. When perched, it frequently calls with a very shrill, nasal, loud *cheeh-cheeh*; *cheeh-cheeh-cheeh* etc, which is almost explosive in quality. Also, harder *cha-cha-cha* notes are often heard. The alarm call is a hard *chack*, usually repeated and sometimes drawn into series *chack-cha-cha-cha-cha*. Also see Dusky Thrush.

Note: Intermediates between Naumann's and Dusky Thrushes are frequently seen, showing the full range of intermediate characters.

Range: Breeds in C-E Siberia, S of Dusky Thrush. Winters mainly in China.

Status: Rare vagrant in Europe. Records of this form have been recorded from: Britain (Jan-Mar 1990*), France (Sept 1845, Sept 1901, Feb 1985), Belgium (Oct 1951), Finland (Apr 1988), Poland (6), East Germany (Dec 1958-Jan 1959, Mar 1975), West Germany (6), Czechoslovakia (one early 19th century and Mar 1963), Austria (one in 19th century, Feb 1976, Apr 1984), Hungary (winter 1820), and Italy (2).

L 24cm (9.5"). Asia. Rare vagrant (mainly autumn/winter), although more often recorded than nominate race, Naumann's Thrush.

All plumages: Easily identified. Shows bold head pattern and dark upperside with slightly paler fringes, the upperside usually having some rufous admixed. The extensively dark underparts have pale fringes;

underparts gradually becoming darker as the fringes wear narrower. It also has largely pale chestnut wings, both above/below (may be faint on upperside in 1st-years). Occasionally, the chestnut on the upperwing is lacking in individuals which look otherwise normal – these may be intergrades with Naumann's or just variants of Dusky (easily confused with female Black-throated Thrush, p. 350). Further, shows either none or only a very little rufous in the tail, unlike Naumann's.

Adult male: Generally has the most brightly and contrastingly patterned plumage, although many are apparently difficult to tell from adult female. Outermost primary coverts often show rufous outer (and inner) webs with distinct dark tips.

Adult female: Usually slightly duller than the adult male, with less blackish-centred feathers both below and, particularly, above. Also, generally shows a more distinct malar stripe. Apparently never shows an entirely rufous outer web to the outermost primary coverts, and the dark tips to the inner webs are generally less dark and more diffuse than in the adult male (inner webs can only be seen in the hand).

Juvenile: See Naumann's Thrush (p. 348).

1st-winter/-summer male: Mostly similar to the adult male in normally showing rather blackish centres to the feathers of the upper and underparts. The primary coverts are patterned basically like the female, but the dark tips are generally more blackish and clearcut. It can be aged by the same criteria as for Naumann's Thrush.

1st-winter/-summer female: Resembles the adult female. It can be aged by the same characters as described for Naumann's Thrush.

Voice: Similar to Naumann's Thrush. In flight, shrill *shrree* or *shrrr* notes often heard. The same call is probably also given by Naumann's.

Note: Naumann's × Dusky hybrids are frequently seen.

Range: Breeds in Siberia, N of Naumann's Thrush and the range apparently extends both further W and E than in that race. Also apparently winters further E than Naumann's, mainly in Japan and neighbouring areas. Accidental in Cyprus (Nov 1958, one showed characters intermediate between *eunomus* and *naumanni*).

Status: Rare vagrant in Europe. There are records from: Faeroes (Dec 1947), Britain (8, Sept-Mar), France (Dec 1856, Dec 1910, Nov 1972, and a *naumanni × eunomus* hybrid in Nov 1978, and 3 others where race uncertain), Belgium (4, Nov-Jan; and 2 others where race uncertain), Netherlands (Nov 1899, Feb 1955), Denmark (Oct 1888, Sept 1968), Norway (5, Oct-Mar), Finland (Oct 1980; singing male, 17th May 1983), Poland (2), East Germany (4), West Germany (5+), Austria (3), Italy (*c.* 20), and Yugoslavia.

RED-THROATED THRUSH   *Turdus ruficollis ruficollis*   B **47**

L 25cm (9.75"). Asia. Rare vagrant (Oct-May).

All plumages: Evenly grey-brown above, with largely rufous outer tail-feathers and often has brownish-grey flanks with diffuse, dark streaks. The underwing-coverts are rufous.

Adult male: Further characterized by rufous face, throat and breast. The rufous is fringed narrowly whitish in winter.

Adult female: Streaked with dark on the throat and breast, with a variable amount of rufous mixed in, often forming a mainly rufous pectoral band. The supercilium is often rather distinct. Possibly sometimes very similar to adult male.

Juvenile: Probably resembles juvenile Black-throated (below) except for tail pattern.

1st-winter/-summer male: Initially resembles the adult female but tends to be more patterned on the upper breast and throat. It can be told by the retained juvenile outer (sometimes all) greater coverts with pale edges and whitish tips to the outer web; any new inner and adult greater coverts show diffuse greyish edges and tips. The tail-feathers are normally more pointed than in the adult. The throat and breast pattern becomes more like the adult male during the 1st winter-spring.

1st-winter/-summer female: Generally more streaked/spotted and less rufous on the breast than the adult female. It can be aged by its coverts and tail as in 1st-year male.

Females/1st-winter male are very similar to some, mainly 1st-winter/-summer female Naumann's Thrushes but never show any rufous on the flanks. In Naumann's, the flanks typically show prominent, rounded or triangular rufous spots; sometimes the flanks are diffusely dark-streaked, but there is always some rufous admixed. Often the undertail-coverts of Naumann's also show some rufous markings, not seen in Red-throated.

The head pattern is normally slightly different. The supercilium tends to be less prominent and ear-coverts paler than in Naumann's, but with considerable variation. The ear-coverts do not show a pale patch below the eye, as in Naumann's. The upperparts never show any rufous as in most Naumann's, but some Naumann's are plain above.

Voice: The song resembles Song Thrush, but is apparently slower. The calls are practically identical to those of Naumann's/Dusky Thrush.

Note: Intermediates (hybrids) between Red-throated and Black-throated Thrushes are sometimes seen.

Range: Breeds USSR, chiefly in the Lake Baikal region. Intergrades with Black-throated Thrush in the W part of its range. Winters mainly in China and the E Himalayas.

Status: Rare vagrant in Europe (even rarer than Black-throated). Records of this form have been recorded from: France (Apr 1969), Belgium (Oct 1904), Norway (3), Poland (*c.* 5, Feb-May), East Germany (6, Mar, Oct-Dec), West Germany (*c.* 5), Austria (Mar 1851), and Italy.

BLACK-THROATED THRUSH   *Turdus ruficollis atrogularis*   D 47

L 25cm (9.75"). Asia. Rare vagrant (Oct-May). More frequently recorded than nominate race, Red-throated Thrush.

All plumages: Basically resembles the respective plumages of Red-throated Thrush, but the rufous of the face, throat and breast is replaced by black. It also lacks rufous in the tail.

Juvenile: Very different from adult. There is prominent pale spotting on the upperside; the breast shows large, blackish spots (the upper spots almost form an adult female-like gorget); and the flanks show rather crescentic dark marks.

Female/1st-winter male: Can be confusingly similar to those Dusky Thrushes lacking chestnut upperwing panels (possibly intergrades with Naumann's), but shows finer and more diffuse dark streaks on the flanks, never rufous-tinged. Dusky typically shows large, rounded or triangular, dark spots on the flanks, often with a rufous tinge. The supercilium is usually less prominent than in Dusky and the ear-coverts paler and lacking the pale patch below the eye. The differences in the head pattern are generally more pronounced than between Naumann's and Red-throated. The upperparts are uniform, unlike in many Dusky, which also frequently show some rufous admixed. However, some Dusky are rather plain above.

Voice: Similar to Red-throated.

Note: Red-throated × Black-throated hybrids are sometimes seen, showing intermediate characters.

Range: Breeds in Siberia, from the Urals to the Lake Baikal area. In the E parts of its range intergrading with the nominate subspecies. Winters mainly in the Himalayas to Iran.

Status: Rare vagrant in Europe. Records of this form have been recorded from: Britain (20, Oct-Apr), France (6, only 3 documented as this race), Belgium (*c.* 5), Netherlands (Mar-Apr 1981, Oct 1982), Denmark (1822, Nov 1872, Dec 1983), Norway (12, mainly Oct), Sweden (13, Sept, Nov-May), Finland (15, Dec-May), Estonia, Latvia (2), Poland (12+ records in 19th century, after 1945 four records, mostly in winter, but also a flock on 28th Oct 1966), West Germany (30), East Germany (*c.* 12), Czechoslovakia, Austria (7), Italy (18), Greece, Bulgaria, Rumania, and Spain.

AMERICAN ROBIN *Turdus migratorius*   B **47**

L 25cm (9.75"). North America. Rare vagrant.

Adult male: Easily identified. Shows blackish head with white markings above/below the eye and a white-streaked central throat. Deep grey or brownish above. Has orange-red breast/flanks and fore-belly (with narrow pale fringes in fresh plumage), and white lower belly, under-tail-coverts and tips to outer tail feathers. Bill yellow with dark tip.

Adult female: Resembles the adult male but is usually browner on the head and paler on the upper– and underparts.

Juvenile: Easily distinguished from the adult female by e.g. paler and duller plumage with distinct pale streaks to the scapulars, and it has a heavily spotted breast. This plumage is quickly lost and thus unlikely to be seen in Europe.

1st-winter/-summer male: Generally similar to adult male, but sometimes the plumage is closer to the adult female. It can be aged by the distinct, whitish, triangular or square spots to the retained coverts (generally at least the outer greaters). Adults often show pale tips to coverts but not the distinctive pattern of the juvenile and never show a moult contrast. The rectrices are more pointed, paler and greyer than in the adult.

1st-winter/-summer female: Resembles the adult female, but can be aged by the same characters as described for 1st-winter/-summer male.

Voice: The song is rather simple, short and quite slow, built up of clear notes of alternating pitch. The phrases are slightly variable, e.g. *triu tiu teeuee tiyrr teeyh cheeduee*. Calls with a rather shrill, metallic *chek* or *chink*, a rather Blackbird-like *chok* and a rather Redwing-like *zeee*. The alarm call is a shrill, fast *kreekreekreekree.*

Range: Breeds over most of North America. Also locally in Mexico and Guatemala. Winters in much of USA. Vagrant to Greenland.

Status: Rare vagrant in Iceland (2); British Isles (30, Sept-July, including 10 in Ireland); Belgium (Jan-Feb 1965); Norway (Oct 1983); Sweden (24th Apr 1988); East Germany (19th century, Apr 1968, Apr 1972); West Germany (4); Czechoslovakia; and Austria (3).

Family SYLVIIDAE   Warblers, Goldcrests etc.

PALLAS'S GRASSHOPPER WARBLER   *Locustella certhiola*   B **48**

L 13.5cm (5.25"). Asia. Very rare autumn vagrant.

All plumages: Resembles Grasshopper Warbler, but the crown is distinctly more heavily streaked and usually greyer, and the rest of the upperside is obviously more rufous-tinged, especially the rump, and more heavily streaked on the mantle/scapulars. It is also more rufous-tinged on the breast/flanks and undertail-coverts, the latter without dark streaks but usually with paler tips (always dark markings on undertail-coverts in Grasshopper). Furthermore, it has a more prominent supercilium and shows more contrasting and more clearcut tips to the tertials, frequently with a distinct whitish spot on the tip of the inner web. Juvenile may show rather moderately streaked upperside and more poorly marked supercilium. The tail pattern is the best character: the tail is brown, shading to blackish near the tip, with greyish-white tips on all but the central pair of tail feathers (only visible from below unless tail spread, see figure). Normally, Grasshopper shows uniformly brownish rectrices. However, it should be noted that Grasshopper Warbler very rarely shows a tail pattern that approaches Pallas's, but the pale tips are broader, duskier and less clearcut, and the outer tail-feathers are paler.

Tail from above

Could be confused with Sedge Warbler, which has a proportionately shorter, uniformly brown and less rounded tail (outermost tail feather clearly shorter than tips of undertail-coverts in *Locustella*, former clearly longer than latter in *Acrocephalus*); longer primary projection; less heavily streaked mantle; more prominent supercilium; generally paler crown centre; at the most a faintly streaked rump and uppertail-coverts (sometimes heavily spotted in Pallas's); and less distinct pattern on the tips of the tertials.

Adult: The throat and belly are whitish, and there are no, or rarely, very few dark spots on the breast. The autumn moult is very variable but generally conclusive for ageing. Some adults go through a partial moult and thus have very worn remiges and rectrices in the autumn. Many (most?) moult most feathers except a few inner primaries, the secondaries and some coverts (carpal covert and some median and outer greaters are often retained). In these, the primary coverts are not normally moulted, not even when their corresponding primaries are renewed (an exceptional strategy; in the vast majority of birds, the primary coverts are moulted at the same time as their corresponding primaries). Some apparently moult completely.

Juvenile: Resembles the adult, but is yellowish-tinged on the throat/belly, and the breast is usually spotted. All of the remiges are rather fresh, and the tail-feathers are usually slightly narrower and more pointed than in the adult. It appears that the juvenile plumage is of unusually good quality and retained during the migration (if so – exceptional for a passerine).

Some birds are so heavily streaked/spotted on the underparts, that they could be mistaken for Lanceolated Warbler. However, the tail pattern is very different, as Lanceolated shows uniformly brown rectrices (possibly sometimes with paler tips as in some Grasshopper; see above). Additional differences are: the dark markings tend to be more spotty than in Lanceolated, but this is not always clear; it is normally more rufous-tinged above, especially on the rump/uppertail-coverts; the undertail-coverts usually differ significantly, but in some Lanceolated they are unstreaked and show pale tips, and very rarely Pallas's actually have a few streaks on the very innermost feathers.

1st-summer: Apparently indistinguishable from adult by the plumage or relative wear/moult contrasts (all moult completely in winter). If the assumption that the juvenile plumage is not moulted until in the winter quarters is correct, this applies to 1st-winter plumage as well.

Voice: The song is fast and rather simple, consisting of some hard rattles and a characteristic, far-carrying *seewee-seewee-seewee-seewee-seewee*; from a distance only the *seewee*s are heard. The (alarm) calls include a sharp, metallic *pit* and a hard, drawn-out and descending rattle, *trrrrrrrrrrrr*.

Habitat and behaviour: Much as Grasshopper Warbler. Extremely skulking except when singing. Occasionally sings in a short song-flight.

Note: The possibility of the closely related Middendorff's Grasshopper Warbler *L. ochotensis* of easternmost Asia (perhaps better treated as conspecific with Pallas's Grasshopper) turning up in Europe should be borne in mind. It is very similar to Pallas's but very faintly or not at all streaked above.

Range: Breeds in S-C Siberia, Mongolia and neighbouring parts of China. Winters primarily from NE India to SE Asia.

Status: Accidental in Britain (12, Sept-Oct, mainly from Fair Isle/Shetlands). Ireland: Rockabill Lighthouse, Dublin (28th Sept 1908). France: Ouessant (31st Aug 1987). Belgium (28th Sept 1989*). Norway: Utsira (28th Sept 1986, 7th-8th Oct 1988). Poland: near Darlowo (Sept 1989*). West Germany: Heligoland (juvenile 13th Aug 1856).

LANCEOLATED WARBLER *Locustella lanceolata* C **48**

L 12cm (4.75"). Rare autumn vagrant; plus few summer records (Finland).

All plumages: Like a small Grasshopper Warbler, but has a proportionately shorter tail and a usually slightly shorter, deeper bill. Most birds are distinctly streaked on the breast/flanks and thus readily separated from the vast majority of Grasshopper Warblers. However, many birds show very few and very fine streaks (sems to be the usual case in juvenile). These could be confused with the rather frequent Grasshopper Warblers which show a 'necklace' of distinct streaks across the lower throat/upper breast and a few distinct streaks on the flanks. The problem is complicated even further by the fact that Grasshopper can rarely show heavily streaked throat, breast and flanks and may thus resemble a normal Lanceolated.

In moderately heavily streaked Grasshopper Warblers, the breast streaking is centred at the junction of the throat and the breast, thus

Lanceolated Warbler   Grasshopper Warbler

fresh feathers on mantle

rump/uppertail-coverts

Lanceolated Warbler   Grasshopper Warbler

tertials

Pallas's Grasshopper Warbler

higher up but not extending so far down as in sparsely streaked Lanceolated. The sides of the lower breast/upper flanks are generally unstreaked in Grasshopper, but more often streaked in Lanceolated. The throat is on average more streaked in heavily streaked Grasshopper than in Lanceolated.

In fresh plumage it is warmer brown, less olive-tinged above than Grasshopper, but in worn plumage the colour is more greyish in both and very similar. The crown and mantle are usually more heavily streaked than in Grasshopper. In the latter, in fresh plumage the crown and mantle generally look spotted rather than streaked; in worn plumage more streaked like Lanceolated. The back and rump are generally more heavily patterned than in Grasshopper, which is sometimes very poorly marked. The uppertail-coverts range from plain to heavily marked, while they are usually (but not always) unmarked in Grasshopper. In the hand, the pattern of individual feathers of the upperside (especially back, rump and uppertail-coverts) differ (see figure).

The breast is normally whitish in the centre and buffish on the sides, sometimes all whitish and occasionally buffish right across. The flanks and undertail-coverts are normally deeper buff. In Grasshopper, the breast and flanks are generally darker and more olive– or greyish-brown, usually forming a pectoral band, and the undertail-coverts are usually paler. Very rarely there is a rather strongly yellowish-tinge on the throat/belly, which is frequently the case in Grasshopper.

Furthermore, the pattern at the tips of the tertials usually differs clearly between the two species. The dark centres are slightly darker and decidedly more clearcut, particularly on the inner webs, than in Grasshopper (see figure). There is a very slight overlap.

The most reliable difference from Grasshopper is the pattern of the undertail-coverts. Usually, the proximal undertail-coverts are streaked and the distal ones unmarked. Sometimes virtually all are unmarked or all are streaked. Some or all often show whitish tips. In Grasshopper, all of the undertail-coverts show dark markings, but no distinct, contrasting whitish tips. Furthermore, the dark markings are distinctly blacker and more clearcut than in Grasshopper. Also in the hand it can be seen that they are diamond– or drop-shaped isolated spots, whereas in Grasshopper, they are triangular and reaching to the bases of the feathers, 'never ending' (see figure). See also juvenile Pallas's Grasshopper Warbler (p. 352).

undertail coverts

Lanceolated Warbler

Grasshopper Warbler

single feather

Adult: The autumn moult is very variable but normally a reliable ageing character. Apart from head, body, coverts, tertials and tail, most individuals (?) moult the outer primaries and sometimes a few inner secondaries. Some moult most of the flight- feathers but retain the innermost primaries. As in Pallas's Grasshopper Warbler, the primary coverts are not always moulted with their corresponding primaries. Some birds do not moult any flight-feathers before the migration, which are then heavily worn. Some birds probably go through a complete moult on the breeding grounds.

Juvenile: The plumage is looser and fluffier than in the adult. The streaking, both above and below, is more sparse, fainter and more diffuse (breast-sides, flanks and rump area usually poorly streaked or unstreaked) – resembling Grasshopper Warbler even more than in adult and 1st-winter. Apparently normally moulted before the autumn migration, but birds have reached Europe in this plumage several times.

1st-winter: Similar to the adult, but all remiges are rather fresh in the autumn (which is probably the case in some adults too). Iris darker and more grey-brown than adult (also in juvenile).

1st-summer: See Pallas's Grasshopper Warbler (p. 352).

Voice: The song is very similar to Grasshopper Warbler, but is slightly sharper, more metallic and higher-pitched and with marginally more well-spaced syllables. The calls include a sharp, slightly metallic *pit*, often repeated, a rather faint *tack* and a scolding, harsh and slightly shrill *cheek-cheek-cheek-cheek...*

Habitat and behaviour: Similar to Grasshopper Warbler. Exceptionally skulking when not singing, creeping about on the ground in dense vegetation – can be mistaken for small rodent!

Range: Breeds in S and C Siberia to NE China and N Japan. Also said to occur patchily W to Lake Onega, W USSR. Winters from NE India through SE Asia to the Philippines.

Status: Rare vagrant in Britain (47, mid-Sept to early Nov, majority on Fair Isle/Shetland). France: Ouessant, one singing 15th-16th Aug 1986, and another found dead 11th Sept 1986. Belgium (Sept 1988), Netherlands (Dec 1912, Sept 1958), Denmark (3, Oct), Norway (Sept 1980), and a surprising record of one found *c.* 70 nautical miles N of Bjørnøya (Bear Is), Arctic Ocean, 15th Sept 1982. Sweden (13th Oct 1939, 19th Oct 1987, both found dead at Hoburgen lighthouse, on the island of Gotland). Finland (11, only two in autumn, with singing males present in July 1971, June and Aug 1981, June-July 1983, June 1984, June 85, June-July 1985). West Germany (Oct 1909, Sept 1920, Oct 1979), and Yugoslavia (Nov 1907).

GRAY'S GRASSHOPPER WARBLER *Locustella fasciolata*   A **48**

L 16-18cm (6.5-7"). Asia. Accidental – three autumn records.

All plumages: Almost the size of Great Reed Warbler, although a typical *Locustella* warbler in general appearance and build (notably the very rounded tail and long undertail-coverts, the latter reaching well beyond the tips of the shortest, outermost tail feathers). It is characterized by unstreaked brown upperparts, warmest on the rump, uppertail-coverts and tail, and has a grey breast (brownish in easternmost populations and often olive-tinged in juvenile). It also has browner flanks and warm brownish-buff undertail-coverts, sometimes with diffuse pale tips to the longest feathers.

Adult: Shows greyish-white supercilium and whitish throat and belly. At least sometimes shows worn remiges and rectrices in the autumn (moulted in winter).

Juvenile: Resembles the adult, but is generally dirty yellowish-tinged on the supercilium, throat and belly, and more olive-tinged on the breast and sometimes flanks. The remiges and usually the rectrices are rather fresh, the latter slightly narrower and more pointed than in the adult. It is not fully clear whether it is the juvenile plumage that is retained during the migration (cf. Pallas's Grasshopper Warbler). At least in the easternmost populations, young birds in the autumn are usually similar to the adult in plumage.

1st-summer: See Pallas's Grasshopper Warbler (p. 352).

Voice: Its loud, almost bulbul-like song is very unusual for a *Locustella* warbler (although Pallas's Grasshopper also lacks a reeling song). It is very loud, short, and explosive and accelerates towards the end, e.g. *chyt-tut chyt- tut CHYT-CHIT-CHYDUDIDUDU*.

Habitat and behaviour: Favours bushy, not too wet, areas. Extremely skulking and difficult to observe.

Range: Breeds in S Siberia, W to Ob and E to Sakhalin. Also in NE China and N Japan. Winters primarily in Indonesia.

Status: Accidental in France: Ouessant, 1st-year on 26th Sept 1913, and an individual on 17th Sept 1933. Denmark: Lodbjerg Fyr, N Jutland 1st-year on 25th Sept 1955.

AQUATIC WARBLER *Acrocephalus paludicola*   R Br* **48**

L 12-13cm (5"). Rare/local breeder in E Europe. Mainly rare passage migrant in rest of Europe.

All plumages: Resembles Sedge Warbler, but shows a dark crown with a clearcut, narrow, buff median crown-stripe. The mantle is much more heavily streaked, with pale 'braces'. It usually has a rather heavily streaked back/rump and uppertail-coverts and especially adult has distinctly streaked sides to the breast and flanks (breast/flanks less streaked or unstreaked in 1st-winter). Note that Sedge Warbler generally shows a paler median crown-stripe, although never as contrasting, narrow and well-defined as in Aquatic. Adult Sedge Warblers, especially in worn plumage, often show some streaking on the back/rump and uppertail-coverts, and the streaking on the mantle is more pronounced than in fresh plumage, although not nearly so distinct as in Aquatic. Juvenile and 1st-winter Sedge generally show some dark spots on the breast. The lores are normally paler than in Sedge. Also, the tail-feathers are more pointed and the tail more graduated than in Sedge, but this is usually of little importance in the field.

Adult: In the autumn it generally shows quite worn plumage, including rather heavily worn remiges and rectrices (moulted in the winter quarters). The breast sides and flanks are often rather heavily streaked, and the iris is rather warm brown.

1st-winter: In the autumn, the plumage is fresher and buffier than in most adults. The remiges and rectrices are fresh and it shows a rather dark brown-grey iris. The breast-sides and flanks are unstreaked or rather sparsely streaked.

1st-summer: See Paddyfield Warbler (below).

Voice: The song is distinctive, slow and monotonous, alternating between a slightly variable, harsh rattling *cherrrrr* and a more musical *chududududu* or similar. The song does not change speed as dramatically as it does in Sedge Warbler. The song is sometimes given in a short song-flight like Sedge, but unlike that species, it is reported to sing only during the descent. Call is said to be a soft *tak-tak* or *trr-tr*.

Habitat and behaviour: It breeds chiefly in wet areas with sedges. On migration it is found in more diverse habitats, frequently in reed-beds. Behaviour much as other *Acrocephalus* warblers.

Range: In Europe, breeds in a limited number of localities (has declined markedly over several decades) and now considered to be one of the most threatened migratory passerines in Europe. Breeds locally in Poland (1,600-1,800 pairs, Biebrza Marshes now largest breeding site, with *c*. 1,000 pairs), East Germany (*c*. 50 singing males), Czechoslovakia (breeds occasionally), and Hungary (*c*. 200 pairs).

Also, breeds in European USSR from Baltic States to the Black and Azov Seas to central Ob River in W Siberia, where it is generally considered to be rare. Wintering areas in Africa poorly known, probably in W Africa. Vagrant in the Canary Is.

Status: Generally a scarce or rare passage migrant in W Europe. Ringing has shown that in autumn it migrates west and south-west to reach staging sites in the Netherlands, Belgium, S Britain and NW France. Recorded from the British Isles (*c*. 700 to 1985, mainly Aug-early Oct), Channel Islands (80+), France (regular in autumn, early Aug to mid-Sept, with max *c*. 90 ringed in 1987, fewer in spring), Luxembourg, Belgium (500; an exceptional influx between 2nd-25th Aug 1989, when *c*. 200 ringed at Zeebrugge), Netherlands (*c*. 600 with 135 since 1969), West Germany, Denmark (15, Aug-Oct), Norway (6), Sweden (18, Aug-Sept), Finland (3), Switzerland (small passage mid-Apr/mid-May and late July-early Oct; *c*. 250, 1959-83), Rumania, Yugoslavia, Italy (regular migrant), Sicily (4), Malta (1), Greece (5), Portugal, Spain and the Azores.

Has bred France (Marne and Camargue), Belgium (1872, 1875, and 1941), Netherlands (1892, 1904, 1919, and 1941) and probably in other years. West Germany (perhaps no longer breeds, last proved 1972, but suspected near Hamburg 1980), and Austria (bred locally until 1928).

PADDYFIELD WARBLER   *Acrocephalus agricola*   R Br **48**

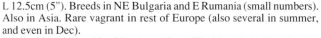

L 12.5cm (5"). Breeds in NE Bulgaria and E Rumania (small numbers). Also in Asia. Rare vagrant in rest of Europe (also several in summer, and even in Dec).

All plumages: Resembles Marsh and Reed Warblers, but is fractionally smaller with a proportionately shorter bill; also shows a little longer and more rounded tail, and has a distinctly shorter primary projection.

The head pattern is characteristic. The crown/nape are often contrastingly greyer, and the sides of the neck are frequently rather pale. Also, the supercilium is usually strikingly more prominent behind the eye than in the other two species (tending towards Sedge Warbler), although it may be less distinct in worn adults. Frequently there is a darker margin above the supercilium, lacking in Marsh/Reed. Furthermore, the ear-coverts tend to be paler with a more contrasting eye-stripe behind the eye. The upperparts tend to be more rufescent, especially when compared to Marsh Warbler, but there is much variation. When fresh, the tertials are slightly more contrastingly patterned than in, particularly, Reed. The tip of the lower mandible is usually dark; very rarely the lower mandible is all pale as in Marsh/Reed. In the hand, easily told from both Marsh and Reed Warblers by its different wing formula, revealing a much more rounded wing and three emarginations instead of only one (see figure, p. 359). Especially when in worn plumage, it may be confused with Booted Warbler (see p. 361). Also, see Blyth's Reed Warbler (below).

Adult: Heavily worn remiges and rectrices in the autumn (moulted in the winter quarters). The iris is rather warm brown or reddish-brown.

1st-winter: Shows fresher remiges, also a darker, more brown-grey iris than the adult.

1st-summer: Indistinguishable from adult (both adults and 1st-years moult completely in winter) except, with experience, by the still darker and more olive grey-brown iris.

Voice: The song is distinctive and most like Marsh Warbler but still clearly different. It is less repetitive and less highly variable; the nasal *bi-zeeh* usually included in the song of Marsh is not heard. The calls include *tack*, a not very hard *trrrr* and a rather harsh and nasal *cheeer*.

Habitat and behaviour: Similar to Reed Warbler. Also breeds in damp, dense vegetation away from open water.

Range: Breeds in small numbers in NE Bulgaria and in the Danube delta, Rumania, also in E Turkey and neighbouring parts of the USSR. Also in Asia E to Mongolia and NE China. Winters chiefly in the Indian Subcontinent and neighbouring areas.

Status: Rare vagrant in Britain (16, mainly Sept-Oct, also May-June, Nov), Ireland: North Slob, Co. Wexford (trapped 3rd Dec 1984), France (Sept 1990*), Belgium (4, June-Sept*), Netherlands (6, Sept-Oct), Denmark (Sept 1987), Faeroes (Oct 1988*), Sweden (8, June-Oct), Finland (9, May-July), Latvia (July 1987, July 1988), West Germany (Heligoland, June 1864), Hungary (Aug 1978), Greece, and Malta (Sept 1986).

BLYTH'S REED WARBLER *Acrocephalus dumetorum*   R Br **48**

L 12.5-14cm (5.25"). Breeds in S Finland and in Asia. Rare vagrant elsewhere in Europe.

All plumages: Very difficult to separate from Marsh and Reed Warbler in the field, particularly the former. The upperparts are usually greyer, generally with a less contrastingly warm rump-area than in Reed (beware of worn adult Marsh/Reed which can be very similar in colour). The underparts are usually paler and with a more greyish-yellow tinge on the breast-sides and flanks, but especially worn adult Marsh/Reed can be very similar in this respect.

The wings are typically more uniformly coloured than in either Marsh or Reed. The alula and the tertials are only marginally darker than the rest of the wing and very indistinctly pale-edged. Marsh and Reed show darker-centred alula and tertials with more contrasting pale edges (particularly in the former). Note that the appearance of the alula and tertials varies slightly with the angle of light and view, so that they can sometimes look rather dark and pale-edged in Blyth's and rather uniform and poorly contrasting in Marsh and Reed. The base colour of the remiges and rectrices is also slightly paler than in Marsh and Reed. The pale tips to the primaries generally visible in Marsh when fresh, are lacking. In 1st-winter the remiges are frequently slightly contrastingly rufous-tinged, unlike in Marsh and Reed.

The tip of the lower mandible often shows a dark smudge, rarely very prominent, unlike either Marsh or Reed. Also, the primary projection is usually distinctly shorter than in Marsh/Reed. In the hand, the wing formula separates from both Marsh and Reed. Note in particular the more rounded wing and two, often three, emarginations (see figure).

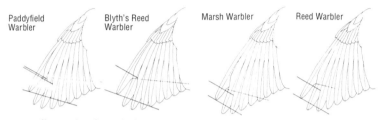

Paddyfield Warbler   Blyth's Reed Warbler   Marsh Warbler   Reed Warbler

Note number of emarginations and where tip and notch fall on the 9th primary

It might also be confused with Paddyfield Warbler. The differences in general coloration, structure (not wing formula; see figure), head and wing pattern are the same as between Paddyfield and Marsh/Reed. However, some individuals show a more prominent supercilium behind the eye than Marsh/Reed, tending towards a very poorly marked Paddyfield. The tip of the lower mandible is only rarely as dark as in a normal Paddyfield; rarely, however, the dark tip is faint or, exceptionally, lacking in Paddyfield.

It is also very similar to Olivaceous Warbler. Olivaceous is normally distinctly paler, particularly above, but this is not always obvious when compared to a worn Blyth's Reed. Olivaceous never shows any warm brown coloration. The edges to the secondaries are often contrastingly pale in Olivaceous, forming a pale panel not seen in Blyth's Reed. The undertail-coverts are obviously shorter, and the tail is more square at the tip (but beware of Blyth's Reed with longest undertail-coverts missing!). The outermost tail-feathers usually (but not always) show pale edges on both webs and pale tips, unlike Blyth's Reed. The lower mandible is usually all pale but extremely rarely shows a little dark at the tip. Olivaceous also has a distinctive habit of nervously twitching the folded tail downwards with small movements.

phalus Hippolais

*adertail and
dertail coverts*

Adult, 1st-winter and 1st-summer: See Paddyfield Warbler (p. 357).
Voice: The song resembles Marsh Warbler's but is distinctly slower, more elaborately repetitive and contains more whistles, usually including a typical *see-ee-hue*, and a recurrent *teck teck*. The calls include a *teck*, which appears to be slightly softer than the corresponding note of Paddyfield Warbler, also a harsh, scraping *cherr*.
Habitat and behaviour: Much as in Marsh Warbler, although it prefers slightly drier and bushier habitat.

Note: In Finland, repeated hybridization has been recorded with Marsh Warbler; hybrid young reared in 1979-81 at Lappeenranta. In 1979, it was found that 3 out of 44 male Blyth's Reed were paired with female Marsh Warblers.

Range: Breeds in S Finland and Baltic States, eastwards across Russia to the Lake Baikal area. During 1930-1940s, Blyth's Reed Warbler became established as a breeding species in SE Finland, and it is now rather wide-spread, with an estimated number of 5,000 singing males. Also in Latvia unusually high numbers were noted in the east in 1981, and more recently some extension has been noted further west. Winters mainly in the Indian region. Accidental in Cyprus.

Status: First recorded in Sweden in June 1958, then *c.* 10 records in 1960s, annual since 1970 and increasing (*c.* 290), with max 53 in 1988; also first confirmed breeding from N of Gävle, Gästrikland in 1984. The vast majority of the records are of singing males in June-July.

Very rare elsewhere: British Isles (16, Aug-Oct, one in May). France (26th Aug 1984). Belgium (19th Sept 1988*), Netherlands (June 1990*), Denmark (8, May-July), Norway (6, June-July, Sept-Oct). Poland (11, including a few singing in June-July 1981-83, perhaps breeding 1983). East Germany (singing, June 1982 and June 1987). Rumania: Danube delta, first recorded in early Aug 1975 (at least 4), and May-June 1976 (9 ringed). Italy (Toscana 1969), Spain (Sept 1972) and Gibraltar (Sept 1973).

THICK-BILLED WARBLER *Acrocephalus aedon* A **49**

18cm (7"). Asia. Two autumn records for N Europe.

All plumages: Almost the same size as Great Reed Warbler, but has a distinctly shorter, deeper bill, and an entirely pale lower mandible (lacking dark tip of most Great Reed). It also has a decidedly shorter primary projection, and a longer, more graduated tail. There is no dark loral stripe and pale supercilium as in Great Reed; the lores are uniformly pale instead. Lacks the dark streaking on the throat/upper breast present in many Great Reed Warblers. In the hand, further told from

Great Reed
Warbler

Thick-billed
Warbler

Great Reed by the clearly different wing formula (see figure).

Adult, 1st-winter and 1st-summer: See Paddyfield Warbler (p. 357).

Voice: The song is rather similar to Marsh Warbler's, but the voice is obviously deeper. The call is a hard, strong *tack*, often repeated.

Habitat: Preference is clearly different from that of most *Acrocephalus* warblers. Throughout the year it favours bushy, scrubby areas, often in forest, and is not associated with wet habitats and reeds etc.

Range: Breeds in S Siberia, N Mongolia and NE China. Winters mainly from E India to SE Asia.

Thick-billed
Warbler

Great Reed
Warbler

Status: Accidental in Britain: Shetland, Fair Isle (6th Oct 1955), and on Whalsay Island (23rd Sept 1971).

BOOTED WARBLER *Hippolais caligata* B **48**

L 12cm (4.75"). Asia, as near as W USSR. Rare vagrant in N Europe (mainly summer/autumn).

All plumages: Could be confused with Olivaceous Warbler, but is slightly smaller, with a distinctly finer/shorter bill; in general shape it is more like e.g. Willow Warbler than Olivaceous Warbler. It generally has a dark tip to the lower mandible (all pale in Olivaceous; exceptionally with a little dark at tip). The upperparts are usually noticeably browner, and the breast/flanks (particularly rear) are usually slightly darker and more buffish. The supercilium is usually prominent (but rather diffuse) behind the eye, and there is frequently a darker shade bordering the upper edge of the supercilium. In Olivaceous, the supercilium usually does not continue behind the eye or only very short and indistinctly, and there is no dark margin above the supercilium.

It could also be confused with a worn Paddyfield Warbler, although it is probably always less warmly coloured, especially above. It has shorter undertail-coverts and a more square-tipped tail, with usually obvious pale edges on both webs and pale tips to the outermost tail feathers (sometimes pale edges and tips indistinct or even lacking). It has also been confused with Bonelli's Warbler, but Bonelli's always shows some greenish in the plumage, at least on the rump area, wings and tail.

The Siberian race of Chiffchaff (*tristis*) is also a potential pitfall, but this differs in e.g. dark bill and legs.

Adult: Generally shows worn remiges and rectrices in the autumn; sometimes these are in moult.

1st-winter: Shows fresher remiges and rectrices than the autumn adult.

1st-summer: See Paddyfield Warbler (p.), although iris colour not known to differ.

Voice: The distinctive song is a short, fast, chattering verse, clearly different from the rather more Reed Warbler-like song of Olivaceous Warbler. Call a hard and slightly harsh *chet*.

Habitat and behaviour: Favours bushier habitat than Olivaceous Warbler. Apparently it lacks the characteristic twitchy, downward tail-movements of Olivaceous.

Range: Nominate race breeds in C-W USSR, in NW almost to Leningrad, in NE to Yenisei and in S to Kirghisia. Subspecies *rama* (taxonomic status unclear) breeds further south, to Iran and Pakistan. The nominate race is reported to winter on the Indian Subcontinent and Sri Lanka.

Status: Rare vagrant in the British Isles (30, Aug-Nov), France (two in Sept 1984, Oct 1985), Belgium (Sept 1988*, Sept 1989*), Netherlands (Oct 1982, Oct 1986, Sept 1988), West Germany (2), Denmark (Sept 1988, 2 in Sept 1989*), Norway (Oct 1978, Sept 1983), Sweden (Sept 1971), Finland (7, of which 5 concern singing males in June 1981, May 1984, June 1986, and June-July 1987; June and Sept 1988) and Estonia (two singing males in June 1987).

MARMORA'S WARBLER   *Sylvia sarda*   R Br **49**

L 12-13cm (5"). Very local in SW Europe. Accidental outside breeding range.

All plumages: Very similar to Dartford Warbler, but the throat and underparts are grey, and lack Dartford's fine white spots on the throat, and it generally shows a less well-defined whitish belly. 1st-winter birds particularly are often slightly brownish-tinged below with some paler mottling on the throat and thus more similar to female/1st-winter male Dartford. The pale at the base of the bill is said to be normally pale reddish, as opposed to horn-coloured in Dartford.

Adult male: Usually greyer than the other plumages, with more brightly coloured bare parts.

Adult female: Slightly more brownish-tinged both above and below than the adult male. Apparently, sexing is sometimes very difficult.

Juvenile: Browner above and below than the adult, with rather greyish-buffish tinge to the belly (fainter to the rest of the underparts). Extremely like juvenile Dartford and perhaps not separable with certainty.

1st-winter/-summer: Differs from the adult in more worn remiges and rectrices. The edges to the primaries are pale brownish-tinged (normally pale greyish in adult), and the outermost tail-feathers show less distinct, less clearcut and duskier edges and tips. However, at least some tail-feathers are often moulted in the autumn, sometimes some primaries and secondaries as well (moult contrast not seen in adult).

Voice: The song resembles Dartford Warbler's, but is clearly higher-pitched, faster, longer and with more slurred trills. The alarm call is a harsh *tcheg*. Also, reported to give a *drrrt*.

Range: Breeds on the Balearic Islands, Corsica, Sardinia, Pantelleria Is, and perhaps locally along the E coast of Spain. Mainly resident, but some winter in Tunisia and Algeria. Gibraltar: very scarce visitor, mainly Aug-Nov, but also winter/early spring. In Sicily: rare and irregular passage migrant and winter visitor (Nov-Mar). In Malta: possibly a resident and irregular breeding species between 1890-1910.

Status: Accidental in Britain: S Yorkshire (singing male present from 15th May-24th July 1982). Mainland France (Apr 1973, Mar 1987, 3 in Mar 1989*). N Italy (occasionally in Liguria and Calabria). Malta: several recent records (1975-76) mainly during Nov-Dec, also in Feb.

MÉNÉTRIES'S WARBLER   *Sylvia mystacea*   A **49**

L 11-13cm (4.5-5"). W Asia. Only one record.

Adult male summer: Resembles male Sardinian Warbler, particularly the paler, Middle East subspecies *momus*. The dark cap to the head is usually not quite so blackish as in Sardinian and normally fades into the grey upperparts and often also rear ear-coverts; the demarcation line is typically more clearcut in Sardinian. The throat is usually pinkish with a white submoustachial stripe, the pink extending onto the breast/flanks. However, occasionally the throat and breast show a very faint pinkish-buff tinge, and rarely this is lacking altogether. Sardinian never shows any distinct pink on the underparts, and the sides of the breast and flanks are normally darker and browner/greyer. The tertials usually show paler centres and less distinct and more diffuse pale edges than in Sardinian.

Some individuals could be confused with adult male or very bright adult female Subalpine Warbler, but the head and tail are darker, and the colour of the throat/breast/flanks is not so deep rufous.

Adult male winter: Generally browner above, with a more brownish-grey head, showing very little or even no blackish. Clearly different from male winter Sardinian (both adult and 1st-winter) which is still plumaged much as in summer.

Adult female: Similar to female Sardinian, particularly the paler race *momus*, but is obviously paler, more sandy coloured above, with contrastingly darker, almost blackish tail and clearly paler, buffish, breast-sides and flanks.

The tertials show noticeably paler centres and more indistinct pale fringes than in Sardinian. The head is generally less contrastingly grey; the lores normally paler; the eye-ring more complete and more conspicuous; and the orbital ring more orange than in Sardinian.

It is even more similar to many female/1st-winter male Subalpine Warblers. Subalpine frequently shows a distinct bluish-grey tinge above and a rufous tinge to the throat/sides of the breast (mainly summer plumage) unlike Ménétries's. The tail pattern is the most reliable difference. In Subalpine, the tail contrasts very little with the upperparts (contrary to Ménétries's), and the pattern of the outermost tail feathers usually differs significantly (but see 1st-winter/-summer female; see figure, p. 364). Also, the flanks tend to be more warmly coloured, particularly at rear, frequently with an orange-brownish tinge, but some are very pale, recalling Ménétries's in this respect. The tertials are on average more contrastingly patterned in Subalpine, but some show plain tertials like normal Ménétries's.

In the hand, the wing formula is an additional help. The 10th primary is normally not longer than the primary coverts in Subalpine but frequently distinctly longer than the primary coverts in Ménétries's. Also, the notch on the 9th primary usually falls approximately equal to (slightly longer to slightly shorter) the tips of the secondaries in the former, and well below in the latter.

1st-winter male: Very similar to 1st-winter female (see below), but frequently shows a few pinkish feathers on the throat/breast.

1st-summer male: Like summer adult male but with browner, more worn wings. Often identifiable by some retained juvenile tail feathers.

1st-winter/-summer female: Similar to the adult female, but the rectrices paler, browner and slightly more pointed than in adult, and the outer three or four pairs are differently patterned; often some rectrices are newly moulted and clearly contrasting with the others. Sometimes, some outer primaries and inner secondaries are new, contrasting with the remaining more worn flight-feathers. The iris is darker and more olive-brown than in adult (rather pale orange-brown in adult).

When the tail is wholly juvenile, the risk of confusion with female/1st-winter male Subalpine Warbler is even greater than in individuals with some new rectrices, since the juvenile tail feathers are paler and contrast less with the upperparts (still usually more than in Subalpine, though), and the pattern of the outermost tail-feathers is often less different from Subalpine (see figure, p.364).

Voice: The song is a dry, chattering warble, clearly different from that of Sardinian and Rüppell's Warbler. It is apparently generally shorter

outer tail-feathers

Ménétries

adult-patterned   juv.

Subalpine

and less varied than in the former and longer than in the latter. The calls include a *dack* and a dry, harsh rattling *tzerrr-r-r-r-r* or *tzerrr*, recalling Spectacled Warbler.

Behaviour: Said to have a characteristic habit of frequently raising and "waving" the tail.

Range: Breeds from SE Turkey and Syria to Afghanistan and Tadzhikistan (USSR). Winters in S Arabia and neighbouring parts of NE Africa.

Status: Accidental in N Portugal: Morais, Macedo de Cavaleiros, 1st-winter male trapped on 13th Sept 1967.

DESERT WARBLER *Sylvia nana*   B **49**

L 12cm (4.75"). Asia and N Africa. Rare vagrant (mainly late autumn).

All plumages: Easily identified by its small size, pale sandy-coloured upperparts and contrastingly rufous rump, uppertail-coverts and central pair of tail feathers (the outermost feathers show much white; see figure). Also, has very pale underparts, pale yellow iris, and pale straw-coloured legs and bill (culmen and tip of lower mandible dark). The N African subspecies is pale rufous-tinged above.

Adult: In autumn often shows fresh plumage without any moult contrasts.

1st-winter/-summer: Appears to be difficult to distinguish from the adult, but especially the primaries, tertials and tail feathers are generally more worn. A moult contrast can often be seen among the tertials.

Voice: The song is short, starting with a harsh trill and is immediately followed by some clear notes. Also has a more varied, clear, 'lark-like' song. The commonly heard call is a scolding, slightly nasal rattle, *djerrr-r-r-r-r*, recalling one of the calls of Blue Tit.

outer tail feathers

Habitat and behaviour: Breeds in desert, frequently in sand dunes with sparse vegetation. Stragglers can be found in any habitat but usually in low vegetation or even on the ground.

Range: Breeds from S and E Iran and W Kazakhstan to C Mongolia and winters from NE Africa to N India (nominate subspecies). Also resident in the Sahara (subspecies *deserti*). Vagrant in Cyprus (3, Mar-Apr).

Status: Rare vagrant in Britain (5, Oct-Jan), Netherlands (30th Oct-3rd Nov 1988), Denmark (Nov 1989*), Sweden (9, Oct-Nov, May), Finland (6, Oct-Nov), West Germany – Schleswig-Holstein (singing male from 21st June-7th July 1981, built 2 nests), Italy (3), and Malta (4, Mar-Apr, Oct). At least the N European records refer to the nominate race.

EASTERN CROWNED WARBLER *Phylloscopus coronatus* A **50**

L 11.5cm (4.5"). E Asia. One 19th century record.

All plumages: Resembles Arctic Warbler, but is darker on the crown (particularly rear), with a well-marked pale median crown-stripe (most distinct at rear, normally not reaching forehead). The eye-stripe is often noticeably darker than in Arctic. It is normally slightly more yellowish-green above, particularly on the edges of the remiges, and generally has a whiter underside with contrasting, pale yellow undertail-coverts. The lower mandible is all pale, lacking the dark tip of most Arctic. Ageing seems to be as in Greenish Warbler (below), but more research is needed.

Voice: The song is a characteristic *tuweeu tuweeu tuweeu tuweeu tswi-tswi zueee*. The first notes are rather clear and the last one drawn-out, harsh and squeaky. Sometimes a shorter version is heard, *psit-su zueee*.

Note: There are some very similar *Phylloscopus* species in Asia, but they are unlikely to reach Europe. The whitish underside with *contrasting* yellow undertail-coverts is unique to Eastern Crowned.

Range: Breeds in Japan, Korea, NE China and extreme SE USSR. Winters chiefly in Malaysia and W Indonesia.

Status: Accidental in W Germany: Heligoland, one collected on 4th Oct 1843.

GREENISH WARBLER (and allies) *Phylloscopus trochiloides* R Br **50**

L 10.5-12cm (4.5"). Breeds in Europe (race *viridanus*). Accidental to neighbouring areas mainly in spring and to W Europe mainly in autumn. Also in Asia.

All plumages: Very similar to Arctic Warbler (see p. 366). See also Yellow-browed Warbler (p. 368).

Differs from Chiffchaff and Willow Warbler in usually having a longer and more distinct supercilium; more prominent and more clear-cut dark eye-stripe; and usually shows one or two distinct wing-bars (may be lacking in very worn plumage). Some eastern Chiffchaffs show a rather distinct wing-bar and could be mistaken for Greenish. However, in these the wing-bar is normally longer and more curved, as well as being more greyish-tinged and less clearcut than in Greenish. Such Chiffchaffs further differ from Greenish in e.g. more grey-brown upperparts and a mainly dark lower mandible.

Three distinct subspecies (often considered separate species, see Appendix) have been recorded in Europe: *viridanus* being the breeding one, while both *nitidus*, 'Green Warbler' and *plumbeitarsus*, 'Two-barred Greenish Warbler' are rare vagrants (see below on Status).

On average, Green has a slightly larger bill than the other two races. It also shows more yellowish-green upperparts and a pale yellow suffusion to the supercilium, ear-coverts, throat and centre of the belly. In fresh plumage the underparts are often even more extensively yellow, but in worn plumage the coloration may be very close to *viridanus*. The greater covert-bar tends to be slightly wider than in *viridanus*, and there is a greater tendency to show a second wing-bar (wing-bars are yellowish when fresh).

Two-barred Greenish is normally slightly darker above and whiter below than *viridanus*, although this is of little importance. When fresh, it shows a clearly broader, greater covert-bar, and there is a distinct

365

median covert-bar. The wing-bars are approximately as prominent as in Yellow-browed Warbler. In worn plumage, the wing-bars are narrower, and the bar on the median coverts may be lacking completely. It is then not safely distinguished from *viridanus*.

Adult: The remiges, rectrices and normally the greater coverts are rather heavily worn by the autumn and later moulted in the winter quarters.

1st-winter: Shows fresh plumage in the autumn.

1st-summer: Indistinguishable from adult by the plumage, since both adult and 1st-year have a complete moult in the winter quarters.

Voice: Has a very distinctive song, which is hurried, high-pitched, liquid, and rather short. It often includes trills, and is reminiscent of the song of an excited Pied Wagtail. The song is quite variable, both individually and geographically, but always recognizable. The call of *viridanus* is a rather loud, disyllabic *tsee-lee*, recalling Pied Wagtail. The calls of *nitidus* and *plumbeitarsus* are usually more trisyllabic.

Range: The race *viridanus* breeds from SE Finland and the eastern Baltic coast in a belt eastwards across Siberia. It intergrades with the nominate race in the Tien Shan and NW India. *Plumbeitarsus* occurs from approximately the River Yenisei through Mongolia to E Siberia and Manchuria (China). The nominate race continues through the Himalayas to C China. *Nitidus* breeds from the Caucasus and Turkey through Iran to Afghanistan.

Nitidus winters mainly in S India and Sri Lanka, *viridanus* and *trochiloides* mainly in the Indian region and *plumbeitarsus* mainly in N SE Asia.

The range of Greenish Warbler has shown some westward expansion since the last century. Numbers in W Finland and E Sweden vary considerably from year to year.

Status: Regular in E Sweden, mainly in May-June, with a total of *c.* 1,185 with high numbers in 1978 (110), 1984 (85), 1987 (*c.* 75) and 1988 (250). There are 18 breeding records. In the remainder of Europe, mainly a rare vagrant in spring and early autumn. British Isles (*c.* 190, majority Aug-Nov, with a peak in late Aug, a few also in May-July), Channel Islands (Nov 1976), France (5), Belgium (2), Netherlands (7 since 1969), Denmark (*c.* 185). Norway (18). Poland (many records, breeding proved in 1958, 1963/64, 1978, and 1982). East Germany (some singing males recorded every year in Mecklenburg *c.* 120 records since 1933), in other parts of GDR only a very rare vagrant (10-15 records). West Germany (*c.* 50, May-June, Aug-Sept) first breeding pair confirmed summer 1990 on Heligoland. Austria and Czechoslovakia (5th record since 1963 of a singing male present in June 1985).

· The Green Warbler has been recorded from Britain: Isles of Scilly, 1st-winter (26th Sept-4th Oct 1983) and W Germany: Heligoland (11th Oct 1867).

Two-barred Greenish Warbler has been recorded from the Isles of Scilly, 1st winter (21st-27th Oct 1987*). Netherlands: Castricum, one trapped (17th Sept 1990*).

ARCTIC WARBLER   *Phylloscopus borealis*   R Br **50**

L 11.5-12.5cm (4.75"). Uncommon breeding species in NE Norway and N Finland. Also breeds eastwards to Alaska. Rare vagrant elsewhere in Europe (mainly autumn).

All plumages: Differs from Willow Warbler and Chiffchaff by much the same characters as described for Greenish Warbler (see above).

Difficult to separate from Greenish Warbler (particularly W subspecies *viridanus*) unless heard. It is slightly larger and more attenuated, with a slightly longer primary projection. The bill is slightly longer and deeper (particularly at the base), but note that some individuals have relatively fine bills and some Greenish strikingly large-looking bills (normally proportionately larger than in e.g. Willow Warbler and Chiffchaff). The tip of the lower mandible is usually dark, whereas it is more faintly marked or unmarked in Greenish, but there is overlap. The tarsus is usually pale brownish-grey, and the toes slightly paler, more yellowish-brown to straw-coloured; often the tarsus too is more straw-coloured. Greenish usually shows darker grey legs/feet, but they may be pale.

Arctic Warbler

small-billed individual

Greenish Warbler

The head pattern usually differs in many subtle ways (see figure). It should be noted that none of the characters marked in the figure is exclusive for either species, but combined they give each species a characteristic head pattern. The breast-sides and flanks are on average more greyish or olive-grey than in Greenish Warbler, often looking slightly streaked. The underside is never so yellowish as in a fresh Greenish Warbler of the race *nitidus*. Compared to Greenish of race *plumbeitarsus* the wing-bars are generally distinctly narrower.

In the hand the wing formula instantly separates from Greenish. Has three emarginations (on the 6th-8th primaries), whereas Greenish has four (5th to 8th). The 10th primary is distinctly shorter (slightly shorter to *c.* 3mm longer than the tips of the primary coverts, as opposed to 5-10mm longer than the primary coverts in Greenish).

Arctic Warbler

Adult: See Greenish Warbler, above, but note that the wing-feathers are surprisingly fresh in the autumn. The iris is deep brown.

1st-winter: See Greenish Warbler. The iris is grey-brown; with experience it looks appreciably duller than in the adult, (can only be judged in the hand). The iris colour is probably valid for ageing the other *Phylloscopus* species described here but this requires confirmation.

1st-summer: See Greenish Warbler.

Voice: Entirely different from Greenish Warbler. The song is a fast trill, *dyryryryryryryryryry* or, differently transcribed, *derererererere-rere*, often suddenly changing pitch and/or speed. The call is a diagnostic short, sharp *dzrt*.

Range: Breeds locally in small numbers in NE Norway and N Finland. Also further E in a belt across N Siberia to W Alaska. Winters primarily in Malaysia, Indonesia and the Philippines.

Status: Rare vagrant in the Faeroes (Sept 1984). Britain: annual since 1964 (160, Aug-Oct, with a peak in Sept, rarely also in July, Nov), Ireland (6, Sept-Oct), France (Ouessant, Oct 1984, Sept 1987, Oct 1988), Netherlands (Nov 1935, Sept 1976, Oct 1980, Oct 1982), Denmark (27th May 1988), Sweden (*c.* 150, breeding proved six times; only 5 from Aug-Oct), Estonia, Poland (Sept 1986), East Germany (Aug 1985), West Germany (Heligoland, 5), Italy (2), Greece (Apr 1965, Apr 1967), Bulgaria (25th Aug 1987), Malta (Oct 1987), and Gibraltar (30th Oct 1984).

PALLAS'S WARBLER *Phylloscopus proregulus* D **50**

L 9cm (3.5"). Asia. Very rare but annual (numbers variable), mainly late autumn.

All plumages: Tiny size; bold head pattern (bright yellow when fresh, especially in front of/above eye), with a conspicuous pale supercilium and median crown-stripe, and dark lateral crown-stripes; double wing-bars; and pale yellow rump. It could only be confused with Yellow-browed Warbler (below). Ageing apparently very difficult on plumage.

Voice: The song is extremely loud for a bird of its size. It is beautiful and varied, rather hurried with clear Canary-like notes and trills. The call is a rather faint, soft, slightly nasal *dju-ee* or, *duee* and is somewhat reminiscent of one of the calls of Greenfinch.

Habits: Goldcrest-like when feeding, frequently hovering on the outside of tree foliage to pick off insects.

Range: Breeds in S Siberia, W to approximately River Yenisei, and in N Mongolia and Manchuria. Winters mainly in S China. Other populations (usually considered conspecific with Pallas's but probably better treated as a separate species) breed in the Himalayas to C China.

Status: Rare autumn vagrant (mainly Oct-Nov), now annual with occasional influxes (see below). Generally arrives later than Yellow-browed Warbler. Very rare in spring, e.g. France, Côte d' Or (18th Mar 1976); Poland (9th May 1977); Sweden, Ottenby (28th May 1978). Spain (17th Apr 1987).

Many records from the British Isles (*c.* 510). Also, Faeroes (Oct 1987), Channel Islands (2), France (8), Belgium (*c.* 20), Netherlands (36), Denmark (*c.* 65), Norway (34), Sweden (*c.* 235), Finland (*c.* 230), Estonia (9), Latvia (8), Poland (14), East Germany (2), West Germany (>50), Czechoslovakia (Oct 1987), Spain (1), and Malta (Nov 1987).

An unprecedented influx occurred in W Europe in Oct 1982. In the British Isles (with 3 records prior to 1958), there were influxes of 18 (1968), 29 (1975), and 33 (1981) all considered remarkable at the time. However, in the autumn of 1982 at least 123 individuals were recorded (cf. grand total of 181 prior to that date). This influx also reached a number of other countries, e.g. Denmark (14), Norway (13), Sweden (48), and Finland (43).

YELLOW-BROWED WARBLER *Phylloscopus inornatus* D **50**

L 10cm (4"). Asia. Rare but regular autumn visitor; the most frequent Siberian vagrant.

All plumages: Resembles Pallas's Warbler, but the head pattern is clearly different. The crown is not as dark, and it lacks or has, at the most, a faint median crown-stripe. The supercilium is less strongly yellow (but can be pale yellowish or even whitish in worn Pallas's). The dark eye-stripe is less marked, and it does not curve down distinctly at the rear end as it frequently does in Pallas's. Also, the rump is concolorous with the upperparts, and the wing-bars are not as yellow as in fresh Pallas's.

The (sub)species *humei*, 'Hume's Yellow-browed Warbler', which is probably better considered a separate species, (see Appendix), has been reported a few times in NW Europe. In fresh plumage *humei* differs from *inornatus* by the following: overall, it generally looks more washed-out than *inornatus*; flight-feathers and centres to greater coverts are slightly paler; upperparts are slightly paler green; the crown is more brownish-grey, lacking any distinct greenish tinge as in *inornatus*. Also, the supercilium in front of/above the eye is pale buffish (not yellowish as in *inornatus*). The tips to the median coverts are generally approximately the same colour as the upperparts and therefore do not form a distinct wing-bar as in *inornatus* (however, there is some overlap, as some individuals show paler tips, as in less well-marked *inornatus*). Note that in worn plumage, both look more grey and white, and that the slight differences in colour are then even more difficult to perceive. In both, the wing-bars and pale edges to the tertials progressively become narrower due to wear, but note that in *humei* the median covert-bar often becomes *more* whitish than in fresh plumage. The bill is on average proportionately slightly shorter than in *inornatus*, and the base of the lower mandible tends to be darker, as do the tarsus and toes. The voice differs significantly (see below).

The wing formula is slightly different. The wing-point is normally 6th-7th (6th may be longest) and 5th and 8th slightly shorter; often 5th≈8th. The 9th = 4th/3rd (closer to 3rd), 3rd/2nd or, less often, 2nd/1st. In *inornatus*, the wingpoint is normally 6th-8th (7th may be longest and 6th may be shortest); 5th is clearly shorter; and 9th≈4th or = 5th/4th, sometimes = 4th/3rd. However, the wing formula of *humei* is sometimes identical to *inornatus*.

There is a risk of confusion between, especially, *humei* and Greenish Warbler and *inornatus* and 'Two-barred Greenish Warbler'. Both *humei* and *inornatus* are characterized by e.g. whitish edges to tertials (may be very indistinct when worn), dark centres to coverts and tertials (distinctly darker than upperparts), and usually by a dark shade at the base of the secondaries. Ageing by plumage apparently very difficult.

Voice: The song of *inornatus* is an almost Goldcrest high/thin, *tsitsitsui itsui-it seee, tsi tsi-u-eee* or similar. The call, rather frequently given (unlike Pallas's Warbler), is a distinctive, loud, penetrating, rather high-pitched *tsuee-eep*, or differently transcribed *tsweet*. The song of *humei* is a thin, buzzing, drawn-out, falling note, *bzzzzzzzzee*, somewhat reminiscent of an extended Redwing's call note. Another type of song is a double *visu-visu*. These two types of song are usually alternated. The call is a *visu*, uttered singly or repeated.

Range: Nominate *inornatus* breeds in taiga in N Siberia, W to the Urals. It winters in S China, SE Asia and the Philippines. The (sub)species *humei* breeds from NW India to the Tien Shan, possibly also in the Altai and Sajan Mountains. It winters mainly in the Indian region. There is a third subspecies in C China, closely related to *humei*.

Status: The most regular Siberian vagrant. Annual in the British Isles and Scandinavia, and those countries bordering North Sea coasts. Smaller numbers reach the Channel Islands and particularly the island of Ouessant (France). Much rarer in C and S Europe. Occurs mainly mid Sept-Oct, exceptionally over-wintering, but very rare in spring. More numerous in some years than others, i.e. large influxes noted in UK and NW Europe in 1967, 1975, 1981, 1982, 1984, 1986, but unprecedented numbers reported in autumn 1985, e.g. British Isles (615 individuals, including 87 in Ireland), France (28), Netherlands (*c.* 100), Denmark (17), Heligoland (12), Norway (50+), Sweden (58), Finland (40), and Latvia (12). The 'lively' Yellow-browed has even reached

Iceland (12 between 1979-1986), Faeroes (13), and Madeira. National totals in Europe are given where known: British Isles (*c.* 2,650 between 1958-1985), France (210+ between 1981-88, including *c.* 75 on Ouessant in autumn 1988), Belgium (*c.* 200), Netherlands (*c.* 500), Denmark (*c.* 190), Norway (many), Sweden (*c.* 365), Finland (*c.* 300), Estonia (22+), Latvia (100+), Poland (*c.* 40), East Germany (17, since 1930), West Germany (many, especially Heligoland with up to 20 per day during 1st week Oct 1988), Czechoslovakia, Austria (3), Hungary (2), Switzerland (5), Italy (15), Sicily (Apr 1931, Dec 1980), Greece, Malta (*c.* 20), Portugal (a number of autumn records, but also occasionally recorded in winter), Spain (4), and Gibraltar (Oct 1984). There are also a number of documented records of *humei* from Britain, France, Belgium, Netherlands (4), Denmark, West Germany, Norway, Sweden (5 to 1989), Finland (3) Poland and Italy. Their arrival appears to be rather late in autumn, usually from mid-Oct to mid-Nov (a few have even over-wintered), often coinciding with the appearance of Pallas's Warblers, rather than with the slightly earlier arrival of most *inornatus.*

RADDE'S WARBLER   *Phylloscopus schwarzi*   D **50**

L 12-13cm (5"). C and E Asia. Rare autumn vagrant.

All plumages: Basically brownish above and pale below, with buffy-brown breast-sides and flanks and usually warmer, rusty-buff, undertail-coverts. The belly often shows a faint yellowish tinge which is very obvious in some autumn birds. The supercilium and eye-stripe are both prominent, and the bill is typically short and heavy. It can only be confused with Dusky Warbler (below). Ageing appears to be difficult by plumage, but adults probably never become as strongly yellowish below as do many (but not all) 1st-winter birds.

Voice: The song is loud. Gives short outbursts of fast, variable trills, e.g. *ty-ty   sui-sui-sui-sui-sui-sui.....   tydydydydydydydy.....ty-ty tyrrrrrrrrrrrrr.....ty-ty suisuisuisuisuisuisuisui.....tuee-tuee-tuee-tuee-tuee.....* The call is a characteristic rather soft, slightly nasal *tyt* or, differently transcribed, *tet,* irregularly repeated, often stuttering, *tyt tyt, tyt, tyt tyt-tyt-tyteryt, tyt.*

Habitat and behaviour: Favours scrubby areas and woodland edge, where it mainly moves about on the ground or at low level.

Range: Breeds in S Siberia, N Mongolia and NE China. Winters chiefly in extreme S China and N SE Asia.

Status: Rare vagrant in Europe (late Sept-early Nov). British Isles (92, especially in Oct), best annual totals were in 1982 (14), 1987 (10) and 1988 (21). Channel Islands (Sark, Oct 1978), France (Oct 1957, Oct 1987), Belgium (4, Oct-Nov), Netherlands (4, Oct), Denmark (7), Norway (Oct 1981, Oct 1987), Sweden, (15), Finland (8), Poland (Sept 1976), West Germany (Heligoland, 4), and Spain (Nov 1966).

DUSKY WARBLER   *Phylloscopus fuscatus*   D **50**

L 12cm (4.75"). Asia. Rare autumn vagrant.

All plumages: Distinguished from the Siberian race of Chiffchaff (*tristis*) by its darker upperparts, never showing any green (normally on back, rump and uppertail-coverts and edges to wings and tail in *tristis*) and generally browner flanks and undertail-coverts. The underwing-coverts and axillaries are warm buffy-brown (pale yellow in Chiffchaff). Usually has a longer, more distinct supercilium and more pronounced dark eye-stripe. Also has a paler lower mandible, paler legs, and very different call (*tristis* calls with high-pitched *eet*).

Easily confused with Radde's Warbler. However, Dusky is slightly smaller/slimmer, with a proportionately smaller head, slightly shorter tail and usually shows a clearly finer bill. Some Radde's are comparatively fine-billed and may be confusing to someone without previous experience. However, the bill is still proportionately deeper and shorter and shows a more decurved tip to the upper mandible than in Dusky (see figure). The tip of the lower mandible is dark, whereas in Radde's the lower mandible is often all pale in spring/summer and rarely also in autumn. The legs are thinner and generally darker than in Radde's. The head pattern usually differs significantly. The supercilium is generally rather narrow and sharply defined in front of the eye, and usually it is whitish in front and distinctly buffish at the rear (often from above the eye). In Radde's, it is usually broader and more diffuse in front of the eye and normally deeper buffish in front than above/behind. Never shows a diffuse darker margin above the supercilium as in many Radde's. Furthermore, lacks the olive tinge above which is shown by many Radde's, particularly on the rump/uppertail-coverts and remiges. Generally shows a less yellowish-buff tinge to the breast sides, flanks and undertail-coverts, and it does not normally show the usually obvious colour contrast between the flanks and undertail-coverts as in Radde's. It never shows more than a trace of yellowish to the belly (not visible in the field), unlike some Radde's in the autumn. Ageing by plumage extremely difficult.

Dusky Warbler

...ually small-billed ...e's Warbler

Voice: The song resembles Radde's, but is distinctly higher-pitched, obviously slower and less varied. It is without strong rattling trills, and has fewer syllables to each phrase. It also lacks the *ty-ty* notes frequently used by Radde's to introduce phrases. Instead, Dusky often begins with a thin *tsirit*. To the experienced ear the call is clearly different from Radde's. Dusky gives a slightly liquid but still rather hard *tett* or *tak* often nervously repeated and even drawn out into a rattling series when alerted.

Habitat and behaviour: It is generally less of a 'ground-dweller' than Radde's but it still usually keeps low. It has some preference for scrub and vegetation associated with wet habitats.

Range: Breeds in Siberia, Mongolia, N Manchuria (China) and Tibet. Winters from India to S China and SE Asia. Accidental in Morocco.

Status: Rare autumn vagrant in Europe. British Isles (77, late Sept-late Nov, once in May), including an exceptional influx of 13 in Oct-Nov 1987. Channel Islands (Sark, Nov 1980). France (Ouessant, Nov 1984, Oct 1986, but influx with 5 or 6 in Oct-Nov 1987; Apr 1988), Belgium (9), Netherlands (11, Oct-Nov). Denmark (13, where first recorded in Oct 1980, but large influx: 2nd-11th records in Oct-Nov 1987!). Norway (Oct 1974, Oct 1984), Sweden (20, including at least 7 in Oct 1987), Finland (23, including 9 records in the autumn influx of 1987), Estonia (Oct 1986, Nov 1987), Poland (Oct 1965, Sept 1986 and three inland: near Kolo, Apr 1984; Bialowieza Forest, June 1984; near Leszno, Dec 1984), East Germany (Oct 1987), West Germany (3), Austria (Nov 1973), and Italy (2).

RUBY-CROWNED KINGLET *Regulus calendula* A **50**

L 11cm (4.25"). North America. Recently recorded in Iceland.

All plumages: Resembles Goldcrest, but lacks dark lateral crown-stripes and shows a broad, broken eye-ring (broken above and below eye). Females are also identifiable by the lack of a colourful crown patch. Beware of juvenile Goldcrest, which shows a plain crown.

Adult male: Shows red or orange patch on the crown (often concealed).

Adult female: No red or orange on the crown.

1st-winter/-summer: Many distinguishable from adult of respective sex by narrower and more pointed tail feathers (more difficult in spring).

Voice: The song is remarkably loud and ringing for a bird of its size. Begins with thin *tee tee tee* notes, followed by rich and liquid *chew-chew-chew cheeda-cheeda-cheeda...* Call is a thin *see see*.

Range: Breeds widely in Canada except extreme northernmost areas, also in NE and W USA. Winters from British Columbia and Maryland south to Guatemala. Vagrant in Greenland (2).

Status: Accidental in Iceland: Heimaey, Westman Is, 1st-winter on 23rd Nov 1987.

Britain: one shot near Loch Lomond, Scotland in summer 1852 has never been formally accepted for inclusion in the British List.

Family MUSCICAPIDAE Old World Flycatchers

BROWN FLYCATCHER *Muscicapa dauurica* A **51**

L 12cm (4.75"). Asia. Accidental (autumn).

Adult: Uniformly brownish-grey above and pale below, with a pale greyish wash on the breast and flanks, sometimes more prominent and occasionally even faintly streaked. The bill is rather large, particularly when viewed from above or below, with a pale inner part to the lower mandible. The head pattern is diagnostic – pale lores, eye-ring and short submoustachial stripe and narrow, dark malar stripe. The coverts and tertials are indistinctly edged and tipped dull rufous when fresh.

Juvenile: Differs from adult in showing large, buffy spots to entire upperside, and has distinct buffy wing-bars and edges to the tertials. This plumage is not retained for long and is unlikely to be seen in Europe.

1st-winter/-summer: Distinguished from the adult by the distinct, clear-cut pale tips to the greater coverts and edges to the tertials (retained juvenile, but feathers bleached and usually appearing whitish; much less distinct in spring/summer, when also a few inner greater coverts and up to all tertials sometimes are new, adult-like). Occasionally some juvenile feathers on the upperparts, especially uppertail-coverts, are retained in the autumn.

Voice: The song is rather faint, and mainly built up of thin, squeaky notes. A short, faint, thin *tzi* and a rather fine, rattling *tse-te-te-te-te* are sometimes heard, the latter probably an alarm call.

Habits: Rather similar to Spotted Flycatcher.

Note: Siberian Flycatcher, *M. sibirica*, with much the same range as Brown Flycatcher, seems a likely candidate for future vagrancy. It is very similar to Brown. It has a distinctly shorter bill with less obvious pale base especially when viewed from the side. When viewed from above/below the edges of the bill are straight or slightly concave

(slightly convex in Brown). The primary projection is obviously longer than in Brown. Siberian usually shows distinctly darker, generally diffusely streaked breast/flanks, but note that Brown with unusually dark and diffusely streaked breast is very close to a pale individual of Siberian. Siberian shows rather indistinctly pale lores, and the lower part of the lores usually look dark (looking like a dark loral stripe); it thus lacks the strikingly pale lores of Brown. Furthermore, Siberian frequently shows a distinct pale half-collar, not seen in Brown. Siberian has dark-centred undertail-coverts, not seen in Brown (not always visible in the field, though). Also shows rusty-brownish underwing-coverts and axillaries (whitish to pale buffish in Brown). In the hand the wing formula is a further aid – the 9th primary is usually > 6th in Siberian < 6th in Brown, occasionally slightly shorter than 6th in Siberian, but the distance from the wing-point to the tip of the 6th primary is ≥ 2.5mm in Sooty and ≤ 2.0mm in Brown; and the 10th is < the tips of the primary coverts in Siberian and > the primary coverts in Brown.
Range: Breeds in S Siberia, NE Mongolia, China and Japan, also in the Himalayas. Winters chiefly in SE Asia and Indonesia.
Status: Accidental in Denmark (24th-25th Sept 1959) and Sweden (27th-30th Sept 1986).

Family PARIDAE   Tits

AZURE TIT   *Parus cyanus*   C **51**
L 12.5-13.5cm (5.25"). W USSR to Siberia and NW China. Rare vagrant (has even bred).
All plumages: Characterized by pale blue and white, 'fluffy' plumage. It could be confused with an aberrant Blue Tit, but is slightly larger, has a proportionately longer tail, lacks a black bib, and shows diagnostic wing and tail pattern.
Adult: Shows bright blue edges to the flight-feathers, lesser, median and greater coverts and primary coverts.
Juvenile: Looser plumaged than the adult, and shows grey lesser and median coverts and grey edges to the greater coverts. The blue edges to the primary coverts and flight feathers are fractionally duller than the adult, but this is of no importance without comparison.
1st-winter: Apparently separable from the adult by plumage only when some juvenile coverts are retained – which seems to be unusual.
Voice: Very variable. One type of song is similar to a slow, deep voiced Coal Tit. Another is similar to a common type of Blue Tit song and a third type is more similar to Marsh Tit. The calls are equally variable. Some are remarkably similar to some calls of Great Tit, others to some calls of Blue Tit and even some Willow Tit-like notes can be heard.´
Note: Sometimes hybridizes with Blue Tit (e.g. an individual recorded in Netherlands in Nov 1968).
Range: Breeds from W USSR (W of Moscow) across S Siberia and Mongolia to NE China and in NW China, Tien Shan and neighbouring areas. Mainly resident.
Status: Rare vagrant in Europe. In 19th century, some periodically irrupted westwards to E and C Europe. Fewer records in 20th century.

In Finland, a pair was found breeding for the first time in 1973 near the Russian border, and a bird was seen near Turku in Dec 1974-Mar 1976; in 1975 it was paired with a Blue Tit. There were six more observations in 1973-1975, and a total of 21 individuals have so far been recorded up to the end of 1988. In Latvia, several observations also include the 3rd record of a hybrid Azure × Blue Tit, ringed at Pape Bird Ringing Station (Oct 1981). There are also records from France (winter 1907/8), Sweden (2nd in Nov 1983). Estonia, Poland, (27, Oct-Feb, Apr, more recently in Dec 1977, Mar 1981, and 3-4 in Feb 1982). Czechoslovakia (*c.* 30, Oct-Mar), Austria (10+), Hungary (Dec 1988, Oct 1989), Yugoslavia and Rumania.

Family SITTIDAE   Nuthatches

RED-BREASTED NUTHATCH   *Sitta canadensis*   A **51**
L 10.5cm (4.25"). North America. Accidental in N Europe.
All plumages: Easily identified by small size, prominent white supercilium and dark eye-stripe. Shows buffy to rusty underparts.
Adult male: The glossy black on the crown and eye-stripe contrasts markedly with the grey mantle. The underparts are rich rusty.
Adult female: Differs from the male by its paler, dark grey to dull blackish crown and eye-stripe (the latter often darker than the crown) and paler underparts.
1st-winter: Resembles the adult of its respective sex.
Voice: The calls are nasal, recalling the sound made by a toy horn, a slow *nyak nyak nyak*.
Range: Breeds in Canada, W and NE USA. Many northerly breeders are migratory, wintering as far S as S USA.
Status: Accidental in Iceland: Westman Is, male on 21st May 1970. Britain: Holkham Meals, Norfolk, male from 13th Oct 1989-6th May 1990*.

CORSICAN NUTHATCH   *Sitta whiteheadi*   R Br* **51**
L 12cm (4.75"). Endemic to Corsica.
All plumages: Resembles respective plumages of Red-breasted Nuthatch but larger, paler below and shows pale grey tips to outer tail-feathers (dark tips with whitish subterminal bar in Red-breasted).
Voice: The song is a clear *pu-u-u-u-u-u-u-u-u-u-u*, usually increasing in volume, often decreasing again at the end. One call is a harsh note, recalling the alarm call of Starling.
Habitat: Breeds in mountain conifer forests (especially *Pinus laricio*).
Range and status: Confined to Corsica, where *c.* 2,000 pairs (1981-84).

Family LANIIDAE   Shrikes

BROWN SHRIKE   *Lanius cristatus*   A **52**
L 18-19.5cm (7.75"). Asia. Accidental.
All plumages: Closely resembles the darker forms of Isabelline Shrike, but is slightly larger, more heavily built, with a proportionately larger bill and has a distinctly more graduated tail (difference between tips of

longest and shortest rectrix is 15-25mm in Brown, and 7.5-14.5mm in Isabelline). The tail-feathers are narrower (6.5-9.5mm as opposed to 9-11mm in Isabelline).

It is usually slightly darker above, showing less contrast between the upperparts and the tail (the rump and uppertail-coverts are often rather contrastingly rufous, though). The crown/nape do not usually contrast with the mantle/scapulars as in the *phoenicuroides* race of Isabelline. However, there is occasionally a distinct contrast. The breast-sides, flanks and undertail-coverts are usually deeper buff than in Isabelline. There is no pale patch or, at the most, only a trace of it at the base of the primaries.

The wing formula is approximately as in Isabelline, but the 9th primary tends to be even shorter (usually ≈5th or = 4th/5th, sometimes even = 4th).

Adult male: Shows a distinct blackish face mask and usually no dark markings below. Further differs from Isabelline in often showing a diffuse pale greyish-white band on the forehead (not at all or only indistinctly in Isabelline).

Adult female: Difficult to tell from the male but usually shows a slightly less distinct mask in front of the eye, and usually has some dark chevrons on the underparts.

Juvenile: Shows dark barring above, otherwise like 1st-winter. Best separated from juvenile Isabelline Shrike by the deeper buff colour below, and narrow and rather indistinct pale tips to the remiges and primary coverts.

1st-winter: Differs from the adult in showing distinct dark subterminal bands to the retained juvenile coverts (usually only greaters) and tertials. The face mask is browner and not complete on the lores, the supercilium is less prominent in front (not meeting on the forehead), and the breast/flanks are generally more heavily marked. The underparts tend to be more heavily marked, but above it is on average even less barred than 1st-winter Isabelline (i.e. usually completely unmarked). Isabelline generally shows some fine dark barring at the upper end of the supercilium, not normally seen in Brown. As in juvenile, the pale tips to the remiges and primary coverts are less distinct (of little value in worn birds, though).

1st-summer: Not separable from the adult, since both go through a complete pre-breeding moult.

Range: Breeds in Siberia, W to approximately the Yenisei, Mongolia, NE and E China, and Japan. Winters from India to S China, Indonesia and the Philippines. Vagrant in Alaska (4) and Farallon Is. California (Sept 1984).

Status: Accidental in Britain: Shetland, Sumburgh, adult from 30th Sept-2nd Oct 1985. Denmark: Falster, 1st winter trapped on 15th Oct 1988*.

ISABELLINE SHRIKE *Lanius isabellinus* B **52**

L 17-18.5cm (7"). Asia. Rare vagrant in N Europe (mainly autumn).
All plumages: Similar to Brown Shrike (see p. 374).
Adult male: The nominate race is characterized by a blackish face mask (usually paler on the anterior lores) and pale sandy upperparts with contrasting rufous rump, uppertail-coverts and tail. Also has pale buf-

fish, usually unmarked, breast/flanks and generally a whitish patch at the base of the primaries.

In the subspecies *phoenicuroides*, the mantle and scapulars are usually darker grey-brown, contrasting with a more or less prominently rufous forehead, crown and nape. The lores are generally blacker (forming a complete face mask); the flight-feathers darker; the rump to tail deeper rufous; and the underparts slightly more whitish, with a more pinkish tinge. A third race, *speculigerus*, is somewhat intermediate.

Adult female: In *isabellinus* the sexes are rather difficult to separate, but the female usually shows slightly paler ear-coverts and some dark crescents on the breast/sides flanks, and the pale patch at the base of the primaries is indistinct or lacking altogether. Female *phoenicuroides* is more easily distinguished from the male. The forehead-nape generally contrasts less or not at all with the mantle, and the face mask is incomplete. It further differs by the same characters as described for *isabellinus* above. Females are generally more difficult to assign to a subspecies than are males.

Females are normally distinctly paler and more grey-brown above and show a more contrastingly rufous rump, uppertail-coverts and tail than female Red-backed Shrike, and the underparts are normally obviously less marked. Red-backed is often rather rufous on the upperparts and coverts, with contrasting grey forehead to nape and back to uppertail- coverts. In some, only the nape is greyer. The crown/nape and upperparts are plain in Isabelline; in many Red-backed they show some distinct barring.

The autumn moult is very variable (same in adult male). Some go through a complete moult, whereas others only moult partially before the migration. Some are intermediate between these extremes, with suspended moult of remiges; cf. 1st-winter.

Juvenile: Similar to 1st-winter (see below) but with distinct dark barring above. Extremely similar to juvenile Red-backed (see below).

1st-winter: Resembles the adult female of its respective race (the subspecies are often difficult to separate), but the upperparts frequently show some distinct barring (juvenile feathers), and the underparts are generally more heavily marked than the adult female. There is usually no pale patch on the primaries. Any retained juvenile median and greater coverts and tertials show distinct dark subterminal bands, lacking in the adult (in most individuals these feathers are retained throughout the autumn). The remiges and rectrices are all rather fresh in the autumn, a further distinction from those adults which have only moulted partially. Occasionally the rectrices and inner secondaries and all of the coverts and tertials are renewed in the autumn, making ageing more difficult. The fact that there are two generations of feathers separates those birds from an adult which has moulted completely (in which the feathers belong to the same generation). However, the contrast between the different feather generations is not so pronounced as in those adults which have not moulted completely, since the old-generation feathers are less worn than in those adults. Further distinctions from all adults irrespective of the stage of moult is that, if not too worn, the primary coverts usually show distinct pale tips and dark subterminal markings (no or very narrow pale tips in adult and no dark subterminal markings), and when reasonably fresh, the remiges usually show more distinct pale tips than the adult.

Most are easily told from 1st-winter Red-backed Shrike by the paler and greyer upperside and coverts, with contrasting rufous rump, uppertail-coverts and tail; unmarked or very faintly barred upperside (normally strongly barred in Red-backed); and generally less heavily marked breast/flanks. However, some individuals of the race *phoenicuroides* (and juveniles of both races), are extremely similar to rather normal Red-backed. The nape is not greyer as it generally is in Red-backed, and the ear-coverts are apparently never deep rufous as in some Red-backed. Does not normally show any distinct rufous on the coverts, centres to the tertials, scapulars and lower mantle as in most Red-backed. The underside of the rectrices is more rufous, but this is often difficult to judge. However, some individuals are so close, that they can only be reliably distinguished by wing formula (below).

The 9th primary = 5th/6th or ≈5th in Isabelline and = 7th/6th (sometimes 6th) in Red-backed. Also, there are three emarginations (8th-6th), as opposed to two (8th-7th) in Red-backed.

1st-summer: At least the majority are indistinguishable (most individuals moult completely in winter, but more research needs to be done).

Note: Isabelline and Red-backed Shrikes have often been considered conspecific, together with the Brown Shrike – under the name of Red-backed when this and Isabelline have been grouped together or under Brown Shrike when all three have been grouped together.

Range: Breeds from Iran and Kazakhstan to N China and Mongolia. The race *phoenicuroides* breeds in the W parts to approximately the Tien Shan, east of which *speculigerus* continues. The nominate race (and the similar *tsaidamensis*) breeds in NW and N China. The winter quarters are in E Africa to India, *phoenicuroides* apparently mainly in Africa and S Arabia, *speculigerus* probably in NE Africa to W India and *isabellinus* apparently throughout the range, although perhaps mainly in the Indian region.

Status: Rare vagrant in the British Isles (30, including 7 in Oct 1988, mainly mid Aug-mid Nov, also Mar-May), France (Ouessant, Sept 1982, Aug 1986, Sept 1987), Belgium (Sept 1989*), Norway (Sept 1973, Sept-Oct 1974, Oct 1975), Sweden (Nov 1967, Oct 1984, 2 in Oct 1988), Finland (May 1980, Oct 1980, Oct 1987, June 1989*), Poland (Sept 1981, Sept 1984), and West Germany (Heligoland, Oct 1854, Sept 1980).

LONG-TAILED SHRIKE *Lanius schach* A **52**

L 22-23cm (9"). Asia. One record in spring for E Europe.

All plumages: Unmistakable large shrike with long, rather narrow dark tail.

Adult: Subspecies *erythronotus* shows a grey crown/nape and anterior upperparts, with contrasting orange-brown scapulars, lower mantle, back, rump and uppertail-coverts. Also has blackish wings, often with a little whitish at the base of the primaries, and whitish underparts with an orange-brownish wash on the flanks and undertail-coverts. Female tends to show less whitish at the base of the primaries than male.

Juvenile: Easily distinguished from the adult by more brownish-grey upperside with distinct dark and pale barring, less extensive dark face mask, dark chevrons on breast/flanks, and dark subterminal bands and pale fringes to the coverts and tertials. Usually lacks a pale patch at the base of the primaries.

1st-winter/-summer: Distinguished from the adult by its browner and more worn remiges and primary coverts which contrast with the blackish and fresher coverts/tertials. Sometimes some outer greater coverts and one to all tertials are also unmoulted and clearly contrasting.

Range: Breeds in much of S Asia, W to Iran. Resident. Has straggled once to both Turkey (autumn) and Israel (winter). Other distinctive races occur east to China, Indonesia and New Guinea.

Status: Accidental in Hungary: Fehértó on 21st Apr 1979.

Family CORVIDAE   Crows

DAURIAN JACKDAW   *Corvus dauuricus*   A **51**

L 33cm (13"). C and NE Asia. Two records in spring for N Europe.

All plumages: Resembles Jackdaw in size and shape. Has diagnostic dark iris (whitish in adult, greyish in young Jackdaw).

Adult: Differs significantly from Jackdaw by its contrasting black and greyish white plumage (may recall Hooded Crow). Shows diagnostic whitish streaks on the ear-coverts and supercilium. Partially albinistic Jackdaws may be confusing but they would never show exactly the same pattern as Daurian.

1st-winter/summer: Most are very similar to Jackdaw, but have a darker nape, whitish streaks on the sides of the head and a faintly outlined darker bib (extension as in adult). A few are apparently similar to adult, but show duller and less glossy wing-feathers, progressively becoming more brownish (some coverts may be new and contrasting). Also, tail-feathers slightly narrower and more pointed than in adult.

Range: Breeds in S-C Siberia, Mongolia and N and C China. Northern birds are migratory, wintering mainly in China.

Status: Accidental in Finland: Uusikaarlepyy in May 1883. Sweden: near Umeå from 26th-28th Apr 1985. Both individuals were pied morphs.

Family STURNIDAE   Starlings

ROSE-COLOURED STARLING   *Sturnus roseus*   D **52**

L 20.5-22.5cm (8.5"). Breeds regularly E Rumania. Also in Asia. Sometimes in spring irrupts into other parts of E Europe, breeding in many places (sometimes in large numbers). Rare vagrant elsewhere (mainly May-Oct).

Adult male: Unmistakable in spring-autumn. The plumage is pink and black and there is a conspicuous crest (27-45mm). The head is glossed purplish, and the wing-feathers are strongly glossed blue-green. In winter plumage (generally attained in winter quarters) the pink is partially concealed by dusky, while the head and undertail-coverts show narrow, pale fringes. The culmen of the bill is dark in winter.

Adult female: Resembles the adult male, but the dark parts are slightly browner, showing less gloss, and in winter the pink areas are generally

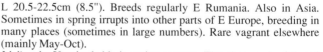

more extensively dusky. The crest is distinctly shorter (17-30mm, most 20-26mm).

Note that partially albinistic Starlings can show a pattern of dark and pale recalling Rose-coloured, but such aberrant Starlings do not show any pink (also the case in some heavily worn Rose-coloured), obviously lack a crest, and it would be exceptional if the pattern of dark/pale exactly matched Rose-coloured.

Juvenile: Much paler than juvenile Starling and told even from aberrant, pale (leucistic) Starlings by their slightly heavier and more decurved-looking, pale brownish-yellow bill with dark culmen and tip to lower mandible (all-black in Starling). Also has pale lores and finely spotted lower foreneck/sides to the upper breast (dark lores and no distinct spots in Starling). The rump is usually contrastingly pale. Unlike Starling (and most other passerines), the juvenile plumage is normally moulted in the winter quarters, and it is frequently seen in Europe still in full juvenile plumage in Sept-Nov.

1st-winter/-summer: After a complete moult in the winter quarters, the immature male resembles a winter adult female. The immature female is usually even duller and duskier with no or little pink visible. As in the adult, the plumage progressively becomes more black and pink as the dusky tips and pale fringes wear narrower. Odd juvenile wing-feathers are often retained after the moult, readily enabling ageing. The crest is 24-34mm long in the male and 13-19mm long in the female. Some individuals are still very dusky in spring/summer, and apparently, juvenile bill pattern is often retained.

Range: Breeds from E Rumania east through S USSR to Kazakhstan and Iran. Winters in India south to Sri Lanka. Periodically migrates beyond normal breeding limits. Vagrant to Canary Is and Madeira.

Status: Mainly rare vagrant in N and C Europe (especially late May-July, also autumn). Recorded from Iceland (11), Faeroes (7), British Isles (350, average 8 per year, *c.* 25% juveniles), Channel Islands (4), France (30+), Belgium (35+), Netherlands (27), Denmark (35), Norway (37), Sweden (68, nearly all adults), Finland (*c.* 40), Estonia, Latvia, Poland (formerly an irregular visitor, but only 6 since 1946), East Germany (*c.* 15 since 1930), West Germany, Czechoslovakia, Austria, Switzerland (7), Yugoslavia (many, including several thousand passing through Buljarica Marsh, Petrovac, in late May 1989), Greece (many), Albania, Italy, Sicily (9), Malta, Portugal, and Spain.

In July 1984, an extensive influx was noted in N Greece, including one flock of 500+, and there were above-average sightings in N Europe (late May-Aug) from Britain, France, Scandinavia, Poland, and Austria.

DAURIAN STARLING *Sturnus sturninus*   A **52**

L 18cm (7"). Eastern Asia. Accidental.

Adult male: Shows pale grey head and underparts, with more creamy to buffish belly and undertail-coverts, the latter even pale rufous sometimes. Also has a dark spot on the nape; purplish-black mantle; green gloss to blackish wings and tail; pale bar on median coverts and usually also on inner greater coverts and tips to tertials; pale bar on scapulars; and buffish to pale rufous rump. There is a broad, pale brown wing-bar on the basal parts of the outer secondaries and primaries.

Adult female: Duller and more brownish in general coloration, especially on top of the head and on the mantle.

Juvenile: Said to be brownish above and pale below, with faint dark streaking on the breast.

1st-winter/-summer: 1st-winter is like the adult of its respective sex, but the inner *c.* four secondaries and outermost tertial are usually retained. They are brown and distinctly pale-edged and contrast with the rest of the flight-feathers. These retained juvenile flight-feathers are normally moulted during late winter, so that the 1st-summer plumage is usually indistinguishable from the adult.

Note: The female is very similar to the female Red-cheeked Starling *S. philippensis* (breeding Japan and Sakhalin, wintering Indonesia and Philippines). This lacks the pale bar on the scapulars and the pale tips to the tertials and inner greater coverts of most Daurian.

Range: Breeds SE USSR from SE Transbaikalia to Lower Amur, south to NE Manchuria (China). Winters mainly from S China to Malaysia and Indonesia.

Status: Accidental in Britain: Shetland, Fair Isle, male (7th-28th May 1985). Norway: Lillestrøm, near Oslo, 1st-winter male (29th Sept 1985).

Family PASSERIDAE Sparrows and allies

DEAD SEA SPARROW *Passer moabiticus*   B **59**
L 12cm (5"). Middle East to Iran. One record.

Adult male summer: Small sparrow with diagnostic head pattern. Shows grey forehead, crown, nape and ear-coverts and a whitish supercilium turning buffish at rear. Shows a rather small and well-defined black bib and whitish submoustachial stripes which are bright yellow on the sides of the neck. The lesser coverts are black with whitish tips, forming a narrow whitish bar (lesser coverts often concealed). Median and greater coverts are mainly contrastingly chestnut. The bill is black.

Adult male winter: The grey on the head is largely covered by brown tips, and the black bib and yellow patch on the neck are normally less conspicuous. Also, the bill is much paler.

Adult female: Very similar to female House Sparrow, but is distinctly smaller and often "cuter-looking" due to its proportionately slightly larger head and smaller bill. The plumage is slightly paler. Sometimes shows some yellow on the side of the neck.

1st-winter male: Difficult to separate from adult male winter with certainty, but generally less brightly and contrastingly patterned, with browner head, paler lores, less distinct black bib and yellow neck-patch.

Voice: Higher-pitched than House Sparrow.

Range: Patchily distributed in Turkey, Cyprus (recently discovered breeding at least 1980-85, and would appear to be a continuation of westward spread in Turkey), the Middle East, Iraq, Iran and W Afghanistan.

Mainly resident, although some populations are presumed migratory as absent from breeding areas from mid-Nov until March..

Status: Greece: a flock of *c*. 20 birds observed on the E coast of the island of Rhodes in early Oct 1972.

Family VIREONIDAE Vireos

PHILADELPHIA VIREO *Vireo philadelphicus*   A **54**

L 12cm (4.75"). North America. Two recent autumn records.

All plumages: Shows olive-green upperparts, usually with a greyer crown/nape. Has pale yellowish underside, with belly usually more whitish. Typical face pattern shows a dark eye-stripe, rather diffuse whitish supercilium and often a diffuse pale crescent below the eye. It also has a stout bill with slightly hooked tip. Ageing difficult by plumage, but 1st-winter tends to show more pointed tail-feathers than adult.

Voice: The song resembles Red-eyed Vireo but is thinner, higher-pitched and distinctly slower, e.g. *tiuvit...tidiu...tsiuvit...*

Range: Breeds mainly in C to E Canada. Winters in Central and N South America.

Status: Accidental in Ireland: Galley Head, Co. Cork (12th-17th Oct 1985); Britain: Isles of Scilly (10th-13th Oct 1987).

RED-EYED VIREO *Vireo olivaceus*   C **54**

L 15cm (6"). North America. Rare vagrant. Appears with some regularity in the British Isles (late Sept-Oct).

All plumages: Easily recognized by its distinctive head pattern with prominent whitish supercilium, grey crown, dark lateral crown stripe and dark eye-stripe. Has greenish upperparts and pale underside. Note strong bill with hooked tip and iris colour.

Adult: Has bright red iris. In the autumn, the flight feathers are generally either heavily worn, or some fresh (moult of remiges takes place in winter quarters, or the moult is suspended during the migration).

1st-winter: Has brown or reddish-brown iris. All of the flight-feathers are usually the same age (little worn in autumn).

Voice: The song consists of short, clear notes repeated at short intervals, e.g. *teeduee tueedee tuee teeudeeu....* It is slightly reminiscent of a faster version of the song of some thrushes, e.g. Eye-browed Thrush.

Range: Breeds in North America. Winters in the northern half of South America. Vagrant to Greenland and Morocco.

Status: Rare autumn transatlantic vagrant. British Isles: 57, mainly late Sept-mid Oct, especially SW Britain and S Ireland, with exceptional influxes of 13 (1985) and 11 (1988). Also, recorded in Iceland (4), France (Oct 1983, Oct 1985, Oct 1988* two), Netherlands (two in Oct 1985), West Germany (Heligoland, Oct 1957), and Malta (Oct 1983).

Family FRINGILLIDAE   Finches and allies

RED-FRONTED SERIN   *Serinus pusillus*   A **53**

L 11cm (4.5"). W to C Asia. Accidental in Greece.

Adult: Resembles Serin in size and build. Readily identified by its mostly blackish head and breast with a red patch on the forehead. Shows narrow, pale fringes to black parts in fresh winter plumage.

Juvenile: Clearly different from the adult. Shows a diagnostic mainly pale chestnut head, breast and wing-bars.

1st-winter/-summer: Basically like the adult, but many birds retain much chestnut on the head and show little red on the forehead. The juvenile outer greater coverts are usually retained, pale chestnut on the edges and tips (orange-or greenish-yellow in adult and on new, adult-type, coverts) and with clearly more sharply defined dark centres, especially at tips. In spring they are heavily worn, but still contrasting with inners (no moult contrast in adult).

Voice: Song described as a soft, pleasant, rippling twitter. Calls with a soft, tinkling trill, *firrrrrrrrr*, softer than the corresponding call of Serin; also gives a soft *dUeet*.

Range: Breeds in mountainous regions from W Turkey to Tarbagatai and the Tien Shan to Kashmir and Ladakh. Mainly resident (undertakes altitudinal movements), but also occurs in winter in mountains of Near East, N Iraq, S Iran, S Afghanistan, NW Himalayas. Accidental in Cyprus.

Status: Accidental in Greece: second record concerned several flocks of 5-10 birds on Chios in Jan-Feb 1987.

ARCTIC REDPOLL   *Carduelis hornemanni*   R Br **53**

L 13-15.5cm (5-6"). Circumpolar. In Europe breeds only N Norway, Sweden and Finland. Rarely seen far S of breeding area but sometimes irruptive.

All plumages: Very similar to Redpoll, with which it has often been considered conspecific. In classic individuals the plumage is very pale, with little or no streaking on the breast-sides and flanks. Shows white, unstreaked rump and sometimes back and very narrow or no dark central streak on the longest undertail-coverts. Redpoll is usually distinctly darker above and heavily streaked on the breast-sides, flanks and rump, and shows a rather broad, dark central streak to the longest undertail-coverts (see figure, p. 383). Arctic's plumage normally looks softer and fluffier. It also generally appears to have a more rounded and compact body (shorter neck), and the bill is usually proportionately shorter with a straighter culmen than in Redpoll.

Some individuals (apparently mainly 1st-years) are considerably darker above and more heavily streaked on the breast-sides/flanks and thus very similar to pale Redpolls (in both species the plumage is paler when fresh and darker when worn). In these birds the rump is often faintly streaked, and the dark central streak to the longest undertail-coverts may be fairly broad (see figure, p. 383). Such individuals may be extremely difficult to separate from some Redpolls.

Adult male: Normally has the palest and least streaked plumage, and shows pale pink breast and often pale pink rump – paler pink than in male Redpoll.

382

undertail-coverts

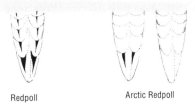

Redpoll

Arctic Redpoll

Adult female: Normally shows no pink on the breast or rump. The latter is sometimes faintly streaked.

1st-winter/-summer: Resembles the adult female, but the tail-feathers are normally more pointed and more worn than in the adult. Males usually show at least some pink on the breast, but it may be lacking altogether.

Voice: Very similar to Common Redpoll. Some studies suggest that the calls are separable, but more research is needed.

Note: Birds said to show characters intermediate between Arctic Redpoll and Common Redpoll have been claimed many times. According to some authors, such individuals are often 1st-year Arctic Redpolls.

Range: Race *exilipes*, breeds in northernmost Sweden, Norway, Finland (rare breeder), and across northernmost USSR, to Alaska and N Canada. The slightly larger *hornemanni* breeds on Ellesmere and Baffin Islands and N Greenland.

Status: Rare vagrant. Iceland, Faeroes (2), British Isles (170, mainly from late Sept-Feb), France (9), Belgium (6), Netherlands (9 since 1980), Estonia, Denmark, East Germany (18 since 1930, Oct-Apr), West Germany (*c*. 10), Poland (22 records, but largest ever influx in winter 1989, mainly on Baltic coast, including flock *c*. 100 together with *c*. 1,000 Redpolls, inland near Szczecinek, Pomerania during 15th-21st Jan), Estonia, Latvia, Czechoslovakia (15+), Austria, Hungary (3), and Rumania (15+). It seems likely that the Arctic Redpoll is more numerous than indicated by the number of records, since usually only 'classic' individuals have been accepted.

TWO-BARRED CROSSBILL *Loxia leucoptera*   R Br **53**

L 15cm (6"). NE Finland, N-C Asia, N North America and West Indies. Irregular visitor (mainly late summer-winter).

All plumages: Best distinguished from other crossbills by the broad, white wing-bars and tips to the tertials. However, note that some individuals of other species of crossbill show prominent wing-bars and tips to the tertials, although never as wide as in a normal Two-barred. The greater covert-bar obviously tapers more towards the outer end, and the median covert-bar appears to be positioned obliquely in relation to the greater covert-bar, whereas in abnormal other crossbills, the wing-bars are positioned rather more parallel and are of uniform width. Note that in individuals which have all the juvenile coverts retained, these are sometimes so heavily worn that the white tips are very narrow, and such individuals can be very difficult to tell from a Crossbill with distinct wing-bars. However, Two-barred are slightly smaller, slimmer and proportionally longer-tailed and usually show a slightly weaker

Two-barred Crossbill
1st-winter with retained
juv. wing-coverts and
tertials

Crossbill
extreme ad. with prominent
wing-bars and pale
markings to tertials

typical
ad.-patterned   juv.

tertials

greater covert

bill. Under good light conditions, wing-bars can often be seen also on the underwing.

Adult male: The plumage normally shows a slightly more pinkish-red tinge than in an adult male Crossbill. As in adult males of other crossbills, the plumage can be mottled yellowish-green and red.

Adult female: Usually shows some streaking on the breast and flanks, not normally seen in Crossbill; also tends to be more yellowish, particularly on the rump.

Juvenile: Easily distinguished from the adult by the dull, heavily streaked plumage. Juveniles may be seen from early in the spring to late in the autumn.

1st-winter/-summer male: Much like the adult male, but usually with the outer greater coverts retained from juvenile. These are clearly shorter, more worn, with narrower white tips than the newly moulted inners. Also some juvenile tertials are often retained. The pattern of the greater coverts and tertials differs between juvenile and adult (see figure).

1st-winter/-summer female: See 1st-winter male, but the tertial pattern is sometimes similar in juvenile and adult.

Voice: The repertoire includes a bouncing *glip-glip*, softer and less metallic than the corresponding call of Crossbill. Frequently calls with a characteristic *chet- chet*, reminiscent of a Redpoll, as well as a nasal *eeeaat*, recalling a subdued version of the song of Trumpeter Finch.

Habits: Similar to other crossbills, but prefers larch to pine and spruce, and is often found feeding in rowans and birches.

Range: Breeds in N-C Asia, N North America and in the mountains of Hispaniola, West Indies. Resident or nomadic, in some years irrupting to areas far outside its normal range. Vagrant in Greenland.

Status: Rare and irregular visitor to most of Europe. Frequently wandering to Scandinavia (normally from late July), where large irruptions of this species seem to occur at regular seven-year intervals. In some years arrives with invasions of Crossbills. Sweden: large numbers noted in autumn/winter 1979 (*c.* 650), 1985 (*c.* 800), 1986 (*c.* 600), and 1987 (750+). Breeding has been recorded a few times, most recently in 1987. Finland: frequent visitor, breeding annually in the NE parts, but widespread breeding noted in 1987. Norway: many records; between 1956-86, there were four great invasion years i.e. 1959, 1966, 1979 and 1986 (Aug-Nov, usually with maximum in Sept). One pair bred successfully in Nord-Trøndelag in 1982, also a nesting attempt was recorded near Bergen in Apr 1987.

Elsewhere there are records from the Faeroes (4), British Isles (90+, most July-Feb), France (8), Belgium (30+), Netherlands (6), Denmark (many), Estonia, Latvia, Poland (formerly an irregular visitor, 10 records in 20th century), East Germany (16 records of up to 12 birds since 1930), West Germany (50+), Czechoslovakia, Austria, Hungary, Switzerland (3), Italy (20), Yugoslavia, Bulgaria (Nov 1983), and Rumania.

SCOTTISH CROSSBILL   *Loxia scotica*   R Br*

L 16.5cm (6.5") Endemic to N Scotland. In the past considered conspecific with either Crossbill or Parrot Crossbill. Now considered a separate species.

Two-barred
Crossbill

Crossbill

Scottish Crossbill

Parrot Crossbill

All plumages: Very difficult to distinguish from Crossbill and Parrot Crossbill, since the bill is intermediate in size. The bill length is 17.4-20.2mm (to feathering) and the depth 11.0-13.4mm (at feathering). The corresponding measurements for Parrot Crossbill are 18.5-22.0mm and 12.5-15.0mm and for Crossbill 16.5-21.0mm and 9.5-12.3mm.

Voice: Vocal differences between Crossbill, Parrot Crossbill, and Scottish Crossbill are not yet fully understood but are currently being investigated.

Habitat and Behaviour: Prefers Scots pines, occurring most often in old native pinewoods. Habits similar to Crossbill, but seldom seen in parties of more than 15-20 birds, unlike the latter where flocks of 80-100 or more are not unusual.

Range/status: Restricted to N Scotland, mainly in NE and central Highlands. Total population approximately 1,500 individuals.

TRUMPETER FINCH *Bucanetes githagineus*   R Br **53**

L 13-14cm (5.25"). Rare and local breeder in SE Spain. Also breeds N Africa and W Asia. There are a few records from N Europe.

All plumages: Small, compact finch with a short, stout conical bill.

Adult male: Shows some pink on the head and body, most pronounced in summer, and pink edges to wings/tail. The bill is pale reddish in summer, more horn-coloured in winter.

Adult female: Very nondescript, mainly rather plain, pale grey-brown.

1st-winter/-summer male: Similar to the adult male, but usually shows at least some retained juvenile flight feathers and/or primary coverts with buffish edges (more worn than the newly moulted ones). The primary coverts are not always moulted in sequence with their corresponding primaries (cf. adult Pallas's Grasshopper Warbler).

1st-winter/-summer female: Can usually be aged by showing a moult contrast in the wings, but the difference is less striking than in males.

Voice: The song is a peculiar, drawn-out, nasal, buzzing note recalling a toy horn. The call, often given in flight, is a rather soft, nasal *wehp*.

Habitat: Desert or semi-desert areas.

Range: Breeds locally in SE Spain, where breeding first presumed in 1968, following recent colonization of arid terrain around Almeria. By 1971 had become a potentially numerous breeding resident in SE Spain. Range expansion: Cartagena Mts, breeding confirmed spring 1988.

Also breeds in N Africa (including Sahara), Canary Is, Middle East, and N Arabia to Pakistan. Resident, but may undertake movements in periods of drought. Vagrant in Cyprus (6, Mar-Apr, 1 in Dec).

Status: Accidental in Britain (6, May-June, Aug-Sept), Channel Islands (Alderney, Oct-Nov 1973), Denmark (June-July 1982), Sweden (June

1966, June 1971), West Germany (July 1987) and Austria (autumn 1907). Origin of these birds is perhaps hard to assess. Elsewhere: Greece, Italy (possibly regular migrant) with maximum 10 at Linosa Is (May 1967) and *c*. 20 near Siracusa, Sicily (July 1977), Gibraltar (very scarce migrant), and Malta (very scarce visitor – almost annual, but large influx noted in 1977, with flocks of up to 50 in late June-July).

PALLAS'S ROSEFINCH   *Carpodacus roseus*   A 53

L 16cm (6.25"). Asia. Accidental. Only two records in 19th century and two recent records.

Adult male: Easily identified by the largely pinkish-red plumage, with glistening pinkish-white on the forehead and throat. Shows heavily streaked mantle/scapulars and has broad, pale, double wing-bars and edges to the tertials.

Adult female: Readily distinguished from female Scarlet Rosefinch by its obviously more heavily streaked head, mantle/scapulars and underparts, and pink on the forehead, throat/breast, back/rump, and often also on the uppertail-coverts. In some individuals the pink on the forehead and particularly on the throat/breast is rather indistinct. The pale edges to the tertials are more distinct than in Scarlet (most pronounced near tips in Scarlet).

1st-winter/-summer: Appears to be indistinguishable from the adult female by plumage.

Voice: The call has been reported to bear some resemblance to the high piercing note of Dunnock.

Range: Breeds in C and E Siberia (range imperfectly known). It winters in the S parts of the breeding range to Mongolia, NE China and Korea and a few in Japan.

Status: Accidental in Britain: Orkney, N Ronaldsay, female or 1st-summer male (early June to 14th July 1988*); Denmark: Blåvandshuk, W Jutland, adult male (12th Oct 1987), Czechoslovakia (1); Hungary (Dec 1850). Since not particularly migratory and known to occur as a cage bird in Europe, it is quite possible that the records (particularly the recent ones) relate to escapes.

LONG-TAILED ROSEFINCH   *Uragus sibiricus*   A 58

L 13-15cm (5.5"). Asia. Recently seen in Finland (spring).

All plumages: A rather small, long-tailed finch with a short, bullfinch-like bill. Shows prominent double wing bars, pale edges to the tertials and has three pairs of outer tail feathers white.

Adult male: Unmistakable. Mostly pinkish-red (paler in winter, especially on head/mantle), with heavily streaked mantle and scapulars. In worn plumage, especially, the supercilium, ear-coverts and throat are contrastingly pale pink.

Adult female: Heavily streaked on the mantle/scapulars and more finely streaked on the head and underparts. The rump-area is usually pink and unstreaked, and sometimes there is a hint of pink on the ear-coverts, throat and breast.

1st-winter/-summer male: Rather variable, some are mostly like the adult male, and some are like the adult female, but usually with a little more pink on the head/breast. A moult contrast can usually be seen among the greater coverts, a few outer, juvenile, ones being browner-centred and more worn. The juvenile tertials are also often retained.

1st-winter/-summer female: Like the adult female but probably never shows any pink on the head and breast, and a moult contrast similar to that of 1st-year male can often be found.

Voice: The song is a hurried, short, rather clear, repeated verse, which could be transcribed *tsitsuitsu tuitsi-tuitsi-tuitsi-tuitsi*. Calls with a slightly metallic *pink*.

Range: Breeds in S Siberia and N Mongolia east to Sakhalin and Japan, Ussuriland, also in NE, NW, central China and SE Tibet.

Status: Accidental in Finland: Kustavi, immature male, 25th-27th Apr 1989*.

EVENING GROSBEAK *Coccothraustes vespertinus* A **53**

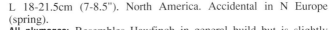

L 18-21.5cm (7-8.5"). North America. Accidental in N Europe (spring).

All plumages: Resembles Hawfinch in general build but is slightly larger. The huge bill is greenish-yellow to yellow.

Adult male: Unmistakable. Contrastingly patterned in brown, yellow, black and white. The large white area in the wing is even more conspicuous in flight.

Adult female: Mostly greyish above and pale below, generally with some yellowish-green on the side of the neck and often elsewhere. Wing pattern resembles the adult male, but shows less white on inner wing, and has a white patch at base of the primaries. The primaries, uppertail-coverts and tail are broadly tipped white, unlike the male.

1st-winter/-summer male: Similar to the adult male, but shows slightly browner and more-worn flight-feathers and primary coverts. The latter usually show narrow paler tips, and the outer primaries frequently show pale edges. Usually has dusky edges to the inner webs of the tertials and often whitish tips to the outer rectrices. The outer greater coverts may be unmoulted and contrast with the inners. Some of the retained coverts may show distinct, pale yellowish spots on their tips. Also has more pointed and worn tail-feathers.

1st-winter/-summer female: Resembles the adult female but shows the same moult contrast in the wings and the same shape of the tail-feathers as 1st-winter male.

Voice: The song is similar in pattern to Hawfinch's, rather simple and mainly consisting of call-notes, a rather irregular *brreit, breeit, pcheeu*. It calls with a slightly hoarse and metallic *pcheeu*.

Range: Breeds in the S half of Canada and in W and NE USA. Northern populations are migratory, some wintering as far south as S USA.

Status: Accidental in Britain: St Kilda, Outer Hebrides, male (26th Mar 1969); Highland, Nethybridge, female (10th-25th Mar 1980). Norway: Østfold, male (2nd-9th May 1973), Sør-Trondelag, male (17th-26th May 1975).

Family PARULIDAE . American Wood Warblers

BLACK-AND-WHITE WARBLER *Mniotilta varia*   B 54

L 11.5-13cm (4.75"). North America. Accidental in N Europe (mainly autumn).

All plumages: Readily identified by black-and-white, heavily striped plumage. Note white median crown-stripe and supercilium, bare face and dark-spotted undertail-coverts. Shows white spots on tips of outer tail feathers.

Adult male summer: Shows black throat, rather extensive black on the ear-coverts and blackish streaking on the sides of the breast/flanks. The primary coverts, alula and remiges contrast very little with the centres of the greater coverts.

Adult male winter: As summer, with white (often dark-spotted) throat.

Adult female: Distinguished from the adult male by much paler ear-coverts and obviously paler and more diffuse streaking to the sides of the breast/flanks. The rear flanks are generally pale brownish. In summer, also by its white throat.

1st-winter/-summer male: Resembles the adult male but the primary coverts, alula and remiges are slightly but still appreciably browner than the greater coverts. In 1st-winter the ear-coverts are paler (like female). Tail-feathers more pointed than in adult (see figure).

1st-winter/-summer female: Resembles the adult female, but the primary coverts, alula and remiges are slightly browner than the greater coverts, although the contrast is less pronounced than in 1st-winter/-summer males. Tail-feathers more pointed than in adult (see figure).

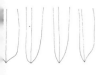

Voice: The song is very high-pitched and thin. Often begins with *chik*, followed by a shuttling *s(u)ee-s(u)ee-s(u)ee-s(u)ee-s(u)ee-s(u)ee-s(u)ee uee uee tee-tee-tee*; *t' seet-t' seet-t' syyt-t' syyt-t' syyt-sisi* or similar, and slightly reminiscent of the song of Treecreeper. Also *t' seet-t' seet-t' seet-t' seet-t' seet-t' seet*. The call is a hard *tik* and a thin *tzit*.

ad.   1st-year

typical outer and central tail-feather in wood warblers

Behaviour: Has distinctive nuthatch-like habit of creeping along branches and often up and down tree trunks.

Range: Breeds in E USA and Canada. Winters from SE USA to N South America.

Status: Accidental in Iceland (1), Faeroes (July 1984), Britain (9, Sept-Dec, once in Mar), and Ireland (Cape Clear, Co Cork, 18th Oct 1978; Loughermore Forest, Co Derry, 30th Sept-2nd Oct 1984).

GOLDEN-WINGED WARBLER *Vermivora chrysoptera*   A 54

L 11.5-12.5cm (4.5-5"). North America. Recently in Britain (one successfully over-wintered).

All plumages: A very distinctive warbler, which is not likely to be confused with any other species. Note the dark throat and eye-mask; uniformly blue-grey upperparts; unstreaked, whitish or pale grey underparts; yellow or greenish-yellow patch on the forehead/fore-

388

crown; and very broad yellow wing bars, almost forming a panel on the coverts. The outer tail feathers show much white.

Adult male: The face mask and throat are black (tipped grey when fresh in autumn), and the patch on the forehead/forecrown is bright yellow.

Adult female: The black parts are grey, and the patch on the forehead/forecrown is greenish-yellow.

1st-winter/-summer: Like adult of respective sex and only told with care by the more pointed rectrices (see figure).

Voice: The song has a buzzing-like quality; typically gives a *zee* followed by several short *bee* notes, given at a lower pitch. Call is a *chip*.

Range: Breeds in NE USA, range just extending into SE Canada. Winters from Central America south to N Colombia and N Venezuela.

Status: Accidental in Britain: Larkfield, Maidstone, Kent, male from 24th Jan-10th Apr 1989. This individual presumably arrived in Europe the previous autumn and fortuitously survived because of an unusually mild winter.

TENNESSEE WARBLER *Vermivora peregrina* A **54**

L 12cm (4.75"). North America. Accidental in N Europe (autumn).

All plumages: Especially 1st-winter birds could be confused with some *Phylloscopus* warblers, but the very pointed bill with pale grey lower mandible is diagnostic. Some birds, possibly only adults, show a rather prominent whitish patch on the outermost tail-feather.

Adult male: Shows grey crown/nape and ear-coverts. Also has a rather diffuse and not very long, whitish supercilium. Upperparts are green, and underparts are mainly whitish, with a trace of yellow. In winter, the grey of the head is often (perhaps usually) partly replaced by greenish.

Adult female: Resembles the adult male summer, but shows some greenish on the crown. Also, has a slightly yellowish-tinged supercilium and ear-coverts and more yellowish-tinged underparts. In winter plumage it is even greener on the head and more yellow below and thus very similar to 1st-winter (see below). There is possibly some overlap between the plumage of the adult male and female in summer, and in winter many males are indistinguishable from female .

1st-winter: Green above and mainly yellowish below (belly and under-tail-coverts usually whitish). Shows a rather ill-defined yellowish supercilium and dark eye-stripe, and often has a rather distinct pale wing-bar. Difficult to tell from the adult (female), but the rectrices are slightly more pointed.

1st-summer: Resembles the adult of its respective sex and is very difficult to distinguish. The slightly more pointed and more worn rectrices and outer primaries may be of some help.

Voice: The song is a *psit psit psit psit-psit-psit-psit-psit-psit-sit-sit-sit-sit-sit-sit-sit-sit-sit-sit-sit-sit-sit-sit*, with the second part of the song slightly lower-pitched than the first ('accelerating and changing gear').

Range: Breeds in Canada and northeastern USA. Winters from Mexico to N South America. Vagrant to Greenland.

Status: Accidental in Iceland (1); Faeroes (21st-29th Sept 1984); Britain, Shetland, Fair Isle (from 6th-20th and another on 24th Sept 1975), Orkney (5th-7th Sept 1982).

NORTHERN PARULA   *Parula americana*   B **54**

L 11.5cm (4.5"). North America. Accidental.

Adult male: Easily identified by small size and bright, very characteristic plumage. Shows a largely greyish-blue head and upperparts
with contrasting yellowish-green mantle. Also shows a bright yellow
throat/breast with a dark band across the lower throat, deep rufous
breast band and often patches of rufous on the upper flanks. The lores
are normally blackish. In fresh winter plumage, head and upperparts
are greenish-tinged and the dark lores and dark/rufous pattern of the
throat/breast is less distinct. The alula, primary coverts and remiges
show distinct bluish edges (secondaries very faintly greenish-tinged
when fresh) and hardly contrast with the greater coverts. Shows white
spots on outer tail feathers.

Adult female: In spring/summer readily identified from male as it lacks
or only shows a very indistinct dark band across the lower throat and an
indistinct rufous band across the breast. It also usually shows pale lores
with a narrow dark streak. In the autumn, some bright individuals can
be confused with less well-marked 1st-winter males. Sometimes, even
the edges of the remiges are greenish-tinged (usually bluish, though).
The alula and primary coverts have distinct bluish edges (cf. 1st-winter
male, below), and the tail feathers are more rounded at the tips.

1st-winter/-summer male: Basically like the adult male but with more
greenish edges to the central alula feather and primary coverts. On the
latter the pale edges are also more indistinct than in the adult. The primaries are faintly, and the secondaries distinctly, greenish-tinged. The
edges to the alula, primary coverts and remiges contrast with the bluish
edges to the newly moulted greater coverts. The tail-feathers are also
slightly more pointed (see figure), and especially in spring/summer

ad.   1st-year
(extremes)

they are generally slightly more worn than in the adult.

1st-winter/-summer female: Like dult female, but central alula feather,
primary coverts and remiges distinctly greenish-edged, contrasting
with bluish-edged greater coverts. Tail as in 1st-year male (see figure).

Voice: The song is a very fast, buzzy, metallic trill that ends abruptly
with a short *zeep*.

Range: Breeds in E USA and SE Canada. Winters chiefly in S Florida,
Mexico, Central America and the West Indies. Vagrant to Greenland.

Status: Accidental in Iceland (4); Britain (13, Sept-Nov); Ireland: Co
Cork, Firkeel (19th-24th Oct 1983), Dursey Is (25th Sept 1989) and
France (Ouessant, 17th-27th Oct 1987).

YELLOW WARBLER   *Dendroica petechia*   A **55**

L 13cm (5"). Americas. Accidental.

All plumages: Basically greenish above and yellow below, with an unmarked, 'mild' face, often with a yellow eye-ring. The inner webs to
the outer rectrices are largely yellow, which is diagnostic (from below,
tail looks yellow with dark edges and tip). Indistinct, yellow wing-bars
often formed. See also female Wilson's Warbler (p. 402).

Adult male: Shows largely yellow head with greenish rear crown/nape.
In autumn the forehead/crown and ear-coverts are also washed greenish. Shows distinct reddish-brown streaks on breast/flanks.

1st-year
♀
(extremes)

Adult female: Duller than the adult male, with greenish forehead/fore-crown. Shows indistinct, reddish-brown streaks on breast/flanks (often lacking altogether, usually in winter).

1st-winter male: Very similar to the adult female, but the yellowish edge of the juvenile central alula feather is usually duller and the dark centre often obviously more brownish than on the newly moulted carpal covert and greater coverts. The tertials are apparently not normally moulted and are more worn, with more whitish edges than in the adult (yellowish in latter). The rectrices are usually more pointed than in the adult (see figure), generally with less extensive and contrasting yellow on the outer feathers.

1st-summer male: Similar to the adult male, but shows more worn alula and primary coverts with less distinct yellowish edges. The remiges and rectrices are also generally more worn than in the adult. Note that both 1st-summer and adult summer show newly moulted inner greater coverts, contrasting with the outers.

1st-winter/-summer female: Resembles the adult female but tends to be even duller. In 1st-winter usually, and in 1st-summer often lacks the reddish-brown streaking below. Other differences are as for 1st-winter male. The outer tail feathers are generally even less extensively yellow than in the latter (see figure).

Voice: The song is a clear, variable, *suee-suee-suee-suee tu-tu-tu-eeh* (recalling Treecreeper), *suee-suee-suee-suee uee-duee-duee*, and similar, sometimes recalling a fast and short Willow Warbler song. The call is a rather full, soft *tsep*.

Range: Breeds in North America, except the most S and SE parts and most northern areas. Also breeds in West Indies and from Mexico to N South America. North American populations winter from S Mexico to N South America.

Status: Accidental in Britain: Gwynedd, Bardsey Is on 29th Aug 1964; Lerwick, Shetland from 3rd-4th Nov 1990*.

CHESTNUT-SIDED WARBLER *Dendroica pensylvanica* A 55

L 13cm (5"). North America. One record in autumn.

All plumages: Shows broad, pale yellowish wing-bars and white spots on outer tail-feathers.

Adult male summer: Unmistakable. Diagnostic head pattern with greenish-yellow crown, and black eye-stripe, supercilium, nape and 'moustachial stripe'. Has obvious chestnut stripe on breast-sides/flanks.

Adult male winter: The plumage is very different from summer but still distinctive. Mainly bright green above with faint streaking (extensive blackish centres mostly concealed), and unstreaked below with some distinct chestnut on the flanks. Further characterized by very distinctive facial pattern, showing grey ear-coverts and lores sharply contrasting with bright green crown and a distinct whitish eye-ring.

Adult female summer: Resembles the adult male summer but is duller, with a less distinct head pattern and shows reduced chestnut on the flanks. May be very similar to 1st-summer male.

Adult female winter: Similar to adult male winter but with little or no chestnut on the flanks. Tends to show less extensive and slightly duller blackish centres to upperparts (can only be judged in the hand).

ad.   1st-year
(extremes)

1st-winter male: Very similar to adult female winter, but usually has slightly more pointed tail feathers (see figure). Many are intermediate.
1st-winter female: Like 1st-winter male, but with apparently never any chestnut on the flanks, and the dark centres to the upperparts tend to be less distinct. Note that most 1st-winters cannot be sexed, and it is usually difficult to distinguish between 1st-winter and adult winter.
1st-summer: Resembles the adult summer of its respective sex, but tends to be slightly duller. Some males can be confused with adult females. The shape of the rectrices is as in 1st-winter birds, although this may be even more difficult to judge because of heavy wear (generally more worn than in adult). The primary coverts, alula and remiges are browner and more worn and generally contrast slightly more with the greater coverts than in the adult. Both adult and 1st-summer generally show a moult contrast among the greater coverts.
Voice: The song is a clear, variable verse, e.g. *seeseesee-tititutiu...tuee-tuee-tuee-tuee-tutitui*.
Range: Breeds in SE Canada and NE USA. Winters in Central America. Vagrant in Greenland (Sept 1974).
Status: Accidental in Britain: Shetland, Fetlar, 1st-winter on 20th Sept 1985.

BLACK-THROATED BLUE WARBLER *Dendroica caerulescens*   A **55**
L 12-14cm (5.25"). North America. Recently recorded in Iceland (autumn).
Adult male: Unmistakable. Has dark blue upperside; black sides to the head, throat, sides of breast and upper flanks, and contrasting white underparts. Shows conspicuous white patch at base of primaries. Outer tail feathers usually show conspicuous whitish patches (see figure).
Adult female: Distinctive, showing rather dark, uniformly greyish olive-green upperparts, pale dusky yellow underside and a usually prominent whitish patch at the base of the primaries. The head pattern is also typical, showing well-defined dark ear-coverts and a narrow, whitish supercilium and broken eye-ring.
1st-winter/-summer male: Like adult male, but with a slight greenish tinge above when fresh in the autumn, and the alula, primary coverts and remiges have greyish or greenish edges, contrasting markedly with the blue-edged greater coverts. Sometimes the lores and chin are pale.
1st-winter/-summer female: Like adult female, with slightly duller and more brownish-tinged edges to the alula, primary-coverts and remiges, contrasting very slightly with the more greenish-tinged greater coverts. The pale patch at the base of the primaries is occasionally lacking altogether. The rectrices are slightly more pointed than in the adult.
Voice: The song is a lazy *zwee-azwee-a zwee-a zweee*. The call is a rather soft, full *'tsep'*.
Range: Breeds in SE Canada and NE USA. Winters primarily in the West Indies.
Status: Accidental in Iceland: Heimaey, Westman Is, adult male from 14th-19th Sept 1988.

BLACK-THROATED GREEN WARBLER *Dendroica virens* A 56

L 13cm (5"). North America. Accidental (autumn).

All plumages: Green, unstreaked or very faintly streaked upperside. Shows a prominent yellow supercilium, neck sides and at least sides of the throat, surrounding more greenish-tinged ear-coverts. The central throat ranges from all-black (adult male) to pale with only a little dark on the sides of lower part (1st-winter female). Shows double, broad, whitish wing-bars, and mostly white outer tail-feathers (see figure).

Adult male: Shows black chin, throat and upper breast (with narrow pale fringes in winter plumage) and rather heavy blackish streaking on the flanks.

Adult female: Resembles the adult male, but shows less black on the throat and generally less-blackish streaks on the flanks.

1st-winter male: Very similar to the adult female, but shows slightly paler and browner primary coverts and alula, contrasting slightly with the blacker centres to the greater coverts (hardly any contrast in adult). The tail feathers tend to be slightly more pointed (see figure).

1st-summer male: Resembles the adult male, differing in the same way as between 1st-winter male and adult female. The remiges, rectrices and primary coverts are generally more worn than in the adult.

1st-winter/-summer female: Resembles the adult male but differs in the same way as for 1st-winter male, although less clearly. In 1st-winter plumage it generally shows a less-dark throat/upper breast than the 1st-winter male; also tends to show less-blackish streaking on the flanks. On average it shows less white on the inner web of the third outermost rectrix. Many 1st-winters are probably not reliably sexed.

1st-year ♀
(extremes)

Voice: The song is a characteristic, *tzzee tzzyy tee-tee-tyh* or similar, often preceded by fast, irregular, ticking notes; the *tzzee* and *tzzyy* recall the drawn-out final note in Yellowhammer's song.

Note: There are two other North American warblers, Townsend's *D. townsendi* and Golden-cheeked *D. chrysoparia*, that could be confused with Black-throated Green. On geographical grounds they are unlikely to occur in Europe. The former is best told by its distinctly darker ear-coverts and yellow breast, the latter by yellower ear-coverts with dark eye-stripe.

Range: Breeds from C to E Canada, NE USA and in the mountains of E USA. Winters mainly in Mexico, Central America and the West Indies. Vagrants have reached Greenland on 3 occasions.

Status: Accidental in Iceland: one found dead on board ship, 19th Sept 1984. West Germany: Heligoland, adult male, 19th Nov 1858.

BLACKBURNIAN WARBLER *Dendroica fusca* A 56

L 13cm (5"). North America. Accidental (autumn).

Adult male summer: Unmistakable. Shows bright orange throat, crown patch, supercilium and neck sides, contrasting strongly with the black ear-coverts and rest of the crown/nape. The upperparts are black with distinct pale stripes on the mantle, and the coverts show a prominent white panel. The outer two-three pairs of tail feathers are mostly white (see figure, p. 394)

Adult male winter: The plumage is basically duller, with yellow rather than orange and dark grey rather than black (i.e. black centres are partly concealed by paler fringes), and the white wing panel is reduced to

ad. ♂   1st-year ♂

1st-year ♀

(extremes)

broad, double wing bars. The pattern of the head and upperparts is still very distinctive and characteristic.

Adult female: In summer plumage differs from the adult male in its more yellow head pattern, olive-grey or grey base colour above and shows double white wing bars. In winter plumage it is more difficult to tell from the adult male winter. However, the feathers of the ear-coverts and upperside have paler, olive-greyish instead of blackish, centres, and the streaks on the underparts are generally slightly fainter.

1st-winter male: Like the adult male winter but generally does not show quite so blackish-centred feathers above and on the ear-coverts. There is also a contrast between the newly moulted, blackish-centred, greater coverts and the retained juvenile, slightly browner-centred, alula, primary coverts and flight feathers. The moult contrast also distinguishes 1st-winter male from adult female. Shows slightly more pointed tail feathers than in the adult (see figure).

1st-summer male: Differs from the adult male in the moult contrast described above (note, however, that both adult and 1st-summer usually show a moult contrast among the greater coverts). Sometimes, also shows double wing bars rather than a distinct wing panel.

1st-winter/-summer female: Like adult female, but generally even duller and shows a moult contrast in the wings as in 1st-year male but less pronounced. The rectrices are also slightly more tapered (see figure).

Voice: The song is a rather thin, high *trip-trip-trip-trip, tzeeer see see, te-siti siti sip...* Call a rich *chip*.

Range: Breeds in SE Canada and E USA. Winters in Central and South America. Accidental in Greenland.

Status: Accidental in Iceland: At sea, 1st-winter female found exhausted on trawler, *c*. 65km N of NW Iceland in Oct 1987. Britain: Skomer Is, Dyfed on 5th Oct 1961, and Fair Isle, Shetland, 1st-winter male on 7th Oct 1988.

CAPE MAY WARBLER *Dendroica tigrina*   A 55

L 13cm (5"). North America. One record of a singing male in June.

Adult male summer: Easily identified. Shows greenish to more greyish upperparts and a variably streaked mantle, which may look rather plain when fresh (heavily streaked when worn). Also, has contrasting yellow back/rump and yellow underside with heavily streaked breast/flanks. Shows blackish crown and a yellow supercilium (may be chestnut above/behind eye) and sides to the neck, framing the chestnut ear-coverts. Has bold white wing panel. Note also tail pattern (see figure).

Adult male winter: As adult summer but lacks or only shows very little chestnut on the ear-coverts, and black of crown is largely concealed by green fringes.

Adult female: Much less yellow and less distinctly streaked below than the adult male. Less heavily marked above (notably on crown), with more yellowish-green rump area than in the adult male. Also, lacks chestnut on the ear-coverts and shows two whitish wing-bars rather than a whitish wing panel.

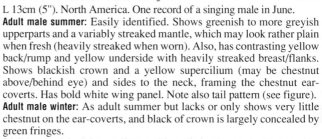

ad. ♂   1st-year ♀

1st-winter/-summer male: Similar to the adult male, but normally lacks or shows less chestnut on the ear-coverts (1st-winter and 1st-summer, respectively). Also tends to show less extensive dark centres to the crown and mantle. The primary coverts, alula and remiges are slightly paler and browner and contrast with the blacker centres to the greater coverts. In 1st-summer birds especially, primary coverts, alula and remiges are also generally slightly more worn than the adult. It generally shows slightly more pointed rectrices (normally more worn than adult in spring/summer; see figure, p. 394).

1st-winter/-summer female: Resembles the adult female but is distinguished by the same wing/tail characters as for 1st-winter and adult males, although the contrast in the wing is less obvious than in males. The third outermost rectrix normally lacks white (adult female usually has a small whitish spot).

Some 1st-winter females are very grey and white, without any noticeable yellow on the underparts or neck sides and only show a little yellowish-green on the rump. They might be confused with Yellow-rumped Warbler, but are easily distinguished by e.g. different shape and head pattern, greyer, not so brown, and less heavily streaked upperparts, not so distinct and bright yellow rump, and lack the yellow patch at the breast sides shown by most Yellow-rumped.

Voice: The song is a very high-pitched, *seet seet seet seet seet*, with the volume increasing slightly. The call is a rather hard, high-pitched, thin *tsip*.

Range: Breeds from NW-C to E Canada and extreme NE USA. Winters chiefly in the West Indies.

Status: Accidental in Britain: Paisley, Strathclyde, singing male (17th June 1977).

MAGNOLIA WARBLER   *Dendroica magnolia*   A 55

L 13cm (5"). North America. One record in autumn from Britain.

All plumages: Shows diagnostic tail pattern, with broad, blackish tips and a white subterminal bar to all except the central pair of tail feathers (see figure). Folded tail from below shows broad blackish terminal bar and broad white subterminal bar.

Adult male summer: Very distinctive. Shows black lores and ear-coverts, contrasting with grey crown/nape and a distinct white supercilium above and behind the eye. Has mostly black upperparts with a contrasting yellow rump. The underside is yellow with black streaks on the breast/flanks, and the wings show a bold white pattern.

Adult male winter: The black on the upperparts is mostly concealed by greenish, and the head/neck (except throat) are greyish. There is less white on the greater coverts than in summer plumage, forming a distinct wing-bar rather than a white panel.

1st-year ♀
(extremes)

The combination of greyish crown/nape/ear-coverts with a pale eye-ring, greenish mantle and scapulars (generally rather poorly marked), yellow rump, yellow underside with more or less distinct streaking on the breast/flanks and distinct, whitish double wing-bars easily distinguishes all birds in winter plumage from other North American warblers.

Adult female summer: Similar to the adult male summer, but separable by the less black lores and ear-coverts, green mantle and scapulars with blackish streaks, slightly finer and fainter dark streaking on the breast/flanks, and generally less white on the greater coverts. Some are very similar to less advanced 1st-summer males.

Adult female winter: Generally shows narrower, blackish centres (streaks) to the mantle/scapulars (can only be judged in the hand) and slightly finer and fainter streaking below than in the adult male winter.
1st-winter: Very similar to the adult female winter but has slightly paler and browner alula, primary coverts and flight feathers, contrasting more with more blackish-centred, newly moulted, greater coverts (contrast often most easily noted between central alula and carpal covert/outer greater coverts). Shows slightly more pointed rectrices (see figure, p. 395).

1st-winter males tend to have more extensive and more blackish centres to the mantle/scapulars and uppertail-coverts and more blackish streaking on the underparts than the 1st-winter female. Some even approach the adult male. Only the extremes are safely sexed.
1st-summer: Resembles the adult summer of its respective sex, but on average it is slightly duller, with browner and more worn alula, primary coverts and remiges. Also shows more pointed and more worn rectrices. Both adult and 1st-summer show a moult contrast among the greater coverts.
Voice: The song is clear, variable and rather fast, e.g. *vitiu-vitiu-vitiu-vitiu-viTIU...seeu-seeu-veeSU...visu-visu-viSUtitititiTIU....* The call is a rather hard, high-pitched *dzip*.
Range: Breeds in large parts of Canada and in NE USA. Winters in Mexico, Central America and the West Indies. Vagrant to Greenland.
Status: Accidental in Britain: Isles of Scilly, on 27th-28th Sept 1981.

YELLOW-RUMPED WARBLER *Dendroica coronata* B 56

L 14cm (5.5"). North America. Accidental (mainly late autumn).
Adult male summer: Easily identified by its blue-grey, distinctly streaked upperside with contrasting yellow rump and yellow patch on the crown (latter may be concealed). Shows whitish underside with distinct blackish streaking (usually forming complete breast band) and a yellow patch on the sides of the breast/upper flanks. Also note distinctive head pattern. The three outermost pairs of tail-feathers show white spots (see figure).
Adult male winter: Basically as in summer, but is browner on the head and upperparts, with less obvious streaking above/below. It is very similar to 1st-winter males and females in winter plumage (see below).

All birds in winter plumage are separable from other North American warblers by combination of brown upperparts (generally rather distinctly streaked), clearcut yellow rump, whitish underside with streaked breast/flanks (of variable prominence) and usually a yellow patch on the breast sides. Note also its distinctive head pattern (yellow crown patch is usually concealed and may be lacking at least in 1st-winter female). The bill is comparatively short and the tail relatively long.

nominate race

Adult female summer: Browner above than the adult male summer, with paler and browner ear-coverts, and shows less heavy streaking on the breast (often not forming a complete breast band).
Adult female winter: Generally not safely separable from the adult male winter, but tends to be slightly duller and browner. Usually shows smaller blackish centres to the mantle, scapulars and uppertail-coverts

and on average less prominent streaking on the underparts. The fringes to the uppertail-coverts tend to be browner than in the adult male.

1st-winter: Similar to a winter adult female, but has marginally contrastingly paler and browner alula, primary coverts and remiges (generally most obvious between central alula and carpal covert/outer greater coverts). 1st-winter female tends to show less distinct streaking above/below than male of same age and may even lack yellow on the breast sides. 1st-winter female is further said generally to show white on the outermost two pairs of tail feathers (normally three in 1st-winter male). Although the extremes may be sexed, most 1st-winter birds are not reliably sexed.

1st-summer: Resembles the adult summer of its respective sex, but has browner and more worn remiges, primary coverts and alula. On average, the plumage is also slightly duller. Both 1st-summer and adult normally show newly moulted inner greater coverts.

Voice: The song is a clear *tuee tuee tuee tuee tuee tuee tuee-tu-du-du-du*, or similar. The call is a rather hard *tick*, *tyck* or *tip*. Also may give a sharp, thin *tsi*.

Note: Western birds, subspecies *auduboni*, 'Audubon's Warbler', usually show at least some yellow on the throat, and the pale throat normally does not reach onto the sides of the neck as in the nominate race. Furthermore, it shows more white in the tail (white on four to five outer tail-feathers). In summer they also have less contrastingly dark ear-coverts/lores, but lack the nominate race's supercilium, and usually show more white in wings.

Range: Breeds in Alaska, Canada, W and extreme NE USA. Winters in much of E and S USA and along the Pacific coast of USA.

Status: Accidental in Iceland (7), and British Isles (17, mainly Oct, but once in Sept and twice in May-June and a wintering bird was in Devon from 4th Jan-10th Feb 1955). The records are usually comparatively late in the season, which reflects its late migration in North America.

PALM WARBLER *Dendroica palmarum* A 56

L 13cm (5"). North America. Accidental in Britain (once in spring).

Adult summer: Easily identified by olive-brown, rather faintly streaked upperparts, contrasting with chestnut forehead/crown and greenish-tinged back/rump and uppertail-coverts. Shows a distinct yellow supercilium and yellow underside with a fine, generally chestnut malar stripe and streaking on breast/flanks. The wing-bars are comparatively indistinct. The outer tail-feathers show white spots (see figure).

Adult winter: Browner above and generally slightly paler yellow below and on the supercilium than in summer. Some are very dull on the supercilium and underparts, with contrasting yellow undertail-coverts. The chestnut of the crown is concealed by brown, and the streaks on the underside are less chestnut.

1st-winter/-summer: Apparently very difficult to distinguish from adult.

Voice: The song is a slightly harsh, buzzing, mechanical trill, e.g. *suee-suee-suee-suee-suee-suee-suee*, sometimes very fast and then often recalling one variant of the song of Yellowhammer (except for the last note). Call, a rather hard *tsep* or *chik*.

Behaviour: Usually terrestrial. Habitually pumps its tail.

Range: Breeds from C-NW to E Canada and extreme NE USA. Winters from SE USA to central America and the West Indies.
Status: Accidental in Britain: Cumbria, Walney Is, remains of a male found on tide-line on 18th May 1976.

BLACKPOLL WARBLER *Dendroica striata* B **56**

L 13cm (5"). North America. Rare vagrant in NW Europe (autumn).
Adult male summer: Unmistakable. Shows a solidly black cap, white ear-coverts and underparts, with heavy blackish streaking to the breast-sides and flanks, and black sides to the throat. The upperparts are brownish-grey with strong, blackish streaking on the mantle/scapulars. Shows double wingbars and whitish edges to the tertials. The outer two or three pairs of tail-feathers show large, white spots.
Adult male winter: Has greyish-green upperside with faint to moderate dark streaking, and dull yellowish throat/breast, fading on the flanks and becoming whitish on the undertail-coverts. Shows faint streaking below, mainly on the breast-sides. Usually shows an indistinct, dull yellowish supercilium and dark eye-stripe. Has double, whitish wing-bars and whitish edges to the tertials. Also, pale to rather dark brown tarsus, usually pale brown toes and yellowish-brown soles. It is extremely similar to 1st-winter male and females in winter plumage.
Adult female summer: Easily distinguished from the male summer by the greyish-green crown and ear-coverts, with distinct dark streaking on the former, and lack of black throat-sides.
Adult female winter: Not safely distinguished from the winter adult male by plumage, but on average is more finely streaked above.
1st-winter: Resembles the adult winter, but can be told by its slightly contrastingly paler and browner alula, primary coverts and remiges. Also generally shows more pointed rectrices. The 1st-winter male is on average slightly more distinctly streaked above than the adult or 1st-winter female, but it is generally not safely distinguished (except from the former in the hand).
1st-summer: Resembles the adult summer of its respective sex, but separable with care by more worn and more contrastingly brown alula, primary coverts and remiges. Also, normally shows more pointed and more worn rectrices than the adult. Both adult and 1st-summer normally show a moult contrast among the greater coverts.
Voice: The song is an exceptionally high-pitched *si-si-si-si-si-si-si-si-si-si-si-si-si-si-si*, increasing and fading in volume. The call is a rather hard *tsip*, similar to Cape May Warbler.
Note: The Bay-breasted Warbler *D. castanea*, is a possible future candidate for vagrancy to Europe. In winter plumage it is very similar to Blackpoll, but is generally slightly more vividly greenish above, and the underside is rather evenly pale buffish, often unstreaked, and frequently shows pale chestnut on the flanks. Also, shows hardly any supercilium or eye-stripe; has pale bluish rather than yellowish-greenish edges to the remiges; and Garden Warbler-like grey tarsus, toes and soles. In the hand, easily separated by its emarginated 6th-8th primaries (only 7th-8th in Blackpoll).
Range: Breeds from W Alaska across C Canada to Newfoundland. Winters in South America.

Status: Rare vagrant in Iceland (6). British Isles (26, Sept-Oct, 17 of these records are from the Isles of Scilly), Channel Islands, Sark (Oct-Nov 1980) and France (Ouessant Oct 1990*).

AMERICAN REDSTART   *Setophaga ruticilla*   B 57

L 13cm (5.25"). North America. Accidental (autumn).

All plumages: Shows diagnostic tail pattern. Has distinctive jizz and habits (see below).

Adult male: Glossy black with pale belly to undertail-coverts and shows extensive orange on the wings/tail and breast sides.

Adult female: Dull greyish-green above with a greyish head. Whitish below with a yellow to pale orangey patch at the breast sides. Shows some yellow to the bases of the secondaries, also often to the bases of the primaries and yellow on the tail.

1st-winter/-summer male: Resembles the adult female, but often shows some blackish mottling, primarily in 1st-summer plumage. Seems to show prominent yellow at the base of the primaries more often than the adult female.

1st-winter/-summer female: Very similar to the adult female but does not regularly show any orange tinge to the breast side patches. It generally lacks or shows very little yellow on the inner web of the third innermost tail-feather (usually all-yellow inner half in adult female). Often lacks the yellow patch on the secondaries (also some adult females?).

Voice: The song is a high-pitched, lisping *see-see-see-see-see see-sir* (the *see* immediately preceding the *sir* is slightly higher than the other notes). Call, a rather hard clicking *tsip* and a rather thin *tzit*.

♂   1st-year
♀

Habitat and Behaviour: Arboreal. Moves about in tree foliage with a rather flitting action, often springing at insects in the air. The wings are often slightly drooped and the tail is frequently slightly raised and often fanned.

Range: Breeds from SE Alaska, W Canada and NW USA across S Canada to Newfoundland and in E USA. Winters from extreme SE USA to N South America.

Status: Accidental in Iceland (1), Britain (5, Oct-Dec), Ireland, Co Cork (Oct 1968, Oct 1985), France (Ouessant, Oct 1961), and near the Azores (5th Oct and 14th Oct 1967).

OVENBIRD   *Seiurus aurocapillus*   A 57

L 14-15.5cm (5.75"). North America. Accidental in British Isles (autumn to winter).

Adult: Unmistakable. Mainly greenish-brown above and shows a brownish-orange median crown-stripe, bordered by blackish stripes. Has pale underparts with heavy, rather 'pipit-like' streaking on breast/flanks.

Juvenile: More buffish below with more indistinct streaking than subsequent plumages. Also shows an indistinct crown pattern, faintly streaked upperparts and distinct double wing-bars. This plumage is very unlikely to be recorded outside the breeding areas.

1st-winter: Separable from the adult in showing narrow, rufous tips to the unmoulted tertials (when not too worn) and has slightly more pointed rectrices.

Voice: The song is a monotonous *pitsu-pitsu-pitsu-pitsu-pitsu-pitsu-pitsu- pitsu-pitsu*; *seteet-seteet-seteet-seteet-seteet-seteet-seteet-seteet-seteet*; *titiu-titiu-titiu-titiu..*, or similar, somewhat recalling the song of Marsh Tit. The call is a clicking *tsek* or *tsyt*.

Habitat and behaviour: Terrestrial, usually skulks in rather dense scrub. Typically walks on the ground searching among leaf litter. Has a characteristic habit of bobbing its rear body/tail.

Range: Breeds from C-NW to E Canada (including Newfoundland) and in E USA. Winters from Mexico to South America and in the Caribbean. Vagrant in Greenland.

Status: Accidental in Britain: Shetland, Out Skerries (7th-8th Oct 1973); Devon, Wembury, one found freshly dead (22nd Oct 1985); Formby, Merseyside, tideline wing found (4th Jan 1969). Ireland: Lough Carra Forest, Co. Mayo, one found dead (8th Dec 1977), Dursey Is. Co Cork (24th-25th Sept 1990*).

NORTHERN WATERTHRUSH *Seiurus noveboracensis* A 57

L 15cm (6"). North America. Accidental (autumn, once in spring).

Adult: Very distinctive, dark grey-brown above and pale, usually dull yellowish (sometimes whitish) below with distinct dark streaks. Shows a distinct pale, generally yellowish, supercilium. Readily separated from Ovenbird by its different head pattern.

1st-winter: See Ovenbird, above.

Voice: The song is a *ti ti tiu-tutututu...tit tit tit tiu-tududududiu*, or similar. Call, an explosive, sharp, metallic *pzint*.

Habitat and behaviour: Much as Ovenbird, but favours wet areas.

Note: The Louisiana Waterthrush, *S. motacilla* (E USA), could possibly reach Europe as a vagrant. It is very similar but slightly larger and has a slightly heavier bill. Also, the supercilium is whitish (sometimes also in Northern), and generally there are no fine dark spots on the throat as in most Northern. Has slightly more sparse and fainter streaking below and mainly whitish underparts, contrasting with buffish rear flanks to undertail-coverts.

Range: Breeds from W Alaska across Canada to Newfoundland and in extreme NE USA. Winters from Mexico to South America and in the Caribbean. Vagrant in Greenland.

Status: Accidental in Britain: Isles of Scilly (Sept-Oct 1958, Oct 1968, Sept-Oct 1982 and Aug 1989), Lincolnshire (22nd Oct 1988), Ireland: Cape Clear, Co Cork (10th-11th Sept 1983), Channel Islands: Jersey (17th Apr 1977), France: Ouessant (17th Sept 1955).

COMMON YELLOWTHROAT *Geothlypis trichas* A 57

L 11.5-13cm (4.75"). North America. Accidental in Britain (Jan-Apr, June, Oct-Nov).

Adult male: Unmistakable. Shows a bold black face mask and a pale grey band bordering it above. Mainly greenish-brown above and yellow on the throat and central upper breast. Shows brownish breast-sides and flanks, and 'dirty' yellowish undertail-coverts.

Adult female: Similar to the male but lacks the black and grey head pattern. There is usually a rather indistinct pale yellow eye-ring, often broken. The upper breast is often sullied pale brownish.

1st-winter/-summer male: Shows at least a trace of the black mask and grey band on the head, although in very fresh 1st-winters this is only visible at very close range. Some individuals are already well advanced in 1st-winter plumage (approaching adult male), but there is apparently always some brown and whitish mixed in on the ear-coverts, and usually there is a pale eye-ring. In 1st-summer the head pattern is sometimes just like the adult male. The primary coverts generally look darker because of less distinct greenish edges (almost lacking) than in the adult, and they contrast more with the greenish-edged, newly moulted, greater coverts; also the greenish edges to the alula are very indistinct (distinct in adult). The rectrices are slightly more pointed than in the adult.

1st-winter/-summer female: Similar to the adult female, but tends to be duller, at least in 1st-winter. Sometimes, only the throat is yellowish and washed with pale brownish. Rarely, the throat is buffish rather than yellowish. The same characters for wing/tail as described for the 1st-winter/-summer male are also valid.

Voice: The song is a slightly variable, short phrase, e.g. *visitu visitu visitu visi...visitiu-visitiu-visitiu*, or similar. It calls with a rather soft, tongue-clicking *tep* or *trep*.

Habitat and behaviour: Favours dense undergrowth, thickets, brush, reeds etc. Generally rather secretive.

Range: Breeds from SE Alaska across the S half of Canada to Newfoundland and in all of the USA to S Mexico. Winters in the S parts of USA to N South America and in the Carribean. Vagrant in Greenland.

Status: Accidental in Britain: Devon, Lundy Is, 1st-winter male (4th Nov 1954); Isles of Scilly, 1st-winter male (2nd-17th Oct 1984); Shetland, Fetlar, male (7th-11th June 1984); and Kent, near Sittingbourne, 1st-winter male (6th Jan-23rd Apr 1989).

HOODED WARBLER *Wilsonia citrina*   A 57

L 13cm (5.25"). North America. Accidental in Britain (once in autumn).

Adult male: Unmistakable. Has contrasting black hood, yellow ear-coverts and forehead (rather like a yellow-faced, Pied Wagtail). Also has greenish upperparts and yellow underparts. Shows a large amount of white on the outer tail-feathers (see figure).

Adult female: Greenish above including wings/tail and yellow below. Has yellow face, generally extending diffusely onto the forehead. Some show blackish mottling on the head, sometimes rather extensively but never as complete as in the male. The tail pattern is similar to the male. Also see female Wilson's Warbler (p. 402).

1st-winter/-summer: Resembles the adult of its respective sex, and is generally not reliably aged by plumage.

Voice: The song is a short, softly whistling *vitiu vitiu vu viTIU*; *du-du-diu dududidudiu*, etc. Call is a somewhat metallic *tsyp*.

Range: Breeds in E USA. Winters mainly from Mexico to C Panama.

Status: Accidental in Britain: Isles of Scilly, female on 20th-23rd Sept 1970.

.dividual variation

WILSON'S WARBLER *Wilsonia pusilla* A **57**

L 12cm (4.75"). North America. Recently in Britain (autumn).
Adult male: Easily identified by glossy black cap, yellow face, forehead and underside, and greenish upperside. The tail is unpatterned.
Adult female: Resembles the male but either lacks black cap or shows some dull blackish mottling, particularly on the forecrown (mainly in western populations).

It could be confused with a female Hooded Warbler, but is slightly smaller, with a proportionately smaller bill. It also shows a less well-defined border between the greenish rear crown/nape and the yellowish ear-coverts. Furthermore, it lacks a dusky loral stripe, and has no white in the tail.
1st-winter/-summer: Resembles the adult of its respective sex, but separable with care by its slightly more pointed rectrices (slightly more worn especially in summer).
Voice: The song is a slightly variable *tsit-tsit-tsit-tsit-tsitsitsitsitsi...tsi-tsi-tsi-tsi-tsy-tsy-tsy-tsy...*, or similar. Call, a sharp *chip*.
Range: Breeds in most of Alaska south to California and across Canada to Labrador and Newfoundland. Winters chiefly from Mexico to W Panama. Vagrant in Greenland (Sept 1975).
Status: Accidental in Britain: Rame Head, Cornwall, male on 13th Oct 1985.

CANADA WARBLER *Wilsonia canadensis* A **57**

L 13cm (5.25"). North America. Accidental on Iceland (once in autumn).
All plumages: Uniformly blue-grey above including wings/tail. Yellow below with a band of dark streaks across the breast. Also, shows a whitish or pale yellowish eye-ring and a yellowish streak on the lores. The legs are strikingly pale. Unlikely to be confused with any other species.
Adult male: Shows black face markings, black streaks on the breast and bluish edges to the primary coverts and remiges (not contrasting with the greater coverts).
Adult female: Similar to the adult male but slightly duller with greyer face markings and streaking on the breast.
1st-winter/-summer: Resembles the adult of its respective sex but tends to be duller; 1st-winter male and adult female may be rather similar. In some females the streaks on the breast are very faint (also in some adult females?). The primary coverts and remiges are distinctly more grey-brown than the greater coverts, and the rectrices are slightly more pointed than in the adult.
Voice: The song is a fast, short, rather thin and irregular phrase. The call, *check*, recalls one of the familiar calls given by House Sparrow.
Range: Breeds in C and E Canada, NE USA and in the mountains of E USA. Winters in N South America.
Status: Accidental in SW Iceland: male caught when flew into a car on 29th Sept 1973.

Family THRAUPIDAE   Tanagers

SUMMER TANAGER   *Piranga rubra*   A **58**

L 17-19cm (6.75-7.5"). North America. Accidental in Britain (once in autumn).
All plumages: Rather large with a stout, quite pale bill.
Adult male: Unmistakable. Has all rosy-red plumage.
Adult female: Unmarked, yellowish-brownish olive above including wings/tail. Has paler, brownish-yellow to orangey-yellow underside. The rectrices and remiges (especially outer primaries) often show brownish-red edges. Some show a substantial amount of reddish to the plumage. See female Scarlet Tanager, below.
Juvenile: Shows more brownish general coloration than the adult female and is rather heavily streaked above/below, with distinct pale, double wing-bars. Most unlikely to be seen in Europe in this plumage, since it is moulted early.
1st-winter male: Resembles the adult female, but tertials are usually retained, juvenile, with rather distinct paler tips to outer webs, lacking in the adult. The tail feathers are obviously more pointed than in the adult.
1st-summer male: Usually red with scattered yellowish patches and has mostly yellowish-green edges to the wings. Some have most coverts, tertials and some flight feathers new and with red edges. The tail feathers are often renewed red.
1st-winter/-summer female: Difficult to distinguish from 1st-winter male, but tends to be duller. Differs from adult female by the same characters as for 1st-winter male.
Voice: The song is a short series of slightly harsh, but still clear notes, delivered rather slowly and deliberately. Calls with a *chiduduk.*
Range: Breeds in the E and S parts of the USA (except in extreme NE and SW). Winters from Mexico to C South America.
Status: Accidental in Britain: Bardsey Is, Gwynedd, 1st-winter male from 11th-25th Sept 1957.

SCARLET TANAGER   *Piranga olivacea*   A **58**

L 17.5cm (6.75"). North America. Accidental in N Europe (autumn).
Adult male summer: Bright red with contrasting black wings and tail. Unlikely to be confused with any European species.
Adult male winter: Basically like the adult female (see below), but has black scapulars, wings and tail. During the moult to winter plumage the head and body show a mixture of red, green and greenish-yellow.
Adult female: Greenish above and greenish-yellow below with slightly darker wings/tail. It is very similar to female Summer Tanager. However, the bill is clearly smaller and tends to be darker. It is generally more greenish-tinged, both above and below, with slightly darker wings. The underwing-coverts are whitish with a dark leading edge (uniformly brownish-yellow, pink or pale orange in Summer Tanager). Generally shows a complete eye-ring (broken in Summer Tanager).
Juvenile: See Summer Tanager. Best separated by colour of underwing-

coverts. Most unlikely to be recorded in Europe in this plumage.

1st-winter male: The plumage resembles a mixture of both adult male winter and female. The scapulars, lesser, median and at least the inner greater coverts and sometimes one to all tertials are black. These contrast with the paler and greenish-edged/fringed remainder of the wings.

1st-summer male: Similar to the adult male summer, but shows a distinct contrast between mostly black coverts and usually tertials and tail and the browner remainder of the wing.

1st-winter/-summer female: Similar to the adult female, but the tertials are usually retained, juvenile, more worn and show whitish tips to the outer webs (adult lacks whitish tips). The outer greater coverts are sometimes unmoulted (brown-grey with greenish edges and pale yellowish to whitish spots on the tips of the outer webs). These contrast with the newly moulted inners, which are more fresh and generally slightly longer, showing slightly darker centres and greenish edges and tips. The rectrices are more pointed than in the adult. In some 1st-winters, all of the coverts and tertials have been renewed, in some 1st-summers the rectrices too. In these individuals, the primary coverts and remiges usually contrast more with the coverts than in the adult.

Voice: Song is similar to Summer Tanager. The call is a slightly cross-bill-like *chip*, often immediately followed by a harsh, guttural *durr*.

Range: Breeds in E USA (not in S) and extreme SE Canada. Winters mainly in NW South America.

Status: Accidental in Iceland (at least two records). Britain: Isles of Scilly, 1st-winter male (4th Oct 1970), 1st-winter male (28th Sept-3rd Oct 1975), female (12th-18th Oct 1982); Cornwall, Nanquidno, 1st-winter male (11th Oct 1981). Ireland: Copeland Is, Co. Down, female (12th Oct 1963); Firkeel, Co. Cork, 1st-winter female (12th-14th Oct 1985), adult male (18th Oct 1985).

Family EMBERIZIDAE   Buntings and allies

RUFOUS-SIDED TOWHEE   *Pipilo erythrophthalmus*   A **58**

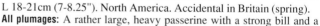

L 18-21cm (7-8.25"). North America. Accidental in Britain (spring).

All plumages: A rather large, heavy passerine with a strong bill and a relatively long tail.

Adult male: Distinct from any European bird. Black above and on the throat/breast, with contrasting whitish belly. Has orange-brown flanks and lower breast sides, buff undertail-coverts and distinct white markings on the primaries and outer tail-feathers.

Adult female: The plumage is basically like the male, but brown where the male is patterned with black.

Juvenile: Similar to the adult female, but shows rather heavy streaking above/below. The male has more-blackish remiges and rectrices than the female. This plumage is lost quickly and therefore most unlikely to be encountered in Europe.

1st-winter/-summer: Resembles the adult of its respective sex, but has contrastingly paler and browner alula, primary coverts and remiges. It also has a duller, browner iris (colour changes during the course of the 1st autumn to red as in adult).

Voice: The song is a variable verse, generally built up of a few distinctive notes, followed by a run of fast ones, e.g. *tuee-tuee tee-tee-tee-tee-tee*, with the first note rather harsh. It calls with a rather harsh *towhee* (same quality as the first note of the song), which has given the species its English name. Also gives a soft *heu* and a slightly metallic *tsyt*.

Range: Breeds in much of USA and extreme S Canada and in Mexico and Guatemala. Mainly resident, but northern populations migratory.

Status: Accidental in Britain: Devon, Lundy Is (7th June 1966). One present at Spurn, Humberside (5th Sept 1975-10th Jan 1976), belonged to one of the western races and was considered more likely to have been an escape.

SAVANNAH SPARROW *Passerculus sandwichensis* A 59

L 14cm (5.5"). North America, Mexico and Guatemala. Accidental in Britain (two recent records).

Adult: Superficially similar to females of some Palearctic buntings, e.g. Reed, Yellow-browed and Black-faced Buntings, but lacks white in the tail and has a clearly different pattern to the central and longest tertials (cf. plates). Note the usually yellowish supercilium, particularly in front of the eye and the distinct, narrow, pale median crown-stripe. The NE subspecies *princeps* ('Ipswich Sparrow'), which at least the first record was considered to be, is slightly larger, paler and greyer above, and more finely streaked below than other E subspecies. Most likely to be confused with Song Sparrow (p. 406).

1st-winter/-summer: Distinguished from the adult with care by the slightly narrower, more pointed and more worn rectrices.

Voice: Song begins with a few accelerating notes, followed by a drawn-out, buzzing note (the latter reminiscent of a drawn-out version of the final note of Yellowhammer's song), e.g. *tsi tsi tsi-tsi-tsi-dzzzzzzzzzz-iti*. The calls include a thin *tsi* and a rather hard *tsep*.

Range: Breeds in Alaska and Canada (including the northernmost parts of the mainland), from W to NE USA, Mexico and Guatemala. Winters along the coasts and in the S parts of USA, south to Central America.

Status: Accidental in Britain: Portland, Dorset (11th-16th April 1982); Shetland, Fair Isle, 1st-winter (30th Sept-1st Oct 1987).

FOX SPARROW *Passerella iliaca* A 59

L 16-19cm (6.5-7"). North America. Accidental (spring).

Adult: The rather large size and heavy bill are distinctive features. Note also in particular the greyish-brown upperside with rufous streaking and contrasting rufous rump, uppertail-coverts and tail; grey supercilium and neck sides; mainly rufous ear-coverts; and rather rufous wings, especially secondaries and greater coverts. Shows very heavily streaked underparts, some of the markings almost triangular in shape. The streaks usually rufous at least on the breast, often also on flanks.

1st-winter/-summer: See Savannah Sparrow above.

Voice: The song is slightly variable and rather short, with clear notes; a rather harsh, buzzing *churrr* and a *chik* are often included.

Note: There is much geographic variation within this species. Only the eastern form is described here.

Range: Breeds from W Alaska across C Canada to Newfoundland and in W USA. Winters along the W coast and in E USA. Vagrant in

Greenland.
Status: Accidental in Iceland (1). Ireland: Copeland Is, Co. Down (3rd-4th June 1961). West Germany (May 1949, Apr 1977). Italy: Liguria (1936).

SONG SPARROW   *Melospiza melodia*   **A 59**
L 15-16cm (6"). North America. Accidental in Britain and Norway (spring).
Adult: Superficially similar to some female buntings, mainly Reed and Black-faced, but differs in the same way as Savannah Sparrow (p. 405). It is slightly larger than the latter with a distinctly longer and slightly rounded tail (slightly notched in Savannah). The supercilium is pale buffish-grey to greyish (never shows any yellow). The general impression is of a darker, more rufous-brown bird than Savannah.
1st-winter: Generally not possible to distinguish from adult by plumage. Note that the skull is not fully pneumatized until early in the 2nd year.
Voice: Song variable. Usually begins with a few clear notes followed by a trill, e.g. *his his his tirrrrrrrrrrrrr-etesch.* Calls include a rather House Sparrow-like, slightly harsh *chepp* and a fine, high-pitched *tsii.*
Range: Breeds mainly in the S half of Canada and the N half of USA, except on the W coast, where it reaches further south, into N Mexico. The northern populations are chiefly migratory, wintering as far south as S USA and N Mexico.
Status: Accidental in Britain: Shetland/Fair Isle (Apr-May 1959, Apr-June 1979, Apr 1989); Spurn, Yorkshire (May 1964); Bardsey Is, Gwynedd (May 1970); Isle of Man (May-June 1971). Norway (May 1975). It is most remarkable that all of the records are from spring-summer.

WHITE-CROWNED SPARROW   *Zonotrichia leucophrys*   **A 59**
L 15-17cm (6.25"). North America. Accidental.
Adult: Easily identified by its distinctive black-and-white striped head pattern and uniformly grey ear-coverts, sides of the neck, throat (may be diffusely whitish) and breast. Also, has brownish, unstreaked flanks and mainly pinkish bill. See White-throated Sparrow (p. 407).
Juvenile: Most similar to 1st-winter, but easily distinguished by e.g. distinctly and finely streaked breast/flanks and noticeably different head pattern (i.e. dark framing to the ear-coverts, no grey sides to the neck, and dark malar stripes). The bill is darker on the upper mandible and on tip of the lower. Very similar to juvenile White-throated Sparrow (p. 407). Most unlikely to be recorded outside breeding range.
1st-winter: Basically like the adult, but shows reddish-brown lateral crown-stripes and eye-stripe, pale brownish-tinged median crown-stripe and supercilium and brownish ear-coverts.
Voice: The song is rather variable, e.g. *eeh uuh-uuhtree-tree-tuu, uuh eeh-eeh tee-tee-trree,* or similar. Call, a rather sharp, metallic *pzit,* reminiscent of alarm call of Pied Flycatcher. Also gives a thin, high, *tssiip* or *tssiep.* Calls similar to those of White-throated Sparrow.
Range: Breeds from Alaska across N Canada to Labrador and in the Rocky Mountains. Winters mainly in the southern half of USA, in the west also further north to SW Canada. Vagrant in Greenland.
Status: Accidental in Iceland (1). Britain: Shetland, Fair Isle (15th-16th

May 1977), Hornsea Mere, Yorkshire (22nd May 1977). France: Barfleur, Manche (25th Aug 1965). Netherlands (Dec 1981-Feb 1982), and West Germany (uncertain provenance).

WHITE-THROATED SPARROW *Zonotrichia albicollis* B 59
L 15-17cm (6.25"). North America. Rare vagrant. More frequent than other American sparrows.

Adult: Polymorphic. Some show a black and white head pattern, bright yellow on the fore-supercilium and have uniformly grey ear-coverts and breast. Others show a reddish-brown and pale brownish head pattern, dirty yellowish fore-supercilium, and brownish-grey ear-coverts and breast, the latter with diffuse mottling.

'White-striped morph' is rather similar to the White-crowned Sparrow, but easily distinguished by yellow supercilium in front of the eye and conspicuous white throat, generally with dark framing (at least below). The bill is more horn-coloured with a mainly dark upper mandible.

Juvenile: Very similar to juvenile White-crowned Sparrow but generally shows more rufous-tinged upperparts, more whitish belly to undertail-coverts and more prominent supercilium in front of the eye. It could also be confused with Song Sparrow, but shows a more prominent pale median crown-stripe, less strong malar stripes and finer streaking on the underparts. Most unlikely to straggle to Europe in juvenile plumage (lost early).

1st-winter: Resembles the adult, but on average is less black and white (especially females). Shows a distinctly duller, less reddish-brown iris at least until early in the 2nd year.

Voice: The song consists of a few, clear, high-pitched notes. Usually begins with two clear notes, followed by a triplet, e.g. *uuh eeh eeh-eeh-eeh*. The calls are similar to those of White-crowned Sparrow.

Range: Breeds from C-NW Canada to Newfoundland and in extreme NE USA. Winters in E and SW USA to N Mexico.

Status: Rare vagrant in Europe. Iceland (5), Britain (11, Apr-June, 4, Oct-Jan), Ireland: Cape Clear, Co Cork (Apr 1967), Co. Antrim (Dec 1984-May 1985), Netherlands (Sept 1967, Oct 1967, Apr 1977, June 1989*), Denmark (May 1976), Sweden (Dec 1963), Finland (June-July 1967, June 1972), and Gibraltar (18th-25th May 1986). It is interesting to note that spring-summer records predominate (cf. other North American sparrows and Dark-eyed Junco).

DARK-EYED JUNCO *Junco hyemalis* B 58
L 14-16cm (5.75"). North America. Accidental (mainly spring).

Adult male: Easily identified by its plain, dark grey plumage with white belly and undertail-coverts and a large amount of white on the outer tail-feathers. The bill is pinkish with a fine dark tip.

Adult female: Generally paler, more brownish-washed than adult male.

Juvenile: Basically brownish with paler belly and undertail-coverts and distinct streaking both above and below. Moults early and thus most unlikely to be seen in Europe in this plumage.

1st-winter/-summer male: Basically like the adult male (sometimes more similar to the adult female in autumn/winter). It usually shows retained juvenile tertials, which are more worn and with browner edges than in the adult and generally shows whitish tips to the outer webs. Sometimes, there are also a few retained juvenile outer greater coverts, which are more worn and browner and with distinct buffish to whitish tips to the outer webs (indistinct paler tips can sometimes be seen in adult). Also, the alula and primary coverts are browner with less bluish-tinged edges. During the 1st autumn-winter the iris is greyish-brown to brown (deep red-brown in adult), and the rectrices are more pointed than in adult.

1st-winter/-summer female: Resembles adult female but tends to be even paler and browner. Differs in the same way as 1st-year male.

Voice: The song is a fast, rattling trill, reminiscent of the song of some Yellowhammers but lacks the drawn-out final note. The alarm call is a slightly liquid *chek*. Other calls include a squeaky, clicking twitter.

Note: There are several distinctly different races of Dark-eyed Junco. The one described here ('Slate-coloured Junco') is the northern one, the only one to have occurred in Europe.

Range: Breeds in Alaska and Canada (not in the northernmost parts) to Newfoundland and in NE USA. Also (other forms) in W USA. Winters over much of USA and in S Canada.

Status: Accidental in Iceland (1), British Isles (12, Apr-June; 3, Dec-Mar), Netherlands (Feb 1962), Norway (4th Dec 1987), Poland (4th May 1963), and Gibraltar (18th-25th May 1986 – coinciding there with the arrival of a White-throated Sparrow). An exceptional vagrancy pattern for a North American bird!

BLACK-FACED BUNTING *Emberiza spodocephala* A **60**

L 13.5-15cm (5.5"). Asia. Accidental in N Europe (three records in Nov, one in May).

Adult male summer: Easily distinguished from other buntings by its greenish blue-grey hood and black face mask.

Adult male winter: Generally shows a slightly duller head and breast, with distinct streaking on the sides of the crown/nape. Some individuals are more female-like, see 1st-winter male for differences.

Adult female: Distinguished from other female buntings by the lack of distinct field-marks rather than by any special characters. Note the rather dull grey-brown coloration, relatively dull and indistinct supercilium (often less conspicuous than the submoustachial stripe) and rather indistinct pale median crown-stripe. The centre of the breast is streaked comparatively faintly, and there is usually a pale yellowish wash on the belly (not always visible in the field). It also has a distinctly pinkish and dark bill, with nearly straight culmen. In summer, some females are a little more male-like, with rather faint supercilium, less distinct streaking on crown, and greyish, very faintly streaked breast.

Reed Bunting differs in e.g. diagnostic rufous lesser and tips to median coverts and Pine Bunting and dull Yellowhammers by e.g. a rufous back, rump and uppertail-coverts.

Cirl Bunting shows a slightly different head pattern, with more distinct supercilium, more contrastingly patterned ear-coverts and very faint (if any) malar patch and median crown-stripe; often shows some chestnut on the scapulars and sides of the breast; usually has finer and more clearcut streaking below (especially on the flanks) and has a more swollen bill with blue-grey on the lower mandible. See also Yellow-browed and Yellow-breasted Buntings (p. 411 and p. 414).

1st-winter ♂

1st-winter male: Very variable. Some are very female-like, but usually the supercilium is less distinct, crown and sides of the neck are tinged blue-grey (often also the ear-coverts and breast, although fainter), and the crown has rufous/blackish spots and very indistinct pale median crown-stripe. Some individuals show a little blackish on chin and lores, unlike females. Some hardly distinguishable from female in the field, but in the hand the pattern to the crown/nape can be seen to differ (see figure). Some are very similar to typical adult males.

crown feather

    The extensive individual variation found in adult and 1st-winter males makes ageing (and sometimes sexing) difficult. On average, 1st-winter males are less 'male-like', i.e. duller than adults. In the hand, the tail-feathers can be seen to be more pointed (see figure), and with practice the iris is more grey-brown than in the adult (reddish-brown in latter; can only be judged in the hand). It should be noted that adults only exceptionally acquire fully pneumatized (ossified) skulls, but in the autumn/early winter, 1st-years are distinctly less pneumatized than the adults.

central tail-feather

1st-summer male: Difficult to separate from the adult male. Generally shows more pointed and more worn tail-feathers.

1st-winter/-summer female: Tail, iris and skull differ in same way as between 1st-winter and adult male. As in the adult male, ageing is more difficult in spring/summer.

Voice: The song is a characteristic, rather variable, quick, short, ringing phrase. The call is a sharp *tzit*, slightly finer compared to the call of most other buntings with similar call.

Range: Breeds in S and SE Siberia and NE China. Also in Japan and C China. Three different subspecies, but only nominate described here. Winters mainly in Japan and S China and neighbouring areas.

Status: Accidental in the Netherlands: Westenschouwen, 1st-winter male (16th Nov 1986). West Germany: Heligoland (5th Nov 1910, 23rd-26th May 1980). Finland: Dragsfjärd, male (2nd Nov 1981).

ad.   juv.

PINE BUNTING *Emberiza leucocephalos*   D **60**

L 17cm (6.5"). Asia. Rare vagrant, mainly late autumn/winter, often in flocks of Yellowhammers.

Adult male: Unmistakable. Shows diagnostic head pattern of chestnut, white and black, and a rufous breast-band. In winter, the head pattern is less distinct, but the basic pattern is still obvious.

Adult female: Almost identical to female Yellowhammer, but completely lacks yellow and greenish coloration. In Yellowhammer there is always some yellow at least on the throat, supercilium, belly, edges to the primaries, and on the underwing-coverts. There is also at least some yellowish-green on the crown (usually concealed) and on the lesser coverts, and often a faint greenish tinge to the mantle. Rarely, Yellowhammer does not show any obvious yellow to the plumage, but the belly apparently never becomes as pure whitish as it does in Pine Bunting. In Pine the upper breast is generally more dark-spotted ('necklace'), and when fresh the throat is generally pale buffish. It never shows a greyish-green breast band as is regularly seen in male Yellowhammers and sometimes in females as well. On average, the undertail-

409

coverts are more finely streaked than in Yellowhammer, and sometimes they are unstreaked, which is perhaps never the case in Yellowhammer (can only be judged in the hand). At least some adult females show rufous breast and flanks with pale fringes – a pattern which is never seen in Yellowhammer. In summer, some females are easily recognized as they show a whitish patch on the central crown and some chestnut on the supercilium and throat – ghosting the head pattern of the male.

It might possibly be confused with female/winter male Rustic Bunting. However, Rustic has more conical bill, shorter tail and small erectable crest. Also shows e.g. more distinct head pattern; rufous lesser coverts and usually some obvious rufous on nape; whiter and more distinct wing-bars; and very different call (close to Little Bunting).

1st-winter/-summer: Resembles the adult of its respective sex. Best distinguished by more pointed tail-feathers, although of less value in spring/summer, since these feathers by then are often very worn (generally more than in the adult) and the shape difficult to judge. Also, the tertials are often unmoulted and contrastingly more worn and bleached compared to the newly moulted greater coverts.

Voice: The song and calls appear identical to those of Yellowhammer.

Note: Rather frequently hybridizes with very closely related Yellowhammer. Hybrids show a wide range of intermediate characters.

Range: Breeds in Siberia south of the Arctic Circle, west to Urals and in N Mongolia and possibly in NW Manchuria and N Tibet. Winters chiefly in N and NE China, NW India and in and around Afghanistan. A few winter regularly as far west as Israel. Accidental in Cyprus.

Status: Rare vagrant in Europe. Iceland (1), British Isles (18, Jan, Apr, Aug-Nov), France (14, Sept-Feb), Belgium (13), Netherlands (24), Denmark (Nov-Dec 1973), Norway (5), Sweden (Jan 1959, Jan 1963, June 1966, Feb 1967 and Oct 1988), Finland (Nov 1968, Nov 1986, Apr 1988), West Germany, Austria, Czechoslovakia, Hungary (Jan 1986), Yugoslavia (13, Oct-Jan), Greece (2), Bulgaria, Italy, Malta (2), Spain, and Gibraltar (pair on 2nd May 1987).

MEADOW BUNTING *Emberiza cioides* A **60**

L 15-16cm (6.5"). Asia. Accidental.

Adult male: Easily recognized by its diagnostic head pattern. Also shows unmarked rufous breast and flanks and has rufous back/rump and uppertail-coverts. The lesser coverts are bluish-grey (often concealed) and the tail is comparatively long.

Adult female: Basically like the adult male, but the head pattern is less contrasting and clearcut, with brown or even no loral and malar stripes and less chestnut ear-coverts. In some individuals the whitish patch below the eye is rather poorly marked. Others have rather pale ear-coverts with a broad, diffuse, dark eye-stripe behind the eye and a trace of a malar stripe (see figure, p. 411). The underparts are paler.

Juvenile: Resembles the adult female, but is generally paler on the underparts with distinctly streaked breast/flanks, and is also streaked on the back/rump and uppertail-coverts. The head pattern is quite different from either the adult or 1st-winter female, i.e. shows pale brown ear-coverts with a dark eye-stripe behind the eye and a dark rear border and often a pale spot at rear (see figure); there is also frequently a rather

juv.

distinct dark malar stripe.

It is very similar to the juvenile of the very closely related Rock Bunting, and is best separated by its generally much broader, orange-brown edges to the central pair of tail-feathers (slight overlap, though). The belly tends to be paler. Juvenile plumage is very unlikely to be seen in Europe (since it is moulted early in the autumn).

1st-winter/-summer: See Pine Bunting (p. 409).

Voice: The song is a rather short, hurried, variable phrase. It often begins with a short, single, stressed note, *tit* or *tiu*. The calls are quite variable, including a thin *tzi*, often rapidly repeated, *tzi-di-di* or *tzi-di-di-di-di*, sometimes harder, *tse-tse-tse* or thinner *hsit-sit-sit*. At least eastern Rock Buntings may call very similarly.

Range: Breeds in China, Mongolia, Japan and the southernmost parts of Siberia. Mainly resident.

Status: Accidental in Finland: Korppoo, Utö, Turku archipelago, singing male (20th-27th May 1987). Italy: Veneto (2 records of uncertain provenance in 1910).

YELLOW-BROWED BUNTING   *Emberiza chrysophrys*   A **61**

L 14-15cm (5.75"). Asia. Accidental in Britain and the Netherlands (Oct).

All plumages: Shows a very striking head pattern with dark lateral crown-stripes, a distinct whitish median crown-stripe and a very prominent supercilium. The latter is usually yellow, turning whitish at the rear end, but sometimes (only in juvenile and some 1st-winter females?) appearing whitish in the field with no perceptible yellowish tinge. The ear-coverts range from black (male summer) to dull brownish with distinct dark framing (other plumages); apparently invariably shows a distinct whitish spot at the rear. Shows whitish underparts with some brownish on the breast-sides and flanks and comparatively fine streaking. Also shows rather chestnut-tinged scapulars, central mantle, back/rump and uppertail-coverts. The bill is distinctly dark and pinkish with almost straight culmen.

Birds lacking distinct yellowish on supercilium could be confused with a female Black-faced Bunting. However, this has a much less distinct head pattern, usually yellowish-tinged belly (not always easily seen in the field); more heavily and diffusely streaked breast sides and flanks, and duller brownish upperparts (lacks the chestnut tinge).

Adult male summer: Shows blackish lores, ear-coverts (with white spot at rear), lateral crown-stripes and bright yellow on the supercilium.

Adult male winter: Shows a more brownish head pattern and has slightly less bright yellow on the supercilium – very similar to females and 1st-winter male (see below).

Adult female summer: Distinguished from male summer by its browner head pattern and generally slightly duller yellow on supercilium.

Adult female winter: Very difficult to separate from the adult male winter. Generally shows marginally less-black and slightly less extensive centres to the feathers on the sides of the crown.

1st-winter/-summer: Resembles the adult of its respective sex and plumage, and is accordingly very difficult to sex in the autumn-winter. Even in spring, some males can be confused with female, since the summer plumage is not yet fully developed. At least in autumn/winter, 1st-winters show slightly more pointed and more worn rectrices than the adult and have a slightly more greyish-brown iris (reddish-brown in adult; difficult to use without experience). At least in some adults, the skull apparently does not become fully pneumatized, although in the autumn/early winter 1st-year birds show distinctly larger 'windows' than the adult.

Voice: The song is a short, characteristic phrase, usually beginning with a typical, clear, full, drawn-out note, often followed by two higher-pitched, drawn-out, clear notes, e.g. *huuu huee-huee tititirr* or *huu tee-tee tu-tu-tu*. The call resembles that of Little Bunting.

Range: Breeds in Siberia, mainly NE of Lake Baikal. Winters in SE China. Vagrant in Ukraine (Jan 1983).

Status: Accidental in Britain: Norfolk, Holkham Meals (19th Oct 1975) and Shetland, Fair Isle (12th-23rd Oct 1980). Netherlands: Friesland, Schiermonnikoog (19th Oct 1982).

LITTLE BUNTING   *Emberiza pusilla*   R Br **61**

L 13-14cm (5.25"). Breeds in small numbers in NE Norway, N Finland and sometimes in N Sweden. Also in Siberia. Frequent vagrant in rest of Europe (mainly autumn).

All plumages: Reminiscent of a rather small, short-tailed female Reed Bunting, particularly in the autumn. It differs in having a proportionately slightly longer bill with almost straight culmen (slightly convex in Reed); narrower, more distinct and generally rufous-tinged median crown-stripe (usually lacking in Reed in summer); and rufous tinged ear-coverts, lores and anterior supercilium. It also usually shows a more contrasting pale eye-ring, lacks a moustachial stripe (distinct in Reed, all the way to the base of the bill) and generally has a more distinct pale spot on the rear ear-coverts. Shows grey-brown lesser coverts (rufous in Reed), and more prominent wing-bars, especially on the median coverts (rufous tips in Reed when fresh). The tarsus and toes are never dark as in many Reed Buntings.

Adult male: It is generally not possible to distinguish males with any certainty from other plumages in the field (not even in the hand from adult female). An individual with a very black and extremely bright and extensively reddish-brown head pattern is likely to be a male.

Adult female: Generally not safely distinguished from the adult male even in the hand, but individuals with very dull head pattern are likely to be females.

1st-winter/-summer: In the hand, distinguished from adult by its slightly more worn and more pointed tail-feathers. Shape of the rectrices is often difficult to judge in spring/summer because of heavy wear (normally more in 1st-summers than in adults). Also told from adult in autumn/winter by its more grey-brown iris (reddish-brown in adult). Extremes may be tentatively sexed, but the majority not reliably.

Voice: The song is a characteristic, rather short, slow phrase, somewhat recalling the songs of both Ortolan and Reed Bunting. The call is a sharp *tzit* or *tzic*, very different from the soft, thin *tseeu* and harsh *bzy* of Reed Bunting.

Range: Breeds in small numbers in NE Finland, although 'hundreds of pairs in the north' were recorded in 1987. Rare breeder in NE Norway and sometimes (perhaps annually) in N Sweden. Range extends across

N Siberia. Winters in Asia from NE India and Himalayas to S China.
Status: Frequent vagrant in NW Europe, mainly autumn, fewer in spring, occasionally wintering. There are records from Iceland (2nd in Oct 1980), Faeroes, British Isles (*c.* 500, mainly Sept-Oct, fewer Nov-May), Channel Islands (*c.* 5), France (many 19th cent, 16 since 1981), Belgium (35+), Netherlands (44), Denmark (22), Norway (many), Sweden (*c.* 175), Estonia (4), Latvia (2), East Germany (13 since 1930, Oct-Apr), West Germany (especially Heligoland), Poland (9), Austria, Hungary (Nov 1988), Switzerland (12), Italy, Sicily (Sept 1958, Dec 1970), Yugoslavia (Feb 1985, Nov 1986), Greece, Bulgaria, Malta (19), and Spain (3 in Nov-Dec 1986 were first in 20th century).

CHESTNUT BUNTING *Emberiza rutila* A **61**

L 13-15cm (5.5"). E Asia. Only a few records.
All plumages: Shows mainly yellow underparts and has rufous back/rump and uppertail-coverts. There is little or no white in the tail. Note the rather small size, shortish tail and conical bill with almost straight culmen.
Adult male: Unmistakable. Uniform bright rufous on the head, central breast, upperparts and coverts. The sides of the breast and flanks are rather lightly streaked. In autumn-winter the rufous is partly obscured by narrow pale fringes, especially on the supercilium and throat.
Adult female: Rather similar to female Yellowhammer, but differs in smaller size, shorter tail, slightly different bill shape and only shows very little or no whitish in the tail. It is also less heavily streaked on the breast and flanks (distinctly streaked in juvenile but still with finer and more clearcut streaks than in Yellowhammer), and the throat is never yellow. Often shows rufous on the lesser coverts, crown and scapulars, sometimes also on the ear-coverts, nape, breast and median coverts. See also Yellow-breasted Bunting (p. 414).
Juvenile: Differs from the adult female (individuals with rufous only on back, rump and uppertail-coverts) mainly in showing rather dense blackish streaking on the breast and flanks and streaked back, rump and uppertail-coverts. The pattern of the median and greater coverts (particularly former) differs slightly from the adult (see figure). See juvenile Yellow-breasted Bunting (p. 414). Moulted before the autumn migration and thus very unlikely to be seen in Europe. However, the Norwegian record concerned a juvenile.
1st-winter male: Rather variable. Some are very similar to the adult male. The upper throat generally shows little or no rufous, unlike in the adult male. Shows fine dark spots to the crown and, slightly more prominently, to the mantle (very fine spots present in some adult males), and the olive-tinged fringes are broader and generally less clearcut. Often some of the lesser coverts are olive, unlike in the adult. The median coverts often show obvious dark centres; in the adult (and many 1st-winters as well) the dark centres are small and generally not visible. At least the outer greater coverts show rather narrow olive-tinged edges and prominent dark centres (inners are sometimes rather broadly rufous-edged though). In the adult, the greater coverts show broad rufous edges, sometimes with the dark centre visible on the outer feathers. The juvenile tertials are usually retained and show clearly narrower rufous edges than in the adult male (in the latter the entire outer

median coverts

ad.-patterned

greater coverts

ad.-patterned

web is normally rufous on the inner two pairs, slightly narrower on the outermost pair); also, the juvenile tertials are more worn and whitish near the tips on the outer webs.

Other 1st-winter males show heavily streaked, olive-tinged mantle and scapulars with very little or no rufous, and more distinctly streaked crown. There is also less rufous on the throat/breast and coverts. These individuals are very similar to bright adult females and are generally not safely distinguished in the field. In the hand, they can be distinguished by the usually retained juvenile tertials, which are more worn and with paler outer edges (turning whitish near the tips). Note that the shape of the tail feathers cannot be used for ageing (pointed in all).

1st-summer male: Resembles the adult male, but can usually be distinguished by the same characters as for 1st-winter (except throat pattern).

1st-winter/-summer female: Resembles the adult female. It is possible that it never shows any rufous on the head, breast, mantle/scapulars and coverts in 1st-winter and generally not in 1st-summer either. The juvenile tertials are generally retained (see 1st-winter male).

Voice: The song is basically quite similar to e.g. Black-faced Bunting, but is very variable and often somewhat reminiscent of both Pallas's Warbler and Tree Pipit. The call is very similar to Little Bunting.

Range: Breeds in SE Siberia, N Mongolia and NW Manchuria. Winters mainly in SE Asia.

Status: Accidental in Europe. There are four autumn records more in keeping for a vagrant Siberian species: Netherlands (female, 5th Nov 1937), Norway (juvenile, 13th-15th Oct 1974), Yugoslavia (1st-winter male, 10th Oct 1987) and Malta (1st-winter male, Nov 1983).

There are also four records in June from Britain: Foula, adult male (9th-13th June 1974); Isle of May, female (11th June 1985); Fair Isle, 1st-summer male (15th-16th June 1986); Bardsey Is, 1st-summer male (18th-19th June 1986). These late spring records from the UK concern individuals that might equally be wild but some are known to be imported regularly, albeit in small numbers from Hong Kong as a cage bird (cf. Red-headed Bunting).

YELLOW-BREASTED BUNTING   *Emberiza aureola*   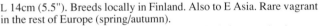 R Br **61**

L 14cm (5.5"). Breeds locally in Finland. Also to E Asia. Rare vagrant in the rest of Europe (spring/autumn).

Adult male summer: Easily recognized by its black face-mask, chestnut upperside, yellow underparts and chestnut breast-band. Also has Chaffinch-like, broad white wing-bars.

Adult male winter: Basically as summer, but with rather broad, pale fringes to the entire upperside, obscuring most of the chestnut. The breast-band is also obscured, the black face mask is reduced to dark framing to the ear-coverts, and there is a distinct supercilium. The pattern is thus reminiscent of the adult female, but the upper wing-bar is obviously broader than in most adult females, the breast-band is usually faintly evident, and the crown, mantle and scapulars lack or show less distinct blackish streaks. In the hand, the typical male pattern can easily be seen on the upperside and as the plumage becomes more worn, this becomes apparent also in the field.

Adult female: Shows distinctive head pattern, with dark, heavily streaked sides to the crown, distinct pale median crown-stripe, prominent supercilium, and usually distinct dark framing to the ear-coverts. There is usually no or only a very faint malar stripe. It is further characterized by its mostly yellowish underparts (sometimes washed very faintly) and only sparsely streaked central (and sometimes sides of) breast. The back/rump and uppertail-coverts are often rather rufous and usually at least indistinctly streaked. In some individuals the upper wing-bar is quite broad and there may be an incomplete chestnut breast-band, as well as some chestnut on the crown.

Especially females that are less yellow could be confused with female Black-faced Bunting. However, shows a more prominent pale median crown-stripe and supercilium, generally more strongly dark-framed ear-coverts and less prominent dark malar stripe and malar patch. Also, more distinct wing-bars and generally streaked rump-area, often showing some rufous.

Can also be similar to some female Chestnut Buntings. However, shows a more distinct head pattern, with more prominent median crown-stripe, supercilium and dark framing to the ear-coverts. The malar stripe tends to be more poorly marked though. Often shows a yellow throat, but only rarely has yellow undertail-coverts (usually whitish to pale buffish), whereas in Chestnut the throat is never yellow, but the undertail-coverts are always yellow. Furthermore, the crown/nape and mantle/scapulars are less olive-tinged, the rump area is streaked and less rufous and the underparts are generally more heavily streaked (streaks often olive-tinged in Chestnut). The wing-bars, especially the upper, are normally more whitish and contrasting, and there is also much white in the tail.

Juvenile: Differs from the adult female mainly by the densely and finely streaked breast and flanks and the slightly different pattern to the median and greater coverts, particularly the former (see figure under Chestnut Bunting, p. 413). Also, the underparts are generally buffish rather than yellowish. Similar to juvenile Chestnut Bunting, but especially the head and tail pattern differs in the same ways as in adult female (see above). Surprisingly, juvenile plumage is at least often not moulted until in the winter quarters. This may be the usual strategy, but further research is required.

1st-winter male: Differs from the adult male winter in showing fine dark subterminal spots to the crown (see figure), much less chestnut and more heavily streaked mantle/scapulars (at most rather finely streaked in adult), often broken breast-band, generally clearly less white on the median and lesser coverts (some close to adult male though) and less chestnut edges to the greater coverts. In the autumn, shows fresher remiges and rectrices than the adult, since the latter moult these feathers in their winter quarters (on the breeding grounds in the E Asian populations). Note that the shape of the rectrices is of no help in ageing (often very pointed in adult).

r   ♀

wn feather

In the hand, distinguished from most females (adult and 1st-winter) by the extensive chestnut centres to the crown/nape and usually to at least the sides of the breast. Also, often shows more extensive white on the median and lesser coverts. However, the plumage of some adult females can approach 1st-winter males. In western birds the wear of the remiges is a good feature for separating adult females from 1st-winter males. In eastern birds (in which adults moult the remiges before the autumn migration) the primary coverts are slightly more pointed, worn and frayed at the tips in 1st-winter.

1st-summer male: Usually differs from the adult male summer by the same characters as for 1st-winter. Also, tends to show a duller head pattern than the adult.

1st-winter/-summer female: Very similar to the adult female, but in the autumn shows fresher remiges in western populations and slightly different primary coverts in eastern (see 1st-winter male). See above for differences from 1st-winter male.

Voice: The distinctive song consists of a series of clear, ringing notes that ascend except for the ending, e.g. *tru-tru-tree-tree-tri-tri-iih-tiu.* It most resembles the song of Ortolan Bunting. The call *tzip*, is a little reminiscent of the call of Spotted Flycatcher; generally not easily distinguished without experience from the call of e.g. Little Bunting.

Range: Breeds across C Finland (*c.* 300 pairs). Also across Siberia to Kamchatka and in Japan, Mongolia and Manchuria. Winters from NE India and S China to Malay Peninsula. Accidental in Cyprus.

Status: Rare vagrant in rest of Europe (spring/autumn). Iceland (1), British Isles (146 mainly late Aug-mid Oct, especially Fair Isle); Channel Islands, Guernsey (Sept 1978); France (Oct 1974, Dec 1987, Oct 1988), Belgium (Sept 1928), Netherlands (8), Denmark (Aug 1984), Norway (21), Sweden (24, mainly June), Latvia (May 1985), Estonia (3, May-June), Poland (5), West Germany (<10), Czechoslovakia, Greece, Italy (*c.* 20), Malta (5), and Spain (Oct 1969).

PALLAS'S REED BUNTING   *Emberiza pallasi*   A **62**

L 13-14cm (5.25"). NE European USSR, but mainly from E Siberia. Two autumn records for Britain.

All plumages: Very similar to Reed Bunting but is slightly smaller (near size of Little Bunting). The bill shows a straight culmen (slightly convex in Reed, although this can be difficult to determine and the culmen is occasionally straight in some E races of Reed) and, except for males in summer plumage, has pale pinkish lower mandible (more greyish in Reed, and generally less contrasting with the upper mandible). Also, the plumage generally looks paler, especially on the rump, and there is little or no streaking on the breast/flanks (except in juvenile and in some non-juvenile females). However, some E races of Reed Bunting are equally pale with very little streaking below. The most reliable plumage character is the colour of the lesser coverts, although this is often very difficult to see in the field. In Pallas's the lesser coverts are brownish (juvenile and females) to bluish-grey (most males), and in Reed they are rufous. The wing-bars, especially the upper, are generally paler and more distinct than in Reed, but when fresh the difference may be rather slight. The tarsus and toes are usually pale, rarely slightly darker; in Reed they are frequently dark (though often pale).

Adult male summer: Shows the same basic head and breast pattern as Reed Bunting. The mantle/scapulars are usually slightly more contrastingly patterned than in Reed and generally show paler and less brownish base colour and marginally blacker and more clearcut streaks. The dark centres to the coverts and tertials are also generally marginally blacker and more sharply defined than in Reed, further adding to the more contrastingly patterned plumage. There is often a trace of warm buffish on the nape (from winter plumage), not seen in Reed.

Adult male winter: Basically similar to the winter female. In the hand the feathers of the forehead, crown, throat and centre of the breast are mostly black with pale fringes and the basal parts of the feathers on the lower nape are white. In females, the feathers of the forehead/crown are basically brownish with brownish-blackish streaks, the throat is only dark on the sides (malar stripes and malar patches), and there is no or very little white on the nape. See 1st-winter male. The differences from Reed Bunting described under adult female also apply to the adult male winter.

Adult female: Further differs from female Reed Bunting by slightly different head pattern. The crown looks uniformly pale rufescent-brown, sometimes with slightly darker sides. In Reed in fresh plumage (autumn-winter), the centre of the crown is paler and more greyish, and a rather obvious pale median crown-stripe and darker lateral crown-stripes are thus usually formed. The nape and sides of the neck are generally the same colour as the crown, i.e. less greyish-tinged than in Reed (not always obvious, though). The supercilium tends to be less distinct, and the ear-coverts are more uniformly patterned, with no or less distinct darker framing and normally showing a contrasting dark spot in the rear lower corner. However, some eastern Reed Buntings show similarly patterned ear-coverts. Also, the underside is generally slightly more buffish-tinged than in Reed, especially in fresh plumage.

Juvenile: Generally looks darker overall, with more streaked back/rump and uppertail-coverts and heavily streaked breast/flanks. The pattern of the median (in particular) and greater coverts is also noticeably different from the adult (see figure under Chestnut Bunting, p. 413). It is very similar to juvenile Reed Bunting and also more similar than the other plumages to female Reed Bunting. The main distinguishing features are the bill, the colour of the lesser coverts and call. It would seem very unlikely for a juvenile to reach Europe, since they usually moult before the migration, but, in fact, the second European record was of a bird in full juvenile plumage (cf. Richard's Pipit).

1st-winter/-summer: Resembles the adult of its respective sex, but is distinguished in the hand by its more pointed and more worn rectrices (shape often difficult to judge in spring/summer), and sometimes by retained juvenile tertials (more worn and bleached than adult and any newly moulted tertials and also contrasting with the greater coverts, which are new). Also, has more grey-brown rather than reddish-brown iris, at least throughout the 1st winter (very subtle; can only be judged in the hand). In 1st-summer male the plumage is generally slightly less advanced than in adult male summer.

Voice: The calls are very characteristic and completely different from the calls of Reed Bunting. Especially when perched it usually calls with a slightly variable *tsleep*, recalling one of the calls of Tree Sparrow. In flight, often gives a call somewhat resembling Richard's Pipit but very much fainter.

Range: Distribution imperfectly known, but now known to breed in W Palearctic (since at least 1981), west to source of River Seyda in Bol'shezemel'skaya tundra (NE European USSR). Mainly breeds in E Siberia W to Yenisei and in the Altai, N Mongolia and possibly locally in N China. Winters chiefly in E China.

Status: Accidental in Britain: Fair Isle, Shetland, adult female (29th Sept-11th Oct 1976), and juvenile (17th-18th Sept 1981).

RED-HEADED BUNTING   *Emberiza bruniceps*   ? **62**

L 16-17cm (6.5"). C Asia. Vagrant – status clouded by many avicultural escapes.

All plumages: A large, rather heavy and relatively large-billed and long-tailed bunting which lacks any pure white in the tail.

Adult male summer: Unmistakable, with slightly variable, bright rufous hood extending onto the centre of the breast (crown and upper throat may be more yellowish). Has yellow, unstreaked underparts and rump, and greenish-tinged, finely streaked upperparts.

Adult male winter: Acquires pale fringes to the rufous ear-coverts and throat/breast and has more brownish forehead, crown/nape and upperparts; the typical pattern is still usually discernible.

Adult female: Greyish-brown, faintly streaked above and more or less yellowish below (at least on the undertail-coverts), without, or with only very little streaking. It is extremely similar to the very closely related Black-headed Bunting. The mantle and scapulars are generally slightly more greyish-tinged (some are notably brownish though), on average with slightly more distinct and more sharply-defined dark streaks. At least in summer, there is frequently some rufous on the forehead, ear-coverts, throat and breast centre and some greenish-yellow on the crown – thus showing a trace of the male's pattern. Black-headed is on average more distinctly streaked on the forehead and crown, and these parts, together with the ear-coverts, are often quite dark, ghosting the pattern of the male. There is probably never any rufous on the head/breast and rarely any greenish-yellow on the crown.

The mantle/scapulars and rump probably never show any rufous, which is commonly seen in Black-headed. The rump and uppertail-coverts are usually greenish-yellow, which is sometimes the case in Black-headed as well. The bill averages marginally shorter and deeper than in Black-headed.

Only typical individuals are safely identified, and the differences are generally even less pronounced in autumn/winter than in spring/summer. The reported hybridization SE of the Caspian Sea further complicates the issue.

Juvenile: Upperside generally shows more extensive dark centres than in subsequent plumages, and breast and flanks are distinctly streaked.

1st-winter: Resembles the adult female, except that in the autumn it generally shows fresher remiges and rectrices (may be surprisingly heavily worn though!). Some juvenile scapulars are frequently retained, often also the longest uppertail-coverts, and differ markedly from those of the adult and newly moulted feathers in being more worn and paler on the fringes, and generally show obviously larger dark centres. The majority of the greater coverts and tertials are usually juvenile, sometimes also some median coverts. These are clearly more worn and bleached than any newly moulted feathers. Note that adults sometimes moult a few coverts/tertials before the autumn migration, then showing a moult contrast. However, the retained adult coverts/tertials are much more worn than the juvenile.

Sexing is apparently not possible, but males tend to be more yellow below. The 1st-winter is generally not safely distinguished from 1st-winter Black-headed Bunting.

1st-summer: Not separable from adult (both moult completely in winter).

Voice: The song is a rather harsh, ringing, short, monotonous phrase, which usually begins with a few, full *zrit* notes. It is very similar to the song of Black-headed Bunting. The calls comprise *tliip* and *tlyp* (both rather House Sparrow-like), a rather harsh *jyp* and a *prrit*.

Note: Red-headed and Black-headed Buntings are often considered conspecific. Hybridization has been described from the area SE of the Caspian Sea where their respective ranges overlap.

Range: Breeds from N and SE of the Caspian Sea, through S USSR and Afghanistan to NW China. Winters chiefly on the Indian Subcontinent.

Status: Rare vagrant in Europe. Numerous records, but particularly in N Europe most have been attributed to escaped cagebirds, where until fairly recently it was imported in large numbers. General vagrancy seems very likely, and records should be collected so that perhaps some kind of pattern can be assessed in the future.

It has been reported from the following countries: Iceland, Faeroes, British Isles (many), France, Channel Is, Belgium, Netherlands, Denmark, Norway, Sweden, West Germany, Czechoslovakia, Switzerland, Italy, and Spain.

DICKCISSEL   *Spiza americana*   A **63**

L 16cm (6.25"). North America. Only one record from Norway.

Adult male: Easily identified by its distinctive greyish, black, white and yellow head pattern, and has reddish-brown lesser and median coverts. The black throat patch acquires pale fringes in winter.

Adult female: Rather nondescript. Shows distinctive head pattern with brownish-grey crown/nape and rather faint streaking on the crown, uniformly brownish-grey ear-coverts with a pale crescent below the eye, usually yellowish supercilium, and distinct malar and submoustachial stripes, the latter often partly yellowish. Usually has a yellowish breast; normally at least some chestnut on the lesser and median coverts (sometimes lacking); finely streaked flanks and sometimes breast, and large bill.

1st-winter: Resembles the adult female, but shows no or less yellow on head and breast, 1st-winter female also less rufous on coverts. The juvenile tertials are usually retained (1-2 pairs are sometimes new), more worn and show narrower, more sharply defined and paler (generally whitish) edges and tips than the adult. The edges to the alula are whitish to pale buffish and contrast with the browner edges to the newly moulted greater coverts/carpal covert. In the adult the edges to the alula are the same colour as on the greater coverts/carpal covert. The tail feathers are rather pointed at all ages, but they are extremely acute in 1st-year and generally slightly more worn than in the adult.

The 1st-winter male tends to be more yellow and less streaked on the breast than 1st-winter female, and there are sometimes a few blackish feathers on the throat. The lesser and median coverts are generally more chestnut, with less extensive dark centres to the latter than in 1st-winter female. Typical males show almost entirely chestnut lesser and median coverts, whereas classic females lack chestnut on the lesser coverts and show pale chestnut tips and extensive dark centres to the median coverts.

1st-summer: Resembles the adult of its respective sex, but the same characters as for 1st-winter are usually valid but more difficult to judge.

Voice: Song is a variable *zic zic zre-zre-zre*; *zic-zic serrr-si-si*, or similar. Call a buzzing *brrrt*, somewhat reminiscent of Long-tailed Tit.

Range: Breeds on the plains of EC USA. Winters primarily from Mexico to N South America.

Status: Accidental in Norway: Maløy, Sogn og Fjordane on 29th July 1981.

ROSE-BREASTED GROSBEAK   *Pheucticus ludovicianus*   B **62**

L 18-21.5cm (7-8.5"). North America. Rare vagrant (mainly autumn).

All plumages: A rather large, heavy passerine with a massive, pale bill.

Adult male summer: Easily recognized by black head, mantle and scapulars; mostly white rump area; black wings and tail, the former with double white bars and a prominent white patch at the base of the primaries, and the latter with much white on the tips of the outer 2-4 pairs. Also, has white underparts with a bright pink patch in the centre of the breast and bright pink underwing-coverts.

Adult male winter: Resembles females/1st-winter male, but the centres to the mantle and scapulars are normally blacker. The back and rump are often white with dark barring, and there is more pink on the throat/breast (usually none in females). Further, the base colour of the wings and tail is black, usually with considerably more white at the base of the primaries, and there is prominent white in the tail.

Adult female: Distinctive head and wing pattern, streaked mantle and scapulars and breast/flanks. The underwing-coverts are yellow, a mixture of yellow and pink or sometimes even entirely pink.

1st-winter male: Resembles females, but the breast tends to be less streaked. The white patch on the primaries is accentuated by a blackish

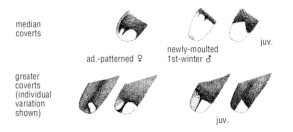

median coverts

ad.-patterned ♀

newly-moulted 1st-winter ♂

juv.

greater coverts (individual variation shown)

juv.

shade at the distal end, and compared to 1st-winter female, the white patch is generally larger. The underwing-coverts are always pink (cf. adult and 1st-winter females respectively). Often there is also some pink on the throat/breast and some decidedly black-centred feathers on the mantle and scapulars, not seen in females. Any newly moulted greater coverts are blacker than in the female, and any newly moulted median coverts show more white.

Frequently, median coverts and some inner greater coverts are moulted, fresher, longer and usually show a different pattern than retained juvenile feathers (see figure, p. 420; but slight overlap). Sometimes, all of the coverts are moulted, then contrasting with the primary coverts. The rectrices are narrower and less truncated than in the adult.

1st-summer male: Resembles the adult male, but is easily distinguished by the distinct contrast shown between the brownish primary coverts/remiges and the blacker greater coverts. Also, usually at least one pair of tertials is juvenile and sometimes some to all of the tail-feathers.

1st-winter/-summer female: Differs from the adult female by the same characters for upperwing and tail as for 1st-winter male. The underwing-coverts are yellow or yellow with some pinkish admixed.

Voice: The song is soft, full-toned, clear and rather short. It calls with a rather squeaky, metallic *kick* or *kink*.

Range: Breeds from C-NW Canada to SE Canada and NE USA. Winters from C Mexico to NW South America. Vagrant in Greenland.

Status: Rare vagrant in the British Isles (21, all Oct, except one in Dec-Jan; all have been immatures); Channel Islands (Sark Sept 1975, Guernsey Oct 1987); France, Ouessant (Oct 1985); Norway (May 1977, Oct 1977); Sweden, (10th Oct 1988); Spain, Benidorm (Oct 1982); Yugoslavia (Oct 1976), and Malta (Apr 1977, Oct 1978, Oct 1979).

INDIGO BUNTING *Passerina cyanea*   B **63**

L 12-13cm (5"). North America. Accidental in N Europe (spring/autumn).

Adult male summer: The brilliant blue plumage prevents confusion with any European species of similar size and build.

Adult male winter: The plumage is browner, due to rather extensive brownish fringes to most of the feathers of the head, body, coverts and tertials. Some blue usually 'shines through' here and there and is always evident on the primary coverts and remiges.

Adult female: Uniformly pale rufous-brown above and paler below with a brownish wash on the breast/flanks. Shows some indistinct streaking on the breast. Also, has rather indistinct paler brownish wing-bars and edges to the tertials. The edges to the primary coverts, central alula, rectrices (especially basal parts) and generally remiges show a pale greenish-blue tinge. The colour to the edges of the remiges varies slightly with the angle at which they are seen, and they may look more brownish. The lesser coverts also generally show some pale greenish-blue. A few bluish feathers are sometimes also present elsewhere.

1st-winter: Resembles the adult female, but most of the greater coverts are usually retained from juvenile, and show more sharply defined and paler tips than adult and any newly moulted greater coverts. Sometimes, some median coverts are retained as well, differing from adult and newly moulted medians by pointed dark centres and paler tips. Also, shows brown-edged primary coverts and central alula. The remiges normally show brownish edges, but sometimes look more greenish/bluish-tinged as in adult female. Also, shows more pointed tail-feathers than adult, at least in some without greenish-blue edges.

From Nov-Dec (sometimes earlier) the outer, sometimes all, primaries are renewed, and then contrasting with the more worn retained remiges with less bluish-tinged edges. Males also acquire scattered blue body feathers.

It is perhaps most similar to a female/1st-year male Scarlet Rosefinch. However, it is decidedly smaller, more rufous-tinged and plainer above, generally less distinctly streaked below, browner on the flanks, and generally shows less distinct wing-bars and has a proportionately longer and less bulbous bill.

1st-summer: Resembles the adult of its respective sex but generally shows a moult contrast among the remiges. 1st-summer male usually shows some brown mottling.

Voice: The song is rather high-pitched, clear, quick and variable, somewhat resembling a rather slow Greenish Warbler. Call, loud *pwit* or *pwit pwit*.

Note: The Blue Grosbeak *Guiraca caerulea*, from North America has been recorded a few times in N Europe, although these have generally been considered more likely to have been escapes. It is considerably larger than Indigo, with a larger bill. It also shows rufous double wingbars, most prominent in the male.

Range: Breeds chiefly in E USA. Winters mainly from S Mexico to Panama and in the Caribbean.

Status: Accidental in Iceland (2nd record in Oct 1985). Britain: Shetland, Fair Isle (Aug 1964), Essex (Sept 1973), Norfolk (Oct 1988). Ireland: Cape Clear, Co. Cork, 1st-winter (Oct 1985). Netherlands (June-July 1983, Mar 1989*). Denmark (Aug 1987, Feb 1990*). Sweden (Apr-May 1989*). Finland (May 1982, May 1989* two). Yugoslavia (singing male, June 1978, considered an escape). Kept as a cage-bird, so escapes always possible.

Family ICTERIDAE   Bobolink, Grackles, and New World Blackbirds, Orioles etc.

BOBOLINK   *Dolichonyx oryzivorus*   B **63**

L 16-18cm (7"). North America. Rare vagrant (majority in autumn).

All plumages: Shows exceptionally pointed tail-feathers and a rather large bill.

Adult male summer: Very distinctive and unlikely to be confused with any other species. The black head and underparts, buffish nape and black upperparts with pale streaking in the centre of the mantle, also whitish scapulars and back, rump and uppertail-coverts are diagnostic.

Adult male winter: Resembles the adult female and 1st-winter birds. In the hand usually distinguished from the adult female by the slightly longer wing (> 91mm; < 93mm in female) and often by a few extensively blackish feathers on the underparts.

Adult female: Very distinctive. Note characteristic head pattern, with dark lateral and pale median crown-stripes, prominent supercilium, rather plain face with darker eye-stripe behind the eye and no dark malar stripes. Shows heavily streaked upperparts, with rather prominent 'braces' on the mantle and distinct streaking on the flanks and, less prominently, on the breast sides. The wing-feathers have distinct pale edges/fringes, but the wing-bars are comparatively indistinct. The general coloration is decidedly buffish.

1st-winter: Similar to the adult female and adult male winter, but the tertials are usually unmoulted (some may be moulted), more worn and with more whitish outer edges and tips and usually show more extensive dark centres than the adult. Also, in the hand the edge to the central alula can be seen to be whitish, contrasting with the browner edges to the newly moulted greater coverts/carpal covert (no contrast in adult). The primary coverts show whiter tips, and the tail-feathers are even more pointed and more worn than in the adult.

The 1st-winter male differs from 1st-winter female in the same way as the adult male differs from the adult female (see above).

1st-summer: Not safely separable from the adult, because both adult and 1st-year have a complete pre-breeding moult. Adults are rather unique among Holarctic passerines in moulting completely twice annually.

Voice: The song is very distinctive. Produces rather short, variable phrases with a very characteristic voice, including both very deep-throated and very high-pitched, thin, 'squeezed' notes. The call is a soft *pint*.

Range: Breeds on the plains across N USA and S Canada. Winters in South America.

Status: Rare vagrant in the British Isles (14 Sept-Oct, including 8 on the Isles of Scilly), France: Ouessant (15th-16th Oct 1987). Norway, near Oslo (Nov 1977). Italy: Tuscany (18th Sept 1989). Gibraltar (male, 11th-16th May 1984).

COMMON GRACKLE   *Quiscalus quiscula*   A **64**

L 28-34.5cm (12.5"). North America. Accidental in Denmark (once in spring).

All plumages: Rather large, all-dark passerine with characteristic shape (notably bill and long, keel-shaped tail).

Adult male: Black with variable gloss and shows a pale yellowish iris.

Adult female: Resembles the adult male but is distinctly smaller (wing *c.* 120-136mm, *c.* 131-151mm in male), slightly duller and less-black, especially on the underparts.

Juvenile: Entirely dull brown with a rather dark iris. Moults completely or nearly so at an early age and is unlikely to be recorded in Europe.

1st-winter/-summer: Both sexes are usually more similar to the adult female in plumage, but some juvenile feathers are often retained, more worn and obviously browner than the rest. The colour of the iris apparently quickly becomes pale like the adult.

Voice: Calls are generally hoarse, shrill and grating, including *chak*, *chek* and a *cheer*.

Note: There are other, more or less similar, species (e.g. corvids, grackles and starlings) both in America and Africa which might turn up in Europe as escapes.

Range: Breeds Canada and USA, E of Rocky Mts. Winters in E USA (not N parts).

Status: Accidental in Denmark: Grevinge, Zealand (Mar-Apr 1970). Origin hard to assess.

YELLOW-HEADED BLACKBIRD *Xanthocephalus xanthocephalus*   A **64**

L 20-26cm (8-10"). North America. Accidental in N Europe (May-Oct).

Adult male: Black, with contrasting yellow head, neck and breast, and shows a small black face-mask. There is a large white patch on the primary coverts, and it has prominently white-tipped outer greater coverts and central alula.

Adult female: Dark grey-brown with yellowish supercilium, throat and breast, and often shows dark malar stripes. The lower breast/upper belly are often mottled with whitish.

1st-winter male: Resembles the adult female but shows distinct whitish tips to the primary coverts and central alula, often also on the outer greater coverts. Also has slightly narrower and more tapered rectrices. Wing-length > 128mm (cf. 1st-winter female).

1st-summer male: Still most like female, but often shows more adult male-like head pattern.

1st-winter/-summer female: Differs from the adult female by the same characters of wing and tail as for 1st-year male. Tends to show less yellow than a male of the same age, especially in 1st-summer plumage. It is also much smaller than the male (wing < 127mm).

Voice: The song is a peculiar mixture of variable sounds, in some parts recalling the songs of Fieldfare, Great Reed Warbler and Trumpeter Finch, respectively.

Range: Breeds in W North America, north to C Canada. Winters in SW USA and Mexico. Regularly strays to the E coast of USA, mainly in autumn and winter. Has been recorded at sea in Atlantic *c.* 300 miles NE of New York City. Vagrants have twice reached Greenland, Nanortalik (Sept 1840) and Särdloq (Aug 1900).

Status: Accidental in Iceland (23rd-24th July 1983), Britain (several records currently under consideration, including a male present on Fair Isle, Shetland in Apr 1990), France (Aug-Sept 1979), Denmark (Oct 1918), Norway (May 1979), Sweden (May 1956).

NORTHERN ORIOLE *Icterus galbula*   B **64**

L 17-19cm (7.5"). North America. Accidental in N Europe (mainly autumn).

All plumages: A relatively large, quite slim passerine with a rather long and very pointed bill.

Adult male: Has very striking black-and-orange plumage. The E, nominate, subspecies, 'Baltimore Oriole' has black head and neck, orange lesser and median coverts and a whitish greater covert-bar. The W subspecies, *bullockii*, 'Bullock's Oriole' has orange sides to the head/neck and black forehead to hindneck, eye-stripe and 'bib' and a large white wing-panel.

Adult female: Very variable. The dullest females are faintly tinged orange-yellow on the head (more greenish on top/sides) and on most of the underparts. The mantle and scapulars are greyish-brown and show indistinct dark mottling, with more yellowish-green back/rump, upper-tail-coverts and tail. Other individuals are brighter and more orange-tinged on the head, underparts and rump area and more yellow/greenish-brown on the mantle/scapulars. All show double, whitish, wing-bars and whitish edges to the tertials

Some females show a pattern rather more similar to an adult/1st-summer male, but not quite so strikingly coloured, and generally show prominent green/yellowish-brown fringes to the mantle/scapulars, less extensively orange lesser and median coverts, and have a duller and more diffuse black and orange tail pattern. They further differ from less advanced 1st-summer males in the same way as between 1st-summer male and adult male (see below).

'Bullock's' is more greyish on the mantle/scapulars and generally more yellow, less orange-tinged, on the head and underparts, with whitish belly and greyish flanks. However, some female-type Northern are very similar. In 'Bullock's' the head pattern often mirrors that of the adult male.

1st-winter male: Resembles the adult female (not adult male-like type). Generally shows a moult contrast among the greater coverts (new feathers are fresher and slightly darker-centred with slightly more greyish-tinged and marginally more diffuse pale tips) or, if all the greater coverts have been renewed, between the greater coverts and the alula/primary coverts. At least some of the tertials are often retained. The rectrices are also more tapered than in the adult.

1st-summer male: Usually similar to the adult male, but shows contrasting brown alula, primary coverts, remiges, often a few outer greater coverts, and one to all pairs of tertials. The median coverts are occasionally retained (whitish instead of orange), sometimes also the odd tail-feather. Some are said to be less advanced and show a mixture of black and orange on the head and upperparts. Apparently, 'Bullock's' is normally less advanced.

1st-winter/-summer female: Similar to the adult female, but is usually duller and at least in 1st-winter lacks the strong blackish mottling shown by some adult females. The wing and tail are as in 1st-winter male, from which it is difficult to tell, but tends to be less bright.

Voice: The song is a rather short series of clear, fluty, rather well-spaced and irregularly delivered notes, e.g. *tiu, heeu, huee, tiu-tiu*. Call a hard, rattling *cher-r-r-r-r* and a nasal *ueht*.

Range: Breeds in most of USA and in S Canada. Winters chiefly from Mexico to N South America, occasionally further north in USA. Vagrant to Greenland.

Status: Accidental in Iceland (3+ records). Britain (16, Sept-Dec, May, plus 1st-winter female wintering at Roch, Dyfed from 2nd Jan-23rd Apr 1989 and, like the Golden-winged Warbler and Common Yellowthroat in Kent, it completed a remarkable trio of wintering N American passerines during that period). Netherlands (Oct 1987), Norway (male, Utsira, 28th Sept 1986). The majority of records appear to refer to 'Baltimore'.

British Rarities

The number and variety of rare species identified annually in the British Isles is often astonishing. There seems to be no limit to the new species that may turn up and subsequently qualify for admission to the British and Irish List.

However, a number of species that were previously considered British rarities have subsequently been dropped – either because of the increase in the number of individuals being recorded or, as in the case of Ferruginous Duck, because of the large number of escapes involved. These are:

Cory's Shearwater	Sabine's Gull
Purple Heron	Ring-billed Gull
White Stork	Richard's Pipit
Snow Goose	Tawny Pipit
Red-crested Pochard	Cetti's Warbler
Ferrugineous Duck	Savi's Warbler
Crane	Aquatic Warbler
Kentish Plover	Icterine Warbler
Pectoral Sandpiper	Melodious Warbler
Buff-breasted Sandpiper	Yellow-browed Warbler
Long-tailed Skua	Serin
Mediterranean Gull	Scarlet Rosefinch

Times and places

A rare bird can be discovered on almost any day of the year, although there are obvious peak periods when rarities are more frequent, during the spring and autumn migrations. During the peak migration periods, the more common migrants, scarcer species, and a good sprinkling of rarities, are scattered more widely throughout the British Isles (both coastal and inland), from Fair Isle and Shetland, southwards to the Yorkshire, Norfolk and Kentish coasts, west to the Isles of Scilly, and reaching Cape Clear Island, Co. Cork.

During the peak periods, heavy falls of migrants often occur in periods of bad weather. This is especially so on the North Sea coasts, when large numbers of migratory birds are forced off course by strong north-easterly or easterly winds. Often by the following morning many hundreds or thousands of tired birds (many flying all night and often beyond midday) eventually reach our shores and drop down quickly to shelter.

The prime example of this phenomenon was the vast fall of north European migrants on the east coast of Norfolk and Suffolk on 3rd September 1965, probably by far the heaviest ever recorded in Britain. It was estimated that more than half a million birds came down along 24 miles of Suffolk coastline between

Sizewell and Hopton on that one day. Evidently most of these birds were part of the stream of migrants travelling south-south-west from Scandinavia towards Spain and Portugal. They had been disorientated, concentrated and forced down by overcast conditions and heavy rain.

Winds with an easterly component in spring and autumn often bring rarities. By keeping a watchful eye on weather patterns during peak migration times, one can often predict to some extent an overnight fall of migrants, or the arrival of certain diurnal migrants during the following few days.

As well as the European migratory species, there are also rarer migrants which reach us from very much further east in Siberia. Some of these species are annual and occur in varying numbers each autumn, such as Richard's Pipit, Yellow-browed and Pallas's Warblers. Others occur in smaller numbers as vagrants, and not necessarily every year, such as Olive-backed Pipit, Pechora Pipit, Citrine Wagtail, Pallas's Grasshopper Warbler, Lanceolated, Radde's and Dusky Warblers. A high percentage of these species often consist of migration-inexperienced young birds.

In spring, various scarce visitors to the British Isles, such as Wryneck, Hoopoe, Bluethroat, Icterine Warbler, Red-backed Shrike, and Ortolan Bunting, often turn up with falls of predictable common migrants. This particularly on our south and east coasts, but also in some numbers as far north as Shetland. Occasionally other rarer species such as Little Bittern, Red-footed Falcon, Alpine Swift, Bee-eater, Red-rumped Swallow, Woodchat Shrike, Bonelli's Warbler or Subalpine Warbler may arrive then.

In the autumn, a period of gales and strong westerly or north-westerly winds coinciding with the southward return of Nearctic waders will inevitably produce a string of familiar rarities in Britain and Ireland, such as Baird's, Buff-breasted, Pectoral and White-rumped Sandpipers, and Wilson's Phalarope.

However, of all the Nearctic species on the British and Irish list, perhaps the most remarkable are the American wood warblers, such as the tiny, colourful Northern Parula, the strikingly patterned Black-and-white Warbler, or the gaudy American Redstart. Especially in autumn, many migratory species of North American birds can be displaced very much further east by hurricanes and powerful westerly airstreams. Most of them perish in the Atlantic. The tiny fraction that reach us often draw large crowds of birdwatchers to see them. Individuals of these American warblers have often been watched feeding actively in tree cover, sometimes in the company of migrating Chiffchaffs and Goldcrests or even alongside one of the Siberian *Phylloscopus*, such as the Yellow-browed Warbler.

News of rarities

Most birdwatchers build up their own network of friends to pass on the latest birding information, so that news of the unusual bird tends to travel fast. The greatest source of information, however, is available by telephone from the Bird Information Service called BIRDLINE (0898 700 222, or enquiries on 0263 741139). They will tell you about the latest rarities in the British Isles, on recorded messages which are often updated several times a day. Those who find a rarity can also phone in the news (hotline number 0263 741140).

There are also Regional Bird Lines for the South-east, East Anglia, Midlands,

North-east, North-west and Scotland; others are expected to cover the South-west and South Wales, thereby completing the coverage for Britain. These regional birdlines are very useful in providing local information on migratory or certain resident species present in the area; supplying details of how to reach a particular site if you are already in the area or intending to visit (be prepared to jot down an OS map grid reference quickly). They are also useful in the study of one's own area, especially when time is limited or travel difficult.

An alternative information service is National Bird News (N.B.N.): (telephone 0898 884 500), which also aims to provide the fastest daily Rare Bird News anywhere in the UK, with its Twitch-Line (0898 884 501). Three other lines are also available: B.T.O. News Line; I.C.B.P. World Bird Line; and even a Butterfly Line. These other lines are mainly concerned with conservation issues, while a percentage of all profits of N.B.N. goes to conservation projects.

Other birds rare in Britain

The main part of this book covers the birds considered rare in Europe as a whole. But there are some further 80 species which, although not qualifying for inclusion as not rare in the rest of Europe, are undoubtedly rarities for Britain and Ireland. Most of those listed below breed in various areas to the south or south-east of the British Isles, often around the Mediterranean. We give for each the total number of individuals accepted up to the end of 1989, with the year of the last accepted sighting in brackets and an indication of the months of sighting. A few exceptional records for 1990 are included.

Since not rarities for mainland Europe, these birds are all covered in all the main field guides. We include for each a reference to two standard works:

P = *A Field Guide to the Birds of Britain and Europe* Peterson, Mountfort & Hollom (4th Ed. 1983), followed by the relevant **plate** number.

H = *The Birds of Britain and Europe, with North Africa and the Middle East* Heinzel, Fitter & Parslow (1972), followed by the **page** number.

Little Bittern *Ixobrychus minutus* **P 5 H 39.** 313, (1989): Mainly Apr-June, also July-Sept. (Yorkshire, pair bred successfully in 1984).

Night Heron *Nycticorax nycticorax* **P 5 H 39.** 406, (1989): All months, especially Apr-June.

Squacco Heron *Ardeola ralloides* **P 6 H 37.** 120, (1988): Apr-Oct.

Cattle Egret *Bubulcus ibis* **P 6 H 37.** 51, (1988): All months.

Little Egret *Egretta garzetta* **P 6 H 37.** 603, (1989): All months, most Apr-Sept.

Great White Egret *Egretta alba* **P 6 H 37.** 44, (1989): Apr-Nov, especially May-July.

Black Stork *Ciconia nigra* **P 6 H 43.** 74, (1989): Mar-Nov, mostly May-Aug.

Glossy Ibis *Plegadis falcinellus* **P 6 H 41.** Many earlier records (54 between 1958-89): All months.

Black Kite *Milvus migrans* **P 21, 22 H 73, 89.** 134, (1989): especially Apr-June; July-Nov.

White-tailed Eagle *Haliaeetus albicilla* **P 25, 26 H 71, 88.** Many before last breeding record of *c*. 1916. Following recent re-introduction programme in W Scotland, 6 pairs nested in 1987 (two successfully). Elsewhere in British Isles, 18 records (1958-89) of birds of presumed genuine continental origin.

Egyptian Vulture *Neophron percnopterus* **P 20 H 83**. 2, (Oct 1825, Sept 1868).

Griffon Vulture *Gyps fulvus* **P 71 H 85**. 3, (spring 1843, two in June 1927).

Lesser Kestrel *Falco naumanni* **P 27, 28 H 95**. 21, (1987): Feb-Nov.

Red-footed Falcon *Falco vespertinus* **P 27, 28 H 95**. 446, (1989): mainly Apr-Oct, especially May-June.

Gyr Falcon *Falco rusticolus* **P 28 H 91**. Many earlier records (93 between 1958-89): Sept-May.

Little Crake *Porzana parva* **P 31 H 115**. 99, (1987): All months, especially spring/autumn.

Baillon's Crake *Porzana pusilla* **P 31 H 115**. Many earlier records, also bred 19th century (6 between 1958-89).

Little Bustard *Tetrax tetrax* **P 32 H 113**. 107, (1989): All months, especially late autumn/winter.

Great Bustard *Otis tarda* **P 32 H 113**. many, formerly bred to 19th century. (21 between 1958-87).

Black-winged Stilt *Himantopus himantopus* **P 36, 37 H 119**. 242, (1989). Bred successfully 1945, 1987, failed 1983. Mainly Apr-Sept.

Collared Pratincole *Glareola pratincola* **P 36, 39 H 143**. 75, (1989): Feb-Nov, especially Apr-July.

Broad-billed Sandpiper *Limicola falcinellus* **P 40 H 127**. 148, (1989): May-Sept.

Great Snipe *Gallinago media* **P 39, 39 H 141**. 244, (1989): All months.

Slender-billed Gull *Larus genei* **P 44 H 147**. 5, (1987): Apr-Sept.

Gull-billed Tern *Gelochelidon nilotica* **P 47, 49 H 159**. 238, (1989): Apr-Oct. Essex, pair bred 1950 (probably also in 1949).

Caspian Tern *Sterna caspia* **P 47, 49 H 159**. 199, (1989): Apr-Nov.

Whiskered Tern *Chlidonias hybridus* **P 48, 49 H 163**. 106, (1989): Mainly Apr-Sept.

White-winged Black Tern *Chlidonias leucopterus* **P 48 H 163**. 567, (1989): Mar-Nov, mainly May-Sept.

Great Auk *Pinguinus impennis.* Extinct: no records since about 1840.

Great Spotted Cuckoo *Clamator glandarius* **P 54 H 175**. 30, (1989): Mar-May, July-Oct.

Scops Owl *Otus scops* **P 52 H 179**. 81, (1989): Apr-Nov.

Eagle Owl *Bubo bubo* **P 52 H 177**. Several in 18th, 19th centuries (status uncertain due to escapes).

Snowy Owl *Nyctea scandiaca* **P 52 H 177**. Many (94 between 1958-89), pair bred successfully 1967, 1968.

Hawk Owl *Surnia ulula* **P 53 H 181**. 11, (1983): Aug-Mar.

Tengmalm's Owl *Aegolius funereus* **P 53 H 181**. 57, (1986): May-June, Oct-Mar.

Red-necked Nightjar *Caprimulgus ruficollis* **P 54 H 185**. 1, (Oct 1856).

Pallid Swift *Apus pallidus* **P 57 H 187**. 6, (1984): May, Nov.

Alpine Swift *Apus melba* **P 57 H 187**. 429, (1989): Mar-Nov.

Bee-eater *Merops apiaster* **P 54 H 189**. 464, (1989): Apr-Nov. Bred Sussex 1955 (3 pairs, 2 successfully).

Roller *Coracias garrulus* **P 54 H 189**. 215, (1989): Apr-Nov, especially May-July.

Calandra Lark *Melanocorypha calandra* **P 56 H 203**. 3, (Apr 1961, Apr 1978, Apr 1985).

Short-toed Lark *Calandrella brachydactyla* **P 56 H 201**. 350, (1989): Apr-Jan, especially May & Sept-Oct.

Lesser Short-toed Lark *Calandrella rufescens* **P 56 H 201**. 4 records involving a total of 42 birds (last record in 1958): Jan-May (all in Ireland).

Crested Lark *Galerida cristata* **P 56 H 205**. 19, (1982): Mar-June, Sept-Jan.

Crag Martin *Ptyonoprogne rupestris* **P 57 H 207**. 3, (June, July 1988, Sept 1989).

Red-rumped Swallow *Hirundo daurica* **P 57 H 207**. 188, (1989): Mar-Nov.

Red-throated Pipit *Anthus cervinus* **P 58 H 209**. 219, (1989): Apr-June, Aug-Nov.

Alpine Accentor *Prunella collaris* **P 73 H 221**. 35, (1978): Mar-June, Aug-Jan.

Rufous Bush Robin *Cercotrichas galactotes* **P 63, H 255**. 11, (1980): Aug-Oct, Apr.

Thrush Nightingale *Luscinia luscinia* **P 60 H 255**. 90, (1989): May-Oct.

Black-eared Wheatear *Oenanthe hispanica* **P 60 H. 245**. 46, (1989): Mar-Nov, especially Apr-June, Aug-Oct.

Black Wheatear *Oenanthe leucura* **P 60 H 249**. 4, (1954): Aug-Oct.

Rock Thrush *Monticola saxatilis* **P 60 H 243**. 24, (1989): Feb-June, Oct-Nov.

Fan-tailed Warbler *Cisticola juncidis* **P 62 H 227**. 4, (1985): Apr-Sept.

River Warbler *Locustella fluviatilis* **P 62 H 223**. 12, (1989): May-Sept.

Moustached Warbler *Acrocephalus melanopogon* **P 62 H 227**. 10, (1979): Apr-Aug. Pair bred Cambridge in 1946.

Great Reed Warbler *Acrocephalus arundinaceus* **P 62 H 225**. 156, (1989): Apr-Nov, especially May-June.

Olivaceous Warbler *Hippolais pallida* **P 64 H 229**. 14, (1985): Aug-Oct.

Subalpine Warbler *Sylvia cantillans* **P 63 H 235**. 248, (1989): Mar-Nov, especially May-June, Sept-Oct.

Sardinian Warbler *Sylvia melanocephala* **P 63 H 233**. 18, (1988): Apr-Oct.

Rüppell's Warbler *Sylvia rueppelli* **P 63 H 233**. 3, (Aug-Sept 1977, June 1979, Oct 1990).

Orphean Warbler *Sylvia hortensis* **P 63 H 233**. 5, (1982): July-Oct.

Bonelli's Warbler *Phylloscopus bonelli* **P 64 H 237**. 107, (1989): Apr-Oct.

Collared Flycatcher *Ficedula albicollis* **P 67 H 241**. 16, (1986): Mainly May-June; Sept-Oct.

Wallcreeper *Tichodroma muraria* **P 66 H 273**. 10, (1985): Jan-June, Sept-Dec.

Short-toed Treecreeper *Certhia brachydactyla* **P 66 H 273**. 7, (1978): Apr-May, Sept-Dec.

Penduline Tit *Remiz pendulinus* **P 68 H 265**. 35, (1989): Jan-Jun, Sept-Dec.

Lesser Grey Shrike *Lanius minor* **P 67 H 219**. 135, (1989): May-Nov.

Woodchat Shrike *Lanius senator* **P 67 H 219**. 558, (1989): Mar-Oct.

Nutcracker *Nucifraga caryocatactes* **P 69 H 305**. 403, (1987): Mainly Aug-Feb.

Spanish Sparrow *Passer hispaniolensis* **P 73 H 299**. 3, (June 1966, Oct 1972, Oct 1977).

Rock Sparrow *Petronia petronia* **P 73 H 301**. 1, (June 1981).

Citril Finch *Serinus citrinella* **P 71 H 293**. 1, (Jan 1904).

Parrot Crossbill *Loxia pytyopsittacus* **P 72 H 297**. 231, (1987): All months. Bred successfully in 1983-85.

Pine Grosbeak *Pinicola enucleator* **P 72 H 297**. 10, (May 1975): Apr-May, Oct-Nov.

Rock Bunting *Emberiza cia* **P 74 H 275**. 6, (1967): Feb-Aug.

Cretzschmar's Bunting *Emberiza caesia* **P 74 H 279**. 2, (June 1967, June 1979).

Rustic Bunting *Emberiza rustica* **P 73 H 277**. 223, (1989): Apr-June, Sept-Nov.

Black-headed Bunting *Emberiza melanocephala* **P 74 H 277**. 87, (1989): Apr-Oct.

Further Reading :

Baker, K. 1977. Westward vagrancy of Siberian passerines in autumn 1975. *Bird Study* 24: 233-42.

B.O.U. Records Committee: Eleventh Report (Dec 1983) *Ibis* 126: 440-4. Twelfth Report (Apr 1986)*Ibis* 128: 601-3. Thirteenth Report (Dec 1987) *Ibis* 130: 334-7. Fourteenth Report (Apr 1991) *Ibis* 133: in press.

Carruthers, M. P., Cubitt, M. G. & Hall, L. 1989. The dark-rumped petrels in Tyne & Wear. *Birding World* 2: 288-9; 1990. 3: 224-5.

Dymond, J. N., Fraser, P. A. & Gantlett, S.J.M. 1989. *Rare Birds in Britain and Ireland.* Calton. Indispensable. Analyses some 45,000 records of scarce and rare birds in Britain and Ireland for the period 1958-85, and extreme rarities outside the period. Maps show distribution by county, in spring and autumn or at particular times of the year.

Elkins, N. 1988. *Weather and Bird Behaviour.* 2nd ed. Calton.

Mead, C. 1983. *Bird Migration.* Feltham.

Redman, N. & Harrap, S. 1987. *Birdwatching in Britain – a Site-by-Site Guide.* Comprehensive accounts (including information on access, maps etc.).. Bromley.

Rogers, M. J. et al. 1988. Report on rare birds in Great Britain in 1987. *British Birds* 81: 535-96.

Sharrock, J.T.R. 1974. *Scarce migrant birds in Britain & Ireland.* Berkhamstead.

Sharrock, J.T.R. & Grant, P. J. 1982. *Birds new to Britain and Ireland.* Calton.

Snow, D. W. (Ed). 1971. *The Status of Birds in Britain and Ireland.* Prepared by the Records Committee of the B.O.U. Oxford.

See also the excellent series *Where to Watch Birds* published by Christopher Helm.

Appendix

The following are the cases where the nomenclature adopted in this book differs from that of Voous (1977):

Egretta caerulea and ***Egretta tricolor***. Voous: *Hydranassa caerulea* and *Hydranassa tricolor*. We follow the American Ornithologists' Union (1983) and others (e.g. Hancock & Kushlan 1984).

Aquila nipalensis. Voous: *Aquila rapax*. Because of the distinct differences in size and structure, plumage and ecology, the *nipalensis* group (with the subspecies *nipalensis* and *orientalis*) and the *rapax* group (with subspecies *rapax*, *belisarius* and *vindhiana*) have been treated as separate species by several authors (Porter *et al.* 1981, Gensbøl 1984), and this is also the view of the EEC Checklist Committee (Jon Fjeldså, pers. comm.).

Falco peregrinus pelegrinoides. Voous: *Falco pelegrinoides*, although in a footnote he writes: "sometimes treated as conspecific with *F. peregrinus* (author's preference)". See Brosset (1986), who advocates the view that the two forms are treated as conspecific.

Catharacta maccormicki. Voous: *Stercorarius maccormicki*. We follow the American Ornithologists' Union (1983) and Harrison (1983) in separating the skuas into two genera.

Pluvialis dominica and ***Pluvialis fulva***. Voous: *Pluvialis dominica dominica* and *Pluvialis dominica fulva*. This is now the most widely accepted treatment.

Anthus richardi. Voous: *Anthus novaeseelandiae*. *Anthus novaeseelandiae sensu lato* comprises many different subspecies breeding on three continents. It seems to make sense to divide this complex into a number of species, as has been suggested by e.g. Bauer & Glutz (1985).

Anthus rubescens (including subspecies ***japonicus***). Voous: *Anthus spinoletta rubescens* and *Anthus spinoletta japonicus*. The decision to split off *rubescens* and *japonicus* from *spinoletta* is now widely accepted.

Phylloscopus trochiloides nitidus and ***Phylloscopus trochiloides plumbeitarsus***. Voous: *Phylloscopus nitidus* and *Phylloscopus plumbeitarsus*. Both *nitidus* and *plumbeitarsus* are morphologically and vocally very close to the north-western subspecies *viridanus* of Greenish Warbler.

Phylloscopus (inornatus) humei. Voous: *Phylloscopus inornatus humei*. The form *humei* is generally considered a subspecies of *P. inornatus* but there may be sufficient reason for treating *humei* (with subspecies *mandellii*) as a separate species.

Muscicapa dauurica. Voous: *Muscicapa latirostris*. We follow the reasons given by Watson (1986), i.e. Pallas's *Muscicapa dauurica* described in 1811, was in wide use in the Russian literature and precedes *Muscicapa latirostris* Raffles, 1822.

Coccothraustes vespertinus, Passerculus sandwichensis, Passerella iliaca and ***Melospiza melodia***. Voous: *Hesperiphona vespertina*, *Ammodramus sandwichensis*, *Zonotrichia iliaca* and *Zonotrichia melodia* respectively. In these cases we prefer to follow the American Ornithologists' Union (1983).

Bibliography

Listed below are the references that have been consulted and that we can recommend for further studies.

I Identification, moult, taxonomy and distribution

General

American Ornithologists' Union. 1983. (6th ed.). *Checklist of North American Birds*. Kansas.

Bruun, B., Delin, H., Svensson, L., Singer, A. & Zetterström, D. 1986. *Birds of Britain and Europe*. London.

Cornell University, Laboratory of Ornithology. 1975. *A Field Guide to Western Bird Songs*. Boston.

Cramp, S. (Ed.) et al. 1977-. *Handbook of the Birds of Europe, the Middle East and North Africa: The Birds of the Western Palearctic*. Vols I-V. London.

Delin, H. & Svensson, L. 1988. *Photographic Guide to the Birds of Britain and Europe*. London.

Dementiev, G. P. & Gladkov, N. A. et al. 1951-4. *Birds of the Soviet Union*. 6 vols. Israel Program for Scientific Translation, Jerusalem, 1966-70.

Farrand, Jr J. (Ed.) et al. 1983. *The Audubon Society Master Guide to Birding*. 3 vols. New York.

Ferguson-Lees, J., Willis, I. & Sharrock, J. T. R. 1983. *The Shell Guide to the Birds of Britain & Ireland*. London.

Flint, V. E. et al. 1984. *Field Guide to the Birds of the USSR, including Eastern Europe & Central Asia*. New Jersey.

Ginn, H. B. & Melville, D. S. 1983. *Moult in Birds*. B.T.O. Guide No. 19. Tring.

Glutz von Blotzheim, U. N., Bauer, K. M. & Bezzel, E. et al. 1966-. *Handbuch der Vögel Mitteleuropas*. 11 vols. published so far. Wiesbaden.

Heinzel, H., Fitter, R., & Parslow, J. 1972. *The Birds of Britain & Europe with North Africa and the Middle East*. London.

Jonsson, L. 1978-82. *Birds of Lake, River, Marsh and Field; Birds of Sea and Coast; Birds of Wood, Park and Garden; Birds of Mountain Regions; Birds of the Mediterranean and Alps*. 5 vols. London.

Kaufman, K. 1990. *Advanced Birding*. Boston.

Mild, K. 1987. *Soviet Bird Songs* (two cassettes and booklet). Stockholm.

Mild, K. 1990. *Israel and Middle East Bird Songs* (two cassettes and booklet). Stockholm.

National Geographic Society. 1987. *Field Guide to the Birds of North America*, 2nd Edn. Washington, D.C.

Palmér, S. & Boswall, J. 1980-1. *A Field Guide to the Bird Songs of Britain and Europe*. First (gramophone) & second (cassette) edition. Stockholm.

Peterson, R.T. 1980. *A Field Guide to the Birds*. (4th Ed.). Boston.

Peterson, R., Mountfort, G. & Hollom, P. A. D. 1983 (4th Ed.). *A Field Guide to the Birds of Britain & Europe*. London.

Sonobe, K. & Washburn Robinson, J. (eds), et al. 1982. *A Field Guide to the Birds of Japan*. Tokyo.

Stresemann, E. & Stresemann, V. 1966. Die Mauser der Vögel. *Journ. Orn* (Sonderheft) 107:1-448.

Vaurie, C. 1959. *The Birds of the Palearctic Fauna. Passeriformes.* London.

—— 1965. *The Birds of the Palearctic Fauna. Non-Passeriformes.* London.

Voous, K. H. 1977. *List of Recent Holarctic Bird Species.* Brit. Orn. Union. London. (Originally published 1973, 1977 in *Ibis*).

Divers

Appleby, R. H., Madge, S. C. & Mullarney, K. 1986. Identification of divers in immature and winter plumages. *British Birds* 79: 365-391.

Barthel, P.H. & Mullarney, K. 1988. Die Bestimmung der Seetaucher Gaviidae im Winter. *Limicola* 2:45-69.

van Ijzendoorn, E.J. 1985. Divers in winter. *Dutch Birding* 7:49-58.

Seabirds

Harrison, P. 1986. *Seabirds: an Identification Guide.* 2nd edn. Beckenham.

—— 1987. *Seabirds of the World: a photographic guide.* Beckenham.

Lee, David S. 1988. The Little Shearwater (*Puffinus assimilis*) in the western North Atlantic. *American Birds* 42: 213-20.

Herons

Hancock, J. & Kushlan. J. 1984. *The Herons Handbook.* Beckenham.

Yésou, P. 1984. Little Egrets with uncommon bare-parts coloration. *British Birds* 77: 315-16.

Wildfowl

Dean, A. R. and the Rarities Committee. 1989. Distinguishing characters of American/East Asian race of Common Scoter. *British Birds* 82: 615-16.

Madge, S. C. & Burn, H. 1987. *Wildfowl: an Identification Guide to the Ducks, Geese and Swans of the World.* Beckenham.

Birds of prey

Brosset, A. 1986. Les populations du faucon pélerin, *Falco peregrinus* Gmelin, en Afrique du nord: un puzzle zoogéographique. *Alauda* 54: 1-14.

Clark, W. S. & Wheeler, B. K. 1987. *Field Guide to the Hawks of North America.* Boston.

Clark, W. S., Frumkin, R. & Shirihai, H. 1990. Field Identification of Sooty Falcon. *British Birds* 83: 47-54.

Edelstam, C. 1984. Patterns of moult in large birds of prey. *Ann. Zool. Fennici* 21: 271-276.

Forsman, D. 1984. *Rovfågelsguiden.* Helsinki.

—— 1990. Identification of Spotted, Lesser Spotted and Steppe Eagle with special reference to birds in subadult and adult plumages. *Fåglar i Uppland* 17:43-69. (In Swedish with an English summary).

Königstedt, D. & Gleinich, W. 1988. Über die Feldkennzeichen junger Bindenseeadler *Haliaeetus leucoryphus. Limicola* 2:70-73.

Porter, R.F., Willis, I., Christensen, S. & Nielsen, B.P. 1981. *Flight Identification of European Raptors.* 3rd Edn. Calton.

Svensson, L. 1971. *Circus macrourus* and *C. pygargus* – the problem of identification. *Vår Fågelvärld* 30: 106-122. (In Swedish with an English summary).

—— 1975. Spotted Eagle *Aquila clanga* and Lesser Spotted Eagle *A. pomarina* – the problem of identification. *Vår Fågelvärld* 34: 1-26. (In Swedish with an English summary).

—— 1987. Underwing pattern of Steppe, Spotted and Lesser Spotted Eagles. *International Bird Identification. Proceedings* of the 4th International Identification Meeting 1986, p. 12-14.

Rails

Becker, P. & Schmidt, C. 1990. Kennzeichen und Kleider der europäischen kleinen Rallen und Sumpfhühner *Rallus* und *Porzana*. *Limicola* 4:93-144.

Moore, D. R. & Piotrowski, S. H. 1983. Hybrid Coot × Moorhen resembling American Coot in Suffolk. *British Birds* 76: 407-9.

Waders

Alström, P. 1987. The identification of Baird's and White-rumped Sandpipers in juvenile plumage. *Birding* 19: 10-13.

—— 1990. Calls of American and Pacific Golden Plovers. *British Birds* 83: 70-2.

—— & Olsson, U. 1989. The identification of juvenile Red-necked and Long-toed Stints. *British Birds* 82: 360-372.

van den Berg, A. B. 1988. Identification of Slender-billed Curlew, and its occurrence in Morocco in winter of 1987/88. *Dutch Birding*. 10: 45-53.

Britton, D. 1980. Identification of Sharp-tailed Sandpipers. *British Birds* 73: 333-45.

Chandler, R. J. 1989. *North Atlantic Shorebirds*. London and Basingstoke.

Colston, P. R. & Burton, P. 1988. *A Field Guide to the Waders of Britain and Europe with North Africa and the Middle East*. London.

Connors, P. G. 1983. Taxonomy, distribution & evolution of Golden Plovers (*Pluvialis dominica* and *Pluvialis fulva*). *Auk* 100: 607-620.

Dunn, J. L., Morlan, J. & Wilds, C. P. 1987. Field Identification of forms of Lesser Golden Plover. *International Bird Identification*. Proceedings of the 4th International Identification Meeting 1986, p. 28-33.

Grant, P. J. 1983. Spotted Redshanks flying with legs retracted. *British Birds* 76: 136-7.

—— 1986. Four problem stints. *British Birds* 79: 609-21.

—— & Jonsson, L. 1984. Identification of stints and peeps. *British Birds*. 77: 293-315.

Hayman, P, Marchant, J. & Prater, T. 1986. *Shorebirds: an Identification Guide to the Waders of the World*. Beckenham.

Jonsson, L. 1984. Fältbestämning av små *Calidris*- vadare. *Vår Fågelvärld* 43:339-361.

Marchant, J. H. 1984. Identification of Slender-billed Curlew. *British Birds* 77: 135-40.

Nielsen, B. P. & Colston, P. R. 1984. Breeding plumage of female Caspian Plover. *British Birds* 77: 356-7.

Pitelka, F.A. 1950. Geographic variation and the species problem in the shorebird genus *Limnodromus*. *University of California Publications in Zoology* 50:1-108.

Prater, A. J., Marchant, J. & Vuorinen, J. 1977. *Guide to Identification and Ageing of Holarctic Waders*. B.T.O. Guide 17. Tring.

Taylor, P. B. 1982/83. Field identification of sand plovers. *Dutch Birding*. 4: 113-30; 5: 37-66.

Wilds, C. 1982. Separating the Yellowlegs. *Birding* 14: 172-8.

—— & Newlon, M. 1983. The identification of dowitchers. *Birding* 15: 151-66.

Gulls and terns

Gantlett, S. J. M. & Harris, A. 1987. Identification of large terns. *British Birds* 80: 257-76.

Grant, P. J. 1986. *Gulls: a Guide to Identification*. 2nd edn. Calton.

Hayes, H. 1975. Probable Common × Roseate Tern hybrids. *Auk* 92:219-234.

Hedgren, S. & Larsson, L. 1973. *Larus hyperboreus, L. glaucoides*, or aberrant-coloured other gulls – the problem of identifying light-winged gulls in the field. *Vår Fågelvärld* 32:173-98.

Kirkham, I. R. & Nisbet, I. C. T. 1987. Feeding techniques and field identification of Arctic, Common and Roseate Terns. *British Birds* 80: 41-7.

Knox, A. 1987. Taxonomic status of 'Lesser Golden Plovers'. *British Birds* 80: 482-7.

Lauro, A.J. & Spencer, B.J. 1980. A method for separating juvenile and first-winter Ring-billed Gulls (*Larus delawarensis*) and Common Gulls (*Larus canus*). *American Birds* 34:111-117.

Mullarney, K. 1988. Identification of Roseate Tern in juvenile plumage. *Dutch Birding*. 10: 109-20.

—— 1988. Identification of a Roseate × Common Tern hybrid. *Dutch Birding* 10: 133-5.

—— 1988. Identification of adult Roseate Tern. *Dutch Birding* 10: 136-7.

Smith, N. G. 1966. Evolution of some arctic gulls (*Larus*): An experimental study of isolating mechanisms. *Orn. Monogr.* 4. A.O.U. Lawrence.

Swifts

Catley, G. P. & Sharrock, J. T. R. 1978. Partially albino Swifts. *British Birds* 71: 222-3.

Passerines

Alström, P. 1988. Identification of Blyth's Pipit. *Birding World*. 1: 268-72.

—— 1989. Identification of Lanceolated Warbler, *Locustella lanceolata*. *Vår Fågelvärld* 48: 335-46. (In Swedish with an English summary).

—— & Hirschfeld, E. 1989. The identification of three Asiatic *Muscicapa* flycatchers. *Vår Fågelvärld* 48: 127-38. (In Swedish with an English summary).

—— & Mild, K. 1987. Some notes on the taxonomy of the Water Pipit complex. *International Bird Identification*. Proceedings of the 4th International Identification Meeting 1986, p. 47-8.

—— & Mild, K. 1989. Identification of Pechora Pipit. *Birding World* 2: 276-82.

—— & Olsson, U. 1987. Field Identification of Arctic and Greenish Warblers. *International Bird Identification*. Proceedings of the 4th International Identification Meeting 1986, p. 54-9.

—— & Olsson, U. 1988. Taxonomy of Yellow-browed Warblers. *British Birds* 81: 656-7.

Barthel, P.H. & Schmidt, C. 1990. Hinweise zur Bestimmung der Zitronenstelze *Motacilla citreola*. *Limicola* 4:149-182.

van den Berg, A.B. 1982. Moults and basic plumages of Rose-coloured Starling. *Dutch Birding* 4: 136-9.

—— 1984. Field identification of Dupont's Lark. *Dutch Birding*. 6: 102-5.

Dean, A. R. 1982. Field characters of Isabelline and Brown Shrikes. *British Birds*. 75: 395-406.

—— 1985. Review of British status and identification of Greenish Warbler. *British Birds* 78: 437-51.

Elmberg, J. *in prep*. Flight identification of Two-barred Crossbill.

Goodwin, D. 1986. *Crows of the World*. British Museum (Nat. Hist.) 2nd Edn. London.

Hall, B. P. 1961. The taxonomy and identification of pipits (genus *Anthus*) *Bull. Brit. Mus. Nat. Hist.* (*Zool.*), 7: 245-90.

Harrap, S. 1988. Identification of Olivaceous and Booted Warblers. *Birding World* 1: 312-15.

—— & Lewington, I. 1990. Hinweise zur Unterscheidung der Spötter *Hippolais* im Freiland. *Limicola* 4:49-73.

—— & Quinn, D. 1989. The difficulties of Reed, Marsh and Blyth's Reed Warbler identification. *Birding World* 2: 318-24.

Heard, C.D.R. & Walbridge, G. 1988. Field Identification of Pechora Pipit. *British Birds* 81:452-463.

Herremans, M. 1989. Vocalizations of Common, Lesser and Arctic Redpolls. *Dutch Birding* 11: 9-15.

Hirschfeld, E. & Svensson, L. 1985. Field identification of Rufous Turtle Dove, *Streptopelia orientalis. Vår Fågelvärld* 44: 145-52. (In Swedish with an English summary).

Jännes, H. 1988. Identification of Olivaceous Warbler *Hippolais pallida. Lintumies* 23: 66-71. (In Finnish with an English summary).

Jollie, M. 1985. The dimorphism of *Coloeus dauuricus*, the Asian Jackdaw. *Journ. Orn. Berl.*. 126: 303-5.

—— & Lammin-Soila, M. 1989. The separation of first-autumn Citrine Wagtails, *Motacilla citreola*, and "grey and white" Yellow Wagtails, *Motacilla flava. Lintumies* 24: 108-13. (In Finnish with an English summary).

Kaufman, K. 1988. Notes on female Tanagers. *American Birds*. Vol 42. 1: 3-5.

Knox, A.G. 1976. The taxonomic status of the Scottish Crossbill, *Loxia* sp. *Bull. Brit. Orn. Cl.* 96: 15-19.

—— 1979. Partially leucistic Starling resembling Rose-coloured Starling. *British Birds* 72: 79-80.

—— 1988. Taxonomy of the Rock/Water Pipit superspecies *Anthus petrosus, spinoletta* and *rubescens. British Birds* 81: 206-11.

—— 1988. The Taxonomy of Redpolls. *Ardea* 76 (1): 1-26.

Madge, S. C. 1987. Field identification of Raddes's and Dusky Warblers. *British Birds*. 80: 595-603.

Molau, U. 1985. The Redpoll complex in Sweden. *Vår Fågelvärld* 44: 5-20. (In Swedish with an English summary).

Pearson, D. J. 1981. Field identification of Isabelline Shrike. *Dutch Birding*. Vol 3: 119-22.

Pyle, P. et al. 1987. *Identification Guide to North American Passerines.* Bolinas.

Riddiford, N. & Broome, T. 1983. Identification of first-winter Pallas's Reed Bunting. *British Birds*. 76: 174-82.

Robel, D. 1989. Distinguishing juvenile Rose-coloured Starlings, *Sturnus roseus*, from pale Starlings, *S. vulgaris*, in flight. *Limicola* 3: 31-2.

Schulze-Hagen, K. 1989. Notes on Aquatic Warbler, *Acrocephalus paludicola. Limicola* 3: 229-46. (In German with an English summary).

Shirihai, H. Field characters of Sykes's Yellow Wagtail. International Bird Identification. *Proceedings* of the 4th International Identification Meeting 1986, p. 49-53.

—— & Colston, P. R. 1987. Siberian Water Pipits in Israel. *Dutch Birding.* 9: 8-12.

——, Mullarney, K. & Grant, P. J. 1990. Identification of Dunn's, Bar-tailed and Desert Larks. *Birding World* 3: 15-21.

Sluys, R. & van den Berg, M. 1982. On the specific status of the Cyprus Pied Wheatear *Oenanthe cypriaca. Ornis Scand.* 13:123- 28.

Svensson, L. 1984. *Identification Guide to European Passerines.* 3rd edn. Stockholm.

Ticehurst, C. B. 1938. *A Systematic Review of the Genus Phylloscopus.* Brit. Mus. (Nat. Hist.). London.

Ullman, M. 1984. Starlings with sandy-pale plumage like immature Rose-coloured Starling. *Vår Fågelvärld* 43: 42-43. (In Swedish with an English summary).

—— 1986. Stonechats, *Saxicola torquata*, and white rumps. *Vår Fågelvärld* 45: 227-9. (In Swedish with an English summary).

Watson, G. E. in Mayr, E. & Cottrell, G. W. 1986. *Checklist of Birds of the World*, Vol. XI. Cambridge, Mass.

Whitney, B. & Kaufman, K. 1985-7. The *Empidonax* challenge. *Birding* 17:151-158, 17:277-287, 18:153-159, 18:315-327 and 19:7-15.

Williamson, K. 1960. *Identification for Ringers, 1*. The Genera *Cettia, Locustella, Acrocephalus, and Hippolais*. 3rd rev. ed. 1968. B.T.O guide no. 7. Tring.

—— 1962. *Identification for Ringers, 2*. The genus *Phylloscopus*. 2nd rev. ed. 1967. B.T.O guide no. 8. Tring.

—— 1964. *Identification for Ringers, 3*. The genus *Sylvia*. 2nd rev. ed. 1968. B.T.O guide no 9. Tring.

II   Status

Baker, J.K. & Catley, G.P. 1987. Yellow-browed Warblers in Britain & Ireland, 1968-85. *British Birds*. 80: 93-109.

Bannerman, D.A. & Bannerman, W.M. 1983. *The Birds of the Balearics*. Beckenham.

Baumaris, J. & Blums, P. 1969. *Latvijas Putni (Birds of Latvia)*. Riga.

van den Berg, A.B. 1984. Occurrence of Sociable Plover in Western Europe. *Dutch Birding* 6: 1-8.

—— 1988. Slender-billed Curlews at Merja Zerga during winter 1987-8. *Birding World*. Vol 1, No. 5: 175-8.

—— 1989. *Lijst van Nederlandse vogelsoorten (List of Dutch bird species 1989)*. Santpoort-Zuid.

—— 1989. Varia: Bald Ibis. *Dutch Birding* 11: 128-31.

Bernis, F. 1954. Prontuario de la Avifauna Española (incl Aves de Portugal, Baleares y Canaries). *Alauda* 1: 11-85.

Brichetti, P. & Massa, B. 1984. Check-list Degli Uccelli Italiani. *Revista Italiana di Ornitologia*. 54: 3-37.

—— & Foschi, U.F. 1987. The Lesser Crested Tern in the Western Mediterranean and Europe. *British Birds*. 80: 276-80.

'British Birds' List of Birds of the Western Palearctic. 1984. Enlarged and revised edition. Kempston.

British Ornithologists' Union – Records Committee: Thirteenth Report (December 1987). Ibis 130: 334-7.

Bezzel, E. 1985. *Kompendium der Vögel Mitteleuropas, Nonpasseriformes-Pichtsingvögel*. Wiesbaden.

Bloch, D. & Sørensen, S. 1984. Yvirlit Yvir Føroya Fuglar. *Checklist of Faroese Birds*. Tórshavn.

Cardillo, R. et al. 1983. The Western Reef Heron (*Egretta gularis*) at Nantucket Island, Massachusetts. *American Birds* 37: 827-9.

Clapp, R.B. 1971. A specimen of Jouanin's Petrel from Lisianski Island, NW Hawaiian Islands. *Condor* 73: 490.

Cruon, R. & Nicolau-Guillaumet, P. 1985. Notes d'Ornithologie française. *Alauda* 53: 34-63.

—— et al. 1987. Notes d'Ornithologie française. *Alauda* 55: 356-81.

Dennis, J.V. 1986. European encounters of birds ringed in North America. *Dutch Birding*. 8: 41-4.

Dubois, P.J. & Yésou, P. 1986. *Inventaire des Espèces d'Oiseaux Occasionnelles en France*. Secrétariat de la France et de la Flore. Paris.

Durand, A.L. 1963. A remarkable fall of American land-birds on the 'Mauretania', New York to Southampton, Oct 1962. *British Birds*. 56: 157-64.

Dymond, J.N., Fraser, P.A. & Gantlett, S.J.M. 1989. *Rare Birds in Britain and Ireland*. Calton.

European News. *British Birds* (six monthly reports) from May 1977- June 1990. Vols 70-83. Report nos 1-27.

Fernández-Cruz, M. & Aravjo, J. (Eds). 1985. *Situacion de la Avifauna de la Peninsula Iberica, Baleares y Macaronesia*. CODA-SEO. Madrid.

Fjeldså, J. & Jensen, J-K. 1985. "Invasion" af Hvidvingede og Kumlien's Måger *Larus glaucoides glaucoides* og *kumlieni* på Nolsø på Fœrøerne. *Dansk Ornitologisk Forenings Tidskrift* 79: 103-6.

Génsbøl, B. 1984. *Rovfuglene i Europa, Nordafrika og Mellemøsten*. København.

Gollop, J.B., Barry, T.W. & Iversen, E.H. 1986. *Eskimo Curlew. A vanishing species?* Special Publication No. 17 of the Saskatchewan Nat. Hist. Soc. Regina.

Haftorn, S. 1971. *Norges fugler*. Universitetsforlaget, Oslo.

Helbig, A.J. 1985. Occurrence of White-tailed Plover in Europe. *Dutch Birding*. 7: 79-84.

—— 1987. Feldbestimmung des Waldpiepers *Anthus hodgsoni* und sein Auftreten in Europa. *Limicola* 1: 73-85.

Hirschfeld, E. 1986. Rufous Turtle Dove in Europe. *Dutch Birding* 8: 77-84.

Hollom, P.A.D. 1980 (2nd revised Ed.). *The Popular Handbook of Rarer British Birds*. London.

Hoogendoorn, W. & Mackrill, E.J. 1987. Audouin's Gull in the south-western Palearctic. *Dutch Birding*, 9:99-107.

Howey, D.H. & Bell, M. 1985. Pallas's Warblers and other migrants in Britain & Ireland in Oct 1982. *British Birds*. 78: 381-92.

Hudson, R. 1974. Allen's Gallinule in Britain and the Palearctic. *British Birds*. 67: 405-13.

—— 1984. B.O.U. Records Committee: how it works. *British Birds* 77: 247-9.

Irby, L.H.L. 1875. *The Ornithology of the Straits of Gibraltar*. London.

Koskimies, P. 1980. The breeding biology of Blyth's Reed Warbler, *Acrocephalus dumetorum* in SE Finland. *Ornis. Fennica* 57: 26-32.

Lindermayer, R.A. 1860. Die Vögel Griechenlands. Ein Beitrag zur Fauna dieses Landes. *Jb. natwiss. Ver. Passau*, 3: 17-202.

Lippens, L. & Wille, H. 1972. *Atlas des Oiseaux de Belgique et d'Europe Occidental*. Lannoo, Tielt.

Løppenthin, B. 1967. *Danske ynglefugle i fortid og nutid*. Odense.

Mauer, K.A. & van Ijzendoorn, E.J. 1987. Terekruiters in Nederland en Europa. *Dutch Birding* 9: 89-98.

Mayaud, N. 1953. Liste des Oiseaux de France. *Alauda* 21: 1-63.

Merikallio, E. 1958. *Finnish Birds. Their distribution and numbers*. Helsingfors.

Møller, A.P. 1978. *Nordjyllands Fugle* Klampenborg.

Moltoni, E. & Brichetti, P. 1978. Elenco degli Uccelli Italiani. *Rev. Ital. di Orn*. 48: 65-142.

Nadler, T. & Ihle, U. 1988. Beobachtungen am Feldrohrsänger *Acrocephalus agricola* in Bulgarien. *Limicola* 2: 205-17.

Newton, I. & Chancellor, R.D.(eds). 1985. Conservation Studies on Raptors. *I.C.B.P. Tech. Pub*. No 5. Cambridge.

Norderhaug, A & M. 1982. X – *Anser erythropus* in Fennoscandia. *Aquila* 89: 93-101.

Olioso, G. 1987. Les Pouillots Orientaux en France. *Alauda* 55: 122- 39.

Olson, S.L. 1985. The Italian Specimen of *Bulweria fallax* (Procellariidae) *Bull. Brit. Orn. Cl.* 105: 29-30.

Pétursson, G. 1987. Flaekingsfuglar á Íslandi: Máfar* (Rare & vagrant birds in Iceland – Gulls*). *Náttúrufraedingurinn* 57: 57- 79.

Risberg, L. 1990. *Sveriges Fåglar*. Stockholm.

Robbins, C.S. 1980. Predictions of future Nearctic landbird vagrants to Europe. *British Birds*. 73: 448-57.

Rogers, M.J. 1982. Ruddy Shelducks in Britain in 1965-79. *British Birds*. 75: 446-55.

Sharrock, J.T.R. 1974. *Scarce migrant birds in Britain & Ireland*. Berkhamstead.

—— & Sharrock, E.M. 1976. *Rare birds in Britain and Ireland*. Berkhamstead.

—— & Grant, P.J. 1982. *Birds new to Britain and Ireland*. Calton.

Snell, R.R. 1989. Status of *Larus* gulls at Home Bay, Baffin Island. *Colonial Waterbirds*. 12:12-23.

Snow, D.W. (Ed.). 1971. The Status of Birds in Britain & Ireland. Prepared by the *Records Committee of the B.O.U.* Oxford.

Solomonsen, F. 1963. *Oversigt over Danmarks fugle*. København.

Sterbetz, I. 1982. X11 – Migration of *Anser erythropus* & *Branta ruficollis* in Hungary 1971-1980. *Aquila* 89: 107-114.

—— 1987. Demoiselle Cranes (*Anthropoides virgo* L. 1758) in Hungary. *Aquila* 84: 25-8.

Sveriges Ornitologiska Förening. 1978. *Sveriges Fåglar*. Stockholm.

Teixeira, A.M. & Moore, C.C. 1983. The breeding of the Madeiran Petrel *Oceanodroma castro* on Farilhão Grande, Portugal. *Ibis* 125: 382-4.

Thibault, J.C. 1983. *Les Oiseaux de Corse*. Ajaccio.

Tomialojc, L. 1990. *Ptaki Polski* (Birds of Poland – their distribution and abundance, with English summary). 2nd revised Edn. Warsaw.

Toschi, A. 1986. *Avifauna Italiana*. 3 vols. Firenze.

Ullman, M. 1989. Varför är nordliga kungsfågelsångare *Phylloscopus inornatus* och kungsfågelsångare *Ph. proregulus* tidigare än sydliga? *Vår Fågelvärld* 48: 467-75.

Vinicombe, K. 1985. Ring-billed Gulls in Britain and Ireland. *British Birds* 78: 327-37.

Wallace, D.I.M. 1980. Possible future Palearctic passerine vagrants to Britain. *British Birds*. 73: 388-97.

'Western Palearctic News'. 1988-90. *Birding World*. Vols 1-3.

Watson, G.E., Lees, D.S. & Backus, E.S. 1986. Status and subspecific identity of White-faced Storm-Petrels in the western North Atlantic Ocean. *American Birds* 40:401-8.

Wille, H. 1984. De Purperkoet *Porphyrio porphyrio* ten onrechte als Europese dwaalgast miskend. *Wielewaal* 50: 41-47, 220-6, 330-3.

Winkler, R. 1984. Avifauna der Schweiz, eine kommentierte Artenliste. 1. Passeriformes. *Der Orn. Beobachter*. Beiheft 5: 1-59.

—— 1987. Avifauna der Schweiz, eine kommentierte Artenliste. 2. Non-Passeriformes. *Der Orn. Beobachter*. Beiheft 6: 3-97.

III   Rarity reports

We give here the latest published reports for different countries.

Britain

Rogers, M.J. & the Rarities Committee. 1990. Report on rare birds in Great Britain in 1989. *British Birds* 83: 439-96.

Ireland (Eire and Northern Ireland)
O'Sullivan, O. & Smiddy, P. 1989. Thirty-sixth Irish Bird Report, 1988. *Irish Birds* 4: 79-114.

Iceland
Pétursson, G. & Ólafsson, E. 1989. Sjaldgaefir fuglar á Íslandi 1987. *Bliki* 8: 15-46.

Faeroes
Sørensen, S. 1988. Sjaeldne fugle på Faerøerne i 1986 og 1987. *Dansk Ornithologisk Forenings Tidskrift* 82: 101-8.

France
Dubois, P.J. et le Comité d'Homologation National. 1989. Les Observations d'Espèces Soumises à Homologation Nationale en France en 1988. *Alauda* 57(4): 263-94.

Belgium
Van der Elst, D. & Lafontaine, R-M. 1989. Rapport de la Commission d'Homologation Annee 1987. *Aves* 26 (1): 1-14.

Netherlands
de By, Rolf A., & de Knijff, Peter. 1989. Zeldzame en schaarse vogels in Nederland in 1988. *Limosa* 62: 195-206.

van den Berg, Arnoud B & de By, Rolf A. & CDNA. 1989. Rare birds in the Netherlands in 1988. *Dutch Birding* 11: 151-64.

Denmark
Olsen, K.M. 1989. Sjaeldne fugle i Danmark og Grønland i 1988. *Dansk Orn. For. Tidskr.* 83:131-49.

Norway
Bentz, P-G. & Clarke, A.W. 1990. Sjeldne fugler i Norge i 1988. Rapport fra Norsk sjeldenhetskomité for fugl (NSKF), NZF og NOF. *Vår Fuglefauna.* 13: 131-140.

Sweden
Hirschfeld, E. 1989. Sällsynta fåglar i Sverige 1988 – rapport från SOF: s raritetskommitté. *Vår Fågelvärld* 48: 447-63.

Finland
Hario, M., Numminen, T. & Palmgren, J. 1989. Rariteettikomitean hyväksymät vuoden 1988 harvinaisuushavainnot. *Lintumies* 24: 238-56.

Poland
Notaki Ornitologiczne. 1988. Rare birds recorded in Poland in 1986. Avifaunistic Commission Report No 3. *Notaki. Orn.* 29 (3-4), 135-49.

West Germany
Bundesdeutscher Seltenheitenausschuss. 1989. Seltene Vogelarten in der Bundesrepublik Deutschland von 1977 bis 1986. *Limicola* 3:157-196.

Switzerland
Commission de l'Avifaune suisse,- Les observations suivantes ont été homologuées en juillet 1989. *Nos Oiseaux* 1989. Vol 40, fasc 4.

Schmid, H. 1989. Die wichtigsten ornithologischen Ereignisse 1987 und 1988 in der Schweiz. *Der Orn. Beob.* 86: 163-70.

Italy
Brichetti, P., Fasola, M. & C.O.I. 1989. Comitato di Omologazione Italiano. 6. *Rev. Ital. di Orn.* 59: 269-72.

BIBLIOGRAPHY

Spain
Eduardo de Juana, A. y el Comité Ibérico de Rarezas de la S.E.O. 1989. Observaciones Homologadas de Aves Raras en España Informe de 1987. *Ardeola* 36: 111-123.

IV   Principal sources for other countries:

Azores
Bannerman, D.A. & Bannerman, W.M. 1966. *Birds of the Atlantic Islands*, Vol. 3: *A History of the Birds of the Azores*. London.

Le Grand, G. 1983. *Checklist of the Birds of the Azores*. Ponta Delgada.

—— 1983. Bilan des observations sur les oiseaux d'origine Néarctique effectuées aux Açores (jusqu'en janvier 1983). *Arquipélago*. No. 4: 73-83.

Channel Islands
Dobson, R. 1952. *The Birds of the Channel Islands*. London.

Long, R. 1981. Review of birds in the Channel Islands, 1951-80. *British Birds*. 74: 327-44.

East Germany
Heyder, R. 1952. *Die Vögel des Landes Sachsen*. Leipzig. Jena. 2nd Ed.

Klafs, G. & Stubs, J. 1977. *Die Vogelwelt Mecklenburgs*. Avifaunna der DDR. Vol 1. Jena.

Knorre, D. v., Grün, G., Günther, R. & Schmidt, K. 1986. *Die Vögelwelt Thüringens*. Avifauna der DDR. Vol. 3. Jena.

Kuhk, R. 1939. *Die Vögel Mecklenburgs*. Güstrow.

Niethammer, G., Krammer, H. & Wolters, H.E. 1964. *Die Vögel Deutschlands*. Artenliste. Frankfurt/M.

Makatsch, W. 1981. *Verzeichhnis der Vögel der Deutschen Demokratischen Republic*. Leipzig & Radebeul.

Rutschke, E. 1983. *Die Vogelwelt Brandenburgs*. Avifauna der DDR. Vol. 2. Jena.

Austria
Bauer, K. 1989. Vögel und Säugetiere Österreichs. *Österr. Ges. Vogelkunde*. Klagenfurt.

Blum, V. 1983. *Artenliste der Vögel Vorarlbergs*. Voralberg.

Rokitansky, G. 1964. Catalogus Faunae Astriae. *Aves*. Wien.

Schuster, S., Blum, H. et al. 1983. *Die Vögel des Bodenseegebietes*. Konstanz.

Hungary
Keve, A. 1984. *Magyarország Madarainak Névjegyzéke*. Nomenclator avium Hungariae. Budapest.

Lászlo, H. 1984. *Magyarország fészkelö madarai*. Budapest-Dabas.

Czechoslovakia
Ferianc, O. 1977. *Vtáky Slovenska*. Praha.

Hudec, K. 1983. *Fauna CSSR*. Ptáci. Vol 3 (Pt 2). Praha.

—— & Cèrny, W. 1977. *Fauna CSSR*. Ptáci 2. Praha.

Štastny, K. Randík, A. & Hudec, K. 1987. *Atlas – Hnízdního Rozsírení Ptáku V CSSR*. 1973-1977. Praha.

Yugoslavia
Matvejev, S.D. & Vasic, V.F. 1973. *Catalogus Faunae Jugoslaviae* 4/3. Aves. Ljubljana.

Antal, L., Fernbach, J. et al. 1969. *Register of Birds of the Autonomous Province of Vojvodina*. Larus 23: 73-127.

442

Albania

Ticehurst, C.B. & Whistler, H. 1932. On the Ornithology of Albania. *Ibis*: 13th series, 2: 40-93.

Greece

Bauer, W., Helversen, O. von, Hodge, M. & Martens, J. 1969. *Catalogus Faunae Graeciae*. Pt 2. Thessaloniki.

Handrinos, G. & Demetropoulos, A. *1983. Birds of Prey of Greece*. Athens.

Lambert, A. 1957. A specific check list of the birds of Greece. *Ibis* 99: 43-68.

Rumania

Bacescu, M. et al. 1966. *Nomenclatorul Pasailor Din Republica Socialista România*. Bucuresti.

Câtuneanu, I.I. et al. 1978. *Fauna Republichii Socialiste România. Aves (Pasari)*. Vol. 15, fasc. 1. Bucuresti.

Radu, D. 1979. *Pasarile Din Delta Dunarii*. Bucuresti.

Bulgaria

Harrison, J.M. 1933. A contribution to the ornithology of Bulgaria. *Ibis* 13th series, 3: 494-521, 589-611.

Pateff, P. 1950. *The Birds of Bulgaria*. Sofia.

Uhlig, R. 1988. Bestandszahlen aus Bulgarien. *Orn. Mitt. 40 Jahrgang* (5): 134-5.

Malta

Sultana, J. & Gauci, C. 1982. *A new guide to the birds of Malta*. The Ornithological Society. Valletta.

IL-Merill. 1977-1988. *Bulletin of the Ornith. Soc. of Malta*. Report nos 5-25.

Gibraltar

Cortés, J.E., Finlayson, J.C. et al. 1980. *The Birds of Gibraltar*. Gibraltar.

Finlayson, J.C. & Cortés, J.E. 1987. The Birds of the Strait of Gibraltar – its waters and the northern shore. *Alectoris*. No 6. Special Issue. Gib. Orn. & Nat. Hist. Soc.

Portugal

Sacarrão, G.F. & Soares, A.A. 1979. Nomes Portugueses para as aves da Europa com anotações. *Arquivos da Museu Bocage*. Series 2. vol. 6 No 23: 395-480. Lisboa.

Tait, W.C. 1924. *The Birds of Portugal*. London.

Themido, A.A. 1952. *Aves de Portugal*. Memorias e Estudos de Museu Zoologica da Universidade de Coimbra. No 2.

V   General

Alström, P. & Olsson, U. 1987. Some rare species observed in Japan from September to November 1984. *Strix* 6: 105-8.

Alerstam, T. 1982. *Fågelflyttning*. Lund.

Collar, N.J. & Andrew, P. 1988. *Birds to Watch. The ICBP World Checklist of Threatened Birds*. ICBP Tech. Pub. No. 8. Cambridge.

Diamond, A.W. et al. 1987. *Save the Birds*. Cambridge.

Mountfort, G. & Arlott, N. 1988. *Rare Birds of the World*. London.

Index of English Names

Entries in **bold** type are to Plate numbers

Accentor, Black-throated
329, **42**
Siberian 329, **42**
Albatross, Black-browed 29, **2**
Wandering 30, **2**
Yellow-nosed 30, **2**
Auklet, Crested 170, **36**
Parakeet 170, **36**

Bee-eater 268
Blue-cheeked 182, **39**
Bittern 200
American 41, **5**
Least 41, **5**
Little 200
Schrenck's Little 42, **5**
Blackbird, Yellow-headed 424,
64
Bluetail, Red-flanked 332, **43**
Bluethroat 276
Bobolink 422, **63**
Booby, Brown 37, **4**
Masked 37, **4**
Red-footed 37, **4**
Brant, 'Black' 52, **7**
Bufflehead 70, **11**
Bunting, Black-faced 408, **60**
Black-headed 314
Chestnut 413, **61**
Indigo 421, **63**
Little 412, **61**
Meadow 410, **60**
Pallas's Reed 416, **62**
Pine 409, **60**
Red-headed 418, **62**
Reed 314
Yellow-breasted 414, **61**
Yellow-browed 411, **61**
Bustard, Great 228
Houbara 100, **19**
Little 228
Buzzard, Long-legged 80, **13**
'Steppe' 216

Canvasback 62, **9**
Catbird, Gray 328, **42**
Coot 226
American 97, **18**
Crested 98, **18**
Cormorant, Double-crested 38, **4**
Courser, Cream-coloured 101,
20

Cowbird, Brown-headed **65**
Crane 228
Demoiselle 99, **19**
Sandhill 98, **19**
Siberian White 99, **19**
Crossbill, Scottish 384
Two-barred 383, **53**
Cuckoo, Black-billed 175, **37**
Yellow-billed 176, **37**
Curlew, Eskimo 134, **27**
Slender-billed 135, **28**
Dickcissel 419, **63**
Diver, White-billed 27, **1**
Great Northern 192
Dove, Laughing 174, **37**
Mourning 264
Rufous Turtle 173, **37**
Turtle 264
Dowitcher, Long-billed 130, **27**
Short-billed 129, **27**
Duck, American Black 59, **9**
Falcated 56, **8**
Fulvous Whistling 49, **7**
Harlequin 68, **11**
Ring-necked 63, **9**
Ruddy 214
White-headed 72, **12**

Eagle, Imperial 86, **15**
Lesser Spotted 220, 222
Pallas's Fish 75, **13**
Spotted 82, **16**
Steppe 84, **15**
Egret, Snowy 45, **6**
Eider 210
King 65, **10**
Spectacled 66, **10**
Steller's 67, **10**

Falcon, Eleonora's 88, **17**
'Barbary' 93, **16**
Finch, Trumpeter 385, **53**
Flamingo, Lesser 48, **6**
Flicker, Northern 183, **39**
Flycatcher, Acadian 184, **51**
Brown 372, **51**
Frigatebird, Magnificent 40, **4**

Gallinule, Allen's 95, **18**
American Purple 96, **18**
Purple 96, **18**
Godwit, Black-tailed 244
Hudsonian 133, **27**

Goldeneye 214
Barrow's 71, **12**
Goose, Lesser White-fronted
50, **7**
Red-breasted 53, **7**
Snow 51, **7**
'Blue' **7**
Goshawk, Dark Chanting 79,
14
Grackle, Common 423, **64**
Grebe, Pied-billed 28, **1**
Grosbeak, Evening 387, **53**
Rose-breasted 420, **62**
Guillemot, Brünnich's 169, **36**
Gull, Audouin's 154, **32**
Black-headed 252
Bonaparte's 153, **31**
Common 254
Franklin's 150, **31**
Great Black-headed 148, **30**
Grey-headed 154, **32**
Ivory 160, **33**
Laughing 149, **31**
Little 256
Ring-billed 156, **32**
Ross's 159, **33**
Sabine's 151, **33**
Thayer's **65**
White-eyed 147, **30**
'Kumlien's Iceland' 158, **33**
Gyrfalcon 224

Harrier, Montagu's 218
Pallid 76, **14**
Hawk, Swainson's 79, **16**
Hemipode, Andalusian 94, **18**
Heron, Chinese Pond 44, **5**
Great Blue 46, **6**
Green 43, **5**
Little Blue 44, **6**
Tricolored 45, **6**
Western Reef 46, **6**

Ibis, Bald 47, **6**

Jackdaw, Daurian 378, **51**
Junco, Dark-eyed 407, **58**
Kestrel, American 88, **17**
Killdeer 104, **20**
Kingfisher, Belted 181, **39**
Pied 181, **39**
White-breasted 181, **39**
Kinglet, Ruby-crowned 372, **50**

Kite, Black-shouldered 74, **14**
Kittiwake 256
Knot 236
  Great 115, **23**

Lammergeier 75, **13**
Lanner 90, **17**
Lark, Bar-tailed Desert 185, **40**
  Bimaculated 187, **40**
  Black 188, **40**
  Calandra 270
  Dupont's 186, **40**
  Hoopoe 185, **40**
  White-winged 187, **40**

Merganser, Hooded 73, **12**
Murrelet, Ancient **65**

Nighthawk, Common 178, **38**
Nightjar, Egyptian 177, **38**
Noddy, Brown 168, **35**
Nuthatch, Corsican 374, **51**
  Red-breasted 374, **51**

Oriole, Northern 424, **64**
  Northern 'Baltimore' 318
  Northern 'Bullock's' 318
Ovenbird 399, **57**
Owl, Marsh 176, **38**

Parula, Northern 390, **54**
Pelican, Dalmatian 39, **4**
Petrel, Black-capped 32, **3**
  Bulwer's 32, **3**
  Madeiran 35, **3**
  Soft-plumaged **65**
  Southern Giant 31, **2**
  White-faced 35, **3**
  Wilson's 34, **3**
Phalarope, Wilson's 144, **29**
Phoebe, Eastern 184, **51**
Pipit, Blyth's 191, **41**
  Buff-bellied 324, **41**
  Olive-backed 322, **41**
  Pechora 323, **41**
  Red-throated 272
  Richard's 189, **41**
  Tawny 272
  Water 272
Plover, American Golden 108, **22**
  Caspian 107, **21**
  Greater Sand 106, **21**
  Kittlitz's 104, **21**
  Lesser Sand 105, **21**
  Pacific Golden 110, **22**
  Semipalmated 103, **20**
  Sociable 114, **23**
  Spur-winged 113, **22**
  White-tailed 115, **23**

Pratincole, Black-winged 102, **20**
  Collared 230
  Oriental 102, **20**

Redpoll, Arctic 382, **53**
Redstart, American 399, **57**
  Moussier's 334, **42**
Reeve 242
Robin, American 351, **47**
  Siberian Blue 331, **43**
  White-throated 333, **43**
Rosefinch, Long-tailed 386, **58**
  Pallas's 386, **53**
  Scarlet 296
Rubythroat, Siberian 330, **43**
Ruff 242

Saker 91, **17**
Sandgrouse, Chestnut-bellied 171, **36**
  Pallas's 172, **36**
  Spotted 170, **36**
Sandpiper, Baird's 124, **25**
  Buff-breasted 128, **26**
  Common 248
  Least 122, **25**
  Marsh 137, **28**
  Pectoral 126, **26**
  Semipalmated 117, **24**
  Sharp-tailed 127, **24**
  Solitary 140, **28**
  Spotted 142, **29**
  Stilt 127, **28**
  Terek 141, **28**
  Upland 136, **28**
  Western 118, **24**
  White-rumped 124, **25**
Sapsucker, Yellow-bellied 183, **39**
Scaup 212
  Lesser 64, **11**
Scoter, Surf 70, **11**
  'Black' 69, **11**
Serin, Red-fronted 382, **53**
Shearwater, Little 33, **3**
  Manx 196
Shelduck, Ruddy 54, **7**
Shrike, Brown 374, **52**
  Isabelline 375, **52**
  Long-tailed 377, **52**
Skua, Great 250
  South Polar 146, **30**
Sora 95, **18**
Sparrow, Dead Sea 380, **63**
  Fox 405, **59**
  Lark 308
  Savannah 405, **59**
  Song 406, **59**

White-crowned 406, **59**
  White-throated 407, **59**
Starling, Daurian 379, **52**
  Rose-coloured 378, **52**
Stint, Little 238
  Long-toed 121, **25**
  Red-necked 119, **24**
Stonechat 274
  'Eastern' 334, **42**
Swallow, Cliff 189, **38**
  Tree **65**
Swan, 'Tundra' 50, **7**
Swift, Chimney 179, **38**
  Little 180, **38**
  Needle-tailed 179, **38**
  Pacific 179, **38**
  White-rumped 180, **38**

Tanager, Scarlet 403, **58**
  Summer 403, **58**
Tattler, Grey-tailed 143, **29**
Teal, Baikal 57, **8**
  Blue-winged 59, **9**
  Marbled 61, **8**
  'Green-winged' 58, **8**
Tern, Aleutian 165, **34**
  Bridled 167, **35**
  Caspian 258
  Common 260
  Elegant 163, **34**
  Forster's 166, **35**
  Least **65**
  Lesser Crested 162, **34**
  Roseate 164, **35**
  Royal 161, **34**
  Sooty 167, **35**
Thrasher, Brown 328, **42**
Thrush, Black-throated 350, **47**
  Dusky 348, **47**
  Eye-browed 347, **46**
  Grey-cheeked 345, **46**
  Hermit 344, **46**
  Mistle 280
  Naumann's 348, **47**
  Red-throated 349, **47**
  Siberian 342, **45**
  Swainson's 345, **46**
  Tickell's 346, **46**
  Varied 343, **45**
  White's 341, **45**
  Wood 343, **46**
Tit, Azure 373, **51**
Towhee, Rufous-sided 404, **58**
Tropicbird, Red-billed 36, **4**

Veery 346, **46**
Vireo, Philadelphia 381, **54**
  Red-eyed 381, **54**
  Yellow-throated 298

Wagtail, Citrine 325, **41**
  Yellow 272
Warbler, Aquatic 356, **48**
  Arctic 366, **50**
  Black-and-white 388, **54**
  Black-throated Blue 392, **55**
  Black-throated Green 393, **56**
  Blackburnian 393, **56**
  Blackpoll 398, **56**
  Blyth's Reed 358, **48**
  Booted 361, **48**
  Canada 402, **57**
  Cape May 394, **55**
  Chestnut-sided 391, **55**
  Desert 364, **49**
  Dusky 370, **50**
  Eastern Crowned 365, **50**
  Golden-winged 388, **54**
  Grasshopper 286

Gray's Grasshopper 355, **48**
Greenish 365, **50**
Hooded 401, **57**
Lanceolated 353, **48**
Magnolia 395, **55**
Marmora's 362, **49**
Marsh 286
Ménétries's 362, **49**
Olivaceous 286
Paddyfield 357, **48**
Pallas's 368, **50**
Pallas's Grasshopper 352, **48**
Palm 397, **56**
Radde's 370, **50**
Sardinian 288
Tennessee 389, **54**
Thick-billed 360, **49**
Wilson's 402, **57**
Yellow 390, **55**
Yellow-browed 368, **50**

Yellow-rumped 396, **56**
Waterthrush, Northern 400, **57**
Wheatear 278
  Black-eared 278
  Desert 339, **44**
  Isabelline 336, **44**
  Pied 337, **44**
  White-crowned Black 342, **44**
Whimbrel, Little 134, **27**
  'Hudsonian' 134, **27**
Wigeon 206
  American 54, **8**
Willet 144, **29**

Yellowhammer 310
Yellowlegs, Greater 138, **28**
  Lesser 139, **28**
Yellowthroat, Common 400, **57**

Index of Scientific Names

Acrocephalus aedon 360, **49**
  agricola 357, **48**
  dumetorum 358, **48**
  paludicola 356, **48**
Actitis macularia 142, **29**
Aethia cristatella 170, **36**
Alaemon alaudipes 185, **40**
Ammomanes cincturus 185, **40**
Anas americana 54, **8**
  crecca carolinensis 58, **8**
  discors 59, **9**
  falcata 56, **8**
  formosa 57, **8**
  rubripes 59, **9**
Anous stolidus 168, **35**
Anser caerulescens 51, **7**
  erythropus 50, **7**
Anthropoides virgo 99, **19**
Anthus godlewskii 191, **41**
  gustavi 323, **41**
  hodgsoni 322, **41**
  richardi 189, **41**
  rubescens 324, **41**
Apus affinis 180, **38**
  caffer 180, **38**
  pacificus 179, **38**
Aquila clanga 82, **16**
  heliaca 86, **15**
  nipalensis 84, **15**

Ardea herodias 46, **6**
Ardeola bacchus 44, **5**
Asio capensis 176, **38**
Aythya affinis 64, **11**
  collaris 63, **9**
  valisineria 62, **9**

Bartramia longicauda 136, **28**
Botaurus lentiginosus 41, **5**
Branta bernicla nigricans 52, **7**
  ruficollis 53, **7**
Bucanetes githagineus 385, **53**
Bucephala albeola 70, **11**
  islandica 71, **12**
Bulweria bulwerii 32, **3**
Buteo rufinus 80, **13**
  swainsoni 79, **16**
Butorides striatus virescens 43, **5**

Calidris acuminata 127, **26**
  bairdii 124, **25**
  fuscicollis 124, **25**
  mauri 118, **24**
  melanotos 126, **26**
  minutilla 122, **25**
  pusilla 117, **24**
  ruficollis 119, **24**
  subminuta 121, **25**

tenuirostris 115, **23**
Caprimulgus aegyptius 177, **38**
Carduelis hornemanni 382, **53**
Carpodacus erythrinus **53**
  roseus 386, **53**
Catharacta maccormicki 146, **30**
Catharus fuscescens 346, **46**
  guttatus 344, **46**
  minimus 345, **46**
  ustulatus 345, **46**
Catoptrophorus semipalmatus 144, **29**
Ceryle alcyon 181, **39**
  rudis 181, **39**
Chaetura pelagica 179, **38**
Charadrius asiaticus 107, **20**
  leschenaultii 106, **20**
  mongolus 105, **20**
  pecuarius 104, **20**
  semipalmatus 103, **20**
  vociferus 104, **20**
Chersophilus duponti 186, **40**
Chettusia gregaria 114, **23**
  leucura 115, **23**
Chlamydotis undulata 100, **19**
Chondestes grammacus **59**
Chordeiles minor 178, **38**

Circus macrourus 76, **14**
Coccothraustes vespertinus 387, **53**
Coccyzus americanus 176, **37**
  erythrophthalmus 175, **37**
Colaptes auratus 183, **39**
Corvus dauuricus 378, **51**
Cursorius cursor 101, **20**
Cyclorrhynchus psittacula 170, **36**
Cygnus columbianus columbianus 50, **7**

Dendrocygna bicolor 49, **7**
Dendroica caerulescens 392, **55**
  coronata 396, **56**
  fusca 393, **56**
  magnolia 395, **55**
  palmarum 397, **56**
  pensylvanica 391, **55**
  petechia 390, **55**
  striata 398, **56**
  tigrina 394, **55**
  virens 393, **56**
Diomedea chlororhynchos 29, **2**
  exulans 30, **2**
  melanophris 30, **2**
Dolichonyx oryzivorus 422, **63**
Dumetella carolinensis 328, **42**

Egretta caerulea 44, **6**
  gularis 46, **6**
  thula 45, **6**
  tricolor 45, **6**
Elanus caeruleus 74, **14**
Emberiza aureola 414, **61**
  bruniceps 418, **62**
  chrysophrys 411, **61**
  cioides 410, **60**
  leucocephalos 409, **60**
  pallasi 416, **62**
  pusilla 412, **61**
  rutila 413, **61**
  spodocephala 408, **60**
Empidonax virescens 184, **51**

Falco biarmicus 90, **17**
  cherrug 91, **17**
  eleonorae 88, **17**
  peregrinus pelegrinoides 93, **16**
  sparverius 88, **17**
Fregata magnificens 40, **4**
Fulica americana 97, **18**
  cristata 98, **18**

Gavia adamsii 27, **1**
Geothlypis trichas 400, **57**
Geronticus eremita 47, **6**
Glareola maldivarum 102, **20**

nordmanni 102, **20**
Grus canadensis 98, **19**
  leucogeranus 99, **19**
Gypaetus barbatus 75, **13**

Halcyon smyrnensis 181, **39**
Haliaeetus leucoryphus 75, **13**
Heteroscelus brevipes 143, **29**
Hippolais caligata 361, **48**
Hirundapus caudacutus 179, **38**
Hirundo pyrrhonota 189, **38**
Histrionicus histrionicus 68, **11**
Hoplopterus spinosus 113, **22**
Hylocichla mustelina 343, **46**

Icterus galbula 424, **64**
Irania gutturalis 333, **43**
Ixobrychus eurhythmus 42, **5**
  exilis 41, **5**

Junco hyemalis 407, **58**

Lanius cristatus 407, **58**
  isabellinus 375, **52**
  schach 377, **52**
Larus atricilla 149, **31**
  audouinii 154, **32**
  cirrocephalus 154, **32**
  delawarensis 156, **32**
  glaucoides kumlieni 158, **33**
  glaucoides thayeri 65
  ichthyaetus 148, **30**
  leucophthalmus 147, **30**
  philadelphia 153, **31**
  pipixcan 150, **31**
  sabini 151, **33**
Limnodromus griseus 129, **27**
  scolopaceus 130, **27**
Limosa haemastica 133, **27**
Locustella certhiola 352, **48**
  fasciolata 355, **48**
  lanceolata 353, **48**
Loxia leucoptera 383, **53**
  scotica 384
Luscinia calliope 330, **43**
  cyane 331, **43**

Macronectes giganteus 31, **2**
Marmaronetta angustirostris 61, **8**
Melanitta nigra americana 69, **11**
  perspicillata 70, **11**
Melanocorypha bimaculata 187, **40**
  leucoptera 187, **40**
  yeltoniensis 188, **40**
Melierax metabates 79, **14**
Melospiza melodia 406, **59**

Mergus cucullatus 72, **12**
Merops superciliosus 182, **39**
Micropalama himantopus 127, **26**
Mniotilta varia 388, **54**
Molothrus ater 65
Motacilla citreola 325, **41**
Muscicapa dauurica 372, **51**

Numenius borealis 134, **27**
  minutus 134, **27**
  phaeopus hudsonicus 134, **27**
  tenuirostris 135, **28**

Oceanites oceanicus 34, **3**
Oceanodroma castro 35, **3**
Oenanthe deserti 339, **44**
  isabellina 336, **44**
  leucopyga 341, **44**
  pleschanka 337, **44**
Oxyura leucocephala 73, **12**

Pagophila eburnea 160, **33**
Parula americana 390, **54**
Parus cyanus 373, **51**
Passer moabiticus 380, **63**
Passerculus sandwichensis 405, **59**
Passerella iliaca 405, **59**
Passerina cyanea 421, **63**
Pelagodroma marina 35, **3**
Pelecanus crispus 39, **4**
Phaethon aethereus 36, **4**
Phalacrocorax auritus 38, **4**
Phalaropus tricolor 144, **29**
Pheucticus ludovicianus 420, **62**
Phoenicopterus minor 48, **6**
Phoenicurus moussieri 334, **42**
Phylloscopus borealis 366, **50**
  coronatus 365, **50**
  fuscatus 370, **50**
  inornatus 368, **50**
  proregulus 368, **50**
  schwarzi 370, **50**
  trochiloides 365, **50**
Pipilo erythrophthalmus 404, **58**
Piranga olivacea 403, **58**
  rubra 403, **58**
Pluvialis dominica 108, **22**
  fulva 110, **22**
Podilymbus podiceps 28, **1**
Polysticta stelleri 67, **10**
Porphyrio porphyrio 96, **18**
Porphyrula alleni 95, **18**
Porphyrula martinica 96, **18**
Porzana carolina 95, **18**
Prunella atrogularis 329, **42**
  montanella 329, **42**

Pterocles exustus 171, **36**
   senegallus 171, **36**
Pterodroma hasitata 32, **3**
   mollis **65**
Puffinus assimilis 33, **3**

Quiscalus quiscula 423, **64**

Regulus calendula 372, **50**
Rhodostethia rosea 159, **33**

Saxicola torquata 334, **42**
Sayornis phoebe 184, **51**
Seiurus aurocapillus 399, **57**
   noveboracensis 400, **57**
Serinus pusillus 382, **53**
Setophaga ruticilla 399, **57**
Sitta canadensis 374, **51**
   whiteheadi 374, **51**
Somateria fischeri 66, **10**
   spectabilis 65, **10**
Sphyrapicus varius 183, **39**
Spiza americana 419, **63**
Sterna aleutica 165, **34**
   anaethetus 167, **35**
   antillarum **65**
   bengalensis 162, **34**
   dougallii 164, **35**
   elegans 163, **34**

   forsteri 166, **35**
   fuscata 167, **35**
   maxima 161, **34**
Streptopelia orientalis 173, **37**
   senegalensis 174, **37**
Sturnus roseus 378, **52**
   sturninus 379, **52**
Sula dactylatra 37, **4**
   leucogaster 37, **4**
   sula 37, **4**
Sylvia mystacea 362, **49**
   nana 364, **49**
   sarda 362, **49**
Synthliboramphus antiquus **65**
Syrrhaptes paradoxus 172, **36**

Tachycineta bicolor **65**
Tadorna ferruginea 54, **7**
Tarsiger cyanurus 332, **43**
Toxostoma rufum 328, **42**
Tringa flavipes 139, **28**
   melanoleuca 138, **28**
   solitaria 140, **28**
   stagnatilis 137, **28**
Tryngites subruficollis 128, **26**
Turdus migratorius 351, **47**
   naumanni eunomus 348, **47**
   naumanni naumanni 348, **47**
   obscurus 347, **46**

   ruficollis atrogularis 350, **47**
   ruficollis ruficollis 349, **47**
   unicolor 346, **46**
Turnix sylvatica 94, **18**

Uragus sibiricus 386, **58**
Uria lomvia 169, **36**

Vermivora chrysoptera 388, **54**
   peregrina 389, **54**
Vireo flavifrons **54**
   olivaceus 381, **54**
   philadelphicus 381, **54**

Wilsonia canadensis 402, **57**
   citrina 401, **57**
   pusilla 402, **57**

Xanthocephalus xanthocephalus 424, **64**
Xenus cinereus 141, **28**

Zenaida macroura **37**
Zonotrichia albicollis 407, **59**
   leucophrys 406, **59**
Zoothera dauma 341, **45**
   naevia 343, **45**
   sibirica 342, **45**